go to page 43

Dude Dude

V

THE WORLD AROUND US

UNITED STATES
AND ITS NEIGHBORS

The Statue of Liberty, standing in New York Harbor, is an important part of the story of our country. The photograph is a close-up of Miss Liberty. She has been a symbol of freedom to the world for more than 100 years.

BARRY K. BEYER

JEAN CRAVEN

MARY A. McFARLAND

WALTER C. PARKER

MACMILLAN/McGRAW-HILL SCHOOL PUBLISHING COMPANY

NEW YORK   CHICAGO   COLUMBUS

PROGRAM AUTHORS

Dr. Barry K. Beyer
Professor of Education and American Studies
George Mason University
Fairfax, Virginia

Jean Craven
Social Studies Coordinator
Albuquerque Public Schools
Albuquerque, New Mexico

Dr. Mary A. McFarland
Instructional Coordinator of Social Studies,
 K–12 and Director of Staff Development
Parkway School District
Chesterfield, Missouri

Dr. Walter C. Parker
Associate Professor, College of Education
University of Washington
Seattle, Washington

CONTENT CONSULTANTS

Reading
Dr. Virginia Arnold
Senior Author, *Connections* Reading Program
Richmond, Virginia

Economics
Dr. George Dawson
Professor of Economics
Empire State University
Bellmore, New York

Special Populations
Dr. Jeannette Fleischner
Professor of Education
Teachers College
Columbia University
New York, New York

Multicultural
Jo Bonita Perez
Consultant
Los Angeles County Schools
Downey, California

Curriculum
John Sanford
Director of Curriculum
Acalanes Union High School District
Lafayette, California

Multicultural
Dr. Joe Trotter
Professor of History
Carnegie Mellon University
Pittsburgh, Pennsylvania

History
Dr. David Van Tassel
Founder of United States History Week
Professor of History
Case Western Reserve University
Cleveland, Ohio

Geography
Nancy Winter
Member of the Executive Board of the
 National Council for Geographic Education
Social Studies Teacher
Bedford, Massachusetts

International Education
Gary Yee
Principal
Hillcrest School
Oakland, California

GRADE-LEVEL CONSULTANTS

Judith Eddy
Elementary Teacher
Saint Anthony Grade School
Charleston, West Virginia

Brian Hunger
Fifth Grade Teacher
Huntley School
Huntley, Illinois

Kayte Russell
Fifth Grade Teacher
Holy Spirit School
San Diego, California

Kathleen Sullivan
District Superintendent
Archdiocese of New York
Staten Island, New York

M. Monte Tatom
Chapter 1 Reading and Writing Instructor
Booker T. Washington Middle School
Mobile, Alabama

CONTRIBUTING WRITER

Diane Hart
Menlo Park, California

Roberta Jackson
Alexandria, Virginia

ACKNOWLEDGMENTS

The publisher gratefully acknowledges permission to reprint the following copyrighted material:
Excerpt from AMERICA by Ruth Tooze. Copyright © 1956 by Ruth Tooze. © renewed 1984. Reprinted by
permission of Viking Penguin Inc. Excerpts from I HAVE A DREAM by Martin Luther King, Jr. Copyright ©
1963 by Martin Luther King, Jr. Reprinted by permission of Joan Daves.

Macmillan/McGraw-Hill School Division
866 Third Avenue
New York, New York 10022

Printed in the United States of America
ISBN 0-02-145905-3
9 8 7 6 5 4 3 2 1

CONTENTS

UNIT 4 The American Colonies 174

UNIT 9   The United States in the Twentieth Century   472

UNIT 10   Canada and Latin America   540

Building Citizenship

PEOPLE WHO MAKE A DIFFERENCE

Neighborhood Youth Center / 41
The Loving Cup / 235
Getting Out the Vote / 357
The Friendly Supper Club / 423
Houses for the Poor / 449
You Can Make a Difference / 533

POINT/COUNTERPOINT

Who Has the Right to the Land? / 98
Early 1800s: Did the Spanish Missions Improve
   the Way of Life of the California Indians? / 148
Revolution or Loyalty? / 296
Union or Secession? / 404
1901: Should Women Work Outside the
   Home? / 490

Primary Sources

Poor Richard's Almanac / 233
The Declaration of Independence / 294
The Constitution / 330
The Seneca Falls Declaration of
   Independence / 396
Chief Joseph's Speech of Surrender / 443
''I Have a Dream'' / 523

Building Skills

Charts, Graphs, Diagrams, and Time Lines

Maps

USING YOUR TEXTBOOK

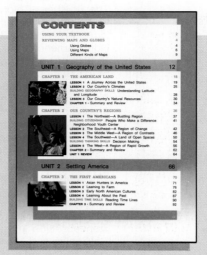

TABLE OF CONTENTS
Lists all parts of your book and tells you where to find them

Your textbook contains many special features that will help you read, understand, and remember the people, geography, and history of the United States.

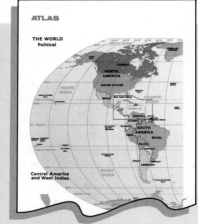

REVIEWING MAPS AND GLOBES
Reviews skills that will help you use the maps in your book

ATLAS
Maps of the United States and the world

LESSON OPENER
Important vocabulary, people, and places introduced in the lesson

Lesson introduction

Asks you to think about what you already know from previous lessons or your own experience

Question you should keep in mind as you read the lesson

LESSON
4 The Road to Victory

READ TO LEARN

Key Vocabulary	Key People	Key Places
territory	George Rogers Clark	Fort Vincennes
traitor	John Paul Jones	Northwest Territory
	Francis Marion	West Point
	Nathanael Greene	Yorktown
	Charles Cornwallis	

Read Aloud

In June 1778 General Washington got a message from his best spies in Philadelphia—the women hired to wash the red-coats' clothes. The British had ordered their laundry to be returned at once, "finished or unfinished." This could mean only one thing. They were leaving the city. Now it was Washington's turn to chase an army across New Jersey.

By July the British were back in New York City. Washington camped nearby, where his army could control the Hudson River. "It is not a little pleasing," he wrote, "that after two years . . . both armies are brought back to the very point they set out from." From now on the war would be fought in other places.

Read for Purpose

1. **WHAT YOU KNOW:** Where were the first battles of the American Revolution fought?
2. **WHAT YOU WILL LEARN:** What battles led to the end of the Revolution?

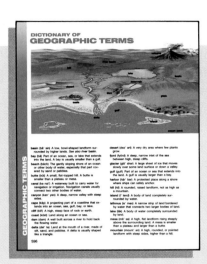

DICTIONARY OF GEOGRAPHIC TERMS

Definition and pronunciation of major geographic features

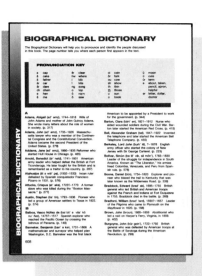

BIOGRAPHICAL DICTIONARY

Identification and pronunciation of important people discussed in your book and page where each is introduced

GLOSSARY

Definition and pronunciation of all Key Vocabulary and page where each is introduced

GAZETTEER

Location and pronunciation of the major places discussed in your book and page where each is shown on a map

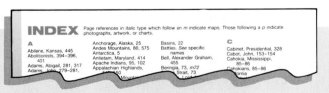

INDEX

Alphabetical list of important people, places, events, and subjects in your book and pages where information is found

REVIEWING
MAPS & GLOBES

Using Globes

Key Vocabulary

continent   equator
ocean   prime meridian
hemisphere

In social studies this year, you will be reading the story of the United States. As you read, you will find that maps and globes can be of great help to you. Maps and globes show many of the places around us. They help you to see where these places are in relation to one another. They show where the United States is in relation to the rest of the world.

Globes can help you understand what the earth actually looks like. Globes are models, or small copies, of the earth. Like the earth, globes are spheres (sfērz). A sphere is an object that is shaped like a ball. Because globes have the same shape as the earth, they give an accurate idea of the shapes and sizes of places. They also show directions and distances between places.

Continents and Oceans

Globes show the **continents** and the oceans. A continent is a very large body of land. The earth has seven continents. They are North America, South America, Europe, Africa, Asia, Australia, and Antarctica. All of these continents, except Australia and Antarctica, are divided into countries.

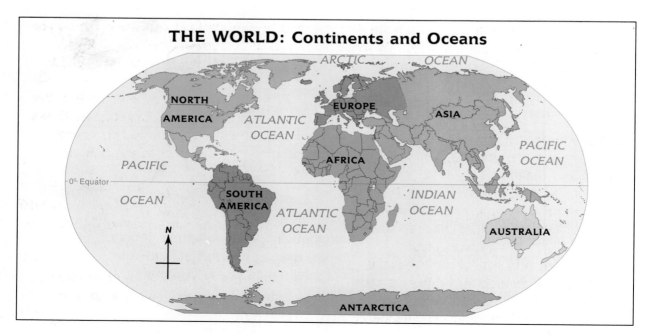

THE WORLD: Continents and Oceans

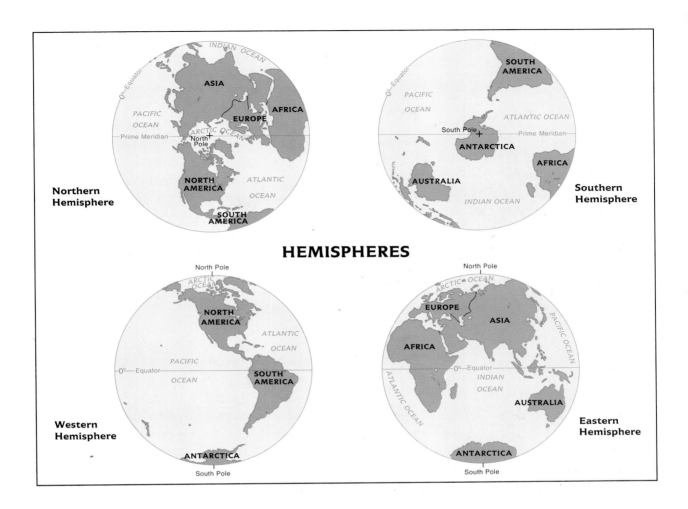

HEMISPHERES

You can see from the map on page 4 that the continents are separated by large bodies of water. These are the oceans. The earth has four oceans: the Atlantic, the Pacific, the Indian, and the Arctic.

Hemispheres

No matter how you turn the globe or where you stand to look at it, you can see only half of it at a time. Since the globe is a sphere, what you see is half a sphere. Another word for half a sphere is hemisphere. *Hemi* means "half."

The maps above show you that the earth can be divided into different hemispheres. It can be divided along the equator into the Northern Hemisphere and the Southern Hemisphere. The equator is an imaginary line lying halfway between the North Pole and the South Pole.

The earth can also be divided into the Eastern and Western Hemisphere. These hemispheres are separated by another imaginary line known as the prime meridian.

1. What does the word *hemisphere* mean?
2. What oceans surround the United States?
3. What is the equator?
4. What are two things you can learn about the earth from looking at a globe?

5

Using Maps

Key Vocabulary

cardinal directions   scale
intermediate directions   symbol
north pointer   map key

Maps are drawings that show all or part of the earth's surface. They are drawn on flat sheets of paper. Maps are easier to use than globes. They can be folded and carried. They can be printed on pages in books. The entire world can be shown on a single map. And it can be seen at one time. This makes it easy to compare different parts of the world.

If you look through this book, you will find a great many maps. These maps can help you better understand what you read in each chapter. However, maps use a special language to give information. In order to use maps you must be able to "read," or interpret, them.

Directions

How can you find directions on a map? You know that north is the direction toward the North Pole. When you face north, south is directly behind you, east is to your right, and west is to your left.

North, south, east, and west are the main, or **cardinal directions**. The letters **N, S, E**, and **W** stand for the cardinal directions.

Northeast (**NE**), southeast (**SE**), southwest (**SW**), and northwest (**NW**) are called the **intermediate directions**. *Intermediate* means "between." Northeast is the direction halfway between north and east. Southeast is halfway between east and south, southwest is halfway between south and west, and northwest is halfway between north and west.

The North Pole is not shown on all maps. However, most maps have a **north** pointer indicating which way north is on the map. If you know which way north is, you can easily find the other cardinal directions and the intermediate directions.

Find the north pointer on the map of Georgia below. In what direction is Albany from Atlanta? In what direction would you travel going from Savannah to Augusta?

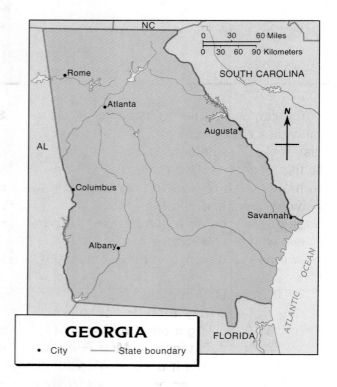

Scale

Maps are never as large as the part of the earth that they show. They are always smaller. **Scale** tells us how much smaller. Scale explains the relationship between real distances on the earth and distances on the map.

On the maps in this book, scale is indicated by two lines—one for miles and the other for kilometers. Find the scales on **Map A** on page 7. The scale shows that one inch on the map stands for 190 miles on the earth. How many kilometers do two centimeters stand for?

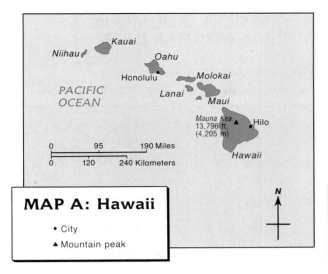

MAP A: Hawaii
- City
▲ Mountain peak

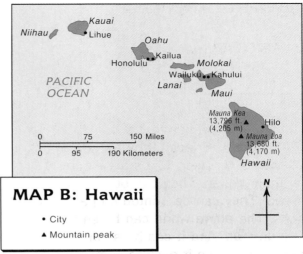

MAP B: Hawaii
- City
▲ Mountain peak

You can use a ruler to measure the distance between places on a map. You can also make a scale strip like the one below to find distances. Use the scale on **Map A** to mark the strip. Now find the distance between Honolulu and Hilo. Place the edge of the strip on a line between these cities, with the "0" below one of them. Now read the distance in miles below the other city.

Maps are drawn at many different scales. Look at **Map B** on this page. Hawaii appears larger on **Map B** than it does on **Map A**. An inch on **Map B** stands for fewer miles than it does on **Map A**. How many miles does one inch stand for on **Map B?** How many kilometers do two centimeters stand for?

Even though scale changes, real distances do not. You can check this by finding the distance in miles between Honolulu and Hilo on **Map B.** If you do this correctly, you will get the same number of miles as you did before.

Symbols

Maps show information by **symbols**. A symbol is anything that stands for something else. Symbols commonly used on maps include lines, dots, circles, squares, stars, letters, and numbers. Color is a special map symbol. It may be used by itself or in combination with lines, dots, or other pattern symbols. Different colors are often used to distinguish one country from another, or one state from another.

On many maps, the same symbols may stand for the same things. For example, on most maps, water is shown in blue. A black dot (•) stands for a city, a star (★) stands for a state capital, and a star in a circle (✪) stands for a national capital. Boundaries between states and countries are shown by different kinds of lines.

If you look at the maps in this textbook, you will see how these symbols are used. When you understand map symbols you know a little bit more about the language of maps.

0	95	190	285	380	475 Miles
0	120	240	360	480	600	720 Kilometers

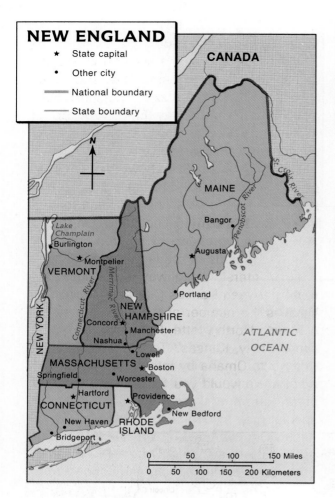

NEW ENGLAND

- ★ State capital
- • Other city
- ▬▬ National boundary
- ▬▬ State boundary

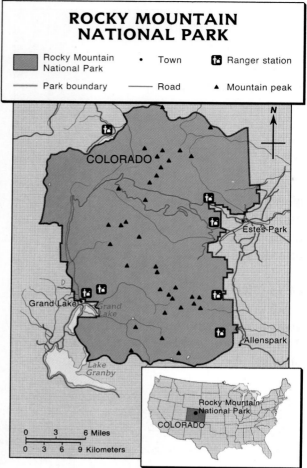

ROCKY MOUNTAIN NATIONAL PARK

- ▨ Rocky Mountain National Park
- • Town
- 🅟 Ranger station
- ▬ Park boundary
- ▬ Road
- ▲ Mountain peak

Look at the map of New England above. What color is used to show the state of Massachusetts? What color is used to show the state of Connecticut? What is the capital of Maine? Is New Haven a capital?

A symbol that stands for one thing on one map may stand for something else on another map. For this reason, it is important to read the **map key**. The map key tells you what each symbol on the map stands for. What four items are shown on the map key for New England?

Look at the map of Rocky Mountain National Park on the right. This park is part of our country's national park system.

It contains some of the most beautiful views in the Rocky Mountains. Thousands of tourists visit it every year. Check the map key. What does the color green show? What does a square show? How is the park boundary shown? What symbol stands for a mountain peak?

1. What advantages do maps have over globes?
2. What are the cardinal and intermediate directions?
3. What does a map scale show?
4. What does a map key tell you?

8

Ha Ha
you
turned
Here
For nothing

Different Kinds of Maps

Key Vocabulary

transportation map
city map
grid
product map

You are already familiar with maps that give you general information about continents, countries, and states. There are other kinds of maps that give special information about a particular subject.

Map Titles

When you use a map, the first thing you should do is look for the map title. The title tells what information the map shows.

Transportation Maps

Transportation maps are special maps designed to help travelers. They show the routes that connect places. Transportation maps may show subway, bus, plane, or train routes. Road maps are the most commonly used transportation maps.

The road map below shows Kansas and parts of the sourrounding states. Some of the cities in this area and the main roads that connect them are indicated. On this map, roads are shown by colored lines. How many kinds of roads are shown?

What interstate highway is the shortest route between Kansas City and Denver? What is the number of the highway that connects North Platte, Nebraska, and Garden City, Kansas? To travel from Denver to Omaha by interstate highway, what route would you first follow?

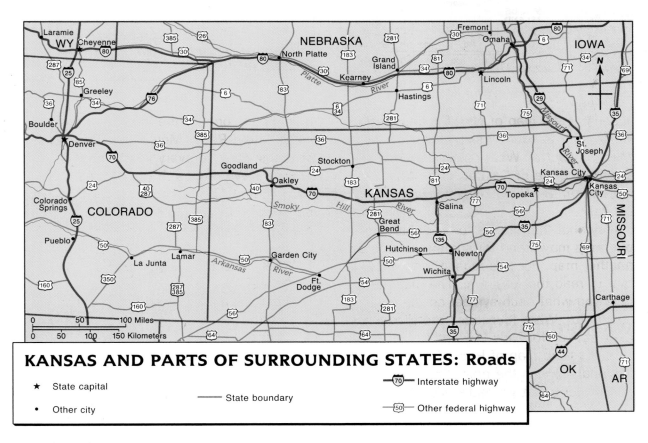

KANSAS AND PARTS OF SURROUNDING STATES: Roads

★ State capital

• Other city

—— State boundary

—70— Interstate highway

—50— Other federal highway

City Maps

City maps are special maps that help people find their way in unfamiliar cities. They usually show such things as streets, parks, and places of particular interest.

Look at the city map of Washington, D.C., below. How are parks shown on this map? What color is used to show places of interest?

The map of Washington, D.C., has a grid. A grid is made up of two sets of lines that cross each other to make squares. One set of lines crosses the map from top to bottom. The other set crosses the map from left to right. Each square on the map can be identified by a letter and a number. For example, the square in the upper left-hand corner of the map is A–1.

A grid makes it easy to find places on a map or to give their location. For example, the Jefferson Memorial is located in D–2. Can you find it on the map? What places of interest are shown in C–3? What street leads from the White House to the Capitol? Now give the letter and number of the square in which Union Station is located.

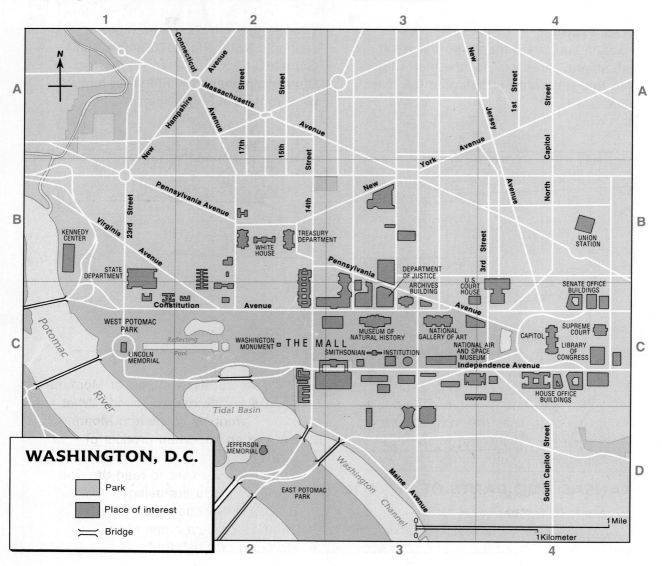

WASHINGTON, D.C.

Park

Place of interest

Bridge

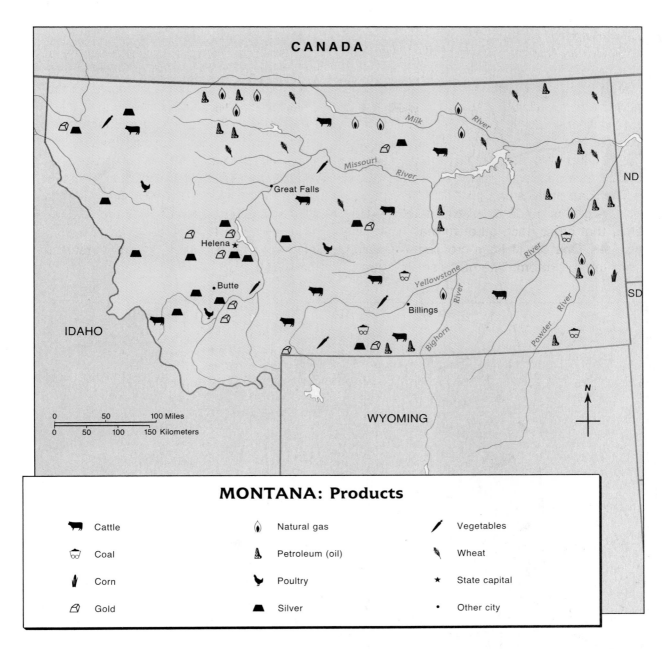

MONTANA: Products

Cattle		Natural gas		Vegetables	
Coal		Petroleum (oil)		Wheat	
Corn		Poultry		State capital	
Gold		Silver		Other city	

Product Maps

Product maps are another kind of special map. They show the most important goods that are produced in an area. Product maps also tell you the kinds of jobs people have.

The map above shows the important products of Montana. As you can see, it uses symbols to show different resources and products. Check the map key to see what these are. In what part of Montana is most of the petroleum found? What are the major products of eastern Montana? Is clothing an important product of Montana?

1. Why is it important to read the title of the map you are using?
2. What is a transportation map?
3. What do product maps show?
4. How is a grid helpful?

11

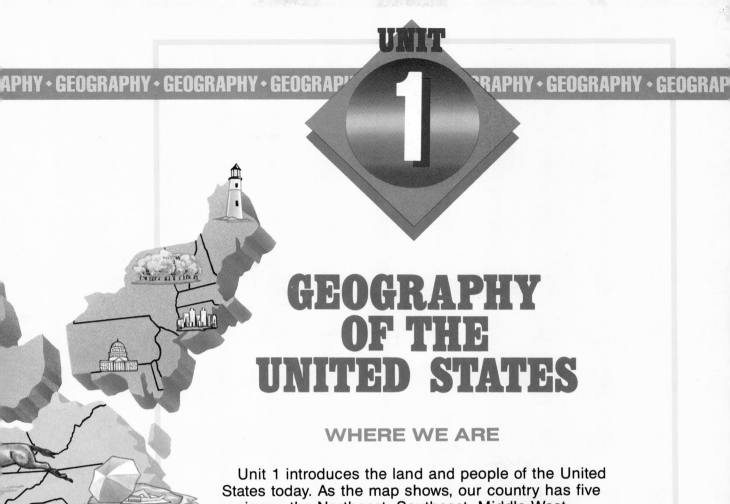

UNIT 1

GEOGRAPHY OF THE UNITED STATES

WHERE WE ARE

Unit 1 introduces the land and people of the United States today. As the map shows, our country has five regions—the Northeast, Southeast, Middle West, Southwest, and West. The states in each of these regions have much in common. They share similar landforms, climate, and natural resources. In this unit you will learn what makes each region of the United States special.

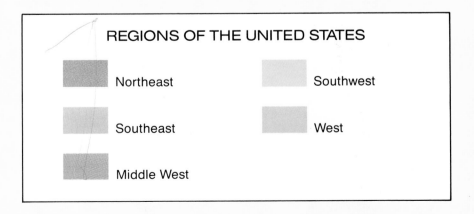

REGIONS OF THE UNITED STATES

Northeast	Southwest
Southeast	West
Middle West	

CALIFORNIA

Capital ★
Sacramento
Population:
27,663,000
Area:
158,706 sq mi;
411,049 sq km

TABLES
ON THE STATES

COLORADO

Capital ★
Denver
Population:
3,296,000
Area:
104,091 sq mi;
269,596 sq km

STATE	FLAG	FACTS

ALABAMA

Capital ★
Montgomery
Population:
4,083,000
Area:
51,705 sq mi;
133,915 sq km

CONNECTICUT

Capital ★
Hartford
Population:
3,211,000
Area:
5,018 sq mi;
12,997 sq km

ALASKA

Capital ★
Juneau
Population:
525,000
Area:
591,004 sq mi;
1,530,700 sq km

DELAWARE

Capital ★
Dover
Population:
644,000
Area:
2,045 sq mi;
5,295 sq km

ARIZONA

Capital ★
Phoenix
Population:
3,386,000
Area:
114,000 sq mi;
295,260 sq km

FLORIDA

Capital ★
Tallahassee
Population:
12,023,000
Area:
58,664 sq mi;
151,939 sq km

ARKANSAS

Capital ★
Little Rock
Population:
2,388,000
Area:
53,187 sq mi;
137,754 sq km

GEORGIA

Capital ★
Atlanta
Population:
6,222,000
Area:
58,910 sq mi;
152,576 sq km

HAWAII

Capital ★
Honolulu
Population:
1,083,000
Area:
6,471 sq mi;
16,759 sq km

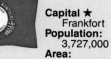

KENTUCKY

Capital ★
Frankfort
Population:
3,727,000
Area:
40,410 sq mi;
104,660 sq km

IDAHO

Capital ★
Boise
Population:
998,000
Area:
83,564 sq mi;
216,432 sq km

LOUISIANA

Capital ★
Baton Rouge
Population:
4,461,000
Area:
47,752 sq mi;
123,677 sq km

ILLINOIS

Capital ★
Springfield
Population:
11,582,000
Area:
56,345 sq mi;
145,934 sq km

MAINE

Capital ★
Augusta
Population:
1,187,000
Area:
33,265 sq mi;
86,156 sq km

INDIANA

Capital ★
Indianapolis
Population:
5,531,000
Area:
36,185 sq mi;
93,720 sq km

MARYLAND

Capital ★
Annapolis
Population:
4,535,000
Area:
10,460 sq mi;
27,092 sq km

IOWA

Capital ★
Des Moines
Population:
2,834,000
Area:
56,275 sq mi;
145,753 sq km

MASSACHUSETTS

Capital ★
Boston
Population:
5,855,000
Area:
8,284 sq mi;
21,456 sq km

KANSAS

Capital ★
Topeka
Population:
2,476,000
Area:
82,277 sq mi;
213,098 sq km

MICHIGAN

Capital ★
Lansing
Population:
9,200,000
Area:
58,527 sq mi;
151,586 sq km

MINNESOTA

Capital ★
St. Paul
Population:
4,246,000
Area:
84,402 sq mi;
218,601 sq km

NEW JERSEY

Capital ★
Trenton
Population:
7,672,000
Area:
7,787 sq mi;
20,169 sq km

MISSISSIPPI

Capital ★
Jackson
Population:
2,625,000
Area:
47,689 sq mi;
123,515 sq km

NEW MEXICO

Capital ★
Santa Fe
Population:
1,500,000
Area:
121,593 sq mi;
314,925 sq km

MISSOURI

Capital ★
Jefferson City
Population:
5,103,000
Area:
69,697 sq mi;
180,516 sq km

NEW YORK

Capital ★
Albany
Population:
17,825,000
Area:
49,108 sq mi;
127,190 sq km

MONTANA

Capital ★
Helena
Population:
809,000
Area:
147,046 sq mi;
380,848 sq km

NORTH CAROLINA

Capital ★
Raleigh
Population:
6,413,000
Area:
52,669 sq mi;
136,413 sq km

NEBRASKA

Capital ★
Lincoln
Population:
1,594,000
Area:
77,355 sq mi;
200,350 sq km

NORTH DAKOTA

Capital ★
Bismarck
Population:
672,000
Area:
70,702 sq mi;
183,119 sq km

NEVADA

Capital ★
Carson City
Population:
1,007,000
Area:
110,561 sq mi;
286,352 sq km

OHIO

Capital ★
Columbus
Population:
10,784,000
Area:
41,330 sq mi;
107,044 sq km

NEW HAMPSHIRE

Capital ★
Concord
Population:
1,057,000
Area:
9,279 sq mi;
24,032 sq km

OKLAHOMA

Capital ★
Oklahoma City
Population:
3,272,000
Area:
69,956 sq mi;
181,186 sq km

16

OREGON

Capital ★
Salem
Population:
2,724,000
Area:
97,073 sq mi;
251,419 sq km

UTAH

Capital ★
Salt Lake City
Population:
1,680,000
Area:
84,899 sq mi;
219,889 sq km

PENNSYLVANIA

Capital ★
Harrisburg
Population:
11,936,000
Area:
45,308 sq mi;
117,348 sq km

VERMONT

Capital ★
Montpelier
Population:
548,000
Area:
9,614 sq mi;
24,900 sq km

RHODE ISLAND

Capital ★
Providence
Population:
986,000
Area:
1,212 sq mi;
3,140 sq km

VIRGINIA

Capital ★
Richmond
Population:
5,904,000
Area:
40,767 sq mi;
105,586 sq km

SOUTH CAROLINA

Capital ★
Columbia
Population:
3,425,000
Area:
31,113 sq mi;
80,582 sq km

WASHINGTON

Capital ★
Olympia
Population:
4,538,000
Area:
68,139 sq mi;
176,479 sq km

SOUTH DAKOTA

Capital ★
Pierre
Population:
709,000
Area:
77,116 sq mi;
199,730 sq km

WEST VIRGINIA

Capital ★
Charleston
Population:
1,897,000
Area:
24,232 sq mi;
62,760 sq km

TENNESSEE

Capital ★
Nashville
Population:
4,855,000
Area:
42,144 sq mi;
109,152 sq km

WISCONSIN

Capital ★
Madison
Population:
4,807,000
Area:
56,153 sq mi;
145,436 sq km

TEXAS

Capital ★
Austin
Population:
16,789,000
Area:
266,807 sq mi;
691,030 sq km

WYOMING

Capital ★
Cheyenne
Population:
490,000
Area:
97,809 sq mi;
253,326 sq km

THE AMERICAN LAND

FOCUS

O beautiful for spacious skies,
For amber waves of grain.
For purple mountain majesties,
Above the fruited plain!

These words from the song "America, the Beautiful" describe the American land. It is a land of great variety, from tall mountains to flat farm fields. It is a land rich in timber, oil, and minerals. But most important, it is our home. In this chapter we will take a closer look at the American landscape. You will be amazed by what you see.

1 A Journey Across the United States

READ TO LEARN

Key Vocabulary

geography	tributary
landform	plateau
plain	canyon
mountain range	basin

Read Aloud

It is an early fall morning at a New Jersey airport. You are about to begin a journey. Your pilot gets ready by warming up her small plane. For the next few days, the two of you will fly across the land that makes up the United States.

Read for Purpose

1. **WHAT YOU KNOW:** What kinds of land features are found in the part of the country where you live?
2. **WHAT YOU WILL LEARN:** What are the major landforms found in the United States?

A JOURNEY ACROSS OUR COUNTRY

On your trip across the United States you will learn about the geography (jē og′ rə fē) of our country. Geography is the study of the earth and the way people live on it and use it. Your study of our country's geography will begin with a look at its many different kinds of landforms. Landforms are the shapes of the earth's surface.

THE ATLANTIC COASTAL PLAIN

Your trip begins on the eastern edge of North America. The first landform you fly over is part of a long coastal plain. A plain is a large area of flat or gently sloping land. A coastal plain lies beside a large body of water.

The Atlantic Coastal Plain reaches from Maine to Florida. In the north, the Atlantic Coastal Plain is narrow. Farther south, it widens to include most of Georgia and all of Florida. If you followed the coastal plain to the south, it would lead you to the Gulf of Mexico. There it is known as the Gulf Coastal Plain.

THE APPALACHIAN MOUNTAINS

Flying west, you soon leave the Atlantic Coastal Plain behind. You are now flying over the Appalachian

Mountains. These low, rounded hills and mountains stretch from Alabama to Canada. The Green Mountains, Alleghenies, Catskills, Blue Ridge, and Great Smokies are all a part of the **mountain range** known as the Appalachian Mountains. A mountain range is a series of many mountains.

On the western side of the mountain range you see the Ohio River. Can you find this river on the map on page 21? Like Indians long ago, you decide to follow it to the "father of waters," the mighty Mississippi River.

THE INTERIOR PLAINS

As the Ohio River flows westward, it follows a winding path across the Interior Plains. Ahead, the land is flat for as far as you can see.

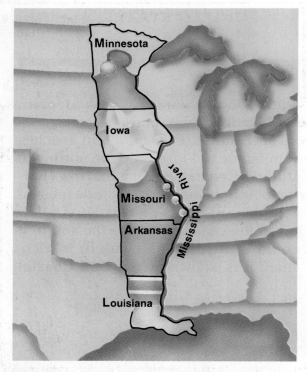

MAP SKILL: Find "Mimal" on the map. What does Mimal help you recall?

The Interior Plains are so wide that they are divided into two parts. The eastern part is called the Central Plains. The western part is known as the Great Plains.

Once the Central Plains were covered with trees and grass as tall as a horse. Later the trees were cut down and the grass was plowed under. Now you see farm fields of wheat and corn that look like a checkerboard on the plains.

The Ohio River finally reaches a long, winding silver ribbon that cuts through the Central Plains. It is our country's longest river—the Mississippi. The Mississippi River begins as a small stream in northern Minnesota. At the place where it empties into the Gulf of Mexico, the Mississippi is almost one mile (1.6 km) wide.

To see how the Mississippi River grows, look at the map on page 21. How many **tributaries** (trib′ yə târ ēz) of the Mississippi can you find? A tributary is a stream or river that flows into a larger river. Major tributaries of the Mississippi River include the Missouri, the Ohio, the Arkansas, and the Red rivers.

Now look at the map on this page. If you follow the Mississippi River you will see that it forms the outline of an elf known as "Mimal." His name comes from the first letter of the names of states that are on the west bank of the Mississippi River: **M**innesota, **I**owa, **M**issouri, **A**rkansas, and **L**ouisiana.

Continuing west from the Mississippi River you fly over the Ozark Plateau (pla tō′). A **plateau** is an area of flat land that is higher than the surrounding land. The Ozark Plateau is the only high area of the Central Plains.

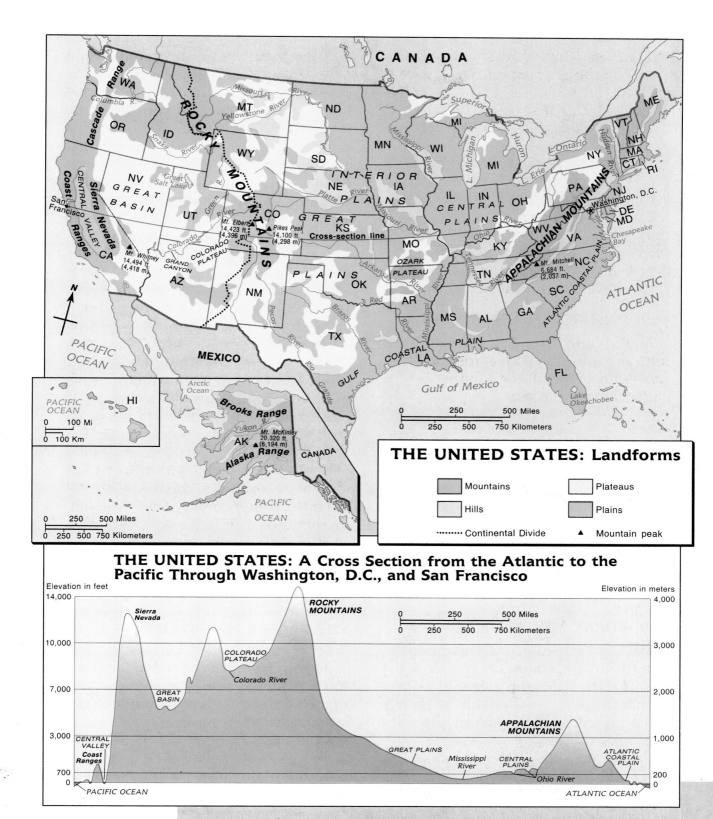

THE UNITED STATES: Landforms

Mountains	Plateaus
Hills	Plains
·········· Continental Divide	▲ Mountain peak

THE UNITED STATES: A Cross Section from the Atlantic to the Pacific Through Washington, D.C., and San Francisco

MAP SKILL: How many landforms are shown on the map? Use the cross-section diagram to see some of the landforms in another way. What is the tallest **mountain range** in the United States?

21

Rafting on the Colorado River is a popular pastime among visitors to the Grand Canyon.

capped peaks sparkle in the bright sun. The poet Katherine Lee Bates was overwhelmed by the beauty of the Rocky Mountains. As you read the words to "America, the Beautiful" on page 23, try to imagine the scenes that she describes.

As you fly west, you soon see a spectacular sight. It is the Grand Canyon. A **canyon** is a deep valley with steep sides. The Grand Canyon took millions of years to form. It was carved by the rushing waters of the Colorado River. Little by little, the river has worn away the rock and carried it downstream.

THE GREAT BASIN

As you leave the Rocky Mountains, the color of the land changes from green to brown. You are now flying over the Great Basin. A **basin** is a low region surrounded by higher lands. The land in the Great Basin looks like a crumpled paper bag, with rows of low hills separating dry, dusty valleys.

This is desert country, where very little rain falls during the year. When the rain does come, it sometimes evaporates before hitting the ground. Old-timers say that even the rabbits here have to carry canteens with water.

THE PACIFIC MOUNTAINS AND VALLEYS

As you approach the end of the Great Basin you see a welcome sight—the rugged Sierra Nevada mountains rise steeply out of the desert. *Sierra Nevada* means "snowy mountains" in Spanish. Soon you see snowy peaks and deep-blue mountain lakes. One hundred and forty years ago, people in horse-drawn wagons struggled for weeks to cross the Sierra Nevada. Flying across the mountains takes about an hour.

West of the Ozark Plateau the plains become drier. Soon you are flying over the Great Plains. The Great Plains area was once a huge grassland. Millions of buffalo roamed across the land from Canada all the way to Texas. Today you see mostly wheat fields instead of short, thick grass.

THE ROCKY MOUNTAINS

Your plane begins to climb. Ahead of you the Rocky Mountains rise from the plains. The Rockies are the longest mountain range in the United States. They stretch from Alaska through Canada, and southward into Mexico.

Pine and fir trees color the slopes of the Rocky Mountains a deep green. The tallest peaks rise more than 14,000 feet (4,200 m) into the air. On the highest peaks the snows of winter never melt completely. These treeless, snow-

AMERICA, THE BEAUTIFUL

Music by Samuel Ward
Words by Katharine Lee Bates

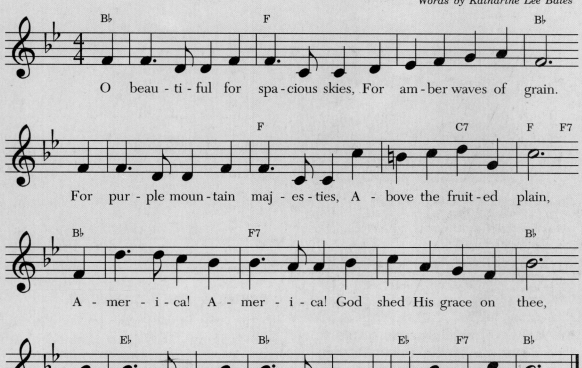

O beau - ti - ful for spa - cious skies, For am - ber waves of grain.

For pur - ple moun - tain maj - es - ties, A - bove the fruit - ed plain,

A - mer - i - ca! A - mer - i - ca! God shed His grace on thee,

And crown thy good with broth - er - hood, From sea to shin - ing sea.

Hawaii is the southernmost state of the United States. This picture shows the mountainous coastline of Oahu, one of the islands that make up Hawaii.

Now you pass over the green fields of California's Central Valley. This is one of the richest farming areas on earth.

At last you cross the Coast Ranges. These low, rolling hills hug the Pacific coast from California to Canada. Beyond the hills is the Pacific Ocean. You have now reached the western edge of the continent.

ALASKA AND HAWAII

To see Hawaii, you will have to cross over the Pacific Ocean. Flying 2,400 miles (3,840 km) southwest from California, you reach the Hawaiian Islands. The islands are really the tops of underwater mountains.

Finally, your plane heads north across the Pacific toward Alaska. The land here is also full of mountains, with the Brooks Range in the north and the Alaska Range in the south. Between these two mountain ranges lies the Yukon River Valley.

AMERICA THE BEAUTIFUL

On your imaginary journey across the United States you have seen how the country changes from coast to coast and beyond. You have seen some of the landforms that make our country so varied and beautiful. But the best way to get to know "America, the Beautiful" is to see as much of it as you can for yourself.

Check Your Reading

1. Where does the Mississippi River begin? Where does it end?
2. In what part of the United States are the highest mountains found?
3. **GEOGRAPHY SKILL:** Name four landforms found in the United States.
4. **THINKING SKILL:** Compare the landforms found on the East Coast of the United States to those found on the West Coast.

24

2 Our Country's Climates

READ TO LEARN

Key Vocabulary

climate   precipitation   altitude
temperature   temperate zone

Read Aloud

The winter of 1977 was so warm in Anchorage, Alaska, that bears in its zoo refused to hibernate, or spend part of the winter sleeping. At the same time, sun lovers in Miami, Florida, were freezing. For the first time in its history, Miami had snow. People in Florida and Alaska wanted to know what was going on.

Read for Purpose

1. **WHAT YOU KNOW:** What month is usually the coldest where you live? The warmest?
2. **WHAT YOU WILL LEARN:** How does climate vary in different parts of the United States?

WEATHER AND CLIMATE

During the winter of 1977 Anchorage and Miami had something in common. Both cities were having strange weather. Weather is the condition of the air at a given time and place. One day the weather may be hot or cold, damp or dry, calm or windy. Weather affects how you live day to day. Your decision to wear heavy clothes, light clothes, or a raincoat each morning depends mostly on the weather.

The cities of Anchorage and Miami have very different climates. Climate is the weather that a place has over many years. Climate affects long-range plans such as what crops to plant in an area.

The two most important parts of a place's climate are temperature and precipitation (pri sip ə tā′ shən). Temperature is the amount of heat or cold in the air. Precipitation is the moisture that falls to the earth as rain or snow.

TEMPERATURE

Three factors greatly affect the temperature of a place during the year. They are its distance from the equator, its height above sea level, and its distance from the ocean.

You read on page 5 that the equator is located halfway between the North Pole and the South Pole. Temperatures are highest near the equator, where the sun's rays are very strong. Temperatures are lowest near the poles.

The United States, except for the states of Alaska and Hawaii, lies about halfway between the equator and the North Pole. This area is one of the earth's **temperate zones**. Climate in the temperate zone is not as hot as near the equator nor as cold as at the North and South poles.

Even in the temperate zone, distance from the equator affects climate. In the northern half of our country, winters are cold. In the southern half, winters are usually mild.

Altitude (al' tə tüd), or the height of a place above sea level, is another factor that affects climate. Places at high alti-

MAP SKILL: Use this map to identify the climate in your state. Is your state in Humid or Arid America?

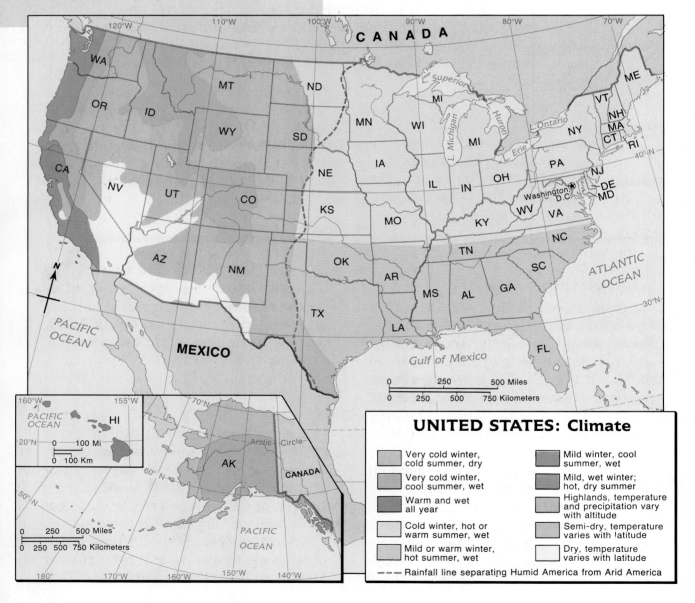

UNITED STATES: Climate

- Very cold winter, cold summer, dry
- Very cold winter, cool summer, wet
- Warm and wet all year
- Cold winter, hot or warm summer, wet
- Mild or warm winter, hot summer, wet
- Mild winter, cool summer, wet
- Mild, wet winter; hot, dry summer
- Highlands, temperature and precipitation vary with altitude
- Semi-dry, temperature varies with latitude
- Dry, temperature varies with latitude
- ----- Rainfall line separating Humid America from Arid America

tudes generally are cooler than places nearer sea level even though they are at the same distance from the equator. The higher up you go, the cooler the air becomes. That's why mountains are usually cooler than nearby lowlands.

The distance of a place from the ocean is the third factor affecting temperature. Ocean waters heat up in summer and cool off in winter more slowly than the land. In summer, ocean breezes keep places near the coast cooler than inland areas. In winter, ocean winds can warm coastal areas.

PRECIPITATION

On the map on page 26 you can see a line running from North Dakota south through Texas. East of this line, more than 20 inches (50 cm) of precipitation falls each year. This part of the country is often called Humid America. Humid means damp or wet. The Atlantic Coastal Plain, the Central Plains, and the Appalachian Mountains are part of Humid America.

West of the line, much of the country gets less than 20 inches (50 cm) of precipitation each year. This half of the country is called Arid America. Arid means dry. The Great Plains and Great Basin are part of Arid America.

In Humid America, there is precipitation throughout the year. Forests grow well here. Farmers have enough water for their crops. There is enough precipitation to fill thousands of lakes and rivers.

Most of Arid America is covered with grass. There are few large rivers and lakes. Forests grow only in the mountains or along the Pacific Coast, where there is more precipitation.

In Arid America, farmers cannot depend on rainfall for growing crops.

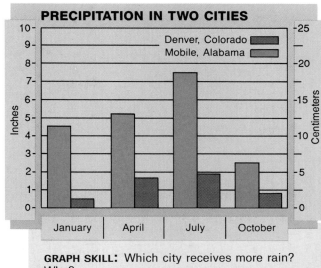

PRECIPITATION IN TWO CITIES

Denver, Colorado
Mobile, Alabama

January   April   July   October

GRAPH SKILL: Which city receives more rain? Why?

Those who did so in the past often met with disaster. Their crops were ruined by long periods with little or no rain. Today, farmers bring water to their crops during dry periods. Canals and ditches carry water from distant rivers and lakes to the fields.

OUR CLIMATE

As you probably know, climate is important. It affects the clothes we wear and the games we play. It influences the kinds of work we do and the amount of time we spend outside. In short, it influences our lives.

Check Your Reading

1. What are the two most important parts of a place's climate?
2. How does precipitation in the eastern part of the United States differ from that in the western part?
3. How do farmers in Arid America get water to their crops?
4. **THINKING SKILL:** What are the three questions you could ask to find out about a place's climate?

27

Understanding Latitude and Longitude

Key Vocabulary

latitude	degrees
longitude	meridians
parallels	grid

Did you notice the two sets of lines that cover the climate map on page 26? The lines that run east and west are called lines of latitude. The lines that run north and south are called lines of longitude. Together, latitude and longitude help you locate places on the earth.

Using Latitude

Look at the lines of latitude on the globe below. Lines of latitude are also called parallels. This is a good name be-

cause lines of latitude are always parallel, or the same distance apart. Lines of latitude never meet.

The starting line for measuring latitude is the equator. The equator is a line of latitude. Find the equator on the globe. You can see that it is labeled 0°. We call this zero degrees. A degree is a unit of measurement for latitude and longitude. The symbol ° stands for degrees. Latitudes north of the equator are labeled **N** for "north." Those south of the equator are labeled **S** for "south."

Using Longitude

The globe on the bottom of this page shows lines of longitude. Lines of longitude are also called meridians. The starting line for measuring longitude is the **prime meridian**. The prime meridian is a line of longitude. Find the prime meridian on the globe. The longitude of the prime

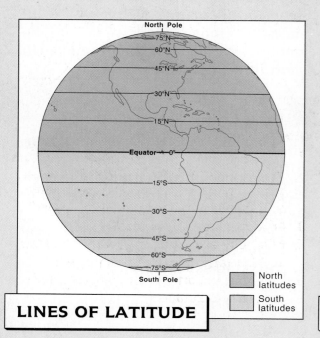

LINES OF LATITUDE

North latitudes

South latitudes

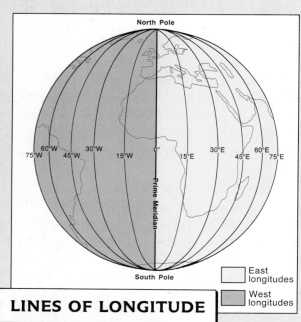

LINES OF LONGITUDE

East longitudes

West longitudes

GLOBAL GRID

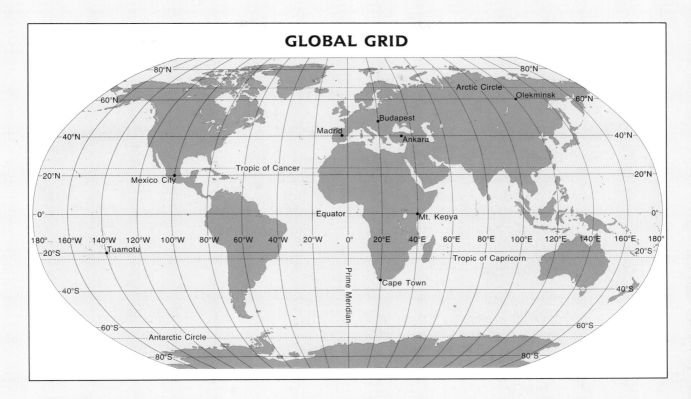

meridian is 0°. Meridians west of the prime meridian are labeled **W**. Those east of the prime meridian are labeled **E**. Since 180° east is the same as 180° west, the label for 180° longitude is marked either **W** or **E**.

All meridians meet at the South Pole and the North Pole. Meridians are farthest apart at the equator. Distances between meridians become smaller as you move from the equator toward the poles.

Finding Places on a Map

Lines of latitude and longitude together form a grid. A grid is a set of crisscrossing lines. On a map, a grid makes it easy to find any place in the world if you know its latitude and longitude. For example, the location of Mexico City can be given

at 20°N, 100°W. To find Mexico City on the map above, first put your finger on the point where the equator and the prime meridian cross. Now move your finger north to the parallel labeled 20°N. Next move your finger west along this parallel to the point where it crosses the meridian labeled 100°W. Did you find Mexico City?

Reviewing the Skill

1. What are lines of latitude and longitude? What do they help you do?
2. What city on the map is directly south of Budapest? What latitude is it near?
3. At what longitude is Madrid?
4. What city shown on the map is located at 60°N latitude, 120°E longitude?
5. Why is it important to understand latitude and longitude?

3 Our Country's Natural Resources

READ TO LEARN

Key Vocabulary

natural resource   mineral
fossil fuel   region

Read Aloud

Imagine trying to live on the moon. The moon has no air to breathe and no water to drink. No plants grow in the moon's soil. There are no forests to supply lumber. There is no oil or coal to burn for heat or to power machines. How long do you think you could live without air, water, or soil?

Read for Purpose

1. **WHAT YOU KNOW:** Does the state you live in have forests, oil, or coal? If so, how have they influenced the kinds of work that people do there?
2. **WHAT YOU WILL LEARN:** What are our country's most important natural resources?

NATURAL RESOURCES

Air, water, and soil are all examples of **natural resources**, or things found in nature that we need and use. The moon has so few natural resources that living there would be very difficult. Fortunately, our country is rich in natural resources.

SOIL

Do you know how much you eat each day? Most Americans eat about four pounds (1.8 kg) of food every day. Multiply this amount by 240 million Americans and you can understand why good soil is an important resource. Without it, the United States could not grow enough food to feed all its people.

The United States has some of the richest land for farming in the world. Good soils and different climates make it possible to raise an amazing number of different crops. The Interior Plains are covered with fields of wheat and corn. Peanuts grow well in Georgia's sandy soil. The wet soil of Massachusetts is good for growing cranberries.

Today the United States grows more food than any other country. Farmers grow more food than we can use. Much of the extra food is sold to other countries, but much is also wasted.

FORESTS

Look around you. How many things do you see made of wood or paper?

Americans use more wood and paper than any other country in the world. All of these products come from another natural resource, forests.

As you can see on the map on this page, large parts of the United States are covered with forests. Trees from forests supply lumber for buildings and furniture. The United States is the second largest lumber producer in the world.

Forests also supply wood for making paper. The wood is ground up and mixed with chemicals to make a thick soup called pulp. Wood pulp is made into cardboard, tissues, and other paper products. The paper in this book came from our forests.

FOSSIL FUELS

In the past, trees were an important source of fuel. Fuel is anything that is burned to produce power or heat. People once burned wood to keep warm and to cook their food. Today, **fossil fuels** are used for heating and cooking. Fossil fuels come in three forms— petroleum or oil, natural gas, and coal. They are called fossil fuels because they were formed from fossils, or the remains of plants and animals that lived long ago. Fossil fuels usually are found deep under the ground.

The United States has large amounts of all three fossil fuels. The map on this page shows where they are found. Our country is one of the largest oil producers in the world. It also has huge amounts of natural gas. The United States has more coal than any other country in the world.

MINERALS AND METALS

Fossil fuels are not the only resources found in the earth. As the map shows, the United States is also rich in

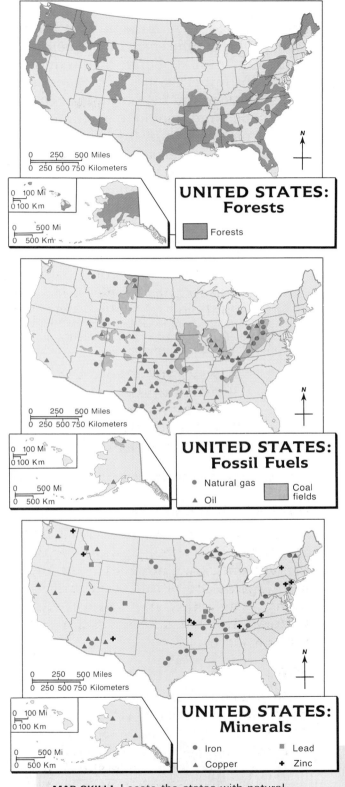

MAP SKILL: Locate the states with natural resources.

many **minerals**. A mineral is a substance found in the earth that is neither plant nor animal. Some of our most important minerals are metal ores, or rocks that contain useful metals. Ores are crushed and treated to separate the metal from the rest of the rock.

There are large deposits of iron and copper in Minnesota and Michigan. Minnesota's Mesabi Range has been mined for iron ore for more than 100 years.

Iron, copper, and zinc are mined in the Appalachian Mountains. These mountains also have huge coal deposits. The coal is used as a fuel to melt down the iron ore needed to make steel. Your desk may be made of steel from an Appalachian steel mill.

In 1848 gold was found in the foothills of the Sierra Nevada. Soon people were searching for gold from the Rocky Mountains to the Coast Ranges. Most of these people did not find gold. But they did find other valuable metals such as copper, silver, lead, and zinc. Uranium (ū rā′ nē əm) ore, which was discovered later, is also buried in the western mountains. This metal is the fuel used in nuclear power plants and weapons.

Petroleum is drilled from the ocean floor off the coasts of Texas and Louisiana. Workers live on drilling platforms like this one.

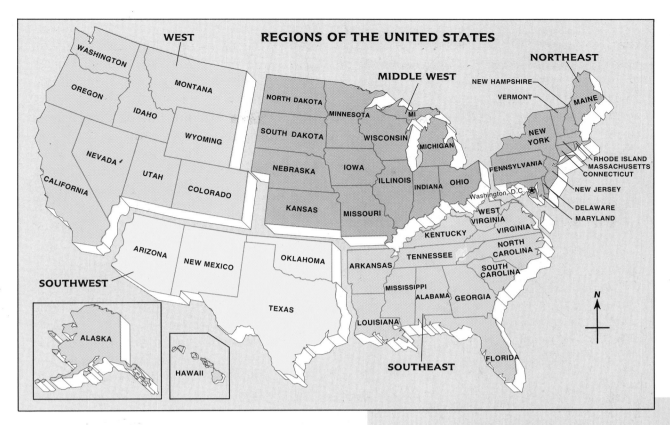

REGIONS OF THE UNITED STATES

WEST · MIDDLE WEST · NORTHEAST · SOUTHWEST · SOUTHEAST

MAP SKILL: Which regions of the United States have the most states? In which region is your state located?

UNITED STATES REGIONS

In Chapter 2 you will learn about the five **regions** of the United States—the Northeast, Southeast, Middle West, Southwest, and West. A region is a large area that has common features. The states that make up each region share similar landforms, climate, and natural resources. For example, the climate of much of the Southeast is wet and warm. Find each of the five United States regions on the map on this page. In which region do you live?

OUR GREAT LAND

The United States, as you have read, is a land rich in natural resources. It has good soils and climates for growing crops. It has forests and fossil fuels. It also has many valuable minerals. As you read about each region, you will see how people have used these riches to make the United States a good place in which to live.

Check Your Reading

1. Name three products that can be made from wood pulp.
2. Name four natural resources found in the United States.
3. **GEOGRAPHY SKILL:** Look at the fossil fuels map of the United States on page 31. Which part of the country has the most oil fields? The most coal? The most natural gas?
4. **THINKING SKILL:** What do you think the moon would be like if it had air, water, and soil?

IDEAS TO REMEMBER

■ The United States has many different landforms, including mountains, hills, plateaus, and plains.

■ The United States has a variety of climates, influenced by distance from the equator, altitude, and distance from the ocean.

■ The natural resources of the United States include forests, fossil fuels, and metals and minerals.

REVIEWING VOCABULARY

altitude	mineral
climate	natural resource
fossil fuel	plateau
geography	precipitation
landform	region

Number a paper from 1 to 10. Beside each number write the word or term from the list above that matches the statement.

1. Something that we need and use from nature, such as soil and water
2. The height of a place above sea level
3. A feature of the earth's surface, such as mountains or plains
4. A large area that has common features
5. A substance, formed from the remains of plants or animals, that is burned to produce power or heat
6. The weather a place has over many years
7. The study of the earth and the way people live on it and use it
8. An area of flat land that is higher than the surrounding land
9. A substance found in the earth that is neither plant nor animal
10. The moisture that falls to the earth as rain or snow

REVIEWING FACTS

Number a paper from 1 to 10. Write whether each statement below is true or false. If it is false, rewrite the statement to make it true.

1. The Appalachians are the longest mountain range in the United States.
2. The longest river in the United States is the Ohio River.
3. The Interior Plains are divided into two parts—the Central Plains to the east and the Great Plains to the west.
4. The Rocky Mountains extend north through Canada to Alaska and south into Mexico.
5. The Grand Canyon was formed by miners in search of valuable minerals.
6. All parts of the United States are attached to one another.
7. The states that make up the United States all have the same climate.
8. Distance from the equator, altitude, and distance from the ocean all affect the climate of a place.
9. The United States has only two major natural resources—forests and coal.
10. The United States has four regions—the Northeast, the Southwest, the Middle West, and the Southeast.

WRITING ABOUT MAIN IDEAS

1. **Writing a Letter:** Think about what you have just read in your imaginary journey across the United States. Write a letter to a fifth grader in another country and tell why "America, the Beautiful" is a good description of the United States.

2. **Writing a Letter:** Imagine that you are writing to a pen pal in another part of the United States. In your letter describe the climate in your area. Explain how the distance from the equator, altitude, and distance from the ocean affect your climate.

3. **Writing a List:** Name three important natural resources of the United States. Give two reasons why each one is important.

BUILDING SKILLS: UNDERSTANDING LATITUDE AND LONGITUDE

Use the map on this page to answer these questions.

1. What steps would you follow to find 60°N latitude, 150°W longitude on the map?

2. Which line of latitude forms the southern rim of the Aleutian Islands?

3. What is the easternmost city in the state of Alaska? At about what line of longitude can it be found?

4. Locate Juneau on the map. Is it north or south of 60°N latitude?

5. Locate Mt. McKinley on the map. At what line of longitude is it found?

6. When is it useful to know about latitude and longitude?

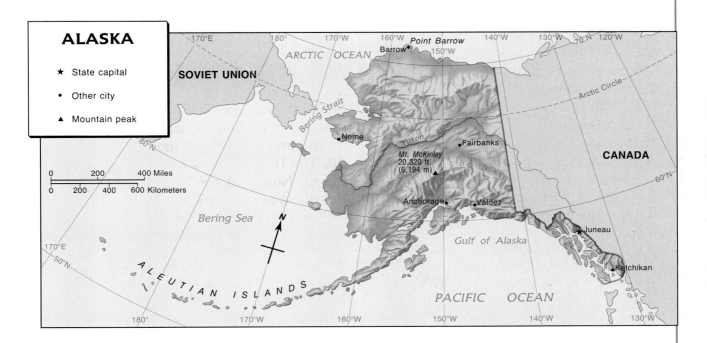

ALASKA

★ State capital
• Other city
▲ Mountain peak

CHAPTER 2

OUR COUNTRY'S REGIONS

FOCUS

America is people.
Young people, old people,
People from every country of the globe.

The writer Ruth Tooze wrote these words about America.
You know that the United States has people of different ages
and backgrounds. But did you know that the people in each
region of our country also differ from one another? In the last
chapter you looked at the United States as a whole. Now let's
divide our country into regions and take a closer look at the
people who live and work in each one.

1 The Northeast–A Bustling Region

READ TO LEARN

 Key Vocabulary

manufacturing
government
megalopolis

Key Places

Piedmont
New York City
Washington, D.C.

Read Aloud

What do you see in your mind when you think of the Northeast? Tiny New England villages? Large cities? Peaceful forests? Noisy factories? All of these images are correct. The Northeast has a little bit of everything.

The Northeast region is actually made up of two sections—the New England states and the Middle Atlantic states. In this lesson, you will study both of these sections and see how they are alike and how they are different.

Read for Purpose

1. **WHAT YOU KNOW:** What are the most important businesses in the part of the country where you live?
2. **WHAT YOU WILL LEARN:** Why is the Northeast described as a bustling region?

THE NEW ENGLAND STATES

The northernmost part of the Northeast is known as New England. It includes the states of Connecticut, Rhode Island, Massachusetts, New Hampshire, Vermont, and Maine.

From the air, New England looks like a series of wrinkles. It is a rocky land with only a thin cover of soil. Winters here are long and cold. People in Vermont sometimes say that their climate is "nine months snow and three months poor sledding."

Forests cover most of the New England states. In the fall, the leaves of maple and birch trees turn bright shades of red, yellow, and orange. Every fall, thousands of people visit New England to see the trees showing off their colors.

The people of New England have learned to use nature's gifts. From the forest they cut down trees for wood and paper. They bring in fish from the sea. From their hills they mine granite and marble for buildings in faraway cities.

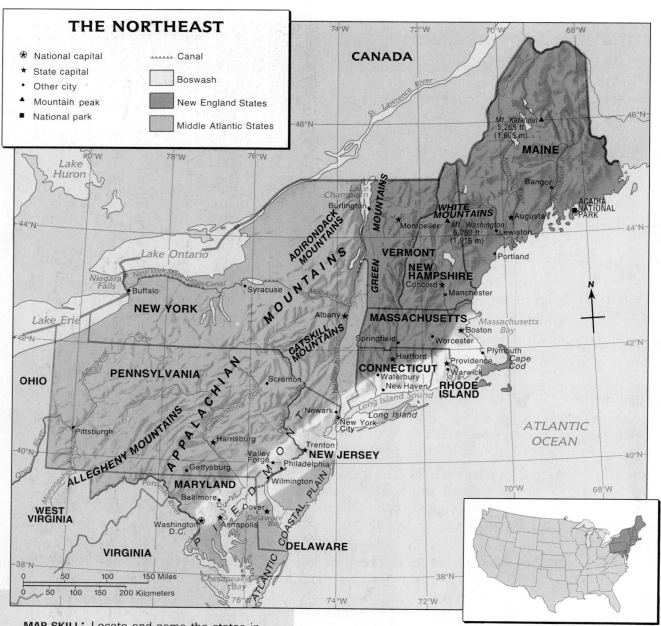

THE NORTHEAST

- ⊛ National capital
- ★ State capital
- • Other city
- ▲ Mountain peak
- ■ National park
- ⋯⋯ Canal
- Boswash
- New England States
- Middle Atlantic States

MAP SKILL: Locate and name the states in the Northeast. Which Middle Atlantic state shares a border with three New England states?

THE MIDDLE ATLANTIC STATES

The Northeast region also includes the Middle Atlantic states—New York, Pennsylvania, New Jersey, Maryland, and Delaware. You can see from the map on this page that these states stretch out along the Atlantic Coastal Plain.

The coastal plain, which you read about in Chapter 1, extends inland from the seashore. Then, suddenly, the land rises. To the west you will find the **Piedmont** (pēd' mont), the rolling hills at the foot of the Appalachian Mountains. In Italian, *piedmont* means "foot of the mountain."

THE MANUFACTURING BELT

The Northeast is one of the country's most important manufacturing regions. Manufacturing means making things by machinery. The Middle Atlantic states have so many factories that they are known as the country's Manufacturing Belt.

One reason so much manufacturing is done in the Northeast is that more people live here than in any other region of the country. Businesses are located here to be near large numbers of skilled workers. These people produce machines, clothing, paper, cameras, computers, and many other products.

SERVICES AND COMMUNICATIONS

Many people in the Northeast have jobs providing services. Instead of manufacturing goods, they help other people or businesses. For example, they might help customers in restaurants, hotels, stores, and banks. Or they might work in medicine, government, or education. Can you think of two kinds of jobs in which people work in medicine?

Other people make a living by providing us with information. The Northeast is a center of communications. Many of the country's largest newspapers and radio and television stations are located here. They tell us about what is happening in the Northeast and around the world.

MAJOR CITIES

The Northeast has more large cities than any other region. New York City is the country's largest city, with more than 7 million people. It is a center of trade, banking, art, television, fashion, theater, and other businesses.

Streets in New York City often are crowded with people and traffic. What attracts people to cities like New York?

Another major city in the Northeast is our country's capital, Washington, D.C. Find Washington, D.C., on the map on the opposite page. Note that the city is not part of any state. Our capital was built on land given to the country by Maryland and Virginia when George Washington was our country's President.

39

The White House (above) and the Capitol (right) are in Washington, D.C.

Every year millions of visitors crowd the streets of our nation's capital. They come to see their national **government** at work. A government is the group of people in charge of ruling a country, state, or city. Visitors tour the White House, where the President lives, and the Capitol, where the senators and representatives make our country's laws.

MEGALOPOLIS

New York City and Washington, D.C., are part of a huge **megalopolis** (meg ə lop' ə lis). A megalopolis is a group of cities that have grown so close together they seem to form one city.

Many people call the megalopolis that includes New York and Washington, D.C., **Boswash**, because it extends from Boston to Washington, D.C. Boswash is a 400-mile-long (640-km) strip of cities, suburbs, and towns. Once these communities were separated by farms and forests. But as they increased in size, they spread out and grew together. Today one fifth of all Americans live in Boswash.

A BUSTLING REGION

The Northeast is a busy place. Of the five regions that you will read about, it has the most people, the most factories, and the most large cities. Why do you think so many people like living in such a busy place?

Check Your Reading

1. Name three kinds of jobs in which people provide information to others.
2. Name two major businesses in the Northeast.
3. **GEOGRAPHY SKILL:** What landforms are found in the Northeast?
4. **THINKING SKILL:** Review this lesson and list all the characteristics of a megalopolis.

NEIGHBORHOOD YOUTH CENTER

Two police officers in a poor neighborhood in New York City were worried about some of the teenagers there. Many of them had left school. They did not have any goals or skills. With time on their hands and no place to go, they began causing trouble on the streets of their neighborhood. Two police officers wanted to show them that there was something better than life on the streets.

One of the officers, George Hankins, had been a champion boxer in the United States Army. He knew that the same effort and training that went into becoming a good athlete could give a boy or girl confidence and direction. So Hankins and his partner, George Pearson, decided to set up a boxing club in the neighborhood.

"Teach those troublemakers to fight?" said some other New York City police officers. "You must be crazy!" But Hankins and Pearson used their own savings to buy boxing gloves and equipment. They started the Fort Apache Youth Center and Boxing Club at a local school. Hankins even left the police force to run the new youth center.

Within a short time, local businesses began to give money to the center. Then one day, a Fort Apache boxing student saved the life of a local police officer.

Members of the police force who had once doubted the center now supported it. The youth center was a success.

Today the Fort Apache Youth Center has its own building. Boys still train on the boxing and exercise equipment. But now there are girls at the center, too. Hankins and Pearson have expanded activities to include an after-school program to help children with their reading and math. Hot meals are provided for children whose parents work. There are sewing and painting classes, weekend dances, and field trips.

Each week 300 boys and girls come through the doors of the Fort Apache Youth Center. To many, it is a second home. Hankins and Pearson are like fathers to those who use the center. As the young people enter, they pass a sign that says, "WE DO NOT SAY WE CAN'T. WE SAY WE WILL TRY."

2 The Southeast—A Region of Change

READ TO LEARN

Key Vocabulary

agriculture
economy
industry

Key Places

Williamsburg
Birmingham

Read Aloud

In 1919 the people of Enterprise, Alabama, built a statue to honor a bug. In a small park in the middle of town stands a large goddess holding a boll weevil above her head. The insect looks like some ugly space creature that you might see in a science-fiction movie.

A few years earlier, boll weevils had begun munching on cotton plants throughout the Southeast. The cotton fields around Enterprise were destroyed. Why, then, do you think the town of Enterprise honored this nasty bug? The answer may surprise you. It is part of the story of change in the Southeast.

Read for Purpose

1. **WHAT YOU KNOW:** What kinds of changes do you see happening in the area where you live?
2. **WHAT YOU WILL LEARN:** How has farming changed in the Southeast?

THE LAND OF COTTON

Find the 12 states in the Southeast on the map on the opposite page. They are Virginia, West Virginia, Kentucky, Tennessee, North Carolina, South Carolina, Georgia, Florida, Alabama, Mississippi, Arkansas, and Louisiana.

For more than 100 years, the most important crop grown in the Southeast was cotton. Cotton needs six months of warm weather and plenty of summer rain. The climate of this region meets these needs perfectly. It is hot during the spring and summer, and mild during the winter. Most of the rain falls in the summer.

When boll weevils began destroying cotton fields in the Southeast, farmers knew they would have to make some changes. They no longer could grow only cotton. The boll weevil forced them to diversify, that is, to produce a variety of crops.

DIVERSIFIED AGRICULTURE

Today a wide variety of crops are grown in the Southeast, making it a region of diversified agriculture, or farming. The flat land along the Atlantic coast and the gulf coast is part of the coastal plain. Many kinds of fruits and vegetables grow well here.

Now find the Mississippi River on the map. The Mississippi River Valley is wide and flat where the river empties into the Gulf of Mexico. Rice, cotton, and sugarcane grow well in the wet lowlands along the banks of the river.

To the east, the Appalachian Mountains rise between the Atlantic Coastal Plain and the Mississippi River. Dairy

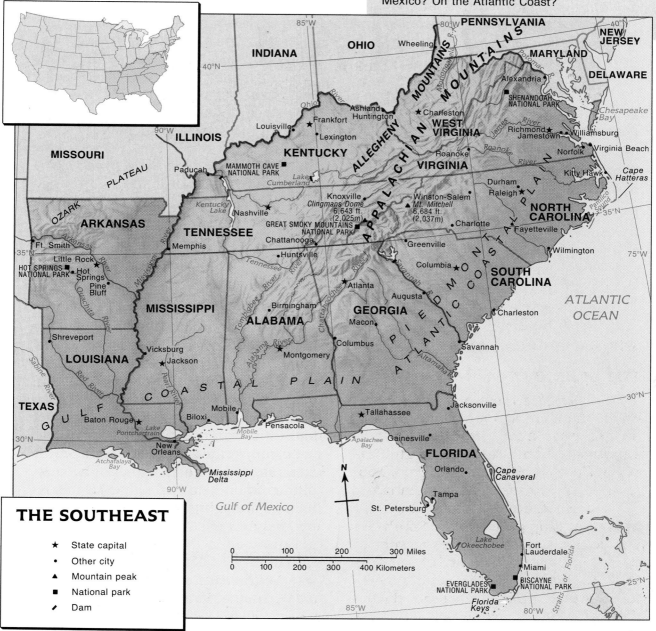

MAP SKILL: Locate and name the states in the Southeast. Which cities are on the Gulf of Mexico? On the Atlantic Coast?

THE SOUTHEAST

★ State capital
• Other city
▲ Mountain peak
■ National park
✐ Dam

43

cattle, peaches, and tobacco are raised on the gentle hills of the Piedmont. Corn and apples grow well in the steep valleys of the Appalachian Mountains. West Virginians joke about farmers in their state who "work on land so steep that they keep falling out of their cornfields."

Diversified agriculture saved farmers in the Southeast and in towns like Enterprise. Thanks to the boll weevil, people began planting vegetables and fruits where once only cotton had grown. Many farmers also began to raise cattle, hogs, and chickens. As farmers diversified, they made more money than ever before. That's why the town of Enterprise has a statue of the ugly little boll weevil.

INDUSTRY IN THE SOUTHEAST

Diversified agriculture is only part of the economy in the Southeast. An economy is the way people use resources to make and sell goods and services. Once, the Southeast was mostly rural. Most people lived on farms, and agriculture was the most important part of the economy. Today most people here live in cities and work in factories or offices.

Many industries have come to the Southeast to be near the region's natural resources. An industry is a branch of business or manufacturing that makes a product or service. All the companies that produce cloth, for example, make up the textile industry.

The coal-mining industry is centered on rich coal deposits in the Appalachian Mountains. Iron deposits brought the steel industry to Birmingham, Alabama. The city is near the coal, limestone, and iron that are needed to make steel. Large deposits of oil and natural gas in Mississippi, Arkansas, and Louisiana are made into gasoline, jet fuel, and other valuable products.

Furniture factories and paper mills were started in the Southeast because of the region's forests. Other industries use the crops grown nearby. For example, textile mills from Virginia to Georgia turn cotton into thread, and thread into cloth and clothing. A North Carolina textile mill makes enough denim each year to wrap around the entire world twice.

Steel making is an important industry in the Southeast. Which natural resources are needed to make steel?

44

Visitors to Williamsburg can see how people lived in the early years of our country. What would it have been like to live then?

TOURISM

Warm, sunny beaches, thick forests, and beautiful rivers and lakes bring many visitors to the Southeast. Each year thousands of tourists come to Florida to see Walt Disney World and the Kennedy Space Center at Cape Canaveral.

One of the country's best-known historic sites is in the Southeast. The town of Williamsburg, Virginia, has been restored to show visitors what life was like in the 1700s. They can see how early Americans dressed, the kinds of work they did, and what their homes looked like. Visiting Williamsburg today is like going back in time more than 200 years!

THE CHANGING SOUTHEAST

Visitors to the Southeast find a region that is changing rapidly. The "land of cotton" is now a region of diversified agriculture and industry. What has not changed is the natural beauty of the Southeast. It is still there for all Americans to enjoy.

 Check Your Reading

1. What kinds of crops are grown in the Southeast?
2. What do you think attracts industry to the Southeast?
3. What kinds of activities attract tourists to the Southeast?
4. THINKING SKILL: Classify all the goods produced in the Southeast. What do the groups you made tell you about life in that region?

45

3 The Middle West—A Region of Contrasts

READ TO LEARN

Key Places

Great Lakes   Chicago
Illinois Waterway   Detroit

Read Aloud

. . . The miles of fresh-plowed soil,
Heavy and black, full of strength and harshness . . .

These words by the American writer Willa Cather describe the farmland of the Middle West. The flat plains stretch for more than 1,000 miles (1,600 km) from the Appalachians to the Rocky Mountains. They are covered with some of the best soil on the earth. This soil makes the plains a good farming region. The Middle West is also an industrial region. The states that border the Great Lakes are as important for their factories as for their farmland.

Read for Purpose

1. **WHAT YOU KNOW:** In Chapter 1, you read about the major landforms of the United States. What landforms cover the Middle West?
2. **WHAT YOU WILL LEARN:** Why is this region known as "America's breadbasket"?

THE SECTIONS OF THE MIDDLE WEST

You can see from the map on the opposite page that the Middle West is made up of two large areas. The Great Lakes states are Ohio, Indiana, Illinois, Michigan, Wisconsin, and Minnesota. The Plains states are North Dakota, South Dakota, Nebraska, Iowa, Missouri, and Kansas. As you read this lesson, you will see how these sections are alike and how they are different.

THE GREAT LAKES

Look again at the map of the Middle West. As you can see, the Great Lakes are in the northeast corner of this region. These five lakes are so large that they hold one fourth of all the fresh water in the world—enough to cover every inch of the United States with 12 feet (3.7 m) of water.

The Great Lakes are part of a great water transportation system. Ships can travel on the Great Lakes all the way from Minnesota to New York State. The

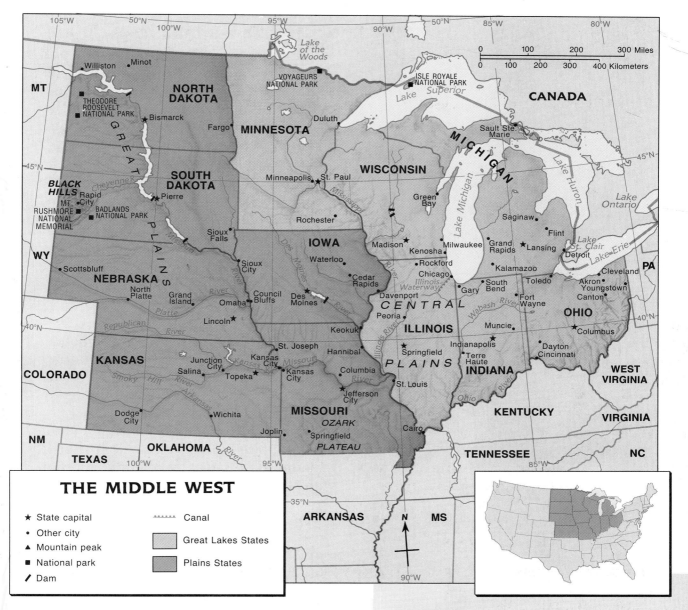

THE MIDDLE WEST

★ State capital
• Other city
▲ Mountain peak
■ National park
⟋ Dam

⋯⋯ Canal
░ Great Lakes States
▓ Plains States

MAP SKILL: Locate and name the states clustered around the Great Lakes. Name the states located on the Great Plains.

lake farthest to the east, Lake Ontario, is connected to the Atlantic Ocean by the St. Lawrence River.

Although some Great Lakes ports lie far inland, ships can carry goods from these ports to any port in the world. This is made possible by a series of canals built by the United States and Canada. One canal connects Lake Superior and Lake Huron. Another one connects Lake Erie and Lake Ontario.

The Great Lakes are also linked to the Mississippi River by the Illinois Waterway. This is a water road running through the middle of the United States. Ships and barges using the Illinois Waterway can travel from the Great Lakes all the way to the Gulf of Mexico.

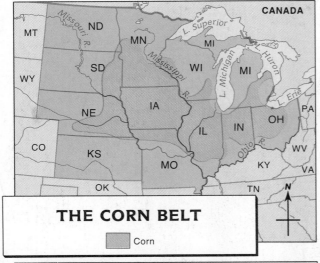

THE CORN BELT

☐ Corn

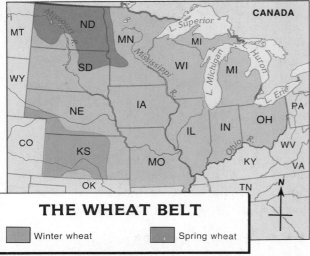

THE WHEAT BELT

☐ Winter wheat   ☐ Spring wheat

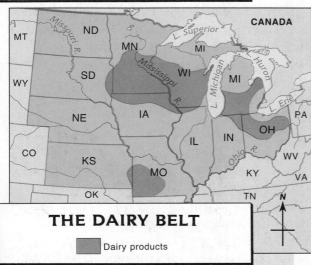

THE DAIRY BELT

☐ Dairy products

MAP SKILL: Locate the states where corn and wheat are grown. Which states are leading dairy producers?

GREAT LAKES INDUSTRY

Manufacturing is an important part of the economy of the Great Lakes states. For example, the area is a major steel-making center. The steel industry is located here because of the region's natural resources and low-cost water transportation.

You learned in Chapter 1 that iron and coal are needed to make steel. Iron comes from mines in Minnesota and Wisconsin. It is carried by boat across the Great Lakes to steel-manufacturing centers such as Cleveland, Ohio, and Gary, Indiana. Coal from nearby coal fields is shipped to the steel plants by river or rail.

Steel manufacturing has helped make Chicago, Illinois, our country's third-largest city. Much of the world's steel and machinery come from factories around Chicago.

Detroit, Michigan, is the center of the automobile industry. Much of the steel made in the Great Lakes area ends up in American cars.

THE CORN BELT

Farms cover most of the Plains. So much corn, wheat, and soybeans are grown here that the Plains are called "America's breadbasket."

The most important crop in the humid Central Plains is corn. The states from Ohio to the central part of Nebraska are called the Corn Belt. Find the Corn Belt states on the map on this page.

Much of the corn raised on the Central Plains "walks to market." It is used to feed farm animals such as hogs and beef cattle that are raised for sale. The animals are fed on corn until they are fat and ready to be shipped to market. Farmers can make more money selling

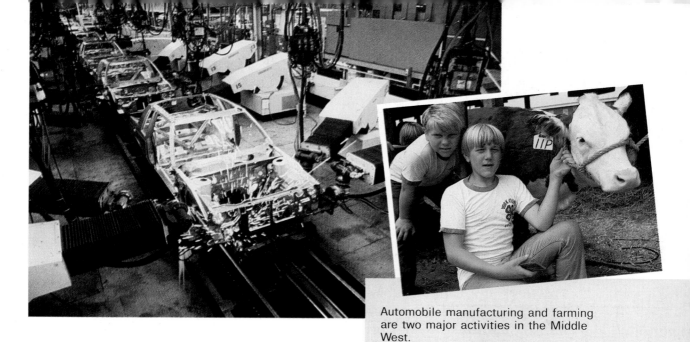

Automobile manufacturing and farming are two major activities in the Middle West.

animals for meat than they can selling corn. More meat is produced in the Corn Belt than in any other part of the country.

THE DAIRY BELT

North of the Corn Belt lies the Dairy Belt. As the map on the opposite page shows, Minnesota, Wisconsin, Michigan, and Ohio are the Dairy Belt states. Dairy farmers need to be near cities so their fresh milk can reach customers quickly. They also need plenty of farmland so they can raise crops to feed their cows during the winter.

The Dairy Belt meets both these needs. The area is close to customers in the large cities on the shores of the Great Lakes. At the same time, there is plenty of good farmland where hay and oats can be grown for feed.

THE WHEAT BELT

Wheat grows well in the dry climate of the Great Plains. This area is the nation's Wheat Belt. Find the Wheat Belt states on the map on the opposite page. Every year farmers here gamble with the weather. If there is enough rain, the wheat will grow. But summer hailstorms or thundershowers can ruin the wheat crop.

Plains farmers worry about insects or disease, which can destroy crops. And crop prices can rise or fall suddenly. So farmers must know much more than how to grow crops.

A REGION OF CONTRASTS

The Middle West is both quiet and fast-paced. You can drive for miles without seeing much activity. Or you can drive through busy cities.

 Check Your Reading

1. Why is industry in the Middle West located near the Great Lakes?
2. Why has the Middle West been called "America's breadbasket"?
3. What problems do wheat farmers face in the Middle West?
4. **THINKING SKILL:** Compare and contrast life for a family living in the Corn Belt and life for a family living near the Great Lakes.

4 The Southwest—A Land of Open Spaces

READ TO LEARN

Key Vocabulary

aqueduct

Key Places

Colorado Plateau   Phoenix

Read Aloud

In 1877 a man set out to look for gold and silver in the Arizona desert. His friends said he would not come back alive. "Instead of a mine," warned one person, "you'll find a tombstone." The man went anyway and soon discovered silver. He named the place where he struck it rich Tombstone.

One hundred years ago, the Southwest seemed wild and dangerous. Most Americans thought only people looking for adventure would want to live there. But today it is one of the fastest-growing regions of the country.

Read for Purpose

1. **WHAT YOU KNOW:** Is the part of the country where you live growing in any way? Why or why not?
2. **WHAT YOU WILL LEARN:** Why has the Southwest become one of our fastest-growing regions?

LANDFORMS AND CLIMATE

You can see from the map on the opposite page that the Southwest has only four states. They are Oklahoma, Texas, New Mexico, and Arizona. You should see from the map that western Oklahoma and Texas are part of the Great Plains. In New Mexico, the land rises to form plateaus and mountains. The southern end of the Rocky Mountain range covers much of this state.

The state of Arizona lies on the Colorado Plateau. Most of this high country is fairly level. Tall mesas dot the plateau. A mesa is a flat-topped hill with steep sides. The Colorado Plateau also has hundreds of deep canyons. In Chapter 1, you read about the most famous canyon of all—the Grand Canyon.

The eastern edge of the Southwest is part of Humid America. You know from Chapter 1 that more than 20 inches (50 cm) of precipitation falls in this part of the country every year. There are so many lakes and rivers in eastern Oklahoma that people there say, "If we ever tip over, Texas will be flooded."

But most of the Southwest lies in Arid America, where less than 20 inches (50 cm) of precipitation falls each year. The soil is sandy and rocky. There is more cactus and sagebrush here than forests or grasslands.

CHANGES IN THE SOUTHWEST

For a long time the population of the Southwest grew slowly. Many people thought it was too hot and dry to be a good place to live. Then three *a's*—**aqueducts** (ak' wə duktz), air conditioning, and automobiles—changed life here.

Lack of water once made it impossible for large numbers of people to live in the Southwest. Today water is brought to dry areas by aqueducts. Aqueducts are pipes or canals that are used to carry water long distances from lakes and rivers. People in Arizona and New Mexico drink water brought by aqueducts from the Colorado River. Farmers use this water to raise fruits and vegetables in the desert. Yet too little water remains a problem in the Southwest. People there must be careful not to waste water.

Summer temperatures in much of the Southwest often rise to more than 100°F. (38°C). Doing just about anything is uncomfortable in such heat. Air conditioning, which came into use during the 1950s, allows people to live and work in comfort even when the weather is very hot.

Once travel in the Southwest was hard and even dangerous. There were wide stretches of desert where there was no water for miles. People here felt cut off from the rest of the world. Automobiles changed this by making travel quicker and safer.

MAP SKILL: Locate and name the states of the Southwest. Which state is located on the Gulf of Mexico?

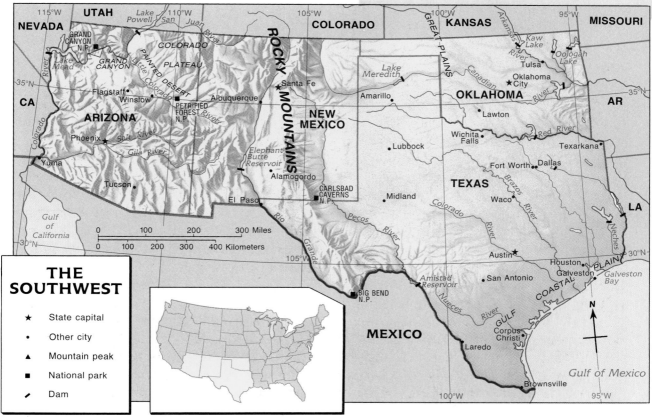

THE SOUTHWEST

★ State capital
• Other city
▲ Mountain peak
■ National park
⬈ Dam

The three *a*'s have made the Southwest a good place to live. In the past 30 years, millions of people have moved here to get away from cold weather and crowded cities.

CITIES OF THE SOUTHWEST

Most people who come to the Southwest want to enjoy its wide open spaces. But they also want to live near cities where there are jobs and stores. Automobiles make this possible. People can live in communities spread out around cities, but they can get to work or shops by car.

Phoenix, Arizona, is one of the Southwest's spread-out cities. One hundred years ago it was just a small group of buildings. Today Phoenix covers an area of more than 324 square miles (839 sq. km) and is the ninth-largest city in the United States.

WATER AND ENERGY

The future growth of the Southwest depends on water and energy. People need water to live. They need energy to run their factories, air conditioners, and cars.

Luckily, Texas, Oklahoma, and New Mexico have large deposits of oil and natural gas. New Mexico is also rich in the uranium that nuclear power plants use to make electricity.

Some people in the Southwest are experimenting with solar, or sun, energy as a source of power. Energy from the sun can be used to heat or cool homes and offices. Today, scientists are looking for better ways to change solar energy into electricity.

Phoenix, Arizona, lies in the Salt River Valley, a flat region surrounded by low mountains. What else can you learn about Phoenix from the picture below?

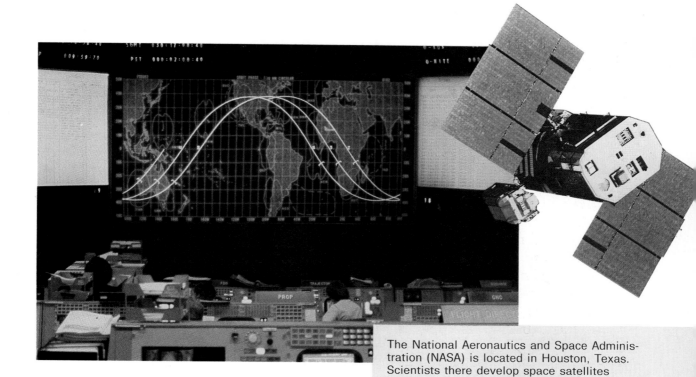

The National Aeronautics and Space Administration (NASA) is located in Houston, Texas. Scientists there develop space satellites like the one shown on the right.

Finding enough water may be harder than finding enough energy. As one farmer says, "You can make gasoline out of cow manure if you have to. But you can't make water."

NEW INDUSTRIES

Many industries in the Southwest are located near natural resources. Texas and Oklahoma are centers of the oil industry. Mining is important in New Mexico and Arizona. Copper, lead, and zinc are some of the minerals that are found here.

Other industries have come to this region because so many people like living in the Southwest. Some Southwest industries make computers and robots. Others make lifesaving equipment for hospitals or rockets to explore space. These industries need large numbers of trained workers. The mild climate and beautiful scenery of the Southwest help businesses to attract such workers.

A LAND OF OPEN SPACES

In the past 30 years, many people have moved to the Southwest. They are attracted by the warm climate. Here they find mountains for hiking and camping. There are lakes for swimming and boating. And there is room for people to spread out and enjoy this broad, open country.

Check Your Reading

1. Name three resources that are used to create energy in the Southwest.
2. How did the three *a*'s make the Southwest a more pleasant place to live?
3. **GEOGRAPHY SKILL:** Describe the landforms and climate of the Southwest.
4. **THINKING SKILL:** Predict what would probably happen if more rain fell in the Southwest.

Decision Making

Key Vocabulary
decision
alternative

What will you wear today? What television program will you watch this weekend? These are just two of the many **decisions**, or choices, that you make every day. Decision making is choosing from a number of **alternatives** to achieve your goal. An alternative is another way of doing something.

Your decisions affect the way you live. Often they influence the lives of people around you. Good decisions are made when you carefully plan what you will select or do.

Trying the Skill
In Lesson 4 you read how one man's decision to dig for gold and silver led to the founding of Tombstone, Arizona. Below is a story of another decision made during the gold and silver mining days of the Old West. Read to find out how that decision was made.

The people in this valley need the wood that my sawmill will produce. I want to finish building the mill. If word gets out that there is gold buried in the mountains nearby, my workers will leave to go and dig for it. My mill will never be finished. I don't want a lot of gold seekers living on my land. I'm going to keep the news of the gold a secret.

1. What did the mill owner consider in making his decision?
2. What alternatives did he come up with?
3. What did he identify as the probable results of each alternative?

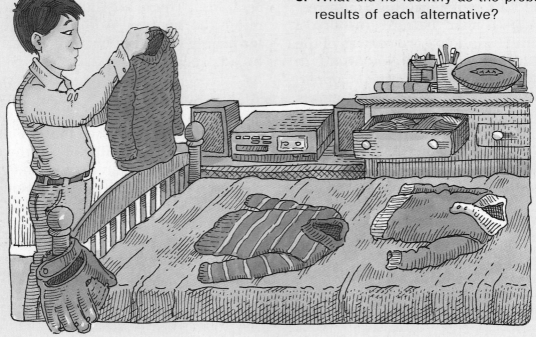

HELPING YOURSELF

The steps on the left help people make good decisions. The example on the right shows one way you might have identified how the man in the story made his decision.

One Way to Make a Decision	Example
1. Identify and clearly define the goal to be achieved.	The man's goal is to finish building his mill. Then he will be able to provide enough wood for the people in his valley.
2. Identify alternatives by which the goal can be achieved.	We know that the mill owner has already found gold. He can tell his workers about the gold or he can keep it a secret.
3. Predict the results of each alternative.	The mill owner predicts that if his workers find out about the gold, they will quit. If they do not know about the gold, they will finish building the mill.
4. Judge each result by determining if it helps or harms you and others.	If the workers quit, the mill owner knows that his mill will never be built. If that happens, he will not achieve his goal.
5. Choose the best alternative.	The best alternative for the mill owner is to keep the gold a secret.

Applying the Skill

Read the following story. Are the steps for making a decision followed?

Uranium is used to produce energy in nuclear power plants. It is my job to find uranium ore. I could search for the uranium on foot. But exploring that way would take time. Another way would be to fly a plane at low altitudes to find areas that might have uranium. But flying costs a lot of money. There has to be a cheaper way, so that nuclear energy won't cost so much.

A third alternative could be to load equipment in a helicopter and fly over areas already identified as having uranium. This choice might save both time and money.

1. What was the goal of the miner?
   a. to get rich quick
   b. to find uranium ore
   c. to fly around the Southwest

2. Which alternative did he *not* consider?
   a. using a helicopter
   b. searching on foot
   c. setting off underground explosions

3. What outcome did the miner think was the most important?
   a. cheap nuclear energy
   b. safety
   c. effect on the environment

Reviewing the Skill

1. What does it mean to make a decision?
2. Name some steps you could take that would help you make good decisions.
3. Why is it important to consider many alternatives when making a decision?

5 The West—A Region of Rapid Growth

READsss TO LEARN

Key Vocabulary

volcano
rain shadow

Key Places

Columbia Plateau
Cascade Range
Seattle

Continental Divide
Prudhoe Bay
Los Angeles

Read Aloud

A few years ago the farmers of Lynndyl, Utah, had the chance to choose their future. Lynndyl could remain a farming area. Or it could become the home of a large coal-burning power plant. But the town could not do both.

Why do you think the farmers had to choose between farming and a new power plant? The reason was water. For years farmers had used water from the nearby Sevier (sə vir′) River to raise cattle and alfalfa. But a new power plant would also need large amounts of water. There was not enough water to run the new power plant and to farm.

Read for Purpose

1. **WHAT YOU KNOW:** Why do you think water is so important for everyday living?
2. **WHAT YOU WILL LEARN:** Why is water such a valuable resource in this region?

HIGH AND DRY

Like the Southwest region, most of the West is dry. The first question that must be asked when people plan new homes, farms, factories, or mines is: Where will the water come from?

You can see from the map on the opposite page that the West is made up of two sections—the Mountain states and the Pacific states. Much of both of these areas is mountainous. Find the Rocky Mountains on the map. They stretch from Alaska, through Canada, and south into Montana, Idaho, Wyoming, and Colorado. Large parts of Idaho and eastern Oregon and Washington lie on the flat, dry Columbia Plateau.

South of the Columbia Plateau lies the Great Basin of Utah and Nevada. Small ranges of hills dot the basin. On a map they might look like rows of caterpillars crawling toward Canada.

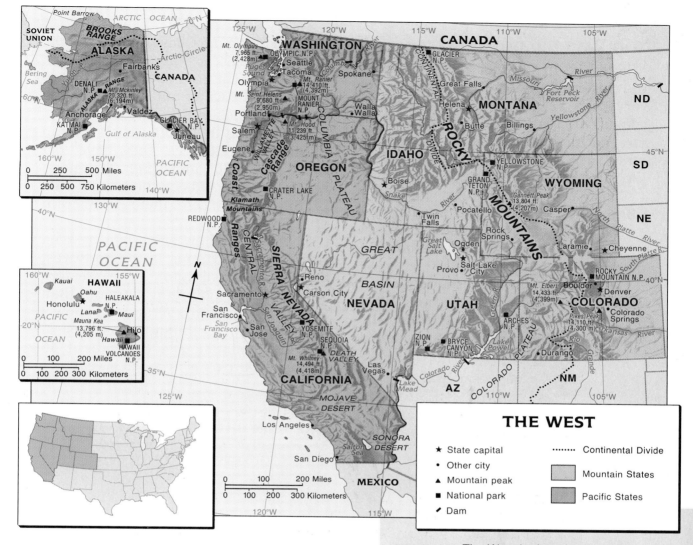

MAP SKILL: The West is dotted with many national parks. Use the legend and the map to locate the parks. Which parks are located in Utah and Wyoming?

MOUNTAINS, VALLEYS, AND VOLCANOES

You can see from the map that the mountains of the Pacific Coast form a giant H. The first upright line of the H is formed by the Coast Ranges, low hills next to the Pacific Ocean.

The second upright line of the H begins with the **Cascade Range** of Oregon and Washington and ends with the Sierra Nevada of California. The Klamath Mountains form the crossbar. Inside the H there are two large valleys—Oregon's Willamette Valley and California's Central Valley.

Hawaii is also mountainous. The Hawaiian Islands were made long ago by **volcanoes**. A volcano is an opening in the earth through which melted rock, ashes, and gas are forced out. These materials rise from deep inside the earth to the surface. As the hot rocks and ashes cool, they form a mountain. The islands of Hawaii are the tops of volcanoes that were built up from the floor of the Pacific Ocean.

THE RAIN SHADOW EFFECT

You read in Chapter 1 that much of the western half of the United States is very dry. Yet some places, like the coastal areas of Washington and Oregon, get rain all year long. It rains so much here that a local joke says, "People don't tan in summer, they rust."

These coastal areas get plenty of rain, while inland areas are dry because of the **rain shadow** effect. As you read about the rain shadow, study the diagram below.

Here is how the rain shadow effect works: Moisture-bearing winds blow across the Pacific Ocean. When the winds reach the coast, they are pushed upward along the Coast Ranges. As the moist air rises, it quickly cools. Since cool air cannot hold as much water as warm air, the water falls as rain on the western slopes of the hills.

By the time the winds reach the top of the Coast Ranges, they have lost much of their moisture. Therefore, much less rain falls on the eastern side of the hills, where there is a "rain shadow."

The rain shadow effect can be seen near Mount Olympus in the northwest corner of Washington. The western slopes of the mountain get more than 200 inches (500 cm) of rain and snow a year. **Seattle**, Washington, just east of Mount Olympus, gets only about 40 inches (100 cm) of rain each year.

DIAGRAM SKILL: This diagram shows the rain shadow effect. On which side of the mountain—west or east—would you be more likely to need a raincoat? Where would you find drier weather?

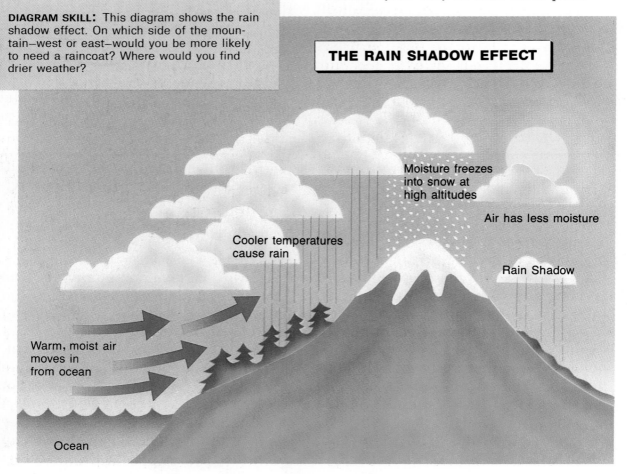

THE RAIN SHADOW EFFECT

Moisture freezes into snow at high altitudes

Air has less moisture

Cooler temperatures cause rain

Rain Shadow

Warm, moist air moves in from ocean

Ocean

Cattle ranchers work outdoors in all kinds of weather. The ranch above is located in Colorado.

THE MOUNTAIN STATES

The Mountain states—Wyoming, Montana, Idaho, Nevada, Utah, and Colorado—cover almost one fourth of the area of the 48 connected states. But only 6 of every 100 Americans live in this large region. Most towns here are small and far apart.

The beauty of the Rocky Mountains draws millions of tourists to these states. Many have their picture taken standing along the Continental Divide. Find the line showing the Continental Divide on the map on page 57. You can see that it zigzags along the high ridges of the Rockies. Rain falling east of the Continental Divide eventually flows to the Atlantic Ocean. Rain falling west of the Continental Divide flows into the Pacific.

RANCHING AND MINING

Only a few places in the mountains have enough water to grow crops. There is much cattle and sheep ranching because these animals do not need as much water. Most ranches are large,

since it takes from 20 to 25 acres (8 to 10 ha) of good grassland to feed just one cow.

The Mountain states have a vast supply of minerals and fossil fuels. For example, the town of Butte, Montana, is said to sit on "the richest hill on earth." Under Butte lies one of the world's largest copper deposits. Gold,

Fishing is a major industry in the Pacific states. Owners of fishing boats often sell their catch to food processing plants. There, workers clean the fish as shown at right, can it, and ship it to markets.

silver, lead, and other minerals are mined in the Mountain states as well. The region is also rich in coal, oil, and natural gas.

THE PACIFIC STATES

The Pacific states are California, Oregon, Washington, Alaska, and Hawaii. These states are known for their beautiful mountains and beaches.

Alaska and Hawaii are the only states that do not border any other state. Alaska lies in the northwest corner of North America. If you look at the map in the Atlas on pages 586–587, you can see that Canada separates Alaska from the rest of the country.

Alaska has the most land of any state. But only Vermont and Wyoming have fewer people. Alaska is also our most northern state. Summers here are short and cool. Winters are long and cold.

The island state of Hawaii lies in the Pacific Ocean, 2,100 miles (3,379 km) southwest of California. Hawaii is our most southern state. The climate here is warm all year.

FORESTS, FARMS, AND FISHING

The land and sea play important roles in the economy of the Pacific states. Forests cover large parts of every state. Oregon is the leading lumber state in the country. Next are California and Washington.

Farming is a big business in every Pacific state except Alaska, where the growing season is very short. Farmlands in California are among the richest in the world. Fruits and vegetables from this state end up on dinner tables and in lunch boxes across the country. From Hawaii's farms come pineapples, sugarcane, and coffee.

The fishing industry plays an important role in the economy of all the Pacific states. Alaska leads the country in the amount of fish caught each year. Factories here freeze or can salmon, crab, shrimp, and other fish as fast as fishing boats can bring them in.

INDUSTRY IN THE PACIFIC STATES

The Pacific states have a great variety of industries. As in the Mountain states, some industries are near valuable natural resources. In 1968 a huge oil deposit was found near **Prudhoe Bay** in northern Alaska. Despite its bitter cold climate, Prudhoe Bay is now an important source of oil.

A sunny climate brought the movie industry to **Los Angeles**, California. Most early movies were made outdoors. The warm, dry climate of this area was ideal for making movies.

A REGION OF RAPID GROWTH

The West is growing quickly. A few years ago California passed New York to become the state with the most people. Los Angeles is now the country's second-largest city. People move to this region to enjoy its scenery and climate.

They find jobs in its many factories that make airplanes, computers, and communications equipment.

As these states grow, the question we started with becomes more important than ever: Where will the water come from?

Movie-making helped make California famous. Here, a director "shoots" a scene for a movie. Some California studios are open to visitors.

Check Your Reading

1. What is the rain shadow effect? How does it determine the ways people use their land?
2. What is one major worry of people beginning businesses in the West?
3. In the early days of film, what made Los Angeles a good place to make movies?
4. **THINKING SKILL:** In what ways is the Southwest like the West?

IDEAS TO REMEMBER

■ The Northeast section of the United States—New England and the Middle Atlantic states—is a region of bustling cities and important manufacturing centers.

■ Diversified agriculture, industries, and tourism have brought change to the Southeast region.

■ The Middle West is a region of farms, fast-paced cities, and busy industrial centers.

■ Once a sparsely populated desert region, the Southwest today is one of the fastest-growing regions in the United States.

■ The West is a region of great mountain ranges, wide open spaces, big cities, and diverse industries.

REVIEWING VOCABULARY

aqueduct	manufacturing
agriculture	megalopolis
economy	piedmont
government	rain shadow
industry	volcano

Number a paper from 1 to 10. Beside each number write the word or term from the list above that best completes each sentence.

1. Boswash is an example of a _____.
2. An island can be formed by a _____ that built up from the floor of the ocean.
3. The leaders in charge of ruling your state work for the state _____.
4. An area of gently rolling hills at the base of mountains is called a _____.
5. Because of the _____ effect, coastal areas get plenty of rain while inland areas are drier.
6. Farming is an important part of the _____ in the Middle West.
7. The shoe _____ is made up of all the companies that make and sell shoes.
8. The Southeast is a region of diversified farming, or _____.
9. A large pipe or _____ carries water from lakes or rivers to dry areas.
10. Many people in the Northeast have jobs in _____, where goods are made by machinery.

REVIEWING FACTS

1. What two sections, or groups of states, make up the Northeast?
2. Why is the word *bustling* used to describe the Northeast?
3. Why did the Southeast become a region of diversified agriculture?
4. Name three natural resources found in the Southeast that have caused industries to develop there.
5. What natural resource has made it possible for the Middle West to become the nation's "breadbasket"?
6. What bodies of water make it possible for ships to travel from the Middle West to New York? From the Middle West to the Gulf of Mexico?
7. Why is it important for dairy farmers to live near cities?
8. Why do many people consider the Southwest a desirable place to live?
9. Why are cattle and sheep ranching important in the Mountain states?
10. Name three major industries in the West. Why did each one develop there?

WRITING ABOUT MAIN IDEAS

1. **Writing a Paragraph:** Imagine that you have enough money to start a small business. In what region would you choose to set up your business? Write a paragraph discussing how your choice of location might influence the kind of business you would decide to start.

2. **Writing a Commercial:** Review the lesson in this chapter that discusses the region where you live. Using that information and any other facts about the area that you have, write a television commercial encouraging people to move to or visit your region.

3. **Writing a Letter:** Imagine you are taking a trip through the United States. Write a letter to a friend describing some of the sights you have visited in each region.

BUILDING SKILLS: DECISION MAKING

1. What is another word for decision?
2. What steps could you follow to make good decisions?
3. Think of a decision you must make soon. For example, are you deciding whether or not to join a certain club? Review the steps below to reach a decision.
4. What might happen if you left out one of the decision-making steps?
5. How can knowing how to make good decisions be helpful?

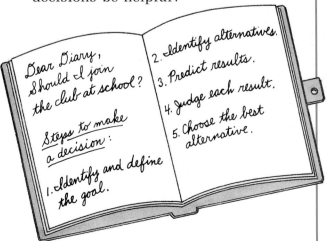

Dear Diary,
Should I join the club at school?

Steps to make a decision:
1. Identify and define the goal.
2. Identify alternatives.
3. Predict results.
4. Judge each result.
5. Choose the best alternative.

REVIEWING VOCABULARY

agriculture	industry
climate	mineral
economy	natural resource
geography	plateau
government	precipitation

Number a paper from 1 to 10. Beside each number write the word or term from the list above that matches the statement.

1. The study of a place and the way people live in it
2. The group of people in charge of ruling a city, state, or nation
3. Things that we need and use from nature, such as trees and water
4. The weather in a place over a long period of time
5. A branch of business or manufacturing that produces a product or service
6. Moisture that falls to the earth as rain or snow
7. The way people use resources to produce and sell goods and services
8. Farming
9. An area of flat land that is higher than the surrounding land
10. A substance found in the earth that is neither plant nor animal

◀═▶ WRITING ABOUT THE UNIT

1. **Writing Sentences:** Which of these places probably has a wetter climate: (a) the eastern slope of the Coastal Ranges or the western coast of the state of Washington; (b) the states on the Atlantic Coastal Plain or the states in the Great Basin? In a few sentences explain your answers.

2. **Writing an Essay:** Write a short essay on how the regions of the United States depend on one another. Give two or three examples of the products or resources one region may need from another region. Remember to give your essay a title.

3. **Writing a Poem:** Choose one region of the United States discussed in this unit. Review the information on its landforms, resources, climate, and economy. Then write a poem that captures the spirit of the region.

4. **Making a Puzzle:** Make up a crossword puzzle based on the information in this unit. Use at least ten words in the puzzle. Write a clue for each one.

ACTIVITIES

1. **Playing "Which Region Am I?":** Divide the class into five teams. Each team should prepare clues for playing "Which Region Am I?" The teams should take turns guessing which region is being described.

2. **Making a State Map:** Make a map of your state showing its natural resources, major products, and main cities. Use the maps in this unit and the Atlas maps on pages 590–591 and 592–593 to help you. Show the location of your community on your map.

3. **Working Together to Trace Natural Resources:** With a partner, list at least three items in your classroom. Then do research to see what natural resources went into making each item. Use the maps on page 31 to see where those resources can be found.

GLOBAL GRID

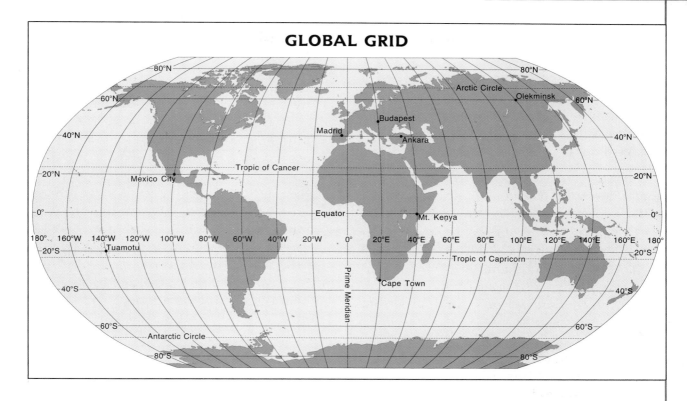

BUILDING SKILLS:
UNDERSTANDING LATITUDE
AND LONGITUDE

1. If you know the latitude and longitude of a place, how can you find that place on a map?

2. Use the map to give the latitude and longitude of Mt. Kenya.

3. What city is found at 20°N, 100°W?

4. What two lines of latitude shown on the map cross Australia?

5. How do parallels of latitude help you understand the climate of a place?

LINKING PAST, PRESENT, AND FUTURE

One way to make sure we have enough natural resources in the future is to be careful not to waste them today. Choose one natural resource and then develop a plan to help the people in your community use that resource wisely. Write a short essay describing your plan and explaining how you will convince others to follow it.

UNIT 2

SETTLING AMERICA

WHERE WE ARE

The map shows you that we are in North America. Thousands of years ago many Indian groups lived here. Each of these groups had its own way of doing things. From the plants and animals around them, the Indians built homes and made tools. Depending upon where they lived, some Indians were hunters and gatherers. Others were farmers. In Unit 2 you will read how the first Americans learned to adapt to the areas in which they lived.

INDIAN GROUPS OF NORTH AMERICA

- Arctic
- Subarctic
- Northwest Coast
- California
- Basin and Plateau
- Southwest
- Plains
- Eastern Woodlands
- Middle America
- Caribbean
- Northern Mexico

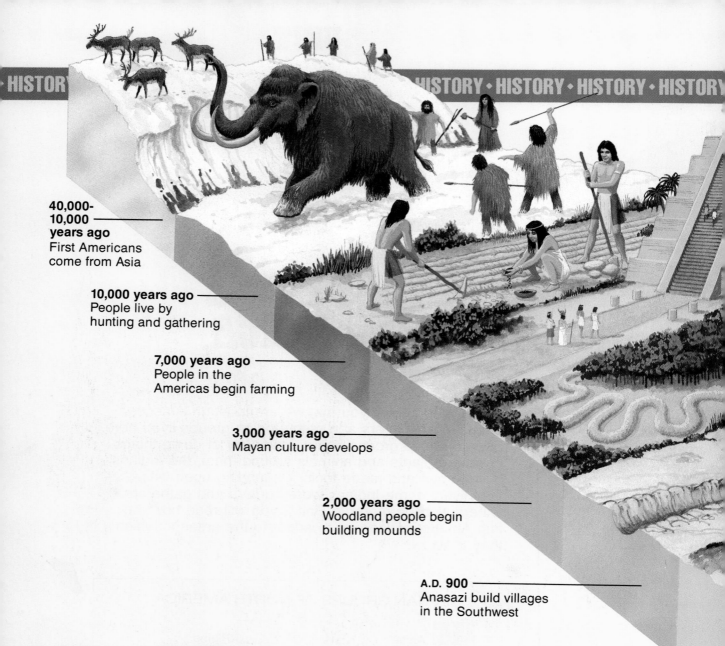

**40,000-
10,000
years ago**
First Americans
come from Asia

10,000 years ago
People live by
hunting and gathering

7,000 years ago
People in the
Americas begin farming

3,000 years ago
Mayan culture develops

2,000 years ago
Woodland people begin
building mounds

A.D. 900
Anasazi build villages
in the Southwest

A.D. 1438
Incas build empire
in Peru

A.D. 1570
Iroquois League
is formed

WHAT HAPPENED

The time line shows that the
first people to live in North America
came from Asia. They traveled across
a narrow strip of land that once connected
the two continents. The earliest people in
America were hunters and food gatherers. Then
the Indians of northern Mexico began farming. They
also built great cities and long roads. Much later farming
spread to the Southwest and to the Eastern Woodlands. In
this unit you will discover how farming changed the way the
first Americans lived.

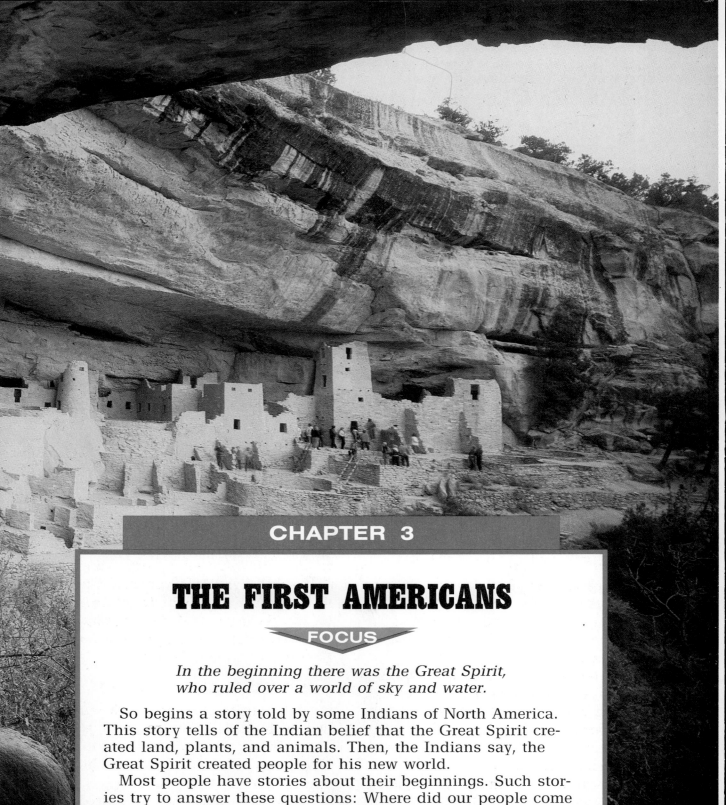

CHAPTER 3

THE FIRST AMERICANS

▼ FOCUS

*In the beginning there was the Great Spirit,
who ruled over a world of sky and water.*

So begins a story told by some Indians of North America. This story tells of the Indian belief that the Great Spirit created land, plants, and animals. Then, the Indians say, the Great Spirit created people for his new world.

Most people have stories about their beginnings. Such stories try to answer these questions: Where did our people come from? How did they live in the past? In this chapter we will try to answer these questions for the first Americans.

1 Asian Hunters in America

READx TO LEARN

Key Vocabulary

Ice Age   strait
glacier   land bridge

Key Places

Bering Strait
Beringia

Read Aloud

The story of the first people to settle in America begins many thousands of years ago. Little is known about the first Americans, but their story is very important. For these earliest Americans are the ancestors of the American Indians. Knowing their story, with all its triumphs and defeats, helps us to better understand our own history.

Read for Purpose

1. **WHAT YOU KNOW:** What might life have been like for the first people to live in America?
2. **WHAT YOU WILL LEARN:** Who were the first Americans, and how did they live?

THE ICE AGE

The geography of the earth was very different when the first people came to America. This was a time known as the **Ice Age**. It began more than 70,000 years ago.

The Ice Age was a long, cold time when thick sheets of ice, or **glaciers**, covered most of the earth. Places that are deserts today were covered by lakes and swamps. Huge animals roamed the plains and forests.

Only animals with thick fur coats could live through the long, cold winters of the Ice Age. Great herds of grass-eating animals such as caribou (kar′ ə bü), moose, deer, and elk roamed near the edge of the glaciers. Although their heavy coats protected these animals against the cold, they faced other dangers. Meat-eating animals, such as the saber-toothed tiger, often hunted them for food.

SURVIVAL OF THE HUNTERS

Groups of hunters also followed the animal herds. How were these people able to survive in this very cold world? Two important discoveries helped make their survival possible.

First, these early people discovered how to make and use fire. In a world without matches, this was a tremendous discovery—maybe the greatest

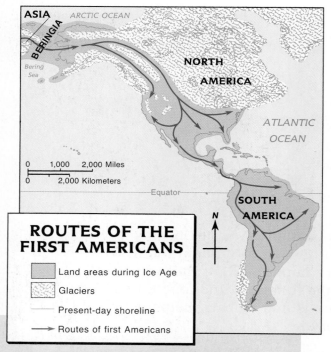

ROUTES OF THE FIRST AMERICANS

Land areas during Ice Age

Glaciers

Present-day shoreline

Routes of first Americans

MAP SKILL: Glaciers like the one shown below covered much of the earth during the Ice Age. Use the map above to locate the area covered by glaciers. How far south did they extend?

discovery up to that time. During the Ice Age, hunters stayed near their campfires to escape the cold and to cook their food.

Second, the earliest people survived because they had learned how to make weapons and tools. By day they hunted animals with their spears. They got most of their food from the animals they hunted. They also got clothing from the animals' thick fur skins.

A LAND BRIDGE TO A NEW WORLD

It was the hunt that probably brought the first group of people to America. But how did these hunters reach North America?

During the Ice Age the earth was much colder than it is today. Much of the earth's water was frozen in glaciers like the one shown in the picture on page 72. In fact, so much water was turned into ice that the water levels of the oceans had dropped. At times the oceans were more than 300 feet (90 m) lower than they are today. Places once covered by shallow seas became dry land.

Look at the map on page 72. Notice how close Asia is to North America. Today the Bering Strait separates Asia from North America. A strait is a narrow waterway that connects two larger bodies of water. At its narrowest point, the Bering Strait is only 56 miles (90 km) wide.

When the ocean dropped during the Ice Age, the floor of the Bering Strait became dry land. It formed a wide land bridge joining Asia and North America. This land bridge is called Beringia (ber' ən gē ə).

Beringia was a wide marshy plain. As herds of animals moved there to graze on grasses and other plants, they were followed by Asian hunters looking for food. Then one day some of the hunters wandered from Beringia to explore the hills of what is now Alaska. Without knowing it, they had become the first Americans.

THE FIRST AMERICANS

These wandering hunters were the ancestors of present-day Indians. They may have come to North America as long as 40,000 years ago. Eventually, they traveled south from Alaska. By about 10,000 years ago, when the water from melting glaciers again covered Beringia, people spread from the Arctic to the southern tip of South America.

These Alaskans are descendants of the first people to come to the Americas. The earliest Americans carved drawings into rocks and boulders like those shown below. What kinds of drawings can you see in the large rock?

These spear points were carved by the first Americans. How do you think the points were attached to the spears?

You can trace the routes of the first Americans as they traveled from the Arctic throughout North and South America on the map on page 72.

The first Americans lived by hunting. Their hunting spears had points made of hard stones such as flint. The hunters also used tools made of bone or flint to scrape meat and hair from animal skins. The skins could then be made into warm clothing.

Food was not hard to find. Indian legends tell of coming to a land "full of game," with animals "as tall as the high branches of a cottonwood tree." The biggest animals were huge, hairy elephants called mammoths. The largest mammoths were 14 feet (4.3 m) tall at the shoulder—tall enough to look into a second-floor window.

HUNTING A MAMMOTH

We know a little about the way the first Americans hunted these huge animals because the hunters left behind a few clues about their work. In Clovis, New Mexico, for example, the leg bones of a mammoth were found standing in what had once been a swampy lake. The rest of the mammoth's bones were found nearby. Stone tools such as spear points and knives were also found.

With a little imagination, we can picture the mammoth hunt. The hunters probably hid by the shores of the lake. They swatted the annoying flies and mosquitoes while waiting for a mammoth to come and drink.

Suddenly the beast was there. The hunters ran toward it, yelling wildly and throwing their spears. The startled mammoth backed into the lake. Soon it was sinking into the muddy bottom. The more the animal struggled to free itself, the deeper it sank into the mud.

Now the hunters moved in. Again and again they attacked with their spears. The mammoth's cries of pain thundered across the lake. Then there was quiet.

Using sharp flint knives, the hunters cut the mammoth apart. They dragged the pieces away from the lake. They then cut off the meat and cleaned the skin. Only the mammoth's legs remained, standing upright in the deadly mud.

Ancient animal bones and flint tools have been found all over North and South America. They tell us that no animal was too large, too small, or too fast to escape the weapons and traps of the first Americans.

THE END OF THE ICE AGE

About 10,000 years ago, the Ice Age ended. As the climate grew warmer, many of the big Ice Age animals became extinct. We do not know why these animals died out. Maybe the changing climate made it harder for some animals to find food.

The first Americans also may have played a part in the disappearance of

 Early American hunters kill a mammoth. Nothing of the mammoth was wasted by the hunters. They used its tusks to make tools and weapons.

the big animals. Over thousands of years they got better and better at making weapons and at hunting. Maybe it was the hunters, and not hunger, that killed the last mammoths and other Ice Age animals.

As the large animals disappeared, the hunters had to find other sources of food. They began to use a new tool in their camping places. It was a smooth, hand-sized rock called a grinding stone. You will read in the next lesson how this new tool marked the beginning of a new way of life.

Check Your Reading

1. Why was there once a land bridge between Asia and North America?
2. What two discoveries allowed the first Americans to survive the cold world of the Ice Age?
3. Why did Asian hunters come to America?
4. **THINKING SKILL:** How might the history of America have been different if Beringia had never existed?

2 Learning to Farm

READ TO LEARN

Key Vocabulary

surplus   civilization
specialize   empire

Key Places

Tenochtitlán
Cuzco

Read Aloud

For some of the first Americans, the end of the Ice Age meant the end of a life based on hunting. After thousands of years, the big animals had disappeared. Now people had to find new sources of food.

Gradually, they learned to gather and cook wild plants and seeds. Some of them learned how to grow their favorite plants. As you will read in this lesson, these early farmers would build America's first towns and cities.

Read for Purpose

1. **WHAT YOU KNOW:** How did the first Americans obtain food to eat?
2. **WHAT YOU WILL LEARN:** How did farming change the way of life of the first Americans?

NEW SOURCES OF FOOD

When the big Ice Age animals died out, the American hunters had to find other things to eat. Some began chasing smaller animals. Others became gatherers who roamed the land in search of food. They ate seeds, nuts, wild fruits, and roots.

Gatherers needed different knowledge and skills than hunters did. They had to know what plants could be eaten and where they could be found. They learned to weave baskets for carrying and storing their foods.

Gatherers also needed new tools. They carried stone knives for cutting up plants. They learned to make smooth stones for grinding hard seeds into flour.

GROWING FOOD

About 7,000 years ago, people in what is today Mexico began to experiment with planting seeds. For the first time they were learning how to farm. Their first crops were squash and chili peppers. Then they added beans and corn to their gardens.

Their most important crop was corn. When first grown, the corn plants became tiny inch-long cobs. Over thousands of years, farmers improved corn until it reached the size we know today. They learned how to grow corn in dry deserts, on high mountains, and in hot rain forests.

Farmers all over America also learned to grow potatoes, sunflowers, tomatoes, and pumpkins. They raised fruits such as pineapples and papayas. They grew chicle for chewing gum, cacao beans for hot chocolate, and tobacco to smoke in their pipes.

A NEW WAY OF LIFE

As farmers learned to grow more food, they gave up the wandering life of the gatherer. They no longer had to roam constantly in search of food. Instead, they settled in villages near their fields and built permanent houses. Once settled, they began to make clay pots and other things that would have been too heavy for them to carry when they wandered from place to place.

The people grew more food as they learned more about farming. Some farming people were able to grow a **surplus** (sûr′ plus) of food. A surplus is an amount greater than what is needed. People with a surplus of corn, for example, could trade their extra food for something else they needed, such as flint.

Having extra food meant that fewer people were needed to farm the land. Not everyone had to spend time planting seeds and taking care of the crops. People could **specialize** (spesh′ ə līz), or spend most of their time doing one kind of job. Specializing meant that people could do the work for which they had the most talent or skill. For example, instead of farming, some people might make clay pots for the village or weave threads into cloth of beautiful colors. With more time for

this kind of work, the way of life of the early Indians began to change greatly.

THE MAYAN CIVILIZATION

The most successful early farmers were an Indian group called the Mayas. The Mayas created America's first **civilization** (siv ə li zā′ shən). A civilization is a community that has developed special skills in farming, building, trade, government, art, and science.

About 3,000 years ago the Mayas lived in small villages in what is today the south of Mexico and Guatemala (gwä tə mä′ lə). Each village was made up of houses with fields all around

The Mayas built small temples on top of tall pyramids. Mayan building methods are shown in the picture below.

Painting by T.W. Rutledge. © National Geographic Society

them. As their villages grew, buildings were added where the people could pray to their gods.

Some 1,700 years ago, the Mayas were building large cities. They built huge temples as tall as a 20-story building. There were also large public squares, ball courts, and palaces. Mayan buildings were carved and painted with beautiful stone figures. Find the Mayas on the map below.

NOBLES AND PRIESTS

Mayan cities were ruled by nobles and priests. The nobles collected taxes and made the laws. The priests helped the people please the many gods they worshiped. No farmer would plant, no artist would create, without the blessings of a priest.

Mayan priests were also scientists. By studying the stars, they created the most accurate calendar known until modern times. They were good at mathematics as well. Hundreds of years before other people, the Mayas understood the use of the number zero in counting and writing numbers.

The Mayas were the first people in the Americas to develop a system of writing. They wrote books on history, religion, science, and mathematics. They collected legends, songs, poems, and plays. Sadly, only four Mayan books survive today.

AN ABANDONED CIVILIZATION

Around 1,000 years ago, the Mayas abandoned their cities. Buildings were left half-finished. Weeds grew in the ball courts. Vines covered the temples.

Why the Mayas left is still a mystery. Did they have to leave because of an earthquake or to escape from their enemies? Did Mayan farmers grow tired of paying taxes to their rulers? We may never know the answer.

THE AZTEC EMPIRE

Other Indian civilizations appeared and disappeared north of the empty Mayan cities. Then, Indians called the Aztecs created a great empire in central Mexico. An empire is made up of lands and people ruled by one group or leader. The Aztecs built their huge empire by taking the lands of the Indians they defeated in war.

Once the Aztecs had been a wandering people in the north of Mexico. Then they moved south, attacking others as they went. Around 1215 they invaded

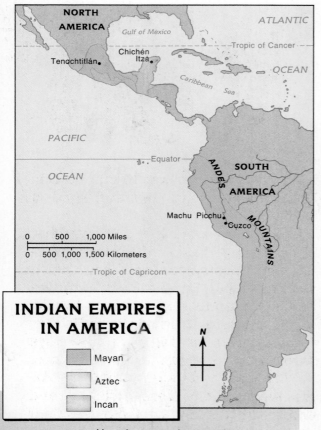

INDIAN EMPIRES IN AMERICA

- Mayan
- Aztec
- Incan

MAP SKILL: Use the map above to locate Chichén Itzá. Was this a city in the Mayan, Aztec, or Incan empire?

The Aztec city of Tenochtitlán was built on an island in the center of a lake. What can you tell about the city and the Aztecs from the picture above and the artwork below?

the Valley of Mexico. From there they sent their armies out in every direction.

Over the next 300 years, the Aztecs conquered many Indian groups. By 1500 the Aztec empire covered half of Mexico. At one time, the Aztecs ruled more than 12 million people. The population of the United States did not reach 12 million until the 1830s—over 300 years after the Aztecs ruled.

AZTEC LIFE

War was important in Aztec life. The Aztecs went to war to get more land. But war was also part of their religion. The Aztec warriors saw fighting as a kind of worship. They also fought wars to capture prisoners.

During a religious ceremony, the unlucky prisoners were offered to the Aztec gods as human sacrifices. A human sacrifice is a person who is killed during a religious ceremony. The Aztecs believed that their gods needed to be fed all the time. They believed that if the gods grew weak from hunger, the sun would not rise and crops would not grow. The Aztecs be-

lieved that the only way to prevent this from happening was to offer the gods a human life.

The Aztecs were not just warriors. They were artists, craftworkers, traders, and priests, too. Every Aztec child went to school. There students studied history, citizenship, religion, music, and crafts. Girls learned the skills they would use in raising a family. Boys were trained to fight in future battles.

When they were not fighting, the Aztecs were building roads, bridges, and cities. The greatest Aztec city was their capital, Tenochtitlán (tā nôch' tē tlän). Only 400 years ago, Tenochtitlán was one of the largest cities in the world.

THE INCAS OF PERU

Far to the south of Tenochtitlán, the Incan people were building another empire in the Andes (an' dēz) Mountains of South America. From 1100 to 1500, Incan armies conquered a vast empire. The Incan empire stretched for more than 2,000 miles (3,200 km) along the western Andes.

The Incan capital was the city of **Cuzco** (kü' skō) in modern-day Peru. There the Incan ruler lived in an elegant palace. The walls of some rooms in the palace were covered with gold. There was even a golden garden filled with life-sized plants, all made of gold.

The long, narrow Incan empire was held together by 10,000 miles (16,000 km) of paved roads. Incan runners used the roads to carry messages from Cuzco to faraway places in the empire. After 2 miles (3.2 km), a runner passed along his message to a fresh runner. In this way, the Incas could send messages all over their empire at about 10

The Incas were skilled builders, as the remains of Machu Picchu (*below*) show. The Incas also created beautiful artwork like the carved llamas. What else did the Incas accomplish?

Andean farmers still terrace the mountain slopes in the style of the early Incas. At right, a Peruvian boy plays the flute. What does his clothing tell you about the climate of Peru?

miles (16 km) per hour. Incan armies used the same roads when marching to war.

The Incas were good farmers. Where the land was mountainous, they built terraces in the hillsides. These flat areas of soil were held in place on the side of the mountain by stone walls.

On this new farmland Incan farmers raised potatoes and corn. Their surplus food was kept in government storehouses that were built along the roads, a day's march apart. The food in each storehouse could feed 25,000 soldiers. Imagine how much food had to be stored in one place to feed that many people.

The Incas were also good at many crafts. Weavers made beautiful cloth from fine soft wool. Metalworkers made gold jewelry that is still beautiful today.

THREE GREAT CIVILIZATIONS

The Mayas, Aztecs, and Incas all created great civilizations. What gave them the time to develop these civilizations was their ability to farm. Rather than having to move from place to place, these farming communities could build cities, form governments, and develop the arts and sciences.

 Check Your Reading

1. Why were hunters and gatherers unable to settle in one place?
2. Where did farming begin?
3. How did the Incas farm the mountains of Peru?
4. **THINKING SKILL:** Classify all the people mentioned in this lesson into two or more groups.

81

3 Early North American Cultures

READE TO LEARN

Key Vocabulary

culture
irrigation

Key Places

Four Corners
Pueblo Bonito
Cahokia

Read Aloud

The first people living in what is now the United States were the hunters and gatherers you read about in the first two lessons. Then, thousands of years ago, farming spread north from Mexico. People learned to plant the "three life-giving sisters"—corn, beans, and squash. Like their neighbors to the south, their lives changed as they learned to farm.

Read for Purpose

1. **WHAT YOU KNOW:** Why was the introduction of farming so important in America?
2. **WHAT YOU WILL LEARN:** Who were the first people to farm in what is now the United States? How did they grow food in the desert?

THE ANASAZI

The first farmers in what is now the United States were the people of the Southwest. It was hard to find enough food in this dry desert region. The development of farming meant that the people there, like the Mayas of Mexico, could settle in one place. They no longer had to wander from place to place in search of food.

The Anasazi (än ə sah′ zē) lived in the vast desert of the Southwest region. Today their land is known as the Four Corners—the place where the states of Arizona, New Mexico, Utah, and Colorado meet. Find the Anasazi on the map on page 83.

Here in the desert the Anasazi created a culture (kul′ chər) based on farming. A people's culture is their way of life—their beliefs, crafts, religion, and customs. People who share a culture speak the same language, follow the same traditions, and eat the same kinds of foods.

Farming was never easy in the Four Corners area. The Anasazi people always had to worry about water. They could not depend on getting enough rainfall to water their crops. And so they developed a system of irrigation (ir ə gā′ shən) to water their fields. Irrigation means bringing water to dry

MAP SKILL: The picture above shows the remains of Pueblo Bonito. Use the map below to locate the village. To which culture did it belong?

ANCIENT CULTURES OF THE UNITED STATES

Anasazi

Woodland People

Important mound areas

—— Present-day boundary

fields from rivers or lakes by means of ditches.

Irrigation made farming possible in the desert. But sometimes there was not enough rainfall to grow crops even with the use of ditches. So the Anasazi learned to store surplus crops during the years when the rains came. Then there would be food to eat during the years that were dry. Food storage was a major step forward for these farmers.

PUEBLO BONITO

The Anasazi created a new way of building. They built villages that looked like large apartment houses. Some villages sat on top of mesas. Other villages were built into caves in the sides of canyons.

What was life like in these villages? Imagine that you lived hundreds of years ago with the Anasazi. Your home might have been the largest Anasazi town, which Spanish explorers called Pueblo Bonito (pweb' lō bə nēt' ō). In Spanish, *pueblo* means "town" or "village" and *bonito* means "beautiful."

The Anasazi began building Pueblo Bonito in a canyon in about the year 900. As the village grew, new rooms were added. By the year 1100, Pueblo Bonito towered five stories above the canyon floor.

In 1150 a long drought dried up the irrigation ditches in the homeland of the Anasazi. Plants withered and died. Because of the drought, the Anasazi were forced to leave their villages. They wandered north, south, and east in search of better lands to farm. For

The dog figure is a water container. The striped animal may be a wildcat. Both were made by the Anasazi.

many years the only sound heard in the empty villages was the desert wind.

THE WOODLAND PEOPLE

Farming also changed the culture of Indians living in the eastern part of what is now the United States. Thousands of years ago, forests covered this large region. People were able to live in the woodlands by hunting animals and gathering roots and seeds. Then farming spread to the woodlands.

Woodland farmers, unlike desert farmers, did not have to worry about water. Rain fell often in the woodlands. But farmers there had a different problem. The land did not get enough sunlight. Trees covered their land, leaving the ground in deep shade.

Woodland farmers had to find a way to clear out trees to make sunny places in the forest. Their stone axes were not strong enough to cut down tall trees. And so they came up with another way to clear out the trees.

The woodland farmers found they could kill a tree by cutting its bark all the way around the trunk. Once the trees in a place were dead, they were burned down. The ashes made the soil more fertile. Now the farmers could plant their crops among the burned-out tree stumps.

THE MOUND BUILDERS

About 2,000 years ago, a group of woodland people began to bury their dead under mounds, or piles, of soil. Mound building spread all over the Eastern Woodlands. Over 10,000 mounds have been found in the Ohio River Valley alone.

The first mounds were built by food gatherers. They built tombs for their dead out of logs, and then covered

them with soil. Year after year, new tombs were built over old ones. The mounds grew larger with each burial.

About 1,300 years ago, a woodland farming people known today as the Mississippians began building villages. These villages became centers of trade, government, and religion. They were surrounded by farmlands.

CAHOKIA

Cahokia (kə hō′ kē ə) was the largest village built by the Mississippians. It is located near the Mississippi River in present-day Illinois. Today you can see Cahokia's ruins if you visit Caho-

kia Mounds State Park in southern Illinois.

Let's walk through Cahokia as it was long ago. At its center is a huge earth mound 100 feet (30.5 m) tall and covering about four city blocks. At the top of this enormous mound is a temple from which priests watch over the activities of the people in the village. There are more than 100 smaller mounds around the temple mound. The Cahokian leaders live on top of some of these smaller mounds.

85

The Cahokians made the eagle (*above*) from copper. They sculpted the frog from stone and polished it until it gleamed. The objects were created as decorations or were buried with the dead.

Cahokia is protected by a high wall made of foot-thick logs. Inside the walls, life is centered in the busy marketplace. Here traders offer goods from places hundreds of miles away. They bring copper nuggets from what is today Wisconsin and sheets of shiny mica rock from present-day Virginia.

These treasures are traded for goods from Cahokia's workshops and for crops from nearby farms. Cahokian craftworkers make tools, leather goods, and pottery. They weave fine cloth and create beautiful jewelry.

Trade has made some Cahokians very rich. When they die, they will be buried in a mound with much of their wealth. One rich man, for example, was buried wearing a robe covered with 12,000 shell beads.

By 1600 the Mississippian culture was dying. Many of the mound cities were empty. What happened to the Mississippians was an unsolved mystery for many years. Today historians think they know what happened.

When the Spanish reached the lands bordering the Mississippi River in the 1540s, they brought with them a disease called smallpox. The Mississippians had no resistance to the germs that caused this terrible new disease. Thousands of people became sick and died. Finally, only the mounds of the Mississippians remained.

THE FARMING LIFE

As you have been reading, the development of farming had a major impact on the way of life of the first Americans. Indians living in what is today the United States learned to prepare the soil, plant different crops, and build irrigation ditches. In doing so, they developed new and more complex cultures.

 Check Your Reading

1. How did the Anasazi make sure that they always had enough food to eat?
2. How did the woodland people clear land for farming?
3. Why did the Mississippians build earth mounds?
4. **THINKING SKILL:** In what ways was the life of a gatherer different from the life of a farmer?

4 Learning About the Past

READ TO LEARN

Key Vocabulary

history	primary source	artifact
historian	secondary source	archaeologist

Read Aloud

In this chapter you have been reading about the first Americans. You have learned how different groups of people lived many, many years ago. But perhaps you have wondered where the stories of the Mayas or the Mississippians come from, or how we know about the giant mammoths or the golden palaces in Cuzco. As you read this lesson, you will find out how we learn about the mysteries of the past.

Read for Purpose

1. **WHAT YOU KNOW:** How do you think we learn about the past?
2. **WHAT YOU WILL LEARN:** How do historians study the past?

PEOPLE AND HISTORY

History (his′ tər ē) is the study or record of what happened in the past. It tells us how people lived years ago. History is made by people. The first hunters to cross Beringia from Asia to North America were making history. So were the people who built Pueblo Bonito. You are making history today. The way you live and the things you do are part of the history of our time.

We learn about history from people who study the past. It is the job of historians (his tôr′ ē ənz) to try to find out what happened long ago. They also study why things happened as they did. Some historians write books, like this one, about the people and events they have studied.

Historians are much like detectives. The job of the historian is to find any clues left by people in the past. From these clues, the historian tries to understand what happened and why.

CLUES FROM THE PAST

Primary sources (prī′ mâr ē sôrs′ əz) are the most valuable clues from the past. A primary source is something that comes from the time that is being studied. It gives historians facts about how people lived and thought.

Primary sources take many forms. Often primary sources are written rec-

An Indian elder passes down the history of his people by telling a story to a young boy. This storytelling is an example of oral history.

ords. These can be laws and other official papers such as court records and birth certificates. Newspaper and magazine articles also are primary sources. Still other primary sources are letters, diaries, and other eyewitness accounts. An eyewitness is someone who was there and saw what happened. Such eyewitness accounts help historians find out what actually happened and why.

Oral or spoken histories are also primary sources. Historians studying events that happened in the recent past can talk to people who took part in them. Often historians tape-record their stories. These oral histories can then be used by other historians.

Pictures are another kind of primary source. Drawings and photographs can tell us what people and places looked like long ago. In the 1900s, movies and videotapes have recorded many events as they happened.

Historians also study **secondary sources** (sek′ ən dâr ē sôrs′ əz). A secondary source is an account of the past written by someone who was not an eyewitness to those events. Most history books, like the one you are reading now, are secondary sources. Historians and students alike look at secondary sources to learn about the past.

UNCOVERING THE PAST

Except for the Mayas, most of the people you have read about in this chapter left no written records. They did not have writing. So we must use other kinds of clues to find out how the first Americans lived. The best clues we have are the things they left behind.

Many things made by the first Americans have rotted away over time. But some objects have survived. These include stone tools, campsites, buildings, weapons, clay pots, and jewelry. These objects, left behind by people who lived long ago, are called **artifacts** (är′ tə fakts).

Scientists who search for and study artifacts are called archaeologists (är kē ol′ ə jists). Archaeologists look for places where people may once have lived. Then they dig up the place, looking for signs of early people.

Archaeologists dig very carefully. Every bit of dirt is sifted to look for artifacts. Tiny pieces of bone or pottery can provide important information about life long ago.

Often archaeologists find remains at different depths under the ground. For example, they might dig up a broken clay pot near the surface. Digging deeper, they might uncover a flint tool. From these discoveries archaeologists might conclude that the person who used the flint tool lived before the person who used the clay pot. Why do you think archaeologists would reach this conclusion?

You can see that we owe a great debt to the archaeologists whose discoveries help us to know about early civilizations. Without their work we would know little of the lives of the first Americans.

WHY WE STUDY HISTORY

Why do historians go to all this trouble to learn about the past? They do so for the same reasons that people tell stories about their beginnings. They are looking for answers to the same questions: Where did our ancestors come from? How did they live in the past? How do their actions help explain our lives today?

As you study our country's history, you will be finding answers to these questions. But you also will be reading a wonderful story. It is a story full of adventure and tragedy, heroes and vil-

Archaeologists at a "dig" like the one shown above have to work carefully and slowly. What kinds of training do you think you would need to become an archaeologist?

lains, glory and sadness. It is the story of a great country and its people. You are part of this great country. This is the story of your past.

Check Your Reading

1. How do artifacts help us to learn about the past?
2. Why do historians study the past?
3. Name two examples each of a primary source and a secondary source.
4. **THINKING SKILL:** What kinds of artifacts do you think archaeologists would find if they dug up one of Cahokia's burial mounds?

Reading Time Lines

Key Vocabulary

time line   B.C.
decade   A.D.
century

As you were learning about the first Americans, you read such phrases as "during the Ice Age" or "about 7,000 years ago." These phrases told you when important events took place. To understand the story of our country, you need to know when things happened.

Time lines are a helpful way to keep track of events. A time line is a diagram that shows when important events took place. A time line lets you see events in the order in which they happened. You can also tell how much time passed between events.

Making a Time Line

A time line is divided into equal parts. Each part shows a time period such as 5, 10, or 500 years. The date and name of each important event is written in the period in which it happened. A time line is read from left to right. The earliest date is on the left. The latest date is on the right.

Make a time line for your life. Divide it into two-year periods. Make the year you were born the first date. Include the year you began school, the year you entered the fifth grade, and at least two other important events. Use the sample below as a guide, but include only events from your own life.

Decades and Centuries

Some time lines are divided into ten-year periods. A ten-year period is called a decade. The decade of the 1970s began in 1970 and ended at the end of 1979. What decade are we living in now?

Many time lines are divided into 100-year periods. A 100-year period is called a century. Look at the Century Time Line on the next page. The period which includes year 1 to year 99 is called the first century. The next period, which includes year 100 to year 199, is called the second century.

The jagged line shows that a long period of time has been left out. The next century you see is the nineteenth century. It lasted from 1800 to 1899. What is the next century shown?

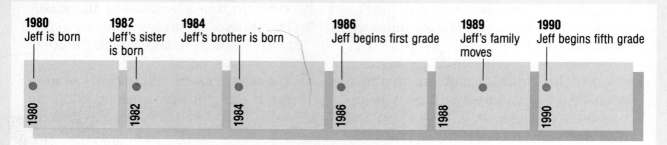

1980 Jeff is born

1982 Jeff's sister is born

1984 Jeff's brother is born

1986 Jeff begins first grade

1989 Jeff's family moves

1990 Jeff begins fifth grade

1980   1982   1984   1986   1988   1990

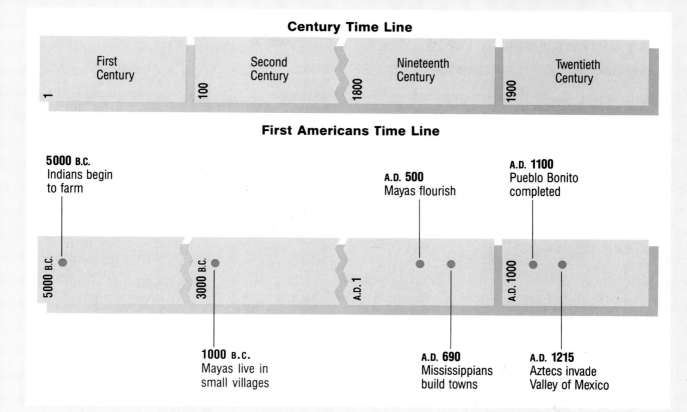

Century Time Line

| First Century | Second Century | Nineteenth Century | Twentieth Century |

1   100   1800   1900

First Americans Time Line

5000 B.C.
Indians begin
to farm

A.D. 500
Mayas flourish

A.D. 1100
Pueblo Bonito
completed

5000 B.C.   3000 B.C.   A.D. 1   A.D. 1000

1000 B.C.
Mayas live in
small villages

A.D. 690
Mississippians
build towns

A.D. 1215
Aztecs invade
Valley of Mexico

The Meaning of B.C. and A.D.

We use a system of dating events that divides time into B.C. and A.D. The letters B.C. stand for "before Christ." The year 300 B.C. means 300 years before the birth of Jesus Christ. The letters A.D. stand for *anno Domini*, Latin words meaning "in the year of the Lord." The year A.D. 100 means 100 years after the birth of Christ. The letters A.D. are often left out before a date, but B.C. is always included.

Look at the First Americans Time Line above. To read B.C. dates, count backward from 1. *With B.C. dates, the higher the number the earlier the date.* That means 5000 B.C. is *earlier than* 1000 B.C. Remember that the earliest date on the time line is on the left.

To read A.D. dates, count forward from 1. For example, Pueblo Bonito was completed about A.D. 1100. This is earlier than A.D. 1215—when the Aztecs invaded the Valley of Mexico. Remember that the latest date on the time line is on the right.

Reviewing the Skill

1. What is a time line? What does a time line help you to do?
2. What years are included in the twentieth century?
3. What is the earliest event named on the First Americans Time Line?
4. Did the Mayas flourish before or after Pueblo Bonito was built?
5. Why is it important to know how to read time lines?

IMPORTANT EVENTS

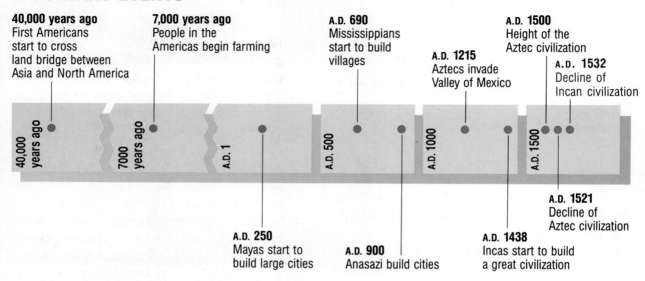

40,000 years ago
First Americans start to cross land bridge between Asia and North America

7,000 years ago
People in the Americas begin farming

A.D. 690
Mississippians start to build villages

A.D. 1215
Aztecs invade Valley of Mexico

A.D. 1500
Height of the Aztec civilization

A.D. 1532
Decline of Incan civilization

A.D. 250
Mayas start to build large cities

A.D. 900
Anasazi build cities

A.D. 1438
Incas start to build a great civilization

A.D. 1521
Decline of Aztec civilization

40,000 years ago | 7000 years ago | A.D. 1 | A.D. 500 | A.D. 1000 | A.D. 1500

IDEAS TO REMEMBER

■ During the Ice Age people came to America by crossing a land bridge that joined Asia with North America.

■ The ability to farm gave the Indians of Mexico and Peru the time and energy to develop rich civilizations.

■ In what is now the United States, groups of Indian peoples learned to farm in the Southwest and in the Eastern Woodlands.

■ Historians learn about the past by studying written records, artifacts, paintings, pictures, interviews, and oral histories.

REVIEWING VOCABULARY

archaeologist   glaciers
artifact   history
civilization   Ice Age
culture   irrigation
empire   specialize

Number a paper from 1 to 10. Beside each number write the word from the list above that best completes the sentence.

1. The study or record of what happened in the past is called ____.
2. An ____ is a scientist who studies objects left behind by people who lived long ago.
3. During the ____ only animals with thick coats of hair could survive.
4. The Anasazi used ____ to bring water to their crops in the desert.

5. The Aztecs created a great ____ in central Mexico, where they ruled many other Indian peoples.

6. A ____ is a community that has developed its own special skills in farming, building, trade, government, and art.

7. A long time ago thick sheets of ice called ____ covered most of the earth.

8. A people's ____ is their way of life, including their beliefs, crafts, religion, and customs.

9. When people ____, they can work at jobs for which they have the most talent or skill.

10. An ____ is an object such as a tool or a weapon left behind by people who lived long ago.

REVIEWING FACTS

1. How did the first people reach North America? Why did they come?

2. Why were fire and the development of weapons important to Ice Age people?

3. What new style of homes did the Anasazi build? Where did they build these homes?

4. List two important accomplishments of (a) the Mayas, (b) the Aztecs, and (c) the Incas.

5. What is a primary source? A secondary source? Give an example of each.

WRITING ABOUT MAIN IDEAS

1. **Writing a Paragraph:** Write a paragraph describing the first people to experiment with the planting of seeds. Tell who these people were as well as where and when they lived.

2. **Writing a Paragraph:** Write a paragraph stating why you would have preferred to live with the Mayas, the Aztecs, or the Incas. Give at least two reasons for your choice.

3. **Writing a Friendly Letter:** Imagine you are taking part in an archaeological "dig" at Cahokia Mounds State Park. Write a letter to a friend describing your experiences as a member of the archaeological team. Tell your friend about some of the activities in which you take part.

BUILDING SKILLS: READING TIME LINES

1. When you read a time line, how can you tell how much time has passed between two events?

2. Look at the time line on page 92. Refer to it as you answer these questions.
   a. What is the earliest event shown?
   b. What is the most recent A.D. event shown?
   c. Which Indian group invaded the Valley of Mexico in 1215?
   d. About how many years ago did the Anasazi build their desert cities?

3. Name two ways that time lines can be helpful when you study history.

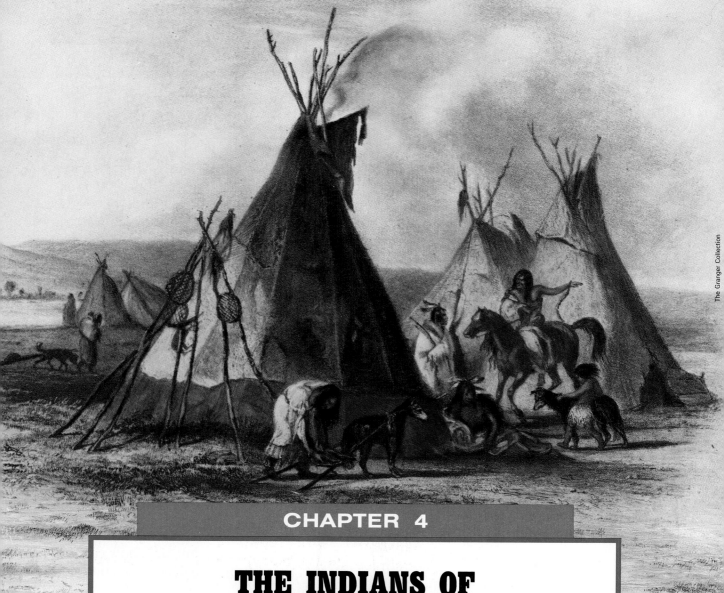

CHAPTER 4

THE INDIANS OF NORTH AMERICA

FOCUS

I am an old woman now. The buffaloes and black-tailed deer are gone. Our Indian ways are almost gone. Sometimes I find it hard to believe I ever lived then.

These words were written by a Hidatsa woman almost 100 years ago. The Hidatsa were just one of many Indian groups that once lived in North America. Some of the groups and the old ways are gone now. But they have not been forgotten.

READ TO LEARN

🔲 Key Vocabulary

environment

🔲 Read Aloud

By 1500, there were hundreds of Indian groups living in North America. As you learned in the last chapter, some Indians lived by hunting and gathering. Others raised crops and lived in villages.

Each Indian group had its own language, customs, and type of shelter. Indian groups in different places dressed differently. They prayed to different spirits in different ways. Look at the map in the Unit Opener on pages 66–67. It shows how some Indian groups lived a long time ago.

🔲 Read for Purpose

1. **WHAT YOU KNOW:** Do you think that the way of life of a person living in a warm, dry area would be the same as that of someone living in a place that was cold and wet? Explain your answer.
2. **WHAT YOU WILL LEARN:** How were North American Indians alike and how were they different?

DIFFERENT ENVIRONMENTS

How would you explain the many different ways of life of the North American Indians? You might begin by looking at the different environments (en vī′ rən mənts) found in North America. Your environment is everything that surrounds you. It includes the plants, animals, climate, and soil where you live.

North American Indians learned to live in many kinds of environments. Some lived in dense forests. Others lived in deserts or on the Great Plains.

In each environment they found different plants and animals for food. Each environment offered different materials that the Indians made use of for shelter and clothing.

The Apache Indians of the Southwest hunted animals and gathered wild plants for food. They wore clothing made of animal skins and lived in shelters made of skins or twigs. They believed their different environments were a gift of Usen (ū′ sən), the Great Spirit. The famous Apache chief Geronimo explained the way the Apaches

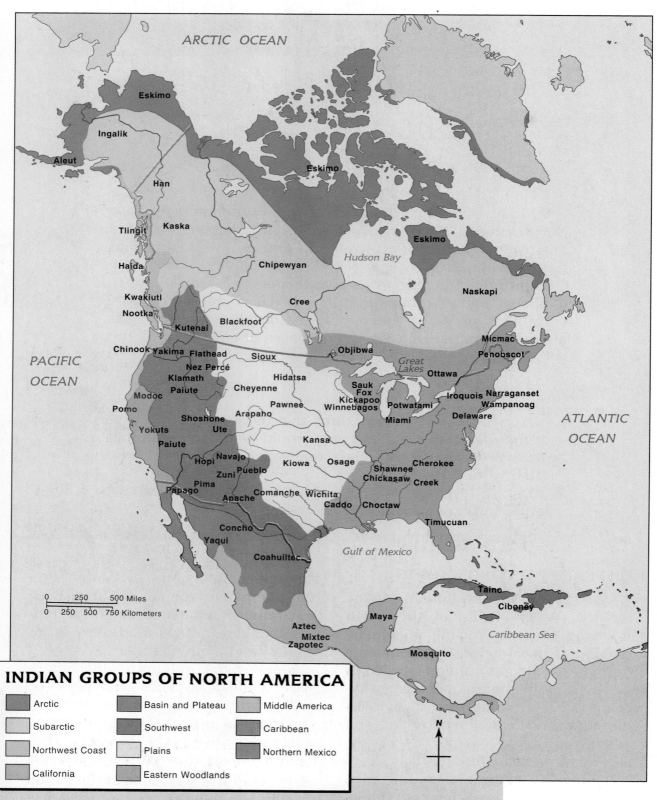

INDIAN GROUPS OF NORTH AMERICA

ARCTIC OCEAN

PACIFIC OCEAN

ATLANTIC OCEAN

Hudson Bay

Gulf of Mexico

Caribbean Sea

Great Lakes

Eskimo

Ingalik

Aleut

Han

Tlingit

Kaska

Haida

Chipewyan

Kwakiutl

Nootka

Cree

Naskapi

Kutenai

Blackfoot

Micmac

Penobscot

Chinook Yakima Flathead

Sioux

Objibwa

Ottawa

Nez Percé

Hidatsa

Sauk

Fox

Iroquois Narraganset

Klamath

Paiute

Cheyenne

Kickapoo

Winnebagos

Potwatami

Wampanoag

Modoc

Pawnee

Miami

Delaware

Pomo

Arapaho

Shoshone

Ute

Yokuts

Kansa

Paiute

Hopi Navajo

Kiowa

Osage

Cherokee

Zuni Pueblo

Shawnee

Pima

Chickasaw

Creek

Papago

Comanche Wichita

Apache

Caddo

Choctaw

Concho

Timucuan

Yaqui

Coahuiltec

Taino

Ciboney

Maya

Mosquito

Aztec

Mixtec

Zapotec

0   250   500 Miles
0   250   500   750 Kilometers

Legend

- Arctic
- Subarctic
- Northwest Coast
- California
- Basin and Plateau
- Southwest
- Plains
- Eastern Woodlands
- Middle America
- Caribbean
- Northern Mexico

N

MAP SKILL: Use the map to locate the different Indian groups of North America. Which states and cities in the United States were named for Indian groups?

The activities of the North American Indians involved the use of their environment. How does this picture show the Indians using their **environment**?

believed that Usen gave each Indian group exactly what it needed to survive.

> For each group of people Usen created, he also made a home. . . . For each people, he placed whatever would be best for their welfare. When Usen created the Apaches, he also gave them their homes in the West. He gave them such grain, fruits, and game as they needed to eat. . . . He gave them a pleasant climate. All they needed for clothing and shelter was at hand.

Not all Indians in the same environment lived in the same way. For example, in the Southwest some Indians farmed while others gathered wild vegetables, seeds, and roots for food. Each group developed ways to survive with what nature provided.

A LOVE FOR THE LAND

While they lived in different ways, the North American Indians shared a deep love for their land. Many Indians spoke of "mother earth." Children of one Indian group, the Creek, were taught to view the land as part of themselves. Read these words of a Creek leader:

> The mountains and hills, that you see, are your backbone. And the gullies [ditches] and creeks, which are between the hills and mountains, are your heart veins.

For Indians, land was not something people could own. It could not be bought and sold. For how could people give up part of themselves?

The culture of each Indian group was different. But all North American Indians respected the land that gave them life.

Check Your Reading

1. Name one way the Indians of North America were alike.
2. How did the way of life of each Indian culture group differ?
3. What explained these differences?
4. **THINKING SKILL:** Look at the picture above. Describe some of the activities of Indian women.

Who Has the Right to the Land?

In the year 1492 a small group of Indians saw an amazing sight. Strange-looking men with pale faces waded out of the Atlantic Ocean onto their island home. Using sign language, the strangers told the Indians that they had come from a faraway land across the sea. The Indians welcomed the men as brothers and shared all that they had with them.

The strangers were sailors from Europe. This first meeting between Europeans and Indians was friendly. But soon more Europeans would cross the Atlantic Ocean to settle in America. As the number of settlers grew, a long conflict began over who had the right to the American land. On one side were the Indians who did not believe that land, or any natural resource, should be owned. Instead, many Indian groups lived on the land and shared its wealth. On the other side were the European settlers who came to America in search of a piece of land to call their own.

Both: The Granger Collection

98

POINT ☆▷

The Indian View

Who had the right to the land? To the Indians the answer was clear. Here Chief Weninock of the Yakima Indians explains the Indian view.

God created the Indian country, and it was like he spread out a big blanket. He put the Indians on it. Then God created fish in the river and put deer in the mountains. The Creator gave the Indians life. As soon as we saw the game and fish, we knew they were made for us. For the women God made roots and berries to gather. The Indians grew and multiplied as a people.

When we were created, we were given our land to live on. From that time on this was our right. We had the fish, berries, and game before the white man came. This was the food on which we lived. We were not brought here from a foreign country. We were put here by the Creator.

● According to Chief Weninock, who gave the land to the Indians?

COUNTERPOINT ▷☆

The European View

Europeans believed they had a right to the land. Governor John Winthrop was the leader of early English settlers in New England. Here he explains why his people had a right to Indian land there.

The whole earth is the Lord's garden. He has given it to all his people so that they can increase and multiply. The Bible tells us to use the land to support our growing numbers. It tells us to tame the wilderness, to turn empty wasteland into fruitful farmland.

The Indians of New England do not plow the land. They do not fence in farm fields. They do not raise cattle or build permanent homes and towns. If we leave the Indians enough land for their needs, we have a right to take the rest. There is plenty of land here for both of our people to use.

● According to Governor Winthrop, what did the Bible tell the New England settlers?

UNDERSTANDING THE POINT/COUNTERPOINT

1. Why did Chief Weninock believe the Indians had the right to the land?
2. Why did John Winthrop believe the settlers had the right to the land?
3. Which side do you think made the stronger case? Why?

Understanding Cause and Effect

Key Vocabulary

cause
effect

Sometimes events affect other events. A sudden rainstorm may force you to cancel a picnic. Something that makes something else happen is a **cause**. What happens as a result of a cause is called an **effect**. In this example, the rainstorm was the cause of canceling the picnic (the effect).

Finding cause and effect connections is important in solving problems in everyday life. It is also important in understanding the history of our country. You can use what you learn about cause and effect to better understand what happened in the past.

Trying the Skill

Read the following paragraph. What cause-and-effect connection is described?

Like the Anasazi, the Pueblo Indians lived in apartment-like houses made of stone or sun-baked bricks. To the Spanish, these tall buildings looked like villages. So the Spanish called these homes *pueblos*, their word for "town" or "village."

1. What effect is described?
2. What is the cause?
3. How did you tell the difference between the cause and the effect?

HELPING YOURSELF

The steps on the left can help you find the cause-and-effect connections when you read something. The example on the right shows one way to apply these steps to the paragraph on page 100.

One Way to Find Causes and Effects	Example
1. Recall the definition of *cause* and *effect*.	A cause is something that makes something else happen. An effect is what happened as a result of a cause.
2. Recall clues to causes and effects: • words that signal causes, such as, *as a result of*, *since*, *because* • words that signal effects, such as, *so*, *therefore*, *as a result*	Word clues that can help you find causes and effects are *because*, *so*, and *as a result of*.
3. Search each sentence for these word clues.	When you reread the paragraph you find the word *so*. The words that follow tell you what the Spanish did as a result of seeing the Indian homes.
4. If you cannot find any word clues, arrange the events in the order they happened. Then see if you can find any links among them. Causes always come before effects.	When you put the events in order you find that the Spanish had a word for villages before they saw where the Indians lived. What they saw was a cause or reason for naming these Indian homes.
5. State the causes and effects that you find.	Naming the Indian villages *pueblos* is the effect of what the Spanish saw and knew.

Applying the Skill

Now use what you have learned about cause and effect to help you understand the paragraph below.

The first people of Pueblo Bonito did not know the importance of trees. They cut them for building and making fires. As a result, rain water no longer seeped into the ground but flowed off into narrow ditches. The farmers' fields dried up and their crops failed. As a result, the people left the area to find food.

1. What happened first in the paragraph?
   a. People moved away.
   b. People cut the trees down.
   c. Rain failed to seep into the ground.

2. What word clues helped you to find effects?
   a. *as a result*
   b. *did not know*
   c. *but*

3. What was the main cause for people leaving Pueblo Bonito?
   a. There was no rain.
   b. The crops failed.
   c. The trees were all cut down.

Reviewing the Skill

1. What is the difference between a cause and an effect?
2. What are some steps you can follow to find cause and effect in a paragraph?
3. Why is it important to know the difference between causes and effects?

READ TO LEARN

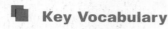 **Key Vocabulary**

kachina

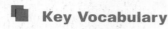 **Read Aloud**

Let the heavens be covered with banked-up clouds. . . . Let thunder be heard over the earth.

So begins a Pueblo Indian prayer. The Pueblo were one of many Indian groups that lived in the Southwest. You read in Chapter 3 that the Southwest is a land of great beauty, but with little water. Day after day, the sun beats down from a bright sky. Most rain comes in two seasons. Winter storms water the desert and cover the mountains with snow. Rain comes again in summer when thunderstorms make the sky black. For the Southwest Indians, these rains meant life.

 Read for Purpose

1. **WHAT YOU KNOW:** Based on what you know about the climate of the Southwest, why do you think rain was so important to the Indians of that region?
2. **WHAT YOU WILL LEARN:** How did the religion of the Pueblo reflect their need for water?

THE PUEBLO INDIANS

Hundreds of years ago, 20 to 30 different Indian groups lived in the Southwest. Some, like the Pima, were farmers. Others, like the Apache, were hunters and gatherers.

In Chapter 3 you read about the Anasazi Indians. They were probably the ancestors of the group of Southwest Indians that we call the Pueblo. Like the Anasazi, the Pueblo Indians lived in apartment house villages made of sunbaked bricks. To the Spanish, these tall buildings must have looked like villages. So they called the houses *pueblos,* the Spanish word for "village" or "town."

Although not all Pueblo Indians spoke the same language, and each village had its own leaders, these Indians had much in common. They planted the same crops of corn, squash, beans, and cotton. They irrigated their dry lands by building canals from nearby rivers and lakes. And, like many Pueblo today, they looked forward to the coming of the **kachinas** (kä chē′ nəz).

The **kachinas**, as shown in the painting and the doll figure, performed ritual dances in Hopi villages. What do the Hopi believe about the kachinas?

THE DANCING KACHINAS

The Pueblo Indians believe kachinas are the living spirits of much-loved ancestors. Each spring, they believe that the kachinas borrow men's bodies and come down from their home in the sacred mountains.

Imagine yourself living among the Hopi, who are one group of Pueblo Indians. It is a hot spring day. The entire Hopi village is gathered around a dusty courtyard. It feels like a holiday.

"The kachinas are coming!" At this cry all eyes turn in the same direction, straining to see the dancers. You hear the sound of rattles and drums coming closer. Then the kachinas appear.

A parade of masked figures moves through the pueblo. The colorful kachinas take many forms—animals, birds, and clowns. For six months the kachinas live in the Hopi village. They teach the people how to live. The Hopi believe the kachinas bring the rains and make sure that crops planted each spring will grow.

THE HOME DANCE

Today you and your friends are very excited, for the Hopi kachinas are dancing the Home Dance. Tonight the kachinas will return to their mountain home.

The courtyard is filled with dancing kachinas. They dance and sing for hours. Not wanting to be forgotten after they leave, they give dolls to the children. Each doll looks like one of the kachinas.

At sunset the kachinas leave the village. You want to follow them. But an old man stops you. "You cannot go on," he says. "They are they, and we are we. They have their own ways, and we have ours."

The Pueblo Indian village of San Geronimo de Taos in New Mexico is the oldest inhabited dwelling in the United States. At the left, present-day Hopi women take part in a ceremony. What did the Hopi often pray for?

THE PUEBLO RELIGION

Like most North American Indians, the Pueblo Indians were deeply religious. Their religion was part of their everyday life. The Hopi, for example, believed that the kachinas brought rain and helped crops grow. They believed too that the kachinas cured the sick and helped the villagers defeat their enemies.

The Pueblo religion taught people how to live each day. Children were taught to be gentle and polite. Adults were expected to settle arguments peacefully. In everything they did, the Pueblo tried to please the spirits.

RELIGION AND SURVIVAL

You have read that in the hot dry Southwest there was always a need for water. Every summer, the Indians living there depended on the rains to help their crops grow.

Each Pueblo religious ceremony, with its lively songs and dances, was a prayer that rain would fall. The Pueblo Indians believed that the rains would come only if the spirits were pleased. Then the desert would bloom and their people could live in the dry land for another year.

Check Your Reading

1. Who were the ancestors of the Pueblo Indians?
2. Describe the special kind of houses built by the Pueblo Indians.
3. Who were kachinas? Why were they important in the religion of many Pueblo Indians?
4. **THINKING SKILL:** Predict what actions the Hopi Indians might take if there were little or no rainfall.

3 The Eastern Woodland Indians

READ TO LEARN

Key Vocabulary
league

Key People
Deganawida
Hiawatha

Read Aloud

Think not forever of yourselves, O Chiefs, nor of your own generation. . . . Think of our grandchildren and of those yet unborn, whose faces are coming from beneath the ground.

These were the words of an Indian holy man named Deganawida (də gä′ nä wē də). Today he is remembered as "the Peacemaker." But in his day, the sounds of war were heard all over the Eastern Woodlands.

Read for Purpose

1. **WHAT YOU KNOW:** Do you know anyone who is good at settling arguments and making peace? How does he or she go about this?
2. **WHAT YOU WILL LEARN:** How did the Iroquois Indians end fighting among their people?

WOODLAND LIFE

Several different Indian groups lived in the Eastern Woodlands. These Indians were farmers, hunters, and food gatherers. Most groups lived in settled villages. The forests of the Eastern Woodlands provided logs and bark for houses. Around the villages there were log walls that protected the Indians from attack.

You read in Chapter 3 that the first Eastern Woodland Indians found a way to clear land in the forest for farming. Women raised corn, beans, squash, and tobacco in their fields. They gathered nuts, berries, and roots from the forests. Men hunted and fished. They also went to war.

War was part of life in the Eastern Woodlands. The Cherokee Indians, who lived in present-day Georgia, said, "We cannot live without war." They called war "our beloved occupation."

From Maine to Florida, warriors talked of "taking up the tomahawk." The tomahawk was a small ax used in battle. War gave young men a chance to prove their strength and courage. The Creek Indians, who lived in what is now Alabama, called a boy by his "baby name" until he saw battle. Only after his first fight did a young man receive the "adult name" he would use for the rest of his life.

The Eastern Woodland Indians loved many kinds of sports, which they called the "younger brother of war." The roughest game they played was lacrosse. In this game, each player had a stick with a cup at one end. The object of the game was to carry a ball past the other team to a goal post. Games often went on all day.

THE IROQUOIS

The most feared Eastern Woodland Indians lived in what is today New York State. Their enemies called them the Iroquois (ir' ə kwoi), a name that meant "terrifying man." The Iroquois were divided into five different groups that spoke the same language.

In spite of the importance of warriors, women played a major role in Iroquois life. They could not be priests or healers, but it was the women who decided which men would be chiefs.

The Iroquois lived in villages of 50 or more longhouses. Each house was about 80 feet (24 m) long and about 25 feet (7.6 m) wide. It was made of poles covered with elm bark. Four cooking fires were kept burning in the main hall of each longhouse. Smoke curled out of holes in the roof.

About eight to ten families lived together in a longhouse. Inside, the Iroquois proudly displayed their wampum (wom' pəm). These were small polished beads made from shells or porcupine quills. The Iroquois strung the beads into necklaces or wove them into belts. They also used wampum as a form of money.

The Seneca lived in the Eastern Woodlands in what is now New York State. They were the largest of the five groups that formed the Iroquois League. What do these pictures tell you about the Seneca way of life?

WOODLAND WARFARE

The Iroquois were skilled warriors. It was said that they moved quickly and quietly "like foxes through the woods." Then they would "attack like lions and disappear like birds."

Most battles were short. The purpose of war was not to kill the enemy. Instead, each warrior hoped to come home with a prisoner tied to his "slave strap." Some prisoners were adopted by families that had lost men in battle. Others were sacrificed to honor the soul of a fallen warrior.

By the early 1500s, the five Iroquois groups were always at war with each other. "Everywhere there was misery," said one Iroquois leader.

THE GREAT PEACE

It was during this time of warfare that the holy man Deganawida had a vision. He saw a mighty tree of "Great Peace." It was held in the ground by five strong roots—the five Iroquois groups.

Deganawida went from village to village to talk about his "Great Peace." But he stammered, and people could not understand him. In his travels he met Hiawatha (hī ə woth′ ə), an Indian warrior. Hiawatha shared the holy man's dream and from then on spoke for him. Together they persuaded the Iroquois to stop fighting each other. They brought about the "Great Peace."

THE IROQUOIS LEAGUE

About 1570, leaders from the five groups joined to form the Iroquois League (lēg). A league is a union of people who join together for a common purpose. Hiawatha talked of the purpose of the Iroquois League in these words:

Into our bundle we have gathered the causes of war. We have cast this bundle away. . . . Our great-grandchildren shall not see them.

Hiawatha meant that the Iroquois League would help to make peace

A chief of the Iroquois League speaks to members of a council in this picture. What was the purpose of such councils?

everywhere so that all wars among the Iroquois would end. The League was led by a council of 50 leaders, who were chosen by the women of each group. The council met each summer to deal with any problems among the Indians. United in peace, the Iroquois soon became the most powerful Eastern Woodland people.

LIVING WELL

The Eastern Woodland Indians lived well in their environment. They got food to eat and wood for houses from the forest. They hunted and fished in their unspoiled wilderness. Rough games and war gave young men a chance to prove that they were brave. But among the Iroquois, making peace became as important as making war.

Check Your Reading

1. How did the Eastern Woodland Indians get their food?
2. Describe the role of women in the Iroquois culture.
3. What was the Iroquois League? How did it bring peace to the Iroquois Indians?
4. THINKING SKILL: How was the way of life of the Eastern Woodland Indians similar to that of the Southwest Indians? In what ways was it different?

4 The Plains Indians

Key Vocabulary

nomad

Read Aloud

The environment of the Great Plains was very different from that of the Eastern Woodlands. In the Plains there were open spaces. The ground was covered with short, tough grass. Rivers dried up during the summer months, and freezing winter winds brought terrible storms. By 1500 only a few Indian groups lived on the Plains. But as you will read in this lesson, that soon changed.

Read for Purpose

1. **WHAT YOU KNOW:** Use what you learned in Chapter 1 to describe the landforms and climate of the Great Plains.
2. **WHAT YOU WILL LEARN:** How did horses change the way Indians lived on the Great Plains?

THE BUFFALO

Give me one buffalo or more.
Help me to fell [kill] *the buffalo.*

So sang the Indians of the Great Plains. They were **nomads** (nō′ madz), or wanderers with no permanent homes. They lived by following the buffalo across the Plains. Millions of these shaggy beasts roamed the grasslands. At times the Plains were absolutely blackened by buffalo as far as the eye could see.

The Plains nomads got everything they needed to live from the buffalo. From birth until death, the Indians wore clothes made of buffalo hides. Buffalo meat was their main food. They made buffalo horns into spoons.

The buffalo also provided shelter. Buffalo skins were sewn together to make a cone-shaped tent called a tepee (tē′ pē). The tent was held up by tall poles, and a hole at the top allowed smoke from fires inside to escape.

TRAVELING ON THE PLAINS

Before 1600 the Plains Indians followed the buffalo on foot. They called the old times "the dog days," because those were the days "when we had only dogs for moving camp."

The problem with buffalo was that they never stayed in one place. When the herds moved, the buffalo hunters had to follow if they wanted to eat. This meant moving their camp.

Moving camp was hard work. Everyone walked, carrying as much as he or she could. The heaviest load was the tepee, which was hauled along by dogs. The poles of the tepee were tied together to make an A-shaped frame called a travois (trə voi′).

Using dogs to carry these loads was often a problem. Sometimes dogs fought or ran off after rabbits. The most a dog could carry was 40 to 50 pounds (18 to 23 kg). On a good day a dog was able to travel only 5 or 6 miles (8 or 10 km).

THE FIRST HORSES

In the 1600s a new animal appeared on the Plains. Spanish settlers in America brought horses to the Southwest. Some escaped and eventually reached the Great Plains, where they ran wild. At first, the Indians called horses "mystery dogs" and sometimes killed them for food.

Soon, though, the Indians tamed the mystery dogs and put them to work. A horse, they found, could carry four times as much as a dog and go twice as far in a day. They also learned how to ride these wonderful new animals.

HUNTERS ON HORSEBACK

The horse quickly changed life on the Plains. With horses, hunting buffalo became easier. A hunter on a horse could ride into the middle of a herd. By getting so close to the herd he could use his bow and arrows to shoot three

Dogs, then horses, were used by the Indians to haul the travois. The pointed end of the travois was tied to a harness on the horse's back while the legs of the travois dragged on the ground. What do you think it was like to ride on a travois?

The Buffalo Hunt was painted by Charles M. Russell. How did hunting buffalo by horseback change the lives of the Plains Indians?

or four buffalo in one day. This would feed a family for months. Hunger, often part of life in the dog days, faded into memory.

The horse attracted more Indians to the Plains. The Cheyenne, Blackfoot, and Sioux (sü) abandoned their woodland villages. The Comanche left their homeland in the Rocky Mountains. Some of these Indians gave up farming completely to follow the buffalo.

Like the Eastern Woodland Indians, Plains warriors went to war to prove that they were brave. But instead of bringing home prisoners, Plains warriors brought back enemy horses. The more horses a warrior captured, the more honor he had among his people.

A CHANGING WAY OF LIFE

On the Great Plains, the buffalo provided food, clothing, and shelter. But in the dog days, the nomadic hunting life was too hard to attract many Indians. Then horses came to the Plains. With horses the Plains Indians created a new way of life. Where there had once been few Indians, now there were many.

Check Your Reading

1. Why was the buffalo important to the Plains Indians?
2. How did the way of life of the Plains Indians influence the type of shelter they built?
3. What changes did the horse bring to life on the Plains?
4. **THINKING SKILL:** How was the life of the Plains Indians similar to the life of the Pueblo Indians? How was it different?

111

5 Hunters and Gatherers of the West

READ TO LEARN

Key Vocabulary

totem pole
potlatch
tundra

Key Places

Arctic Plains

Read Aloud

Don't you ever, you in the sky, Don't you ever get tired
Of having the clouds Between you and us?

While the Southwest Indians prayed for rain, Indians in the Pacific Northwest prayed for sunshine. Their rain-drenched homeland was one of many different environments west of the Rockies. Few of the Indians living in the West were farmers. Instead, they ate whatever they could find by hunting, gathering, and fishing.

Read for Purpose

1. **WHAT YOU KNOW:** Who do you think would worry least about having enough food—farmers, hunters, or food gatherers? Explain why.
2. **WHAT YOU WILL LEARN:** Why was life hard for some Indians of the West and easy for others?

THE NOMADS OF THE GREAT BASIN

On your journey in Chapter 1, you learned that the Great Basin forms a giant bowl between the Rocky Mountains and the Sierra Nevada. This is a harsh, dry land, broken by row after row of hills. The little rain that falls here quickly sinks into dry desert sands.

This was not an easy environment. Yet the Shoshone (shə shō′ nē), Paiutes (pī′ ütz), and other Indian groups made the Great Basin their home. Like the Plains Indians, they were nomads. They moved across the desert, always looking for food.

To survive, the nomads had to know every source of food the Great Basin offered. Men hunted insects, lizards, and larger animals such as gophers and rabbits. Women gathered seeds, roots, nuts, and berries. The nomads made use of over 100 kinds of plants. As much food as possible was stored in baskets for winter.

THE CALIFORNIA INDIANS

The Indians of California lived in the area between the Pacific Ocean and the Sierra Nevada. Compared to the Great Basin, California was a land of plenty. More than 100 small Indian groups lived in California's sunny valleys. They spoke many languages, and had different customs and beliefs. But for all of them, life was good.

Food was easy to find. From rivers and the ocean the Indians gathered fish and shellfish. In the forests there were elk, deer, and smaller game to hunt. Women gathered roots, seeds, nuts, and berries.

With so much food, the California Indians were able to live in villages. Men spent much of their time taking part in religious ceremonies. Women liked to weave beautiful baskets. Some baskets were so tightly woven they could hold water.

War was not part of life in California. Despite their differences, most California Indians lived in peace with each other. When different groups came together, it was to trade goods, not to fight.

The California Indians were skilled basket weavers. Many of their baskets were for everyday use. Others were given as gifts or used in religious ceremonies.

THE NORTHWEST COAST INDIANS

The Pacific coastline from northern California to Alaska is both rugged and beautiful. Ocean waves crash against rocks and cliffs. Forest-covered hills seem to drop into the Pacific. The climate is mild with fog and rain much of the year.

Along this coastline lived the most fortunate Indians in North America. Here the forest and sea provided a huge amount of foods unknown elsewhere.

The Northwest Coast Indians lived in villages facing the Pacific. From the ocean they harvested fish and sea mammals such as otters and whales. Twice a year the rivers were crowded with salmon. In a few weeks, a family could catch and dry 1,000 pounds (454 kg) of salmon. This was enough to last for months.

From the forest the Indians used the wood of cedar trees to build large barnlike houses. They hollowed out logs and turned them into ocean-going canoes. And they wove beautiful rugs and blankets from cedar bark fiber.

The Northwest Coast Indians also used tall trees from the forests to carve very special poles called totem poles. These painted carvings often showed the history of a family. Totem poles were placed in front of a family's home as a sign of wealth.

Northwest Coast Indian houses and totem poles were decorated with images of birds and animals.

A chief of the Northwest Coast Indians (*center left*) holds a potlatch, or lavish display of wealth. What took place during a potlatch?

THE POTLATCH

The most important person in the villages of the Northwest Coast region was the "big man" or chief. To prove his greatness, the big man spent years gathering valuable goods. Everyone in the village helped. People spent their free time making baskets, blankets, carved boxes, or jewelry.

When he felt rich enough, the big man invited the chiefs of other villages to a potlatch (pot' läch). This was a special feast at which the big man showed off his wealth by giving it all away! A potlatch was a kind of contest. To win, you had to give away more than the others could. The prize was an important place among the big men.

Imagine that you are going to a potlatch with your village chief. Travel by foot through the tangled forest is nearly impossible. So you decide to paddle a canoe down the nearest river.

The guests are welcomed to the big man's village with songs and speeches. The next few days are filled with dances, plays, games, and feasts. At every meal you stuff yourself to honor your host.

On the last day, the gift-giving begins. The guests sit around the fire in the big man's home. He makes a

speech about the greatness of his family. Then, at a signal, fish oil is poured on the fire. Your host says he was worried that his guests were cold. But you know he is showing off that he has oil to burn.

Each guest is called up to receive a gift. When all the gifts are gone, the big man folds up his own blanket. "Who wishes to take it?" he asks. His words are a challenge. Who, he is asking, will give the next potlatch? Who can match what I have given away today?

THE ESKIMOS OF THE FAR NORTH

Far to the north of the potlatch givers, in the land called the **Arctic Plains**, lived the Eskimos. They called themselves the Inuit, which means "the people." The Eskimos learned to survive in the most challenging envi-

Kayaks (*below*) are used by the Eskimos for hunting and for transportation. An Eskimo artist (*above*) uses a modern tool to sculpt a stone figure.

ronment of all—the tundra (tun' drə). The tundra is a huge frozen plain.

Summers are cool in the Far North. As the days warm, the top few inches of the tundra thaw. Mosquitoes and small plants thrive. Birds and herds of caribou and musk oxen come north to feed on the tundra. Whales, walruses, and seals fill the Arctic waters. For a short time, hunting is good.

All too soon, winter returns. Temperatures drop to below freezing and stay there for months. It is so cold that the ocean freezes. Most of the birds and animals leave.

SURVIVAL IN THE ARCTIC

To survive in this cold land, the Eskimos made use of everything at hand. From animal skins they made warm clothing. They carved fishhooks and many kinds of handy tools out of bones and walrus tusks. Whale ribs became roof beams and sled runners.

On hunting trips during the winter, some Eskimos used the snow itself to make temporary homes called igloos. Working with a long bone knife, they cut blocks of packed snow. The blocks were stacked to form a dome-shaped house. A block of ice near the top let in light. Inside their igloos, the Eskimos were protected from winter storms. Whale oil burning in stone lamps kept them warm through the coldest nights.

Cooperation was as important to the Eskimos as competition was to the Northwest Coast Indians. There were no "big men" in Eskimo villages. Instead, they looked to the best hunters or wisest elders for advice. No one went hungry as long as someone had food. For the most admired people were those who were willing to share.

Igloo-building is taught by one generation to another. Here, two people fit together blocks of packed snow to form the igloo. How did the Eskimos keep the inside of the igloo warm?

LIVING IN HARMONY WITH NATURE

Wherever Indians lived, they lived in harmony with their environment. They used what nature offered to create many successful ways of life.

Farmers, hunters, fishers, and gatherers all saw themselves as part of nature. They knew the beauty of their world. They also knew it could be a hard place to live. And after thousands of years in North America, they left the land as wild and beautiful as it had appeared to the first Americans.

 Check Your Reading

1. Why was life hard for the nomads of the Great Basin?
2. How did the Indians of the Northwest Coast use their wealth?
3. Why was cooperation important for the Eskimos?
4. **THINKING SKILL:** Recall the information in this lesson and list several characteristics of the life of the Eskimos.

117

IMPORTANT EVENTS

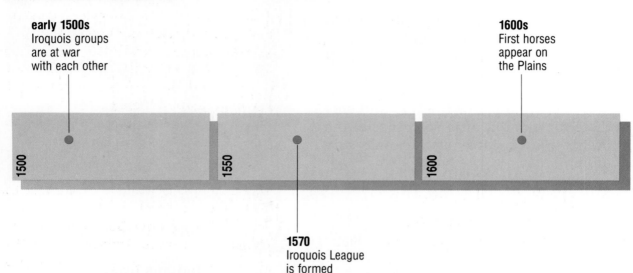

early 1500s
Iroquois groups are at war with each other

1600s
First horses appear on the Plains

1500

1550

1600

1570
Iroquois League is formed

PEOPLE TO KNOW

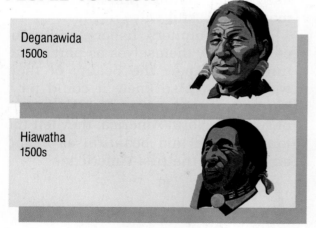

Deganawida
1500s

Hiawatha
1500s

IDEAS TO REMEMBER

■ By 1500 hundreds of different Indian groups lived in North America.

■ The Indians of the Southwest depended upon the rains to help their crops grow.

■ From the forest, the Eastern Woodland Indians obtained food to eat and wood for shelter.

■ The Plains Indians used the buffalo for their food, clothing, and shelter.

■ The California Indians and the Northwest Coast Indians hunted, fished, and gathered roots, nuts, and fruits.

REVIEWING VOCABULARY

Number a paper from 1 to 5. Beside each number write **C** if the underlined word in the sentence is used correctly. If it is not, write the word that would correctly complete the sentence.

1. The Iroquois <u>Pueblo</u> was made up of five groups that joined together to bring peace to the Eastern Woodlands.
2. The Pueblo Indians of the Southwest believe that <u>kachinas</u> are the living spirits of their ancestors.
3. Your <u>culture</u> is everything that surrounds you, including animals, plants, climate, and soil.
4. The Plains Indians were wanderers, or <u>nomads</u>, who followed the buffalo.
5. The Inuit live in the <u>Great Basin</u>, a huge frozen plain.

REVIEWING FACTS

1. How were the Indians of North America alike? How were they different?
2. Why did the Plains Indians build tepees instead of permanent homes? What were tepees made of?
3. Why did the Northwest Coast Indians live in permanent villages?
4. What did the Eastern Woodland Indians use to build their houses?
5. How did the religion of the Pueblo Indians reflect the importance of rain in their lives?
6. Why is Deganawida remembered as "the Peacemaker"?
7. How did Hiawatha help to bring peace to the Iroquois?
8. What was the role of women in Iroquois life?
9. Why did more Indians move to the Great Plains after horses appeared? Where did the horses come from?
10. Name one way in which the environment of the Great Basin Indians was like that of the Inuit. Name one way in which it was different.

✏ WRITING ABOUT MAIN IDEAS

1. **Making a Chart:** Make a chart of the Indian groups you read about in this chapter. Across the top, list these headings: *Environment*, *Type of Homes*, *Way of Getting Food*, *Special Characteristics*. At the left, list these Indian groups: *Southwest*, *Eastern Woodland*, *Plains*, *California*, *Northwest Coast*, *Inuit*. Now fill in the information to complete your chart.
2. **Writing a Myth:** Imagine you are a Plains Indian telling the younger children of your group about the importance of the buffalo to your people's way of life. Create a myth about the buffalo that would make this point clear to your listeners.

BUILDING SKILLS: UNDERSTANDING CAUSE AND EFFECT

1. What steps can you follow to help you find cause-and-effect connections?
2. Reread "Religion and Survival" on page 104. Name two cause-and-effect connections in the paragraphs.
3. Give an example of a cause and an effect that a third grader would understand.

REVIEWING VOCABULARY

archaeologist	environment
artifact	history
civilization	irrigation
culture	nomads
empire	specialize

Number a paper from 1 to 10. Beside each number write the word from the list above that best completes the sentence.

1. The Mayas and Incas each created a _____ with large cities, a complex government, and highly developed arts and sciences.
2. The Plains Indians were _____ who traveled from place to place in search of food.
3. An _____ studies the lives of early people by digging up and studying the things they left behind.
4. A _____ of the United States would describe what happened in our country in the past.
5. Early people had to adapt their lives to suit their _____, or surroundings.
6. An example of an _____ might be a clay pot, jewelry, or a tool.
7. The celebration of Thanksgiving is part of the American _____.
8. The Aztecs built a huge _____ in Mexico by conquering and taking the lands of other Indians.
9. The Anasazi developed a system of _____ to water their crops.
10. When fewer men and women were needed to grow food, some people could _____, or do work for which they had the most skill.

WRITING ABOUT THE UNIT

1. **Writing Captions:** Choose a photograph from this unit that you find interesting. Then write your own caption for the picture. Your caption should explain what the picture is about.
2. **Writing a Travel Brochure:** Choose one of the Indian groups discussed in this unit and write and design a travel brochure telling why people would enjoy visiting those Indians. The brochure should describe their language, customs, tools, and special beliefs.

ACTIVITIES

1. **Researching Place Names:** Many states, streets, rivers, and lakes in the United States have Indian names. Find examples in your state. From what group or groups did the names come? What do the names mean?
2. **Making an Oral Presentation:** Ask your librarian to help you find a book of Indian legends. Choose one legend to tell to the class. Explain the meaning of the legend.
3. **Working Together as Archaeologists:** Form a group with several other students. Together, fill up a box with different layers of artifacts. You should include some objects you use today as well as things people might have used in the past. Remember that objects near the top were probably made more recently than articles buried farther down. After you have finished, each group should talk about the objects in its box.

First Americans Time Line

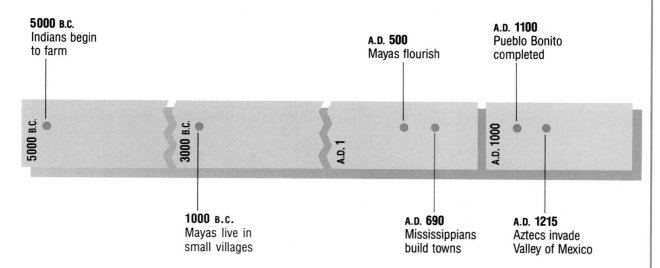

5000 B.C.
Indians begin
to farm

1000 B.C.
Mayas live in
small villages

A.D. 500
Mayas flourish

A.D. 690
Mississippians
build towns

A.D. 1100
Pueblo Bonito
completed

A.D. 1215
Aztecs invade
Valley of Mexico

5000 B.C.   3000 B.C.   A.D. 1   A.D. 1000

BUILDING SKILLS: READING TIME LINES

1. On a time line, how can you tell which events happened earliest?
2. Use the time line of the first Americans to answer these questions.
   a. When was the village of Pueblo Bonito completed?
   b. Which development came first—Mayas settled in small villages or the Mississippians built towns?
   c. What is the most recent event shown on the time line? About how long ago did it take place?

LINKING PAST, PRESENT, AND FUTURE

The lives of the Plains Indians were greatly changed by the arrival of horses. What developments have brought great changes to Americans today? What future developments might bring other important changes?

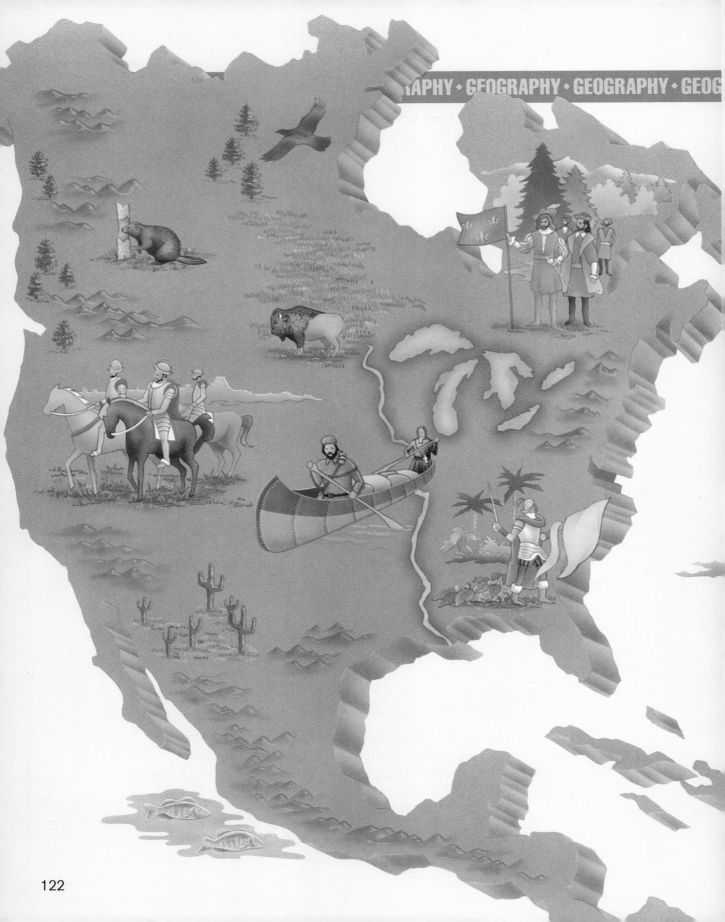

UNIT 3

EUROPEANS COME TO AMERICA

WHERE WE ARE

North and South America are separated from Europe and Africa by a vast body of water called the Atlantic Ocean. European explorers coming to the Americas had to guide their small ships across thousands of miles of this ocean. In Unit 3 you will read about many of the explorers who made this long journey. You can see some of these explorers on the map of North America. They were brave men and women with a spirit of adventure.

123

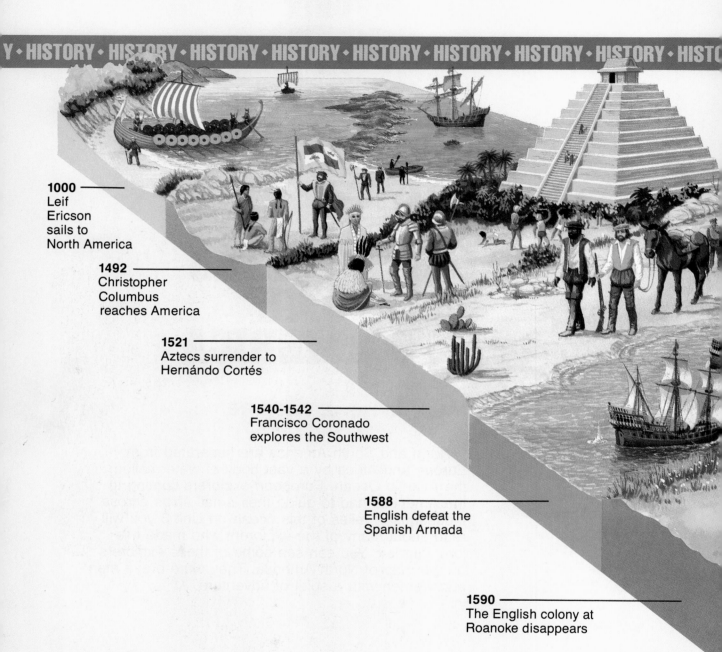

1000
Leif
Ericson
sails to
North America

1492
Christopher
Columbus
reaches America

1521
Aztecs surrender to
Hernándo Cortés

1540-1542
Francisco Coronado
explores the Southwest

1588
English defeat the
Spanish Armada

1590
The English colony at
Roanoke disappears

1608
Samuel de Champlain
founds Quebec

WHAT HAPPENED

The time line shows that the
Vikings were probably the first Europeans
to reach North America. But their settlements
here did not last. In the years that followed,
Europeans looking for a sea route to Asia explored
and settled the Americas. In this unit you will read
what these explorers accomplished.

124

CHAPTER 5

EUROPEANS REACH AMERICA

FOCUS

[We feared] the air for its fury, the water for the waves, and the earth for the reefs and rocks.

The sailor who wrote these words was describing the Atlantic Ocean. To many it was the "green sea of darkness." Mapmakers filled its waters with pictures of sea monsters.

For thousands of years, the Atlantic Ocean was a barrier between peoples. In this chapter you will learn how Europeans began to explore the ocean. You will see what they discovered on the Atlantic's far shore. For people on both sides of the ocean, this discovery changed life forever.

1 The Vikings Reach Vinland

READ TO LEARN

Key Vocabulary

saga

Key People

Eric the Red
Leif Ericson

Key Places

Iceland
Greenland
Vinland
Newfoundland

Read Aloud

From the fury of the Vikings,
Good Lord deliver us!

A thousand years ago, this prayer was said across Europe. No one felt safe from Viking warriors. These daring and adventurous people had attacked towns from Russia to Italy.

Around A.D. 800, many Viking sailors left their homes in northern Europe. Today that land is known as Scandinavia, which includes the countries of Norway, Sweden, and Denmark. Much of Scandinavia is too rocky to farm. So the Vikings set out in their long boats in search of new lands to settle.

Read for Purpose

1. **WHAT YOU KNOW:** Why do you think people might move away from their home?
2. **WHAT YOU WILL LEARN:** Who were the Vikings? What brought them to Vinland?

EXPLORING BY SEA

The Vikings were the best shipbuilders in Europe. They used their boats to fish and trade, and to raid towns all across Europe.

The Vikings also used their boats to explore the rough waters of the northern Atlantic. They first sailed west to Iceland, where many families settled. From there, a group led by Eric the Red decided to explore even farther to the west. Around A.D. 980 they came to a land of ice-covered mountains. Eric named this land Greenland. He hoped the name would attract people to settle there.

ARRIVAL AT VINLAND

The Vikings liked to tell long stories about their great deeds. These stories were called sagas. Some of their sagas told about the discovery of a place called Vinland.

127

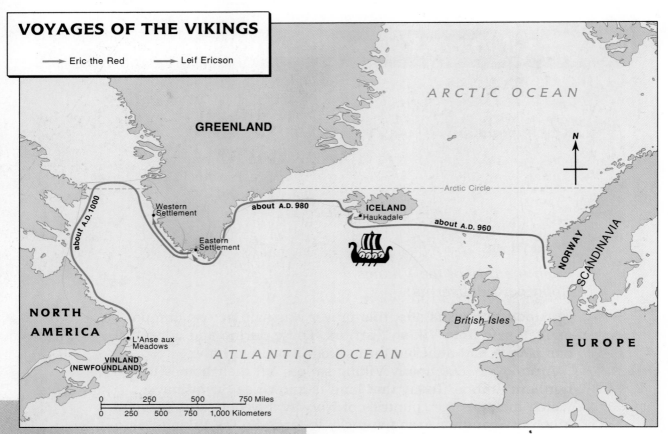

VOYAGES OF THE VIKINGS

→ Eric the Red → Leif Ericson

MAP SKILL: Locate Scandinavia and North America on the map. Use the map to describe the stages of the Vikings' journey from Norway to Vinland.

According to the sagas, Vinland was first found in a fog by Bjarni Herjulfsson (byär′ nē här yōl′ sən), a young man who was sailing west from Iceland to Greenland when his boat got lost in thick fog. As the fog lifted, Bjarni saw a flat, wooded land. It was the Atlantic coast of North America.

"Is this Greenland?" the crew asked. "No," said Bjarni, "for there are said to be glaciers in Greenland." Bjarni had gone too far west. So he sailed back to Greenland and told the others about the new land he had seen.

Bjarni's story fired the imagination of Eric the Red's son, Leif Ericson. Around the year 1000, Leif and his crew sailed west from Greenland. They spent the winter exploring the new land that Bjarni had talked about.

One day a German sailor in Leif's crew came to Leif, rolling his eyes in excitement. "I have news!" he said. "I have found vines and grapes." "Can this be possible?" asked Leif, who had never seen grapes. "Certainly," answered the sailor, "for I was born where grapes grow." Leif named the new land Vinland, the land of wine and vines. Find Vinland on the map.

VIKINGS SETTLE IN VINLAND

Leif returned to Greenland filled with tales about Vinland. About five years later, a Viking named Thorfinn Karlsefni (tü′ fin cärl sev′ nə), and his wife Freydis, convinced many Greenlanders to move to Vinland.

Viking ships and helmets were beautiful as well as useful. What do they suggest about Viking life?

After the Greenlanders had settled in Vinland, they were approached by black-haired men in skin boats. The strangers were probably Indians in birch-bark canoes. The frightened Greenlanders attacked, killing several of the Indians.

According to the sagas, the Indians later came out of the forests to fight back. They shot razor-sharp arrows at the Vikings, who fled in terror. Freydis could not believe her eyes. "Why are you running?" she shouted. She picked up the sword of a dead Viking. As the Indians rushed toward her, she spun around to face them, sword across her chest. Her surprising action stopped the attackers in their tracks. They turned and ran away.

VINLAND IS FORGOTTEN

Soon after the Indian attack, the Viking settlers returned to Greenland. The sagas say that Vinland was "an excellent land." Yet the Greenlanders feared they "could never live there in safety and freedom from fear."

Sagas of Vinland were told around the fire during long winter nights in Greenland. But as the years went by,

the new land became a dim memory. Nearly 500 years would pass before Europeans would again come to North America.

Today we know that the Greenlanders probably settled in Newfoundland (nü' fənd lənd), a large island off the coast of Canada. In 1960 archaeologists uncovered the remains of Viking houses there. These artifacts suggest that the sagas about Vinland are based on real events.

Check Your Reading

1. Who were the Vikings? What did they find in Vinland?
2. How do we know that the Greenlanders probably settled in Newfoundland?
3. **GEOGRAPHY SKILL:** How did the geography of Scandinavia encourage the Vikings to become skilled sailors?
4. **THINKING SKILL:** Beginning with the Vikings' journey from Scandinavia, list all the events mentioned in this lesson in the order in which they occurred.

2 The Search for a Sea Route to Asia

READ TO LEARN

Key Vocabulary

navigation
cape

Key People

Marco Polo
Prince Henry
Bartholomeu Dias
Vasco da Gama

Key Places

Asia   Portugal
China   Africa
India   Cape of Good
          Hope

Read Aloud

"Thanks be to God for pepper!" This was the feeling of many Europeans 500 years ago. Today we sprinkle pepper on our food without a thought. In the 1400s, though, Europeans spent fortunes on this spice. Pepper was worth its weight in silver.

Why was a spice worth so much? The food eaten by most Europeans in the 1400s was dull and tasteless. Pepper and other spices were used to preserve meat and to make food taste better. But only the rich could afford such fashionable dishes as sugar and pepper toasted on bread.

Unfortunately, pepper did not grow in Europe. If Europeans wanted this delicious spice, they would have to get it from somewhere else.

Read for Purpose

1. **WHAT YOU KNOW:** Why do you think pepper was so expensive for Europeans to buy?
2. **WHAT YOU WILL LEARN:** Why did Europeans want to find a sea route to Asia?

THE ADVENTURES OF MARCO POLO

The spices that made food taste good came from Asia. But few Europeans had ever traveled there and lived to tell the tale. One who did was a merchant from Venice, Italy, named Marco Polo.

In 1271, when Marco Polo was just 17 years old, he went with his father and uncle to China. In his travels through China, Marco Polo found a huge, rich country with many wonders. Some of these wonders included flaming springs and amazing black rocks that burned longer than wood. Marco Polo did not know it then but the flaming springs were oil fields, and the burning rocks were coal fires.

After nearly 25 years, the Polos returned to Venice. They had been away for so long that no one recognized them. And nobody believed their stories about Asia and its riches.

The Polos invited their friends to a feast. As their shocked guests watched, they ripped apart their ragged traveling clothes. A fortune in jewels fell out of pockets hidden in the rags.

Marco Polo wrote a book about his travels. Some people found his story too fantastic to believe. When he lay dying in 1324, friends asked him if he had stretched the truth in some places. He answered, "I did not write half of what I saw."

THE SPICE TRADE

After hearing the fascinating stories of travelers such as Marco Polo, Europeans were eager to buy goods from Asia. At the time, trade with Asia was in the hands of Asian and Italian merchants. Asian traders brought silks and spices from India and China overland to the city of Constantinople. Italian merchants sailed from Venice and Genoa to Constantinople. There they traded European goods such as lumber, wheat, and wool for gold, silk, and spices.

The Italians sold the goods they had bought to merchants all across Europe. Every time the goods changed hands, the prices went up.

As the demand for Asian goods grew, the Italian traders became rich and powerful. Leaders of other European countries looked at the Italians with envy. If only they could find a sea route to Asia. Then they could buy goods directly from Asian traders. Such trade would bring new wealth and power to their countries.

Marco Polo left Venice in 1271 to begin his voyage to China. Venice was a rich trading city at that time and had many merchant ships.

PRINCE HENRY THE NAVIGATOR

The country of Portugal led the way. Its leader, Prince Henry, was the first European ruler to look for a sea route to Asia. In the early 1400s he set up a school for sailors. They studied geography and navigation, the science of determining a ship's direction and location. The new science of navigation meant that sailors could be more accurate as they guided their ships across the ocean.

Prince Henry had three goals. First, he wanted to learn more about unknown lands. Second, he wanted to bring the Christian religion to the people of Africa and Asia. Finally, Prince Henry wanted to find a sea route around Africa to Asia. He hoped that Portugal would grow rich trading for gold and spices.

Year after year, Prince Henry sent out his ships to explore the west coast of Africa. Each captain traveled a little farther south and reported back what he had seen. Mapmakers used this information to fill in Henry's maps of Africa. Although Henry never sailed to Africa himself, he became known as Prince Henry the Navigator.

AROUND THE CAPE OF GOOD HOPE

To people in the 1400s, the Atlantic Ocean was a scary "sea of darkness." They thought the ocean was filled with giant, man-eating monsters. For many years, Prince Henry's sailors refused to sail far out into the Atlantic. They had heard the sea boiled there.

When the sailors finally sailed down the west coast of Africa, they found the waters did not boil. By the 1450s, Portuguese ships had begun trading with several African kingdoms.

MAP SKILL: Why do you think Dias hugged the west coast of Africa in his voyage of 1487–1488? Why did Da Gama sail farther out into the ocean on his voyage?

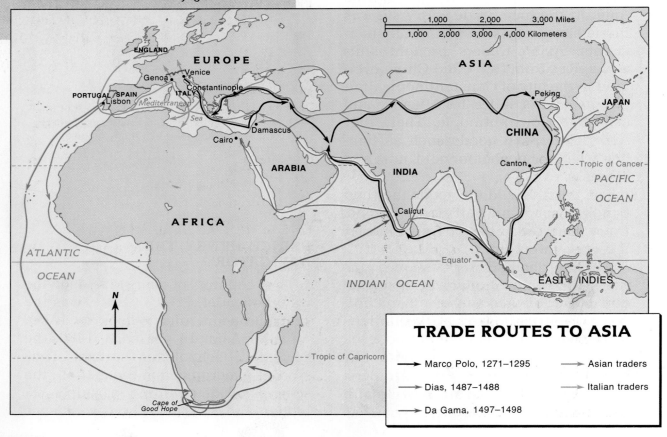

TRADE ROUTES TO ASIA

→ Marco Polo, 1271–1295   → Asian traders

→ Dias, 1487–1488   → Italian traders

→ Da Gama, 1497–1498

When Prince Henry died in 1460, the voyages down the coast of Africa did not stop. In 1487, King John of Portugal asked a Portuguese ship captain, Bartholomeu Dias (bär tu̇ lu̇ mā′ u̇ dē′ əs), to find a way around the southern tip of Africa.

Dias was sailing south along the African coast when his ships were caught in a great storm. For nearly two weeks they were driven south, with no sight of land. They feared they would drown. When the storm finally passed, Dias sailed east to find land. Instead, he found nothing but ocean.

At last Dias realized what had happened. The storm had driven his ships around Africa into the Indian Ocean. Turning back, Dias saw a great cape on the southern tip of Africa. A cape is a pointed piece of coastline that juts out into the sea. Dias called it the Cape of Storms. But when King John heard Dias's report, he knew this cape held the promise of a sea route to Asia. He renamed it the Cape of Good Hope.

THE ROUTE OF VASCO DA GAMA

In 1497 a sailor named Vasco da Gama left Portugal with four ships. His orders were to sail to India. Da Gama sailed around the Cape of Good Hope and across the Indian Ocean to India. Trace the routes of both Dias and Da Gama on the map on page 132.

Da Gama had finally found the sea route to Asia. But the journey was long and hard. Of the 170 men who began the voyage, just 50 came home two years later.

A NEW ROUTE TO ASIA

The search for a sea route to Asia had taken the Portuguese over 60

When Vasco da Gama and his crew arrived in India, they were greeted by the people of Calicut.

years. During that time, they had learned much about Africa and Asia. And for Portugal's sailors, the "sea of darkness" had become a highway to the riches of Asia.

Check Your Reading

1. Why were Europeans interested in trading with Asia?
2. Why did they want to find a sea route to Asia?
3. **GEOGRAPHY SKILL:** What discovery was made by Dias as a result of a storm at sea?
4. **THINKING SKILL:** How did the travels of Marco Polo lead to the discovery of a sea route to Asia?

3 Columbus Reaches America

READ TO LEARN

Key Vocabulary

expedition

Key People

Christopher Columbus
King Ferdinand
Queen Isabella
Amerigo Vespucci

Key Places

Indies
Spain
Caribbean Sea
San Salvador
West Indies

Read Aloud

"Tierra! Tierra!" Land! Land! A lookout on a small ship raised this cry on the morning of October 12, 1492. His shout marked the European discovery of "a new world."

Read for Purpose

1. **WHAT YOU KNOW:** Why did most Europeans know nothing about North and South America before 1492?
2. **WHAT YOU WILL LEARN:** Why did Christopher Columbus want to sail west across the Atlantic Ocean?

CHRISTOPHER COLUMBUS

The leader of the expedition described above was an Italian seaman named Christopher Columbus. An expedition is a journey made for a special purpose. The purpose of Columbus's expedition was to find another, shorter way to Asia.

Columbus was born in Genoa, Italy, and went to sea as a boy. At the age of 25, he was shipwrecked off the coast of Portugal. Clinging to a piece of wood, he swam several miles to shore.

When Columbus arrived in Portugal, he did not know how to read or write. So he decided to settle in Lisbon to study. He was soon reading books on geography and navigation. He also studied by sailing on Portuguese ships. In time, Christopher Columbus became an expert navigator.

Columbus came to believe that the best route to Asia was not south but west. He dreamed of sailing west across the Atlantic Ocean to reach Japan and China. Columbus thought that the Indies (the islands of Southeast Asia) were just 3,000 miles (4,827 km) west of Europe. They are, in fact, more like 10,000 miles (16,090 km) away!

For years Columbus pleaded with King John of Portugal to pay for a trip across the Atlantic. In 1484 the king

Christopher Columbus (*above*) led three ships west across the Atlantic Ocean in search of the Indies. One of them, the *Niña*, is shown at the left. What qualities made Columbus great, in your opinion?

asked a group of experts for advice. They told him that Asia was much farther away than Columbus thought. Such a long voyage was impossible, they said. The king agreed and sent Columbus away.

THE IMPOSSIBLE VOYAGE BEGINS

Columbus then traveled to Spain and asked King Ferdinand and Queen Isabella to pay for his trip. After six years, Queen Isabella decided Spain had much to gain if Columbus succeeded and little to lose if he failed. She raised the money for his voyage.

Early in August 1492, Columbus and a crew of 90 men left Spain with three ships—the *Niña*, the *Pinta*, and the *Santa Maria*. Their course was simple: "West! Nothing to the north. Nothing to the south."

CROSSING THE SEA OF DARKNESS

The farther west they sailed into the "sea of darkness," the more afraid Columbus's sailors became. To calm their fears, Columbus tricked them. He kept two books, or ships' logs, describing the voyage. Each day he wrote the real distance he thought they had traveled in a secret book. In the other book he wrote shorter distances. He showed the sailors the second book so they would not know how far they were from home.

But the sailors still worried. They were afraid they would never see their homes again. By October 10, nerves were at the breaking point. The men demanded that Columbus turn back. Columbus listened to the crew and then made his decision. He agreed to return home if they did not find land in two days. It was just enough time. On October 12, land was sighted at last.

A NEW LAND

If you trace Columbus's route on the map on page 137, you can see that he never reached Asia. He had come to an island in the **Caribbean** (kâr ə bē′ ən) **Sea**. With tears of joy he claimed the island for Spain and gave it the name **San Salvador**—Holy Savior.

After two days on the island Columbus set sail again to find the riches of Japan and China. In two weeks he reached the island of Cuba. But there were no palaces of gold.

For three months, Columbus continued to search for the mainland of Asia. Instead he found more islands. The people he met ate foods he had never seen before, such as corn. And they smoked a strange plant called tobacco. Disappointed, Columbus returned to Spain.

THE RETURN TO SPAIN

In 1493 Columbus and his crew were welcomed home as heroes. King Ferdinand and Queen Isabella were sure his discovery would make Spain the richest country in Europe.

Columbus was so sure the islands he found were near Asia that he named them "the Indies." He called the people he had met "Indians." Even though he was wrong, the names stuck. Today these Caribbean islands are known as the **West Indies**. And the native peoples of the new lands he found are called Indians.

Columbus made three more voyages across the Atlantic. But he never found the fabulous places that Marco Polo had written about. And yet, he would not give up his dream. Columbus died in 1506 still believing he had found some unknown part of Asia.

This painting of Columbus landing at San Salvador hangs in the United States Capitol Building in Washington, D.C. Why does the United States honor Columbus?

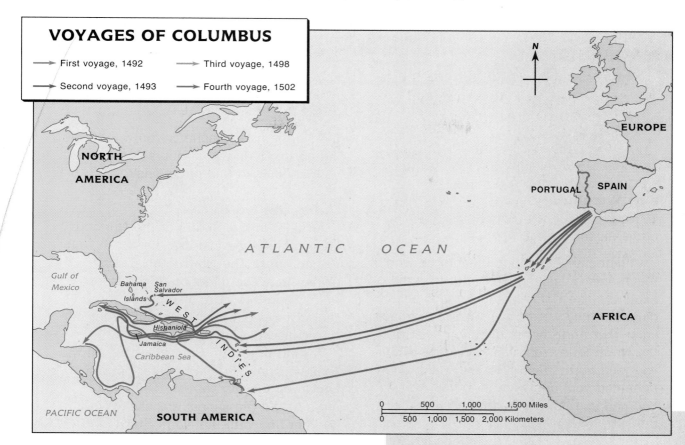

VOYAGES OF COLUMBUS

→ First voyage, 1492
→ Second voyage, 1493
→ Third voyage, 1498
→ Fourth voyage, 1502

EUROPE

NORTH AMERICA

PORTUGAL SPAIN

ATLANTIC OCEAN

Gulf of Mexico

Bahama Islands San Salvador

Hispaniola

Jamaica

Caribbean Sea

WEST INDIES

AFRICA

PACIFIC OCEAN

SOUTH AMERICA

0	500	1,000	1,500 Miles
0	500 1,000 1,500	2,000 Kilometers	

How many voyages to the West Indies did Columbus make? Which of these voyages took him farthest south?

AMERICA IS NAMED

Other explorers followed Christopher Columbus across the Atlantic Ocean. One was an Italian named Amerigo Vespucci (ə mâr′ ə gō ves pü′ chē). After exploring South America, Vespucci realized that the lands Columbus had reached were not part of Asia. They were part of a giant continent unknown to Europeans.

A German geographer was excited by Vespucci's news. In 1507 he published a new map of the world and named the new land "Americhland," in honor of Amerigo Vespucci. From that map came the name America.

WHY WE HONOR COLUMBUS

We honor Columbus because he introduced Europe to a new world. He was the first person to show the way across the Atlantic Ocean. When he returned safely, other explorers were willing to cross the sea.

 Check Your Reading

1. What was Columbus's plan for reaching Asia? Why did he think it would work?
2. Why did King Ferdinand and Queen Isabella treat Columbus as a hero?
3. GEOGRAPHY SKILL: How did the American continents get their name?
4. THINKING SKILL: Recall the story of Columbus's voyage to America. List all the events of this lesson in the order in which they occurred.

137

Finding Directions

Key Vocabulary

North Star   Big Dipper
Little Dipper   compass

Christopher Columbus thought he would reach Asia by sailing west. But how did explorers like Columbus know in which direction they were traveling? You already know that north is the direction toward the North Pole. You also know that when you face north, east is to your right, south is behind you, and west is to your left. You can use the north arrow to find directions on a map.

But how do you find directions if you do not know where you are? Three things can help you. They are the sun, the North Star, and a compass.

Using the Sun

As you know, the sun is in the east in the early morning. If you stand outside at that time and face your shadow, you will be facing west. Late in the afternoon, the sun is in the west. If you face your shadow at that time, you will be facing east. If you face your shadow at noon in the Northern Hemisphere, you will be facing north. During what hours can you use your shadow to find directions?

Using the North Star

At night in most parts of the Northern Hemisphere, you can use the North Star to find north. The North Star always shines from the direction of the North Pole. Therefore, it is also called the Pole Star. This bright star is part of a star pattern called the Little Dipper.

To find the North Star, you can use the "pointer stars" in another star pattern known as the Big Dipper. The pointer stars of the Big Dipper are always in a straight line with the North Star.

Find the Big Dipper, the pointer stars, the Little Dipper, and the North Star below. Notice that the North Star is at the end of the handle of the Little Dipper. During what hours can you use the North Star to find directions?

As the earth turns, the Big Dipper and the Little Dipper rotate around the North Star. The Big Dipper is easy to recognize in the night sky. Its "pointers" will always help you find the North Star.

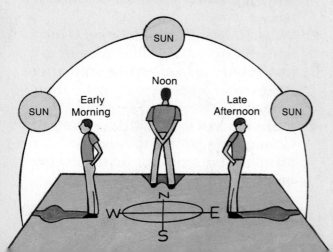

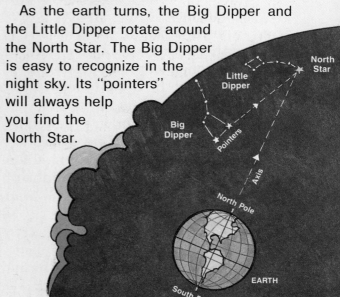

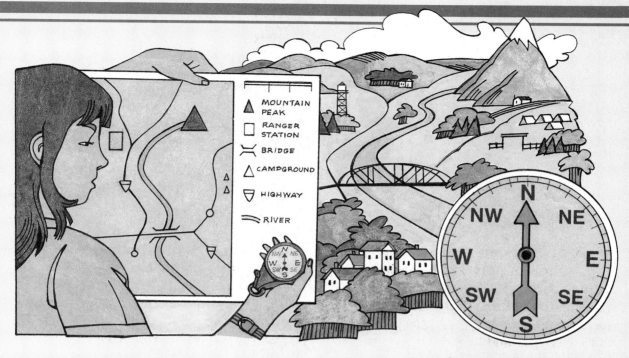

Using a Compass

You will not be able to use the stars and sun at all times, however. When they are not visible, you need a compass to find directions. A compass is an instrument with a magnetic needle that always points north when the compass is held level. Around the needle are shown the cardinal directions: N (north), E (east), S (south), and W (west)—and the intermediate directions: NE (northeast), SE (southeast), SW (southwest), and NW (northwest).

Hold the compass steady. Then, if you turn your body until the letter *N* lines up with the needle, you and your compass will be facing north.

Using a Compass and a Map

If you have a compass and a map, you can easily find your way from one place to another. First, turn the compass so that the letter *N* lines up with the needle. Then, turn the map so that the north

arrow on the map points in the same direction as the compass needle. You have now oriented yourself and the map. To orient means to line up with the compass.

In the drawing above, the girl has oriented herself and her map. If she is at the bridge, in what direction should she go to get to the ranger station?

Reviewing the Skill

1. How do you find directions if you do not know where you are?
2. If you face your shadow in the early morning, in what direction are you facing?
3. To which star pattern does the North Star belong?
4. Which star pattern helps you locate the North Star?
5. What direction does the needle of a compass face when the compass is in a level position?
6. Why is it important for you to be able to use a compass and a map?

4 A Voyage Around the World

READ TO LEARN

Key Vocabulary

isthmus

Key People

Vasco Núñez de Balboa
Ferdinand Magellan

Key Places

Isthmus of Panama
Strait of Magellan
Pacific Ocean
Philippine Islands

Read Aloud

One late summer day in 1522, a sorry-looking ship limped into a port in Spain. The worm-eaten *Victoria* could barely float. Its few surviving crew members looked like living skeletons. But what a story they had to tell! They had done what no one had done before. They had sailed around the world.

Read for Purpose

1. **WHAT YOU KNOW:** Why do you think explorers wanted to sail around the world?
2. **WHAT YOU WILL LEARN:** What did Europeans learn from Magellan's voyage?

BALBOA FINDS A NEW OCEAN

After Columbus's voyage, Spain thought it had found a sea route to Asia. Then came the bad news. A new land blocked the way to Asia. Or did it?

A Spanish explorer named Vasco Núñez de Balboa (bal bō′ ə) tried to find out. In 1513 he landed his ship on the Isthmus of Panama in Central America. An isthmus (is′ məs) is a narrow strip of land that connects two larger pieces of land. You can see on the map in your Atlas on page 595 that the Isthmus of Panama connects North and South America.

Balboa led his men across the jungle-covered isthmus. On the west side they found a huge blue ocean. Balboa claimed all of it for Spain. Now it was clear that Asia lay beyond yet another large body of water.

FERDINAND MAGELLAN

In 1518 a Portuguese sea captain named Ferdinand Magellan went to King Charles of Spain with a plan. Magellan thought he could reach Asia by sailing around South America and then west across the ocean Balboa had found.

King Charles supported his plan. In 1519 Magellan left Spain with 5 ships and about 250 men. As they sailed south along the east coast of South

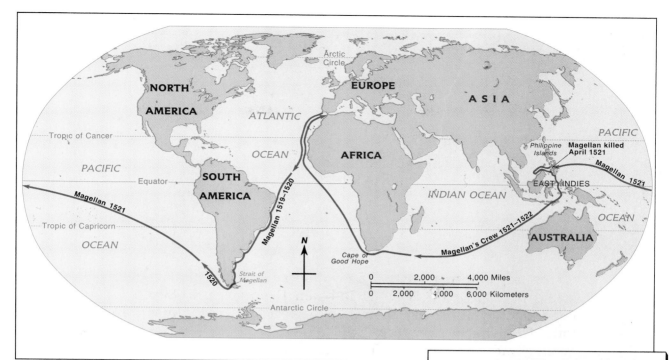

MAP SKILL: Trace Magellan's voyage on the map. In what direction did he sail? In what year did he sail around South America?

America, one of Magellan's ships was wrecked.

A year after setting sail, Magellan found a strait connecting the Atlantic with Balboa's ocean. But it was so stormy and rocky that one ship turned back to Spain. Magellan led his other three ships safely through the 350-mile-long (563-km) strait. Today that passage is known as the Strait of Magellan. You can follow Magellan's route on the map above.

CROSSING THE PACIFIC OCEAN

The ocean Balboa had found was a welcome sight after the stormy strait. Magellan named the ocean *El Pacifico,* which means "peaceful" in Spanish. "Well was it named [the Pacific Ocean]," wrote Antonio Pigafetta, a crew member. For the next three months "we met with no storm."

They also met with no land. Food and water ran low. Their remaining meat became rotten. Of the experience Antonio Pigafetta wrote:

We ate old biscuits that were nothing but dust and worms . . . we drank water that was yellow and stinking. We also ate ox hides . . . and sawdust.

At last Magellan reached the Marianas Islands. With fresh food and water, he sailed on to the Philippine Islands. There he was killed in a local war. Pigafetta wrote sadly, "They killed our mirror, our light, our comfort and our true guide."

THE VOYAGE HOME

By now Magellan's three ships were in sad shape. One had to be left in the Philippines. Two ships sailed on to the East Indies. There the crews traded everything they had for spices. The

141

Magellan and some of his crew explored the area around the southernmost tip of South America. What did Magellan find as a result of his explorations in this area?

overloaded *Trinidad* began to leak and could not go on.

The *Victoria* sailed home alone. It followed the Portuguese route across the Indian Ocean and around Africa. Many men died as supplies of food and water ran out.

In 1522, three long years after leaving Spain, the *Victoria* returned home with 17 half-dead sailors. Their cargo of spices paid the cost of the entire expedition.

A SMALLER WORLD

One hundred years had passed since Prince Henry the Navigator began sending ships out to sea. In that time, Europeans had found a sea route to Asia. They had discovered "a new world" across the Atlantic Ocean. And they had sailed around the world. Once, the oceans had kept distant people apart. Now they were beginning to bring people together. It was becoming a smaller world.

Check Your Reading

1. What body of water did Balboa reach? What country did he claim it for?
2. What did Magellan's voyage prove about the location of Asia?
3. **GEOGRAPHY SKILL:** Where is the Strait of Magellan located?
4. **THINKING SKILL:** How did Balboa's voyage of exploration lead to a voyage by Magellan?

5 Spain's American Empire

READ TO LEARN

Key Vocabulary

conquistador
colony
slave
missionary
mission

Key People

Hernándo Cortés
Francisco Pizarro
Juan Ponce de León
Hernando de Soto
Francisco Coronado
Junípero Serra

Key Places

Peru
Florida
New Spain
California

Read Aloud

In 1519 Indians along the east coast of Mexico saw a scary sight. Pale strangers arrived in "wooden houses on the water." Some thought the strangers were gods. Others saw them as enemies and attacked. But the Indians' stone weapons were no match for Spanish steel and gunpowder. Soon these Indians would become part of Spain's growing empire in North and South America.

Read for Purpose

1. **WHAT YOU KNOW:** Why do we celebrate Christopher Columbus's birthday today?
2. **WHAT YOU WILL LEARN:** What did Spanish explorers achieve in North and South America?

THE CONQUISTADORS

The "pale strangers" seen by the Indians were Spanish soldiers called conquistadors (kon kēs' tə dôrz), or conquerors. The conquistadors came to America to conquer new lands for Spain. They also hoped to find gold and glory for themselves.

The first conquistadors followed Columbus to the West Indies. They turned the islands Columbus had discovered there into Spanish colonies. A colony is a place ruled by another country. From the West Indies, the conquistadors moved on to the mainland of North and South America.

Hernándo Cortés was one of the most famous conquistadors. In 1519 he led about 500 soldiers to Mexico. Helped by thousands of Indians, he conquered the Aztec empire. The Indians who fought with Cortés hoped to free themselves from Aztec rule. But they soon found they had only traded rule by the Aztecs for rule by Spain.

143

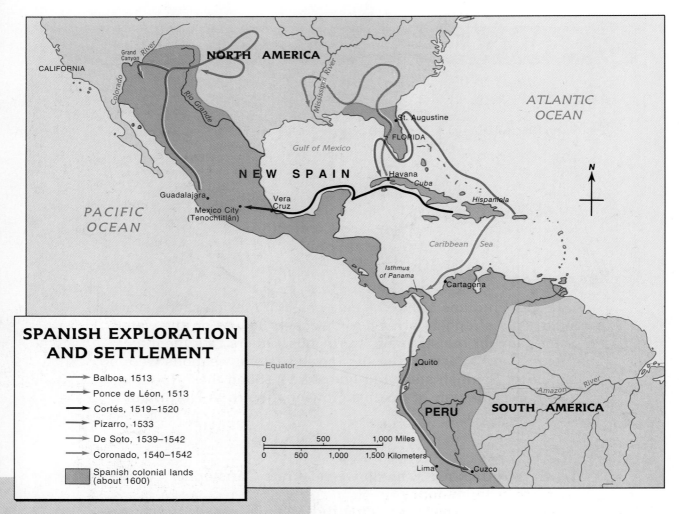

SPANISH EXPLORATION
AND SETTLEMENT

→ Balboa, 1513
→ Ponce de Léon, 1513
→ Cortés, 1519–1520
→ Pizarro, 1533
→ De Soto, 1539–1542
→ Coronado, 1540–1542
▢ Spanish colonial lands (about 1600)

MAP SKILL: Which Spanish explorer won lands for Spain in Peru? Which Spanish explorer saw the Grand Canyon?

In 1533 soldiers under **Francisco Pizarro** (pi zär′ ō) conquered the Incan empire of **Peru.** There he found a fortune in gold and silver. Soon the riches of the Incas were pouring into Spain.

EXPLORING NORTH AMERICA

Tales of treasure lured other conquistadors to the lands north of Mexico. You can follow their routes on the map above.

Juan Ponce de León crossed the Atlantic Ocean with Columbus and set- tled on the island of Puerto Rico. There he heard stories of a fountain with waters that "make old men young again." In 1513 Ponce de León sailed north from Puerto Rico. He discovered a land of birds and flowers. He named it **Florida,** which means "land of flowers" in Spanish. But he never found his fountain of youth.

Hernando de Soto led 600 men to Florida in 1539. He had heard tales of the Seven Cities of Gold, where houses were covered with jewels and the streets were paved with gold. De Soto's men crossed the Appalachian Mountains and explored the Mississippi River Valley. But nowhere did they find

Coronado (*below*) and his men explored the American Southwest. What can you tell about their experiences from the painting above?

gold. In 1543, 311 ragged men straggled back to Mexico. They were the lucky survivors of De Soto's search for the Seven Cities of Gold.

While De Soto explored the Southeast, Francisco Coronado searched for the golden cities in the Southwest. In 1540 Coronado led an army into the land of the Pueblo people. He visited many Indian villages. But nowhere did he find jeweled houses or golden streets.

Coronado's men explored the Southwest for two years. They gazed into the Grand Canyon and followed buffalo herds across the Great Plains. But they returned to Mexico with neither jewels nor gold.

SPAIN'S GROWING EMPIRE

The hunt for treasure took Spain's conquistadors north to San Francisco Bay and south to the Strait of Magellan. Everywhere the Spanish went, they claimed new lands for Spain. This

growing empire was divided into two huge colonies—New Spain and Peru. Find both colonies on the map.

Spain gave the people who came to live in its colonies land and slaves to work for them. A slave is someone who is owned by another person. Many Indian slaves died of overwork. Millions more died of diseases that came to

145

A SPANISH MISSION

River

Cornfields

Vegetable garden

Indian village

Kitchen

Workshops

Priests' quarters

Patio

Fountain

Mission church

Soldiers' quarters

Candle making

Tannery

DIAGRAM SKILL: The Spanish **mission** was the center of many different kinds of activities. Use the diagram to locate the parts of the mission and describe the activities of each.

America with the Spanish. Illnesses such as measles and smallpox wiped out whole villages. So many Indians died that it was said, "The Spaniard's very shadow kills the Indians."

As the Indians died, Spanish colonists looked to other places for workers. They began buying slaves along the west coast of Africa. Most Africans became slaves when they were captured by other Africans in wars. Now they were shipped to America.

SPANISH MISSIONARIES

Many of the Spanish priests who came to America cared deeply about the Indians. These priests had come to New Spain to serve as missionaries. Missionaries are people who teach their religion to others with different beliefs. Often missionaries were the first Spanish settlers in an area. Many missionaries learned the local language so they could teach the Christian religion in words the Indians would understand.

Wherever the missionaries went, they built settlements called missions. Look at the diagram of a Spanish mission on page 146. You can see that a mission usually included a church, houses, farms, and a kitchen. As a mission grew, workshops and schools were added.

One of the best-known Spanish missionaries was Father Junípero Serra (hū nē′ pə rō ser′ rə). In 1769 Serra walked from Mexico to a place the Spanish called California. He was a short man who limped when he walked. But to the priests who came with him, he was a giant in courage and determination. His dream was to bring Christianity to the California Indians.

Father Serra began building a chain of missions from San Diego Bay north to San Francisco Bay. By 1823 there were 21 missions, each about a day's journey apart. The mission priests tried to teach the Indians new skills and a new religion. But they also forced them to do all the work that kept the mission going. The Indians grew the crops the Spanish ate, and they made the cloth, soap, and other products that the Spanish used every day. You can read two views of the Spanish missions on pages 148 and 149.

OUR SPANISH CULTURE

For 300 years Spain ruled an empire that included most of South America, Central America, and large parts of North America. The Spanish left their mark on the lands that they settled. For example, they built over 2,000 towns in the land that became the United States. Some, like San Francisco, California, have grown into major cities.

Today our Spanish heritage can be seen in Spanish-style homes with thick brick walls and red tile roofs. It can be heard in music anytime a Spanish guitar is played. And whenever we bite an orange, sip lemonade, or nibble olives, we are tasting some of the many foods brought to America from Spain.

Check Your Reading

1. What did Spanish explorers hope to find in North America?
2. How did the Spanish change life for the American Indians?
3. **GEOGRAPHY SKILL:** How far north did Coronado explore?
4. **THINKING SKILL:** How did conquistadors bring about the growth of Spain's American empire?

Early 1800s: Did the Missions Improve the Way of Life of the California Indians?

In the last lesson, you read that Father Junípero Serra and other Spanish missionaries hoped to convert the California Indians to the Christian religion. In each mission, the Indians were taught about the beliefs and practices of Christianity. This also meant giving up their old ways in order to live like Spaniards.

Between 1769 and 1833 over 50,000 Indians lived for a time at missions. They learned to farm and ride horses in addition to many other new skills. At the same time, they began to lose touch with their Indian traditions. Many people claimed that this change benefited the Indians. Others argued that it was destroying the Indian way of life.

POINT

The Case for the Missions

Frederick Beechey, a British sea captain, visited some California missions in 1825. Later he wrote:

The object of the missions is to make Christians out of as many of the Indians as possible and to teach them how to lead a good life. The missions also teach them some trade so that they may in time be able to provide for themselves and become useful members of civilized society.

Beechey heard reports that Indians were forced to move to the missions by Spanish troops. Even if such reports were true, wrote Beechey:

The change according to our ideas of happiness would seem to be good for the Indians. They lead a far better life in the missions than in the forests. In the forests they go about with no clothes and depend solely on wild acorns for food.

● What did Beechey think was the purpose of the missions?

COUNTERPOINT

The Case Against the Missions

Some Indians showed what they thought of mission life by running away. Georg Heinrich von Langsdorff, a German visitor to California, wrote in 1812:

An irresistible desire for freedom sometimes breaks out in mission Indians. They love the wandering life—a life of fishing and hunting. In their eyes this life seems better than all the advantages they enjoy at the mission.

Love of freedom was not the only reason Indians ran away. Many feared the diseases brought to America by Europeans. Others left because they hated mission life. Here an Indian named Julio Cesar explains why.

When I was a boy the treatment given the Indians at my mission was not good. For our work in the fields we were paid nothing. We were given only our food and once a year a blanket.

● Why did many Indians run away from the missions?

UNDERSTANDING THE POINT/COUNTERPOINT

1. Why did Frederick Beechey believe the missions were good for the Indians?
2. Why did Julio Cesar believe the missions hurt the Indians?
3. Which side do you think made the stronger argument? Explain your answer.

IMPORTANT EVENTS

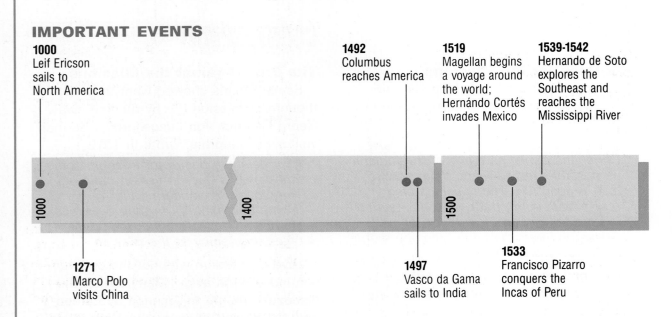

1000
Leif Ericson
sails to
North America

1492
Columbus
reaches America

1519
Magellan begins
a voyage around
the world;
Hernándo Cortés
invades Mexico

1539-1542
Hernando de Soto
explores the
Southeast and
reaches the
Mississippi River

1000

1400

1500

1271
Marco Polo
visits China

1497
Vasco da Gama
sails to India

1533
Francisco Pizarro
conquers the
Incas of Peru

PEOPLE TO KNOW

Christopher Columbus 1451-1506

Vasco da Gama 1460?-1524

Bartholomeu Dias ?-1500

Leif Ericson early 1000s

Prince Henry 1394-1460

Ferdinand Magellan 1480-1521

Junípero Serra 1713-1784

IDEAS TO REMEMBER

- The Vikings reached North America about 1,000 years ago, but their settlements there did not last.
- Portugal was the first European nation to find a sea route to Asia.
- On October 12, 1492, Christopher Columbus and his crew reached America and claimed the lands they found for Spain.
- In 1522 Ferdinand Magellan's crew completed a voyage around the world.
- For over 300 years Spain ruled an empire that included most of South America and large parts of North America.

REVIEWING VOCABULARY

colony   navigation
expedition   slave
missionary

Number a paper from 1 to 5. Beside each number write the word or term from the list above that matches the statement.

1. A journey made by a person for a special purpose
2. A person owned by another person
3. The science of determining a ship's direction and location
4. A place ruled by another country
5. A person who teaches his or her religion to others with different beliefs

REVIEWING FACTS

1. How did the Vikings come to settle in Vinland? Why did they leave there?
2. Why did Prince Henry become known as Prince Henry the Navigator? What were his three goals?
3. Why do we still honor Christopher Columbus today?
4. What problems did Magellan and his crew face?
5. What areas did each of these Spaniards explore: Juan Ponce de León, Hernando de Soto, Francisco Coronado?

◀◀▆▶ WRITING ABOUT MAIN IDEAS

1. **Writing a Paragraph of Contrast:** Write a paragraph comparing early sea exploration with modern-day space travel. The paragraph should include at least two similarities and two differences.

2. **Writing a Journal Entry:** Imagine that you are with one of the explorers discussed in this chapter. Write an entry in your journal describing an experience during your travels. Try to paint a lively picture of the sights, sounds, and smells of an adventure at sea, for example. Or you might imagine what it was like to discover a new place and find out about the people living there.

3. **Making a List:** When Spain took control of New Spain and Peru, some people were helped and others were hurt. Make a list of the people or groups who were affected by Spanish settlement in the Americas. Beside each item on the list, write a sentence explaining how the people were helped or hurt.

4. **Writing Directions:** Look at the map on page 144. Choose one explorer and write a description of his route, including the directions he traveled and the approximate distances. For example, "The explorer traveled about 100 miles (160 km) northeast, then he turned west," and so on.

BUILDING SKILLS: FINDING DIRECTIONS

1. How would you use a compass and the North Star to find out which way is east?
2. If you were facing north, where would south be?
3. If you were facing south, where would west be?
4. If you were facing east, where would north be?
5. Why was the invention of the compass so important for sailors?

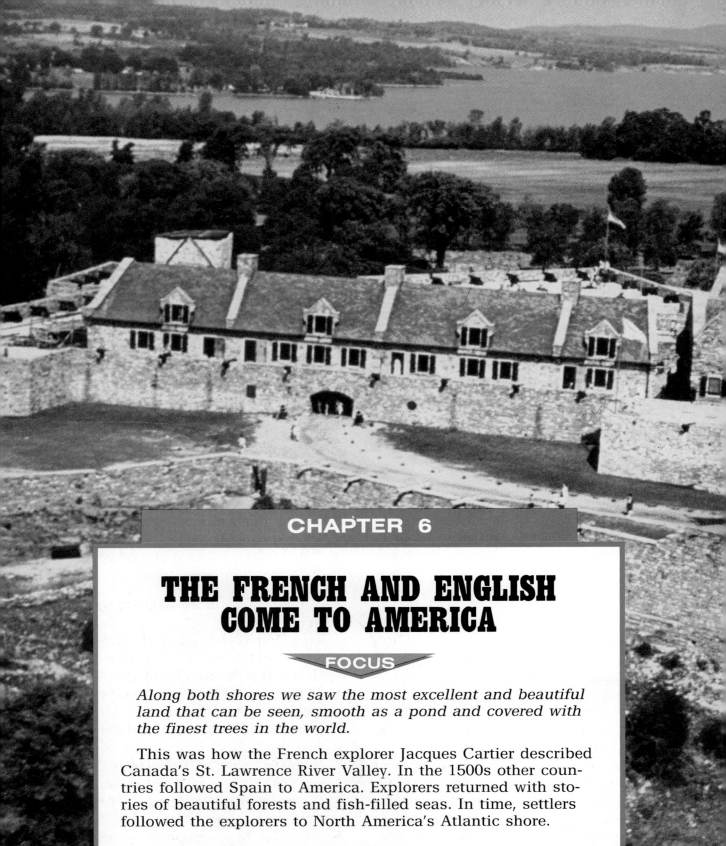

CHAPTER 6

THE FRENCH AND ENGLISH COME TO AMERICA

FOCUS

Along both shores we saw the most excellent and beautiful land that can be seen, smooth as a pond and covered with the finest trees in the world.

This was how the French explorer Jacques Cartier described Canada's St. Lawrence River Valley. In the 1500s other countries followed Spain to America. Explorers returned with stories of beautiful forests and fish-filled seas. In time, settlers followed the explorers to North America's Atlantic shore.

1 The Search for the Northwest Passage

READ TO LEARN

Key Vocabulary
Northwest Passage

Key People
John Cabot
Giovanni da
   Verrazano
Jacques Cartier
Donnaconna
Henry Hudson

Key Places
Grand Banks
Canada
St. Lawrence River
Montreal
Hudson River
Hudson Bay

Read Aloud

"China!" "Spices!" The magic words spread quickly through the town of Bristol, England, one August day in 1497. The first English ship to cross the Atlantic Ocean was back. Crowds rushed to the docks to hear the news. Everyone hoped that the English explorers had found a new sea route to Asia.

Read for Purpose

1. **WHAT YOU KNOW:** What treasures did Europeans hope to find in Asia?
2. **READ TO LEARN:** Why were explorers searching for a North-west Passage to Asia? What did they find instead?

THE VOYAGE OF JOHN CABOT

The captain of the first English ship to cross the Atlantic was an Italian named John Cabot. After hearing about Columbus's voyages, Cabot believed that he could reach Asia by sailing west. England's King Henry VII allowed him to try and gave him money for the voyage.

When Cabot returned to England in 1497, he reported that he had found a large island. He had not seen anyone on the island. But there were signs that people came there to hunt and fish. The waters off the island were so full of codfish they could be scooped up with baskets.

King Henry hoped that "the newe founde lande" was part of Asia. Only later did the English learn that the island they called Newfoundland was off the coast of North America. The rich fishing waters Cabot found are now called the Grand Banks.

In 1498 Cabot sailed across the Atlantic with five ships. But this time, the ship he was on disappeared. An Englishman wrote that Cabot had "found his new lands nowhere but on the very bottom of the ocean."

THE NORTHWEST PASSAGE

Cabot's voyage proved to Europeans that two large continents blocked the western sea route to Asia. You read in Chapter 5 that Ferdinand Magellan finally found a passage around South America in 1520. But the voyage through the storm-tossed Strait of Magellan was difficult and dangerous.

Explorers from many countries began looking for a Northwest Passage to Asia. They hoped to find a waterway through North America that linked the Atlantic and Pacific oceans.

In 1524 King Francis I of France sent an Italian, Giovanni da Verrazano (jō vän′ nē da vâr rät sän′ ō), to lead an expedition to find the Northwest Passage. Trace his route on the map below. As you can see, Verrazano explored the Atlantic coastline from present-day North Carolina northward to Maine.

CARTIER SEARCHES FOR THE PASSAGE

Ten years after Verrazano's voyage, King Francis tried again. This time he sent Jacques Cartier (zhäk kär tē ā′) to find the Northwest Passage. Cartier's hopes rose as he sailed into the huge Gulf of St. Lawrence. Ahead he saw miles of water that seemed to say, "This is the way to China."

Along the shore, Cartier met a group of Hurons led by Chief Donnaconna. Cartier kidnapped two of the Indian

MAP SKILL: Use the map below and the map key to trace the voyages of Jacques Cartier. What body of water did Cartier explore in 1534? In 1535?

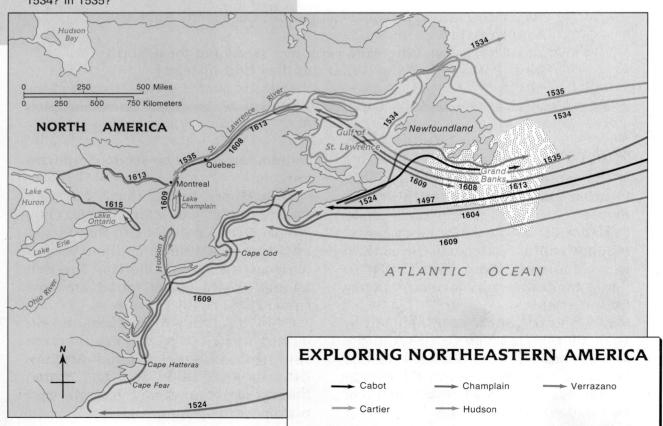

EXPLORING NORTHEASTERN AMERICA

→ Cabot   → Champlain   → Verrazano
→ Cartier   → Hudson

chief's sons and took them back to France. He wanted the young Indians to learn French so that they could translate for him when they returned to America.

CARTIER'S SECOND VOYAGE

In 1535 Cartier sailed back to America with the two Hurons. Now able to speak French, they told him that the Gulf of St. Lawrence led to a great river. This river, they said, went far into their country, which they called "Canada."

The map on page 154 shows that Cartier sailed into the gulf and up the St. Lawrence River. About 1,000 miles (1,600 km) inland from the sea, he stopped at a large Huron village. The Indians took Cartier up a nearby hill, which he named "Mount Royal." Today Canada's largest city, Montreal, spreads over this area.

From Mount Royal, Cartier could see great rapids on the river. There his search for a Northwest Passage ended. No boat could travel through those swirling, tumbling waters.

Cartier and his crew spent the winter camped along the St. Lawrence River. Never had they known such cold. Many of the men were sick. Cartier wrote that "some lost all their strength." Their gums were so rotten that their "teeth all fell out."

The Hurons saved the French, who were suffering from a disease called scurvy. They showed Cartier how to cure the disease by drinking a tea made of ground tree bark. At first the sick men said they would rather die than drink the bitter-tasting tea. But those who tried it became well. Cartier wrote that all the doctors of Europe "could not have done as much in a year as this tree did in a week."

The explorer Jacques Cartier was born in the French seaport of St. Malo. He gained his first sailing experience fishing in the North Atlantic.

THE THIRD VOYAGE

In the spring of 1536, Cartier and his men kidnapped Chief Donnaconna and took him back to France. The Huron chief thrilled King Francis with stories of a kingdom called Saguenay (sag' ə nā). Donnaconna said that Saguenay was a land of gold, rubies, and spices. Some of its people, he said, had wings instead of arms and flew like bats from tree to tree!

Cartier returned to Canada in 1541. He hoped to find the kingdom of Saguenay and to start a colony in Canada. To this end, the French colonists built a settlement along the St. Lawrence River. But they never found Saguenay. After another cold Canadian winter, the settlers gave up and decided to return to France.

155

Henry Hudson, waving his hat, explored the shores of the river that today bears his name. What present-day states does the Hudson River flow through?

HENRY HUDSON

The search for the Northwest Passage continued. In 1609 an English sea captain named Henry Hudson led an expedition to America for the Netherlands. He explored New York Harbor and the river that today bears his name—the Hudson River. Hudson's voyage gave the Netherlands a claim to the Hudson River Valley.

A year later, Hudson explored northern Canada for England. He sailed into a huge bay. Fearing death in these icy waters, the crew begged Hudson to turn back. When he refused, they put Hudson, his son, and eight others in a rowboat and left them in Hudson Bay. They were never heard from again.

THE SEARCH CONTINUES

For over 100 years, Europeans searched for the Northwest Passage. They discovered fine harbors and great rivers. They claimed large areas of land for England, France, and the Netherlands. But they never found a passage to China.

Check Your Reading

1. What was the Northwest Passage?
2. Why were French and English explorers interested in finding a new route to Asia?
3. **GEOGRAPHY SKILL:** What island did John Cabot reach on his voyage to America? What group of people had probably settled there earlier?
4. **THINKING SKILL:** How was Saguenay like the Seven Cities of Gold?

2 England and Spain Compete

READ TO LEARN

Key People

Queen Elizabeth I
Francis Drake
King Philip II

Read Aloud

"Strike sail!" shouted a voice out of the darkness. "Strike sail or we'll send you to the bottom!"

Captain San Juan de Anton could not believe his ears. Who could be telling him to lower his sails? Only Spanish ships sailed here off the coast of Peru. Anton called back angrily, "Come on board and strike sail yourself!"

A cannon thundered. One of Anton's sails came crashing down. Englishmen swarmed onto his ship like angry hornets. Now Anton knew the truth. He had been attacked by England's most daring sailor, Francis Drake.

Read for Purpose

1. **WHAT YOU KNOW:** In 1550, which European nation had a large empire in America?
2. **WHAT YOU WILL LEARN:** Why did English seamen attack Spanish ships?

THE SEA DOGS

Some 80 years had passed between Cabot's voyage to America in 1497 and Drake's attack on Captain Anton in 1577. For a time, England had lost interest in the Americas and the search for a Northwest Passage.

Then, in 1558, a young woman named Elizabeth became queen. Queen Elizabeth I was determined to make England a strong country. During her rule, English ships again began to sail across the Atlantic.

In 1567 two cousins, John Hawkins and Francis Drake, led several English ships to the West Indies. They had brought slaves from Africa to sell to Spanish colonists there. One day a storm blew their ships into a Mexican port. At first the Spanish there seemed friendly, but then they attacked the English without warning. Only two English ships escaped. John Hawkins reported that the Spanish "slew all our men ashore without mercy."

From that time on, English seamen looked on Spain as a deadly enemy. Whenever they could, they attacked Spanish treasure ships carrying gold and silver from America to Spain.

King Philip II of Spain called those who attacked his ships pirates. But the English seamen proudly called themselves "sea dogs." When they attacked, they were as fast and fierce as a dog stealing a bone!

FRANCIS DRAKE

No one hated Spain more than Francis Drake. In 1572 he began attacking towns in New Spain where gold and silver were stored. He captured Spanish ships and took their treasure. One month he captured a Spanish ship almost every day. When Drake returned to England, he was a very rich man.

A VOYAGE AROUND THE WORLD

In 1577 Drake began his boldest voyage yet. He sailed his ship, the *Golden Hind*, through the Strait of Magellan into the Pacific Ocean. The Spanish towns along the west coast of South America had no protection. No one thought an English ship would dare to sail into the Pacific. Drake attacked town after town without a fight.

Between towns, Drake captured several Spanish ships. His greatest prize was Captain Anton's treasure ship. One of Drake's men wrote:

> *We found in her great riches, as jewels and precious stones, 13 chests full of silver coins, 80 pounds of gold, and 26 tons of silver.*

It took three days to load that treasure onto the *Golden Hind*.

Queen Elizabeth I, shown above in a portrait and below greeting Sir Francis Drake, led England in the late 1500s.

Sir Francis Drake raided Spanish ships and took treasures such as the gold lizard shown here. The Spanish mined gold and silver in their colonies in the Americas.

Now it was time to go home. But Drake knew Spanish warships would be waiting for him if he went back the same way he had come.

Instead, Drake decided to sail up the west coast of North America. He stopped near San Francisco Bay in what is today California and claimed this land for England.

From California, Drake headed west across the Pacific and Indian oceans. Then he sailed around Africa and back to England. Three years after leaving England, the *Golden Hind* returned. It was only the second ship to sail around the world.

ENGLAND GROWS RICH

King Philip was furious. He demanded that Queen Elizabeth hang Drake as a pirate and return his stolen treasure to Spain. Instead, the queen honored Drake by making him a knight. As he knelt before her on the deck of his ship, Elizabeth touched his shoulder lightly with a gleaming sword. Then she said, "I bid thee rise, Sir Francis Drake."

Drake and the other sea dogs had helped make England rich with Spanish treasure. But in Spain, King Philip grew more angry with each attack. He promised to destroy the sea dogs, even if it meant going to war with England.

 Check Your Reading

1. Under what ruler did England challenge Spain?
2. How did the sea dogs help make England rich?
3. **GEOGRAPHY SKILL:** Who was the first English person to sail around the world? Where in North America did he visit?
4. **THINKING SKILL:** Sequence the events that led to the knighthood of Francis Drake.

3 England's First Settlement

READ TO LEARN

Key Vocabulary

armada

Key People

Sir Walter Raleigh
John White
Virginia Dare

Key Places

Roanoke Island

Read Aloud

Queen Elizabeth used the treasure captured by Sir Francis Drake and the other sea dogs to build a strong navy. She feared that these warships would be needed soon. The queen's spies in Spain told her that King Philip was getting ready to attack England.

Philip had his own spies in England. They warned him that the English were planning to start a colony in North America. The Spanish king was determined that they should not succeed. When the time was right, he was sure he would defeat England. Then Spain alone would control the Americas.

Read for Purpose

1. **WHAT YOU KNOW:** Why were the Spanish angry with Francis Drake?
2. **WHAT YOU WILL LEARN:** Why was the English defeat of the Spanish Armada important?

THE ROANOKE COLONY

King Philip's spies were right. In 1584 Queen Elizabeth gave Sir Walter Raleigh (rô' lē) permission to begin a colony in America called Virginia. A year later, Raleigh sent 108 men to America. They built a fort on Roanoke Island near the coast of present-day North Carolina. But a year later, after nearly starving, most of the men returned to England.

In 1587 Raleigh sent 117 more settlers, including many women and children, to Roanoke Island. They were led by John White. White's daughter, Eleanor Dare, had a baby after they arrived. Virginia Dare was the first English child born in America. A week later, White said good-by and sailed back to England for supplies.

THE SPANISH ARMADA

When White reached England, he found a country getting ready for war. No ships could be spared to carry supplies to America.

English ships met the Spanish Armada in a famous sea battle in 1588. What was the outcome of this battle?

In 1588 King Philip II ordered his armada, or large fleet of ships, to set sail for England. The Spanish king bragged that no one could defeat his mighty armada.

Although England had only half as many ships as Spain, the English navy attacked fearlessly. Dozens of Spanish ships were sunk or burned. Then a great storm destroyed the rest of King Philip's armada. For England the defeat of the Spanish Armada was a great victory.

THE LOST COLONY

John White was not able to return to Roanoke until 1590. But when he reached the island, all the settlers had vanished. The only clue White found was the word "CROATOAN," which someone had carved on a post. This was the name of a nearby island where friendly Indians lived.

White's ship turned toward the island. But bad weather blew the ship away from land. What happened to the "lost colony" remains a mystery.

SPAIN'S GREAT LOSS

By 1590 England still had not begun a successful colony in North America. But after England's great victory over Spain in 1588, it was only a matter of time. For Spain, the defeat of its armada meant more than the loss of a battle. Without its mighty fleet, Spain could no longer keep other countries from building colonies in North America.

Check Your Reading

1. Who started the English colony at Roanoke?
2. What did John White find when he returned to Roanoke in 1590?
3. What did the defeat of the Spanish Armada mean to Spain? To England?
4. THINKING SKILL: Place the events of the history of Roanoke in the order in which they occurred.

161

Identifying Fact and Opinion

Key Vocabulary

fact
opinion

It is not always easy to know if what people say is really true. Separating **facts** from **opinions** helps you decide what to believe.

A fact is something that we know for certain. It can always be proven to be true. An opinion is a personal view or belief. It cannot be proven to be true.

For example, a friend might say to you, "Mrs. Jackson's test has two essay questions. They are really hard." The first sentence states a fact. It can be proven that there are two essay questions on the test. The second sentence states an opinion. Everyone might not agree that these questions are hard.

Trying the Skill

Read the following paragraph. Which of the sentences state facts? Which state opinions?

The ships of the Spanish Armada carried 163 long-range cannons. King Philip II probably could not afford any more. They also carried 326 close-range guns called periers. The English ships had only 55 long-range cannons and 43 periers. But they also had 1,874 light, long-range guns. To add to the odds, English guns were the best in the world.

1. What facts and opinions did you find?
2. How did you find them?

HELPING YOURSELF

The steps on the left are one way to tell the difference between facts and opinions. The example on the right shows how these steps can be used to find facts and opinions in the paragraph on page 162.

One Way to Distinguish Facts from Opinions	Example
1. Recall the meaning of a *fact* and the meaning of an *opinion*.	A fact is something that can always be proven. An opinion is a personal view or belief.
2. Recall clues to facts and opinions. <ul><li>*Fact*: has been or could be proven true.</li><li>*Opinion*: a personal belief, often indicated by clues like *I think* or *probably*, or adjectives like *best*, or verbs like *should*.</li></ul>	Look for word clues like *I think* or *probably* as you read.
3. Examine each sentence carefully to find clues to facts or opinions.	You could check old records to see how many guns and cannons belonged to Spain and England. The words *probably* and *best* tell you that the author is giving an opinion.
4. Tell whether each statement is a fact or an opinion.	The statements in the paragraph that can be proven by actual evidence are facts. The sentence that includes the word clue *probably* is an opinion. The last sentence is also an opinion. There is no evidence to support it.

Applying the Skill

In 1864 a Croatan Indian, George Lowrie, made this speech about the lost colony of Roanoke. Identify the facts and opinions in his speech.

Our people lived in Roanoke, in Virginia. When the English came, we treated them kindly. We took them to live with us. We took the English religion and laws. We were told that if we did that, we would prosper. They misled us badly.

1. Which of the following sentences states a fact?
   a. The Croatan lived in Roanoke.
   b. The English were liars.
   c. The Croatan treated the English kindly.

2. Which of the following sentences is an opinion?
   a. The Croatan lived in Roanoke.
   b. The Croatan adopted English laws.
   c. The English misled the Croatan.
3. Is the following sentence a fact or an opinion: "Before the English arrived, the life of the Croatan Indians was easy"? Explain your answer.

Reviewing the Skill

1. What is a fact? What is an opinion?
2. What are two things you could look for to distinguish facts from opinions?
3. Why is it important to be able to distinguish facts from opinions?

4 The French Begin New France

Key People

Samuel de Champlain
Louis Joliet
Jacques Marquette
Robert La Salle

Key Places

New France
Quebec
Louisiana
New Orleans

Read Aloud

As you read in Lesson 1, Jacques Cartier had come to America in the 1530s looking for gold and jewels. Only later did the French realize that the real riches of this land were its fish and furs. Every spring, boats left France to fish in the Grand Banks. Each fall, the boats returned filled with salted and dried codfish for the dinner tables of Europe.

French fishermen also traded with the Indians for beaver furs. Europeans wanted the skins of this soft, furry animal to make warm hats and coats. It seemed to most French people that North America indeed had a lot to offer.

Read for Purpose

1. **WHAT YOU KNOW:** What did the defeat of the Spanish Armada mean to other countries in Europe?
2. **WHAT YOU WILL LEARN:** Why did the French want to settle in North America?

BUILDING A NEW COLONY

Fashion made beaver furs almost as valuable as gold to the French. To be in style, a European gentlemen wanted hats made of beaver fur. And the best beaver skins came from Canada. Hat makers in France simply could not get enough of them.

Each year French fur traders sailed to Canada to trade with the Indians. A knife costing one gold coin in France could be traded for a fur robe in Canada. In France, the robe might be sold for 200 gold coins. Fur traders could make a fortune in one year.

As trade grew, the king of France decided to start a colony in Canada. In 1608 **Samuel de Champlain** (də sham plān'), the geographer and explorer, was chosen to start the colony of **New France**.

Champlain built a trading post called **Quebec** (kwi bek') along the

Champlain and French settlers arrive at Quebec (*above*). French traders in Canada (*below*) exchanged guns and tools for furs.

banks of the St. Lawrence River. Later a second trading post was built along the river at Montreal.

Champlain was a strong leader. Through hard work, courage, and skill, he helped make New France a success. For that reason, he is called "the Father of New France."

THE FRENCH AND THE INDIANS

Champlain worked hard to make friends with the Indians of eastern Canada. After all, the success of the fur trade in New France depended upon the French and the Indians working together. The French got furs from the Indians. In exchange, the Indians got guns and tools that were made in France.

In 1609 Champlain agreed to help a group of Hurons fight against their powerful enemy—the Iroquois. You read in Chapter 4 that the Iroquois were feared woodland warriors. The Hurons and the Iroquois spoke similar languages and had similar ways of living. But they were rivals in the fur trade.

With the help of the French and their guns, the Hurons defeated their enemies. The astonished Iroquois had never seen or heard gunfire before, and they soon ran away in fear. From that day on, the Iroquois were the bitter enemies of the French.

The Hurons, on the other hand, remained friends and trading partners of the French. Fur traders went to live in Huron villages and learned the Huron language. They learned from the Hurons how to build canoes and how to travel long distances on rivers and

French trappers lived with the Hurons and learned how to survive in the wilderness. What does this picture tell you about the lives of trappers?

lakes. The Hurons taught the traders how to trap and hunt, what to eat, and what to leave alone.

Missionaries from France also lived with the Indians and learned their ways. French priests worked hard to spread the Christian religion. But, unlike the Spanish, French missionaries did not force the Indians to work in and live near the missions.

The fur trade changed the way many Indians lived. Hunters laid aside their bows and arrows for guns. The sound of gunfire was heard all over the once quiet forests. The sharp crack of metal axes replaced the dull thud of stone hatchets. Deerskins were scraped with shiny metal knives, and brass kettles hung over village campfires. Indian women wore colorful dresses made of French cloth.

NEW FRANCE EXPANDS

The first Europeans to settle in New France were fur traders. Each spring they went into the forests to trade for furs. In time, a few farmers also came. But farming in the cold climate of New France was not easy. Most French settlers were more interested in trading furs than in growing crops.

Over the years, Champlain used Quebec as the base for exploring expeditions that went deeper and deeper into the North American wilderness. While searching for a Northwest Passage to Asia, he became the first European to see what we now call the Great Lakes.

EXPLORING THE MISSISSIPPI RIVER

A French explorer named Louis Joliet (lü′ ē jō′ lē et) and a priest named Jacques Marquette (zhäk mär ket′) made a remarkable voyage. They began at the Great Lakes, where a group of Indians showed them how to reach the Mississippi River. You can trace the route of Marquette and Joliet on the map on page 167.

Marquette and Joliet hoped that they had, at last, found the waterway to Asia. They paddled down the Mississippi River for hundreds of miles. But the river would not go in any direction but south. At the point where the Arkansas River flows into the Mississippi, they finally turned back. By then they were sure that the Mississippi River flowed into the Gulf of Mexico, not the Pacific Ocean.

This news set a fur trader named Robert La Salle to dreaming. In his mind he saw a vast French empire stretching from Quebec to the Gulf of Mexico. In 1682 La Salle led an expedition of canoes down the Mississippi River. They found the land along the river to be "the most beautiful country in the world."

CLAIMING LOUISIANA

At the mouth of the Mississippi, La Salle raised a cross and "took possession of that river, of all rivers that enter it and of all the country watered by them." He had claimed the entire Mississippi River Valley from the Great Lakes to the Gulf of Mexico for France.

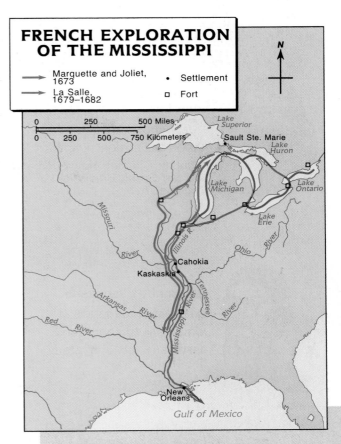

FRENCH EXPLORATION OF THE MISSISSIPPI

→ Marquette and Joliet, 1673
→ La Salle, 1679–1682
• Settlement
□ Fort

MAP SKILL: Marquette and Joliet, shown below, explored the Mississippi River in 1673. Use the map above to trace their journey. Where did they decide to turn back?

EXPLORERS OF NORTH AMERICA

John Cabot

EXPLORATION DATES: 1497

NATION SAILED FOR: England

RESULTS: Claimed Newfoundland and the Grand Banks for England

Samuel de Champlain

EXPLORATION DATES: 1608-1615

NATION SAILED FOR: France

RESULTS: Set up first French colonies in North America

Giovanni da Verrazano

EXPLORATION DATES: 1524

NATION SAILED FOR: France

RESULTS: Explored parts of the Atlantic Coast

Henry Hudson

EXPLORATION DATES: 1609

NATION SAILED FOR: Netherlands

RESULTS: Claimed the Hudson River Valley for the Netherlands

EXPLORATION DATES: 1610-1611

NATION SAILED FOR: England

RESULTS: Claimed the Hudson Bay region for England

Jacques Cartier

EXPLORATION DATES: 1534-1542

NATION SAILED FOR: France

RESULTS: Claimed Newfoundland and the St. Lawrence River Valley for France

Marquette and Joliet

EXPLORATION DATES: 1673

NATION SAILED FOR: France

RESULTS: Explored part of the Mississippi River Valley

Sir Walter Raleigh

EXPLORATION DATES: 1584

NATION SAILED FOR: England

RESULTS: Established Virginia

Robert La Salle

EXPLORATION DATES: 1682

NATION SAILED FOR: France

RESULTS: Reached the mouth of the Mississippi River

CHART SKILL: Use the chart to learn about some of the explorers of North America. Which two countries did Hudson sail for?

La Salle (*right*) meets the Caddo Indians on his trip through the Mississippi River Valley. Which country did La Salle claim this region for?

La Salle named this huge region **Louisiana** after his king, Louis XIV.

Claiming Louisiana was not the same as keeping it. Slowly the French built a chain of forts, trading posts, and farming villages from the Gulf of Mexico to Canada. Around the Great Lakes, the forts were needed to protect settlers from the Iroquois. Farther south, the French were worried about the Spanish in Florida.

In 1718 the French founded **New Orleans** at the mouth of the Mississippi River. This was a perfect place for trading. Soon the village became a thriving seaport.

THE GROWTH OF NEW FRANCE

No explorers found a Northwest Passage to Asia. Still, the money earned from fish and furs encouraged the French to stay in America. The colony of New France began with a tiny trading post at Quebec. It grew slowly as French farmers and fur traders began to settle in America.

When La Salle claimed Louisiana for France, the colony of New France more than doubled in size. France now claimed North America's two greatest river valleys—the valleys of the St. Lawrence and the Mississippi rivers. On a map, at least, the French colony looked very impressive.

Check Your Reading

1. What riches did the French find in North America?
2. Why did the French want to keep peace with the Indians?
3. **GEOGRAPHY SKILL:** What is the origin of the name Louisiana? What is Louisiana today?
4. **THINKING SKILL:** Compare how the Spanish and the French treated the Indians in North America.

IMPORTANT EVENTS

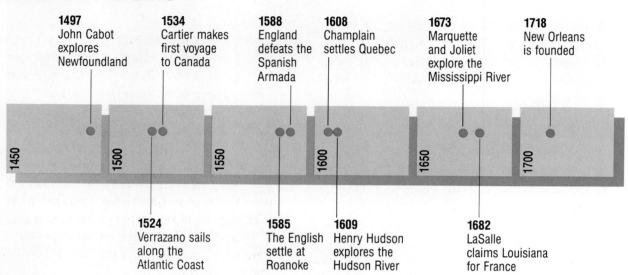

1497
John Cabot explores Newfoundland

1534
Cartier makes first voyage to Canada

1588
England defeats the Spanish Armada

1608
Champlain settles Quebec

1673
Marquette and Joliet explore the Mississippi River

1718
New Orleans is founded

1450 · 1500 · 1550 · 1600 · 1650 · 1700

1524
Verrazano sails along the Atlantic Coast

1585
The English settle at Roanoke

1609
Henry Hudson explores the Hudson River

1682
LaSalle claims Louisiana for France

PEOPLE TO KNOW

Jacques Cartier 1491-1557

Samuel de Champlain 1567-1635

Queen Elizabeth I 1533-1603

Henry Hudson ?-1611

Jacques Marquette 1637-1675

Sir Walter Raleigh 1552?-1618

Giovanni da Verrazano 1480?-1527

IDEAS TO REMEMBER

- The English, the French, and the Dutch all tried to find a Northwest Passage to Asia.
- In 1585 the English tried to start a settlement in America on Roanoke Island.
- After years of challenging Spain on land and sea, England defeated the Spanish Armada in 1588.
- France built an American empire that included present-day Canada and Louisiana.

REVIEWING VOCABULARY

Number a paper from 1 to 5. Beside each number write **C** if the underlined word in the sentence is used correctly. If it is not, write the word that will correctly complete the sentence.

1. Spain used its strong <u>army</u> to try to defeat England.
2. Henry Hudson, among others, explored America looking for a <u>Westward Trail</u>.
3. English seamen who attacked Spanish ships called themselves <u>sea dogs</u>.
4. When John White returned to Roanoke Island in 1590 the only clue as to the fate of the settlers was the word "<u>Croatoan</u>" carved on a post.
5. Each year French traders journeyed to Canada to trade goods for <u>gold</u>.

REVIEWING FACTS

Number a paper 1 to 4. Beside each number write the letter of the phrase from the right column that goes with the numbered word in the left column. Then write a sentence explaining how the word and phrase go together.

1. New Orleans
2. Roanoke Island
3. beaver hats
4. Spanish Armada

a. first English colony in North America
b. stylish item that turned the fur trade into a big business for France
c. ships defeated by the English navy
d. French trading center at the mouth of the Mississippi River

WRITING ABOUT MAIN IDEAS

1. **Writing a Journal Entry:** Imagine you were with Henry Hudson when he was left in Hudson Bay. Write a journal entry about what happened next.
2. **Writing a Letter:** Suppose you were King Philip II of Spain. You have just learned that Queen Elizabeth I has made Francis Drake a knight. Write a letter of protest to the queen explaining how you feel about her action and why.
3. **Writing a Paragraph:** Write a paragraph describing what might have happened when beaver hats went out of style in Europe.
4. **Making a List:** Imagine you were an explorer like Joliet or La Salle. Make a list of the things you would bring with you as you traveled down the Mississippi River.

BUILDING SKILLS: IDENTIFYING FACT AND OPINION

1. Identify the facts and opinions in the paragraph below.

   In 1682 we paddled down the Mississippi River in canoes. Our leader was Robert La Salle. As we sailed along we passed the most beautiful country in the world. Finally we reached the mouth of the Mississippi. La Salle then claimed for France the best land in all of North America.

2. Tell a situation in your own life where it would help you to be able to tell the difference between facts and opinions.

REVIEWING VOCABULARY

armada   missionary
colony   slave
expedition

Number a paper from 1 to 5. Beside each number write a sentence using one of the vocabulary words from the list above. The sentence should show that you understand the meaning of the word.

WRITING ABOUT THE UNIT

1. **Writing a Descriptive Paragraph:** What sort of people became explorers in the 1500s and 1600s? Make a list of words and phrases that you think would describe people who became explorers. Then write a description of a typical explorer. Use the information in this unit to strengthen your description.

2. **Writing an Essay:** Write a short essay comparing the French and the Spanish in America. Mention at least three of the following areas: how they gained control of the land, what their goals in America were, how they got along with the Indians, and what types of settlements they established.

3. **Writing a Story:** Choose one of the pictures in this unit that shows an important event. Then write an account of what is shown in the picture. Your account should be written like a story, using facts where possible and reasonable guesses where necessary.

ACTIVITIES

1. **Writing a Saga About the Vikings:** Write a saga about the Vikings in Vinland. The saga may be in verse or prose. Remember that the sagas were meant to inform as well as to entertain.

2. **Reviewing Facts About Explorers:** Prepare a set of flash cards about the explorers discussed in this unit. On one side of each card write the name of an explorer. On the other side write one or two important facts about his explorations. Then, with a partner, use the flash cards to review information about the explorers.

3. **Drawing a Diagram:** Learn more about the ships that sailed in the 1500s and 1600s. Then draw a diagram of one of the ships. Remember to label the important features of the ship.

4. **Making Modern-day Connections:** The French and Spanish explored many areas of what is now the United States. They gave names to the many settlements they established. Use a map of the United States to find at least five places with French names and five places with Spanish names.

5. **Working Together to Act Out a Skit:** With a group of classmates, write and act out a skit showing Queen Elizabeth's knighting of Francis Drake. Include as much information about the event as possible.

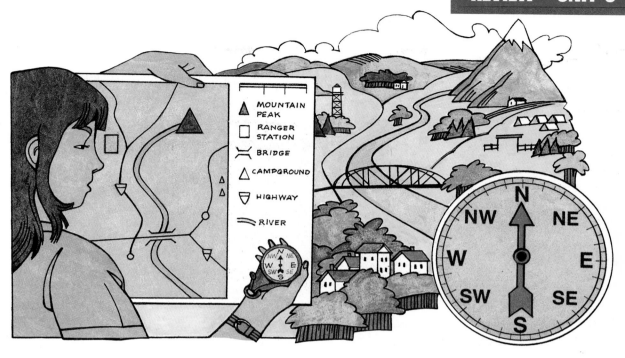

BUILDING SKILLS: FINDING DIRECTIONS

1. Look at the large compass face above. Which are the cardinal directions? Which are the intermediate directions?

2. How can you use a compass together with a map to find your way from one place to another?

3. Look at the picture above. If the girl is standing on the bridge, in what direction should she go to get to the campground? The mountain peak?

 **LINKING PAST, PRESENT, AND FUTURE**

Marco Polo and Christopher Columbus traveled to parts of the world where no Europeans had ever been. In this unit you read how they tried to learn from the people they met in these new lands. What chances do you think people of today have for similar experiences? What chances might people of the future have?

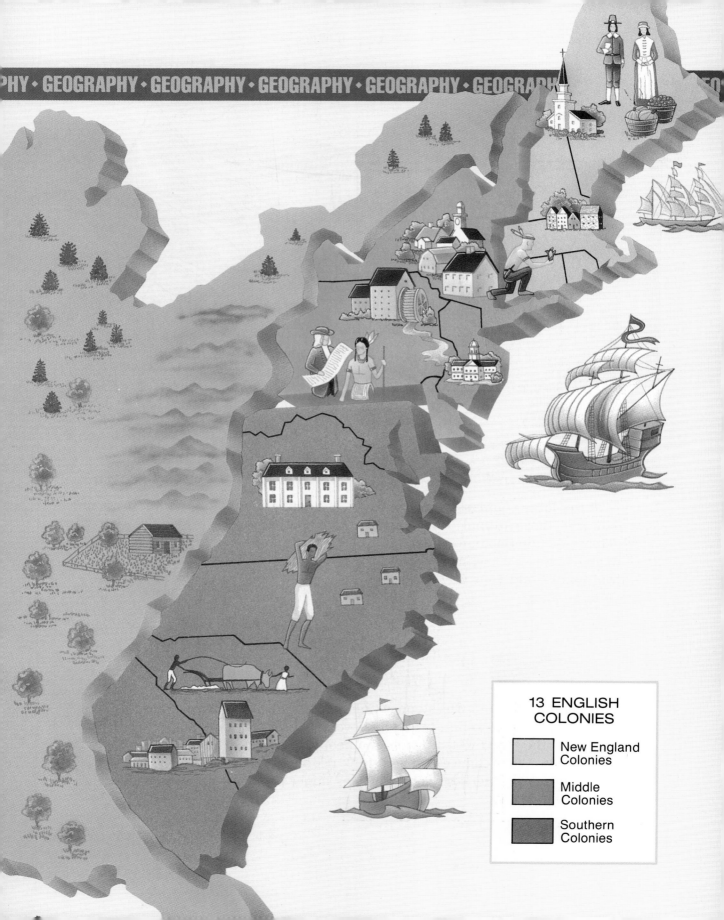

13 ENGLISH COLONIES

New England Colonies

Middle Colonies

Southern Colonies

THE AMERICAN COLONIES

WHERE WE ARE

The map shows that there were 13 English colonies stretching along the Atlantic Coast. They were divided into three groups—the New England Colonies, the Middle Colonies, and the Southern Colonies. In Unit 4 you will read how settlers in each group of colonies adapted to their environments and built very different ways of living.

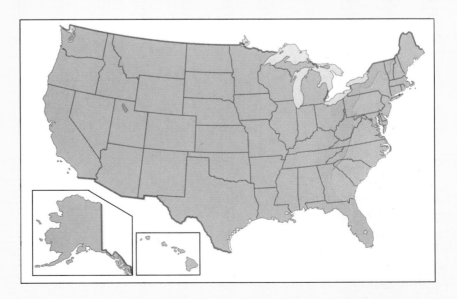

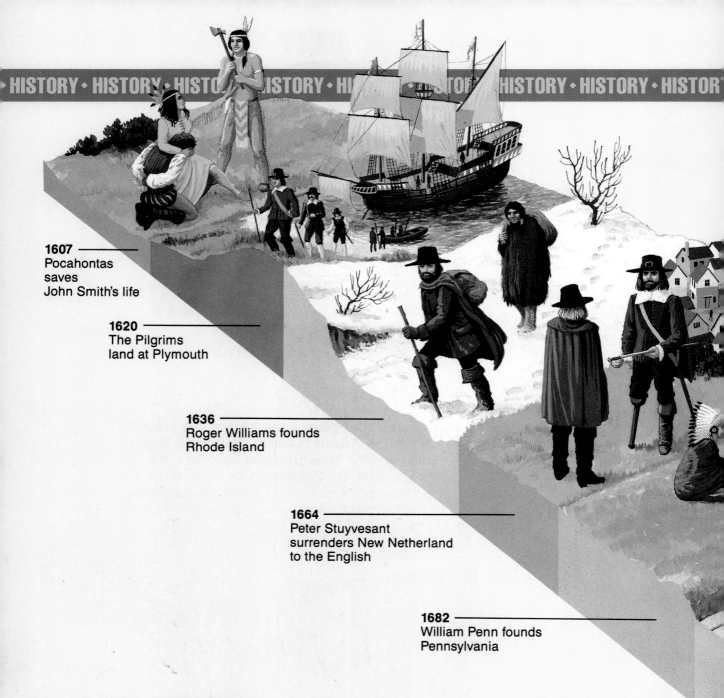

1607 ——————
Pocahontas
saves
John Smith's life

1620 ——————
The Pilgrims
land at Plymouth

1636 ——————
Roger Williams founds
Rhode Island

1664 ——————
Peter Stuyvesant
surrenders New Netherland
to the English

1682 ——————
William Penn founds
Pennsylvania

1732 ——————
Ben Franklin begins
writing and printing
Poor Richard's Almanac

WHAT HAPPENED

In 1607 a group of English settlers
landed in what became Jamestown,
Virginia. John Smith and Pocahontas helped
this settlement to survive. Soon thousands of
colonists settled along the Atlantic Coast. They came from
many places and settled in America for different reasons.
Each group left its own special mark on the development of
our country.

176

CHAPTER 7

SETTLEMENT OF THE ATLANTIC COAST

FOCUS

We hope to plant a nation
Where none before hath stood.

These words are from an English song of the early 1600s. It was inspired by a new attempt to build a colony in North America. Twenty years earlier, England's first colony at Roanoke had vanished into mystery. Now England was ready to try again. This time, it would succeed.

1 Jamestown

READ TO LEARN

Key Vocabulary	Key People	Key Places
stock	John Smith	Chesapeake Bay
	Powhatan	Jamestown
	Pocahontas	

Read Aloud

Captain John Smith pointed his gun at the Indian. He had come to Virginia to build a colony, not to fight Indians. Clutching his Indian guide in front of him, he stepped slowly backward toward his canoe. Arrows flew all around him. "He is a chief!" shouted his guide. The warriors shouted back that if the white chief wanted to live, he should drop his gun.

Suddenly Smith slipped, and he found himself waist-deep in freezing mud. Cold and tired, he threw away his gun. Smith wondered if he would ever live to tell his story.

Read for Purpose

1. **WHAT YOU KNOW:** What European countries had already established colonies in America?
2. **WHAT YOU WILL LEARN:** What problems did the first colonists in Jamestown have to overcome?

A NEW COLONY

The new English colony John Smith had come to build was the idea of a group of London merchants. They hoped to make money by establishing a colony in America. They began by forming a business called the Virginia Company of London. Then they sold shares of ownership, or stock, in the company. By selling stock to many people, the merchants were able to share the cost of starting a colony. If the colony did well, the holders of the stock would make money.

The company offered to pay the way of anyone who wanted to go to America. In return, the settlers would have to give the company a part of any gold or silver they found there.

In December 1606 the Virginia Company sent out 3 small ships carrying 144 men and boys. Five months later the ships reached Chesapeake Bay. The colonists settled along a large river flowing into the bay. They named it the James River after King James I.

On a peninsula jutting into the river, the colonists built a tiny settlement called Jamestown. To John Smith the peninsula seemed to be "a very fit place" for "a great city." Instead, it was a place of death.

EARLY PROBLEMS

Jamestown was built on low, swampy land. The water there was salty and not good to drink. It was also a breeding ground for disease-carrying mosquitoes. By summer, many colonists were sick.

They were also hungry. The rivers and forests around Jamestown were full of food. But the colonists did not know how to hunt, what plants to eat, or where to find the best fishing places. Even when their food ran low, the settlers did not plant crops. They were too busy hunting for gold. For months, Smith wrote, there was "no talk, no hope, nor work" except digging for gold.

By fall, over half the colonists had died. A sad survivor wrote:

Our men were destroyed with cruel diseases and by wars with natives [Indians] . . . but for the most part, they died of hunger. There were never Englishmen left in a foreign country in such misery as we were in this newly discovered Virginia.

JOHN SMITH AND POCAHONTAS

Even more people would have died had it not been for the tough old soldier John Smith. When supplies ran low, Smith traveled to nearby Indian villages to trade for food. On one of these trips, he was taken prisoner by the Powhatan (pou ə tan') Indians. You read about Smith's capture on page 179. The Indian chief, who was also called Powhatan, decided that the white man must die.

John Smith (*below*) and Pocahontas (*above*) worked to save Jamestown. Smith was a soldier and knew how to command. Pocahontas knew where and how to find food.

Powhatan's warriors held Smith's head against a rock. Smith saw them raise their clubs to "beat out [my] brains." Suddenly, the chief's 12-year-old daughter, named Pocahontas (pō kə hon′ təs), ran forward. Smith wrote that she "got [my] head in her arms, and laid her own upon [mine] to save [me] from death."

Pocahontas did more than save Smith that first winter. She also saved Jamestown by bringing the colonists food. Smith said that "she next under God" had kept the colonists "from death . . . and utter confusion."

SMITH TAKES CHARGE

In 1608 Smith took over the colony and ran it like an army camp. When more colonists came, he put them to work building houses and clearing land. Many protested that they were gentlemen. Their soft hands were not used to work. Smith told them, "He that will not work shall not eat."

Under Smith's rule Jamestown began to look like a town. Corn was planted. The colony's herd of pigs and goats grew. Then, in the fall of 1609, Smith was hurt in a gunpowder explosion and had to sail back to England to recover. Jamestown's gentlemen were glad to see him go.

THE STARVING TIME

Without Smith, the colony fell apart. The winter of 1610 was a "starving time." Night and day, the colonists heard nothing but the "pitiful . . . outcries of our sick men."

To survive, the colonists ate "dogs, cats, rats, and mice." They even boiled their shoes and ate the leather. By spring only 60 of about 500 colonists were still alive.

The English settlers at Jamestown finally got down to the job of building and farming. How successful were they at first?

For the next few years Jamestown barely survived. Life in the struggling colony was described as "a misery, a death." Few people were willing to go there.

Check Your Reading

1. How did the Virginia Company raise the money it needed to start a colony in America?
2. What problems did the first Jamestown colonists face?
3. How did John Smith help Jamestown survive?
4. **GEOGRAPHY SKILL:** Was the James River peninsula a poor place to start a settlement? Why or why not?
5. **THINKING SKILL:** What are three facts given about John Smith in this lesson?

Reading Historical Maps

Key Vocabulary
historical map

As you know, a map is a way of showing the earth and the places on it. Information on maps may tell you about a place as it is today. Or it may tell you something about what the place was like in the past. Maps that show you information about the past or where past events took place are called historical maps. A historical map of Virginia, for example, might show where the first colonists built Jamestown.

Maps Show Places and Events

Many of the maps you have looked at so far in this book are historical maps. The map below, for example, is a historical map. It shows what America was like during the Ice Age. It shows what parts of America were land and what parts were water. It also shows the areas that were covered by glaciers. This historical map also shows an important past event: the movement of Asian hunters throughout the Americas.

Keys to Understanding Maps

Now look at the map on page 183. What is its title? How does the title help you to know that it is a historical map?

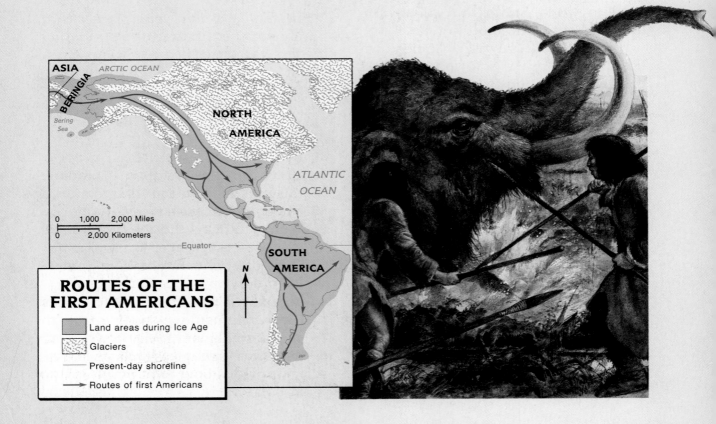

ASIA
ARCTIC OCEAN
BERINGIA
Bering Sea
NORTH AMERICA
ATLANTIC OCEAN
0   1,000   2,000 Miles
0   2,000 Kilometers
Equator
SOUTH AMERICA
N

ROUTES OF THE FIRST AMERICANS
Land areas during Ice Age
Glaciers
Present-day shoreline
Routes of first Americans

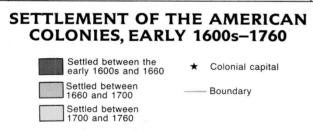

SETTLEMENT OF THE AMERICAN COLONIES, EARLY 1600s–1760

- ■ Settled between the early 1600s and 1660
- ▨ Settled between 1660 and 1700
- □ Settled between 1700 and 1760
- ★ Colonial capital
- — Boundary

The title tells you that the map gives information about settlement in the American colonies. Now look at the map key. It shows that different colors are used on the map to show when areas were settled. For example, areas shaded in brown were settled between the early 1600s and 1660. How are areas that were settled between 1700 and 1760 identified in the map key?

You know that the areas in brown on the map show all the lands that were settled by 1660. The areas in orange, to-gether with those in brown, show you all the lands that were settled by 1700. What colors show you all the lands that were settled by 1760?

You have probably noticed that the names of certain cities appear on the map. The location of these cities is shown by a star. If you check the map key, you will see that this symbol stands for a colonial capital. What city was the colonial capital of Virginia?

Reviewing the Skill

Number a sheet of paper from 1 to 10. Read each statement below. Use the map on this page to decide if it is true or false. Write **T** for "true" or **F** for "false."

1. Up to 1660 most of the settlements were along the Atlantic Coast.
2. All of Connecticut had been settled by 1660.
3. By 1700 there were settled areas in all of the colonies.
4. There were settlements in New Hampshire before there were settlements in North Carolina.
5. There were settlements in the Appalachian Mountains by 1700.
6. Savannah was the colonial capital of Georgia.
7. In general, settlement spread away from the coast, along river valleys.
8. Charles Town was probably settled after 1700.
9. Two different cities served as colonial capitals of Connecticut.
10. There were no unsettled areas in any of the colonies by 1760.

2 Virginia Begins to Grow

READE TO LEARN

Key Vocabulary

representative
House of Burgesses
indentured servant

Key People

John Rolfe

Read Aloud

Earth never did breed
Such a jovial weed.

There were many names for this weed that grew so well in Jamestown. Some called it "sotweed," or "the devil's weed." But most people knew it by its Indian name, tobacco. As you will see, the devil's weed helped tiny Jamestown become a thriving community.

Read for Purpose

1. **WHAT YOU KNOW:** Why did Jamestown have so many troubles at first?
2. **WHAT YOU WILL LEARN:** What changes helped Virginia grow?

A COLONY BUILT ON SMOKE

You read in Lesson 1 that the first years at Jamestown were filled with troubles. But life began to get better after 1614. That year, a colonist named John Rolfe married Pocahontas. Their marriage brought peace between the settlers and the Powhatan Indians.

Rolfe also found a way for the colonists to make money. Smoking was just becoming popular in England. So Rolfe worked at growing tobacco until he found a type that was "strong, sweet, and pleasant as any under the sun."

In England, Rolfe's tobacco was worth its weight in silver. King James I hated the "stinking weed." Smoking,

he said, was "hateful to the nose, harmful to the brain, dangerous to the lungs." But his people did not listen. They puffed away on pipes filled with tobacco.

Jamestown soon went tobacco-crazy. The colonists planted it everywhere— even in the streets and in the graveyard.

Then, in 1618, the Virginia Company encouraged settlers to plant even more tobacco by giving them land of their own. Until then, everyone worked on land owned by the company. And as Smith wrote, "Glad was he who could slip from his labor or sleep on the job." When the colonists worked on their

John Rolfe married Pocahontas in 1614. After their marriage, shown above, Rolfe and his wife lived in England where Pocahontas had her portrait painted wearing English clothes.

own land, they did in a day what had once taken a week. Why do you think this was so?

THE START OF SELF-GOVERNMENT

In 1610 the Virginia Company sent a governor to Jamestown to rule over the colonists. Smith thought that this was wrong. He said that "no man will go from [England] to have less freedom [in Virginia]." Finally, in 1618, the company gave colonists the same rights and freedoms that people had in England. One was the right to elect the people who made their laws.

In 1619 the male property owners in the colony elected representatives to the lawmaking body. A representative is someone chosen by a group of people to speak and act for them. The lawmaking body was called the Virginia House of Burgesses (bur' jis iz).

It was a hot summer day in July when the House of Burgesses held its first meeting. The 22 representatives quickly went to work to solve the problems of the colony. For example, they decided how much planters should charge for their tobacco. They decided what taxes were needed to build roads.

The Virginia House of Burgesses was the first elected lawmaking body in America. It gave the colonists valuable experience in self-government.

185

NEW PEOPLE COME TO VIRGINIA

In 1619 the Virginia Company came up with another way to attract settlers to Virginia. It began sending women to Jamestown. As colonists married and began families, they began to like Virginia better. For the first time, one wrote, they began to think of "Virginia as their country."

Virginia began to grow. Many of the newcomers were too poor to pay their way across the ocean. So they came as indentured servants. A poor person who wanted to come to America signed an agreement called an indenture. The person agreed to work without pay for a colonist who paid the cost of the trip. After about five to seven years, the indentured servant was free. Both men and women came to America as indentured servants.

The first women settlers arrived in Jamestown in 1619. What other group first arrived in that year?

A Dutch ship arrived in Jamestown in 1619 with 20 Africans. Europeans had been bringing Africans as slaves to the West Indies for more than 100 years. But the first Africans in Jamestown were treated as indentured servants, not as slaves. After they had worked for a few years, the Africans were freed.

RELATIONS WITH THE INDIANS

As Virginia continued to grow, the Powhatan Indians watched and worried. The settlers were taking over more and more of the Indians' land.

The Powhatan warriors wanted to stop the growth of the colony. They attacked one morning in 1622. Nearly 350 settlers were killed. The survivors fought back hard. A colonist wrote of the Indians, "Either we must clear them or they us out of the country." In two years, most of the Powhatan Indians had been defeated.

THE VIRGINIA COMPANY LOSES CONTROL

Virginia survived the Indian attacks. But King James I was not pleased with how the Virginia Company had run its colony. Thousands of settlers had been sent to Virginia since 1607. But by 1624 fewer than 1,500 were still alive.

King James especially did not like the idea of the colonists ruling themselves. He thought that a king should rule as he wished. So in 1624 he took complete control of Virginia. But King James could not rule the colony all the way from England. Instead, he appointed a royal governor for Virginia. It was the governor's job to see that the king's orders were obeyed in all things.

Making glass was an important craft in early America. Here, a glass maker shows how the Jamestown colonists made glass long ago. The glass pieces shown above were made using this method.

Over the years, the royal governors and the colonists quarreled about nearly everything. But the House of Burgesses still met to solve the problems of the colony.

THE COLONY SURVIVES

As you have read, English settlers had tried to build a new colony in Virginia since 1607. Many times, hunger and disease had almost wiped out the colonists. Indian attacks had taken still more lives.

Yet, the little colony would not die. The colonists found they could make money by selling their valuable tobacco in England. They gained the right to own their own land and to elect their own lawmakers. By the time King James I took control of Virginia in 1624, it was clear that the English colonists were in America to stay. Jamestown had become the first permanent English settlement in America.

Check Your Reading

1. What was the most important product grown in Virginia? Why?
2. Name two changes made by the Virginia Company that helped Virginia to grow.
3. How were people with little money able to come to America?
4. **THINKING SKILL:** What facts helped to shape the way the Indians viewed the colonists?

3 The Pilgrims Come to New England

Read Aloud

Alone in the Atlantic Ocean, a ship named the *Mayflower* plunged and struggled through the mountainous waves. The foaming sea crashed down on the ship's deck. And with a boom like a cannon shot, the beam of the main deck bent and sagged like a half-broken match.

Water poured through the broken deck on the frightened passengers below. Winds and waves pounded the ship as the passengers cried out, "Yet, Lord, Thou canst save!" The *Mayflower* and its passengers survived.

These storm-tossed passengers were the Pilgrims. They had left England hoping to find religious freedom in America.

Read for Purpose

1. **WHAT YOU KNOW:** What do you think were some of the dangers and hardships that passengers faced on the voyage from Europe to America?
2. **WHAT YOU WILL LEARN:** Why did the Pilgrims decide to come to America?

THE PILGRIMS

A pilgrim is a person who makes a journey for religious reasons. The journey of our weary Pilgrims began many years earlier in an English town called Scrooby Manor.

In England, everyone was supposed to belong to the Church of England. But many people did not like the official church. They had their own ideas about how to worship God. Some formed their own churches and called themselves Separatists. But this was against English law.

William Bradford was a Separatist living in Scrooby Manor. He wrote a history of the people who worshiped in his little church. From his writing we know the story of the Pilgrims.

Bradford tells us that England was not safe for Separatists. "Some were taken, and clapt [locked] up in prison." Others "had their houses . . . watched day and night." Rather than live in fear, they decided in 1608 to go to the Netherlands. They had heard that in the Netherlands "[there] was freedom of religion for all."

The Separatists found religious freedom in the Netherlands. But they felt like strangers there, and their children were growing up more Dutch than English. Some Separatists decided to start a new life in "those vast and unpeopled countries of America."

The Pilgrims did not have enough money for a ship and supplies. But some London merchants agreed to send them to Virginia to start a new colony there. The merchants expected to be paid with fish, lumber, and furs.

THE VOYAGE OF THE *MAYFLOWER*

On September 16, 1620, the *Mayflower* set sail from Plymouth, in southern England, with 101 passengers. More than half were Pilgrims. The rest were settlers hired by the London merchants. The Pilgrims called them "strangers."

Storms battered the *Mayflower* during its seven-week voyage. In bad weather the passengers were crammed into a small space below deck. For

DIAGRAM SKILL: The diagram below shows a cross section of the *Mayflower*. How many masts and decks did it have?

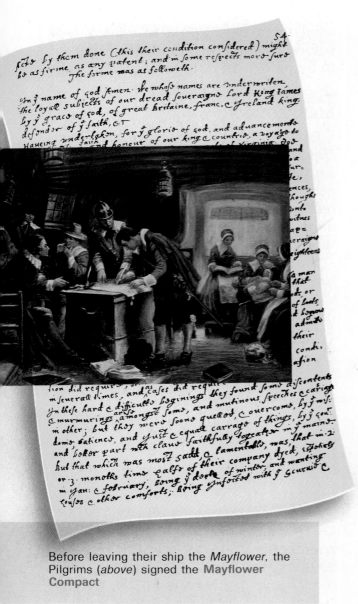

Before leaving their ship the *Mayflower*, the Pilgrims (*above*) signed the **Mayflower Compact**.

weeks they could not cook, wash, or even change clothes.

Halfway across the Atlantic, the ship's main deck beam was crushed by a huge wave. Somehow the deck was propped up, and the small ship sailed bravely on.

Storms blew the *Mayflower* off course. When land was sighted in November, the Pilgrims found they were far to the north of Virginia. The place they had reached had been named **New England** by John Smith. A few years earlier Smith had explored the Atlantic Coast north of the Hudson River.

Sick of stormy seas, the Pilgrims decided to go no farther. On finding a safe harbor near the tip of **Cape Cod**, they "fell upon their knees and blessed the God of heaven."

Relief at seeing land was mixed with fear. Bradford explains why:

> They had now no friends to welcome them, no inns to . . . refresh their weatherbeaten bodies. . . . Besides, what could they see but a hideous and desolate wilderness, full of wild beasts and wild men? . . . What could now sustain [support] them but the spirit of God and His grace?

THE MAYFLOWER COMPACT

The Pilgrims now faced a new problem. Virginia's government had no power in Cape Cod. The Pilgrims feared that without laws and government, the new colony would not be able to survive.

Before going ashore, the Pilgrims drew up a compact, or agreement. In the **Mayflower Compact** the Pilgrims agreed to set up a government and make "just and equal laws" for the good of the colony. Each man signed the Mayflower Compact and promised to live by those laws. The women on the *Mayflower* were not allowed to sign the Compact. But they too were expected to follow the laws.

Today we believe that people should make their own laws and elect their leaders. But in a time of kings and queens, this was a bold idea. Like the House of Burgesses in Virginia, the Mayflower Compact helped to establish the idea of self-government in America.

190

PLYMOUTH COLONY

For four more weeks the Pilgrims sailed along the windy shores of Cape Cod. Finally, they chose a place on Massachusetts Bay for their colony. It had a good harbor and streams with fresh running water. The Pilgrims named their colony Plymouth, in honor of the city in England from which they had sailed. Find Plymouth on the map on page 194.

All winter long the Plymouth colonists cut down trees and built houses. But as the weeks went by, fewer and fewer were able to work. Everyone was weak from hunger. And with hunger came sickness and death. By the time spring finally arrived, half the colonists had died.

HELP FROM THE INDIANS

One day an Indian walked into Plymouth. To the astonishment of the colonists he said, "Welcome!" and asked for a drink. His name was Samoset, and he had learned English from English fishermen. Several days later, Samoset returned to Plymouth with the nearby Wampanoag (wom′ pən ō ag) Indians and their chief, Massasoit (mas ə soit′). With Samoset's help, the Pilgrims and Massasoit worked out a peace agreement that lasted for 50 years.

One of the Indians that Samoset brought to the Pilgrims was named Squanto. Years earlier, Squanto had been kidnapped and sold as a slave in Spain. He escaped to England, where he lived for several years. On his return home, he found that all his people had died of a disease brought by fishermen from Europe. The land where Squanto and his people had grown up now lay empty.

Squanto taught the Pilgrims how to fertilize the soil by planting a fish in the ground with corn seeds. The oil from the fish made the soil rich.

Squanto stayed in Plymouth and became "the tongue of the English." He taught the Pilgrims how to catch fish and dig up clams. He knew where to find herds of deer and wild turkeys. Squanto showed the Pilgrims how to put fish in the ground with corn seeds to help the corn grow tall. William Bradford called him "a special instrument sent of God for their good."

THE FIRST THANKSGIVING

With Squanto's help, the Pilgrims had a good harvest in the fall of 1621. Their hunters came home with turkeys, ducks, and geese. They decided to set aside a day for feasting and giving thanks to God.

191

November 1621 marked the first Thanksgiving. Here the Pilgrims celebrate their plentiful harvest. The Indians brought them wild turkeys.

The colony worked hard to put the feast together. Smells of roasting birds filled the air. Squanto was sent to invite Massasoit. When the chief arrived with 90 Indians, the Pilgrims looked worried. They did not have enough food for so many people. Massasoit could not speak English, but he could read faces. He sent his best hunters into the woods. They returned with plenty of food for everyone.

For three days the Pilgrims and the Indians celebrated. Between meals they played games and held races. It was our country's first Thanksgiving celebration. More than 200 years later, in 1863, President Abraham Lincoln declared Thanksgiving a national holiday.

THE SWEETNESS OF THE LAND

Plymouth grew slowly. There were still hungry times. But each fall the harvest was larger. Soon the Pilgrims "began to taste the sweetness of the land."

In time, others would join the small colony. They, too, would be seeking religious freedom.

Check Your Reading

1. Why did the Pilgrims come to America?
2. How did the Indians help the Pilgrims?
3. **GEOGRAPHY SKILL:** How was the geographic location of the Plymouth colony similar to the location of Jamestown? How was it different?
4. **THINKING SKILL:** Recall all the things done by the Pilgrims and place them in their correct order.

4 The Massachusetts Bay Colony

READ TO LEARN

Key People   **Key Places**

John Winthrop   Boston

Read Aloud

God sifted a whole nation that he might send choice grain into this wilderness.

These words were written by a leader of the next group to seek religious freedom in America, the Puritans. The Puritans saw themselves as "God's chosen people." But to many in England, they were "most dangerous enemies."

Read for Purpose

1. **WHAT YOU KNOW:** Why did the Pilgrims come to America?
2. **WHAT YOU WILL LEARN:** Why did the Puritans decide to come to America?

THE PURITANS

The Puritans were deeply religious people. They looked to the Bible as their guide for living. They believed that everything a person needed to know about God's plan for the world could be found in the Bible. That is why they were called "the people of the Book."

Like the Pilgrims, the Puritans were critical of the Church of England. They were against any church practices that were not described in the Bible. For example, Puritans would not celebrate Christmas or Easter because these were not holidays found in the Bible.

But unlike the Pilgrims, the Puritans did not leave the Church of England. Instead, they tried hard to "purify" the official church. For this they were often sent to jail, whipped, and even hanged. And so they began to think about leaving England. They looked across the sea and saw in Plymouth "one small candle" burning with the light of hope and freedom.

MASSACHUSETTS BAY COLONY

In 1629 a group of Puritans formed the Massachusetts Bay Company. They got permission from King Charles I to build a colony in New England. A year later, the company sent 1,000 colonists to New England on 17 ships. Each family brought enough food for 18 months. The colonists also brought farm animals, tools, books, clothing, and guns. No group had come to America better prepared.

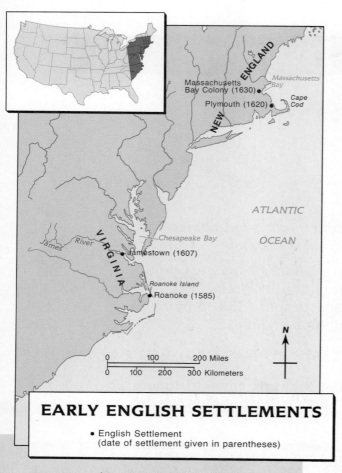

EARLY ENGLISH SETTLEMENTS

- English Settlement
  (date of settlement given in parentheses)

MAP SKILL: Locate the early English settlements on the map above. Which settlement was founded first? Which one was founded last?

The company chose John Winthrop to lead the new Massachusetts Bay Colony. Winthrop spoke to the Puritan colonists about the job ahead. "We shall be as a city upon a hill," he said. "The eyes of all people are upon us." Winthrop expected the Puritans to show the world how God wanted people to live.

The Puritans settled on Massachusetts Bay beside the Charles River. Find their colony on the map above. They called their first settlement Boston. That first year they had "all things to do, as in the beginning of the

world." Unlike the early Jamestown colonists, they went right to work.

THE GROWTH OF NEW ENGLAND

Between 1630 and 1643 more than 20,000 Puritans sailed to New England. They came to America for religious freedom. But many also came to escape bad times at home. Making a living in England was getting harder and harder. Poor Puritans hoped to find a better life in a new land.

Massachusetts Bay Colony grew quickly. By 1640 many towns dotted the shores of the new colony. In 1691 the Plymouth Colony started by the Pilgrims became part of the larger colony of Massachusetts.

PUTTING FAITH TO WORK

The Puritans, as you have read, were a people of deep faith. And from that faith came great strength. In New England, the Puritans put their beliefs to work. In their new land, they hoped to show the world how God wanted all people to live.

Check Your Reading

1. Why did the Puritans come to New England?
2. Why was the success of the Massachusetts Bay Colony so important to the Puritans?
3. **GEOGRAPHY SKILL:** Why do you think the Pilgrims and Puritans decided to settle near bays?
4. **THINKING SKILL:** How did the Puritans differ from the colonists who settled Jamestown?

5 New Netherland and New Sweden

READ TO LEARN

 Key People

Key People	Key Places	
Peter Stuyvesant	New Netherland	New Amsterdam
Johan Printz	Fort Orange	New Sweden

 Read Aloud

By the time the Puritans reached the shores of Massachu-setts Bay in 1630, there were already Dutch settlers living along the Hudson River. In 1625 three Dutch ships, the *Horse*, the *Sheep*, and the *Cow*, had sailed from the Netherlands to America. As the names of the ships suggest, the Dutch colonists brought their farm animals with them. One report suggests that the four-footed passengers traveled better than the two-footed ones.

Each animal has its own stall, with a floor of three feet of sand. . . . Each animal has its own servant who takes care of it.

The colonists, along with their animals, were on their way to the Hudson River Valley. Henry Hudson had claimed this region for the Dutch in 1609. Now Dutch settlers hoped to make a home there.

Read for Purpose

1. **WHAT YOU KNOW:** Why do you think the Dutch colonists brought along their farm animals?
2. **WHAT YOU WILL LEARN:** What was life like in the colony of New Netherland?

NEW NETHERLAND

The Dutch called the land claimed by Henry Hudson New Netherland. In 1624 Dutch fur traders had begun a trading post called Fort Orange along the banks of the Hudson River. Today, Fort Orange is the city of Albany, the capital of New York. Later, the Dutch built another trading post called New Amsterdam on Manhattan Island in New York Harbor. Find both of these settlements on the map on page 197.

Like the French in Canada, the Dutch came to America to trade for furs. But the settlers soon realized that they could not survive unless they raised their own food. And so the *Horse*, *Sheep*, and *Cow* were sent to America with farmers and farm animals. Soon a variety of farm products from New Amsterdam joined furs on Dutch ships bound for faraway lands.

Those ships eventually returned to New Amsterdam with settlers from many countries. French people, Italians, Spaniards, Danes, and Jews from Spain and Portugal all settled in New Amsterdam. In 1646 a visitor to the growing settlement found "400 or 500 men of different religions and nations." The settlers spoke 18 different languages.

PETER STUYVESANT—OLD SILVER LEG

Peter Stuyvesant (stī' və sənt) became the governor of New Netherland in 1646. Stuyvesant had lost a leg in battle and marched about on a wooden leg. But his was no ordinary wooden leg. Stuyvesant had decorated it with silver bands. The colonists called him "Old Silver Leg."

Soon they were also calling the new governor "Hardheaded Peter." He was stubborn about everything. But perhaps the colony needed a tough leader. When Stuyvesant arrived, New Amsterdam had no churches or schools. One of every four buildings was a tavern or bar. Knife-fighting sailors made the streets unsafe. Stuyvesant worked hard to bring law and order to the colony.

NEW SWEDEN

Soon Stuyvesant was hearing reports that Swedish settlers had started a colony called New Sweden south of New Netherland. The reports were true. In 1638 Swedish fur traders built a trading post called Fort Christina on the Delaware River.

At first New Sweden was small and weak. Then, in 1643, Johan Printz

Peter Stuyvesant, at the right, was the first governor of New Netherland. He lost his leg in a battle in the West Indies.

(yō' hän printz) arrived to take charge. The new governor was a very large, tall man. People said of him that "Nobody before and nobody since has weighed as much as Johan Printz."

Printz brought 100 settlers with him to New Sweden. About half were woodsmen from Finland. The Finns felt right at home in the eastern woodlands. They were soon chopping down trees and building cabins out of logs. Other settlers copied the Finns' log cabin. It was a strong, snug, and quickly built home.

Under Governor Printz, New Sweden's fur trade grew. Indians liked dealing with the man they called "Big Belly." He paid more for furs than did the Dutch in New Netherland.

When Peter Stuyvesant heard that his colony was losing business to New Sweden, he was furious. In 1655 he sent an army up the Delaware River and defeated the Swedes. New Sweden became part of New Netherland.

TWO SMALL COLONIES

New Netherland and New Sweden had both begun as fur-trading colonies. The Dutch settled in the Hudson River Valley. The Swedes built their forts along the Delaware River. But both colonies remained small. Few Dutch or Swedish people wanted to leave their homelands for an uncertain life in America.

Still, these settlers gave much to our country. The Swedes and Finns brought the log cabin to America. Tiny New Amsterdam would someday grow into New York City, our country's largest city. Dutch words like *sleigh* and *cookie* have become part of our language. And on a cold December night over 300 years ago, a Dutch child was

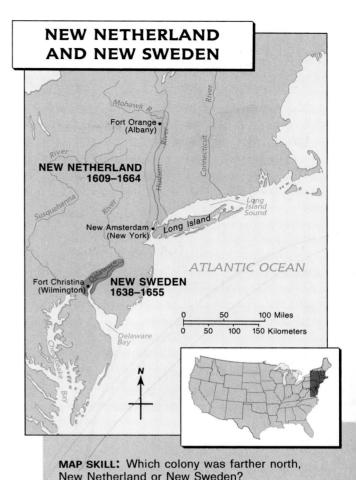

MAP SKILL: Which colony was farther north, New Netherland or New Sweden?

the first person in America to wait up for "Saint Nicholaas." Children in America have been waiting up to see Santa Claus ever since.

Check Your Reading

1. Where did the Dutch settle in America? Where did the Swedes settle?
2. What happened to New Sweden?
3. **GEOGRAPHY SKILL:** Explain how its nearness to water led to the growth of New Amsterdam.
4. **THINKING SKILL:** Name two ways in which the colony of New Netherland differed from the Massachusetts Bay Colony. Why do you think these colonies differed?

197

IMPORTANT EVENTS

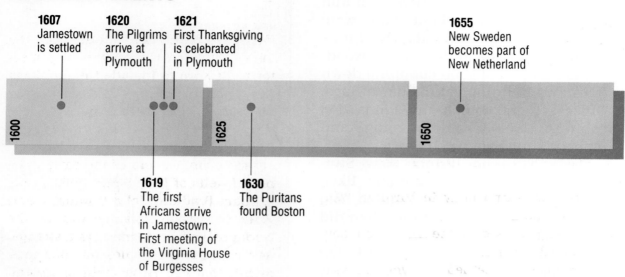

1607
Jamestown is settled

1620
The Pilgrims arrive at Plymouth

1621
First Thanksgiving is celebrated in Plymouth

1655
New Sweden becomes part of New Netherland

1600

1625

1650

1619
The first Africans arrive in Jamestown; First meeting of the Virginia House of Burgesses

1630
The Puritans found Boston

PEOPLE TO KNOW

William Bradford 1590-1657

Massasoit 1580?-1661

Pocahontas 1595?-1617

Powhatan ?-1622

John Smith 1579?-1631

Peter Stuyvesant 1610?-1672

John Winthrop 1588-1649

IDEAS TO REMEMBER

■ In 1607 the Virginia Company started Jamestown, the first permanent English colony in America.

■ The Virginia colony prospered after colonists learned how to grow tobacco.

■ In 1620 the Pilgrims established the colony of Plymouth. It joined the Puritan colony of Massachusetts in 1691.

■ In 1630 the Puritans began the Massachusetts Bay Colony for religious reasons.

■ The Dutch established a colony in New Netherland in 1624.

REVIEWING VOCABULARY

House of Burgesses   pilgrim
indentured servant   representative
Mayflower Compact

Number a sheet of paper from 1 to 5. Beside each number write the word or term from the list above that best completes the sentence.

1. Voters elect a _____ to speak and act for them.
2. The lawmaking body in Virginia was called the _____.
3. The Pilgrims signed the _____ when they reached America.
4. A person who settled in Plymouth was called a _____ because he or she had come to America for religious reasons.
5. An _____ worked without pay for several years to pay off the cost of the trip to the colonies.

REVIEWING FACTS

Number a paper from 1 to 10. Then study the items listed below. Beside each number write **V** if the item has to do with Virginia, **P** if it has to do with Plymouth, **M** if it has to do with Massachusetts, or **NN** if it has to do with New Netherland.

1. Dutch settlers
2. tobacco
3. Squanto
4. John Smith
5. Mayflower Compact
6. Peter Stuyvesant
7. Puritans
8. John Winthrop
9. Thanksgiving
10. Pocahontas

WRITING ABOUT MAIN IDEAS

1. **Writing a Skit:** Write a skit about the main events in the growth of Jamestown. Be sure to include the problems faced by the settlers and the people or ideas that saved the colony.
2. **Writing a Paragraph About Rules for a Peaceful Community:** This chapter discusses many leaders of the early colonies. It tells of John Smith, John Rolfe, William Bradford, John Winthrop, and Peter Stuyvesant. Imagine you are the leader of a new settlement in a strange, new country. Write rules for your community that will preserve the peace and well-being of your people.
3. **Writing a Letter:** Imagine that you were present at the first Thanksgiving celebration. When it was over, you wrote a letter to a friend in England describing the event. Help your friend to picture the celebration and understand why the event took place.

BUILDING SKILLS: READING HISTORICAL MAPS

1. How does a map key help you to understand a historical map?
2. Turn to the map on page 183. Refer to it as you answer these questions.
   a. In which general direction did settlement spread between 1600 and 1760?
   b. What was the colonial capital of Maryland?
   c. What area was located to the south of Georgia?
3. Why are historical maps useful in the study of history?

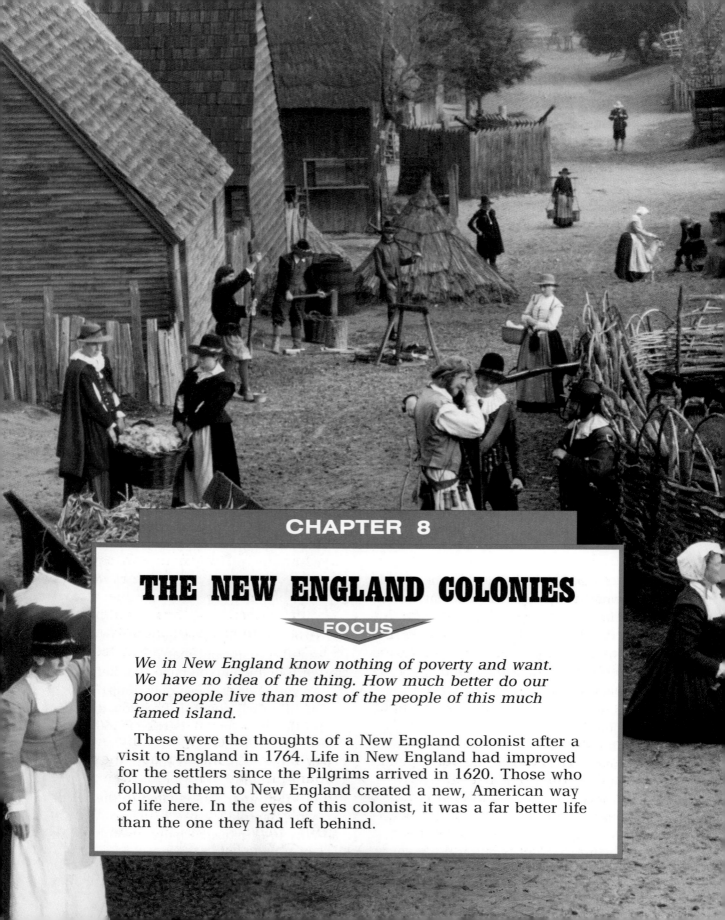

CHAPTER 8

THE NEW ENGLAND COLONIES

FOCUS

We in New England know nothing of poverty and want. We have no idea of the thing. How much better do our poor people live than most of the people of this much famed island.

These were the thoughts of a New England colonist after a visit to England in 1764. Life in New England had improved for the settlers since the Pilgrims arrived in 1620. Those who followed them to New England created a new, American way of life here. In the eyes of this colonist, it was a far better life than the one they had left behind.

1 The Geography of New England

READ TO LEARN

Key Places

Connecticut River Valley

Read Aloud

New England has a harsh climate, a barren soil, a rough and stormy coast, and yet we love it.

Massachusetts Senator Henry Cabot Lodge said this about New England over 100 years ago. But most New Englanders would still agree with him today. New England has never been an easy place in which to live. But for those who grow up there, it has always been a hard place to leave.

Read for Purpose

1. **WHAT YOU KNOW:** What landforms are found in New England?
2. **WHAT YOU WILL LEARN:** How did glaciers change New England's landscape?

A LAND SHAPED BY GLACIERS

Thousands of years before the Pilgrims came, New England was a land of high mountains and a smooth coastline. Then the world entered the Ice Age. You read about the effects of the Ice Age in Chapter 3. Glaciers moved across New England like monstrous bulldozers, reshaping the land.

The great sheets of ice scraped across New England's mountains. As the ice moved, it picked up loose soil and rocks. This rubble was dropped at the edge of the land, near the sea.

The seacoast sank under this heavy load. As the land settled, ocean waves flowed over what had once been a coastal plain. Over thousands of years, the waves cut into the coastline, creating hundreds of harbors and bays.

In some places, the glaciers pushed their loads into the shallow sea. Ocean plants thrived on these underwater banks, or mounds of mountain soil. The undersea gardens attracted millions of fish.

THE LAND LEFT BEHIND

Over time, the earth grew warmer, and the glaciers gradually melted. New England's mountains—the Green Mountains, the White Mountains, and the Berkshires—were left rounded and worn. Pits and hollows dug by the ice filled with water, creating thousands of lakes and ponds.

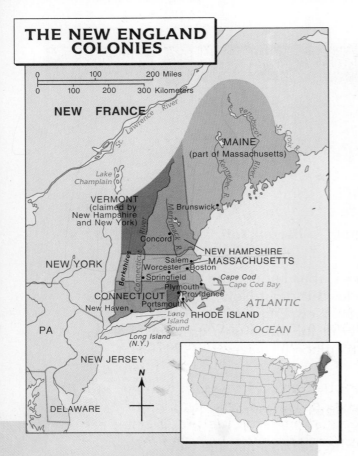

THE NEW ENGLAND COLONIES

NEW FRANCE

MAINE
(part of Massachusetts)

VERMONT
(claimed by
New Hampshire
and New York)

Brunswick

Concord

NEW YORK

NEW HAMPSHIRE

Salem · MASSACHUSETTS
Worcester · Boston
· Springfield

Cape Cod
Cape Cod Bay

CONNECTICUT
New Haven

Plymouth
Providence
Portsmouth

ATLANTIC

RHODE ISLAND

PA

Long Island
Sound

Long Island
(N.Y.)

OCEAN

NEW JERSEY

N

DELAWARE

MAP SKILL: Which of the New England colonies was the largest? The smallest?

Rocks and boulders from mountaintops were cut away by the glaciers and were left in riverbeds. Rivers that once ran smoothly now leaped over rocky waterfalls and rapids on their way to the sea.

The melting glaciers left behind a land littered with rocks and gravel. Most of the soil had been scraped away. The thin layer of dirt left behind covered few treasures. New England is not rich in minerals and has no coal or oil.

Scattered among the hills were pockets of flat, rock-free land. Here, glaciers had blocked river valleys to form huge lakes. Soil brought by streams settled on the lake bottoms. When the

glaciers melted and the lakes drained, deep, rich soil was left behind. New England's largest flat farm region, the **Connecticut River Valley**, was formed in this way. You can locate Connecticut and the other New England colonies on the map.

A "WILD-WOODY WILDERNESS"

The first New England settlers found a "rocky, barren, bushy, wild-woody wilderness." Forest covered most of the land. To the settlers, the trees were a welcome sight. In England, wood was costly. Most English forests had been cut down for firewood. New England seemed a good place for "those that love good fires."

Good fires helped the colonists survive New England's long, cold winters. Summers, they found, were hot, humid, and short. Farmers in New England could count on only four to five months for growing crops.

New England's economy has been shaped by its harsh climate and thin, rocky soil. Farming has never been easy in this part of the country. New England's best crops have come from the forests and the sea.

 Check Your Reading

1. How did glaciers change the geography of New England?
2. Why is farming difficult in much of New England?
3. **GEOGRAPHY SKILL:** What were the names of the New England colonies?
4. **THINKING SKILL:** How did the glaciers affect the geography of New England?

202

2 New England Grows

READ TO LEARN

Key Vocabulary

tolerate
rebel
Fundamental Orders
of Connecticut

Key People

Roger Williams
Anne Hutchinson
Thomas Hooker
Metacom

Key Places

Rhode Island
Portsmouth
Connecticut
New Hampshire
Maine

Read Aloud

We must knit together as one man. . . . We must delight in each other; make others' condition our own; rejoice together, mourn together, labor and suffer together, as members of the same body.

The *Arbella*, a small ship, bobbed up and down in Massachusetts Bay as John Winthrop said these words. In England he had been a rich man. But he had given up his life of comfort to lead the Puritans to New England. Now he faced the greatest challenge of his life—building a new colony on a foreign shore.

At this moment, Governor Winthrop could not know how quickly his new colony would grow. But he did know that he wanted to keep his colonists close together. As you shall see, this was not easy to do.

Read for Purpose

1. **WHAT YOU KNOW:** Why did the Puritans come to America?
2. **WHAT YOU WILL LEARN:** Why did some Massachusetts Bay colonists begin new settlements?

"THE CITY UPON A HILL"

You read in Chapter 7 that the Puritans came to New England in 1630. They had failed to "purify" the Church of England. But in America they hoped to build a colony based on God's laws. Massachusetts, Winthrop said, should become a "city upon a hill." He meant it should serve as a model for all the world to see and follow. Massachusetts, he believed, would show the world how God wanted all people to live.

Winthrop believed that people were not perfect. A wise and strict government was needed to keep the Puritans on the right path. For that reason it was decided that only men who were Puritan church members should choose the colony's leaders.

The men who ran the Massachusetts Bay Colony passed laws based on the Bible. They made sure that any wrongdoings were "seen and made public." To do this, Puritan leaders had to keep a close eye on the colonists. They did not want people settling far from the center of government in Boston.

The Puritans believed that their way was God's way and the only right way. They refused to tolerate ideas that were different from their own. To tolerate means to allow people to hold beliefs even if you disagree. The Puritans believed that tolerating different ideas would lead to wrong deeds. They feared that people would stray from what the Puritans saw as the right way to live.

ROGER WILLIAMS SPEAKS OUT

Not all Puritans liked the way the Massachusetts Bay Colony was run. Some of them chose to move away to start new settlements. Others, like Roger Williams, were forced to leave.

Williams was a Puritan preacher. A friend described him as "the sweetest soul I ever knew." But Williams was stubborn about his beliefs. He did not think the government should tell peo-

Roger Williams (*below*) was the founder of Rhode Island. Here, he speaks with the Narragansett Indians. Williams paid the Indians for the land that became Rhode Island.

ple how to practice their religion. He also said the Puritans had no right to start a colony in America until they had bought the land from its true owners, the Indians.

To the Puritan leaders, these were "dangerous opinions." They tried to show Williams that he was wrong. But Williams would not change his mind. In 1635 he was forced to leave the Massachusetts Bay Colony.

WILLIAMS SETTLES RHODE ISLAND

Williams fled south to the land of the Narragansett (nar ə gan' sit) Indians. He lived with the Indians and learned their ways. Later, he published a guide to the Narragansett language.

In 1636 Williams bought land from the Indians on Narragansett Bay. This was the start of the colony of **Rhode Island**. As Rhode Island grew, Williams insisted that the Indians be treated with respect and that they be paid for their land.

Williams welcomed people of all religions to his colony. And come they did—Baptists, Quakers, Jews, Catholics, and others. An amazed Puritan wrote that never had there been "such a variety of religions on so small a spot of ground."

Rhode Island was the first colony in America to welcome people of all religions. Because of this, Puritans looked down on Rhode Island, calling it "that sewer." But Williams was proud of his colony built on his ideas about religious toleration.

ANNE HUTCHINSON

Not long after Roger Williams was driven out of Massachusetts, another **rebel** began to speak out in the colony.

Like Roger Williams, Anne Hutchinson disagreed with some Puritan ways. What happened to her?

A rebel is someone who will not obey those in charge because he or she has different beliefs about what is right. This time the rebel was a Boston woman named **Anne Hutchinson**.

Anne Hutchinson was smart and energetic. She often met with women in her home to talk about religion. Hutchinson believed that it was more important for a person to pray to God than to go to church. When some of her followers began finding fault with Puritan teachings, the ministers were furious. They brought Hutchinson to trial. In 1637 Anne Hutchinson was banished from Massachusetts. She and her family fled to Rhode Island. There they began the settlement of **Portsmouth** (pôrts' məth).

THOMAS HOOKER BEGINS CONNECTICUT

Thomas Hooker, like Roger Williams, came to Massachusetts to preach. And like Roger Williams, he did not always agree with the colony's leaders. In 1636 Hooker led about 100 followers south to the Connecticut River Valley. In time, this settlement grew into the colony of **Connecticut**.

In 1639 the Connecticut settlers drew up a plan of government. It was called the **Fundamental Orders of Connecticut**. The plan listed the powers of the colony's government. It gave all men who owned land the right to vote. The Fundamental Orders was the first written plan of government in an English colony. Like the Mayflower Compact, it showed that the colonists believed they could govern themselves.

INDIAN WARS

The arrival of Puritan settlers in Connecticut led to conflict with the Indians. In 1637 fighting broke out between the colonists and the Pequots (pē' kwotz). The settlers feared the Pequots because small bands of the tribe had attacked their villages. For their part, the Pequots viewed the settlers as a threat to their rule over the region. The Pequot War ended in tragedy for the Indians. Most of them died when the colonists surrounded their main fort, set it on fire, and killed the Indians as they tried to escape.

For the next 40 years the New England colonists and Indians lived in peace. During those years, settlers moved north into present-day **New**

Thomas Hooker leads his followers into the Connecticut River Valley as shown in this painting.

Hampshire and **Maine**. With each passing year, the Indians saw their hunting lands shrink.

In 1675 the New England Indians joined together in a desperate struggle for survival. They were led by **Metacom**, or King Philip, as the colonists called him. Metacom was a son of Massasoit. You read in Chapter 7 that Massasoit had helped the Pilgrims in Plymouth in 1620. But now his son wanted to drive the colonists out of New England.

Across New England, Metacom's warriors attacked colonial settlements. Flames swept away many homes, including that of Roger Williams. The colonists struck back, wiping out Indian villages and burning their cornfields. Hundreds died on both sides. The struggle, known as King Philip's War, finally ended in 1676 when Metacom was killed.

FOUR NEW ENGLAND COLONIES

As peace returned, the Puritans asked themselves why such a terrible war had happened. For many, there was but one answer. They believed the war was a punishment from God. They had come to New England to build a great Puritan colony where everyone would live by God's laws. But what had gone wrong?

Instead of one "city upon a hill" there were four New England colonies—Massachusetts, Rhode Island, Connecticut, and New Hampshire. And instead of one Puritan religion, there were people with many religions living in New England.

But where Puritans saw failure, others saw success. The New England colonies were growing rapidly. And

The New England Indians attacked colonial settlements in 1675. What was the name of this struggle?

slowly but surely, people with different beliefs were learning to tolerate one another.

Check Your Reading

1. Why did the Puritans banish Roger Williams and Anne Hutchinson from Massachusetts?

2. What is the Fundamental Orders of Connecticut? Why is this document important?

3. How was the colony of Rhode Island founded?

4. **THINKING SKILL:** Look at the picture above. Describe the weapons and strategies Indians used against the colonists in New England.

READ TO LEARN

■ **Key Vocabulary**

village common
town meeting
democracy

■ **Read Aloud**

Life in the New England colonies was shaped by the area's geography. It was also shaped by the ideas the colonists brought with them to America. The result was a new way of life the colonists called "the New England way."

■ **Read for Purpose**

1. **WHAT YOU KNOW:** How do we know that religion was important to the Puritans?
2. **WHAT YOU WILL LEARN:** What was life like in a New England village?

THE NEW ENGLAND VILLAGE

By 1700 dozens of small villages dotted New England. The Puritans had lived in villages in England. Often their new villages were named for those they had left behind.

The colonists laid out their villages carefully. At the center was an open field called the village common, or village green. The common was owned by all the people in the village. Villagers let their cattle graze on this parklike pasture.

As the diagram on page 209 shows, the village common was lined with buildings. At one end was the meeting house. Here the villagers met each Sunday to worship. Most colonists built their homes beside the common.

An inn, blacksmith shop, and school might also be found there. Nearby were farm fields and a wood lot where villagers cut lumber and firewood.

The Puritan village was more than a place to live and work. It was a community of people who shared the same beliefs. Villagers helped each other in many ways. If some ran short of food, others shared whatever they had. If a barn burned down, they joined together to build a new one.

Villagers watched each other to make sure that everyone lived by God's laws. Today we might say that keeping a close watch on our neighbors is snooping. But to the Puritans, it was "Holy Watching" and part of the New England way.

A NEW ENGLAND VILLAGE

Fields

Mill

School

Meeting house

Stocks

Shoemaker

Well

Common

Blacksmith

Barrel maker

DIAGRAM SKILL: The village common was the center of a New England village. Use the diagram to locate the different buildings and activities of the village.

WORKING HARD AND MAKING DO

Hard work was also part of the New England way. The Puritans had to work long hours to make a living out of New England's thin, stony soil. Clearing trees off the land was backbreaking work. Then, before the colonists could plow, they had to clear away rocks from the fields.

New England's growing season was too short for a moneymaking crop like tobacco. The Puritans grew wheat, corn, rye, and pumpkins and other vegetables. They also raised cattle, pigs, and sheep. Most farmers were doing well if they could raise enough crops to feed their families and have a small surplus left to sell.

Everyone in a family worked. Men and women and older children all worked in the fields. In their spare time, men chopped wood, made furniture, and repaired farm tools. Women wove wool into cloth. Then they made clothing for their families. Children knitted socks and hats. There was always more work than time to do it.

The Puritans learned to make use of everything they had. Worn-out clothing was saved for patches and quilts. If a house burned down, the nails were saved to be used again. Nothing was ever wasted. An old saying tells us:

New England says, "Make do or go without."

So they made do.

VILLAGE SCHOOLS

When children were not working at home, they had to go to school. The Puritans believed that everyone should be able to read the Bible. Both Massachusetts and Connecticut had laws saying that every town with 50 families or more must hire a teacher and set up a school. These schools were called grammar or "writing" schools.

Some young children went to private schools called "dame schools." The teacher was a woman who held classes in her home. There, children were taught reading, writing, and a little arithmetic.

For girls, schooling ended with dame school. Puritans did not think girls needed any more education. Older boys went to grammar school for the next six years. Most schools had only one room, which was freezing cold in winter. Boys sat on hard benches studying Latin, Greek, arithmetic, and geography.

To our eyes, a New England school would seem bare. There were no blackboards, globes, or maps. Paper was

Puritans worked hard and lived simply. Notice the Puritan's tall hat and cape.

The Granger Collection

In colonial times, students learned how to read from hornbooks, or pieces of wood covered with a sheet of paper printed with the alphabet. The printed page was covered with a thin sheet of clear animal horn.

much too costly to waste on students. They wrote their lessons on birch bark. Each schoolmaster had one important teaching tool—a birch stick. A Puritan schoolbook tells us why.

The Idle Fool
Is whipped at School.

SUNDAY MEETINGS

On Sunday there was no work or school. Villagers put on their best clothes and walked to the meeting house for religious worship.

Services lasted all day, with a break for lunch. A watchman patrolled the meeting house. He carried a long pole with a wooden knob on one end and a squirrel tail on the other. Children who giggled or talked were silenced with a sharp knock on the head. Older worshipers who fell asleep were tickled awake with the furry tail.

Good preachers were able to keep most people awake during their long sermons and prayers. The villagers had little patience with poor preachers. One villager said of his minister, "I would rather hear my dog bark than hear Mr. Billings preach."

TOWN MEETINGS

Villagers also used the meeting house for **town meetings**. Here, every so often, they talked about the town's needs and problems. Where should the new road be built? What should be done about pigs digging up gardens? How much should the schoolmaster be paid? After everyone had a turn to talk, a vote was taken to decide what to do.

As New Englanders argued and voted, they were learning how to make **democracy** work. Democracy means rule by the people. But democracy in New England town meetings in the early 1700s did not include all the people. While everyone could speak at a town meeting, only men who joined the church could vote.

Each year these voters took part in their democracy by choosing people to fill town public offices. A public office is a position of power and responsibility. The office of fence-watcher, for example, was responsible for keeping pasture fences mended. The constable had the power to arrest lawbreakers. And the town crier yelled out important announcements as he walked around the town.

A NEW WAY OF LIFE

As you have read, life was never easy in New England. The soil was thin and the climate harsh. Yet New England grew, and its people created a new way of life.

New Englanders lived in towns or villages. Here they worshiped God together. They prospered by working hard and wasting little. They taught their children to read and write and to value learning. And in their town meetings they began to learn how to make democracy work. All this was part of the New England way.

Villagers on their way to a New England **town meeting**. Were these meetings truly an example of a **democracy**? Why or why not?

Check Your Reading

1. Why was it important for Puritans to live and work near each other?
2. What did New England children learn at dame school?
3. How were decisions made in New England towns?
4. **THINKING SKILL:** How were New England schools like schools today? How were they different?

4 Fishing and Trading in New England

READ TO LEARN

Key Vocabulary

triangular trade
slave trade

Key People

Olaudah Equiano

Read Aloud

"The abundance of sea-fish are almost beyond believing," wrote one New Englander. "I would scarce have believed it except I had seen it with mine own eyes." It was the sea, not the land, that held New England's greatest riches.

Read for Purpose

1. **WHAT YOU KNOW:** Why were New Englanders unable to make a good living from the land?
2. **WHAT YOU WILL LEARN:** Why was trade important in New England?

TURNING TO THE SEA

The first New England colonists, the Pilgrims, saw the sea as a wall that cut them off from European civilization. Like most early New Englanders, they looked to the land for a living.

As more settlers came, the flat land along the Atlantic Coast and the Connecticut River was turned into farms. Many New Englanders turned as well to the forest and the sea to make a living. Shipbuilding became an important industry. From Rhode Island to Maine, boat builders turned tall trees into ships.

FISHING AND WHALING

Many of those ships were fishing boats. Of all the fish in New England's coastal waters, the most important was cod. New Englanders dried and salted codfish to keep it from spoiling. The dried cod was sold in Europe and the West Indies.

New Englanders also hunted whales off their coast. Whale oil was used in lamps. From just a single whale one might get 500 gallons (1,893 l) of oil.

TRADE DEVELOPS

Many New England ships were used for trade. The sea that had once looked like a wall became a water highway for New England traders. Ships left ports such as Boston and Salem filled with cod, corn, furs, and forest products. They returned with sugar, iron goods, textiles, and slaves.

Many New England sea captains became rich in the triangular trade.

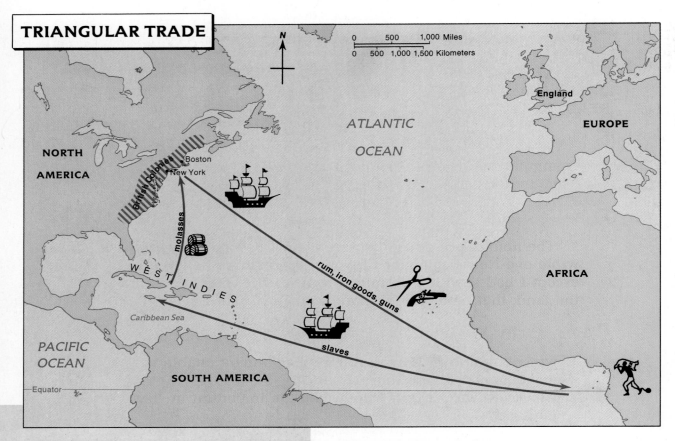

TRIANGULAR TRADE

MAP SKILL: Trace the route of the triangular trade on the map. How long was the route between Africa and the West Indies?

Trace the path of this three-sided trade route on the map above. The first leg of the trip started at ports such as Boston and New York. There, molasses bought from the West Indies was made into rum. Traders then sailed to the west coast of Africa. There, they traded the rum for African slaves.

The second leg of the journey was from Africa to the West Indies. Colonists there wanted to buy African slaves to work in their sugar fields.

The traders sold most of their slaves in the West Indies. Then they filled their ships with molasses and returned to New England. This was the last leg of the triangular trade. In New England

the molasses was made into rum for the next trading trip. Any remaining slaves were sold throughout the English colonies.

New England sea captains viewed the **slave trade**—the buying and selling of slaves—as a business. To make money they had to bring as many slaves to America as they could. They packed slaves into their ships "like books on a shelf." One captain wrote that slaves on his ship "had not so much room as a man in his coffin."

THE NIGHTMARE JOURNEY

For Africans, the voyage across the Atlantic was a nightmare. It began when they were kidnapped from their villages by African slave traders. **Olaudah Equiano** (ol′ ə dä i kwē ä′ no) was a boy of 11 when he was taken from his home in West Africa. Like other captives, he was forced to march to the coast. There he was sold as a slave. Use the map on page 214 to trace the voyage of Africans to the West Indies.

Equiano was put on a slave ship and chained below deck. All around him people were crying. He felt too sick to eat. But when he refused food, he was whipped. In later years, Equiano wrote of the voyage:

> The closeness of the place and the number of us crowded so closely together almost suffocated us. The horrible smells made the air unfit to breathe. This brought on sickness that killed many of us.

As the weeks went by, life below deck got worse. Many slaves died. Day after day the dead were tossed into the sea.

Those who lived through the journey known as the Middle Passage were sold as slaves in America. Ahead was a life of endless toil and little hope.

A GROWING REGION

The first settlers in New England had been farmers. But soon the colonists had learned to use the riches of the forest and the sea.

Shipbuilding, fishing, and trade brought new riches to the people of New England. And as the region grew, coastal towns turned into busy seaports.

Some New England ships followed the triangular trade route. Merchants and shippers grew rich quickly by selling slaves in the West Indies. But for the African slaves the trade route meant a dark, terrible voyage to a faraway, unknown land.

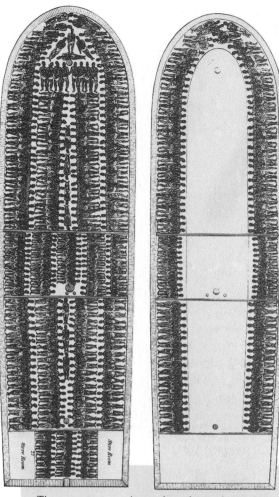

These cross sections show how slaves were carried aboard ships. They were chained both below deck and on top of the deck. They were packed so closely together there was hardly room to move.

Check Your Reading

1. What was the triangular trade?
2. Why did some people in the West Indies buy slaves?
3. **GEOGRAPHY SKILL:** Which ocean did Africans cross on slave ships? Where were most slaves sold?
4. **THINKING SKILL:** Beginning with Boston and New York, put the steps of the triangular trade in their proper order.

215

Determining the Credibility of a Source

Key Vocabulary
source
credibility

Suppose you just received a note in class. It reads: "Amy doesn't want you to come to her birthday party!" Before you get upset, you should determine where the note came from, or what its source was. A source is something that gives information or evidence, such as a book, magazine, or letter. Determining if a source should be believed is the same thing as determining its credibility. Remember, a source that is credible can be believed.

To determine the credibility of the note you would have to find out who wrote it. Then you would have to find out if that person knew Amy well enough to know who she wants at her party. You would also want to know if the person who wrote the note had anything to gain by telling you a lie.

Determining the credibility of a source is one step in deciding if you can trust what it says to be true.

Trying the Skill
Imagine that you want to know more about the shipbuilding industry of colonial New England. Which of the following sources would be the most credible, or believable, on this subject?

A. A made-up story about life in colonial New England, written in only three months by a writer who was born and educated in Tennessee; it is her first book.

B. A book on colonial shipbuilding, written in 1787 by a Connecticut artist whose father was a shipbuilder. His book won a prize from a Boston newspaper in 1788.

1. Which source do you think is more credible?
2. What did you do to determine this?

HELPING YOURSELF

The steps on the left may help you determine the credibility of any source. The example on the right explains one way to apply these steps to the information given on page 216.

One Way to Determine the Credibility of a Source	Example
1. Identify the rules that make a source credible. • The author should be an expert on the subject or very well informed about it. • Most people should regard the author as fair and honest. • The author should have nothing to gain by giving false or wrong information. • The source should agree with other sources of information on the same subject.	The rules to remember are that an author should be respected. He or she should have nothing to gain by giving false or wrong information. Also, the information in the source should agree with other credible sources.
2. Study the source to make sure that these rules have been met. You can get additional information by looking at other books in the library on the same subject.	The author of source **B** probably got helpful information from his father. The prize he won shows that his work was well-regarded. The author of source **A** was more likely to use incorrect information. After all, her story was a work of fiction.
3. Decide how well these rules have been met and tell what you think.	The second book is a more credible source on colonial shipbuilding than the first.

Applying the Skill

Read the following sources and answer the questions below.

A. A description by Olaudah Equiano of his trip to America on board a slave ship

B. A description by a slave ship captain given to officials at the port of Savannah, Georgia, in 1734

C. A New England merchant's account based on what he had heard from sailors who came into his shop

1. Which of the sources above would be most credible on the topic of slave ships in the 1700s?

2. Why is that source most likely to contain truthful information?

3. Which source probably had the most reason to include false information?

Reviewing the Skill

1. What is a source? When is a source credible?

2. What are three rules you could follow to decide if a source is credible?

3. Why is it important to check the credibility of a source?

IMPORTANT EVENTS

1636
Roger Williams
founds Rhode Island;
Thomas Hooker
begins a settlement in
Connecticut

1675
King Philip's War begins

1600

1650

1637
Anne Hutchinson is
banished from
Massachusetts

1639
Fundamental Orders
of Connecticut

PEOPLE TO KNOW

Olaudah Equiano 1750-1797

Thomas Hooker 1586-1647

Anne Hutchinson 1591-1643

Roger Williams 1603?-1683

Metacom ?-1676

IDEAS TO REMEMBER

■ After the Ice Age, New England became
a land with gentle hills, numerous
lakes and ponds, and a rocky, jagged
coastline.

■ The New England colonies grew as the
colonies of Rhode Island and Connecticut were settled.

■ In New England religion played an important part in the lives of the people.

■ Because farming was difficult in New
England, many people turned to fishing, shipbuilding, whaling, and trading
for a living.

REVIEWING VOCABULARY

democracy	town meeting
rebel	village common
slave trade	

Number a paper from 1 to 5. Beside each number write the word or term from the list above that matches the definition.

1. Rule by the people
2. Someone who will not obey those in charge because he or she has different beliefs about what is right
3. An open field in the center of a New England town
4. A gathering of people for the purpose of making decisions for their community
5. The buying and selling of slaves

REVIEWING FACTS

1. Write at least five sentences describing the geography of New England.
2. Why were the colonies of Rhode Island and Connecticut founded?
3. Give examples of "the New England way."
4. What were two ways in which New Englanders showed they believed in the process of self-government?
5. Describe the treatment of slaves during their journey to America.

WRITING ABOUT MAIN IDEAS

1. **Writing a Paragraph of Contrast:** You have read about education in the colonies. Write a paragraph discussing at least three ways in which schooling today is different from schooling in colonial New England.

2. **Writing a Speech:** Imagine that you live in Massachusetts at the same time as Roger Williams. The leaders of the colony want to banish him. Do you think they should? Write a speech that you might give at a town meeting explaining how you think Williams should be treated. In the speech try to convince others to agree with you.

3. **Writing a Letter:** Pretend that you are Roger Williams. It has been a year since you were ordered to leave Massachusetts. Write a letter to a friend in England describing how Rhode Island is different from Massachusetts.

4. **Writing a Paragraph:** Write a paragraph with this topic sentence: "Geography greatly affected the way New England developed." Write at least two more sentences that show why this topic sentence is true.

BUILDING SKILLS: DETERMINING THE CREDIBILITY OF A SOURCE

1. What steps could you follow to decide if a source is credible?
2. Which of the following sources would be most credible on the subject of the trial of Anne Hutchinson? Why?
   a. A diary entry by a judge in Virginia who read about her case.
   b. An eyewitness account of someone who attended the trial of Anne Hutchinson.
   c. A description of the trial written by a descendant of Anne Hutchinson 100 years after the event.
3. What might happen if you believe a source is credible when it is not?

CHAPTER 9

THE MIDDLE COLONIES

▼ **FOCUS**

This [land] is peopled by as happy and free a set of men as any in America.

These words could have been written to describe any one of the Middle Colonies—New York, New Jersey, Pennsylvania, and Delaware. Many thousands of people came to the Middle Colonies in the 1600s and 1700s. They were looking for a better life. Many of the newcomers found what they were looking for. They helped to turn the Middle Colonies into the "breadbasket of America."

1 The Geography of the Middle Colonies

READ TO LEARN

Key Vocabulary

fall line
navigable

Key Places

New Jersey   New York
Delaware   Pennsylvania

Read Aloud

The province of Pennsylvania is a healthy one; for the most part it has good soil, good air and water, lots of high mountains and . . . many rivers. The land is very fertile and all kinds of grain flourish.

This is how a German named Gottlieb Mittelberger described Pennsylvania during a visit in 1748. As you will see, he was right.

Read for Purpose

1. **WHAT YOU KNOW:** Would Mittelberger's description fit New England? Why or why not?
2. **WHAT YOU WILL LEARN:** Why were the Middle Colonies called a region of contrasts?

PLAINS, HILLS, AND RIVERS

The Middle Colonies formed a region of contrasts. You learned in Chapter 1 that New Jersey and Delaware lie on the Atlantic Coastal Plain. Here the land is flat or gently rolling. The other two Middle Colonies, New York and Pennsylvania, stretch across the Appalachian Mountains. This region was once rich in timber and beaver.

You know that the rolling hills between the coastal plain and the Appalachians are called the Piedmont. Many rivers flow through here on their way to the sea. As the rivers drop from the hills to the low coastal plain, they form rapids and waterfalls. For this reason, the dividing line between the Piedmont and the coastal plain is called the fall line. As you will read, the fall line was important in the history of the Middle Colonies.

These same rivers served as gateways to the Middle Colonies. They led colonists inland from the coast to beaver-filled streams, thick forests, and rich farmland. Once settled, colonists used rivers as highways to send furs, lumber, and food to coastal cities where they would then be sold.

221

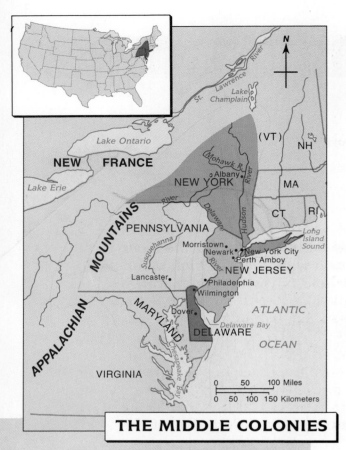

THE MIDDLE COLONIES

MAP SKILL: Locate the Hudson and Delaware rivers on the map. Which colonies do they flow through?

changed. You can locate some of these cities on the map on this page.

FARMING IN THE MIDDLE COLONIES

Like New England, much of New York was once covered by glaciers. The two Great Lakes that border New York—Lake Ontario and Lake Erie—were scooped out by ice sheets. The other Middle Colonies escaped the ice. Farmers on the plains and Piedmont found deep, rich soil.

Farming was far easier here than it was in New England. The Middle Colonies had a six-to-seven-month growing season. Plenty of summer rain watered the farmers' fields. It was hard not to succeed at farming in the Middle Colonies.

THE RICHES OF THE MIDDLE COLONIES

The Middle Colonies, as you have read, offered colonists many resources. There was good farmland on the coastal plain and Piedmont. The forests were rich in lumber and beaver. Navigable rivers flowed through each of the colonies. And rivers tumbling down the fall line provided water power for mills. These were riches that New England farmers must have envied.

Riverboats could not get past the rapids at the fall line. But some colonists found ways to put the falling water to work. All along the fall line, colonists built water-powered sawmills for cutting lumber and grist mills for making flour.

The most important rivers in the Middle Colonies were the Hudson and the Delaware. A look at the map on this page will show you why this is so. Both the Hudson and Delaware are large, **navigable** rivers. That means they are wide and deep enough for ships to use. Each of these navigable rivers ends in a large, protected harbor where ships can load and unload goods. Cities rose up in the places where goods were ex-

 Check Your Reading

1. Why were rivers important to people in the Middle Colonies?
2. How did colonists make use of the fall line?
3. **GEOGRAPHY SKILL:** Describe the geography of the Middle Colonies.
4. **THINKING SKILL:** Why was farming easier in the Middle Colonies than in New England?

2 New York and New Jersey

READ TO LEARN

Key Vocabulary
assembly

Key People
John Peter Zenger

Read Aloud

As you read in Chapter 7, the Dutch built the settlement of New Amsterdam in 1626. In 1664 four English warships sailed into the busy harbor at New Amsterdam. The English captain demanded that the colonists of New Amsterdam surrender.

"Never will I surrender!" replied Governor Peter Stuyvesant. But when the Dutch colonists saw English guns pointed at their town, they refused to fight. Stuyvesant was such an unpopular governor that the colonists would not fight for him. Stuyvesant had no choice and gave the order to surrender. New Amsterdam, with the rest of the Dutch colony of New Netherland, was soon divided to form two of the Middle Colonies—New York and New Jersey.

Read for Purpose

1. **WHAT YOU KNOW:** How did the Dutch lose New Netherland?
2. **WHAT YOU WILL LEARN:** What great freedom was won by John Peter Zenger?

TWO NEW ENGLISH COLONIES

King Charles II of England gave the Dutch colony to his brother James, the Duke of York. The colony of New Netherland was renamed New York. New Amsterdam became New York City.

James gave a large part of his colony to two friends, Lord John Berkeley and Sir George Carteret. They started the colony of New Jersey on land between the Hudson and Delaware rivers.

Berkeley and Carteret hoped to make money by renting land in New Jersey. They offered colonists rich soil and religious freedom. Soon Puritans, Baptists, Quakers, Jews, Germans, Finns, Swedes, and others were farming New Jersey's coastal plain. Use the map on page 222 to locate the colonies of New York and New Jersey.

New York grew slowly at first. Most of the farmland along the Hudson River was owned by a few families. They did not want to sell their land to new settlers. But New York City became a busy seaport that attracted people from many countries.

John Peter Zenger, to the right, was brought to trial (*above*) for criticizing the governor of New York in his newspaper. What was the result of the Zenger trial?

Like the Virginia colonists, the settlers in New York and New Jersey wanted to govern themselves. They fought for and won the right to elect an **assembly**, or lawmaking body. Each colony also had a governor chosen by the king. The governor's job was to see that the laws of England were obeyed.

THE ZENGER TRIAL

In 1731 the king chose William Cosby to be the governor of New York. Many New Yorkers did not like the way Cosby ran the colony. One of them was **John Peter Zenger**, who published a newspaper called the *New York Weekly Journal.* In 1734 Zenger printed a story that accused the governor of being dishonest. Governor Cosby was so angry he had Zenger arrested and put in jail.

At his trial, Zenger was defended by a lawyer named Andrew Hamilton. Hamilton argued that people had the right to find fault with their officials, as long as what they wrote was true. This was not just the case of "a poor printer," he said. "It is the cause of liberty [freedom]!"

John Peter Zenger was found not guilty. The Zenger trial helped establish an important freedom for all Americans—freedom of the press. It gave Americans the right to speak the truth freely without fear of arrest.

"A MIXED MEDLEY"

In 1664 New Netherland had become New York and New Jersey. These colonies welcomed one and all. They offered to this "mixed medley" of people land, religious freedom, and the right to govern themselves.

Check Your Reading

1. What happened to the colony of New Netherland in 1664?
2. Why did the colonies of New York and New Jersey attract new settlers?
3. Why was John Peter Zenger put in jail? What happened at his trial?
4. **THINKING SKILL:** How did Zenger's choice of action in 1734 lead to freedom of the press?

224

3 Pennsylvania and Delaware

The iron door slammed shut. William Penn found himself locked inside a "nasty and stinking" jail. His crime was preaching Quaker beliefs on the streets of London, England's capital.

In the next few years, Penn would see the inside of many English prisons. During one time in jail he was promised freedom if he gave up his Quaker faith. "My prison shall be my grave before I budge a jot," Penn answered. This proud young man soon started two Middle Colonies—Pennsylvania and Delaware.

Read for Purpose

1. **WHAT YOU KNOW:** Why did different groups of people settle in the Middle Colonies?
2. **WHAT YOU WILL LEARN:** Why did William Penn found the colony of Pennsylvania?

WILLIAM PENN BECOMES A QUAKER

William Penn grew up in a rich English family. His father, Admiral William Penn, won many great sea battles for England. He dreamed that his son would do the same.

But William joined a new religious group known as the Society of Friends. The Friends were also called Quakers. This name comes from their belief that they should "quake before the power of the Lord."

Why did the Admiral dislike the Quakers? Part of the answer lies in the Quakers' beliefs, which were very different from those of the Church of England. The Society of Friends was founded in England by George Fox. Fox taught that inside every person shone an "inner light," a spark of God. To know God, he said, people did not need preachers or churches. They had only to listen to God's voice in their heart.

The Quakers believed that all people were equal. They would not take off their hats to show respect to their "betters." Quakers also believed that the Bible's commandment "Thou shalt not

225

kill" meant they should not serve in the army or navy. They would not pay taxes used to pay for war.

Such ideas made many people angry. The government of England said that Quakers were a "dangerous and mischievous people." Thousands of Quakers were put into English jails.

PENN'S "HOLY EXPERIMENT"

In 1681 King Charles granted William Penn land in America. Penn wanted to start a colony where Quakers could live in peace. He called his land Pennsylvania, which means "Penn's Woods."

Although Pennsylvania was very large, it had no seaport. So Penn asked for more land along the Atlantic Coast. In 1682 the Duke of York gave Penn a piece of land on the west bank of the Delaware River. Later, the people of this area would break away from Pennsylvania to become the separate colony of Delaware.

Penn called his new colony a "holy experiment." He offered complete religious freedom to all who came there. He promised settlers that "you shall be governed by laws of your own making." Penn hoped to build a colony where people were "as free and happy as they could be."

PENN VISITS HIS COLONY

In 1682 Penn came to Pennsylvania with 100 colonists. He chose a place on the Delaware River for his first settle-

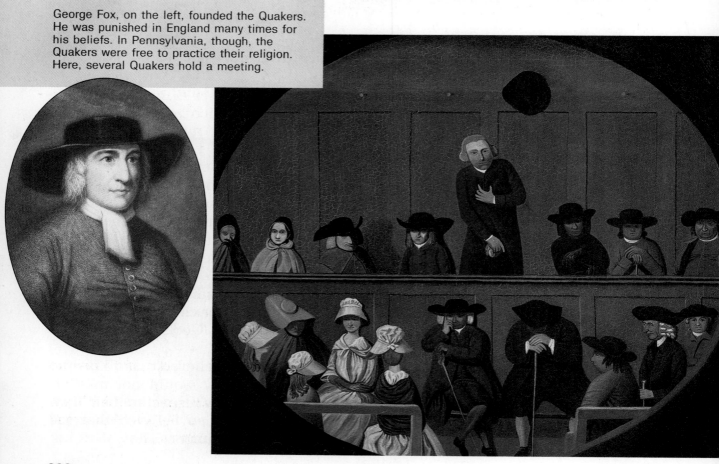

George Fox, on the left, founded the Quakers. He was punished in England many times for his beliefs. In Pennsylvania, though, the Quakers were free to practice their religion. Here, several Quakers hold a meeting.

William Penn bought the land that became Pennsylvania from the Indians. His fair treatment of the Indians led to peace in Pennsylvania for many years.

ment. He named it Philadelphia, which means "brotherly love" in Greek.

Because of his Quaker beliefs, Penn treated the Indians of Pennsylvania as his equals. A colonist wrote that Penn "walked among them, sat with them on the ground, and ate with them of their roasted acorns."

Penn respected the Indians. He was careful to pay them for the land the king had given him. The Indians also respected Penn. They signed a peace agreement with him that lasted for many years.

"THE SEED OF A NATION"

William Penn, as you have read, began Pennsylvania as a "holy experiment." He offered settlers religous freedom and self-government. He treated the Indians in his colony as equals and lived at peace with them.

Penn once wrote that he hoped his colony would become "the seed of a nation." And in many ways it was. Penn's ideas on freedom of religion, government by the people, and the equality of all people took root in Pennsylvania. A great country would one day grow from such ideas.

Check Your Reading

1. Name three beliefs of the Quakers.
2. Why did William Penn want to establish a colony in America for the Quakers?
3. How was the colony of Delaware founded?
4. **THINKING SKILL:** How was William Penn similar to Roger Williams? How was he different?

4 The People of the Middle Colonies

READ TO LEARN

Key Vocabulary

immigrant
frontier
self-sufficient

Read Aloud

The people are a collection of . . . French, Dutch, Germans, Swedes, Danes, Finns, Scotch, Irish, and English. . . . But they . . . live like people of one country.

William Penn wrote this description about Pennsylvania in 1685. Penn wrote many letters to attract settlers to his colony. All over the British Isles and Northern Europe people read his letters with eagerness. They learned that Penn was offering religious freedom, good government, and fertile land at low prices. This good news brought many people to the Middle Colonies.

Read for Purpose

1. **WHAT YOU KNOW:** Why were Quakers treated badly in England?
2. **WHAT YOU WILL LEARN:** What groups of people settled in the Middle Colonies?

THE ENGLISH QUAKERS

Many of the early settlers in New Jersey and Pennsylvania were English Quakers. Like the Puritans that you read about in Chapter 8, Quakers lived in towns and villages. And like the Puritans, they believed that idleness was a sin. Quakers worked hard and did well.

Each month the Quakers held a meeting to deal with problems. Here they might talk about where to build a new road or how to help the poor and sick. Quakers did not vote to decide what to do. Instead, after everyone had spoken, they seemed to agree on a "sense of the meeting."

The Quakers were the first colonists to speak out against slavery. In 1688 the Quakers of Germantown, Pennsylvania, talked about slavery at their monthly meeting. They decided it was wrong to "bring men [here] . . . against their will." This, they said, "we stand against."

THE PENNSYLVANIA DUTCH

In the early 1700s, thousands of Germans came to the Middle Colonies. Most settled in Pennsylvania where land prices were very low. There they started all-German settlements. Since the German word for their language was *Deutsch*, their English-speaking neighbors called them "Dutch." Soon they were known as the Pennsylvania Dutch.

Most German **immigrants** did well in America. An immigrant is someone who leaves one country to come and live in another. An eye for good land and a talent for farming helped the German immigrants to do well. They were said to be the best farmers in the colonies. They knew how to care for their land so that the soil did not wear out. They built stone barns to shelter their animals from the winter cold.

Germans built the first Conestoga wagons. These large covered wagons were used by farmers to haul their crops and livestock to market. The Conestoga wagons worked so well that people called them "the ships of the inland trade."

Germantown, Pennsylvania, was founded by the Pennsylvania Dutch. The painting below shows the market square, or center of town. The Pennsylvania Dutch also built the first Conestoga wagons.

THE SCOTCH-IRISH

By the 1720s, many immigrants from northern Ireland had begun arriving in the Middle Colonies. They were known as the Scotch-Irish. The Scotch-Irish had moved from Scotland to northern Ireland during the 1600s. They had been promised land and freedom to practice their religion in Ireland. But they found little of either. So they moved again to the Middle Colonies, where they found both.

By the time they arrived in the 1720s, the best farmland on the coastal plain and Piedmont was taken. The Scotch-Irish moved farther west into the Appalachian Mountains. There they cleared land along the **frontier**. The frontier is the edge of a settled area. Beyond the frontier lies unexplored wilderness.

Most Scotch-Irish families lived by themselves on small farms carved out of the frontier. They got as much of their food by hunting as from farming.

THE SELF-SUFFICIENT FARM FAMILY

Whether they lived in villages or on lonely frontier farms, most people in the Middle Colonies were farmers. Farm families worked hard to be **self-sufficient**. They took care of almost all of their needs. One self-sufficient farmer boasted:

> *I never laid out (besides my taxes) more than ten dollars a year, which was for salt, nails and the like. Nothing to wear, eat, or drink was purchased. . . . My farm provided all.*

Everyone in a farm family worked hard all year. Fathers and sons plowed and planted the fields. They built houses, barns, and fences. They made furniture and farm tools. They sheared sheep for their wool and butchered hogs for their meat.

Mothers and daughters spent hours making the family's clothing. More hours were spent washing, ironing,

Self-sufficient farm families made everything they needed. They even made toys like the miniature kitchen below and the corn husk doll to the right.

Young colonial children had time for play just like children today. Older children learned skills such as needlework. One girl created this quilt showing scenes of her own life.

and mending. Women weeded the garden and picked fruit from the orchard. They milked the cows and turned the milk into butter and cheese. They collected animal fat to make soap and candles. At harvest time, women worked with men in the fields.

Women also cooked and baked every day. Most food was cooked in iron kettles hung in the fireplace. Empty kettles might weigh as much as 40 pounds (18 kg). Filled with oatmeal or stew, they were much heavier. Many women suffered from sore backs, blistered hands, and burned faces while cooking.

Most self-sufficient farm families raised more grain than they needed. The extra grain was sent to New York or Philadelphia for sale. So much grain was raised here that the Middle Colonies were called "the breadbasket of America."

THE PROMISE OF THE MIDDLE COLONIES

During the 1700s, the Middle Colonies grew rapidly. A French settler named Jean de Crèvecoeur (zhän də krev kər') thought he knew why. He wrote that poor people in Europe were treated like "useless plants." They were "mowed down by want, hunger, and war."

The Middle Colonies promised people land and a chance to get ahead. It was this promise that attracted poor people from many countries. Here, wrote Crèvecoeur, they "have taken root and flourished."

Check Your Reading

1. What groups of people made their homes in the Middle Colonies?
2. Why did some people decide to settle along the frontier?
3. **THINKING SKILL:** What are some of the important differences between family life today and family life in colonial times?

READ TO LEARN

Key Vocabulary

almanac

Key People

Benjamin Franklin

Read Aloud

On a Sunday morning in October 1723, a young man stepped off a boat in Philadelphia. He did not look his best. He was tired, dirty, and hungry. His only clean clothes were stuffed in his pockets. He found a bakery where he feasted on "three great puffy rolls." Then he followed some "clean-dressed people" into a Quaker meeting house. As soon as he sat down, he fell sound asleep.

This sleeping 17-year-old with crumbs on his shirt was Benjamin Franklin. When he came to Philadelphia, the town was growing every day. It seemed just the place for a bright, young man with big plans.

Read for Purpose

1. **WHAT YOU KNOW:** Where is Philadelphia located?
2. **WHAT YOU WILL LEARN:** What was Philadelphia like in the 1700s?

COLONIAL PHILADELPHIA

Benjamin Franklin was born in Boston, the fifteenth child in a family of 17 children. He had worked as a printer's helper in his older brother's print shop. To Benjamin, it seemed as if he did most of the work while his brother made most of the money. So he ran away to Philadelphia.

Luckily, Franklin arrived in dry weather. Philadelphia's dirt streets were dusty, but walkable. In wet weather, the streets turned into swamps. Men waded through the mud in their boots. Women often took off their shoes for fear of losing them in the mud.

To Franklin, Philadelphia seemed noisy and exciting. The streets were filled with people, wagons, and barking dogs. The busiest day of the week was market day. Early in the morning, farmers brought their sheep, cows, and crops into town to sell. All day long, farmers and city people traded goods and bits of news.

A CITY OF OPPORTUNITY

For Franklin, Philadelphia was a city of opportunity. By the time he was 24, he owned a print shop. He also published his own newspaper, called the *Pennsylvania Gazette*.

In 1732 Franklin began writing and printing *Poor Richard's Almanac*. An almanac is a book of facts on many subjects. Franklin filled his almanacs with useful information for farmers. He also included clever sayings, such as the ones shown on this page. After the Bible, *Poor Richard's Almanac* was the best-selling book in the colonies.

Franklin's print shop was one of many workshops lining the streets of Philadelphia. The city's craftworkers made clothes, clocks, hats, wigs, dishes, tools, and other things. Workshops near the Delaware River turned out rope and sails needed by Philadelphia's shipbuilders.

The Delaware River was lined with docks built by merchants. Ships left Philadelphia with furs, lumber, grain, and meat. They returned filled with goods made in England. These included everything from silks and lace to swords and mousetraps.

POOR RICHARD'S ALMANAC

Half Wits talk much but say little.

An open foe may prove a curse; but a pretended friend is worse.

There are lazy minds as well as lazy bodies.

A true friend is the best possession.

No gains without pains.

You may be too cunning for one, but not for all.

Be always ashamed to catch thyself idle.

Great talkers, little doers.

Better slip with foot than tongue.

People who are wrapped up in themselves make small packages.

He that cannot obey, cannot command.

Haste makes waste.

Early to bed and early to rise, makes a man healthy, wealthy and wise.

The doors of wisdom are never shut.

Benjamin Franklin owned his own printing shop in Philadelphia. There, he published books and wrote *Poor Richard's Almanac* each year. Some sayings from *Poor Richard's Almanac* are shown above.

Franklin was an inventor, scientist, and an outstanding citizen of Philadelphia. In this picture he is shown wearing a hat of the volunteer fire fighters, which he organized.

CITY IMPROVEMENTS

If you would not be forgotten
As soon as you are dead and rotten,
Either write things worth reading
Or do things worth writing.

Ben Franklin gave this bit of advice to the many readers of his almanacs. He also followed it himself. He worked hard to improve life in Philadelphia.

Books were very costly in the colonies. So, in 1731, Franklin started America's first public library in Philadelphia. People could borrow books for a small fee. The money collected was used to buy more books.

Fires were a great danger in cities. So Franklin organized the Union Fire Company, the world's first volunteer fire department. Members of the fire company were trained to respond quickly to alarms and to put out fires.

Franklin led efforts to pave Philadelphia's muddy streets. He also led the fight for street lights to make the city safer at night.

THE LARGEST COLONIAL CITY

By 1760 Philadelphia was the largest city in the colonies. It had grown rapidly because it was in the center of a rich farming region. Farm products went from Philadelphia to many parts of the world.

Visitors to Philadelphia were impressed by its "fine appearance" and "well-lighted streets." For such improvements, they had Ben Franklin to thank.

Check Your Reading

1. What was colonial Philadelphia like?
2. What was *Poor Richard's Almanac*?
3. **THINKING SKILL:** If you were living in the 1700s, would you prefer to live in Philadelphia or along the frontier? Explain your answer.

THE
LOVING CUP

Benjamin Franklin worked hard to improve the city of Philadelphia. Throughout our history, in cities and towns across the country, people have tried to make their communities better places to live. One example is a young woman named Julie Leirich (lēr′ ik) who started a program called The Loving Cup to help feed hungry people.

Julie works as a cashier in Los Angeles, California. Every morning on her way to work she would pass homeless people looking through garbage cans for food. Yet Julie knew that every day the store where she works threw out dented cans of food, day-old bread, and unattractive fruits and vegetables. But these foods are still good-tasting and good for you. Julie

and a fellow worker, named Fred Frick, decided to rescue these foods before they reached the garbage bins. Their plan was to bring this food to the needy.

Julie and Fred began to give homeless and hungry people the food that the supermarket would have thrown out. When they told the store manager what they were doing, they were afraid that they would be fired. But instead, the manager was pleased. He even added more food to their project. "It's a wonderful idea," he said, "to find a use for food that would have been wasted."

Soon Julie was picking up extra food from other stores and restaurants. When people in the neighborhood heard about The Loving Cup, they wanted to help. Many of them volunteered to pick up and distribute, or give out, food. Today, over six tons of food are handed out each month. Julie Leirich turned her concern for others into a valuable community service.

235

Understanding Elevation and Relief

Key Vocabulary

elevation

relief

The surface of the earth is not even. It changes from place to place resulting in different landforms. You know that the part of the United States that made up the Middle Colonies has a variety of landforms. There are plains, plateaus, hills, and mountains. In this lesson you will learn how maps can help show changes in the surface of the earth.

Using an Elevation Map

The map below shows elevation (el ə vā′ shən). Elevation is the height of land above sea level. It is usually mea-sured in feet or meters. Elevation at sea level is 0 feet (0 m). Places that are near sea level have low elevations. Places far above sea level have high elevations.

Look at the elevation map of New York. You can see that it uses color to show the height of land areas. The map key tells you which colors are used to show differ-ent ranges of elevation. What ranges of elevation are shown on the map of New York?

The highest parts of New York are shown on the map in orange. Find the orange areas on the map. What moun-tains do they show? Now find the Alle-gheny Plateau. Is this plateau higher or lower than the mountains? Dark green is used on the map to show areas of low elevation. What parts of New York have low elevations? What is the elevation of New York City?

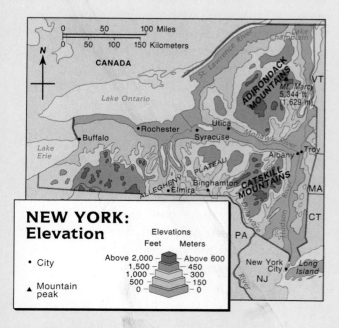

NEW YORK: Elevation

Elevations
Feet — Meters
Above 2,000 — Above 600
1,500 — 450
1,000 — 300
500 — 150
0 — 0

• City

▲ Mountain peak

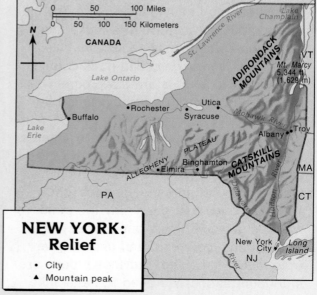

NEW YORK: Relief

• City
▲ Mountain peak

236

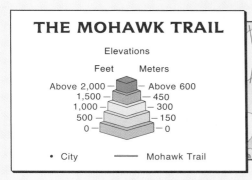

THE MOHAWK TRAIL

Elevations

Feet		Meters
Above 2,000 —		— Above 600
1,500 —		— 450
1,000 —		— 300
500 —		— 150
0 —		— 0

• City ——— Mohawk Trail

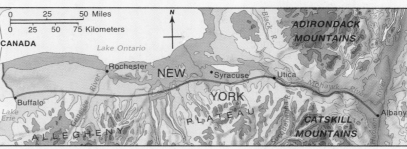

Using a Relief Map

Elevation maps show the heights of land areas. They also show how elevation changes from place to place. The difference in height between land areas is called relief. Level, or flat, land that stretches for long distances has low relief. Land that rises and drops sharply within short distances has high relief.

Mountains are landforms with high elevation and high relief. Hills generally have lower elevations and lower relief than mountains. Plains and plateaus are landforms of low relief. They are found at both low and high elevations. Plateaus drop off sharply on at least one side. Plains do not.

Look at the relief map on page 236. It shows the same area as the elevation map. On this map, shading is used to show relief. The most heavily shaded parts of the map show areas of high relief. Lightly shaded parts of the map show areas of moderate relief—hills and less rugged mountains. Areas of low relief are not shaded at all on the map. The unshaded parts of the map indicate plains.

Using an Elevation and Relief Map

Now look at the map of the Mohawk Trail above. During the 1700s settlers moving west followed its path through the Appalachian Mountains. On this map, both color and shading are used to give a very good idea of both elevation and relief. Check the map key to see what ranges of elevation are shown.

Reviewing the Skill

1. What is the difference between elevation and relief?
2. Which map would you use to find the elevation of Long Island?
3. Why do river valleys provide easy travel routes?
4. Why is it useful to be able to read a map showing elevation and relief when planning a hike?

IMPORTANT EVENTS

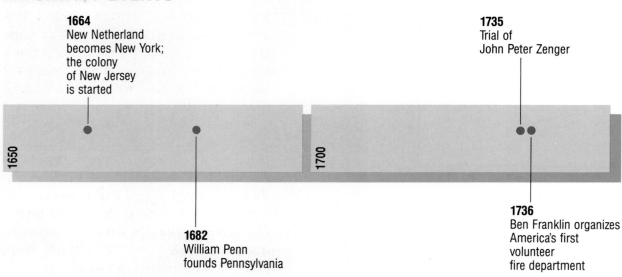

1664
New Netherland
becomes New York;
the colony
of New Jersey
is started

1735
Trial of
John Peter Zenger

1650

1700

1682
William Penn
founds Pennsylvania

1736
Ben Franklin organizes
America's first
volunteer
fire department

PEOPLE TO KNOW

Benjamin Franklin
1706-1790

William Penn
1644-1718

John Peter Zenger
1697-1746

IDEAS TO REMEMBER

- The Middle Colonies were fortunate in having rich farmland, navigable rivers, and good harbors.
- In 1664 the English took over the Dutch colony of New Netherland and created the colonies of New York and New Jersey.
- In 1682 William Penn started the colony of Pennsylvania as a place where Quakers would have religious freedom.
- The Middle Colonies attracted settlers who came from many countries and who held a variety of religious beliefs.
- Benjamin Franklin improved life in the city of Philadelphia by starting a public library, organizing a volunteer fire department, and leading the fight for paved, well-lit streets.

REVIEWING VOCABULARY

assembly   navigable
frontier   self-sufficient
immigrant

Number a paper from 1 to 5. Beside each number write a sentence using one of the words or terms from the list above. The sentence should show that you understand the meaning of the word or term.

REVIEWING FACTS

Read the statements below. Then number a paper from 1 to 5. Beside each number write whether the statement is true or false. If it is false, explain why.

1. The Middle Colonies offered settlers poor farmland and long, harsh winters.
2. The trial of John Peter Zenger established the right of freedom of assembly.
3. Pennsylvania was founded by a Puritan leader named William Penn.
4. Settlers known as the Pennsylvania Dutch came from the Netherlands.
5. Benjamin Franklin set up the first volunteer fire department in Philadelphia.

WRITING ABOUT MAIN IDEAS

1. **Writing an Advertisement:** Choose one colony discussed in this chapter. Then write an advertisement encouraging people to move to that colony. Your advertisement should include at least four features of the colony that would attract new settlers.

2. **Writing a Story:** Many of Benjamin Franklin's clever sayings teach a lesson. Choose one of the sayings on page 233 that teaches a lesson. Then write a story in which your main character learns that lesson. Your story can take place anywhere and at any time—not just in the time of Benjamin Franklin. Use your imagination.

3. **Writing a Summary:** Write a summary of the life and work of William Penn. Begin by making a list of the events in his life. Then identify the things he accomplished. Finally write a brief summary explaining why you think Penn was an outstanding person.

BUILDING SKILLS: UNDERSTANDING ELEVATION AND RELIEF

1. In what ways are elevation and relief maps different?
2. Refer to the map of the Mohawk Trail on page 237 as you answer the following questions.
   a. What areas of low elevation does the Mohawk Trail pass through?
   b. Find the Adirondack Mountains on the map. Is this an area of high or low elevation?
3. Imagine you are hiking along the Mohawk Trail. Write a paragraph describing the elevation and relief you observe along the way.

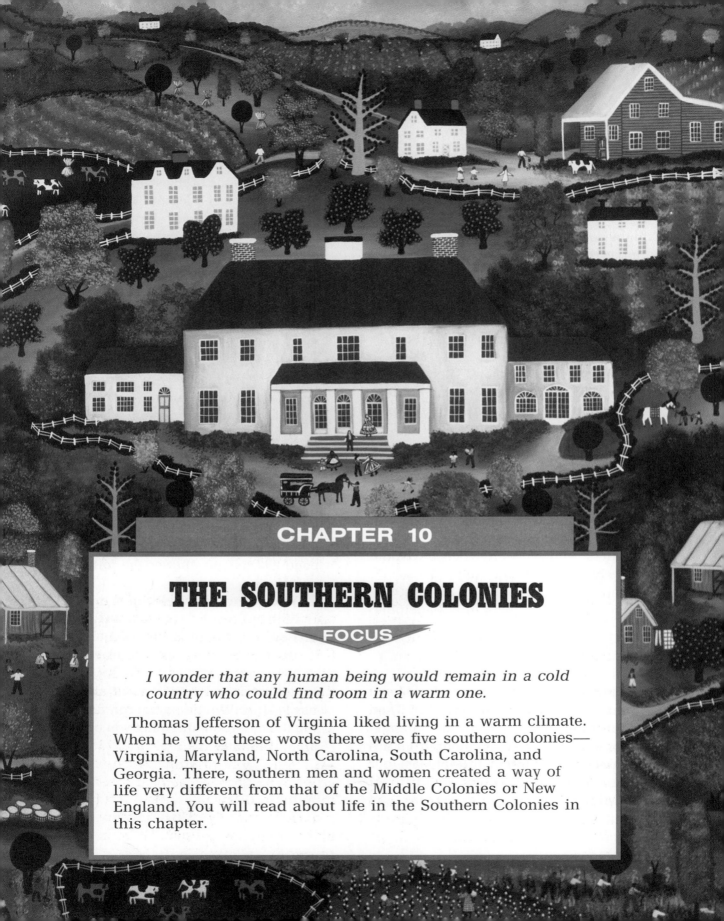

CHAPTER 10

THE SOUTHERN COLONIES

FOCUS

I wonder that any human being would remain in a cold country who could find room in a warm one.

Thomas Jefferson of Virginia liked living in a warm climate. When he wrote these words there were five southern colonies— Virginia, Maryland, North Carolina, South Carolina, and Georgia. There, southern men and women created a way of life very different from that of the Middle Colonies or New England. You will read about life in the Southern Colonies in this chapter.

1 The Geography of the Southern Colonies

READ TO LEARN

Key Vocabulary

tidewater

Key Places

Maryland
Georgia
North Carolina

Outer Banks
Virginia
South Carolina

Read Aloud

O magnet-south! O glistening perfumed South! my South!

The poet Walt Whitman wrote these words in 1860 in a poem called "O Magnet-South." Whitman was not born in the South. Yet it drew him the way a magnet attracts bits of iron. The same was true for the first colonists who settled here in the 1600s. In the Southern Colonies they found a land of great beauty and promise.

Read for Purpose

1. **WHAT YOU KNOW:** Why do you think many people enjoy living in the South?
2. **WHAT YOU WILL LEARN:** Why were the Southern Colonies a good place for growing crops?

THE TIDEWATER REGION

Looked at from the Atlantic Ocean, the Southern Colonies seem to have no solid coastline. That is because the coastal plain from Maryland to Georgia is cut by great bays, broad rivers, and tangled swamps. In many places it is hard to tell where the sea ends and the land begins.

Along North Carolina's coast is a chain of sandy islands called the Outer Banks. Wind and waves are always reshaping these islands. Storms can cut an island in half. The islands change shape so fast that sailors' maps cannot keep up.

The first settlers in the Southern Colonies settled on the coastal plain. Colonists called this area the tidewater. A tidewater is a low-lying coastal plain that is full of waterways. At high tide the ocean flows into the land and the rivers rise. As the tide goes out, the rivers fall.

The climate and soil of the tidewater are ideal for raising warm-weather crops. The growing season lasts seven months in tidewater Virginia. In Georgia and South Carolina it stretches to eight months or longer. There is plenty of rainfall all year.

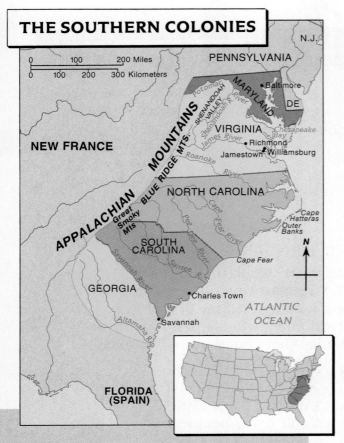

THE SOUTHERN COLONIES

MAP SKILL: Locate the coastal areas of the Southern Colonies. The picture below shows a section of the **tidewater**.

The tidewater forests were filled with animals. Hunters found ducks, deer, bears, buffaloes, and turkeys. Fish filled the many rivers that wound through the tidewater. Clams, crabs, and other shellfish were easy to find. The tidewater was an area of great natural riches.

THE BACKCOUNTRY

The tidewater ends at the fall line. Farther west lies the backcountry—the Piedmont and the Appalachians. Frontier farmers found that the red clay soil of the Piedmont was good for growing corn and tobacco.

Beyond the Piedmont rise the Blue Ridge and Great Smoky mountains. Find these mountains on the map to the left. The Blue Ridge and Great Smoky mountains are the tallest mountains in the Appalachians. In North Carolina's backcountry, more than 40 peaks rise to over 6,000 feet (1,800 m).

A GENTLE WILDERNESS

The people who settled in the Southern Colonies, as you have seen, found a quiet wilderness. The soil was fertile. The woods were full of animals, and fish filled the rivers. The climate was warm most of the year. As the poet Walt Whitman found, it was an easy land to love.

 Check Your Reading

1. Why was the tidewater a good place for growing crops?
2. Was the backcountry a good place for farming? Why or why not?
3. **GEOGRAPHY SKILL:** Locate the tidewater on the map above. How did this area get its name?
4. **THINKING SKILL:** Why were settlers attracted to the tidewater?

2 The Founding of the Southern Colonies

READ TO LEARN

Key Vocabulary
proprietor
cash crop

Key People
George Calvert
Lord Baltimore
James Oglethorpe

Key Places
Charleston

Read Aloud

Virginia was the first of the Southern Colonies. In Chapter 7 you read that the English settlement at Jamestown almost failed. Then John Rolfe learned how to grow tobacco. Soon life in Virginia improved, and other colonies were begun nearby.

Read for Purpose

1. **WHAT YOU KNOW:** Why did the settlement at Jamestown almost fail?
2. **WHAT YOU WILL LEARN:** How did the Southern Colonies begin?

MARYLAND

The second colony started in the South began as the idea of a rich Catholic named George Calvert. In 1632 Calvert decided to build a colony for Catholics in America. At that time, Catholics could not practice their religion openly in England for fear of arrest.

Calvert persuaded King Charles I of England to grant him a large area of land beside Chesapeake Bay. The king named the new colony Maryland after his wife, Queen Mary. Calvert planned to make Maryland a place where Catholics could worship in peace. But he died before he could carry out his plans. His son Lord Baltimore took over the colony.

In 1634 two ships, the *Ark* and the *Dove*, sailed to Maryland with about 300 people. They set to work at once planting crops in the rich tidewater soil. One happy colonist found that beans grew 14 inches (36 cm) in 10 days. Another wrote that the new colony needed nothing "but greater numbers of people to enjoy it."

Such reports attracted many people to Maryland. By the 1640s most of the colonists were not Catholics. A worried Lord Baltimore asked Maryland's assembly to protect the religious freedom of Catholics. In 1649 the assembly passed the Maryland Toleration Act. This law said that no Christian should "be in any ways troubled" for following "his or her religion."

THE CAROLINAS

In 1663 England's King Charles II gave the area south of Virginia to eight friends. The friends named their colony Carolina in the king's honor (*Charles* is *Carolus* in Latin) and became the "Lord Proprietors" of Carolina. A **proprietor** (prə prī′ ə tər) is a person who owns property or a business.

The proprietors hoped to make money by renting and selling land in Carolina. But they did not rule their colony well. Settlers complained to the king about high rents and bad government. In 1729 King George II took over Carolina, and he divided it into two colonies—North Carolina and South Carolina.

North Carolina was first settled by farmers from Virginia. A warm climate and good soil made for an easy life.

One visitor wrote that "surely there is no place in the world where the inhabitants live with less labor than in North Carolina."

South Carolina's first settlement, Charles Town, was built where the Ashley and Cooper rivers meet. Today we know this city as **Charleston**. The land around Charles Town was too swampy for tobacco. But it was good for growing rice and indigo. Indigo is a plant that produces a blue dye. These products became South Carolina's first **cash crops**. A cash crop is a crop grown to be sold for a profit.

GEORGIA

The last Southern Colony was begun as a refuge for poor people. In England, people who owed money could be put in jail. These people often stayed in prison year after year. But as long as they were locked up, they could not earn money to pay off what they owed.

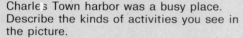

Charles Town harbor was a busy place. Describe the kinds of activities you see in the picture.

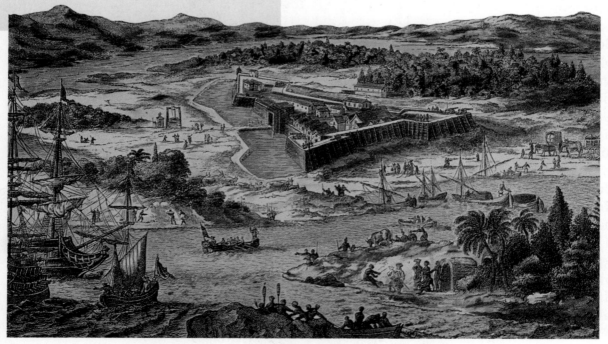

The town of Savannah, Georgia, was set out in a grid pattern of neat plots and streets. James Oglethorpe was the founder of the Georgia colony.

In 1732 King George II granted to a military man named **James Oglethorpe** the land between South Carolina and Spanish Florida. The colony was named Georgia after the king. Oglethorpe planned to put poor people to work in Georgia raising cash crops. "England will grow rich by sending her poor abroad," he said.

Oglethorpe brought 114 settlers to Georgia in 1733. Each was given 50 acres (20 ha) of land and told to raise wine grapes and silkworms. But wine grapes and silkworms grew poorly in Georgia's soil, and many settlers left.

In 1752 King George II took control of Georgia. He gave the colonists more land and let them plant what they wanted. Soon Georgians were raising rice and indigo. The colony began to grow at last.

THE FIVE SOUTHERN COLONIES

The five Southern Colonies had been started for many reasons. Maryland was a refuge for Catholics. The founders of Virginia and the Carolinas hoped to make money. Georgia began as a place where the poor could make a new start. But most settlers came for one reason. The Southern Colonies offered them fertile land to farm.

Check Your Reading

1. What were George Calvert's plans for Maryland?
2. Why did King George II take over Carolina in 1729?
3. Why did James Oglethorpe want to begin a colony in Georgia?
4. **THINKING SKILL:** Although Massachusetts and Maryland were both settled for religious reasons, how did the two colonies differ?

go to page 457

Comparing Line, Circle, and Bar Graphs

Key Vocabulary

graph   circle graph

line graph   bar graph

Since colonial times, the United States government has collected facts and figures that provide information about a particular subject. This information might show how many people live in an area or how much rain fell in a region of the country.

A good way to present facts and figures is to put them into **graphs**. A graph is a diagram that allows you to compare different facts and figures.

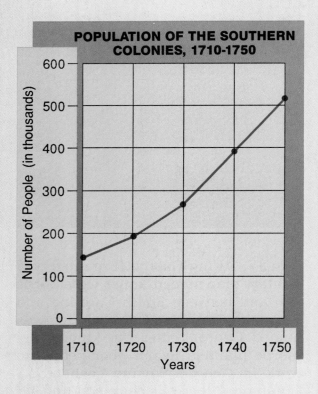

POPULATION OF THE SOUTHERN COLONIES, 1710-1750

Reading a Line Graph

One type of graph is a **line graph**. A line graph shows changes over time. It lets you see trends, or patterns, up or down.

To read a line graph, first look at its title. What is the title of the line graph on this page? Next look at the information along the bottom of the graph. What does it tell you?

Now find the information on the left side of the graph. What does it tell you about the graph?

Notice that for each year on the graph, a dot shows how many people lived in the Southern Colonies. Often a dot falls between the numbers. In 1710 it falls halfway between the numbers 100,000 and 200,000. You can then figure out that

there were about 150,000 people in the Southern Colonies in 1710. About how many people lived in the Southern Colonies in 1730? In 1750?

In a line graph, the dots are joined to form a line. The line shows the trend in population. What trend does the line graph show?

Reading a Circle Graph

A second kind of graph is a **circle graph**. A circle graph shows how something can be divided into parts. Together, all the parts make up the whole. A circle graph is often called a pie graph because the parts look like slices of a pie.

Suppose you wanted to see whether the New England, Middle, or Southern

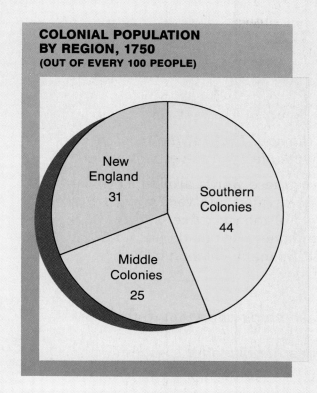

COLONIAL POPULATION BY REGION, 1750
(OUT OF EVERY 100 PEOPLE)

New England 31

Southern Colonies 44

Middle Colonies 25

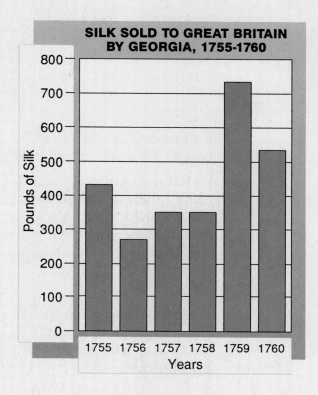

SILK SOLD TO GREAT BRITAIN BY GEORGIA, 1755-1760

Pounds of Silk

Years

Colonies had the most people at a certain time. The circle graph above shows that information clearly. The whole circle graph represents 100 people living in the colonies in 1750. Of every 100 people, 31 of them lived in New England. How many of every 100 people lived in the Middle Colonies in 1750? Which region had the most people?

Reading a Bar Graph

Another kind of graph is a **bar graph**. A bar graph can be used for several purposes. It can show changes over time. It can compare different items. And it can show big contrasts or sudden changes.

The bar graph on this page shows how many pounds of silk were sold to Great Britain by Georgia from 1755 to 1760. Like a line graph, the information on a bar graph is labeled. What information do the numbers alongside the graph show? About how many pounds were sold in 1759?

Reviewing the Skill

1. What is a graph? Name three kinds of graphs.
2. When did the population of the Southern Colonies reach 500,000?
3. In 1750 did the New England Colonies or the Middle Colonies have more people?
4. In 1756 did Georgia sell more or less silk to Great Britain than in 1755?
5. Why do we use different kinds of graphs?

247

3 The World of the Planter

READ TO LEARN

📭 Key Vocabulary   **Key People**

plantation   William Byrd II

📭 Read Aloud

The planters, by the richness of the soil, live [in] the most easy and pleasant manner of any people I have ever met with.

A visitor to North Carolina wrote these words around 1750. By then much of the tidewater was divided into very large farms. Farmers selling a great deal of tobacco, rice, and indigo made good money. With the money they made, they created a way of life that was envied by many colonists.

📭 Read for Purpose

1. **WHAT YOU KNOW:** Why were cash crops important to the economy of the South?
2. **WHAT YOU WILL LEARN:** What was life like on a southern plantation?

THE PLANTATION

In the South, very large farms were called **plantations**. The people who owned these farms were known as planters. Most plantations were on tidewater rivers. Instead of addresses, they had names like Gunston Hall or Claremont Manor.

As the diagram on page 249 shows, the center of plantation life was the "big house." These large homes were planned for warm weather. High ceilings and wide halls helped heat escape during the hot summer months. The kitchen was in a separate building to keep the big house cooler.

The homes of wealthy planters had beautiful furniture from England. Fireplaces in every room had shiny brass tools. The dining table was set with crystal glasses, silver platters, and china dishes.

Almost everything else that planters needed was made or grown on the plantation. Near the big house were gardens and orchards. There were also work buildings, including a laundry house, smokehouse, carpentry shop, and blacksmith shop.

Away from the big house and hidden from view were the workers' cabins. At first most plantation workers were indentured servants. Later, as you will read, planters began to replace indentured servants with slaves.

A SOUTHERN PLANTATION

Tobacco fields

Slave cabins

Stable

Blacksmith shop

Carpentry shop

Vegetable garden

Laundry

Smokehouse

Kitchen

Big house

Dock

Tobacco barn

DIAGRAM SKILL: Almost everything planters needed was made or grown on the plantation. Use the diagram to locate the many buildings and activities of the plantation.

TOWNS AND TRADE

In New England and the Middle Colonies, towns such as Boston and Philadelphia had become centers of trade. The trading centers of the Southern Colonies were the plantations. Some plantations had their own wharves, or docks. Ships from England and the West Indies came right to the plantation to trade slaves and English goods for tobacco. One colonist wrote, "Tobacco is the current coin of Maryland, and will sooner purchase commodities [goods] from the merchant than [will] money."

Without trade, most towns in the South remained small. But Charles Town grew quickly. Because South Carolina's rivers were shallow, large oceangoing ships could not reach plantations that were not on the coast. Instead, many planters had to send their rice and indigo to Charles Town for sale.

Planters came to Charles Town for pleasure as well as business. In the town's shops they found goods not made on the plantation. Here they could buy jewelry, coaches, books, and the latest in clothes. They could go to plays and concerts. Or they could see the first science museum in America.

WORK AND PLAY

Running a plantation was like running a business. William Byrd II, one of Virginia's richest planters, left a diary of his activities each day. Most of Byrd's time was spent looking after his plantation. He told his workers when to plant and harvest. When something broke, he saw that it was fixed. If slaves tried to run away, he punished them. But he also took care of "his people" when they got sick. One of his favorite medicines was "a gallon or two of chicken broth."

Slaves did most of the hard work on southern **plantations**. Planters like William Byrd II (*right*) made sure the plantation was a success.

Fox hunting (*above*) was a popular sport among southern planters. A wealthy southern lady might have bought this decorated fan in Charles Town.

Most plantations were miles from any other farm or town, so guests were always welcome. Families often visited each other for several days or even weeks. A popular saying was, "Ride a mile and stay a week."

During these visits, planters enjoyed horse races and fox hunts. There were other entertainments. While Puritans and Quakers frowned on dancing, many Southerners loved to dance. A shocked visitor from New Jersey wrote that "these Virginians will dance or die."

"THE ART OF ENJOYING LIFE"

In the Southern Colonies the wealthy planters lived in fine houses on their plantations. They wanted to live like English landowners. And with the help of their servants and slaves, many planters succeeded. A preacher from Maryland wrote that southern planters "really have the art of enjoying life, I think, in a manner to be envied."

Check Your Reading

1. Were plantations in the South self-sufficient? Explain your answer.
2. What were some of the responsibilities of a southern planter?
3. Why did towns grow slowly in the Southern Colonies?
4. **THINKING SKILL:** Do you think William Byrd's diary would be a good source to learn about the treatment of slaves? Explain your answer.

4 Slavery in the Colonies

READ TO LEARN

Key Vocabulary

overseer

Read Aloud

The comfortable life of the wealthy planter would have been impossible without slavery. Although slavery existed in all 13 colonies, most slaves lived in the South. Here they worked long and hard for farmers and planters.

Read for Purpose

1. **WHAT YOU KNOW:** What was life like for wealthy southern planters?
2. **WHAT YOU WILL LEARN:** What was life like for slaves in the South?

SLAVES AND SERVANTS

You read in Chapter 7 that the first Africans brought to Virginia in 1619 were sold as indentured servants. After working for a few years, they were freed. Many free blacks started their own farms and businesses.

For many years whites and blacks worked together on farms and plantations. One white servant wrote, "We and the Negroes both alike did fare. Of work and food we had an equal share."

But after 1670 all blacks brought into Virginia were made slaves for life. Their children also became slaves. This change came about because planters had learned an important lesson. They could make more money with slaves than with indentured servants. Servants left after a few years. Slaves had to work for life.

"SLAVE YOUNG, SLAVE LONG"

Slaves were treated as property. Slave families were often broken up with the sale of a father, mother, or child. Slaves went to work by the time they were six and worked for as many years as they were able. As one slave put it, "Slave young, slave long."

Slaves had to depend on their owners for food, clothing, and a place to live. On small farms slaves often lived and ate with their owners. But most slaves lived on plantations. Their life was very different from that of the planter's family in the big house.

On most plantations, the day began at dawn. The overseer came to the slave cabins to make sure the slaves went to the fields. The overseer was hired by the planter to make sure the slaves did their work.

Slaves were bought and sold like cattle at auctions. On the plantations, they lived in crowded one-room cabins like the ones reconstructed at Carter's Grove, Virginia.

Field slaves worked hard. Trees had to be cut down and stumps pulled out. Crops had to be planted, weeded, and picked.

Not all slaves worked in the fields. Some were house slaves who worked as cooks or servants in the big house. Other slaves were weavers, carpenters, or dressmakers. Whatever they did, most slaves worked six or seven days a week.

FIGHTING BACK

Planters liked slaves who worked hard and obeyed orders. Those who did not were punished. William Byrd thought of himself as a kind master. But his diary shows that he whipped slaves for such things as spilling water on a couch or "for doing nothing."

Blacks fought back against slavery whenever they could. Some slaves broke tools or worked very slowly. A few were allowed to earn money by working for other planters. When they had saved enough money, they were able to buy their freedom. Other slaves tried to run away.

"OH, FREEDOM!"

Slavery existed in all the colonies. But most slaves lived in the Southern Colonies wherever rice, indigo, and tobacco were grown. Slaves faced a life of endless work with no rewards.

Few slaves wrote about slavery. It was against the law in most colonies to teach a slave to read or write. But slaves did put their feelings into songs and stories. As this song tells us, the greatest hope of most slaves was some-day to be free.

Oh, freedom; oh freedom
Oh, Lord, freedom over me,
And before I'd be a slave
I'd be buried in my grave
And go home to my Lord and be free.

Check Your Reading

1. How did slaves differ from indentured servants?
2. Describe a day in the life of a slave on a plantation.
3. How did blacks fight against a life of slavery?
4. **THINKING SKILL:** What do you think would have happened if slaves had been allowed to learn how to read and write?

5 George Washington's Virginia

READ TO LEARN

Key People

George Washington

Key Places

Mount Vernon
Shenandoah Valley

Read Aloud

Young George Washington thought he was lucky. He had been given the only bed in the inn. But when he undressed and lay down he "found it nothing but a little straw matted together without sheets." Worse yet, the straw was alive with lice and fleas. George put on his clothes and went to sleep on the floor.

Until then, George Washington had spent his life in the big houses of tidewater Virginia. Now, for the first time, he was seeing Virginia's backcountry. It was a very different world from the one he knew best.

Read for Purpose

1. **WHAT YOU KNOW:** How did people live in tidewater Virginia?
2. **WHAT YOU WILL LEARN:** What was life like for settlers in the backcountry?

TIDEWATER VIRGINIA

George Washington was born on a tidewater plantation in 1732. The Virginia of his childhood was not the scary wilderness the first Jamestown settlers found. Indians no longer hunted in the tidewater forests. The lowlands were now home to wealthy planters and their slaves.

Young George was educated at home. Virginia had few schools because the plantations were so far from each other. George had hoped to finish his schooling in England, but his fa-ther died when he was 11. Instead of going to England, George went to live with his older brother Lawrence at his Virginia plantation, Mount Vernon.

While living at Mount Vernon, George Washington became part of a world where a few wealthy families ran nearly everything. The children of these families grew up visiting each other's homes. They went to dances and fox hunts together. In time they married each other and became the leaders of the colony.

Mount Vernon is located on the Potomac River in Virginia. Today, George Washington's home is open for visitors to see how he lived. A map drawn by Washington is to the left.

BACKCOUNTRY VIRGINIA

When he was 16, George Washington made his first trip to the backcountry. He traveled with friends across the Blue Ridge Mountains to the Shenandoah Valley. Indian stories say that this valley was where the Great Spirit brought the stars together to sing for joy. The name Shenandoah means "Daughter of the Stars."

In that mountain valley Washington met many Scotch-Irish and German settlers. Most of them had followed an Indian trail south from the Pennsylvania backcountry.

Frontier families worked hard just to stay alive. Unlike tidewater planters, they grew only small amounts of food. Most of the time they either hunted or fished.

Frontier women were unlike any Washington had ever met. They did not wear silks and lace and talk of parties. Wives worked with their husbands to make fields out of forest. One woman boasted that she could "hew [cut] with an ax as good as any man."

Cabins in the backcountry lacked the comforts Washington was used to. Most had only one room and little furniture. Washington spent many nights sleeping on a cabin floor with an entire frontier family.

THE TWO VIRGINIAS

George Washington had learned on his journey across the Blue Ridge Mountains that there were two Virginias. One was tidewater Virginia with its elegant homes and people. The other was backcountry Virginia with its small cabins and its rough frontier settlers.

Washington belonged in the tidewater world. But as you will see in the next chapter, he would soon return to the backcountry. There he fired the first shots in what became a great war.

 Check Your Reading

1. Describe George Washington's life as a young boy.
2. Describe life in tidewater Virginia.
3. What was life like in the backcountry?
4. **THINKING SKILL:** Review the lesson and place all the events in the order in which they occurred.

255

IMPORTANT EVENTS

1632
George Calvert founds Maryland

1663
The Carolinas are settled

1733
James Oglethorpe founds Georgia

1620

1640

1660

1720

1649
Maryland Toleration Act is passed

1729
Carolina is divided into North Carolina and South Carolina

PEOPLE TO KNOW

Lord Baltimore 1606-1647

William Byrd II 1674-1744

George Calvert 1580?-1632

James Oglethorpe 1696-1785

George Washington 1732-1799

IDEAS TO REMEMBER

- The land and climate of the Southern Colonies were excellent for growing crops.
- The colonies of Maryland, North Carolina, South Carolina, and Georgia were founded between 1632 and 1733.
- For many people in the Southern Colonies, everyday life centered around the plantation.
- Slaves in the Southern Colonies faced a life of endless work with no rewards.
- In most Southern Colonies life in the tidewater region differed greatly from life on the frontier.

REVIEWING VOCABULARY

Number a paper from 1 to 5. Beside each number write **C** if the underlined word or term in the sentence is used correctly. Write **I** if it is used incorrectly, and then write the word or term that will complete the sentence correctly.

1. A person who owns property or a business is called an <u>overseer</u>.
2. The low-lying plain along the coast of the Southern Colonies is called the <u>Outer Banks</u>.
3. In Georgia rice was a <u>cash crop</u> because planters could sell it for a profit.
4. In the South many people lived on large farms called <u>manors</u>.
5. The person who made sure that crops were planted and harvested and that all things ran smoothly was called the <u>master</u>.

REVIEWING FACTS

Number a paper from 1 to 5. Beside each number write the letter of the answer that best completes each sentence.

1. A settler living in tidewater Virginia found _____.
   a. steep mountains   c. cold winters
   b. fertile soil
2. The founders of the colonies of _____ came to America mostly to make money.
   a. Virginia and the Carolinas
   b. Georgia and Virginia
   c. Georgia and the Carolinas
3. Many planters in the South grew _____.
   a. wine grapes and corn
   b. rice and indigo
   c. tobacco and silkworms
4. Most work in the Southern Colonies was done by _____.
   a. Indians   b. indentured servants
   c. slaves
5. Most of the time frontier families _____.
   a. were required to work for an overseer
   b. were busy growing many kinds of crops
   c. hunted or fished

WRITING ABOUT MAIN IDEAS

1. **Writing a Paragraph:** Write a paragraph describing two ways in which the geography of the South influenced its growth.
2. **Writing an Advertisement:** Write an advertisement about one of the Southern Colonies. The advertisement should include information about why the colony is a good place to settle. Be sure to write an eye-catching introductory sentence for your advertisement.

BUILDING SKILLS: COMPARING LINE, CIRCLE, AND BAR GRAPHS

1. Which type of graph—circle or bar—would better show the number of slaves in Virginia in 1700, 1720, and 1740?
2. Make a line graph and a bar graph based on this information about the population of Charles Town.
   1690—1,000 people
   1700—2,000 people
   1710—3,000 people
   1720—3,500 people
3. Why are different kinds of graphs useful in studying history?

257

REVIEWING VOCABULARY

assembly   navigable
cash crop   plantations
democracy   rebel
immigrant   representative
indentured   self-sufficient
    servant

Number a sheet of paper from 1 to 10. Beside each number write the word or term from the list above that best completes the sentence.

1. Benjamin Franklin was born in America, but William Penn was an ____ from England.
2. A person elected to the House of Burgesses was a ____ of the people who elected him.
3. Laws in the colony of New Jersey were made by the members of the ____.
4. In Georgia rice was a ____, a crop grown for profit.
5. Roger Williams acted as a ____ when he refused to obey the laws of Massachusetts.
6. The land that formed the Middle Colonies has ____ rivers.
7. A person who agreed to work for a period of time in exchange for the trip to America was called an ____.
8. Many colonial farm families were ____ because they took care of almost all of their own needs.
9. Large farms in the Southern Colonies were called ____.
10. At town meetings New Englanders learned how to make ____ work.

WRITING ABOUT THE UNIT

1. **Writing a Letter:** Suppose you are a young person living in colonial New England. You have just received a letter from your cousin in South Carolina describing life there. Now you are writing a letter back to your cousin. Your letter should explain how your life is different from your cousin's.
2. **Writing a Paragraph:** If you had lived in colonial times, where would you have wanted to live—in New England, in the Middle Colonies, or in the Southern Colonies? Write a paragraph giving at least three reasons for your answer.
3. **Writing Paragraphs:** In this unit you learned that the colonies were democratic in some ways but undemocratic in other ways. In one paragraph give two examples of democracy in the colonies. In a second paragraph give two examples of undemocratic practices.

ACTIVITIES

1. **Researching Colonial Education:** Find out more about schools in the New England Colonies. Ask yourself such questions as: "What did the students study? What kinds of books did they use? How long was the school day? How long was the school year?" Prepare an illustrated report or a bulletin board display of your findings.
2. **Making a Map of the 13 Colonies:** Using an outline map of the eastern part of the present-day United States, label the following places: each of the 13 colonies, important colonial cities, and major bodies of water.

3. Working Together to Learn About a Famous Person: Work in small groups to research one of the people discussed in this unit. Read a book or an encyclopedia article to learn more about the person. Share what you learned with your group.

BUILDING SKILLS: COMPARING LINE, CIRCLE, AND BAR GRAPHS

1. Use the line graph to tell the number of people who lived in the Southern Colonies in 1710 and 1750.

2. According to the circle graph which region had the largest population in 1750?

3. Suppose the New England part of the circle graph were a separate circle graph called "New England Population by Colony, 1750." Into how many sections would this new graph be divided? Why?

4. Give an example of another kind of information that could be shown on a bar graph. Explain why you would use a bar graph to show this information.

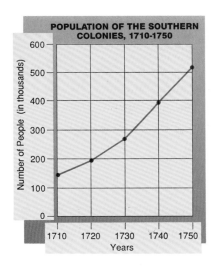

POPULATION OF THE SOUTHERN COLONIES, 1710-1750

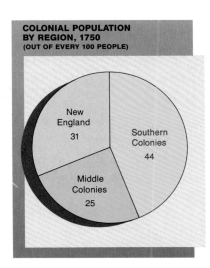

COLONIAL POPULATION BY REGION, 1750 (OUT OF EVERY 100 PEOPLE)

New England 31
Southern Colonies 44
Middle Colonies 25

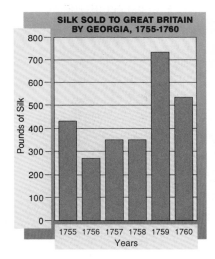

SILK SOLD TO GREAT BRITAIN BY GEORGIA, 1755-1760

LINKING PAST, PRESENT, AND FUTURE

Benjamin Franklin helped to set up America's first lending library and its first fire department. He also led efforts to pave city streets and provide street lighting. No doubt your community today does these same jobs. What other jobs does your community do for its citizens? What jobs do you think cities and towns might do for their citizens in the future?

UNIT 5

THE COLONIES BECOME A NATION

WHERE WE ARE

On July 4, 1776, the 13 colonies declared their independence from Great Britain. As the map shows, in the war that followed battles between American and British soldiers took place throughout the colonies. In Unit 5 you will read how the colonies fought the American Revolution to win their independence. You will also read how they joined together to form a new nation — the United States of America.

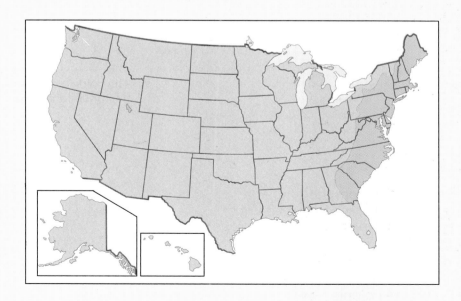

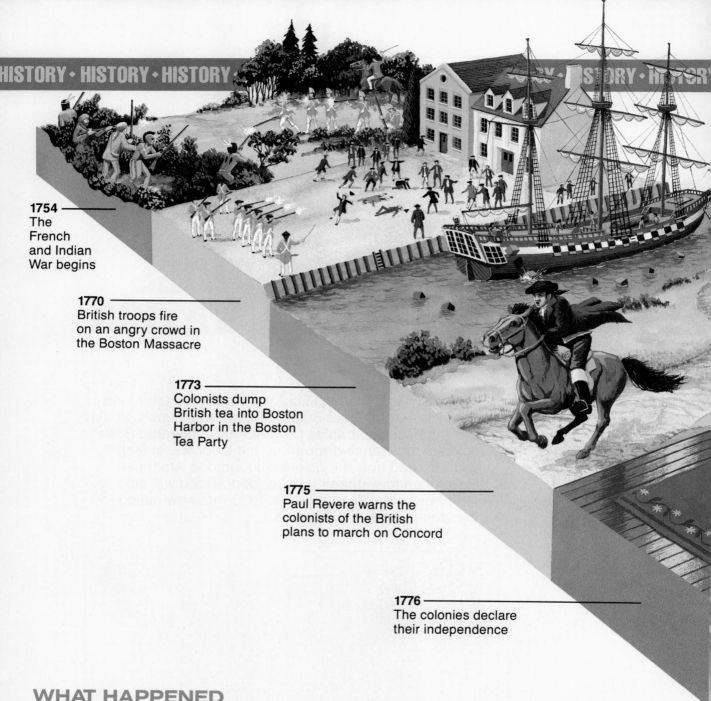

1754
The French and Indian War begins

1770
British troops fire on an angry crowd in the Boston Massacre

1773
Colonists dump British tea into Boston Harbor in the Boston Tea Party

1775
Paul Revere warns the colonists of the British plans to march on Concord

1776
The colonies declare their independence

1781
Washington and the Continental Army defeat the British

WHAT HAPPENED

You can see from the time line that after the French and Indian War, trouble arose between Great Britain and its American colonies. The British thought the colonies should help pay for the cost of the war. But the Americans strongly objected. One quarrel led to another until Great Britain and the colonies were finally at war. In this unit you will read about the events that led to the American Revolution.

CHAPTER 11

THE COLONIES REBEL

FOCUS

Where liberty is, there is my country.

When James Otis of Massachusetts wrote these words about liberty, or freedom, he spoke for many Americans. For the colonists, liberty meant something more important than the freedom to do as they pleased. It meant the right to run their own affairs with their own elected leaders. When that liberty was threatened by Great Britain, the colonists rebelled. They took up arms against the British in a fight for liberty.

1 The Colonies Grow Up

READ TO LEARN

Key Vocabulary

population

Read Aloud

We have an old mother that
peevish is grown;
She snubs us like children that
scarce walk alone;
She forgets we're grown up and
have sense of our own.

When Benjamin Franklin wrote this poem, he saw trouble ahead. To Franklin, Great Britain and its colonies were like a family. At first, the colonies were like small children. They needed the help of their mother country, Great Britain. As the years passed, the colonies grew up. Yet Great Britain still treated them like children. The result was conflict.

Read for Purpose

1. **WHAT YOU KNOW:** How were the 13 American colonies begun?
2. **WHAT YOU WILL LEARN:** How were the colonies governed?

A CENTURY OF GROWTH

One of the most astonishing things about the colonies in the 1700s was their rapid growth. In 1650 there were only about 50,000 colonists in America. Their tiny settlements dotted the Atlantic Coast from New England to Virginia.

By 1700 there were more than 250,000 people in the colonies. The population was five times larger than it had been just 50 years before. The population of a place is the number of people living there.

Why did the population grow so rapidly? One reason was that even more immigrants were coming to America. Before 1700 most colonists had come from England. Now they came flooding in from other countries in Europe. And from Africa came thousands of blacks who were forced to go to the colonies as slaves.

By 1750 there were over 1 million people living in the colonies. Visitors to America no longer found a dark, scary wilderness. Instead, they found

POPULATION OF THE AMERICAN COLONIES, 1610-1750

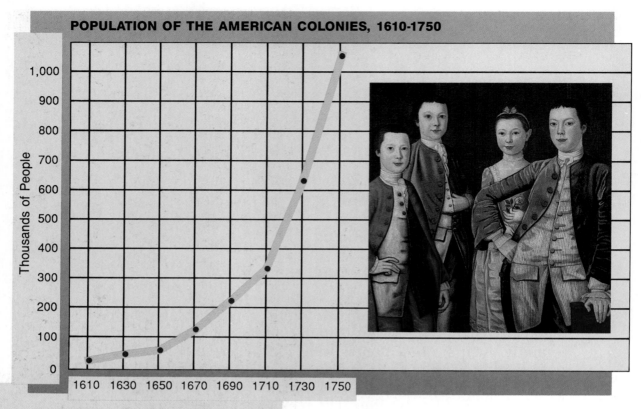

Thousands of People

1,000
900
800
700
600
500
400
300
200
100
0

1610 1630 1650 1670 1690 1710 1730 1750

GRAPH SKILL: What was the population of the colonies in 1650? In 1750?

plantations, farms, villages, and four busy seaports—Boston, New York City, Philadelphia, and Charles Town.

COLONIAL GOVERNMENT

As the colonies grew, they gained experience in governing themselves. In each colony, the colonists elected an assembly like the Virginia House of Burgesses. The assembly passed laws and raised money by setting taxes. It also decided how to spend the tax money.

Each colony had a governor. Most governors were chosen by the king of England. The governor's job was to see that the colony obeyed all British and colonial laws.

The governor was supposed to have great power over the assembly. When he gave orders from the king, the governor expected the assembly to obey. If it did not, he could dissolve, or end, the assembly and send the members home.

Over the years, however, the assemblies found ways to control the governor. For example, they would not pay the governor if he did not do as they wished. As a New Jersey assembly member said, "Let us keep the dogs [governors] poor and we'll make them do what we please."

Assemblies also refused to vote money for things the governor needed unless he went along with the laws they passed. Benjamin Franklin called this practice "the purchase of good laws." To the governors it seemed most unfair.

COLONIAL ELECTIONS

Unlike the governor, the members of the assembly were elected. But only white men who owned property could vote. Most men believed women relied too much on their husbands to make up their own minds about voting.

Voters usually chose wealthy planters, merchants, or lawyers to represent them. Poor people, it was said, should not run a government. Wealthy landowners feared that poor people needed money so badly that they might take bribes. A bribe is money given to a public official to influence that person. Most colonists agreed that government should be run only by men who were rich and successful.

Elections were different from the way they are today. It seemed foolish to office-seekers to make speeches to neighbors and friends. Still, a person trying to win votes might entertain his neighbors. In 1758 George Washington ran for the Virginia House of Burgesses. Before the election he treated voters to all the punch they could drink. Washington won the election and became an assembly member.

Elections took place at the county courthouse or village green. Voting was anything but secret. The people running for office sat at a table with a clerk who counted the votes. Each man came up and announced his choice. Shouts of approval went up from one side. Good-natured hoots were heard from the other. The person who received the vote would then rise, bow, and thank the voter.

GROWTH AND CHANGE

As you have read, much had changed in America between 1650 and 1750. A few struggling settlements

The Granger Collection

Meetings of colonial assemblies were sometimes noisy events as members spoke out about their views.

had grown into 13 thriving colonies. The population of the colonies had increased to over 1 million. And the colonists had learned to govern themselves. As Franklin said, the colonies had "grown up."

Check Your Reading

1. Why did the population of the colonies grow so quickly after 1700?
2. How were colonial assemblies able to control the governors?
3. Why were colonial assemblies important in America?
4. THINKING SKILL: State one fact and one opinion in the first paragraph on this page.

267

2 The French and Indian War

READ TO LEARN

Key Vocabulary

militia

Key People

Edward Braddock

Key Places

Ohio River Valley
Fort Duquesne
Fort Necessity

Read Aloud

In 1754 a tall, young Virginian led 150 men across the Appalachian Mountains into the upper part of the Ohio River Valley. George Washington had grown up since his first back-country adventure. Now he was leading troops into the wilderness.

Washington had been sent by the governor of Virginia. His orders were to build a fort where the Allegheny and Mononga-hela (mə non gə hē′ lə) rivers meet to form the Ohio River. Today the city of Pittsburgh stands on that site. As the Virginians came near the rivers, they met and defeated a small force of French soldiers. Washington wrote home, "I heard the bullets whistle; and believe me, there is something charming in the sound." Those whistling bullets were the first shots of the French and Indian War.

Read for Purpose

1. **WHAT YOU KNOW:** Why did the French get along so well with most Indians?
2. **WHAT YOU WILL LEARN:** What were the results of the French and Indian War?

RIVAL CLAIMS

Washington had been sent to the Ohio River Valley to protect Britain's claims to the region. France also claimed this area. To keep the British out, the French had built a string of forts in the valley. One of them, Fort Duquesne (dü kān′), stood on the exact point where Washington was supposed to build his fort.

Not far from Fort Duquesne, Washington threw together a circle of logs that he called Fort Necessity. There the Virginians were attacked by French troops. This time the sound of bullets had no charm for Washington. His outnumbered **militia** (mi lish' ə) was badly defeated by the French. A militia is a group of volunteers who fight in times of emergency.

Washington lost more than a battle at Fort Necessity. His defeat convinced most of the Indians along the frontier to join the French against the British. The French welcomed the Indians' help. By 1750 New France covered a huge area that stretched from Canada to the Gulf of Mexico. But when the war began, there were only about 65,000 French colonists living there.

GENERAL BRADDOCK'S DEFEAT

In 1755 Great Britain sent an army of 800 soldiers to Virginia. They were led by General **Edward Braddock**. That spring the British troops and about 600 colonists moved slowly toward Fort Duquesne. Washington went along as the general's aide.

As part of their uniforms, the British soldiers wore bright red coats. Washington tried to warn General Braddock that Indians would find it easy to pick off such colorful targets. But the general would not listen. Indians might be a problem for "your raw American militia," said Braddock. "But upon the King's regular and disciplined troops, Sir, it is impossible they should make any impression."

Braddock could not have been more wrong. On July 9 the main part of his army came within 10 miles (16 km) of Fort Duquesne. The British could almost smell victory. Then a thick hail of bullets rained down from nowhere. French and Indian fighters hidden behind the trees had found their bright red targets.

Washington later wrote that the British had panicked. With men dying all

Washington (*above*) was in his early 20s when he led the Virginia **militia**. Why did he warn General Braddock about the British uniforms?

(*above*) The British general, Edward Braddock, was killed in the French and Indian War. (*below*) A cartoon by Benjamin Franklin urged the colonies to unite against France.

JOIN, or DIE.

around them, they ran away "as sheep pursued by dogs." Washington himself had "four bullets through my coat and two horses shot under me." Yet he escaped unhurt. Braddock was not as lucky. He was wounded, and four days later he died. His last words were said to be, "We shall know better how to do it next time."

VICTORY

For the next few years, the war with France went badly for Britain. Colonial assemblies were slow to vote money for war supplies or to raise troops. "I never was among people," wrote one angry governor, "[who] have so little regard to their own safety."

Finally, the British government promised to repay the colonies for most war expenses. Only when it was clear they were not spending their own money did the colonies throw themselves into the war.

In 1759 the war turned in Britain's favor. That year a large army of British

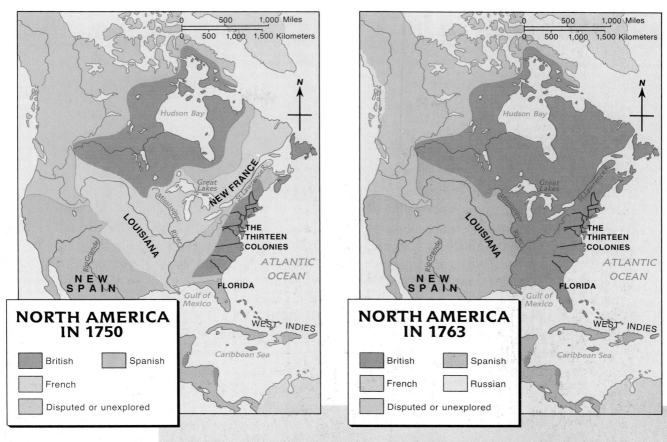

MAP SKILL: What lands in North America did Britain gain as a result of the French and Indian War?

troops invaded Canada. In September the city of Quebec fell. A year later Montreal was captured.

The French and Indian War ended in 1763 in victory for Britain. You can see from the map above that New France was divided between Britain and Spain. Britain claimed all French land east of the Mississippi River. This included Canada and the Ohio River Valley. Spain claimed all of French Louisiana west of the Mississippi.

A TIME TO CELEBRATE

There were victory celebrations on both sides of the Atlantic Ocean. In Great Britain, the English were thrilled to have broken the power of France. In America, the colonists were happy to be rid of the French forever. The future had never looked brighter.

 Check Your Reading

1. What events led to the French and Indian War?
2. Why did the war go badly for Britain at first?
3. **GEOGRAPHY SKILL:** What lands did Britain win from France at the end of the war?
4. **THINKING SKILL:** Place the events described in this lesson in the order in which they occurred.

271

Determining the Accuracy of a Statement

Sometimes people say things that sound true, but you are not sure that what they say *is* really true. At times like this, you have to check the truth, or accuracy, of their statements. When you determine the accuracy of a statement, you are deciding if the statement is correct, or right.

You often have to make a decision based on a statement that you have heard or read. In order to make a good decision, you need to know whether the statement is true. For example, imagine that you want to go fishing on your vacation. You have read that the undersea gardens near New England attract a huge number of fish. Before you use that information as a reason to go fishing there, you first must be sure that it is accurate.

Trying the Skill

It is important to determine the accuracy of a statement when someone is trying to convince you of something. Imagine, for example, that you are British General Edward Braddock in 1755. You are marching on Fort Duquesne with 1,500 British soldiers. Your young aide, George Washington, has just pointed out that your bright red coats make good targets in the woods.

Determine the accuracy of Washington's statement.

1. Was his statement accurate?
    2. How did you go about determining the accuracy of his statement?

HELPING YOURSELF

The steps on the left will help you determine the accuracy of any statement. The example on the right shows one way to use these steps to determine the accuracy of Washington's statement.

One Way to Determine the Accuracy of a Statement	Example
1. Repeat the statement in your own words.	As General Braddock, you might say, "According to Washington, we will lose the battle if we wear our bright red coats."
2. Determine if the statement is generally thought of as true.	General Braddock probably thought that Washington's statement was untrue. After all, Braddock had no experience fighting an enemy in the woods. To the best of his knowledge, Washington's statement had no basis in fact.
3. Check other credible sources to see if they support or agree with the statement.	Since Braddock was in the middle of the Ohio River Valley, it was unlikely that he could check other sources. If he had thought about it more, he might have talked to other British soldiers who had fought against Indians in America.
4. In some cases, do additional research to determine the accuracy of a statement.	Unfortunately, the real Braddock conducted no research. We know that he died as a result of not determining the accuracy of Washington's statement.

Applying the Skill

Apply what you have learned to determine the accuracy of this statement: "Throughout the colonies, people cheered Britain's new king, George III."

1. Which of the following sentences restates the statement about George III?
   a. The colonists were unhappy that a new king was on the English throne.
   b. Everyone living in the English colonies was afraid of the new king.
   c. Almost everyone was pleased with the new king.
2. Name two other credible sources that you might look at to determine if the statement is accurate.

Reviewing the Skill

1. What are two words that mean the same as *accuracy*?
2. What are two things you can do to check the accuracy of any statement?
3. When should you try to check the accuracy of statements?

3 Troubles with Great Britain

READ TO LEARN

Key Vocabulary

proclamation   repeal
Parliament   Townshend Acts
Stamp Act   boycott
treason

Key People

Pontiac   Samuel Adams
George III   Crispus Attucks
Patrick Henry

Read Aloud

The French and Indian War left Great Britain with a very large empire in America. But ruling that empire was much harder than winning it. In this lesson you will read how Britain soon faced problems from the Indians of the Ohio River Valley and from the colonists themselves.

Read for Purpose

1. **WHAT YOU KNOW:** What happened to New France at the end of the French and Indian War?
2. **WHAT YOU WILL LEARN:** What actions by Great Britain angered the colonists?

PONTIAC'S REBELLION

After their defeat in the French and Indian War, the Indians of the Ohio River Valley were worried that they would be pushed off their land. In 1763 an Ottawa chief named Pontiac visited one Indian group after another. His message, which he said came from the Great Spirit, was always the same.

I am the Maker of heaven and earth. . . . The land on which you live I have made for you. . . . Why do you suffer [allow] *the white men to dwell* [live] *among you? . . . You must lift the hatchet against them.*

Pontiac's words united the Indians of the valley. Together they overran British forts and burned backcountry settlements.

King George III of England issued a proclamation, or official announcement, to end Pontiac's Rebellion. This proclamation stated that all land west of the Appalachians would be set aside for Indians "as their hunting grounds." Settlers there were ordered to "remove themselves . . . at once."

The Proclamation of 1763 helped bring peace to the Ohio River Valley. But it angered land-hungry colonists. They saw the land across the Appalachians being closed to them.

Pontiac's Rebellion convinced the British government that 10,000 troops were needed to keep order on the American frontier. But who would pay for such a large army? People in Britain were already heavily taxed to pay the bills left over from the French and Indian War. To the British, the answer seemed clear. The colonists should pay their fair share of defending the North American empire. After all, they lived there.

THE STAMP ACT

In 1765 **Parliament** (par' lə mənt), Britain's lawmaking body, decided to raise money in the colonies. It passed a law called the Stamp Act. This law put a tax on all kinds of documents such as newspapers, calendars, and legal papers. Every document used or sold in the colonies had to have a stamp on it to show that the tax had been paid. Colonists who did not put stamps on such papers could be fined or jailed.

Colonists everywhere began to speak out against the Stamp Act. The stamps are a tax, they argued—only elected representatives in our assemblies should have the right to tax us. We do not elect representatives to Parliament. We have no say in the laws that Parliament makes. Therefore, Parliament has no right to tax us. Cries of "No taxation without representation" floated across the ocean from America to Great Britain.

PATRICK HENRY

Virginia was the first colony to take action against the Stamp Act. The fight was led by a backcountry lawyer named **Patrick Henry**. Henry had failed as a storekeeper and farmer. And in his shabby frontier clothes he did not look much like a lawyer. But he was gifted with a silver tongue. It was

said that when Henry spoke he made people's "blood run cold, and their hair to rise on end."

In a fiery speech to the Virginia House of Burgesses, Patrick Henry said that Parliament could not tax the colonists. Anyone who bought stamps, he said, was an enemy of Virginia.

Henry's words created an uproar. There was a shout of "Treason! Treason!" **Treason** is giving help to the enemies of one's own government. Henry is said to have shouted back, "If this be treason, make the most of it." The Virginia House of Burgesses voted to oppose the Stamp Act.

What was the purpose of stamps like these? How did the colonists react to the Stamp Act?

(*above*) Sons of Liberty tar and feather a stamp agent and pour tea into his mouth. (*below*) Samuel Adams attacked the Stamp Act in his writings.

THE SONS OF LIBERTY

In other colonies, people calling themselves the Sons of Liberty led protests against the Stamp Act. In some cities "liberty boys" burned the hated stamps. Angry groups threatened the agents who were supposed to sell the stamps. After one look at the noisy crowds, most stamp agents quit.

In Boston, protests against the Stamp Act were led by Samuel Adams. Adams filled Boston's newspapers with attacks on the new law. The governor of Massachusetts complained that "Every dip of [Adams's] pen stung like a horned snake."

One day an angry colonist hung a puppet dressed like Boston's stamp agent from a large elm, which became known as the Liberty Tree. Later, a group of "liberty boys" destroyed the stamp agent's office and attacked his home.

THE TOWNSHEND ACTS

Faced with violent protests, Parliament gave in. In 1766 it repealed, or voted to end, the Stamp Act. One angry member of Parliament objected to this action. "You are cowards!" he shouted at government leaders. "You dare not tax America!" Britain's treasurer, Charles Townshend, shouted back, "I dare tax America!"

In 1767 Townshend made good on his word. That year Parliament passed the Townshend (toun' zhund) Acts. These acts taxed many goods brought into the colonies from Britain. Such goods as glass, paper, tea, and paint now cost more to buy.

Once again the colonists spoke out in anger. Sam Adams asked Americans to boycott, or refuse to buy, British goods. The Sons of Liberty pressured merchants not to sell British goods in their stores.

Women calling themselves the Daughters of Liberty made the boycott work. Their spinning wheels hummed day and night. Better to make our own cloth, they said, than to buy an inch of English silk. They brewed "liberty teas" from leaves and berries rather than buy English tea.

Britain was determined not to give in to the colonists. "This is the mother country," said a British leader. "They are the children. They must obey." But as the boycott spread throughout the colonies, British products piled up in colonial stores. English merchants complained that they would fail if the colonists did not buy their goods.

THE BOSTON MASSACRE

In 1768 British troops were sent to Boston to keep order. The people of Boston resented the soldiers. Children called the red-coated troops "lobster backs" and pelted them with eggs. Sam Adams trained his dog to nip at the redcoats' heels. Fist fights broke out between soldiers and colonists.

On March 5, 1770, a Boston crowd began throwing rocks and snowballs at a group of soldiers. Someone shouted, "Fire!" and the troops emptied their guns into the mob. When the smoke cleared, four people lay dead or dying. The first to fall was a leader of the protest, a runaway slave named Crispus Attucks.

These events shocked Boston. Newspapers reported the killings in bold headlines that screamed, "BOSTON MASSACRE." A massacre is the killing of many people who cannot defend themselves. For years March 5 was known as Massacre Day in Boston.

(*above*) Mercy Otis Warren wrote plays and articles against the British. (*below*) A Daughter of Liberty spins her own thread for cloth.

In 1770 British troops fired on a Boston crowd. This event became known as the Boston Massacre. What effect did it have on the colonists in Boston?

"THE SEEDS OF LIBERTY"

In this lesson, you read how Great Britain tried to tighten its grip on the colonies after the French and Indian War. Settlers were not allowed to cross the Appalachians. Parliament passed the Stamp Act and the Townshend Acts to raise money in the colonies.

The colonists protested against "taxation without representation." Benjamin Franklin understood why. "The seeds of liberty," he wrote, "have been planted in America." Great Britain could do nothing to kill them.

 Check Your Reading

1. Why were the colonists unhappy about the Proclamation of 1763?
2. Why was the Stamp Act passed? Why did Americans object to it so strongly?
3. What happened during the Boston Massacre?
4. **THINKING SKILL:** Is John Adams a credible source of information about the Stamp Act? Why or why not?

4 The War Begins

READ TO LEARN

Key Vocabulary

Committee of Correspondence
Boston Tea Party
Intolerable Acts
First Continental Congress
petition
minutemen

Key People

John Adams
Paul Revere

Key Places

Concord
Lexington

Read Aloud

After the Boston Massacre, Britain removed its troops from Boston. All of the Townshend taxes were ended but one, the tax on tea. Calm returned to the colonies. But in just a few years that calm would be shattered by shots "heard round the world."

Read for Purpose

1. **WHAT YOU KNOW:** Why did the Townshend Acts make the colonists so unhappy?
2. **WHAT YOU WILL LEARN:** How did fighting between the colonists and the British begin?

THE COMMITTEES OF CORRESPONDENCE

In 1770 the governor of Massachusetts wrote that "if it were not for two or three Adamses, we should do well enough." But Sam Adams was not his only problem. The governor also had to worry about Sam's cousin John Adams.

The Adams cousins were very different. While Sam Adams had no head for business, John Adams was a successful lawyer. Sam found it easy to talk with all sorts of people. John was stiff and lacked his cousin's charm. But they shared a love of liberty.

Even during this period of calm, the Adams cousins were busy uniting the colonies against Great Britain. John was writing newspaper articles that the governor disliked. And Sam was setting up the first Committee of Correspondence.

Members of the Committee of Correspondence wrote letters telling colonists in other places about important events. By 1774 every colony but Pennsylvania had similar committees. For the first time, wrote John Adams, the colonies were linked together by "a great political engine."

What were the colonists reacting to when they dumped tea into Boston Harbor?

THE BOSTON TEA PARTY

Soon Great Britain gave the committees something new to write about. The colonists had been boycotting English tea since 1770 because it was still taxed. In 1773 the British government tried to trick them into buying the taxed tea by lowering its price. But the colonists did not want taxed tea at any price.

Three ships loaded with tea sailed into Boston Harbor in December 1773. Sam Adams and the Sons of Liberty helped plan a "welcome" for them. One night, colonists dressed like Indians rushed to the waterfront shouting, "Boston Harbor will be a teapot tonight!" With a splash, they dumped 342 chests of tea into the ocean.

King George III was furious when he learned about the Boston Tea Party. In the spring of 1774, Parliament passed several laws to punish the colonists. Boston Harbor was closed to all ships until the colonists paid for the lost tea.

The Massachusetts assembly was dissolved. British troops were sent back to Boston. And the people of the city were ordered to quarter, or house, the hated soldiers in their homes.

The colonists united against what they called these Intolerable Acts. They sent food and money to Boston with the message, "Don't pay for an ounce of the . . . tea." The Committees of Correspondence organized a meeting to decide what to do next.

THE FIRST CONTINENTAL CONGRESS

In September 1774, representatives from every colony except Georgia met together in Philadelphia at the First Continental Congress. The Congress voted to cut off all trade with Britain until the Intolerable Acts were repealed. It also sent petitions to King George III asking for repeal of the acts. A petition is a written request signed by many people.

John Adams saw the First Continental Congress as a kind of school for

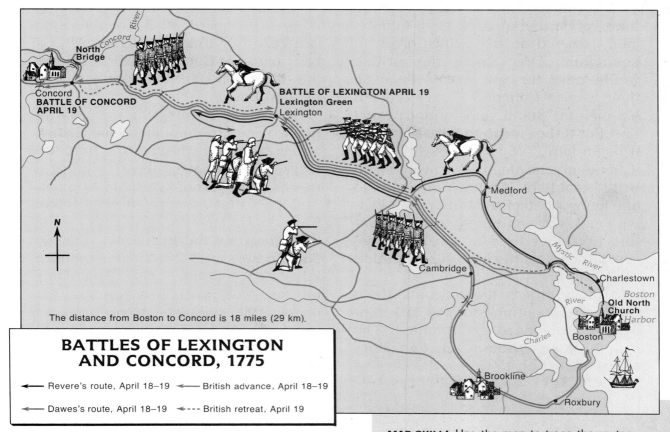

The distance from Boston to Concord is 18 miles (29 km).

BATTLES OF LEXINGTON AND CONCORD, 1775

⟵ Revere's route, April 18–19   ⟵ British advance, April 18–19

⟵ Dawes's route, April 18–19   ⟵--- British retreat, April 19

MAP SKILL: Use the map to trace the routes taken by Paul Revere and William Dawes in 1775.

American leaders. Men came to Philadelphia as Rhode Islanders, New Yorkers, or Virginians. But while working in Congress, they learned to look beyond their own colonies. They began to think like Americans.

After two months, however, Adams was eager to get home. His wife Abigail had written him that the governor of Massachusetts "is making all kinds of warlike preparations. . . . The people are much alarmed."

LEXINGTON AND CONCORD

The governor was not the only one getting ready for war. For months militias across New England had been drilling on village greens. They called themselves **minutemen** because they

were ready to fight the British on a moment's notice.

British spies brought word to Boston that the minutemen had stored guns in the nearby village of Concord. The British planned to capture the weapons in a surprise raid.

The colonists also had spies. When 700 redcoats left Boston after midnight on April 18, 1775, they were being watched. A silversmith named Paul Revere and his friend William Dawes sped through the countryside on horseback. Quickly they spread the word that the British were coming. You can follow the routes taken by Revere and Dawes on the map above.

In the misty light of dawn, Captain John Parker and a group of 70 minutemen gathered on the village green in Lexington. They knew the British would pass through their village on their way to Concord. Parker ordered his men to "Stand your ground! Don't fire! But if they mean to have a war, let it begin here."

Suddenly the green was covered with British soldiers. A shot rang out. No one knew whether it came from a British musket or a minuteman's rifle. But this first shot fired at Lexington became known as the shot "heard round the world."

Without orders the redcoats fired. When the shooting stopped, 18 minutemen were dead or wounded. The British shouted three cheers for victory and marched on to Concord.

The British captured only three cannons in Concord. The colonists had carried off or hidden the rest. After a brief battle at Concord's North Bridge, the British began the weary march back to Boston.

By now the countryside was swarming with angry colonists. One British officer reported "heavy fire from all sides, from walls, fences, houses, trees, and barns." A soldier complained that "even women had firelocks [guns]."

By the time the British were safely back in Boston, 247 redcoats had been killed or wounded. For the Americans the loss was much less serious. Just under 100 colonists were dead or wounded. And riders were galloping throughout the colonies with the news that war had begun.

The minutemen, at the lower left, met the British at Lexington. One minuteman shakes his fist at the British as others retreat or lie wounded.

Patrick Henry gave one of the greatest speeches in our country's history before the Virginia House of Burgesses.

"LIBERTY OR DEATH"

In Virginia, Patrick Henry spoke to the House of Burgesses about the quarrel with Britain. Again and again, he said, the colonists had struggled to protect their liberty. And still Great Britain tried to take away their rights. Now it was time to fight.

"Gentlemen may cry peace, peace!" he said. "But there is no peace. The war is actually begun!" And then, his voice rising, Patrick Henry asked:

Is life so dear, or peace so sweet, as to be purchased at the price of chains and slavery? Forbid it, almighty God! I know not what course others may take; but as for me, give me liberty or give me death!

Check Your Reading

1. Why did colonists in Boston dump tea into the ocean?
2. What were the Intolerable Acts? Why did they make the colonists angry?
3. **GEOGRAPHY SKILL:** Where did Paul Revere's ride begin? Where did it end?
4. **THINKING SKILL:** What is the correct order of the major events described in this lesson?

283

IMPORTANT EVENTS

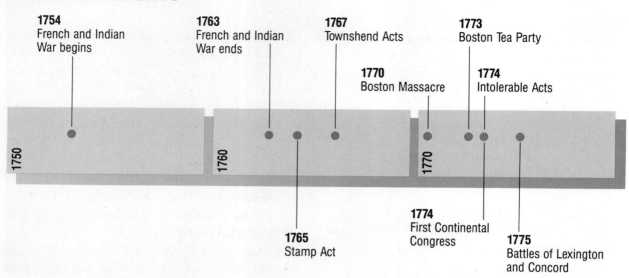

1754
French and Indian War begins

1763
French and Indian War ends

1767
Townshend Acts

1773
Boston Tea Party

1770
Boston Massacre

1774
Intolerable Acts

1750

1760

1770

1774
First Continental Congress

1765
Stamp Act

1775
Battles of Lexington and Concord

PEOPLE TO KNOW

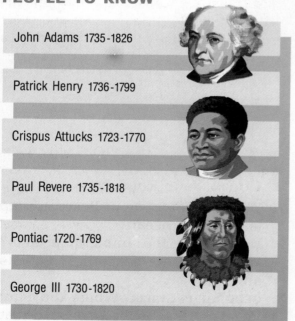

John Adams 1735-1826

Patrick Henry 1736-1799

Crispus Attucks 1723-1770

Paul Revere 1735-1818

Pontiac 1720-1769

George III 1730-1820

IDEAS TO REMEMBER

■ As the English colonies grew in size, they gained experience in governing themselves.

■ The British defeated the French in the French and Indian War, but their victory created new problems in the American colonies.

■ The American colonists grew more and more unhappy as Great Britain took away their freedoms after the French and Indian War.

■ The American colonists fought the British at Lexington and Concord to protect their liberties.

REVIEWING VOCABULARY

boycott

First Continental
   Congress

militia

minutemen

Parliament

petition

population

proclamation

repeal

treason

Number a sheet of paper from 1 to 10. Beside each number write the word or term from the list above that best matches the statement.

1. An official announcement
2. A group of villagers ready to fight the British at a moment's notice
3. To vote to end a law
4. The lawmaking body of England
5. The betraying of one's country by helping an enemy
6. An army of volunteers who fight in emergencies
7. To refuse to buy something
8. A written request
9. The number of people living in a place
10. The first meeting of a group of representatives from the colonies

REVIEWING FACTS

1. Who could vote in colonial America? Why could only those people vote?
2. How did the uniforms of the British affect the outcome of the battle of Fort Duquesne?
3. What were two methods used by colonists to protest the Stamp Act?
4. What were the Townshend Acts?
5. Name two actions taken by the First Continental Congress.

WRITING ABOUT MAIN IDEAS

1. **Writing a Paragraph About Making a Speech:** Imagine you are on a Committee of Correspondence in Massachusetts. Choose one of the following events to write a speech about: the Boston Tea Party, the passage of the Intolerable Acts, or the battles of Lexington and Concord.
2. **Writing a Letter:** Imagine you are a member of the Daughters of Liberty. Write a letter to a cousin in England describing your activities after Parliament passed the Townshend Acts.
3. **Writing Sentences:** In history one event often causes or triggers other events. For example, you could say that the Tea Act caused the Boston Tea Party. Write three cause-and-effect statements based on the information in this chapter.

BUILDING SKILLS: DETERMINING THE ACCURACY OF A STATEMENT

1. What are some steps you could take to determine the accuracy of a statement?
2. Apply what you have learned to determine the accuracy of this statement: "Patrick Henry's fiery speech against the Stamp Act caused an uproar."
   a. Repeat the statement in your own words.
   b. Name one way in which you might check the accuracy of the statement.
3. Why is it important to check the accuracy of statements?

CHAPTER 12

THE AMERICAN REVOLUTION

FOCUS

These are the times that try men's souls. The summer soldier and the sunshine patriot will, in this crisis, shrink from the service of their country; but he that stands it now, deserves the love and thanks of man and woman.

Thomas Paine wrote these words in December of 1776. When the war with Great Britain began, Americans were fighting to protect their rights. But, by 1776, their struggle had grown into a fight for freedom. Paine knew that the war was going badly for the Americans. He reminded the weary soldiers that freedom was worth fighting for, no matter how hard the conflict.

READ TO LEARN

Key Vocabulary

Second Continental
   Congress
independence
Patriot
Loyalist
mercenary

Key People

Benedict Arnold
Ethan Allen
William Howe
Henry Knox

Key Places

Fort Ticonderoga

Read Aloud

"Let them hear the cannon roar," said an English lord, and they will run "as fast as their feet will carry them." King George III declared that once they "have felt a small blow, they will submit."

Both men were talking about the American rebels. They were sure that such "ragtag" troops could not match the king's well-trained soldiers. They soon saw how wrong they were.

Read for Purpose

1. **WHAT YOU KNOW:** Why did fighting break out between the colonists and the British soldiers?
2. **WHAT YOU WILL LEARN:** How did the colonists drive the British out of Boston?

THE FALL OF FORT TICONDEROGA

After the battles of Lexington and Concord, the British army stayed in Boston. The American forces camped around Boston, waiting for the British to move.

Meanwhile, a young New Englander named Benedict Arnold had been appointed to lead 400 soldiers at Fort Ticonderoga (tī kon də rō′ gə) in New York. After arriving there, he joined forces with Vermont's rough and rugged Ethan Allen. Allen led a group of rebels called the "Green Mountain Boys."

Before dawn on May 10, 1775, the Americans attacked Fort Ticonderoga. The British were sleeping peacefully. Allen woke up the commander by banging on his door and shouting, "Come out of there, you old rat!" The Americans captured the fort without firing a shot. Inside, they found something they needed desperately—heavy iron cannons.

THE BATTLE OF BUNKER HILL

A month later, on the night of June 16, British troops in Boston heard strange noises on nearby Charlestown Peninsula. When the sun rose, they could not believe their eyes. The day before, the peninsula had been empty. Now its two small hills—Bunker Hill and nearby Breed's Hill—were alive with Americans. In just one night they had built a fort of dirt and logs on Breed's Hill.

The British knew they had to attack quickly. If the Americans could drag the cannons taken at Fort Ticonderoga up to the hilltops, they would be able to pound Boston and the British ships in the harbor.

On the next day 2,000 of the king's troops lined up at the base of Breed's Hill. General William Howe ordered them to march to the top and take the American fort. The redcoats sweated heavily in the hot June sun as they struggled up Breed's Hill.

In the hilltop fort, fingers tightened on triggers. Fighting to control their fear, the Americans repeated their order—"Don't fire till you see the whites of their eyes." As the red line of troops moved closer, a gray-haired farmer prayed, "I thank thee, O Lord, for sparing me to fight this day."

When the British were almost on top of them, the Americans fired. Huge gaps appeared in the line of redcoats. The surprised British fell back and then made a second attack. Again they were mowed down by American gunfire.

American defenders, on the left, lost to the British in the Battle of Bunker Hill. But the battle proved the colonists would fight.

General Howe regrouped his men and sent them up the hill a third time. Once more, the redcoats' front line was ripped apart by gunfire. As soldiers in the back lines advanced, they tripped over their fallen comrades. But this time the British troops reached the top. By now the Americans had run out of gunpowder and were retreating to safer ground. The cannons captured at Fort Ticonderoga had never left New York.

By evening the British had taken over the Charlestown Peninsula. But as the dead and wounded were counted, General Howe found that victory had been "too dearly bought." He had lost more than 1,000 soldiers that day. The Americans had lost over 400.

Even though most of the fighting took place on Breed's Hill, this bloody conflict was remembered as the Battle of Bunker Hill. After this battle, the British would never again doubt that Americans could and would fight.

THE SECOND CONTINENTAL CONGRESS

While New England went to war, representatives from the colonies were meeting in Philadelphia. This was the Second Continental Congress. John Adams asked the Congress to set up a "Grand American Army" with troops from every colony. To lead this army, Adams suggested "a gentleman whose skill as an officer . . . would command the respect of America." That man was George Washington of Virginia.

The Congress asked Washington to serve as commander-in-chief of the new Continental Army. Washington agreed, saying he would use "every power I possess . . . for the support of the glorious cause."

This hall in Philadelphia was the meeting place of the **Second Continental Congress** in 1775. At that meeting, the Americans decided to set up an army to fight the British.

Adams believed that the colonies should declare their independence, or complete freedom, from Great Britain. But the Congress was not ready to take such a step. Most Americans still thought of the colonies as part of Great Britain. They still felt loyal to King George III. The idea of independence scared them.

The Congress tried to make peace and voted to send another petition to King George III. This petition asked the king to help end the war. It was called the Olive Branch Petition because the olive branch is a symbol of peace.

King George refused to read the petition from what he called an "illegal congress." He saw the actions of the Congress as treason. In Britain the punishment for treason was death.

George Washington, on his white horse, reviews troops of the Continental Army.

WASHINGTON TAKES COMMAND

As George Washington rode toward Boston, he knew that the odds were against him. How, he wondered, could the colonies stand up to Britain—the world's most powerful country? How could rebel farmers defeat the world's strongest army and navy?

Yet Great Britain faced two large problems. One was distance—America lay across a vast ocean. Sending troops and supplies across the Atlantic Ocean was both slow and costly. Britain's second problem was the size of the colonies. To crush the rebellion, the British would have to take control of a huge territory.

Washington also faced great problems. The Continental Army was poorly trained and lacked supplies.

The colonies did not have a navy. Worse still, many people did not support the war. Only about two fifths of the colonists called themselves Patriots and supported the fight against Great Britain. One fifth were Loyalists, people who felt loyal to Great Britain and opposed the war. The remaining two fifths did not take sides and could not be counted on to fight.

Early in July 1775, General Washington took command of the troops camped around Boston. Everywhere he looked he saw "confusion and disorder." Men obeyed only those orders they liked. Washington worked hard to bring order to the army. Soon one soldier wrote, "Everyone is made to know his place and keep it. . . . It is surprising how much work has been done."

THE BRITISH LEAVE BOSTON

For months nothing happened. The British hoped the Patriots would grow tired of their rebellion and go home. To Washington's dismay, many of his troops did just that. The Americans hoped that King George III would pull his troops out of Boston. Instead, he hired German mercenaries to help crush the rebellion. Mercenaries are soldiers hired to fight in another country's war.

Washington desperately needed cannons to drive the British out of Boston. He finally sent a former bookseller, Henry Knox, to get the iron cannons that had been captured at Fort Ticonderoga. Somehow Knox's men loaded 59 huge cannons onto sleds. Then they dragged them for more than 300 miles (480 km) across snowy hills and frozen rivers to Boston.

On March 4, 1776, Boston awoke to a surprise. The day before, nearby Dorchester Heights had been bare hills. Then overnight those hills had sprouted cannons—cannons aimed at the city. The British general announced that if the Americans did not allow him to leave peacefully, he would destroy Boston. Washington wisely agreed to let the British troops move out. A few days later the redcoats sailed for Canada. With them went over 1,000 American Loyalists.

A GOOD BEGINNING

American Patriots were overjoyed by this news. In the past year they had shown the British they could fight. They had formed a Continental Army with George Washington as their leader. And they had driven the British out of the colonies.

One of the problems of the Continental Army was a lack of supplies and guns. Here, Henry Knox and his men haul cannons from Fort Ticonderoga to Boston.

Many people thought the war was over. But Washington knew better. The British would be back. Still, the Patriots had made a good beginning.

 Check Your Reading

1. What difficulties did the British army face at the beginning of the war?
2. How were the Patriots able to take control of Boston?
3. **GEOGRAPHY SKILL:** List and locate the places where fighting took place in the first days of the revolution.
4. **THINKING SKILL:** How could you determine the accuracy of this statement from your lesson: "The Continental Army was poorly trained and lacked supplies."?

2 Declaring Independence

READ TO LEARN

Key Vocabulary

Declaration of Independence
revolution

Key People

Thomas Paine
Thomas Jefferson

Read Aloud

"We must be content," Sam Adams liked to say, "to wait till the fruit is ripe before we gather it." That fruit was independence for the colonies. Adams knew that most colonists hated the idea of cutting their ties with Great Britain. Then, in 1776, a slim book helped change their minds.

Read for Purpose

1. **WHAT YOU KNOW:** Why did Sam Adams believe that the colonies were not ready to become independent?
2. **WHAT YOU WILL LEARN:** What events led to the signing of the Declaration of Independence?

THOMAS PAINE'S *COMMON SENSE*

In January of 1776, a book called *Common Sense* appeared in colonial bookstores. It was written by a newcomer to the colonies named Thomas Paine

Paine wanted to convince the colonists that it was time to become independent. His argument had two parts. First, he argued that King George was not a kindly father who was trying to help the colonists. In Paine's eyes, the king was a "royal brute."

Second, Paine showed the colonists that they had nothing to lose by leaving the British empire. Britain was too far away to rule America, he said. It made no sense for "a continent to be perpetually [forever] ruled by an island." Paine concluded that "'Tis time to part."

In just three months 120,000 copies of Paine's book were sold. "I find *Common Sense* is working a powerful change in the minds of men," wrote George Washington.

THOMAS JEFFERSON

In June of 1776, the Second Continental Congress set up a committee to write a statement on independence. For John Adams, a member of the committee, this was a dream come true. But he asked another committee member to do the writing. "You can write ten times better than I can," he said.

The young man who was so good with words was Thomas Jefferson of Virginia. Jefferson had been born on a plantation. But he was not a typical planter. He did not want to live like an English lord. He even hated to be called "Mister Jefferson." Plain "Tom Jefferson" was good enough for him. Jefferson was a warm but shy man with a brilliant, restless mind. As a member of the Second Continental Congress, he said little. Instead, he spoke with his pen.

THE DECLARATION OF INDEPENDENCE

In the Declaration of Independence, Jefferson explained to the world why the colonies had to separate from Great Britain. He wrote, "We hold these truths to be self-evident," or clear to everyone. The first of these truths is "that all men are created equal." God has given all people certain rights, and "among these are Life, Liberty, and the pursuit of Happiness."

The second truth is that people form governments to "secure these rights." If a government does not do so, "it is their right, it is their duty, to throw off such Government."

Jefferson then listed many things done by "the present King" that took away the rights of Americans. For example, the king would not let the colonies pass laws they needed. And he made them pay taxes that were not approved by their own assemblies. George III was, Jefferson wrote, "unfit to be the ruler of a free People."

Jefferson ended by saying that Americans had tried peaceful means to protect their rights. They had sent many petitions to Britain. But the British "have been deaf to the voice of justice."

Thomas Jefferson was the author of the Declaration of Independence. In it, Jefferson expressed the colonists' belief in the natural rights of all people.

Now the time had come for the Congress to declare "That these United Colonies are, and of Right ought to be, FREE AND INDEPENDENT STATES."

The Declaration of Independence turned the colonial rebellion into a revolution, or a sudden, complete change in government. It told the world that the colonies were breaking all ties with Britain. The Americans' struggle to protect their rights was now a war for independence.

THE DECLARATION OF INDEPENDENCE

In Congress, July 4, 1776. The unanimous Declaration of the thirteen united States of America,

When in the course of human events, it becomes necessary for one people to dissolve the political bonds which have connected them with another, and to assume among the powers of the earth, the separate and equal station to which the laws of nature and of nature's God entitle them, a decent respect to the opinions of mankind requires that they should declare the causes which impel them to the separation.

We hold these truths to be self-evident, that all men are created equal, that they are endowed by their Creator with certain unalienable rights, that among these are life, liberty, and the pursuit of happiness.

That to secure these rights, governments are instituted among men, deriving their just powers from the consent of the governed,

That whenever any form of government becomes destructive of these ends, it is the right of the people to alter or to abolish it, and to institute new government, laying its foundation on such principles and organizing its powers in such form, as to them shall seem most likely to effect their safety and happiness.

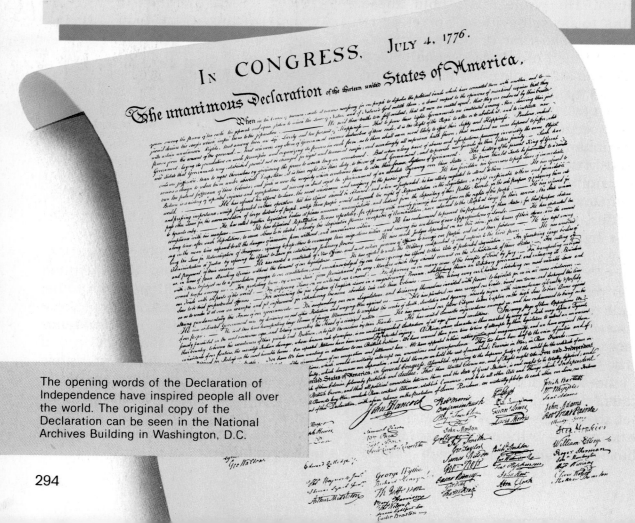

The opening words of the Declaration of Independence have inspired people all over the world. The original copy of the Declaration can be seen in the National Archives Building in Washington, D.C.

The **Declaration of Independence** was signed in Philadelphia in 1776. Here, Jefferson presents the declaration to members of the Continental Congress for their signatures.

On July 4, 1776, the members of the Continental Congress signed the Declaration of Independence. Each man knew that by signing his name he would be a traitor in British eyes. If the Americans lost the war for independence, each of the signers could face the gallows. Benjamin Franklin joked about such fears when he said, "We must all hang together, or we shall all hang separately."

A REVOLUTION BEGINS

As you have read, when the colonies went to war, they were rebelling against actions of the British government. They did not want to separate from Great Britain. Thomas Paine's *Common Sense* helped change the colonists' thinking. He convinced people that independence was not to be feared and that they had nothing to lose by parting from Britain.

On July 4, 1776, the Continental Congress approved the Declaration of Independence. On that day the 13 colonies became the United States of America. From then on Americans were fighting a revolution to overthrow British rule and form a new nation.

Check Your Reading

1. What did Thomas Paine try to show Americans in his book, *Common Sense*?
2. According to Thomas Jefferson, what is the purpose of government?
3. Why did Jefferson think the colonies should be free?
4. **THINKING SKILL:** Find one fact and one opinion on page 293.

Revolution or Loyalty?

Even as the first shots of the American Revolution were fired, the colonists were divided in their support for revolution. As you have read, the Patriots wanted the 13 colonies to be independent from Great Britain. For them, revolution was the only answer to the colonies' problems. Many people, however, remained loyal to King George and his government. These Loyalists sided with Great Britain during the revolution. Still other Americans had not yet made up their minds.

The Second Continental Congress met in 1775 to debate the issue of revolution or loyalty. The delegates agreed to try to make peace with Great Britain. But they also decided to organize an army to defend the colonies against British attack.

POINT ☆\

The United States Should Become Independent

Thomas Paine argued in favor of independence in his book, *Common Sense*.

I dare the strongest supporter of King George to show a single thing the colonies can gain by being connected with Great Britain. We do not need to trade with Great Britain alone. We can sell our corn in any market in Europe.

The harm we suffer by our ties to Great Britain are without number. Thus our duty to the world as well as to ourselves tells us to break this tie. Now our link with Great Britain draws us into European wars and quarrels. It makes enemies of countries who might otherwise seek our friendship. And whenever a war breaks out between Britain and any other country, the trade of America will be ruined.

Everything that is right or natural begs for separation. The blood of the slain [killed], the weeping voice of nature cries, "Tis time to part." Even the distance at which God has placed England and America is proof that the rule of one over the other was never the plan of heaven.

● According to Thomas Paine, how would the American colonies suffer as a result of British quarrels with European countries?

COUNTERPOINT ☆

The United States Should Remain Loyal to Great Britain

A minister named Charles Inglis argued in favor of loyalty to the King of England.

It is time to put aside those hatreds which have pushed Britons to shed the blood of Britons. Peace will be restored. Farming, trade, and industry will be strong again. Now they sicken while this fight goes unsettled. By our connection with Britain, our trade and our coast would again be protected by the greatest sea power in the world.

A few years of peace will restore everything to its former perfect state. People will come again from the different parts of Europe, filling the land and making it more valuable. By a declaration for independence, only the sword will be able to decide the quarrel. War will destroy our once happy land.

Americans have the manners, habits, and ideas of Britons. They are used to a similar form of government. Until very lately, America has been the happiest country in the world. Blessed with all that nature could give, she enjoyed more liberty than any other land. It is not too late to hope that matters may mend.

● Why did Charles Inglis think British seapower was important to the colonies?

UNDERSTANDING THE POINT/COUNTERPOINT

1. Why did Thomas Paine believe that America should separate from Britain?
2. Why did Charles Inglis believe the colonies should remain loyal to Britain?
3. In your opinion, who presents a stronger case? Explain your answer.

3 Fighting for Independence

Key People

Nathan Hale
John Burgoyne
Martha Washington
Thaddeus Kosciuszko

Marquis de Lafayette
Friedrich von Steuben
Haym Salomon

Key Places

Trenton
Saratoga
Valley Forge

Read Aloud

Joseph Martin could not make up his mind. The 17-year-old farm boy sat staring at the paper that would make him a soldier. He was "as warm a Patriot as the best of them." Still, his pen kept tracing his name in the air above the paper. Then someone bumped his hand. The pen "made a woeful scratch on the paper." "Oh," said the clumsy fellow, "he has enlisted." Martin had joined the fight for freedom.

Read for Purpose

1. **WHAT YOU KNOW:** What problems did the Continental Army face in fighting the American Revolution?
2. **WHAT YOU WILL LEARN:** How did the army overcome its problems and keep the Revolution alive?

"THE TIMES THAT TRY MEN'S SOULS"

The British were determined to crush the revolution in the colonies. In the summer of 1776, they landed over 30,000 troops on Staten Island in New York Harbor. One third were German mercenaries hired in Germany. The Americans called them Hessians.

Washington moved most of his army of 20,000 inexperienced soldiers from Boston to New York City. There he divided his forces between Manhattan Island and Long Island.

The British attacked Long Island first, almost trapping the American troops there. Joseph Martin and his fellow soldiers barely escaped. Hidden by fog and darkness, they rowed to Manhattan Island in small boats. They had orders "not to speak, or even cough" as they moved.

Weeks later, the British captured an American spy on Long Island. General Howe ordered him hanged. As the noose was draped around his neck, Nathan Hale said, "I only regret that I have but one life to lose for my country."

Hale's words thrilled Washington's men. But their feelings changed as the British chased them off Manhattan Is-

Washington crossed the Delaware River to attack Trenton on Christmas Day, 1776. In this painting, done years after the event, the artist painted a flag which was not adopted until 1777.

land and across New Jersey. Sick and hungry, many soldiers went home. As Thomas Paine wrote, "These are the times that try men's souls."

In December Washington took his last 3,000 men into Pennsylvania. Unless he could raise more troops soon, he wrote, "I think the game will be pretty near up."

A GLORIOUS DAY AT TRENTON

On Christmas Day of 1776, Washington's ragged army huddled around blazing campfires beside the Delaware River. On the other side of the river, 1,200 Hessians were enjoying a warm holiday in the village of Trenton, New Jersey.

That night the Americans crossed the ice-choked Delaware River in small boats. Then they marched silently through the freezing darkness to Trenton. As the Americans stumbled along, they remembered the password Washington had given them: "Victory or Death!"

In Trenton the Hessians were completely surprised. After a short battle they surrendered. Usually General

Washington kept his feelings to himself. But this time he could not remain silent. "This is a glorious day for our country," he exclaimed.

The news of the victory at Trenton thrilled the country. Thousands of Americans volunteered to fight. The war was not lost after all.

A TURNING POINT AT SARATOGA

In June 1777 British General John Burgoyne (bûr goin') came to America with a plan for winning the war. His idea was to capture New York's Hudson River Valley. New England would then be cut off from the rest of the country. Burgoyne believed that the revolution would fail without men and supplies from New England.

Starting in Canada, Burgoyne's army sailed south on Lake Champlain. First it recaptured Fort Ticonderoga. Then Burgoyne headed through the wilderness toward the Hudson River.

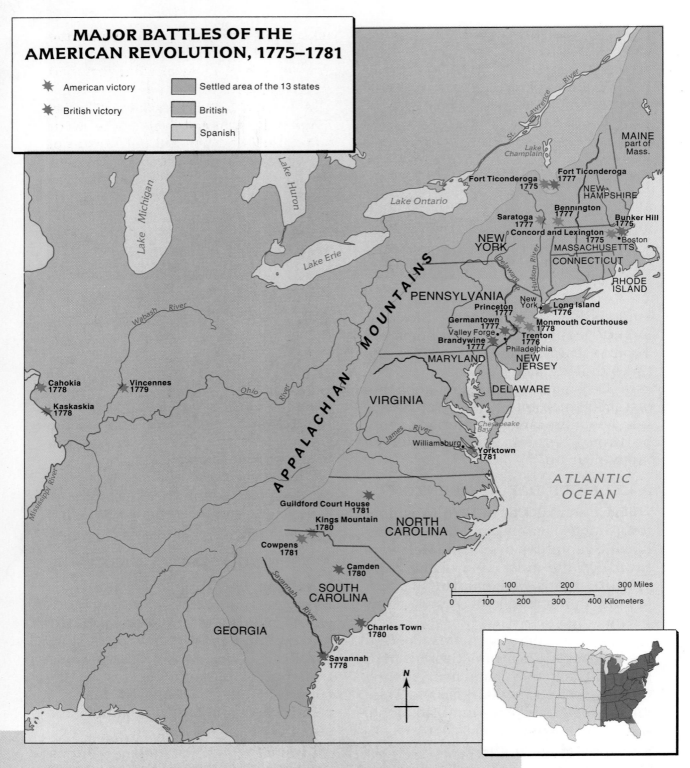

MAJOR BATTLES OF THE AMERICAN REVOLUTION, 1775–1781

★ American victory

★ British victory

Settled area of the 13 states

British

Spanish

MAINE part of Mass.

NEW HAMPSHIRE

Fort Ticonderoga 1777

Fort Ticonderoga 1775

Bennington 1777

Bunker Hill 1775

Saratoga 1777

Concord and Lexington 1775

Boston

MASSACHUSETTS

CONNECTICUT

RHODE ISLAND

NEW YORK

PENNSYLVANIA

Princeton 1777

New York

Long Island 1776

Germantown 1777

Monmouth Courthouse 1778

Valley Forge

Trenton 1776

Brandywine 1777

Philadelphia

NEW JERSEY

MARYLAND

DELAWARE

Cahokia 1778

Vincennes 1779

VIRGINIA

Kaskaskia 1778

Chesapeake Bay

James River

Williamsburg

Yorktown 1781

ATLANTIC OCEAN

Guildford Court House 1781

Kings Mountain 1780

NORTH CAROLINA

Cowpens 1781

Camden 1780

SOUTH CAROLINA

GEORGIA

Charles Town 1780

Savannah 1778

Lake Michigan

Lake Huron

Lake Ontario

Lake Erie

Lake Champlain

St. Lawrence River

Wabash River

Ohio River

Mississippi River

Savannah River

APPALACHIAN MOUNTAINS

| 0 | 100 | 200 | 300 Miles |
| 0 | 100 | 200 | 300 | 400 Kilometers |

N

MAP SKILL: This map shows the major battles of the American Revolution from Fort Ticonderoga in the north to Savannah in the south. Locate Saratoga. Why was this battle a turning point of the war?

On the map, this march looks like a short walk. But Burgoyne had over 600 wagons with him. Thirty of them carried his personal baggage. Even in the wilderness "Gentleman Johnny" Burgoyne ate off silver plates. His men had to cut a road through thick forests and mushy swamps. It took 20 days to move 22 miles (35 km).

This gave the Americans time to prepare a welcome. When Burgoyne finally reached Saratoga, New York, his 6,000-man army was outnumbered. "American militia," the general wrote, "swarmed around . . . like birds of prey." Burgoyne attacked at once. After a fierce fight, Gentleman Johnny was forced to surrender.

The American victory at Saratoga was a turning point in the war. It showed that Americans could defeat a large British force. Great Britain's old enemy, France, then decided to help the new nation. Soon French ships crossed the Atlantic. The United States no longer fought alone.

WINTER AT VALLEY FORGE

The victory at Saratoga cheered Americans, but there were still hard times ahead. In September 1777 the British took over Philadelphia. All through the fall, Washington tried to drive them out. But the redcoats were too strong. Now Washington's army moved to its winter camp at Valley Forge, Pennsylvania.

Joseph Martin wrote that the men who went to Valley Forge lacked blankets, coats, and shoes. Barefoot troops, he said, "might be tracked by their blood upon the rough frozen ground."

Washington begged the Continental Congress for supplies. "What is to become of the army this winter?" he asked. The Congress pleaded with the states to send money and supplies. But the states kept most of what they had for their own militias.

More than 2,000 men died at Valley Forge that winter. Even more went home. But the army did not break up. The main reason it did not was General Washington. His men did not see the angry letters he wrote the Continental Congress. But they knew he cared about them and suffered with them. Washington's quiet strength and belief in the cause of freedom made men proud to stand by him.

AFRICAN-AMERICAN PATRIOTS

At least 5,000 African-American Patriots joined the fight for freedom. Two slaves fought with the militia at Lexington. A free black man named Oliver Cromwell joined the army early in the war. He almost froze to death on the march to Trenton. He suffered with both black and white soldiers at Valley Forge. And he was still fighting when the war ended.

As free blacks and slaves joined the army, some white Patriots asked themselves a painful question. If blacks are willing to fight and die for our freedom, how can we keep them in slavery?

Before the war ended, most New England states had passed laws ending slavery. In other states, some slaves who had fought for their country were freed.

WOMEN SUPPORT THE ARMY

Women supported the fight for freedom in many ways. They kept farms and workshops going while men went off to fight. Some women went off to war with their husbands. Camp wives nursed the sick and wounded. Even

Molly Pitcher helped the Continental Army at the Battle of Monmouth in New Jersey. She loaded cannons and brought water to the troops.

Martha Washington joined her husband at Valley Forge. During that terrible winter her warm smile and soft words comforted many soldiers.

Some women also shared in the fighting. Joseph Martin told this story about Mary Ludwig Hays. The men called her "Molly Pitcher" because she brought them pitchers of water during battles. Once, while helping her husband load his cannon, wrote Martin, "a cannon shot from the enemy passed directly between her legs." But she kept right on working.

HELP FROM FOREIGNERS

People from other countries also helped the Americans. **Thaddeus Kosciuszko** (käs ē əs′ kō) arrived in America from Poland in 1776. He joined the Continental Army and was put in charge of building forts and defenses. Kosciuszko and his engineers built defenses along the Hudson River. Wash-

ington honored Kosciuszko by making him one of his personal assistants.

A young French leader, the **Marquis de Lafayette** (mär kē′ də läf ē et′), joined the army early in the war. Lafayette was a good officer. He used his own money to buy food and clothing for his men.

A German officer named **Friedrich von Steuben** (stü′ bən) drilled the troops at Valley Forge. Serving without pay, he turned American farmers into disciplined soldiers. With his help, the army that left Valley Forge in 1778 was tough and well trained.

The American financial leader, **Haym Salomon**, played a special role. He came to America from Poland and joined the Sons of Liberty. Salomon raised money for the Continental Army.

THE CONTINENTAL ARMY SURVIVES

In the first years of the war, as you have seen, the Continental Army saw both defeats and victories. At times it looked as if the army would fall apart. But the blood and sweat of countless Patriots—men and women, blacks and whites—kept the fight for independence alive.

Check Your Reading

1. Why did the British want to capture the Hudson River Valley?
2. How did women, blacks, and foreigners help the Continental Army?
3. GEOGRAPHY SKILL: Locate Trenton on the map on page 300. Why was the American victory there important?
4. THINKING SKILL: Why did France decide to aid the Americans? What was France's goal?

4 The Road to Victory

READ TO LEARN

Key Vocabulary
territory
traitor

Key People
George Rogers Clark
John Paul Jones
Francis Marion
Nathanael Greene
Charles Cornwallis

Key Places
Fort Vincennes
Northwest Territory
West Point
Yorktown

Read Aloud

In June 1778 General Washington got a message from his best spies in Philadelphia—the women hired to wash the redcoats' clothes. The British had ordered their laundry to be returned at once, "finished or unfinished." This could mean only one thing. They were leaving the city. Now it was Washington's turn to chase an army across New Jersey.

By July the British were back in New York City. Washington camped nearby, where his army could control the Hudson River. "It is not a little pleasing," he wrote, "that after two years . . . both armies are brought back to the very point they set out from." From now on the war would be fought in other places.

Read for Purpose

1. **WHAT YOU KNOW:** Where were the first battles of the American Revolution fought?
2. **WHAT YOU WILL LEARN:** What battles led to the end of the Revolution?

THE FRONTIER WAR

In the summer of 1778, a young frontier fighter named George Rogers Clark left Virginia with 200 men. His goal was to drive the British out of the Ohio River Valley.

That fall Clark captured several British forts along the Ohio River without losing any lives. Then he heard that 500 British troops and their Indian allies were defending Fort Vincennes (vin senz') on the Wabash River.

By now it was winter. Rains had turned most of the Ohio Valley into a freezing swamp. But Clark was determined to strike. "Great things," he wrote, have been done "by a few men." And Clark wanted to do great things.

303

In this painting, the *Bonhomme Richard* defeats the British ship *Serapis*. The ships were so close to each other that their rigging became tied up and their cannons touched.

Clark and his men marched 180 miles (290 km) in just 18 days. Much of the time they sloshed waist-deep through icy water. They held their rifles and gunpowder high above their heads. "Our suffering," Clark wrote, "is too terrible for any person to believe."

Upon reaching Fort Vincennes, Clark divided his men into several groups, each waving its own flag. The British thought they were being attacked by 20 bands of soldiers. They surrendered at once.

Clark's victory gave the United States control of the land north of the Ohio River from the Appalachians to the Mississippi. Later this area became known as the Northwest Territory. A territory is an area of land belonging to a government.

THE WAR AT SEA

When the war began, the United States had no navy. But soon Americans were turning merchant ships into warships and attacking the British at sea. The most daring American seaman was Commodore John Paul Jones. In 1778 Jones was attacking ships off the west coast of England.

In 1779 Jones's ship, the *Bonhomme Richard* (bon əm′ rē shär′), met the British warship *Serapis* (sə rā′ pəs) off the British coast. The *Serapis* pounded the American ship with cannon fire. Looking at the wreckage of the *Bonhomme Richard*, the British captain asked Jones if he was ready to surrender. Jones yelled back, "I have not yet begun to fight!"

The wild battle went on for two more hours. Finally it was the captain of the *Serapis* who had to surrender. One of Jones's men felt that this battle was "the most bloody, the hardest fought . . . between two ships of war of any nation under heaven."

BENEDICT ARNOLD TURNS TRAITOR

The war produced heroes like George Rogers Clark and John Paul Jones. But it also produced traitors. A traitor is a person who turns against his or her country and gives aid to its enemies.

The most famous traitor was Benedict Arnold. As you read in Lesson 1, Arnold had helped capture Fort Ticonderoga. In 1780 Arnold became commander of West Point, a fort on the

Hudson River. But soon he was plotting to turn the American fort over to the British for a large amount of money. Arnold's plan was discovered, but not before he escaped to New York City.

Arnold spent the rest of the war fighting for Britain. He never won the glory he wanted so much. But his name was not forgotten. Today, when we speak of a "Benedict Arnold," we mean a traitor to one's country.

THE WAR MOVES SOUTH

In 1778 the war spread to the South. British troops captured Savannah, Georgia. As the redcoats moved inland, Loyalists turned out to help them. Soon, the British had control of much of North Carolina and South Carolina.

But the rebels did not give up. The war in South Carolina was kept alive by brave men like **Francis Marion** Marion and his band of fighters made hit-and-run raids on British camps. After an attack they faded into the Carolina swamps like ghosts. His enemies called Marion the "Swamp Fox."

Meanwhile, Washington sent a general named **Nathanael Greene** to stop the British forces in the Carolinas. Greene's approach was simple. "We fight, get beat, rise, and fight again." By the spring of 1781, the British general in the South, **Charles Cornwallis** was "quite tired of marching about the country." He gave up chasing Greene and headed for Virginia.

In the South, Francis Marion fought the British with hit-and-run raids. Marion and his soldiers, shown here on a raft, lived off the land and surprised the British at every turn.

Washington, at the right, watches as the British surrender at Yorktown. To honor the soldiers of the war, Washington created a badge of merit which later became known as the Purple Heart. This was the first United States military decoration.

VICTORY AT YORKTOWN

In 1781 Cornwallis led his troops across Virginia to Yorktown, a small town on Chesapeake Bay. More British troops arrived by sea. Cornwallis's force swelled to almost 8,000 men.

Washington decided to prepare a trap for Cornwallis. He made it look as if he were getting ready to attack New York City. Instead, he sent most of his army to Virginia. At the same time, French warships brought French troops to Chesapeake Bay. Altogether, there were 17,000 French and American soldiers.

In early October the trap was sprung. Cornwallis's army was surrounded in Yorktown. French warships blocked any escape by sea. The "awful music" of huge guns pounded Yorktown day and night. Cornwallis surrendered on October 17, 1781. It was the last great battle of the American Revolution.

INDEPENDENCE

In 1783 the last British troops left the United States. In this lesson, you read how Americans met and defeated the British on land and at sea. Now, at last, the new nation was free.

For Joseph Martin and his fellow soldiers, it was time to go home. "We had lived together like a family," Martin wrote. Saying good-by was hard. The same was true for Washington. As he said farewell to his officers, there were tears on every face.

 Check Your Reading

1. How did the bravery of George Rogers Clark pay off?
2. Why is Benedict Arnold regarded as a traitor?
3. **GEOGRAPHY SKILL:** What was the last important battle of the war? Where did it take place?
4. **THINKING SKILL:** How could you determine the accuracy of this statement, "Clark and his men marched 180 miles (290 km) in just 18 days"?

Using Primary and Secondary Sources

You learned in Chapter 3 that a primary source gives first-hand information about a certain time or event. Primary sources let you see how people lived, thought, and felt. When you study a primary source, always ask: *Who? What? When? Where? Who* created the work? *What* does it tell you about a person's life or feelings? *When* was it created? *Where* was it created?

A secondary source is an account of the past written by someone who was not an eyewitness to the event described. Read the two sources that appear here. Then answer the questions that follow. Reading A is taken from a textbook. Reading B is from a person who took part in the Boston Tea Party.

Reading A

In late November and early December 1773, the British ships carrying tea to the colonies sailed into Boston Harbor. Over 300 chests of tea lay waiting to be unloaded from the ships. The colonists were determined not to buy the tea. They wanted the ships to turn back with their cargoes.

The governor of Massachusetts was equally determined to see the tea unloaded. He ordered British patrol boats in Boston Harbor to aim their cannons at the harbor. In this way, the captains of the tea ships could not leave without unloading their cargoes.

In mid-December, at the request of the colonists, one of the captains agreed to go to the governor and beg permission to leave with the tea. A crowd gathered near Boston's Old South Church. For hours the people stood in the cold, waiting for the captain's return.

It was evening when the captain returned. The answer was no. Only moments later, a band of what seemed to be Indians arrived at the wharf and boarded the ships. Silently they brought the cargo on deck—and dumped it overboard.

Reading B

It was now evening, and I immediately dressed myself in the costume of an Indian. After painting my face and hands with coal dust, I went to Griffin's wharf, where the ships lay that contained the tea. At the wharf, we were divided into three parties for boarding the three ships. As soon as we were on board, we demanded that the captain give us the keys to the hatches. We then took all the chests of tea and threw them overboard. In about three or four hours we had thrown overboard every tea chest. We were surrounded by British armed ships, but no attempt was made to resist us.

Reviewing the Skill

1. What is the difference between a primary source and a secondary source?
2. Name one statement in the secondary source that is supported by a description in the primary source.
3. Why is it important to be able to tell the difference between primary and secondary sources?

IMPORTANT EVENTS

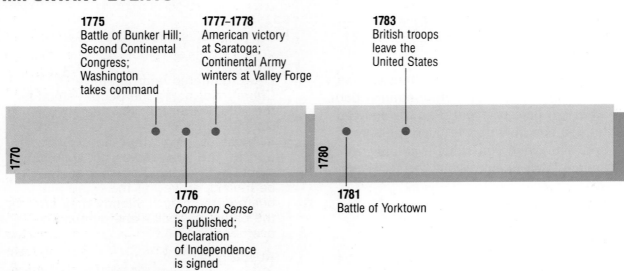

1775
Battle of Bunker Hill;
Second Continental
Congress;
Washington
takes command

1777–1778
American victory
at Saratoga;
Continental Army
winters at Valley Forge

1783
British troops
leave the
United States

1770

1780

1776
Common Sense
is published;
Declaration
of Independence
is signed

1781
Battle of Yorktown

PEOPLE TO KNOW

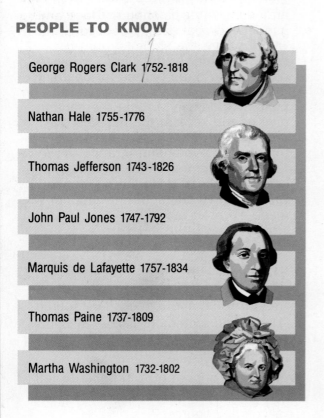

George Rogers Clark 1752-1818

Nathan Hale 1755-1776

Thomas Jefferson 1743-1826

John Paul Jones 1747-1792

Marquis de Lafayette 1757-1834

Thomas Paine 1737-1809

Martha Washington 1732-1802

IDEAS TO REMEMBER

- The fighting in the American Revolution began in New England.
- In the Declaration of Independence the American colonists told the world why they wanted to break away from Great Britain.
- With help from abroad, the Continental Army won some important victories.
- In 1781, after a victory at Yorktown, Virginia, the Americans won the war.

REVIEWING VOCABULARY

independence	territory
mercenary	traitor
revolution	

Number a sheet of paper from 1 to 5. Beside each number write the word from the list above that best completes the sentence.

1. In 1776 Americans had to decide whether to remain colonies of England or to fight for their _____.
2. A person who turns against his or her country is a _____.
3. A soldier paid to fight in another country's war is known as a _____.
4. To overthrow British control of the colonies, Americans had to fight a _____.
5. An area of land belonging to a government is called a _____.

REVIEWING FACTS

Number a sheet of paper from 1 to 5. Beside each number write the letter of the phrase from the lettered column that best matches the name or event in the numbered column.

1. Battle of Saratoga
2. Battle of Yorktown
3. Thomas Jefferson
4. Molly Pitcher
5. Francis Marion

a. Brought water to the soldiers
b. Turning point of the Revolution
c. The "Swamp Fox"
d. Last major battle of the Revolution
e. Wrote the Declaration of Independence

WRITING ABOUT MAIN IDEAS

1. **Writing a Leaflet:** Imagine that you are a recruiting officer for General George Washington and the Continental Army. Write a leaflet in which you try to persuade colonists to join the fight for American independence.
2. **Writing a Newspaper Story:** Choose one battle of the American Revolution. Then write a newspaper story about the battle. Be sure to include a headline.
3. **Writing a Conversation:** Many colonial families were divided over whether America should break away from Great Britain. Write a conversation that might have taken place in a family in which one son was a Patriot and one was a Loyalist. Each speaker should try to convince the other of his opinion.

BUILDING SKILLS: USING PRIMARY AND SECONDARY SOURCES

1. What is the difference between a primary source and a secondary source?
2. Review pages 298, 301, and 302 where the young American soldier Joseph Martin is mentioned.
   a. Which material is a primary source? Which is a secondary source?
   b. From what primary source was this material probably taken?
   c. Give one other example of a primary source used in this chapter.
3. Why are primary sources useful for students of history? Why are secondary sources useful?

REVIEWING VOCABULARY

Number a sheet of paper from 1 to 10. Beside each number write **C** if the underlined word or term in the sentence is used correctly. Write **I** if it is used incorrectly, and then write the word or term that would complete the sentence correctly.

1. To protest the Stamp Act colonists <u>repealed</u> British goods by refusing to buy them.
2. The First Continental Congress sent a <u>proclamation</u> to the king, asking him to end the Intolerable Acts.
3. The Americans fought a <u>revolution</u> to change their government completely.
4. The colonists wanted <u>representation</u>, or complete freedom from England.
5. The <u>population</u> of the colonies grew rapidly after 1700.
6. The British government hired German <u>traitors</u> to help defeat the Americans.
7. <u>In 1765</u> the <u>minutemen</u> decided to raise money in the colonies by passing the Stamp Act.
8. At the end of the French and Indian War, France gave Britain some of its <u>territory</u> in North America.
9. Patrick Henry was accused of <u>treason</u> when he announced that Parliament could not tax the colonies.
10. Representatives in <u>Parliament</u> voted to cut off trade with Britain until the Intolerable Acts were repealed.

✏ WRITING ABOUT THE UNIT

1. **Writing a Conversation:** Imagine that King George III and Thomas Jefferson arrange to have a meeting. They want to discuss their differences of opinion. Write the conversation that might take place between the king and Jefferson.
2. **Writing a Paragraph:** Study the map of Revolutionary War battles on page 300. Choose one battle. Then write a paragraph telling everything you can learn from the map about that battle. Include such information as where and when it took place and who won.

ACTIVITIES

1. **Writing a Character Sketch:** Find out about one of the people listed below and write a character sketch. Your sketch should tell about the person's life. It should also describe what the person was like. For example, you know that John Adams was stiff and formal with people, while his cousin Sam Adams loved to chat with friends.

Samuel Adams	Mercy Otis Warren
Fredrich von Steuben	Nathan Hale
	Martha Washington

2. **Working Together to Find Songs of the American Revolution:** Find a record or songbook of songs about the American Revolution. With other group members prepare a presentation to the class, explaining some of the songs. You might want to sing the songs for the class or play a record or tape of them.

BUILDING SKILLS: USING PRIMARY AND SECONDARY SOURCES

The conversation below took place 67 years after the battles of Lexington and Concord. The two speakers were a historian and 92-year-old Captain Levy Preston, who had fought in the battle. Read the conversation and then answer the questions that follow.

Historian: Captain Preston, why did you go to the Concord fight on the 19th of April 1775? My histories tell me that the men of the Revolution took up arms against "intolerable oppressions [burdens]." What were they?

Preston: Oppressions? I didn't feel them.

Historian: What? Were you not oppressed by the Stamp Act?

Preston: I never saw one of those stamps. I am certain I never paid a penny for one of them.

Historian: Well, what then about the tax on tea?

Preston: Tax on tea! I never drank a drop of the stuff; the boys threw it overboard.

Historian: Well, then, what was the matter? And what did you mean in going to the fight?

Preston: Young man, what we meant in going for those redcoats was this: we always governed ourselves, and we always meant to. They didn't mean we should.

1. What is the difference between a primary and secondary source?
2. Is this a primary or secondary source?
3. a. What is the historian trying to find out from Captain Preston?
   b. What is Captain Preston's answer?
   c. Does this tell you more or less than your textbook about why Americans went to war? Explain your answer.
4. Give two examples of a primary source and two examples of a secondary source.

LINKING PAST, PRESENT, AND FUTURE

Many battle sites of the American Revolution can be visited today. They have been preserved as national landmarks. What do you think is the purpose of preserving battle sites? Do you think the nation should continue to do so in the future? Why or why not?

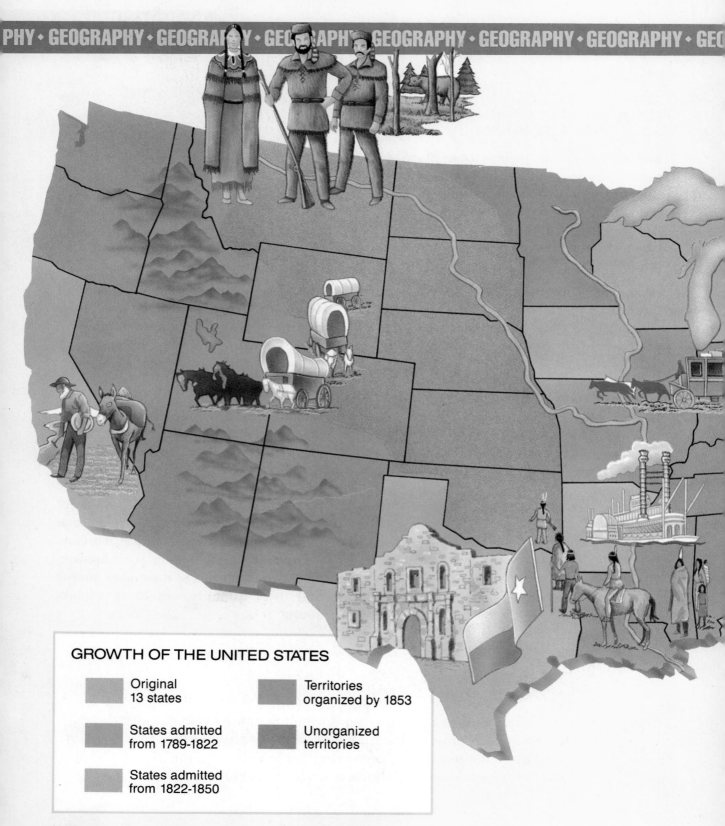

GROWTH OF THE UNITED STATES

Original
13 states

Territories
organized by 1853

States admitted
from 1789-1822

Unorganized
territories

States admitted
from 1822-1850

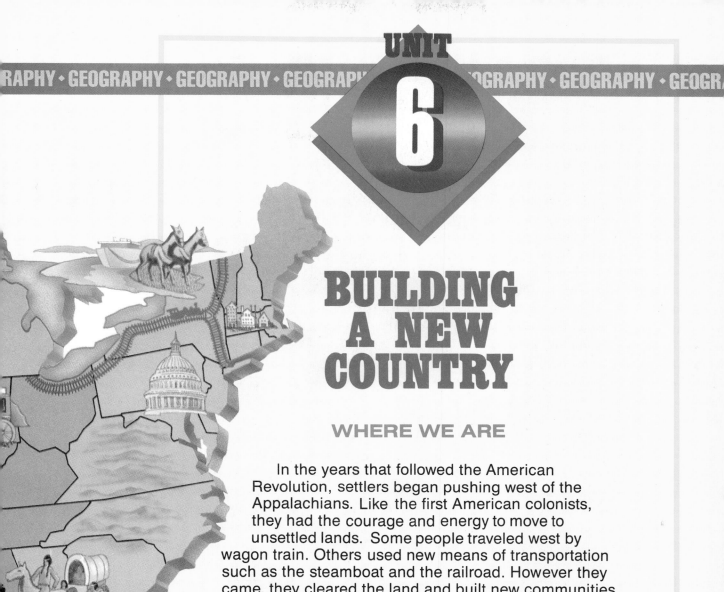

UNIT 6

BUILDING A NEW COUNTRY

WHERE WE ARE

In the years that followed the American Revolution, settlers began pushing west of the Appalachians. Like the first American colonists, they had the courage and energy to move to unsettled lands. Some people traveled west by wagon train. Others used new means of transportation such as the steamboat and the railroad. However they came, they cleared the land and built new communities.

You can see from the map how the United States grew between 1776 and 1853. By then our country was made up of 31 states and several large territories. In Unit 6 you will read how American lands stretched from the Atlantic Ocean to the Pacific.

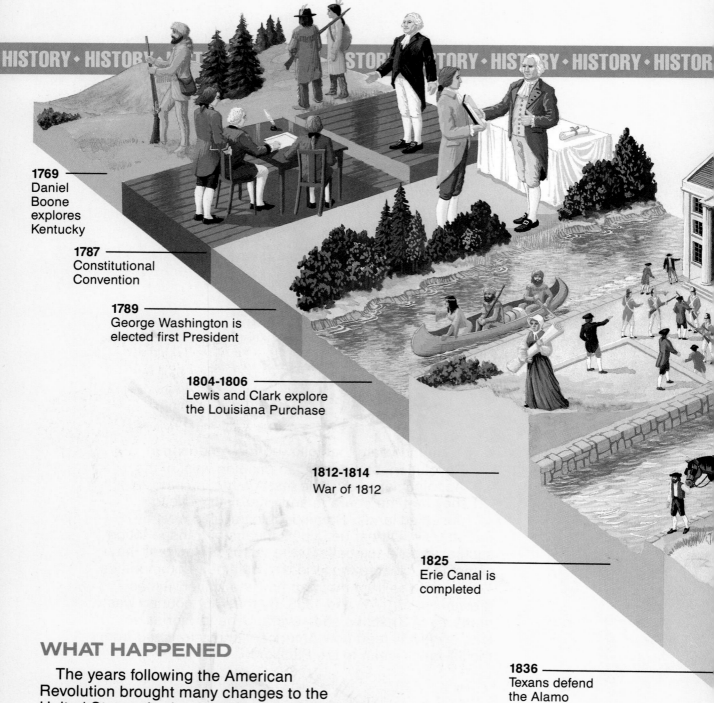

1769
Daniel
Boone
explores
Kentucky

1787
Constitutional
Convention

1789
George Washington is
elected first President

1804-1806
Lewis and Clark explore
the Louisiana Purchase

1812-1814
War of 1812

1825
Erie Canal is
completed

1836
Texans defend
the Alamo

1848
Gold is discovered
in California

WHAT HAPPENED

The years following the American
Revolution brought many changes to the
United States. As the time line shows, George
Washington became the country's first President
in 1789.

As more settlers moved west, new lands were
added to the United States. Lewis and Clark explored
the Louisiana Purchase. By 1848 our country reached all
the way to California. As you read this unit, you will learn how
all of these changes came about.

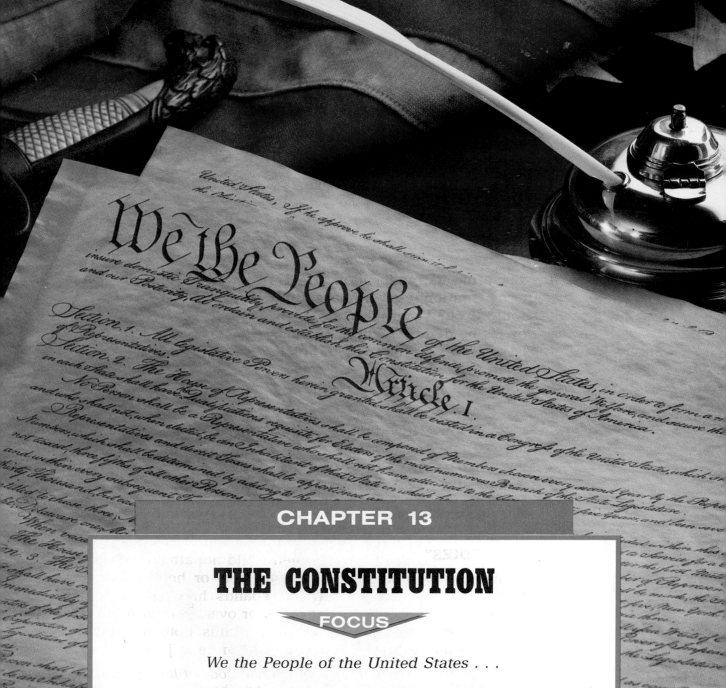

CHAPTER 13

THE CONSTITUTION

FOCUS

We the People of the United States . . .

These are the first words of the Constitution of the United States. The Constitution is the plan of government for our country. When it was written in 1787, most countries were ruled by kings and queens. Those rulers claimed their power came from God. These first words of the Constitution tell us that in our country political power comes from the people. Under our Constitution, the people have ruled the United States for over 200 years.

The Nation's First Government

READ TO LEARN

Key Vocabulary

Articles of Confederation
Northwest Ordinance

Key People

Abigail Adams
Daniel Shays
Alexander Hamilton

Read Aloud

After declaring its independence in 1776, the United States needed a new national government. But what kind of government should it be? What powers should it have? How should these powers be divided? These were not easy questions to answer. The leaders of the new nation had to deal with these questions in the late 1700s.

Read for Purpose

1. **WHAT YOU KNOW:** How did the United States gain its independence from Great Britain?
2. **WHAT YOU WILL LEARN:** What problems did the United States face after the American Revolution?

"REMEMBER THE LADIES"

No one had thought more about what the new government should be like than John Adams. As a member of the Continental Congress, Adams helped write a new plan of government. Many of his ideas came from the books he had read. But he also received plenty of advice from his wife, Abigail.

While John Adams was in Congress, Abigail Adams was raising their four children and running their farm. She was also thinking about what independence could mean for American women.

At that time, women had fewer rights and opportunities than did men.

Women could not attend college. They could not vote or hold public office. And husbands had almost complete legal power over their wives.

Abigail Adams thought that this was wrong. She wrote to John:

In the new code of laws which I suppose it will be necessary for you to make, I desire that you would remember the ladies. . . . Do not put such unlimited power in the hands of husbands.

But the new government of the United States did not "remember the ladies." Not until many years later did women finally gain the same rights as men.

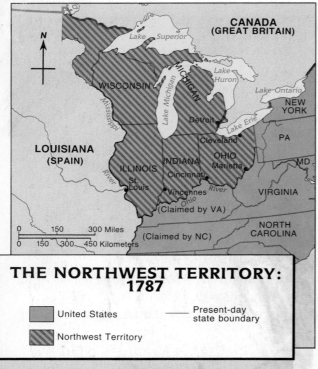

THE NORTHWEST TERRITORY: 1787

United States	Present-day state boundary
Northwest Territory	

MAP SKILL: Locate the Northwest Territory. Which five states were created from this land?

THE ARTICLES OF CONFEDERATION

Most Americans at the time feared a strong central government. They remembered all too well the power that Great Britain had held over them. They wanted to be sure the new American government would protect the rights of the 13 states.

The plan of government approved by the Continental Congress was called the Articles of Confederation. Under this plan, the new country was run by a Congress. Most power, however, remained with the states.

Congress, for example, could declare war. But it had to ask the states to send soldiers for an army. Congress could not tax people in the states. Instead, it had to ask each state for money. And

this, said Robert Morris, who handled the nation's finances, was "like preaching to the dead." The states often ignored requests for money.

Congress could pass laws but had no one to carry them out. It did elect a president, but he had no power. A lawyer once told a sick friend to take that job because it was "the easiest in the Union for an invalid."

As a result, the new government turned out to be almost powerless. Much of the time the states did not even send representatives to Congress.

THE NORTHWEST ORDINANCE

Despite its weakness, Congress was able to plan for the nation's growth. You read in Chapter 12 that the United States won the Northwest Territory from Great Britain during the American Revolution. In 1787 Congress passed a law that provided a way to settle this area.

The Northwest Ordinance divided the Northwest into smaller territories. It promised people who settled there the same rights as all other Americans, except for one. They could not own slaves. When there were 60,000 people in a territory, it could become a state. The map on this page shows the five states that were formed from the Northwest Territory.

This system for settling new territories worked well. Over the next 175 years it helped the United States to grow from a narrow band of 13 states into a vast nation of 50 states.

QUARRELS AND REBELLIONS

By 1787, however, the country seemed more likely to come apart than to grow. The states were quarreling over practically everything, it seemed.

Different money in each state and the rebellion led by Daniel Shays were just two of the country's problems under the **Articles of Confederation**.

Boundaries, trade, and taxes were areas of disagreement. Several states were printing their own money. As a result, paper money used in one state was not good in another.

Rebellion was in the air. In Massachusetts, farmers were tired of seeing state courts seize their land when they could not pay their taxes and debts. Led by **Daniel Shays**, the Massachusetts farmers picked up their rifles and tried to force the courts in their state to close.

George Washington saw these quarrels and rebellions as signs that the nation was in trouble. Things would get no better, he said, as long as the nation had "a half-starved, limping government."

"FIT FOR NEITHER WAR NOR PEACE"

The Articles of Confederation had created a national government with little power. New York lawyer **Alexander Hamilton** said that this government was "fit for neither war nor peace." By 1787 many Americans agreed with him. Something, they said, had to be done before the not-so-United States fell apart.

Check Your Reading

1. Why was Abigail Adams concerned about the role of American women in the new government?

2. What problems were created by the Articles of Confederation?

3. **GEOGRAPHY SKILL:** How did the Northwest Ordinance help the United States to grow?

4. **THINKING SKILL:** Do you think the farmers of Massachusetts would have rebelled if they had thought the government created by the Articles of Confederation was stronger?

Recognizing Point of View

Key Vocabulary
point of view

There's been a fight on the school bus! The principal asks the bus driver and one of the students involved in the fight to describe what happened. Do you think both the bus driver and the student will tell the same story? The difference between the two stories might be caused by their different **points of view**.

Point of view is the way a person looks at or feels about something. For example, we know that the bus driver did not take part in the fight. For that reason, the driver probably saw events differently from the students who were fighting.

Identifying how a person feels about a subject is important. You need to recognize a writer's point of view to determine the accuracy of what he or she says.

Trying the Skill
Below are two reports of Shays's Rebellion. Read both. Then determine the point of view of the first report.

A. Those boys were true Patriots, not traitors! They were fighting to save their homes from unfair taxes. Armed only with pitchforks, they rightly closed down the courts to prevent their land from being taken. Now three lay dead while mercenaries hunt those who escaped through heavy snow as if they were animals.

B. True, I helped pay for the army that Massachusetts leaders raised to put down Daniel Shays and his mob. Look at what happened in Rhode Island! Wicked men in the legislature lent large sums of paper money to landowners. Then they forced the merchants to accept the worthless paper money. I believe that Shays should be tried and convicted of treason.

1. From what point of view was report **A** written?
2. How do you know?

HELPING YOURSELF

The steps on the left will help you recognize a writer's point of view. The example on the right shows one way to apply these steps to the first report that you read.

One Way to Recognize Point of View	Example
1. Identify the subject or topic.	The subject of report **A** is Shays's Rebellion.
2. Identify statements of fact.	To identify statements of fact you might look up the war records of the men who took part in the rebellion or try to find out the number of people killed.
3. Identify parts of the subject that the writer does not talk about but probably could have.	The writer chose not to include the fact that the three rebels died as they were trying to steal weapons from the Massachusetts military.
4. Identify statements of opinion.	Calling the taxes "unfair" or the closing of the courts "right" are opinions.
5. Identify words or phrases that suggest how or what the writer feels or what the writer believes about the subject.	The writer called the state militia "mercenaries." You should recall that mercenaries were hired soldiers who fought against George Washington.
6. Describe the view or position expressed. Tell if the writer is for or against it.	The writer must be telling the story from the point of view of Shays and his men.

Applying the Skill

Now reread report **B**. From what point of view is it told?

1. What is one statement of fact?
   a. Massachusetts leaders raised an army to put down Shays's Rebellion.
   b. Shays's men were an unruly mob.
   c. Daniel Shays was a traitor.
2. Which of the following statements would the writer most likely have left out in order to make his point?
   a. Many people at the time were shocked by Shays's Rebellion.
   b. Shays and his followers threatened the future of the United States.
   c. Farmers like Shays had no way to solve their problems.

3. The writer of report **B** was probably a _____.
   a. poor farmer
   b. merchant
   c. soldier

Reviewing the Skill

1. What is a person's point of view?
2. What are some things you can do to recognize a writer's point of view?
3. When is it important to try to recognize point of view in a statement?

2 The Constitutional Convention

READ TO LEARN

Key Vocabulary

delegate
constitution
legislative branch
executive branch
President

judicial branch
Supreme Court
republic
House of Representatives
Senate

Key People

James Madison

Read Aloud

In May 1787 representatives from 12 states came to the city of Philadelphia. Congress had called a convention to revise, or change, the Articles of Confederation. Not everyone liked this idea. Rhode Island did not send anyone. And Patrick Henry refused to go, saying he "smelt a rat."

Read for Purpose

1. **WHAT YOU KNOW:** Why were people unhappy with the Articles of Confederation?
2. **WHAT YOU WILL LEARN:** What did the delegates achieve at the Constitutional Convention?

THE DELEGATES

The 55 delegates who met in the Philadelphia State House were men of property—bankers, lawyers, planters, and merchants. A delegate is a person chosen by people to represent them. Many of the delegates had fought in the American Revolution. Most had served in their state assemblies. At the age of 81, Benjamin Franklin was the oldest delegate.

George Washington was probably the most reluctant delegate. After the war he had returned to Mount Vernon, hoping never to leave again. But his friends said that the convention would fail without him. It was his duty to go. And Washington was not a man to turn his back on duty.

The best-prepared delegate was a planter named James Madison. He was a short man, "no bigger," someone said, "than half a piece of soap." But he came to Philadephia filled with big ideas for his country.

Madison wanted the delegates to get rid of the Articles of Confederation. The nation needed a strong government to survive, he said. And James Madison had written a plan for just such a government.

THE CONVENTION BEGINS

The convention began on May 25. The delegates' first act was to elect George Washington president of the convention. They also decided to keep their meetings secret. That way they could speak freely without fear of what other people might think.

Fortunately, Madison took notes about everything that happened. "This was a task," he said, that "nearly killed me." From his notes we know what went on each day of the convention.

For several days the delegates looked at the plan Madison had written. They liked it enough to vote against revising the Articles of Confederation. Instead, they would write a new constitution, or plan of government, based on Madison's ideas. From that point on, the meeting in Philadelphia was a Constitutional Convention. And James Madison became known as the "Father of the Constitution."

THE NEW PLAN OF GOVERNMENT

The delegates began planning a government with three branches, or parts. One was a legislative branch, or law-making branch, called the Congress. The Congress would make laws and raise money for the government. The second was an executive branch to carry out the laws and run the government. The executive branch would be headed by a President. The third was a judicial branch that would decide the meaning of laws. This branch would be headed by a Supreme Court.

The summer of 1787 was the hottest that people in Philadelphia could remember. Madison's notes tell us that the delegates' tempers rose with the heat. Most delegates agreed that the

James Madison, called "Jemmy" by his friends, kept the best record of what happened at the Constitutional Convention.

government should be a republic. A republic is a type of government in which the people elect representatives to run the country. Under the new plan of government, the people would elect the members of Congress. But the delegates could not agree on how each state should be represented in the new Congress.

Delegates from large states had their own plan. Edmund Randolph of Virginia said the number of representatives in Congress should be based on each state's population. That way, larger states would have more representatives in Congress than would smaller states.

The delegates from small states disagreed. They wanted each state to have the same number of representatives. Then smaller states and larger states would have equal power in Congress. The argument went on and on until one delegate said that the convention was held together by "no more than the strength of a hair."

After four months of hard work, delegates signed the **Constitution** on September 17, 1787.

An agreement called the Great Compromise saved the convention. In a compromise, each side to a dispute gives up something it wants in order to reach an agreement. In the Great Compromise, the large states and small states agreed that Congress should have two parts, or houses. In the House of Representatives, each state would be represented according to its population. In the other house, the Senate, each state would have two senators regardless of population.

There were other arguments over slavery, trade, and the powers of the government. But by September, the work was done. To George Washington, the new Constitution seemed "little short of a miracle."

A RISING YOUNG NATION

On September 17, the delegates met for the last time. They had worked hard to create a good plan of government for the republic. Tears ran down Ben Franklin's face as he signed the Constitution. Looking at Washington's chair in the State House, he had often wondered if the sun carved on its back was rising or setting. Now, Franklin was happy to say, it was a rising sun— a symbol of a rising young nation.

Check Your Reading

1. Why is James Madison known as the "Father of the Constitution"?
2. What kind of government did the delegates to the Constitutional Convention try to create?
3. What agreement was worked out by the Great Compromise?
4. **THINKING SKILL:** You read that we know what went on at the Constitutional Convention from James Madison's notes. Do you think his notes give us an accurate picture of the convention? Why or why not?

324

3 The New Constitution

READ TO LEARN

Key Vocabulary

Preamble
federal system
checks and balances
veto

Read Aloud

Before the Constitution could go into effect, it had to be approved by 9 of the 13 states. In each state Americans studied the new plan to find out what kind of government it would create.

Read for Purpose

1. **WHAT YOU KNOW:** What three branches of government were created by the Constitution?
2. **WHAT YOU WILL LEARN:** How did the Constitution create a system of checks and balances?

THE PREAMBLE

The first thing Americans saw in the Constitution was its Preamble, or introduction. It begins, "We the People of the United States. . . . " These words told Americans that the Constitution would create a republic. As you know, in a republic, power comes from the people, who elect their own leaders.

The Preamble, which appears on page 330, lists the goals of the nation's government. First, the government should unite the states into a "more perfect Union." It should "establish Justice" and keep peace within the country. It should also defend the country from attack and protect the freedoms of all Americans. These goals are as important to us today as they were to people in 1787.

A FEDERAL SYSTEM OF GOVERNMENT

The Constitution set up a federal system of government in which power is shared between the national government and the state governments.

Our Constitution gives some powers to the federal, or national, government alone. For example, only the federal government has the power to print money or declare war. Other powers, such as setting up public schools and running elections, are left to the states. Still other powers, such as the power to tax, are shared by both the federal and state governments.

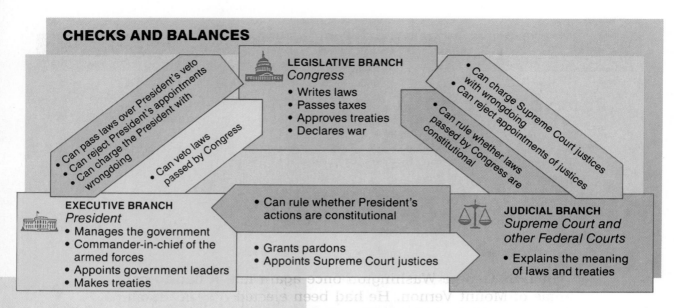

CHECKS AND BALANCES

LEGISLATIVE BRANCH
Congress
- Writes laws
- Passes taxes
- Approves treaties
- Declares war

Can pass laws over President's veto
- Can reject President's appointments
- Can charge the President with wrongdoing
- Can veto laws passed by Congress

Can charge Supreme Court justices with wrongdoing
- Can reject appointments of justices
- Can rule whether laws passed by Congress are constitutional

EXECUTIVE BRANCH
President
- Manages the government
- Commander-in-chief of the armed forces
- Appoints government leaders
- Makes treaties

- Can rule whether President's actions are constitutional

- Grants pardons
- Appoints Supreme Court justices

JUDICIAL BRANCH
Supreme Court and other Federal Courts
- Explains the meaning of laws and treaties

CHART SKILL: Which branch of government explains the meanings of laws?

CHECKS AND BALANCES

The Constitution created a government strong enough to unite the states. But it also included a system of **checks and balances** to keep any branch of the federal government from becoming too powerful. In this system the powers of one branch of government are balanced by the powers of another. Each branch can check, or stop, another branch if it uses its powers wrongly.

Suppose, for example, that Congress passes a law the President thinks is unwise. The President can check Congress by **vetoing**, or refusing to approve, that law. A vetoed law does not go into effect.

Congress can also check the President's power. If two thirds of its members agree, Congress can pass laws over the President's veto. The vetoed law then goes into effect. The flow chart on this page shows several ways each branch of the government can check the power of the other two branches.

THE SUPREME LAW OF THE LAND

The more people studied the Constitution, the more most of them liked it. They saw that it would create a republic. The new federal government would unite the states while sharing power with them. A system of checks and balances would keep the federal government from becoming too powerful.

By June 1788, nine states had approved the Constitution. Since then, the Constitution has provided the framework for our national government. After 200 years, it is still "the supreme law of the land."

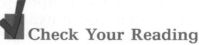

Check Your Reading

1. List three goals of our nation's government.
2. What is a federal system of government?
3. How does the system of checks and balances work?
4. **THINKING SKILL:** What are some alternatives the 55 delegates considered before deciding to write a new Constitution?

4 A New Government

READE TO LEARN

Key Vocabulary

amendment
Bill of Rights
Cabinet
political party

Key People

George Washington

Read Aloud

In 1789 George Washington once again left his beloved home of Mount Vernon. He had been elected the first President of the United States. Now the man who had led the army of the Revolution faced the task of turning the Constitution into a working government. Looking ahead, Washington saw "an ocean of difficulties."

Read for Purpose

1. **WHAT YOU KNOW:** What kind of government was created by the delegates at the Constitutional Convention?
2. **WHAT YOU WILL LEARN:** How did George Washington help to make the new government work?

GEORGE WASHINGTON TAKES OFFICE

George Washington's spirits rose as he traveled toward New York City, the nation's temporary capital. In every town along the way he was greeted by cheering crowds.

One onlooker, young Eliza Quincy, wrote about Washington's welcome to New York City. When he stepped out onto the city hall balcony, she said, there were "shouts of joy and welcome." Then the crowd "hushed in silence." Washington placed his right hand on a Bible and repeated the oath of office taken by every President since that day.

I do solemnly swear [or affirm] that I will faithfully execute the Office of President of the United States, and will to the best of my ability preserve, protect, and defend the Constitution of the United States.

THE BILL OF RIGHTS

The first task of the new Congress was to end fears that a strong government might take away people's rights and freedoms. Ten amendments, or additions, to the Constitution were

George Washington was given a hero's welcome as he traveled to New York City to become the country's first President. Washington was 57 years old when he took the oath of office.

voted by Congress and then approved by the states. These first ten amendments are called the **Bill of Rights**.

Read the summary of the first ten amendments on page 332. You can see that the Bill of Rights lists the most important rights and freedoms of Americans. It protects our right to religious freedom, freedom of speech, and freedom of the press. It also protects each person's right to a fair trial when accused of a crime.

THE PRESIDENT'S CABINET

To help the President run the government, Congress set up three government departments. Each department was in charge of an important govern-

ment activity. The Treasury Department took charge of the government's money. The Department of State took care of dealings with other countries. The War Department took charge of the nation's defense. Each department was headed by an official called a secretary. Congress also set up the Office of Attorney General. It was the attorney general's job to make sure that the country's laws were obeyed.

President Washington met with his secretaries and the attorney general to discuss problems and seek their advice. Together these officials were known as the **Cabinet**. Soon, Cabinet meetings became a regular part of the new government.

THE BEGINNING OF POLITICAL PARTIES

Two members of Washington's Cabinet had very different views of the country's future. Alexander Hamilton, the Secretary of the Treasury, saw a very powerful nation of great cities and busy factories. A strong federal government was needed, he argued, to build and govern such a nation.

Thomas Jefferson, George Washington's Secretary of State, saw another future. He imagined a peaceful land of self-sufficient farmers. Such people had little need for government, he said. For them the best government was that which governed the least.

These two different views led to the rise of **political parties**. A political party is a group of people who share similar ideas about government. Members of a political party work to elect leaders who will carry out their ideas. People who shared Alexander Hamilton's view were called Federalists. Thomas Jefferson's followers called themselves Republicans.

Neither political party trusted the other. One Federalist called Republicans "poison-sucking toads." But both parties had to compromise in Congress to get laws passed.

In one compromise, Congress voted to build the nation's capital city on land between Virginia and Maryland. You read in Chapter 2 that this site is called the District of Columbia and is not part of any state. The new capital city was named Washington.

FIRST IN WAR AND PEACE

George Washington served two terms as President. During his eight years in office, he helped to bring the Constitution to life. In 1797 Washington turned a working government over to the country's second President, John Adams.

Two years later, George Washington was dead. Americans mourned the

Washington and members of his Cabinet meet to discuss an issue. What is the role of the Secretary of State?

man they honored as "the Father of our Country." Washington had led his country through the Revolution, the writing of the Constitution, and the creation of the republic in which we live today. Now, as then, George Washington remains "first in war, first in peace, and first in the hearts of his countrymen."

Check Your Reading

1. What freedoms are given to Americans in the Bill of Rights?
2. What is the President's Cabinet?
3. Why has George Washington been described as "first in war, first in peace, and first in the hearts of his countrymen"?
4. **THINKING SKILL:** How did Hamilton and Jefferson view America's future?

Summary of the
Constitution of the United States

PREAMBLE

We the People of the United States, in Order to form a more perfect Union, establish Justice, insure domestic Tranquility, provide for the common Defense, promote the general Welfare, and secure the blessings of Liberty to ourselves and our Posterity, do ordain and establish this Constitution for the United States of America.

This is the meaning of the Preamble:

The people of the United States made the Constitution for the following reasons: (1) to set up a stronger government and a more united nation than the one that existed under the Articles of Confederation; (2) to ensure peace and justice among the people; (3) to defend the nation against enemies; (4) to help ensure the well-being of all the people; and (5) to make sure that the people of this nation will always be free.

ARTICLE 1
LEGISLATIVE BRANCH

Section 1: The Congress
The legislative branch, or Congress, makes the nation's laws. It is made up of two houses—the Senate and the House of Representatives.

Section 2: The House of Representatives
Members of the House of Representatives are elected for two-year terms. A representative must be at least 25 years old, a citizen of the United States for at least 7 years, and live in the state he or she represents.

The number of representatives a state has depends on the state's population. In order to find out how many people live in each state, the government must do a count of the population every ten years. This count is called a census.

Section 3: The Senate
The Senate is made up of two senators from each state. Each senator is elected for a six-year term. A senator must be at least 30 years old, a citizen of the United States for at least 9 years, and live in the state he or she represents.

The Vice President of the United States is in charge of the Senate but may vote only if there is a tie.

Sections 4–6: Rules
The houses of Congress set their own rules for their members. Each house must

keep a record of its meetings and how each member voted.

To make sure that there is complete freedom of discussion in Congress, senators and representatives cannot be arrested for things they say while doing their jobs.

Section 7: How a Bill Becomes a Law

A suggested law, or bill, becomes a law when both houses of Congress agree to it by a majority vote and when the President signs it. If the President vetoes, or rejects, the bill, it can still become a law if both houses of Congress approve it again by a two-thirds vote.

Section 8: Powers of Congress

The powers of Congress include the power to: collect taxes; borrow money; control trade with other countries and among the states; decide how foreigners can become citizens; coin money; set up post offices; set up courts; declare war; set up an army and a navy; make all laws necessary to carry out powers granted to the government.

Sections 9–10: Powers Denied to Congress and the States

There are certain powers that Congress and the states do not have. Congress cannot, for example, spend money without telling how the money will be spent. The states cannot make treaties with other countries or coin money.

ARTICLE 2
EXECUTIVE BRANCH

Section 1: President and Vice President

The President and Vice President head the executive branch. Along with the people who work with them, their job is to carry out the laws made by Congress. They are elected for four-year terms.

The President and Vice President must be natural-born citizens and at least 35 years old, and must have lived in the United States for at least 14 years.

Sections 2–4: Powers and Duties

The President's powers and duties include: commanding the armed forces; appointing government officials; reaching agreements with other countries; and pardoning crimes. At least once a year, the President must tell Congress how the nation is doing. This is called the President's State of the Union message.

A President who commits a serious crime may be removed from office.

ARTICLE 3
JUDICIAL BRANCH

Section 1: Federal Courts

The judicial branch is made up of the Supreme Court and all other federal, or United States, courts. Federal judges are appointed for life.

Section 2: Duties

The judicial branch has the power to decide the meaning of the Constitution. It may decide if the actions of the other two branches are unconstitutional, or go against the Constitution.

Federal courts have a say in many cases, such as those having to do with the Constitution, federal laws, or disagreements between citizens from different states.

Section 3: Treason

Treason is a crime committed when a citizen of the United States betrays the country, especially in wartime.

ARTICLE 4
THE STATES
Sections 1–4: Dealings Among the States

All states must accept the actions, records, and court decisions of other states. When citizens visit another state, they must be given the same rights as citizens of the state they are visiting.

New states may be added to the United States. The United States government promises to protect the states from enemies.

ARTICLE 5
AMENDMENTS

The Constitution may be amended, or changed, if Congress and three fourths of the states agree.

ARTICLE 6
SUPREME LAW, OATHS
OF OFFICE, DEBTS

The Constitution of the United States is the supreme law, or the highest law, in the nation. Government officials must promise to support the Constitution. In addition, the government promised to pay back all debts owed before the Constitution was adopted.

ARTICLE 7
APPROVING THE CONSTITUTION

The Constitution was to become law when 9 of the 13 original states ratified, or approved, it. Special conventions were held for this purpose, and the process took nine months to complete.

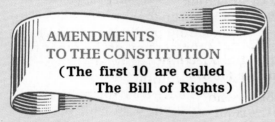

AMENDMENTS
TO THE CONSTITUTION
(The first 10 are called
The Bill of Rights)

AMENDMENT 1
Freedom of Religion, Speech, Press, Assembly, and Petition (1791)

Congress cannot make a law setting up an official religion. It cannot stop people from practicing any religion they choose. Congress cannot take away freedom of speech or of the press. Congress cannot stop groups from assembling, or meeting together, peacefully. It cannot stop people from petitioning, or asking the government, to end an injustice.

AMENDMENT 2
Right to Keep Arms (1791)

The people have the right to keep and carry arms, or weapons.

AMENDMENT 3
Quartering Soldiers (1791)

During peacetime, people cannot be forced to quarter soldiers, or let them stay in their homes.

AMENDMENT 4
Search and Seizures (1791)

People's homes and other property cannot be searched and seized unless the police have a search warrant.

AMENDMENT 5
Rights of Accused Persons (1791)

People who are accused of a crime cannot be forced to testify, or give evidence, against themselves. Their lives, freedom, or property cannot be taken away from them unfairly. The government may take a person's property for public use only if the person is paid for it.

AMENDMENT 6
Jury Trial in Criminal Cases (1791)

People accused of crimes have the right to a public and speedy trial with a jury. They have the right to be told the charges against them. They have the right to have a lawyer.

AMENDMENT 7
Jury Trial in Civil Cases (1791)

In most civil, or noncriminal, cases, people have the right to a jury trial.

AMENDMENT 8
Excessive Bail or Punishment (1791)

Bail must be reasonable for people accused of a crime. Punishments may not be cruel and unusual.

AMENDMENT 9
Other Rights of the People (1791)

The people have rights in addition to those listed in the Constitution.

AMENDMENT 10
Powers of the States and the People (1791)

Powers that are not granted to the national government and not forbidden to the states are left to the state governments or to the people.

AMENDMENT 11
Suing the States (1798)

A state government can be sued only in its own courts.

AMENDMENT 12
Election of President and Vice President (1804)

Electors vote for President and Vice President on separate ballots.

AMENDMENT 13
Abolition of Slavery (1865)

Slavery is abolished, or made illegal, in the United States.

AMENDMENT 14
Rights of Citizens (1868)

Every citizen of the United States is also a citizen of the state in which he or she lives. No state may pass a law limiting the rights of citizens or take away a person's life, liberty, or property unfairly. Every person must be treated equally under the law.

AMENDMENT 15
Voting Rights (1870)

No person may be denied the right to vote because of race.

AMENDMENT 16
Income Tax (1913)

Congress has the right to tax people's incomes.

AMENDMENT 17
Direct Election of Senators (1913)

United States senators are elected directly by the people of their states.

AMENDMENT 18
Prohibition (1919)

The manufacture or transport of liquor is prohibited, or banned, in the United States.

AMENDMENT 19
Women's Voting Rights (1920)

Women cannot be denied the right to vote.

AMENDMENT 20
Terms of Office (1933)

The President and Vice President take office on January 20. Senators and representatives take office on January 3.

AMENDMENT 21
Repeal of Prohibition (1933)

Amendment 18 is repealed, or ended.

AMENDMENT 22
Two-Term Limit for Presidents (1951)

A President may serve only two terms in office.

AMENDMENT 23
Presidential Elections for District of Columbia (1961)

People who live in Washington, D.C., have the right to vote for President and Vice President.

AMENDMENT 24
Poll Tax (1964)

No citizen may be made to pay a tax in order to vote for President, Vice President, senator, or representative.

AMENDMENT 25
Presidential Succession and Disability (1967)

If a President leaves office before the end of term, the Vice President becomes President. If the Vice President leaves office, the President suggests a person to fill the job and Congress must approve. If the President becomes too ill to do the job, the Vice President becomes Acting President until the President recovers.

AMENDMENT 26
Voting Age (1971)

Citizens who are at least 18 years old have the right to vote.

IMPORTANT EVENTS

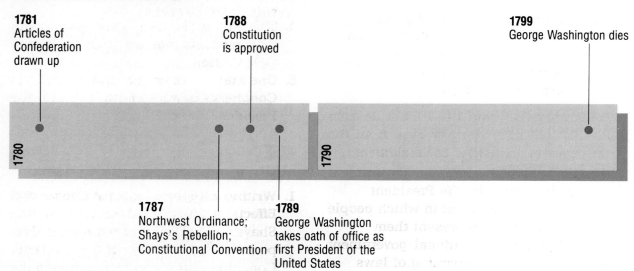

1781
Articles of
Confederation
drawn up

1788
Constitution
is approved

1799
George Washington dies

1780

1790

1787
Northwest Ordinance;
Shays's Rebellion;
Constitutional Convention

1789
George Washington
takes oath of office as
first President of the
United States

PEOPLE TO KNOW

Abigail Adams 1744-1818

Alexander Hamilton 1755-1804

James Madison 1751-1836

Daniel Shays 1747-1825

George Washington 1732-1799

IDEAS TO REMEMBER

- The government that was set up under the Articles of Confederation was weak.
- The delegates at the Constitutional Convention came up with a new plan of government.
- Under the Constitution the federal government is divided into three branches that check and balance each other.
- A new national government took shape under the country's first President, George Washington.

REVIEWING VOCABULARY

amendment	judicial branch
constitution	legislative branch
delegate	political party
executive branch	republic
federal system	veto

Number a paper from 1 to 10. Beside each number write the word or term from the list above that matches the statement.

1. The part of the national government that is headed by the President
2. A type of government in which people elect leaders to represent them
3. The part of the national government that decides the meaning of laws
4. An addition to the Constitution
5. A group of people with similar ideas about government
6. An arrangement where government powers are shared by the states and the national government
7. A written plan of government
8. To refuse to approve a proposed law
9. The part of the national government that passes laws
10. A person chosen by a group of people to represent them

REVIEWING FACTS

Number a paper from 1 to 5. Beside each number write whether the statement is true or false. If it is false, explain why.

1. Under the Articles of Confederation the national government could tax people in the states.
2. The new United States government listened to Abigail Adams and "remembered the ladies."
3. The Constitution set up a national government with two branches.
4. The Preamble lists important rights and freedoms that are protected by the Constitution.
5. One example of checks and balances is Congress's power to pass laws over the President's veto.

WRITING ABOUT MAIN IDEAS

1. **Writing a Report About the Causes and Effects of Shays's Rebellion:** Research Shays's Rebellion and write a brief report about the causes of the rebellion. Conclude your report by discussing the effects of this event.
2. **Writing a Paragraph:** Read the Bill of Rights on page 332. Write a paragraph about how you are affected by the Bill of Rights every day.
3. **Writing a Letter:** Write a letter to George Washington describing the kind of people you think should be selected for his Cabinet. You might want to suggest that he keep in mind their experience, personality, and ideas about government.

BUILDING SKILLS: RECOGNIZING POINT OF VIEW

1. What are some steps you could take to identify the point of view of a writer?
2. Write two sentences about the finished Constitution from the point of view of Abigail Adams and the governor of Rhode Island in 1787.
3. Why is it important to recognize a writer's point of view?

CHAPTER 14

A GROWING NATION

FOCUS

A new world has come into being since the Constitution was adopted.

So said Congressman Henry Clay of Kentucky in 1824. Henry Clay was still a boy when the United States Constitution was approved in 1788. Then he was one of just 3.5 million Americans living in 11 states. By 1824 the United States had undergone changes, however. There were over 10 million Americans living in 24 states. The young nation was growing—and growing fast.

1 Geography of the Growing Nation

READ TO LEARN

Key Vocabulary

pioneer
prairie

Read Aloud

Bring me men to match my mountains,
Bring me men to match my plains.

These are the first lines of "The Coming American," a poem by Sam Walter Foss. In this poem Foss wrote about our country's mountains, forests, and rivers. Such a vast and varied land awaited those with the courage to push past the Appalachian frontier and into the wilderness beyond.

Read for Purpose

1. **WHAT YOU KNOW:** Why did the British try to keep settlers from crossing the Appalachian Mountains before the American Revolution?
2. **WHAT YOU WILL LEARN:** What landforms did settlers find west of the Appalachian Mountains?

BEYOND THE APPALACHIANS

During colonial times, the Appalachians stood like a wall keeping settlers close to the Atlantic shore. Very few Americans had moved into the forests and plains beyond the mountains. After the Revolution, however, pioneers found pathways through these mountains. Pioneers are the first people to settle or enter an area. West of the Appalachians, pioneers moved onto the flat Central Plains.

Looking down on the Central Plains from the Appalachians, pioneers saw an endless stretch of treetops. Hidden below this leafy green canopy was a layer of rich, black soil. The pioneer families who settled here found plenty of good land for farming.

As pioneers moved across the Central Plains, they saw fewer and fewer trees. West of the Mississippi River, these pioneers found miles of gently rolling plains covered with tall, thick grass. These grassy meadows are called prairies. In the battle between trees and grass for growing room, the grasses were clearly winning. Though not as strong or long-lived as trees, grasses will grow in areas where trees wither and die.

Alligators and manatees live in the swamps of the Gulf Coastal Plain.

THE GULF COASTAL PLAIN

While some pioneers moved west onto the Central Plains, others were heading south. There they settled on the Gulf Coastal Plain. You read in Chapter 1 that this wide, well-watered plain borders the Gulf of Mexico from Florida to Texas.

The first American pioneers on the Gulf Coastal Plain found a green world of tangled forests, grassy marshes, and dark swamps. Those bold enough to explore the swamps discovered strange creatures such as alligators and manatees. A manatee is a sea animal with two broad front flippers and a tail shaped like a paddle.

Pioneers on the Gulf Coastal Plain also found dark, fertile soil. An Arkansas storyteller claimed that things grew so well in this soil that planting was "dangerous," at least to his pig. Here he tells why.

The old thief [the pig] stole an ear of corn, and took it down where she slept at night to eat. Well, she left a grain or two on the ground and lay down on them: before morning the corn shot up and . . . killed her dead.

A NEW FRONTIER

As you have read, beyond the Appalachians lay a great wilderness to explore and settle. Vast plains stretched west to the Rocky Mountains and south to the Gulf of Mexico. Here pioneers found forests to clear, swamps to drain, and grasslands to plow. These wide, wild plains were America's next frontier.

Check Your Reading

1. Why did the Appalachian Mountains once keep settlers from moving west?
2. What did pioneers find as they moved west across the Central Plains?
3. **GEOGRAPHY SKILL:** What kinds of landforms did pioneers find south of the Appalachians?
4. **THINKING SKILL:** Classify the land west of the Appalachians into groups. Label each group.

2 Opening the Way West

READ TO LEARN

Key People

Daniel Boone

Key Places

Kentucky
Cumberland Gap
Wilderness Road
Boonesborough

Read Aloud

Hidden under an overhanging rock in the Great Smoky Mountains stands a hut no bigger than a large doghouse. It was once the secret resting place of America's best-known hunter, explorer, and pathfinder—Daniel Boone. Here Boone and other hunters found shelter during long journeys into the wilderness. These were the people who opened the way west.

Read for Purpose

1. **WHAT YOU KNOW:** Where did most Americans live during colonial times?
2. **WHAT YOU WILL LEARN:** What area did Daniel Boone open to settlers?

DANIEL BOONE

Daniel Boone came from a family of pioneers. When Daniel was 16, his family left the Pennsylvania backcountry because they thought it had become too crowded. They moved south to the North Carolina frontier. Young Daniel barely learned how to read and write. His real school was the forest. There he learned how to swing an ax, shoot a rifle, track a bear, and live off the land.

As a young man Boone married, had children, and tried to settle down on a farm. But he missed the freedom and adventure of life in the forest. Soon he was spending more time with his rifle than with his plow.

Boone spent months each year wandering over the eastern slopes of the Appalachians, hunting and trapping. Often he dreamed of crossing the mountains to explore the wilderness on the western side—a land known as Kentucky. Find Kentucky on the map on page 340.

THE LAND OF KENTUCKY

The Cherokee, Shawnee, and Iroquois Indians all looked on Kentucky as a land perfect for hunters. But it was also a battleground where Indians often fought with each other. Their name for this land, *Ken-ta-ke*, means "the dark and bloody ground."

In 1769 Boone and some friends left North Carolina and followed an Indian trail to the west. It took them through a hidden pass in the Appalachian Mountains. The pass they found was a narrow valley which became known as the **Cumberland Gap**.

On the west side of the pass, Boone wrote, they "saw with pleasure the beautiful level of Kentucke." For two years Boone wandered through Kentucky's "vast forests" and hunted its "abundance of wild game."

Boone was determined to bring his family to Kentucky. In 1773 he led a group of five families across the mountains and through the Cumberland Gap. But on the way they were attacked by the Shawnee. Six pioneers were killed. One of them was Boone's son James. The settlers voted to turn back from "the dark and bloody ground."

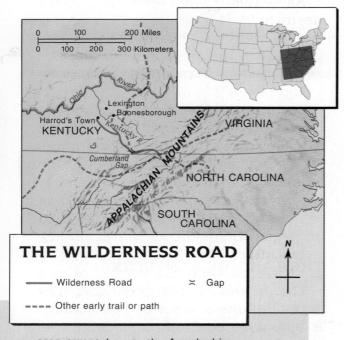

THE WILDERNESS ROAD

Wilderness Road ⪥ Gap

---- Other early trail or path

MAP SKILL: Locate the Appalachian Mountains on the map. What pass did Boone and his friends discover? What lay beyond this pass?

THE WILDERNESS ROAD

In 1775 Boone helped persuade the Cherokee to sell large parts of Kentucky to a land developer. The developer then hired Boone and 30 men to cut a road through the wilderness to the Kentucky River.

Boone led the way, using his ax to blaze, or mark, trees to show the route. His woodsmen followed, cutting down trees and bushes to make a trail. Later, this narrow trail became known as the **Wilderness Road**. You can follow its route on the map on this page.

The group started out in high spirits. But by the time they reached the Kentucky River three months later, they were in "deep gloom." Once again Kentucky had lived up to its name. Along the way they had been attacked by groups of both Shawnee and Cherokee Indians, who still claimed Kentucky's hunting grounds as their own. Boone and his tired men built a settlement called **Boonesborough** beside the Kentucky River. Its first building was a sturdy fort.

Word of the new path across the mountains spread quickly through the backcountry. Pioneers loaded their Conestoga wagons and headed for Kentucky. They soon learned, however, that the Wilderness Road was not a wide, smooth wagon road but rather a rough, stump-filled trail.

For many years, Kentucky-bound pioneers had to carry their belongings across the Appalachians on their backs or on a horse. The trip was long and hard, but few turned back. Some pioneers joked that this was "not because the western country is so good, but because the journey back is so bad."

Daniel Boone was a great pioneer. He explored lands west of the Appalachians and helped to bring settlers there.

During the 1780s, the Wilderness Road was jammed with settlers. By 1792 Kentucky had enough people to become the first state west of the Appalachians. The new state government improved the Wilderness Road, making it wide enough for wagons. Even so, bruised and tired travelers still called the road "the worst on the whole continent."

THE PATHFINDER

By then the Wilderness Road was not the only route across the Appalachians. Other easier ways had been found through the mountains. But Daniel Boone was still honored as "the pathfinder"—the man who had led the way into "the western country."

As Kentucky filled up, Boone felt the desire to head west again. This time he settled west of the Mississippi River. One day a painter came to Boone's cabin to paint his picture. The painter asked Boone if in all his travels he had ever been lost. The pathfinder thought a moment and then answered, "No, but I was right bewildered [confused] once for three days."

 Check Your Reading

1. Why is Daniel Boone known as "the pathfinder"?
2. Why was Kentucky thought of as a "dark and bloody ground"? Why did pioneers want to move there?
3. GEOGRAPHY SKILL: Where did the Wilderness Road lead?
4. THINKING SKILL: Find one fact and one opinion about Daniel Boone in this lesson.

Drawing Conclusions

Key Vocabulary

conclusion

Imagine that you got a 94 on your history test last week. This week, an "A" was written on the top of your report. Today, the teacher excused you from taking a surprise quiz. You might conclude that your studying has paid off.

Drawing a **conclusion** is pulling together pieces of information so that they mean something. A conclusion is an end point of a process. It is a statement that results from thinking about certain information. But it does not repeat any of that information.

Let's compare drawing a conclusion to making your lunch. The sandwich, a piece of fruit, and your drink represent separate pieces of information. All together they are your lunch. But the word *lunch* does not repeat any of the parts included in it. The word *lunch* also gives meaning to the separate pieces that they do not have by themselves.

Trying the Skill

When you read something you should try to remember the facts that the writer tells you. But you should also try to draw conclusions about the information in order to give the facts meaning.

State a conclusion about the early pioneers from the following facts.

- Pioneers moved to the West against the orders of the British government.
- Large mountain ranges separated pioneer settlements from the laws and customs of the East.
- Pioneers built their own homes in the center of their wilderness farms. They banded together only for protection.

1. What conclusion did you draw?
2. What did you do to draw your conclusion?

HELPING YOURSELF

The steps on the left will help you draw conclusions. The example on
the right shows one way to apply these steps to the facts on page 342.

One Way to Draw Conclusions	Example
1. Identify the subject of all the information given.	The subject is the early pioneers of the West.
2. Skim, or quickly read through, the information.	The next step calls for you to read through the information quickly to get the general picture that the facts create.
3. Look for common features.	All the facts give information about the views of the pioneers toward government. For example, they moved west without the government's permission. Pioneers lived far from courts, police officers, and even their neighbors.
4. Write a sentence that tells about the common features and how they are connected to the subject.	One conclusion that you might draw from the information is that the pioneers were independent-minded people.

Applying the Skill

Now apply what you have learned by
drawing a conclusion from the following
list of facts.

A. No hunting is permitted in the Cumberland Gap National Historic Park.

B. There are four campgrounds in the Cumberland Gap Park. Three of these can be reached only by hiking.

C. Water may or may not be available at these Cumberland Gap campsites. When it is available, it should be boiled to make it safe for drinking.

1. What is the subject of all the information given?
   a. national historic parks
   b. wilderness camping
   c. the Cumberland Gap as it is today

2. What common feature does all the information share?
   a. The park has not been developed.
   b. Thousands of people visit the park every year.
   c. The water at the park is unclean.

3. Write a sentence that draws a conclusion from the information given.

Reviewing the Skill

1. What is meant by drawing a conclusion?

2. Name four steps that will help you draw conclusions.

3. Why is it important to draw conclusions about the information you read?

3 The World of Thomas Jefferson

READw TO LEARN

Key Vocabulary

Louisiana Purchase

Key People

Benjamin Banneker
Thomas Jefferson
James Monroe
Meriwether Lewis
William Clark
Sacajawea

Key Places

Washington, D.C.
Missouri River
Snake River
Columbia River

Read Aloud

In 1801 the nation's third President, Thomas Jefferson, moved into the White House. He brought with him his garden tools and his books. During his eight years as President, Jefferson would see Washington, D.C., the new capital city, rise beside the Potomac River. He would also see the nation double in size.

Read for Purpose

1. **WHAT YOU KNOW:** How was the location of the nation's capital decided upon?
2. **WHAT YOU WILL LEARN:** How and why did President Thomas Jefferson double the size of the United States?

WASHINGTON, D.C.—THE NEW CAPITAL

Work had been started on the new capital city while George Washington was President. Washington, D.C., was planned by Pierre L'Enfant, a French architect who had fought with the Americans during the Revolution. In 1791 President Washington asked Benjamin Banneker to help lay out the new city. Banneker, a mathematician, surveyed, or measured, the size and shape of the land. He was the first African-American appointed by a President to work for the government.

By the time Thomas Jefferson became President in 1801, the capital was still little more than a "swamp in the wilderness." Most government buildings, including the White House, were not finished. The street connecting the White House to the Capitol building, where Congress met, was little more than a muddy path through the woods.

Jefferson complained often about the "noise, the heat, the stench [smell] and the bustle" of the growing city. Still, he wanted all Americans to feel that this

President Thomas Jefferson (*bottom left*) saw Washington, D.C., including the Capitol building (*top right*) take shape. Benjamin Banneker (*top left*) surveyed and helped lay out the new city.

new city, like the government it housed, belonged to them. He opened the White House each morning to visitors. While George Washington and John Adams had greeted citizens with a stiff bow, Jefferson warmly shook their hands.

THE LOUISIANA PURCHASE

Soon after taking office, Jefferson learned that Spain had returned Louisiana to France. You read in Chapter 11 that Spain had been given this huge territory in 1763 at the end of the French and Indian War.

The news that France now controlled Louisiana worried Jefferson. A look at this area on the map on page 346 will show you why. Jefferson feared that France, with its strong army and navy, might close New Orleans to Americans. Western farmers sent their crops down the Mississippi River to be sold in that port city.

As President, Jefferson sent his friend James Monroe to France with an offer to buy New Orleans. To his surprise, Monroe returned with an agreement to buy not only New Orleans but all of Louisiana from France. The price was $15 million.

Jefferson could hardly believe the news. Here was a chance to double the size of the United States at the then bargain price of about four cents an acre. But not everyone was in favor of the purchase. Some said the land was worthless. Others worried about the cost. Still, Congress approved the Louisiana Purchase in 1803.

THE LEWIS AND CLARK EXPEDITION

Jefferson was filled with questions about the new territory. His maps showed Louisiana as an empty space stretching from the Mississippi River to the Rocky Mountains. He knew nothing about this land except the tall tales told by trappers.

345

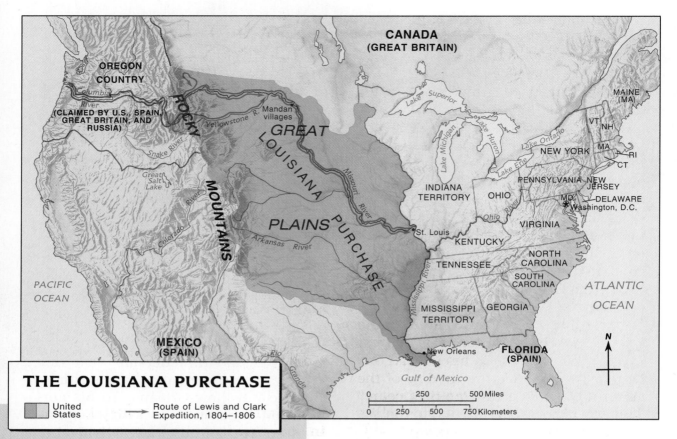

THE LOUISIANA PURCHASE

■ United States

→ Route of Lewis and Clark Expedition, 1804–1806

MAP SKILL: Use the map to locate the route taken by Lewis and Clark. Which rivers did they travel along?

In 1804 Jefferson sent an expedition led by **Meriwether Lewis** and **William Clark** to explore Louisiana. He told them to take notes about everything they saw—landforms, plants, animals, and Indians.

On a rainy May morning in 1804, the Lewis and Clark expedition left St. Louis, Missouri, in three boats. The crew of 47 included soldiers, woodsmen, and trappers. You can follow their route on the map above.

The explorers moved slowly west along the **Missouri River**. It was hard going. Rowing left their hands blistered. Boats caught on hidden snags.

Mosquitoes drew blood. But the explorers were rewarded by views of vast prairies sprinkled with spring flowers.

SACAJAWEA

The expedition spent the winter with the Mandan Indians beside the great bend of the Missouri River. There a French fur trapper and his wife, a Shoshone Indian named **Sacajawea** (sak ə jə wē′ ə), joined the expedition. As a young girl, Sacajawea had been forced to live with the Mandan Indians. Lewis and Clark hoped she would translate for them when they reached Shoshone country.

In the spring of 1805, the explorers continued west along the Missouri River. Now rapids and waterfalls slowed them down. Grizzly bears raided their camps for food.

By August the plains lay behind them. Ahead they saw the snow-covered peaks of the Rocky Mountains "glittering with the reflection of the sun." For Sacajawea, this was the land of her childhood.

One day a group of Shoshone approached. Clark watched as Sacajawea began "to dance and show every mark of extravagant joy." She had found her people, and her brother was now their chief. Sacajawea acted as translator for the expedition. With her help, Lewis and Clark persuaded the Shoshone chief to help them cross the Rockies before the first snows of autumn.

From the Rockies, Lewis and Clark followed the Snake River and then the Columbia River to the sea. "Great joy . . ." Clark wrote in his journal one December day. "We are in view of the Ocean . . . this great Pacific Ocean." The expedition spent the winter on the Oregon coast.

THE EXPEDITION RETURNS

In September 1806, after being away for two years, the ragged, bearded explorers returned to St. Louis. By now most Americans had given them up for dead. But the expedition had lost only one man, who had died when his appendix burst.

Later, Jefferson welcomed Lewis and Clark with "unspeakable joy." He was even happier when he saw the plants, animals, and boxes of notes and maps they had brought back with them.

"A WIDE AND FRUITFUL LAND"

When Jefferson became President in 1801, he had seen the United States as "a rising nation, spread over a wide and fruitful land." By the time he left

Sacajawea accompanied Lewis and Clark on their exploration of the Louisiana Territory. When and where did she join Lewis and Clark?

office in 1809, the country had doubled in size thanks to the Louisiana Purchase. And Lewis and Clark had begun the exploration of the western lands.

Someday, Jefferson knew, pioneers would spread into the new territory. Then it too would become part of America's "wide and fruitful land."

Check Your Reading

1. Describe Washington, D.C., at the time Jefferson became President.
2. How did Sacajawea help Lewis and Clark?
3. GEOGRAPHY SKILL: What was the Louisiana Purchase? Why was it so important to the United States?
4. THINKING SKILL: What kinds of information would you need to determine the accuracy of Lewis and Clark's notes on the Louisiana Territory?

347

4 The War of 1812

READ TO LEARN

Key Vocabulary

neutral
War Hawks

Key People

James Madison
Oliver Hazard Perry
Dolley Madison
Francis Scott Key
Andrew Jackson

Key Places

Baltimore
Fort McHenry

Read Aloud

"Clear out! Clear out!" shouted a man on horseback. He was trying to warn Dolley Madison that British troops were attacking Washington, D.C. She thought back to her first day in the White House as President James Madison's wife. There had been a great party to honor the nation's fourth President. That night people had said she "looked like a queen."

On this August day in 1814, Dolley Madison did not feel like a queen. For two years the United States had been at war with Great Britain. Now the capital city was being invaded.

Read for Purpose

1. **WHAT YOU KNOW:** What was the first war in which America fought Great Britain?
2. **WHAT YOU WILL LEARN:** Why did the United States go to war with Great Britain in 1812?

THE WAR HAWKS

When **James Madison** became President in 1809, Great Britain and France were at war in Europe. Madison tried to keep the United States **neutral** (nü' trəl)—not taking sides. But a group of young western Congressmen did not want to remain neutral. These **War Hawks** pushed the country toward war with Great Britain.

The War Hawks were angry about British attacks on American ships and sailors. Many American trading ships heading for France had been captured by British warships. Thousands of sailors had been kidnapped and made to serve in the British navy.

The War Hawks also blamed Britain for Indian attacks on their frontier settlements. They were sure that the British in Canada were giving the Indians guns. There could be no peace on the frontier, they said, until the British were out of North America.

The War Hawks had another reason for wanting war with Britain. They dreamed of adding Canada to the United States. Amid shouts of "On to Canada" and "Free trade and sailors' rights," Congress declared war on Britain in June 1812.

THE WAR AT SEA

When the War of 1812 began, many people were sure that conquering Canada would be easy, "a mere matter of marching." Instead, all attacks on Canada failed. The Americans were beaten back again and again.

The war at sea went better than the land war. On August 19, 1812, the American warship *Constitution* sank one of Britain's finest warships, the *Guerrière* (gair rē âr'). British cannon-balls seemed to bounce off the *Constitution*'s thick oak sides. "Her sides are made of iron!" yelled a member of the ship's crew. From then on, the *Constitution* was known as "Old Ironsides."

A long string of American sea victories ended in June 1813, when the British captured the American warship *Chesapeake*. The *Chesapeake*'s captain, James Lawrence, died defending his ship. But his last words lived on in history to inspire generations of American sailors. "Don't give up the ship," Lawrence said as the battle raged around him.

On Lake Erie, Captain Oliver Hazard Perry used Lawrence's last words as a

The American ship, the *Constitution*, meets the British ship, the *Guerrière*, in battle. Today the *Constitution* is docked near Boston. It is the oldest warship afloat.

The Granger Collection

motto for his tiny fleet of ships. Perry won control of the lake in a fierce battle with several British ships. When the battle ended, he said, "We have met the enemy and they are ours."

"THE STAR-SPANGLED BANNER"

In the summer of 1814 British troops captured Washington, D.C., and set it on fire. **Dolley Madison** was in the White House when the British invaded the city. A friend came to warn her and take her away. But brave Dolley Madison did not leave without first saving important state papers and a famous painting of George Washington. The First Lady escaped just in time. The dinner she left behind was still hot when British troops broke into the White House.

The next British target was the city of **Baltimore**, Maryland. To reach it,

British ships had to sail past **Fort McHenry**. A huge American flag flew over the fort.

On September 13, 1814, British ships began pounding Fort McHenry with rockets and bombs. A Washington lawyer named **Francis Scott Key** watched the battle over the fort anxiously. As long as the American flag still flew, he knew the fort had not surrendered.

All night long Francis Scott Key watched "the rockets' red glare, the bombs bursting in air." At daybreak he was thrilled to see a tattered American flag still waving over the fort.

Key wrote down what he saw and felt in a stirring poem called "The Star-Spangled Banner." His poem was set to music and later became our national anthem. Read the words of the anthem on the next page.

The British burned the Capitol, the White House, and other buildings when they captured Washington, D.C., in 1814. What did Dolley Madison save as she fled?

THE STAR-SPANGLED BANNER

Music attributed to J. S. Smith

Words by Francis Scott Key

Oh, — say! can you see, by the dawn's ear-ly light,

What so proud-ly we hailed at the twi-light's last gleam-ing?

Whose broad stripes and bright stars, through the per-il-ous fight,

O'er the ram-parts we watched were so gal-lant-ly stream-ing?

And the rock-ets' red glare, the bombs burst-ing in air,

Gave proof through the night that our flag was still there.

O, say, does that — Star-Span-gled Ban-ner — yet — wave —

O'er the land — of the free and the home of the brave?

The Battle of New Orleans was the last battle of the War of 1812. Why was it an unnecessary battle?

THE END OF THE WAR

Early in 1815 the British attacked New Orleans. General Andrew Jackson put together an army of freed blacks, pirates, and Indian fighters to save the city. In one terrible day of fighting, the British lost more than 2,000 men. The Americans lost fewer than 50. One soldier wrote that the battleground "looked at first glance like a sea of blood."

Andrew Jackson's great victory in the Battle of New Orleans thrilled Americans. What they did not know was that the battle should never have been fought. A peace agreement ending the War of 1812 had been signed in Europe two weeks earlier. Today, of course, the world would have known about the peace agreement within hours after the signing. But in 1814 it took several weeks for the news to cross the Atlantic Ocean and reach the United States.

A NEW SENSE OF PRIDE

The War of 1812 settled very little. Still, Americans felt a new sense of pride in their country. Once again they had fought against Great Britain to protect their rights.

This was the last time that the two largest English-speaking nations met on the battlefield as enemies. From that time on they solved their problems with words, not bullets.

Check Your Reading

1. Why did the War Hawks want to fight Great Britain?
2. What happened to the city of Washington, D.C., during the War of 1812?
3. Why did Francis Scott Key write "The Star-Spangled Banner"?
4. **THINKING SKILL:** Arrange the major events discussed in this lesson in the order in which they occurred.

352

5 The World of Andrew Jackson

READ TO LEARN

Key Vocabulary

Trail of Tears

Key People

Andrew Jackson
Osceola
Sequoyah

Key Places

Indian Territory
Oklahoma

Read Aloud

Margaret Smith had lived in Washington, D.C., for many years. She had seen many things in her day. But on the morning of March 4, 1829, she could hardly believe her eyes. An enormous crowd had gathered in the capital city to watch Andrew Jackson become President. Afterward, everyone went to the White House to celebrate.

When the White House doors were opened, the crowd surged in. Punch was spilled. Men with muddy boots stood on satin-covered chairs to see the new President. Poor Jackson, Smith wrote, was nearly "pressed to death" by the crowd. He barely escaped out a back door. "It was," she said, "the People's day." And Jackson was "the People's President."

Read for Purpose

1. **WHAT YOU KNOW:** Which battle in the War of 1812 made Andrew Jackson a hero?
2. **WHAT YOU WILL LEARN:** How did democracy grow during the time Jackson was President?

THE GROWTH OF DEMOCRACY

There was a reason visitors from all over the country crowded into the White House that day. Never before had so many "common people" helped to elect a President.

In the early days of the country, voting was limited to white men who owned property. Only such men, it was said, had enough education and experience to vote wisely.

Along the western frontier, though, a man was not measured by what he owned. There all men, rich or poor, educated or not, faced the same problems and dangers. They believed they should share the same rights, including the right to vote.

The frontier states were the first to give all white men the vote. Soon the older states followed their example. But women, blacks, and Indians could not yet vote. Even so, giving the vote to more men was an important step in the growth of democracy.

"THE PEOPLE'S PRESIDENT"

Andrew Jackson was popular with these new voters. Born on the South Carolina frontier, he later moved to Tennessee. Like so many westerners, he was a "self-made man." He had had little schooling, but he had taught himself enough law to become a lawyer and a judge.

Jackson was also a tireless military leader, often going for days without sleep. "He's tough as old hickory," his men would say. Hickory wood was the hardest living thing they knew. And Jackson was like that wood—strong and unbreakable. The nickname "Old

Andrew Jackson was elected President in 1828. His election was seen as a victory for the "common man."

The Granger Collection

Hickory" followed him from his fighting days.

In 1828 Jackson ran for President. He was the candidate of a new political party called the Democratic Party. The Democrats worked hard to reach the new voters, even those who could not read. They held parades, picnics, and dinners for "Old Hickory." They stuck hickory poles everywhere—on signposts, steeples, and street corners.

"Planting hickory sticks!" complained one newspaper. "What have hickory trees to do with . . . the great contest?" But when the votes were counted, it was clear that the Democrats' campaign had worked.

More than twice as many men voted in 1828 as had voted in 1824. Their votes made Andrew Jackson President. Americans saw this great turnout of voters as a victory for democracy and the "common man."

INDIAN REMOVAL

As President of the United States, Andrew Jackson worked hard to solve the country's problems. None was more difficult than the conflict between settlers and Indians. Jackson had spent years fighting Indians along the frontier. He knew how much suffering this warfare brought to both sides.

Jackson believed the only way to end the fighting was to "remove" all Indians from lands east of the Mississippi River. Unless this was done, he said, the Indians would be destroyed. Their way of life would "disappear and be forgotten." He suggested that the Indians be sent to new homelands on the Great Plains.

Many people were against Jackson's idea. They thought the land west of the Mississippi River was a desert. How, some asked, could Jackson send Indians to certain death in this wasteland?

Despite such arguments, Congress passed the Indian Removal Act in 1830. The act called for the removal of all eastern Indians from their homelands. They would have to move to a new Indian Territory in present-day Oklahoma.

THE TRAIL OF TEARS

Jackson hoped to persuade the Indians to leave their lands peacefully. In a letter to the Creek Indians of Alabama and Florida he wrote:

Friends and brothers, listen. Where you are now, you and my white children are too near to each other to live in harmony and peace. . . . Beyond the great river Mississippi . . . your white brothers will not trouble you . . . and you can live there as long as the grass grows or the water runs, in peace and plenty.

Some Indian groups were persuaded by Jackson to move west. Many Creeks, however, refused to go. They were rounded up by troops and forced to march west in handcuffs.

The Seminole did not want to leave their Florida homeland. Led by a young chief named Osceola (os ē ō′ lə), they fought removal for ten years. Finally, most of the Seminole also were forced to move to the Indian Territory. But some hid in the Florida swamps and never went west.

The Cherokee of Georgia also refused to leave their homeland. The Cherokee had adopted many of the settlers' ways. They had given up hunting to become farmers. A Cherokee named Sequoyah (si kwoi′ ə) had invented an alphabet for his language. Many Cherokees had learned to read and write in their own language. Soon they published a newspaper written in both Cherokee and English.

The Indian Removal Act of 1830 forced all eastern Indians to leave their lands. Men, women, and children had to make a long, hard journey to the new Indian Territory.

The Granger Collection

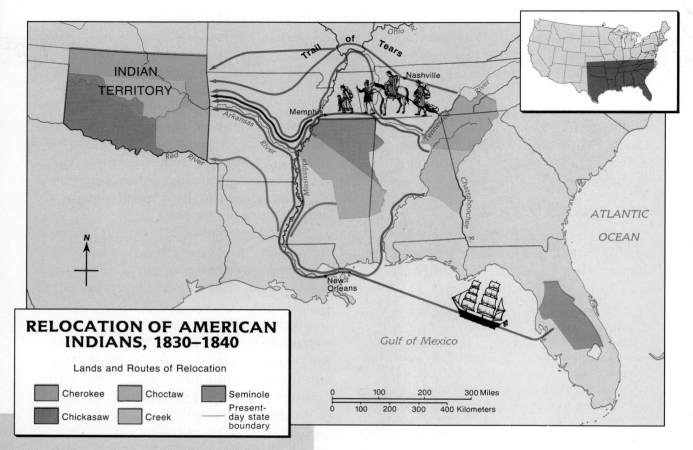

RELOCATION OF AMERICAN INDIANS, 1830–1840

Lands and Routes of Relocation

- Cherokee
- Chickasaw
- Choctaw
- Creek
- Seminole
- —— Present-day state boundary

MAP SKILL: Use the map to trace the routes of the Indians as they moved west. Which group called their route the **Trail of Tears?**

After a long fight, the Cherokee were driven out of Georgia. Those who tried to stay were dragged from their homes and loaded onto wagons. A soldier who helped in the removal called this "the cruelest work I ever knew."

About 15,000 Cherokees made the long journey to the Indian Territory. About 4,000 of them died along the way from cold, sickness, and hunger. The Cherokee who survived would always remember the route west as their **Trail of Tears**.

SUCCESS AND SORROW

After two terms as President, Jackson left office in 1837. By then the frontier had reached the Mississippi River. The country had grown to 26 states.

For most Americans, such growth was a good sign. But the Indians who had lived east of the Mississippi felt differently. For them the growth of the United States had brought only sorrow.

Check Your Reading

1. Why was Andrew Jackson called "the People's President"?
2. Why did more men vote for President in 1828 than in 1824?
3. **GEOGRAPHY SKILL:** What happened to the Indians living east of the Mississippi River?
4. **THINKING SKILL:** Based on Andrew Jackson's letter on page 355, what do you think was his point of view about the Indians?

Getting Out ★★★ The Vote ★★★

When Andrew Jackson was elected President in 1828, only white men were allowed to vote. Today all Americans at least 18 years old can vote. But many people do not bother to vote. They do not believe their vote makes a difference. Beatrice Gallego (gi yā′ gō) knows better. She has worked hard to show people that voting can bring about important changes.

All too often Beatrice watched her children wade to school through streets which were flooded by rain. It made her angry that her Mexican-American neighborhood in San Antonio, Texas, did not get its fair share of storm drains and other city services. Beatrice wanted better conditions

for her family. She wanted good schools, new parks, and libraries.

The neighborhood where Beatrice lived was not the only part of San Antonio with problems. Other communities also needed new schools and new parks. Soon neighborhood groups were formed to improve life in San Antonio.

At first, no one at city hall listened to the demands of these neighborhood groups. Then someone came up with the idea of forming one large, citywide organization. The new group was called COPS, for Communities Organized for Public Service.

Beatrice Gallego was one of the first presidents of COPS. She learned as much as she could about the issues that concerned the groups' members.

Despite the creation of COPS, many in San Antonio still believed that things would not change. "What good is my vote?" they would say. Beatrice answered by explaining the difference that voting could make in their lives. Voters not only choose representatives, she said. They also decide about community projects.

Beatrice and other members of COPS quickly went into action. In two weeks they signed up over 13,000 new voters. Going from house to house, Beatrice registered thousands of people—both young and old. The next election proved her point. COPS members and new voters elected people who shared their goals.

Beatrice is still registering, educating, and encouraging voters. She has helped to make San Antonio a city that understands the rights and responsibilities of voting.

IMPORTANT EVENTS

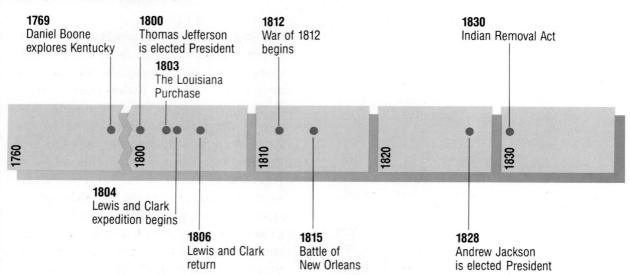

1769
Daniel Boone
explores Kentucky

1800
Thomas Jefferson
is elected President

1803
The Louisiana
Purchase

1812
War of 1812
begins

1830
Indian Removal Act

1760

1800

1810

1820

1830

1804
Lewis and Clark
expedition begins

1806
Lewis and Clark
return

1815
Battle of
New Orleans

1828
Andrew Jackson
is elected President

PEOPLE TO KNOW

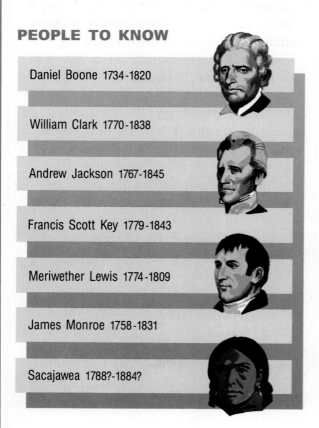

Daniel Boone 1734-1820

William Clark 1770-1838

Andrew Jackson 1767-1845

Francis Scott Key 1779-1843

Meriwether Lewis 1774-1809

James Monroe 1758-1831

Sacajawea 1788?-1884?

IDEAS TO REMEMBER

- Pioneers who settled west of the Appalachians found a land of forests, swamps, and grasslands.
- Led by Daniel Boone, many settlers went to the frontier to start new farms and businesses.
- As President, Thomas Jefferson doubled the size of the United States by purchasing the Louisiana Territory.
- Troubles with Great Britain led to the War of 1812.
- While Andrew Jackson was President, more and more people took part in the government. But the Indians in the East were forced to leave their homes.

2 Getting from Place to Place

READ TO LEARN

Key Vocabulary

flatboat
steamboat
canal
lock

Key People

Robert Fulton
DeWitt Clinton
Peter Cooper

Key Places

Erie Canal

Read Aloud

"Old America seems to be breaking up and moving westward," an English traveler wrote in the early 1800s. Americans were spreading out. And as they did, they needed better ways of getting from place to place.

Read for Purpose

1. **WHAT YOU KNOW:** What happened to the frontier after the American Revolution?
2. **WHAT YOU WILL LEARN:** How did transportation improve during the 1800s?

BUILDING BETTER ROADS

In 1800 most roads in America were narrow, stump-filled paths. When dry, they were so deeply rutted that wagon and stagecoach riders were constantly bouncing up and down. When wet, the same roads became swamps. Wagons and coaches often got stuck in the mud. Then passengers had to jump out and push, the mud oozing over their boots. Sometimes horses almost drowned in muddy pits while wagons sank slowly out of sight.

In the early 1800s, Americans began building better roads. They were wide and paved with crushed rocks. When it rained, they did not become wagon traps. Most were toll roads. Every few miles travelers came to a pike, or pole, across the road. After paying their toll, the pike was turned aside to let them pass. This is why toll roads were often called turnpikes.

STEAMBOATS

Even with better roads, most people preferred to travel by water. River travel was faster and cheaper than going by land.

Many pioneers made part of their journey west on large rafts that are called **flatboats**. Later they used the same boats to ship their crops down the Mississippi River to New Orleans. There was just one problem with flatboats. They could not travel upstream against the river current. To get upstream, flatboats had to be pulled by animals that walked along the shore.

Robert Fulton, a painter turned inventor, built a new kind of boat that could go upstream. It was powered by a steam engine. Fulton named his steamboat the *Clermont*. But it looked so strange that most people called it "Fulton's Folly."

On August 17, 1807, Fulton was ready to take his "furnace on a raft" up the Hudson River from New York City to Albany. When he fired up the *Clermont's* engine, it showered him with sparks and soot. Then, to almost everyone's surprise, the steamboat began to chug upstream.

News of the trial run traveled faster than the boat's 5 miles (8 km) an hour. People lined the river to see the smoke-belching monster. The *Clermont* traveled 150 miles (240 km) to Albany in just 32 hours. Fulton later wrote, "I overtook many boats and passed them as if they had been at anchor. The power of the steamboat is now fully proved." He was right. Soon steamboats were a common sight on lakes and rivers.

THE ERIE CANAL

"Rivers are ungovernable things," wrote Ben Franklin. "Canals are quiet and always manageable." A canal is a narrow waterway dug for boat travel. Unlike rivers, canals go where people build them.

Governor DeWitt Clinton of New York dreamed of building a canal to

Robert Fulton built the first successful steamboat, the *Clermont*. As a child, Fulton made pencils, tools, skyrockets, and even a paddle wheel for a rowboat.

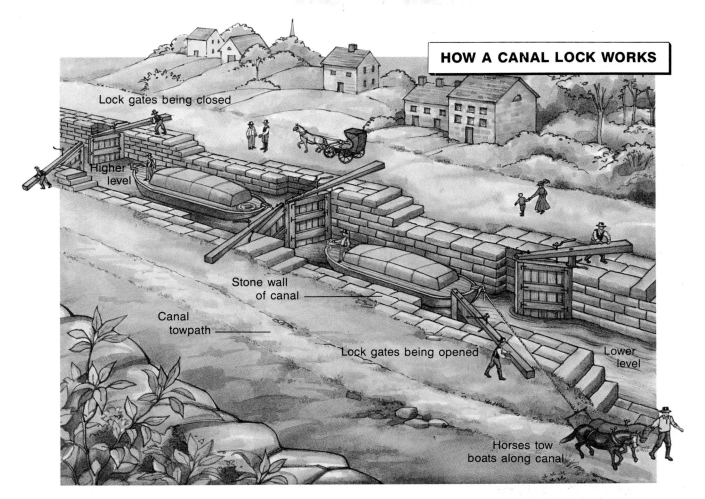

Lock gates being closed

Higher level

Stone wall of canal

Canal towpath

Lock gates being opened

Lower level

Horses tow boats along canal

DIAGRAM SKILL: The Erie Canal joined Lake Erie with the Hudson River. The diagram shows a barge in one of the **locks**. What is a lock?

link the Hudson River with Lake Erie. With such a canal, it would be easy to ship goods from the Northeast to the West. In the early 1800s, the country's only canals were just a few miles long. Clinton's canal would run for hundreds of miles through a swampy, woody wilderness. Thomas Jefferson said that Clinton's idea was "little short of madness."

Madness, perhaps. But Clinton and his fellow New Yorkers decided to make their dream come true. In 1817 work began on the **Erie Canal**. Thousands of workers used picks and shovels to dig a shallow ditch 40 feet (12 m) wide and 363 miles (584 km) long. Since Lake Erie is higher than the Hudson River, they had to build 83 **locks**. A

lock is a kind of water elevator that moves boats to higher or lower levels. The diagram above shows how a canal lock works.

In 1825 "Clinton's big ditch" was finished, and it was an instant success. The cost of shipping dropped dramatically. Before the Erie Canal was built, it cost $100 a ton to send goods by land from Lake Erie to New York City. After 1825, the cost dropped to ten dollars a ton. At that price western farmers could ship their crops to eastern cities. New York City quickly became the country's busiest port.

TRANSPORTATION IN THE EASTERN UNITED STATES, 1860

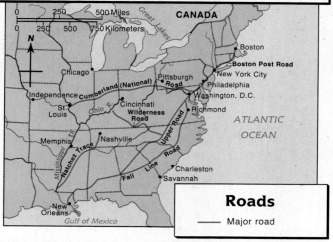

Roads

—— Major road

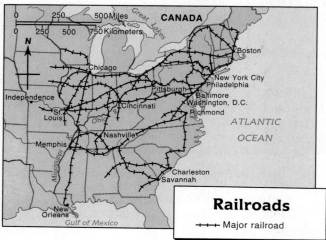

Railroads

+++ Major railroad

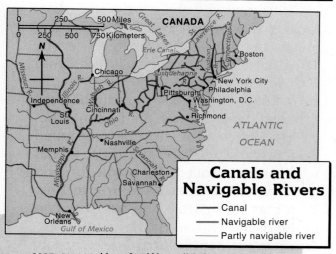

Canals and Navigable Rivers

—— Canal
—— Navigable river
—— Partly navigable river

MAP SKILL: How far West did the country's transportation system extend in 1860?

THE IRON HORSE

The success of the Erie Canal set off a wave of canal building. But by 1860 many of those canals were muddy memories. A new form of transportation took their place—the railroad.

The country's first road made of iron rails was built in 1826. It was used to move large blocks of stone in carts pulled by horses. A Boston newspaper reported that "twenty-one tons was moved with ease by a single horse."

A year later, a group of Baltimore business leaders decided to build a railroad to the Ohio Valley. You can see the route of that railroad on the map on this page. They had seen how the Erie Canal brought farm products from the Central Plains to New York City. They wanted to bring some of that business to Baltimore.

The Baltimore & Ohio Railroad Company was soon laying tracks. Most people thought that horses would pull wagons along the rails. But a self-taught mechanic named **Peter Cooper** had a different idea. "I will knock an engine together in six weeks," he said, "that will pull carriages [train cars] ten miles an hour."

Cooper put together a steam engine on a cart. It was so small that people called it the *Tom Thumb* or the "teakettle on wheels." But the engine did what Cooper had promised and more. On its fifth run in 1830 the *Tom Thumb* reached the amazing speed of 18 miles (29 km) an hour. A horse-drawn train traveled at about 6 miles (10 km) an hour.

Baltimore's local stagecoach companies did not like the idea of competing with steam engines. They set up a race to show that a horse pulling a car on rails could outrun any "iron horse."

Peter Cooper's *Tom Thumb* races a horse in a contest of speed. Who won—the horse or the steam engine? A more recent steam engine is shown at the left.

At the start of the race, the horse dashed ahead while the engine gained speed slowly. But before long, a witness wrote:

> . . . the race was neck and neck, nose and nose—then the engine passed the horse, and a great hurrah hailed the victory.

The cheering ended suddenly when the engine broke down. The horse galloped on to victory. Still, Cooper had proved that steam engines could haul larger loads than horses and move them faster. Soon people were building railroads in many parts of the country. By 1860 Americans could travel by rail between most large cities and as far west as the Mississippi River.

AMAZING PROGRESS

In 1837 David Stevenson, a Scottish engineer, wrote about America's amazing progress in transportation. He described the great changes that had taken place.

> Thirty years ago, the United States had but one steamboat and one short canal. And now its rivers and lakes are navigated by between five and six hundred steamboats, and its canals are upwards of 2,700 miles in length. Ten years ago there were but 3 miles of railway in the country, and now there are no less than 1,600 miles in operation.

Getting people and goods from place to place had never been easier.

Check Your Reading

1. Why was the steamboat an important invention?
2. What happened to shipping prices after the Erie Canal was built? Why did this happen?
3. **GEOGRAPHY SKILL:** What was another name for the Cumberland Road?
4. **THINKING SKILL:** Why can Clinton, Fulton, and Cooper be described as pioneers?

3 The Growth of Factories

READ TO LEARN

Key Vocabulary

cotton gin
mass production

Key People

Eli Whitney
Samuel Slater
Francis Cabot Lowell

Key Places

Waltham
Lowell

Read Aloud

The young man from Massachusetts listened politely to the planters' complaints. Tobacco prices were low, they said. Rice and indigo prices were not much better. Cotton grew well, but cleaning the seeds out of cotton was a big problem. A slave could clean only a few pounds a day. At that rate, there was no money in raising cotton.

As they talked, a solution to their problem took shape in the young man's head. Not only would it give the planters a cash crop, but it would also encourage the growth of the first factories in the United States.

Read for Purpose

1. **WHAT YOU KNOW:** What is a cash crop?
2. **WHAT YOU WILL LEARN:** What inventions led to the growth of factories?

ELI WHITNEY'S COTTON GIN

The young man from Massachusetts was Eli Whitney. In 1792 Whitney went to Georgia to study law. But he found the cotton problem so interesting that he "struck out a plan of a machine in my mind." Six months later he tested his cotton engine, or "gin" for short. One person using Whitney's cotton gin could clean 50 times as much cotton as a person working by hand.

Few machines brought such important changes as the cotton gin. All over the South planters began growing cotton. You can see the result in the graph on page 369. Cotton replaced tobacco as the leading cash crop in the South.

As fields of cotton spread across the South, the demand for slave labor increased. Workers were needed to clear land, plant cotton, and then pick the fluffy white crop. Most planters used slaves to do this work and could not imagine growing cotton without them.

The snowy fiber pouring out of cotton gins also changed life in New England. The country's first factories were built there to turn cotton into cloth.

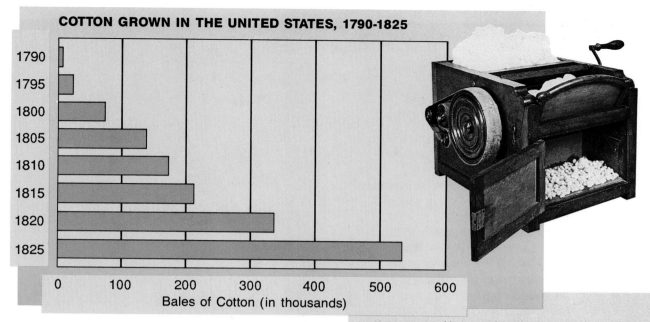

COTTON GROWN IN THE UNITED STATES, 1790-1825

Year	Bales of Cotton (in thousands)
1790	~5
1795	~30
1800	~75
1805	~140
1810	~170
1815	~210
1820	~335
1825	~530

Bales of Cotton (in thousands)

GRAPH SKILL: How much cotton was produced in 1800 as a result of the cotton gin? In 1825?

SAMUEL SLATER'S SPINNING MILLS

At first, most of the South's cotton crop was shipped to Great Britain. The British had invented machines that could spin cotton into thread and weave cotton cloth. They tried to keep these inventions secret. No one was allowed to take the machines or plans for them out of Britain. But a young Englishman named Samuel Slater had other ideas. Slater memorized every part of a spinning machine. Then he left for the United States.

A wealthy merchant named Moses Brown helped Slater build a water-powered spinning mill in Rhode Island. Their first mill began spinning cotton in 1790. Soon they had more mills spinning thread beside New England's rivers.

FRANCIS LOWELL'S FACTORIES

A Bostonian named Francis Cabot Lowell decided that making cloth was a good business. Cotton thread had been spun in one mill and then woven into cloth elsewhere. Lowell decided to combine these steps in one factory.

In 1813 Lowell and his partners built their first factory in Waltham, Massachusetts. The falling waters of the Charles River turned a water wheel beside the factory. Big leather belts moved by the spinning water wheel kept the machines inside working. Raw cotton went into one end of the factory. Woven cloth came out of the other end.

At first Lowell had trouble finding men to work in his mills. So he decided to hire farm girls to run the machines. At the time, few jobs were open to women, so they were willing to work for half as much money as men. Lowell built boarding houses near the factory for the mill girls to live in.

The Waltham factory was so successful that Lowell's partners bought up land by the falls of the Merrimack River. There they decided to build a much larger factory with several mills.

369

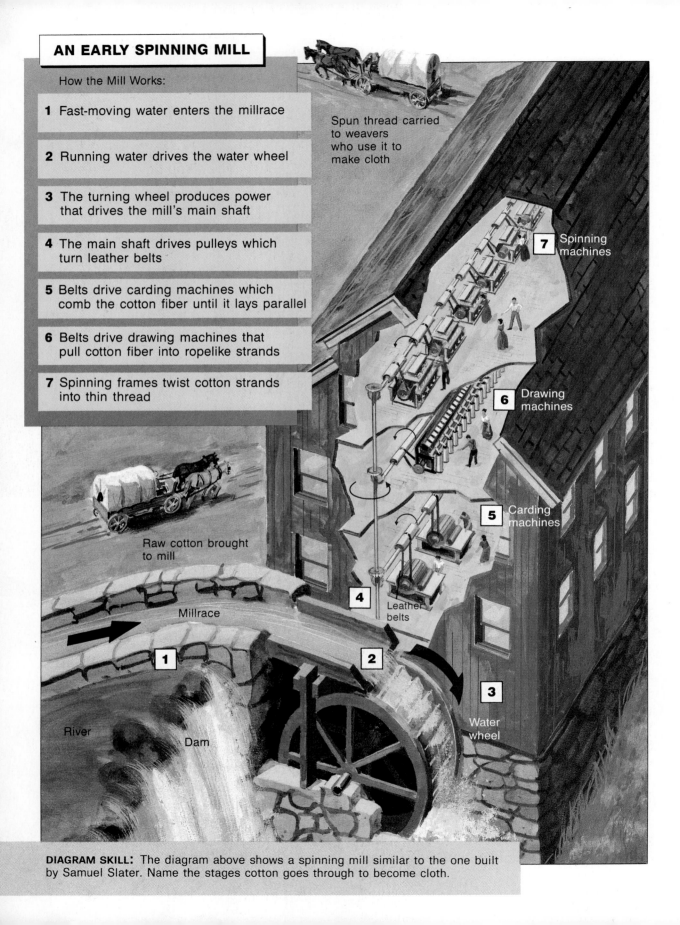

AN EARLY SPINNING MILL

How the Mill Works:

1 Fast-moving water enters the millrace

2 Running water drives the water wheel

3 The turning wheel produces power that drives the mill's main shaft

4 The main shaft drives pulleys which turn leather belts

5 Belts drive carding machines which comb the cotton fiber until it lays parallel

6 Belts drive drawing machines that pull cotton fiber into ropelike strands

7 Spinning frames twist cotton strands into thin thread

Spun thread carried to weavers who use it to make cloth

7 Spinning machines

6 Drawing machines

5 Carding machines

4 Leather belts

Raw cotton brought to mill

Millrace

1

2

3

River

Dam

Water wheel

DIAGRAM SKILL: The diagram above shows a spinning mill similar to the one built by Samuel Slater. Name the stages cotton goes through to become cloth.

They named this new town Lowell. They wanted Lowell to be "a shining example of . . . Yankee ideals; profit and virtue, doing good and doing well."

For a time, Lowell was a shining example. Visitors described the town as "clean" and "healthy." The mill girls seemed "well dressed and lively."

Lucy Larcom was 11 years old when she went to work in Lowell. At first she liked mill work "better than going to school." The hours were long—from 5:00 A.M. to 7:00 P.M. But the work was not hard. Lucy lived in a boarding house. The girls there slept six to a room, two to a bed. In the evening they took classes, heard lectures, or read in the Lowell Library.

Soon Lucy wished she could leave the mill. The price of cotton cloth dropped in the late 1830s. Wages were cut and the workday was made even longer. Workers who complained were fired. As one mill manager said:

> I regard my work-people just as I regard my machinery. So long as they can do my work for what I choose to pay them, I keep them, getting out of them all I can.

MASS PRODUCTION

Eli Whitney, Samuel Slater, and Francis Lowell were pioneers in mass production. Each used machines to do jobs once done by hand. With those machines, workers could produce larger amounts of goods in less time. Soon other Americans followed their example.

FACTORIES BEGIN TO BOOM

You have read how Whitney's cotton gin led to the spread of cotton fields and slavery across the South. Cotton

Women were the first workers in the early textile mills of the United States. Later, children were used as workers in the mills.

soon became the "king" of southern crops. Slater and Lowell moved cloth making out of the home and into the factory. Wherever there were swift-flowing rivers, factories were built to produce many kinds of goods. The pioneers in mass production were changing the American landscape.

 Check Your Reading

1. What changes did the cotton gin bring about in the South?
2. Why were many early factories located on the fall line?
3. What was life like for a mill girl?
4. **THINKING SKILL:** Was Francis Lowell's decision to hire women a good decision? Why or why not?

BUILDING SKILLS
STUDY AND RESEARCH SKILLS

Using the Library

Key Vocabulary

reference book
dictionary
encyclopedia
almanac
atlas
fiction book
nonfiction book
card catalog
call number

Suppose you have to write a report on Robert Fulton. Or maybe you have to find out how many miles of railroad the United States has today. To write a report, to answer a question, or to find a book about imaginary people or events, you need to go to the library.

Kinds of Reference Books

A library has many kinds of reference books. These books give information about a subject. Four handy reference books are: the dictionary, the encyclopedia, the almanac, and the atlas.

A dictionary gives the definitions, or meanings of words. Each word in the dictionary is called an entry. The dictionary shows you how to spell and how to pronounce each entry word. It also divides the word into syllables. Some dictionaries have pictures to help you understand a word's meaning. You might use a dictionary to look up key vocabulary words.

An encyclopedia is a book or set of books that gives information on a number of subjects. If you wanted to find out when Robert Fulton was born or what education he had, you could look in an encyclopedia.

Encyclopedia entries are arranged in alphabetical order. Encyclopedias also have an index volume that lists all subjects that are covered. At the end of most articles is a list of other articles on related subjects.

An almanac is a book that is very useful if you want the most recent information about the United States or other countries. An almanac is published each year and contains information and charts on many subjects. If you want to find out the population of the United States or the highest temperature on record, you would look in an almanac.

Finally, an atlas is a book of maps. It gives information about where cities, rivers, and countries are located. For example, you can look in an atlas to find the latitude and longitude of a city. You have an atlas in the back of your textbook.

Learning About the Card Catalog

Once you are at the library, how do you find the books that will help you? If you want to read a make-believe story you would take out a fiction book. Fiction books are about people and events that are not real. If you want to learn about any subject in American history, you would use nonfiction books. Nonfiction books are about real people, places, and

```
385.09    Nock, Oswald
   N          Railways of the USA.
          New York, Hastings
          House, 1979
             317p. ill.
```

A

```
          Railways of the USA

385.09    Nock, Oswald
   N          Railways of the USA.
          New York, Hastings
          House, 1979.
             317p. ill.
```

B

```
          RAILROADS

385.09    Nock, Oswald
   N          Railways of the USA.
          New York, Hastings
          House, 1979.
             317p. ill.
```

C

events. To find nonfiction books in the library, you have to use either the **card catalog** or a computer.

The computer lists every book in the library. So does the card catalog. Unlike the computer, the card catalog is a collection of cards. Like the computer, it tells you where to find the books you need. Every nonfiction book has at least three cards in the card catalog—one for its author, one for its title, and one or more for its subject. The cards are filed alphabetically in the drawers of the card catalog cabinets.

To tell whether a card is an author, title, or subject card, look at the top line. Is **Card A** an author, title, or subject card?

Each card gives the following information: the book's author, title, place of publication, publisher, date of publication, and length.

At the top of the left-hand corner of every card is the **call number**. The call number tells you where to find a book on the library shelves. The same call number appears on the outside edge, or "spine," of the book. What is the call number of the book on **Card A**?

If you know either the author or title of a book, look in the card catalog or scan through the computer for the author's last name or the first word in the book's title. Otherwise, you can look under the subject.

Look again at the sample catalog cards on this page. Then answer the questions that follow.

Reviewing the Skill

1. How do you find the books you need in a library?
2. What kinds of reference books can you find in the library?
3. What kind of card is Card C?
4. What do you think the *N* after the call number stands for?
5. If you wanted to find more books in the library about American canals, what subject would you look up?
6. Why is it important to know how to use the library?

373

4 A Place Called Texas

READ TO LEARN

Key People

Stephen Austin
Antonio López
  de Santa Anna
Davy Crockett

Jim Bowie
William Travis
Sam Houston

Key Places

Texas
Alamo
San Jacinto River

Read Aloud

South of the Louisiana Territory lay a place called Texas. Much of West Texas is dry grassland and desert. One old-timer said that here you can look farther and see less than in any other part of the world. East Texas is a very different kind of place. There, rolling hills and forests open onto grassy plains with rich black soil. When a pioneer named Moses Austin visited East Texas in 1820, he knew his future lay there.

Read for Purpose

1. **WHAT YOU KNOW:** How did the United States get the Louisiana Territory?
2. **WHAT YOU WILL LEARN:** How did Texas become part of the United States?

"GONE TO TEXAS"

In 1820 **Texas** belonged to Spain. One year later Mexico won its independence from Spain, and Texas became part of Mexico. Moses Austin had died by then. But his son Stephen carried out his dream of starting an American settlement in Texas.

In 1822 **Stephen Austin** led a group of settlers to Texas. The Mexican government gave them land. In return, the settlers agreed to become Mexican citizens and join the Catholic Church— the official church of Mexico. One new-

comer wrote to friends back home that "Everything is bigger here than in the United States."

"Texas fever" swept through the Mississippi River Valley. Restless frontier families packed their wagons and scribbled *G.T.T.* for "Gone to Texas" on their cabin doors. They were joined by land-hungry cotton planters and their slaves. Soon there were more Americans than Mexicans in Texas.

This worried the Mexican government. In 1830 it sent troops to Texas to stop the flood of American settlers. Mexico also wanted to end slavery in Texas. But American settlers there felt strongly about self-rule and resented the soldiers. When Mexican troops attacked a village to take away its guns, it seemed like Lexington and Concord all over again. The Texans rebelled.

"REMEMBER THE ALAMO!"

The President of Mexico, Antonio López de Santa Anna, marched into Texas with 6,000 troops. He was determined to crush the Texas rebels.

Santa Anna reached San Antonio, Texas, early in 1836. There he found a band of 186 Texans just as determined to stop him. They had taken over a mission called the Alamo and turned it into a fort.

The defenders of the Alamo were a tough group. Davy Crockett, a famous bear hunter, frontiersman, and ex-congressman from Tennessee, was there. So was Jim Bowie. He was the inventor of the Bowie knife—a wicked-looking hunting knife known as the "genuine Arkansas toothpick."

These frontiersmen were led by a young lawyer named William Travis. When told to give up the Alamo, Travis replied, "I shall never surrender or retreat." Like General George Washington at Trenton, Travis's motto was "Victory or Death!"

For 11 days Mexican troops pounded the Alamo with cannon fire. They were driven back again and again by deadly rifle fire. But on the twelfth day, Mexican troops overran the fort. Most of the defenders of the Alamo died in the fighting.

In death the defenders of the Alamo were more powerful than in life. As news about the Alamo spread, thou-

The Alamo came under attack by Mexican troops in 1836. What was the result of the fighting?

sands of angry Americans grabbed their rifles and took off for Texas.

The enraged Texans declared their independence. Sam Houston, an old frontier warrior, took command of the tiny Texas army. For weeks Santa Anna chased Houston's force eastward across Texas. But as Houston retreated, his army grew.

On April 21, 1836, in a field near the San Jacinto (san jə sint' ə) River, Houston caught the Mexicans napping. The Texans crept silently toward the sleeping camp. Suddenly, the afternoon stillness was broken by the cry, "Remember the Alamo!"

Sam Houston was wounded in the Battle of San Jacinto. Here, he accepts the surrender of Santa Anna. As a result of Houston's victory, the Lone Star flag (*left*), flew over an independent Republic of Texas.

TEXAS WINS ITS INDEPENDENCE

The Battle of San Jacinto was over in a few minutes. The surprised Mexicans were killed or captured. Santa Anna was found trying to escape, disguised in the uniform of a common soldier. Texas had won its independence.

A new flag with a single star rose over the Republic of Texas. Sam Houston was elected its first president. Most Texans, however, wanted Texas to become part of the United States.

President Andrew Jackson was against statehood for Texas. Mexicans did not yet accept the loss of Texas, and he feared that making Texas a state would lead to war with Mexico. Others did not want Texas to become a state as long as it allowed slavery.

In 1845 Texans again asked for statehood. This time Congress voted yes. The Republic of Texas became the new Lone Star state of Texas.

THE LONE STAR STATE

As you have read, the first Americans arrived in Texas in the early 1820s. But as more and more Americans settled in this Mexican territory, trouble developed. Like other Americans before them, the Texans valued their freedom. They did not want to follow Mexican laws.

In 1836, after a war with Mexico, Texas declared its independence. Nine years later, in 1845, Texas became our 28th state.

 Check Your Reading

1. Why did the Mexican government send troops into Texas?
2. What did Americans mean when they cried, "Remember the Alamo"?
3. Why did President Jackson oppose statehood for Texas?
4. **THINKING SKILL:** How did the Mexican government view "Texas fever"? Why?

5 Winning the West

READ TO LEARN

Key Vocabulary

treaty
gold rush
Forty-Niners

Key People

Brigham Young
James K. Polk

Key Places

Oregon
Utah
Great Salt Lake
Rio Grande

Read Aloud

By the time Texas became a state in 1845, pioneers had pushed the frontier to the edge of the Great Plains. And here they stopped. Everyone knew that farming was hopeless where trees did not grow. The settlers' maps called the plains the "Great American Desert." But from faraway Oregon came tales of tall trees and green valleys. Soon "Oregon fever" was driving pioneers westward once again.

Read for Purpose

1. **WHAT YOU KNOW:** Why did only grasses grow on the Great Plains?
2. **WHAT YOU WILL LEARN:** How were Oregon, Utah, and California settled?

THE OREGON TRAIL

Oregon fever was spread by Mountain Men and missionaries. In 1836 a pioneer named Marcus Whitman and his bride Narcissa traveled west with Henry and Eliza Spaulding. Both couples hoped to teach Christianity to the Northwest Indians. The two wives were the first white women to cross the continent to Oregon. The route they followed across the plains and mountains came to be known as the Oregon Trail.

The Whitmans and other missionaries wrote home about the beauties of Oregon. After reading about rich soil, good harbors, and fish-filled rivers, many Easterners were eager to move west. To begin the journey, most traveled first to Missouri, where they joined up with 50 to 100 other families. Then, for the next six months, they traveled over 2,000 miles (3,200 km) in wagon trains on the Oregon Trail.

Most families began the journey with their covered wagons heavily loaded. Then, as their oxen or mules grew weary, they had to toss things out to lighten the load. The Oregon Trail soon

Pioneers used oxen as well as mules to pull their wagons on the long trip to the West. When they reached a river, everyone's help was needed to guide the wagons across the water.

was littered with furniture and trunks. It also was lined with the graves of those who died along the way.

By the time they reached Oregon, most families had a story to tell. Some had seen buffalo stampedes and prairie fires on the Great Plains. Some had almost frozen to death crossing the Rocky Mountains. And many had nearly died of hunger and thirst in the desert lands beyond.

A young pioneer named John Sager had a tale stranger than most. His parents died on the Oregon Trail, leaving five children and a skinny cow. The children walked 500 miles (805 km) to the mission founded by the Whitmans in Oregon. John, the oldest at 14, carried his baby brother the entire way. The children had lived on nothing but cow's milk and whatever wild fruits they could find along the trail.

When the Sager children came to Oregon in the early 1840s, the territory was claimed by both the United States and Great Britain. In 1846 the two countries agreed to divide Oregon. The American part of the territory became the states of Oregon, Washington, Idaho, and Montana.

THE CALIFORNIA TRAIL

Settlers also traveled west into lands claimed by Mexico. In 1841 a group of pioneers led by John Bidwell left the Oregon Trail west of the Rockies. They were going to the Mexican territory of California.

Bidwell's group headed west across the Great Basin. This dry land, wrote Bidwell, was "glimmering with heat and salt." Water and grass were scarce. When the animals grew weak from hunger and thirst, the settlers had to abandon their heavy wagons.

Once they were across the desert, the pioneers faced the Sierra Nevada. It seemed to Bidwell that "only a bird could get through" the maze of peaks and canyons. They struggled across the mountains on foot.

The Bidwell group finally reached California's Central Valley. Others soon followed them west on the California Trail.

THE MORMONS SETTLE UTAH

A religious group called the Mormons settled in Utah, which was also claimed by Mexico. Like the Pilgrims more than 200 years before, the Mor-

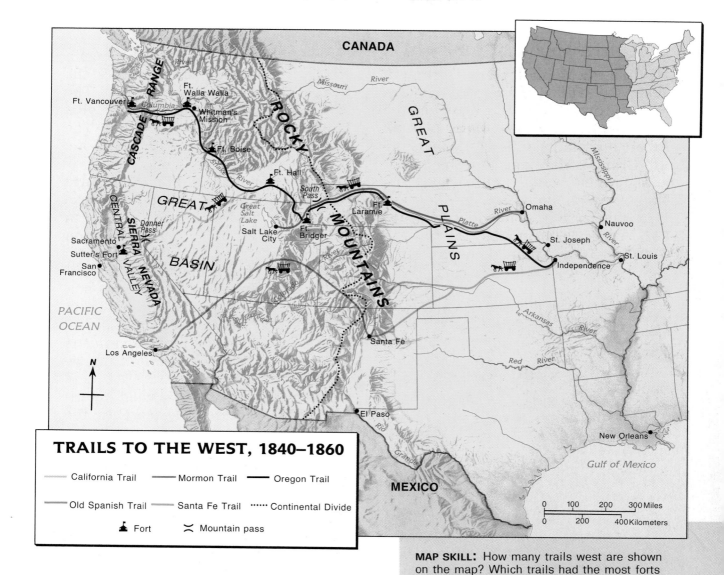

TRAILS TO THE WEST, 1840–1860

— California Trail ■— Mormon Trail ■— Oregon Trail

— Old Spanish Trail — Santa Fe Trail ····· Continental Divide

🛕 Fort ⤬ Mountain pass

MAP SKILL: How many trails west are shown on the map? Which trails had the most forts along their routes?

mons were looking for a place where they could follow their religion in peace. They had been driven from towns in New York, Ohio, Missouri, and then Illinois because of their religious beliefs.

In 1847 Brigham Young led a group of Mormons west into the Great Basin. Upon reaching a dry, sunbaked valley near the Great Salt Lake, he announced, "This is the place." Find the Mormon Trail and the Great Salt Lake on the map above.

The area chosen by Brigham Young was not promising. One woman wrote

that "Weak and weary as I am, I would rather go a thousand miles further than remain." But that was one of the attractions of this desert valley. No one else wanted it.

Thousands of Mormons flocked into the area and settled by the Great Salt Lake. They blocked up nearby mountain streams and dug irrigation ditches to carry water to their fields. In time, the Utah desert became a land of thriving farms.

WAR WITH MEXICO

While the Mormons were settling in Utah, the United States went to war with Mexico. The war began on the border between Texas and Mexico. Americans claimed the border was the Rio Grande. Mexicans said the border was farther north and east at the Nueces (nù ā′ səs) River.

In January 1846, President James K. Polk sent 1,500 troops to the Rio Grande. They camped in an area claimed by both countries. When a Mexican army appeared across the river, a battle of bands broke out. The Americans played "The Star-Spangled Banner" and "Yankee Doodle." The Mexicans answered with patriotic songs of Mexico.

It was not long before songs gave way to battle sounds. Fighting broke out along the Rio Grande. Then, in May, the United States declared war on Mexico.

American troops marched into Mexico in the summer of 1846. Many soldiers never came home. Some died in battle. Many more died of disease. Even so, spirits were high. Americans bragged that "We may be killed, but we can't be whipped."

The war ended in 1847 when American troops captured Mexico City, the capital of Mexico. The final battle took place at an old fort called Chapultepec (chə pùl′ tə pek) Castle. One hundred students from a Mexican military school joined the fighting. *Los Niños*, or "the boys," died defending their country.

Early in 1848 the two countries signed a peace treaty. A treaty is a formal agreement. According to the treaty, Mexico was forced to give up about half of its territory. That land is now Arizona, Nevada, Utah, California, and parts of New Mexico, Colorado, and Wyoming. In return the United States paid Mexico $15 million.

American troops storm the fort of Chapultepec during the Mexican War. What was the outcome of the war?

The Granger Collection

THE CALIFORNIA GOLD RUSH

The ink on the treaty was hardly dry when newspaper headlines shouted, "GOLD, GOLD, GOLD IN CALIFORNIA!" Gold had been discovered in the Sierra Nevada foothills. Across California people dropped what they were

(*left*) The **Forty-Niners** traveled to California in many different ways, according to the artist of this amusing picture. (*right*) Once there, panning for gold was hard work.

doing. "All were off to the mines," wrote a minister, "some on horses, some on carts, and some on crutches." The **gold rush** was on.

In 1849 over 70,000 people left their homes for California. These "**Forty-Niners**" were sure they would strike it rich. One said that "if I don't pick up more than a hatful of gold a day, I shall be perfectly satisfied."

Once they got to California, the Forty-Niners were lucky to find a thimbleful of gold a day. Most gold was well hidden in rocks, mountains, or icy rivers.

Settlements called mining camps sprang up wherever gold was found. These camps had colorful names like Humbug, Roaring Camp, or Rough and Ready. Many people found it easy to make money in the camps by selling eager miners everything from axes to fancy clothes. Some merchants made fortunes selling eggs at $6 a dozen and flour for $400 a barrel.

Theft was a problem in many mining camps. The miners at Old Dry Diggings even changed their camp's name to Hangtown to warn away thieves.

"FROM SEA TO SHINING SEA"

In 1840 the frontier reached the Great Plains and stopped. But, as you have read, wagon trains soon were crossing the western half of the continent. By 1850 the United States had gained vast new territories once claimed by Great Britain and Mexico. The American flag now waved "from sea to shining sea."

Check Your Reading

1. Why did the Mormons settle in Utah?
2. Why did the United States go to war with Mexico in 1846?
3. What brought thousands of people to California in 1849?
4. **THINKING SKILL:** Compare the settlement of Oregon to the settlement of Texas.

IMPORTANT EVENTS

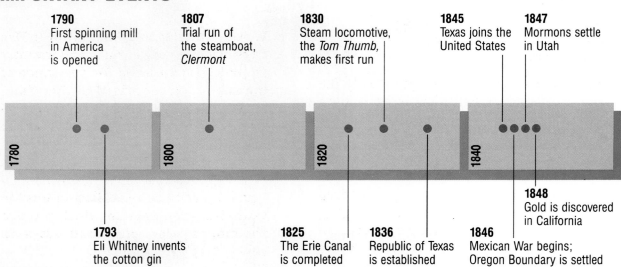

1790
First spinning mill in America is opened

1807
Trial run of the steamboat, *Clermont*

1830
Steam locomotive, the *Tom Thumb,* makes first run

1845
Texas joins the United States

1847
Mormons settle in Utah

1780

1800

1820

1840

1848
Gold is discovered in California

1793
Eli Whitney invents the cotton gin

1825
The Erie Canal is completed

1836
Republic of Texas is established

1846
Mexican War begins; Oregon Boundary is settled

PEOPLE TO KNOW

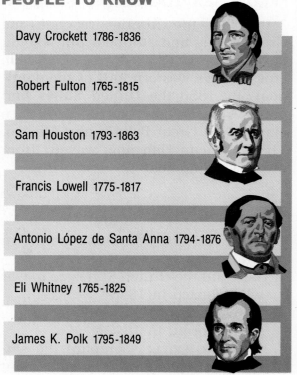

Davy Crockett 1786-1836

Robert Fulton 1765-1815

Sam Houston 1793-1863

Francis Lowell 1775-1817

Antonio López de Santa Anna 1794-1876

Eli Whitney 1765-1825

James K. Polk 1795-1849

IDEAS TO REMEMBER

■ The West is a land of vast plains and deserts, towering mountains, and huge valleys.

■ Canals, steamboats, and railroads all helped make travel in America cheaper and faster during the 1800s.

■ The number of factories in New England increased as Americans learned how to use new machines.

■ Following a war with Mexico, Texas became a republic in 1836 and a state in 1845.

■ "Oregon fever," the Gold Rush, and the desire for religious freedom attracted thousands of settlers to the West.

REVIEWING VOCABULARY

canal	steamboat
cotton gin	treaty
mass production	

Number a sheet of paper from 1 to 5. Beside each number write the word or term from the list above that best completes the sentence.

1. The boat traveled up the _____, which had been built to connect two rivers.
2. The two countries signed a _____ ending the war.
3. After the _____ was invented, cotton became the most important cash crop in the South.
4. One important feature of a _____ is that it can travel upstream.
5. Using _____ methods workers could produce more goods in less time.

REVIEWING FACTS

1. Which areas of the West were probably good for farming? Which areas probably were not?
2. Name two ways in which steam power improved transportation in the 1800s.
3. Write a sentence that gives one result of each of the following facts.
   a. The cotton gin was invented.
   b. Samuel Slater moved to the United States.
4. What did each of these people have to do with the independence of Texas?
   a. William Travis
   b. Sam Houston
5. What new lands were added to the United States in the 1840s?

WRITING ABOUT MAIN IDEAS

1. **Writing Instructions About How to Use a Machine:** Imagine you are an inventor of one of the machines or new kinds of transportation discussed in this chapter. Choose one of these inventions and write a list of instructions about how to use it.
2. **Making a Chart:** Make a chart with the following two headings: "The American Revolution"; "The Texas Revolution." In your chart list ways in which the two revolutions were alike and ways in which they were different.
3. **Writing a Short Story:** Imagine that you have traveled west to settle in a new land. Decide where you went, how you got there, and how you succeeded in your new home. Then write a short story about your experiences as a pioneer.
4. **Writing About a Graph:** Study the graph on page 369 about cotton grown in the United States. Then write a paragraph explaining what you learned.

BUILDING SKILLS: USING THE LIBRARY

1. How would you go about finding a book in the library about the Mexican War?
2. Suppose you wanted to find a book about the Forty-Niners. Name at least two subjects you might look under in the card catalog.
3. Which of these subjects—Brigham Young or Eli Whitney—would be listed first in a card catalog?
4. Why is the library a good place to look when you want to learn more about a subject?

REVIEWING VOCABULARY

amendment	republic
pioneer	treaty
political party	

Number a sheet of paper from 1 to 5. Beside each number write **C** if the underlined word or term in the sentence is used correctly. Write **I** if it is used incorrectly, and then write the word or words from the list above that would complete the sentence correctly.

1. The two countries signed a <u>constitution</u> in which they agreed to end the war.
2. The <u>pioneer</u> found a pathway through the Appalachian Mountains.
3. The Constitution was changed when the <u>treaty</u> was added.
4. Members of a <u>political party</u> usually have similar ideas about government.
5. The United States is a <u>republic</u>; the people elect representatives to run the country.

WRITING ABOUT THE UNIT

1. **Writing an Editorial:** Who do you think was the better President—Thomas Jefferson or Andrew Jackson? Write a newspaper editorial giving three reasons for your choice.
2. **Writing a Poem:** Write a poem about one of these subjects: (a) traveling west to Oregon, (b) the Mexican War, (c) the Constitutional Convention, (d) the Trail of Tears. Your poem should be written as if you had actually lived through the event.

3. **Writing About People:** Write a sentence or two about how each of these people helped factories to grow in the United States: (a) Eli Whitney, (b) Samuel Slater, (c) Francis Cabot Lowell.

ACTIVITIES

1. **Making a Map of the Growth of the United States:** Review the sections in the unit that tell about the growth of the United States. Make a map of the United States, showing all the lands that were added to the original 13 states. Then label each area with its name and the date when it became part of the United States.
2. **Researching Battles:** Find out about an important battle in the War of 1812 or the Mexican War. Prepare a newspaper account of the battle. Include a headline and map or picture.
3. **Writing a Book Report:** Read a book about the California Gold Rush. Then write a report telling about the book.
4. **Working Together to Make a Bulletin Board Display:** Changes in transportation were very important in the first half of the 1800s. With a group of classmates, make a bulletin board display about these changes. Include a map or time line, as well as pictures and captions for your display.

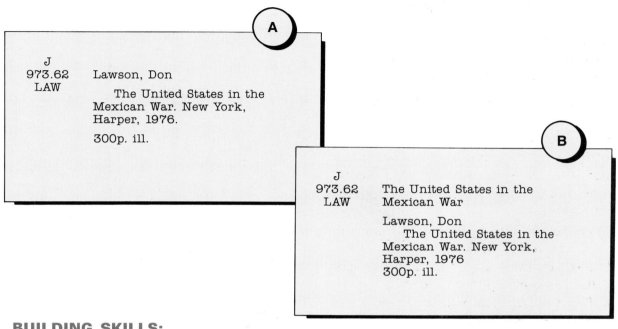

A

J
973.62
LAW

Lawson, Don
       The United States in the
Mexican War. New York,
Harper, 1976.

300p. ill.

B

J
973.62
LAW

The United States in the
Mexican War

Lawson, Don
       The United States in the
Mexican War. New York,
Harper, 1976
300p. ill.

BUILDING SKILLS: USING THE LIBRARY

1. If you were going to do a report on the Mexican War, what steps would you follow to find books in the library?
2. Look closely at the card catalog cards above. Then answer these questions.
   a. What kind of card is Card A?
   b. What is the call number on Card B?
   c. If you wanted to find more information about the Mexican War, what subject would you look up?
3. How can call numbers help you find books in the library?

LINKING PAST, PRESENT, AND FUTURE

In the 1800s many more Americans worked on farms than in factories. Today the opposite is true. There are fewer farms. And many people work in factories. You read in Unit 1 that many Americans work at jobs helping other people. Some are teachers, doctors, or waiters. What kinds of jobs do you think will be needed in the future?

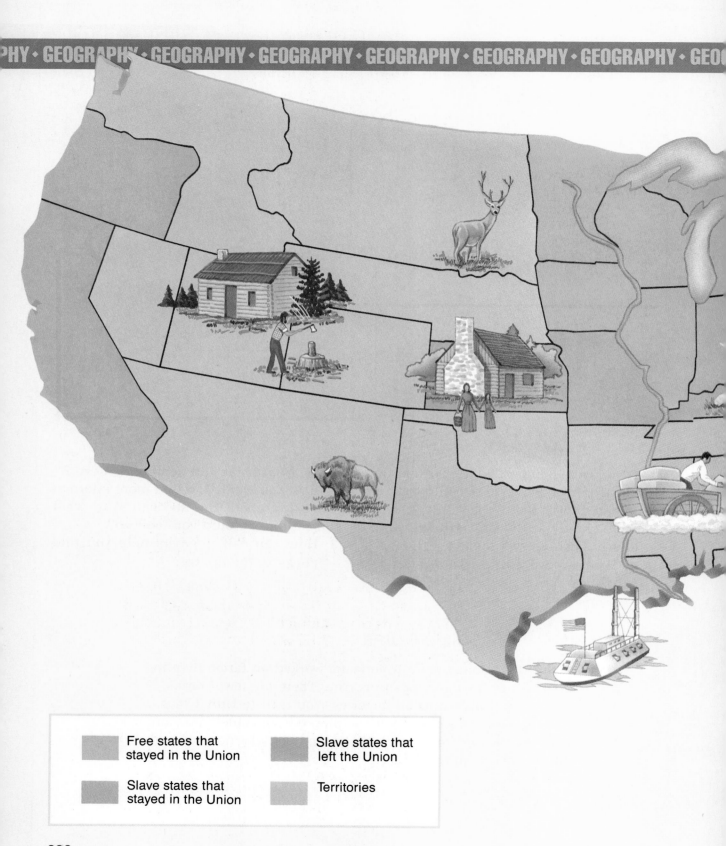

Free states that
stayed in the Union

Slave states that
left the Union

Slave states that
stayed in the Union

Territories

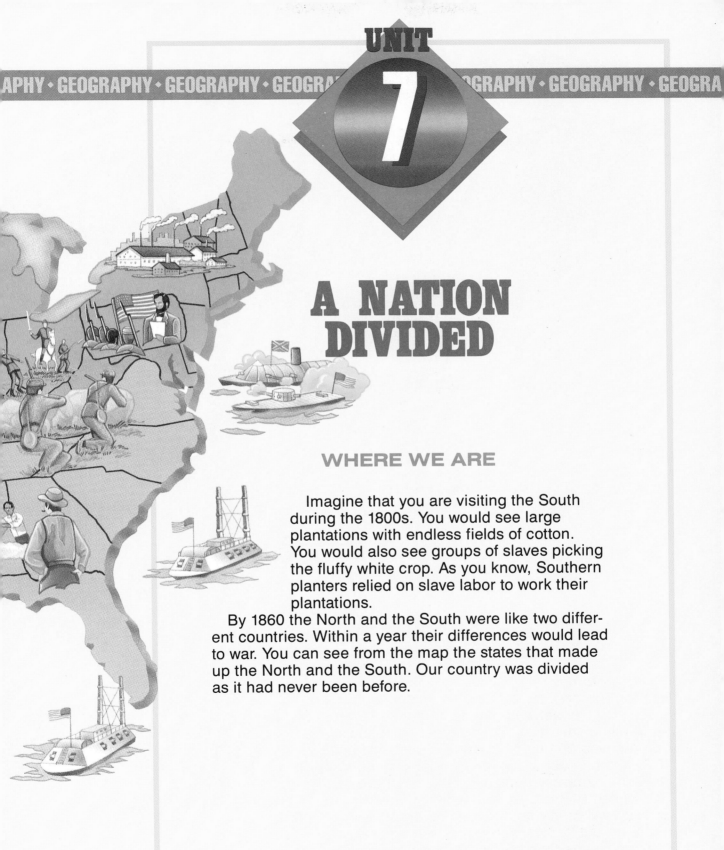

UNIT 7

A NATION DIVIDED

WHERE WE ARE

Imagine that you are visiting the South during the 1800s. You would see large plantations with endless fields of cotton. You would also see groups of slaves picking the fluffy white crop. As you know, Southern planters relied on slave labor to work their plantations.

By 1860 the North and the South were like two different countries. Within a year their differences would lead to war. You can see from the map the states that made up the North and the South. Our country was divided as it had never been before.

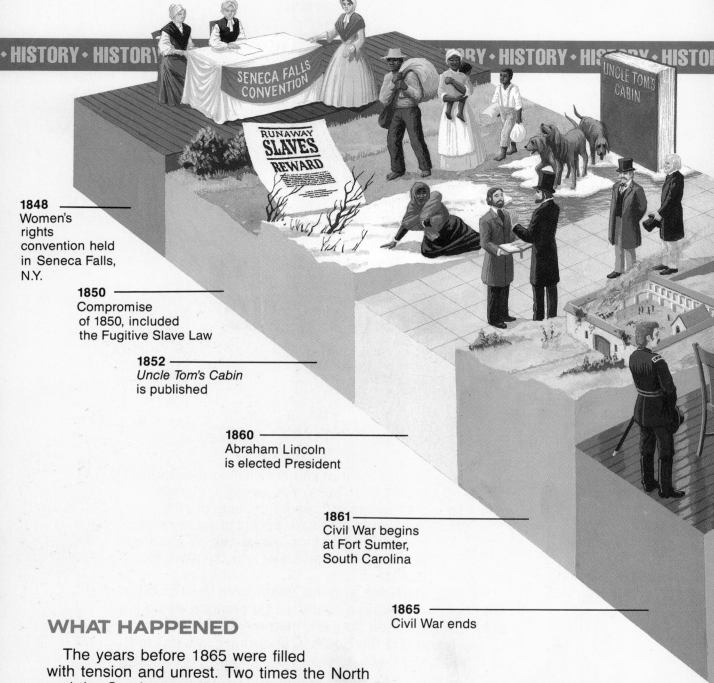

1848
Women's rights convention held in Seneca Falls, N.Y.

1850
Compromise of 1850, included the Fugitive Slave Law

1852
Uncle Tom's Cabin is published

1860
Abraham Lincoln is elected President

1861
Civil War begins at Fort Sumter, South Carolina

1865
Civil War ends

1865
President Lincoln is killed

1865-1877
Reconstruction

WHAT HAPPENED

The years before 1865 were filled with tension and unrest. Two times the North and the South were able to settle their differences. As the time line shows, one of these times was the Compromise of 1850. However, a series of events after 1850 left the country too divided for compromise. The election of Abraham Lincoln was one of these events. The United States was split apart by a bitter war. In this unit you will read about the events that pulled the North and the South apart. You will also read about the steps that Americans took to unite their country again.

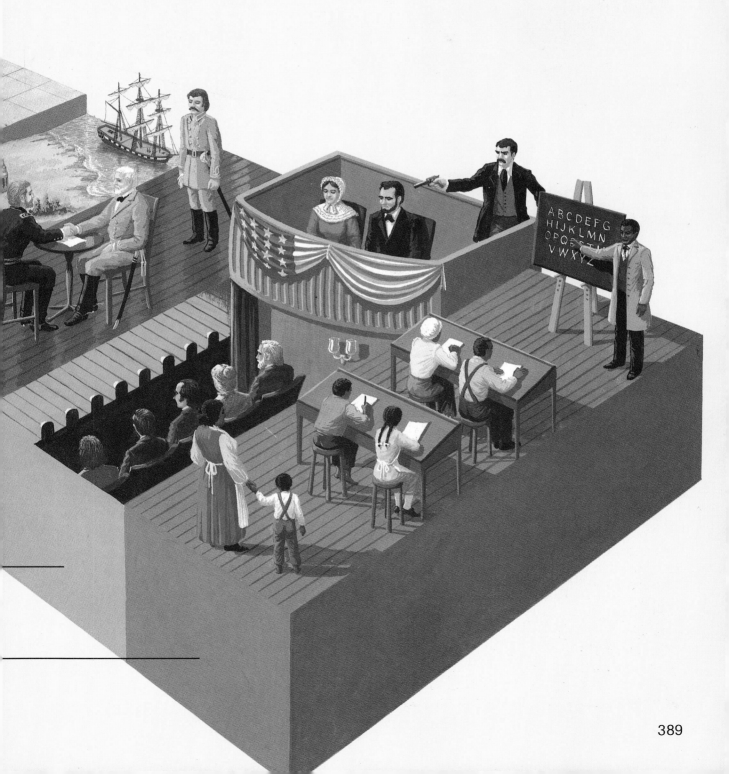

389

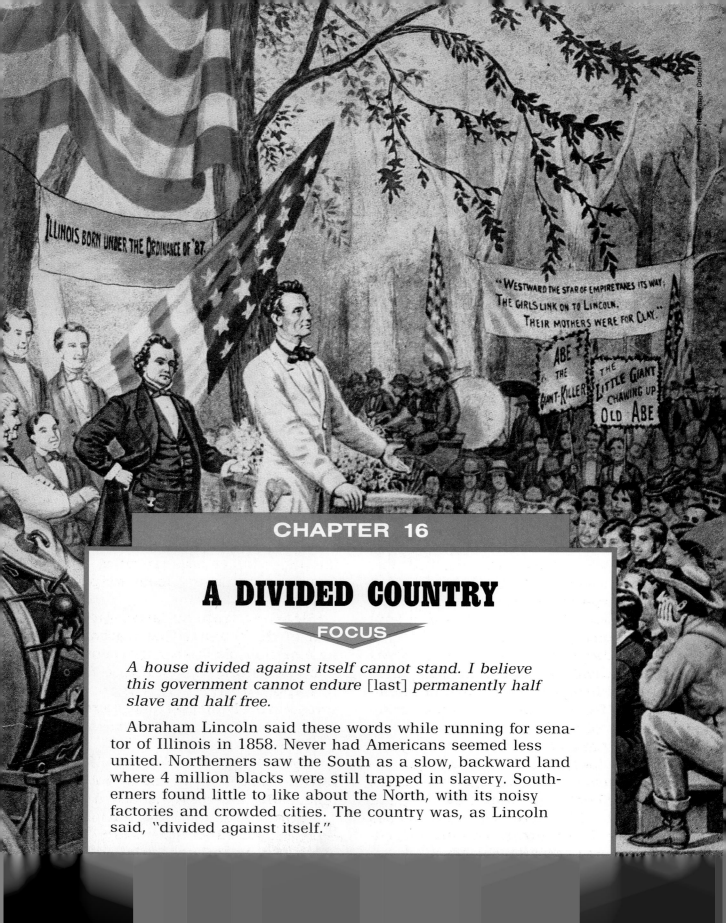

CHAPTER 16

A DIVIDED COUNTRY

FOCUS

*A house divided against itself cannot stand. I believe
this government cannot endure [last] permanently half
slave and half free.*

Abraham Lincoln said these words while running for senator of Illinois in 1858. Never had Americans seemed less
united. Northerners saw the South as a slow, backward land
where 4 million blacks were still trapped in slavery. Southerners found little to like about the North, with its noisy
factories and crowded cities. The country was, as Lincoln
said, "divided against itself."

1 Two Different Worlds

READraw TO LEARN

Read Aloud

People in the North and South spoke the same language. They shared the same beliefs about democracy and self-government. Their grandparents had joined together to fight the British in the American Revolution. And yet, by the 1850s, the North and South seemed like two different worlds existing in one country, the United States. Why were these two parts of our country so different? In this lesson you will see why the North and South had become two different worlds.

Read for Purpose

1. **WHAT YOU KNOW:** Why were the colonies united at the time of the American Revolution?
2. **WHAT YOU WILL LEARN:** In what ways were the North and the South different by the 1850s? How were they alike?

THE NORTH

When Southerners talked about "the North," they meant the Northeast and the Great Lakes and Plains states. They saw the North as a harsh, hurried land. Northerners saw their world differently. To them the North was a land of progress.

Northerners saw signs of progress everywhere. By 1850 there were more than 100,000 factories in the North. These factories turned out an amazing variety of goods.

As growing numbers of workers found jobs in factories, villages became towns and towns grew into cities. In 1790 only two cities, New York and Philadelphia, had more than 20,000 people. By 1860 there were 45 such cities, most of them in the North.

The North also had most of the country's canals and railroads. Trains and boats carried farm products from the plains to busy eastern cities. They returned with factory goods for plains farmers.

The North was the fastest-growing part of the country. One reason was immigration. Each year thousands of immigrants came to the United States by way of New York City. Many of them settled in the Northeast and around the Great Lakes. They hoped to start a new life here.

Most of the newcomers to the United States came from Germany and Ireland. Many Germans headed for the rich farmland of the plains. But most of the Irish stayed in the eastern cities. Years of crop failures in Ireland had

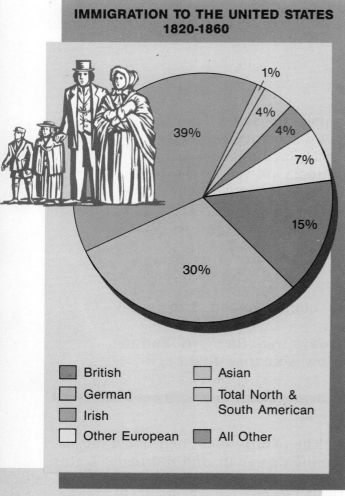

IMMIGRATION TO THE UNITED STATES 1820-1860

1%
4%
4%
7%
15%
30%
39%

- British
- German
- Irish
- Other European
- Asian
- Total North & South American
- All Other

GRAPH SKILL: How many years does the graph represent? What percent of immigrants came from Ireland during that time?

shown them that to farm was to starve. Irish workers helped to build the Erie Canal and the railroads. By the 1840s, poor Irish women were replacing the mill girls in New England's textile factories. The graph above shows the different groups of immigrants that settled in the United States at this time.

THE SOUTH

When Northerners talked about "the South," they meant the slave states from Maryland to Texas. To them, the South was a slow and backward land—a land where most blacks still toiled as slaves. Southern whites had a different view. They saw the South as a warm, beautiful land where they had created a comfortable way of life.

The South was a world of farms and plantations. Here Southerners raised tobacco, sugar, rice, and indigo. But cotton was by far the most important cash crop. By the 1850s cotton was the country's most valuable product.

In the South people talked more softly and moved more slowly than in the North. Southerners did not seem in such a hurry to get ahead. They took time to treat both friends and strangers with kindness.

TWO WAYS OF LIFE

The North and South were joined together in one nation. But as you have read, each had its own way of life. The North was fast becoming a world of cities and factories. The South remained a world of plantations and farms. But the greatest difference between the North and South had to do with slavery. As you will read, this difference would soon tear the country apart.

Check Your Reading

1. Why did Northerners view the North as a land of progress?
2. What was the most important cash crop in the South?
3. Why do you think most immigrants settled in the North, and not in the South?
4. **THINKING SKILL:** What was the point of view of Northerners toward the South?

2 The Attack on Slavery

READ TO LEARN

Key Vocabulary

abolitionist
Underground
    Railroad
Seneca Falls
    Convention

Key People

William Lloyd Garrison
Frederick Douglass
Harriet Tubman
Sarah and Angelina
    Grimké

Lucretia Mott
Elizabeth Cady
    Stanton
Sojourner Truth

Read Aloud

One August day in 1831 the sun turned a "peculiar greenish-blue." To a Virginia slave named Nat Turner, it was a sign. The time had come, he believed, to lead his people out of slavery. Turner's slave rebellion began with six men armed with two axes. In 24 hours there were 70 rebel slaves, and some 60 whites lay dead. Only then was the violence stopped.

In the South, Nat Turner's rebellion seemed like a nightmare come true. But in the North, some people saw Turner as a hero. They decided it was time to speak out against slavery.

Read for Purpose

1. **WHAT YOU KNOW:** Why did Nat Turner's revolt frighten Southerners?
2. **WHAT YOU WILL LEARN:** How did abolitionists work for the freedom of slaves?

THE SOUTH DEFENDS SLAVERY

Slavery had gradually ended in the North after the American Revolution. At the time, many Americans thought that it would also die out in the South. But, as you read in Chapter 15, the growing importance of cotton kept slavery alive. By 1860 one out of four white Southern families owned slaves. Most cotton planters in the South believed that their way of life depended on slave labor.

You read in Chapter 10 how hard life was for slaves in the South. But many slave owners argued that slavery was good for blacks. Our slaves are better off, they said, than workers in the North. Factory workers, planters argued, worked longer and harder than slaves. And while workers in the North always lived in fear of losing their jobs, slaves were taken care of from birth until death.

WILLIAM LLOYD GARRISON

William Lloyd Garrison was not impressed by such arguments. Garrison was one of a growing group of **abolitionists** (ab ə lish′ ə nists)—people who wanted to abolish, or end, slavery. In 1831 he began a newspaper in Boston called *The Liberator*. Garrison promised to be as "harsh as truth" in his attacks on slavery. "I will not retreat a single inch," he said. "And I will be heard."

Garrison was heard. His attacks on slavery made slave owners so angry that his paper was burned across the South. Georgia even offered a $5,000 reward for Garrison's arrest.

Separation of families was just one part of slave life vividly described by the **abolitionist** speaker and writer Frederick Douglass.

Northerners also were upset by *The Liberator*. In his paper Garrison demanded that blacks be treated the same as whites. At that time, most blacks in the North could not vote. Most schools and jobs were closed to blacks. Whatever Northern whites thought about slavery, few believed in equal rights for blacks. Garrison was often attacked by angry white mobs. One newspaper called him "the most mobbed man in the United States."

FREDERICK DOUGLASS

The most powerful abolitionist speaker was **Frederick Douglass**. Born a slave in Maryland, Douglass never saw his father. His mother worked from dawn to dusk in the fields. Later Douglass wrote, "I do not remember ever seeing my mother by the light of day." She died when he was just seven years old.

Douglass burned with a desire to learn how to read. But his owner refused to let him learn. "Learning," he said, "will spoil the best slave in the world." Douglass learned to read despite his owner.

When Douglass was 21, he escaped to New England. Still, he was not safe. If caught, he could be returned to his owner. Many runaway slaves went to Canada to avoid this danger. But Douglass changed his name to keep from being captured. He stayed in the North and became an abolitionist speaker.

Douglass made slavery real to people in the North. Listening to him, they could hear the sobs of a mother torn from her children. They could feel the sting of the overseer's whip. People who came to Douglass's speeches to make fun of him left convinced that slavery was wrong.

HARRIET TUBMAN

Like Frederick Douglass, Harriet Tubman was born a slave. At the age of 28, Tubman learned she was to be sold and separated from her family. So she decided to run away. Harriet Tubman soon found her way to freedom on the Underground Railroad.

The Underground Railroad had no rails or engines. Its "passengers" were runaway slaves. Its "trains" were farm wagons used to hide and move slaves. And its "stations" were homes and farms where slaves were cared for on their journey north. The "conductors" on the Underground Railroad were fearless blacks and whites who led slaves out of the South to freedom in the North or Canada.

Freedom felt so good to Tubman that she became a conductor on the Under-

Harriet Tubman was a leader of the **Underground Railroad**. She guided many runaway slaves to freedom in the North.

ground Railroad. Again and again she went south to help slaves escape. Blacks called her Moses. For like Moses in the Bible, she led her people out of slavery. Slave owners offered $40,000 for her capture. Harriet Tubman was never caught.

WOMEN SPEAK OUT FOR EQUALITY

Tubman was one of many black and white women who joined the attack on slavery. Sarah and Angelina Grimké (grim' kē) grew up with slaves on a South Carolina plantation. They found slavery so cruel that they moved north and became abolitionist speakers. At the time, it was quite daring for a woman to speak in public. Many people came to hear the Grimké sisters just to see what these women were like.

The Grimké sisters asked women everywhere to speak out against slavery. "Women ought to feel a special sympathy for the colored man," Angelina said. "For, like him, she has been accused of mental inferiority and denied a good education."

As women talked about the rights of blacks, they began to think more about their own rights. In 1848 abolitionists **Lucretia Mott** and **Elizabeth Cady Stanton** held the world's first women's rights convention in Seneca Falls, New York.

The women who went to the **Seneca Falls Convention** approved a Declaration of Sentiments on the rights of women. The declaration began by saying that "all men and women are created equal." Read some of the ideas contained in the Seneca Falls Declaration of Sentiments on this page.

A second women's rights convention was held three years later. A former slave, **Sojourner Truth**, listened as men argued that women were weak and needed protection, not equal rights. She answered them:

> Look at me! Look at my arm! I have plowed, and planted. . . . And aren't I a woman? I could work as much and eat as much as a man (when I could get it) and bear the lash as well—and aren't I a woman?

Sojourner Truth won the argument. She certainly was not weak or frail. But the battle for equal rights for women and blacks was just beginning.

"A CAUSE WORTH DYING FOR"

You have read in this lesson that in the 1830s black and white abolitionists began a long attack on slavery. Abolitionist speakers were sometimes mobbed by angry whites. But they would not be silent. For as the Grimké sisters said, "This is a cause worth dying for."

THE SENECA FALLS DECLARATION

*T*he history of mankind is a history of repeated injuries on the part of man toward woman. . . .To prove this, let facts be submitted to a fair world.

Having deprived her of. . .the right to vote, he has oppressed her on all sides.

He has made her, if married, in the eye of the law, civilly dead [without rights].

He has taken from her all right of property, even to the wages she earns.

He has denied her the facilities for obtaining a thorough education. . . .

Now, in view of this denial of the rights of one half the people of this country. . . we insist that they have immediate admission to all the rights and privileges which belong to them as citizens of the United States.

What are some of the rights women were asking for at Seneca Falls?

Check Your Reading

1. What arguments did some Southerners use to defend slavery?
2. How did William Lloyd Garrison and Frederick Douglass attack slavery?
3. Describe how the Underground Railroad worked.
4. **THINKING SKILL:** How did the fight against slavery lead to the women's rights movement in the 1840s?

Writing a Report

Key Vocabulary

source   bibliography

I have a Social Studies report due on the 15th, you suddenly remember. What are you going to do?

Choosing a Topic

First choose a topic that you can cover in a short report. Avoid a topic that is too broad, such as "Slavery in America." Instead, narrow your topic. You could write your report on one part of the slavery story such as "Nat Turner's Rebellion."

Then make a list of the information you will need. For example, who was Nat Turner? Why did he rebel?

Note Taking

Use a separate note card or sheet of paper for each **source**. A source is any book where you find information about a subject. On each card, write the author, the title of the book or the name of the encyclopedia, and the page. On your note cards, write facts or quotations that you might use in your report.

Writing and Revising

Before you begin writing, make an outline. List the ideas you want to include in your report. Then put your ideas in a logical order so that they make sense. After your outline is finished, start to write the report. Remember to include a beginning, a middle, and an end. Reread what you have written. Now prepare a **bibliography**. A bibliography is a list of the sources that you used.

Reviewing the Skill

Read the sample note cards on this page. Then answer the questions that follow.

1. What is the first step in writing a report?
2. What is the source of information on Card A?
3. Do any of the cards have a direct quotation? If so, which?
4. What other questions might a report on Nat Turner's rebellion try to answer?
5. Why does it make sense to first prepare an outline when writing a report?

A

What was Nat Turner's childhood like?
Dorothy Sterling, Forever Free. Garden City, N.Y., Doubleday & Co., 1963. p. 105
taught himself to read and write
had an excellent memory
was interested in science
"All my time, not devoted to my master's service, was spent in making experiments."

B

How did Nat Turner's rebellion get started?
"Nat Turner," Merit Students Encyclopedia, volume 18. pp. 416-417

known to other slaves as "The Prophet"
rebellion began August 21, 1831, when he killed his master and other slaves joined rebellion.

C

How did people react to Turner's rebellion?
William Katz, Slavery to Civil War 1812-1865. New York, Franklin Watts, 1974. p. 9

Because Turner was educated and a preacher, whites in Virginia cracked down on black preachers. They limited movement of blacks and tried to stop them from becoming educated.

3 The Country Pulls Apart

READ TO LEARN

Key Vocabulary

Missouri Compromise
Compromise of 1850
Uncle Tom's Cabin
Kansas-Nebraska Act

Dred Scott Decision
secession
Confederate States
    of America

Key People

Harriet Beecher Stowe
Abraham Lincoln
John Brown
Jefferson Davis

Read Aloud

In 1850 Senator John C. Calhoun of South Carolina was near death. Still, his eyes glowed in his sunken face as a friend read his last speech to the Senate. Calhoun warned that attacks on slavery were pulling the country apart. "The Union is in danger," Calhoun said. "California will become the test question."

Read for Purpose

1. **WHAT YOU KNOW:** How did abolitionists fight against slavery?
2. **WHAT YOU WILL LEARN:** What events drove the North and the South apart by 1861?

FREE STATES AND SLAVE STATES

California! How could this sunny land won from Mexico threaten the United States? In 1850 California asked to join the Union, or the United States, as a free state. Free states did not permit slavery within their borders. The South said no.

By 1850 the North, with its large population, had more votes than the South in the House of Representatives. In the Senate, slave states and free states had the same number of votes. Allowing California into the Union would tip this balance in favor of the free states. It could give them enough votes to make laws against slavery.

Congress had faced this problem before. In 1819 Missouri had asked to join the Union as a slave state. At the time there were 11 slave states and 11 free states. Adding Missouri would have upset this balance. Finally a compromise was reached in 1820. Missouri was admitted as a slave state, and at the same time, Maine joined the nation as a free state.

The **Missouri Compromise** drew an imaginary line through the Louisiana Territory. Slavery was allowed south of

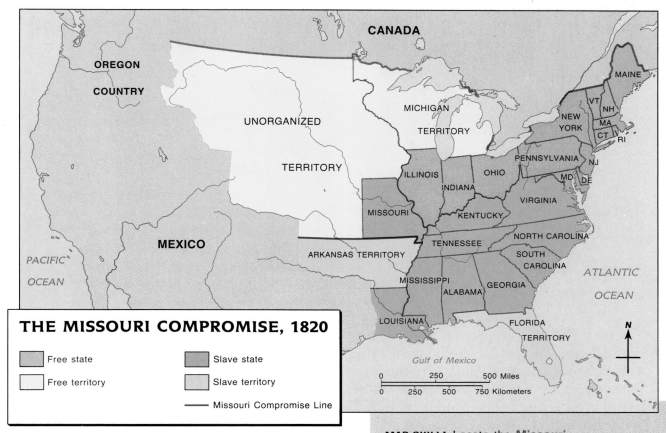

THE MISSOURI COMPROMISE, 1820

- Free state
- Free territory
- Slave state
- Slave territory
- —— Missouri Compromise Line

MAP SKILL: Locate the Missouri Compromise line on the map. On which side of the line was slavery forbidden? What state was an exception?

this line. North of the line, slavery was forbidden, except in Missouri. This compromise kept the number of new slave states and free states the same for 30 years. You can see the Missouri Compromise line on the map above.

In 1850 Congress compromised again. Southerners in Congress agreed to let California become a free state. But they made sure that slaveholders could settle in the rest of the lands won from Mexico. Later the people of those territories would be allowed to decide for themselves whether to become free or slave states.

In return, Northerners in Congress voted for the Fugitive Slave Law. A fugitive is a person who runs away from something. This law said that free states must return runaway slaves, or fugitives, to their owners. This law was important to Southerners because to them slaves were valuable property. The Compromise of 1850 kept the country together. But for how long?

UNCLE TOM'S CABIN

On a cold winter morning in 1851, a writer named Harriet Beecher Stowe was sitting in church. With one ear she followed the service. But in her mind, a picture was taking shape. She saw an image of an old slave dying. This scene became part of a book she wrote called *Uncle Tom's Cabin*. It was the most powerful attack on slavery yet written.

399

The slave Eliza was one of the characters in *Uncle Tom's Cabin*. Here, Eliza and her baby escape from slave catchers. What happened to Eliza?

The novel first appeared in a weekly newspaper in 1851. Each week the newspaper printed part of Stowe's moving story. One week readers suffered with a kind slaveholder who had to sell his old slave, Uncle Tom. Another week readers held their breath as the beautiful slave Eliza ran for freedom, her baby in her arms. Eliza escaped slave catchers by dashing across the ice-filled Ohio River. Weeks later, readers sighed with relief when Eliza found freedom in Canada.

Later still, readers came to hate the cruel slave dealer, Simon Legree. One day Legree demanded that Uncle Tom whip an old woman. Tom replied softly, "I never shall—I'll die first." Readers wept bitter tears as Legree had Uncle Tom beaten to death.

Uncle Tom's Cabin was published as a book in 1852 and quickly became a best seller. More copies were sold than any other book except the Bible. People who had never thought much about slavery before were deeply moved by Harriet Beecher Stowe's story.

The success of *Uncle Tom's Cabin* worried Southern slave owners. They wondered if readers who cheered Eliza's escape would obey the Fugitive Slave Law. The answer was no. The Underground Railroad continued to run despite the new law. Slave catchers who followed slaves north were often attacked by angry mobs. The Compromise of 1850 began to look to Southerners like a bad bargain.

THE KANSAS-NEBRASKA ACT

Southerners were happier about the **Kansas-Nebraska Act** of 1854. This law opened the territories of Kansas and Nebraska to slavery. Both of these territories were north of the imaginary line drawn by the Missouri Compromise. Remember that new states north of this line were supposed to be free states. The Kansas-Nebraska Act allowed the people who settled in these territories to decide for themselves whether to form slave or free states.

Many Northerners were outraged. Frontier farmers were worried that rich Southern planters would grab all the best land and use slaves to farm it. The farmers demanded that the western lands be "free soil." Workers who wanted to move west were also upset. They did not want to compete with slaves for jobs.

Many "free soilers" joined with abolitionists to form a new political party.

They called it the Republican Party. The Republicans believed that "no man can own another man" and "all new states must be free states."

An Illinois lawyer named **Abraham Lincoln** spoke for the new party. The Kansas-Nebraska Act, he warned, was a bad law. People from slave states and free states were already rushing into Kansas. "Knives and six-shooters are seen plainly enough," said Lincoln. "Is it not probable that the contest will come to blows and bloodshed?"

Lincoln was right. Free soilers and slave owners in Kansas were soon at war. Newspapers were full of stories about "Bleeding Kansas."

MAP SKILL: Use the map to locate Kansas and Nebraska. Were these territories north or south of the Missouri Compromise line?

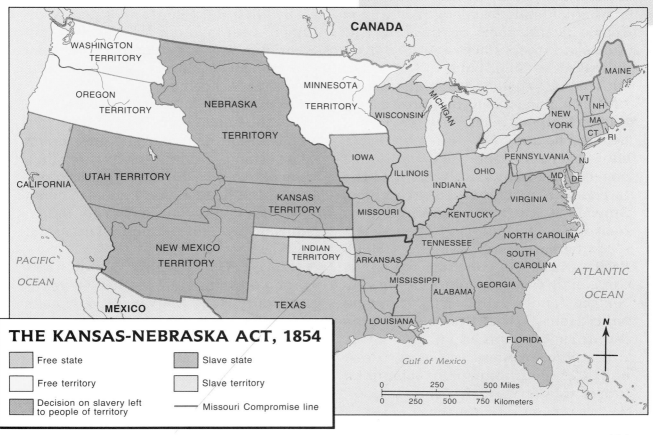

THE KANSAS-NEBRASKA ACT, 1854

- Free state
- Free territory
- Decision on slavery left to people of territory
- Slave state
- Slave territory
- Missouri Compromise line

DRED SCOTT AND JOHN BROWN

In 1857 the Supreme Court tried to end the argument over whether slavery should be allowed in the territories. That year a slave named Dred Scott asked the court for his freedom. Scott had lived with his owner in free territory. He argued that this fact should make him a free man.

The Supreme Court ruled against Scott. Slaves, it said, were property. The Constitution protects the right of Americans to take their property anywhere. Congress could not close some territories to slavery. Slavery, the Court said, could exist anywhere.

Southerners cheered the Dred Scott Decision. But most Northerners opposed the Court's ruling. One newspaper called it "The Decision that Cannot Be Obeyed." A few people even feared that cruel slave dealers like Simon Legree would soon be invading the North with their slaves.

Instead, a small band of black and white abolitionists invaded the South. In 1859 a man named John Brown led a raid on Harper's Ferry, Virginia. Brown believed he had been chosen by God to end slavery. He and his 18 followers hoped to set off a slave rebellion. The raiders were quickly killed or captured. Brown was later hanged in Virginia for treason.

Northerners were divided over John Brown's raid. *The Liberator* called the work of Brown and his followers an "insane effort." But New England writer Henry David Thoreau saw John Brown as "an angel of light."

Southern whites, however, were united in their opinion. To them John Brown was an "angel of destruction."

LINCOLN IS ELECTED

By 1860 the country was deeply divided. Four men ran for President that year. But only one stood firmly against the spread of slavery. That man was Abraham Lincoln.

Northerners admired Lincoln as a self-made man. He had been born in a log cabin in Kentucky and grew up on the Illinois frontier. His schooling, Lincoln wrote, "did not amount to one year." But he read every book he could get his hands on. Later he taught himself law and became a successful lawyer.

Lincoln's belief that slavery was wrong drew him into the new Republican Party. Like Lincoln, Republicans wanted to keep slavery out of the territories. In 1860 the Republican Party chose Lincoln to run for President. Their slogan was "Free Territory for a Free People."

The actions of John Brown in Kansas (*far left*) and later at Harper's Ferry helped further divide the country. By 1861, the North was led by Abraham Lincoln (*left*) and the South by Jefferson Davis (*right*).

Southerners were frightened by the Republican Party. Their newspapers predicted ruin for the South if Lincoln won the election. When the votes were counted, the Southerners' worst fears came true. Abraham Lincoln had been elected President.

Angry Southerners began talking about secession, or leaving the Union. Lincoln called such talk "humbug." But by the beginning of 1861, seven slave states had seceded from the Union.

The states that seceded joined together to form the Confederate States of America. They chose a Mississippi Senator named Jefferson Davis as the President of their new Confederacy.

THE NOT-SO-UNITED STATES

In 1861 Abraham Lincoln became President of the United States. Once, Congress had been able to keep the Union together with compromises. But no longer. *Uncle Tom's Cabin*, Bleed-ing Kansas, and John Brown's raid had left the country too divided for more compromise. Now the North and South pulled completely apart.

 Check Your Reading

1. How was the issue of slavery in the territories settled in 1820? In 1850?
2. Why did the Dred Scott decision please Southerners? Why did it upset Northerners?
3. How did several Southern states react to the election of Abraham Lincoln in 1860?
4. GEOGRAPHY SKILL: How far north did slavery extend as a result of the Missouri Compromise?
5. THINKING SKILL: Classify the events described in this lesson into at least three groups. What do the groups you made tell about the events before the Civil War?

Union or Secession?

By 1860 the North and the South had become two very different places. For many years they had tried to solve their disagreements peacefully. But the issue of slavery only drove them farther and farther apart.

Then came the election of Abraham Lincoln in 1860. You read in Lesson 3 that the South was very upset over Lincoln's victory. Some Southerners feared that Lincoln would free the slaves. Others feared a slave rebellion. Talk of secession grew. No one knew what would happen to the United States in the months ahead.

The Granger Collection

POINT ☆▷

Reasons for Secession

In 1860 a paper in Charleston, South Carolina, explained why it supported secession.

In every way, the whole Northern people have been hostile to us and our most important rights.

Has a man's own brother, born of the same parents, a right to invade his home, to wage war upon him and his family, and take away his property? And if he should do so, the hurt brother has not only a right but a duty to cut off all communication with that unnatural brother, to drive him from his home, and treat him as an enemy and a stranger. Then why should we any longer submit to our tyrant brother—the power-hungry, abolitionist North!

The political policy of the South demands that we should rise up and announce to the world that we must be a free and an independent people. All admit that a final breakup of the Union is inevitable, and we believe the crisis is not far off. Then let it come now; the better for the South that it should be today.

● How did the writer believe the North treated the South?

COUNTERPOINT ▷☆

Reasons for Staying in the Union

In March 1861, when he took the oath of office, Lincoln gave his view about the importance of keeping the Union together.

I believe that the Union of these states is forever. No government ever had a law to bring about its own end. Continue to follow all the laws of the Constitution, and the Union will last forever.

One section of our country believes slavery is right, and ought to be extended. The other believes it is wrong, and ought not to be extended. This is the only real dispute.

Physically speaking we cannot separate. A husband and wife may be divorced and be beyond the reach of each other. But the different parts of our country cannot do this. They have to remain face to face.

In your hands, my countrymen, is the important issue of civil war. You can have no conflict without being yourselves the ones ready to attack. You have no reason to destroy the government, while I shall have the most solemn oath to "preserve, protect, and defend" it.

● What did Lincoln believe was the only dispute between the North and South?

UNDERSTANDING THE POINT/COUNTERPOINT

1. Why did the newspaper writer believe the South should secede?
2. Why did Lincoln believe that the Union was forever?
3. In your opinion, which argument made the stronger case? Explain your answer.

IMPORTANT EVENTS

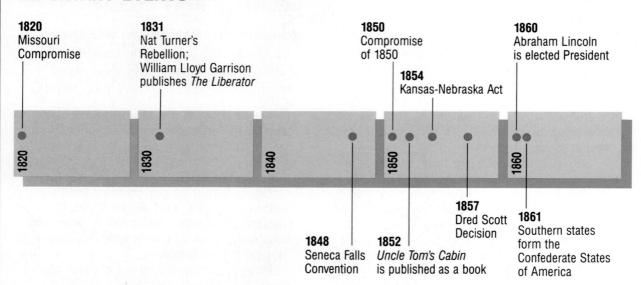

1820
Missouri
Compromise

1831
Nat Turner's
Rebellion;
William Lloyd Garrison
publishes *The Liberator*

1850
Compromise
of 1850

1854
Kansas-Nebraska Act

1860
Abraham Lincoln
is elected President

1820

1830

1840

1850

1860

1848
Seneca Falls
Convention

1852
Uncle Tom's Cabin
is published as a book

1857
Dred Scott
Decision

1861
Southern states
form the
Confederate States
of America

PEOPLE TO KNOW

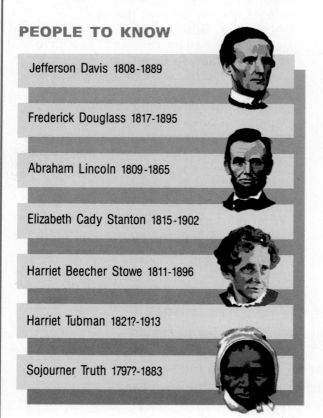

Jefferson Davis 1808-1889

Frederick Douglass 1817-1895

Abraham Lincoln 1809-1865

Elizabeth Cady Stanton 1815-1902

Harriet Beecher Stowe 1811-1896

Harriet Tubman 1821?-1913

Sojourner Truth 1797?-1883

IDEAS TO REMEMBER

■ By 1850 the North and South had developed two very different ways of life.
■ Black and white abolitionists worked hard to bring about an end to slavery.
■ Disputes over slavery grew worse with the publication of *Uncle Tom's Cabin*, the passage of the Kansas-Nebraska Act, and the Supreme Court's decision on the Dred Scott case.

REVIEWING VOCABULARY

abolitionist
Compromise of 1850
Missouri Compromise
secession
Underground Railroad

Number a sheet of paper from 1 to 5. Beside each number write the word or term from the list above that matches the statement.

1. An agreement between the North and South that settled the slavery question in the Louisiana Territory
2. An agreement between the North and South that involved the Fugitive Slave Law and the admission of California as a free state
3. A system of helping slaves escape to freedom in the North or Canada
4. A person who wanted to end slavery
5. A state's withdrawing from the Union

REVIEWING FACTS

Number a sheet of paper from 1 to 5. Beside each number write whether the statement is true or false. If it is false, explain why.

1. The North was filled with farms and plantations.
2. The most important cash crop in the South was tobacco.
3. More people lived in the South than in the North.
4. The Seneca Falls Convention was the first black rights convention.
5. *Uncle Tom's Cabin* was a novel that explained why slavery was needed in the South.

WRITING ABOUT MAIN IDEAS

1. **Writing a Play About Frederick Douglass:** Write a brief play about one or two events in the life of the abolitionist Frederick Douglass. Your play should explain how events shaped Douglass's views.
2. **Writing a Character Sketch:** Choose one of the people discussed in this chapter. Make a list of words that describe that person. Then write a paragraph based on the words in your list.
3. **Finding Cause-and-Effect Statements:** Many events discussed in this chapter had important effects or results. For example, Lincoln's election led to the secession of the Southern states. Write at least four cause-and-effect statements based on information in the chapter.

BUILDING SKILLS: WRITING A REPORT

1. When writing a report why is it important to limit your subject? Why is it important to make an outline? What is a bibliography?
2. Pretend your textbook is one of your sources for a report on Nat Turner's rebellion. Prepare some note cards for your report from this source.
3. Read over your note cards. Then make an outline for a report on Nat Turner's rebellion.

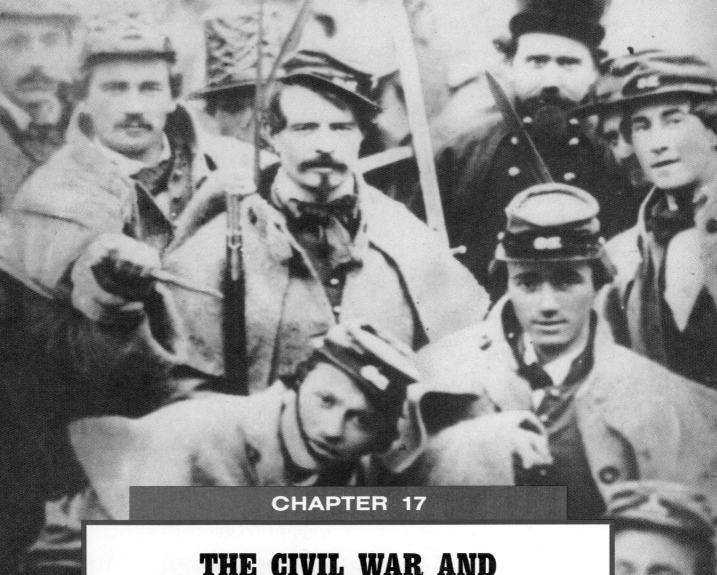

CHAPTER 17

THE CIVIL WAR AND RECONSTRUCTION

FOCUS

Fourscore and seven years ago our fathers brought forth on this continent, a new nation, conceived [formed] in liberty, and dedicated to the proposition [idea] that all men are created equal.

When President Lincoln said these words in 1863, the United States was torn apart by war. Southerners insisted they had a right to secede from the Union. Northerners believed just as strongly that secession was wrong. They fought to save the Union. By 1863 they were also fighting to end slavery.

READ TO LEARN

Key Vocabulary	Key People	Key Places
Civil War	Abraham Lincoln	Fort Sumter
	Winfield Scott	Richmond
	Robert E. Lee	Bull Run
	Thomas "Stonewall" Jackson	

Read Aloud

All through the night of April 12, 1861, the rooftops of Charleston, South Carolina, were covered with people. Through the moonlight they could see the shadowy outlines of Fort Sumter in the harbor. Union troops still held the fort, even though South Carolina had joined the Confederacy. But the troops would not be there much longer.

As dawn brightened the sky, a loud boom startled the city. A fiery red ball burst overhead. Confederate guns had begun to bombard Fort Sumter. The war that so many had feared for so long had begun.

Read for Purpose

1. **WHAT YOU KNOW:** Why did the Southern states secede when Abraham Lincoln was elected President?
2. **WHAT YOU WILL LEARN:** What were the strengths of the Union? Of the Confederacy?

STRENGTHS OF THE UNION

The cannonballs crashing down on Fort Sumter were the first shots of the Civil War. A civil war is an armed fight between groups of people within the same country. The Civil War is also known as the War Between the States.

In 1861 South Carolina, Mississippi, Florida, Alabama, Georgia, Louisiana, and Texas had left the Union and created the Confederacy. These states be-

lieved the North was trying to destroy their way of life. They were ready to fight for their independence.

President Abraham Lincoln opposed secession. He believed that no state had the right to leave the Union. The North, he said, would go to war to keep the United States together.

When the Civil War began, Northerners expected a quick victory. After all, the Union had far more people and wealth than the Confederacy. It could build and supply a bigger army.

You can see from the graph on this page that most of the country's factories were in the North. Those factories would be used to make weapons and uniforms for the Union army. Even though the South was a farming area, the North grew most of the country's food—enough to feed a large army. Finally, the North had most of the country's railroads. They could be used for moving soldiers and supplies.

General **Winfield Scott**, commander of the Union army, thought talk of a quick victory was foolish. Scott knew that the North needed time to build an army and a navy. He also knew that the South would be a very stubborn enemy. Scott thought it would take three years to crush the Confederacy. He was wrong. It would take four.

During those long years many people grew tired of war and pleaded with President Lincoln to "let the South go."

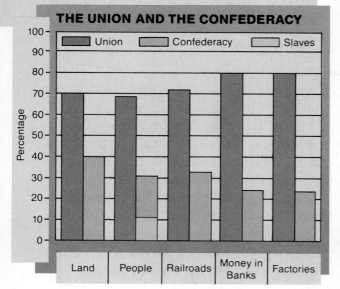

GRAPH SKILL: Compare the strengths of the Union and Confederacy. Which had more people—the North or the South?

THE UNION AND THE CONFEDERACY

Union Confederacy Slaves

Percentage

100 90 80 70 60 50 40 30 20 10 0

Land People Railroads Money in Banks Factories

But Lincoln believed that a united nation was worth fighting for. It saddened him greatly to read the lists of those who died in each battle. Still, he would not let the United States be destroyed. His strong leadership was, perhaps, the Union's greatest strength.

STRENGTHS OF THE CONFEDERACY

After the Union troops at Fort Sumter surrendered, four more slave states left the Union. With 11 states in the Confederacy, Southerners also hoped for a quick victory. If we can hold out against the North for a few months, they said, the North will grow tired of war and quit.

The South's greatest strength was its army. Southern boys grew up riding horses and using guns to hunt. They were better prepared for war than Northerners from cities. Southerners would fight fiercely to protect their homes and their way of life.

The Confederate army was led by many of the country's best generals. When the war began, Lincoln asked **Robert E. Lee** of Virginia, to command the Union army. Lee faced a hard choice. But he decided he could not fight "against my relatives, my children, my home." Lee became the commander of the Confederate army.

THE BATTLE OF BULL RUN

In the spring of 1861 both sides built up their armies. "Oh, but this is grand!" wrote a Union officer. "Troops, troops, tents, tents, the frequent thunder of guns practicing." But Northerners soon grew tired of all the practicing. They wanted to end the war quickly by capturing the capital of the Confederacy—**Richmond**, Virginia.

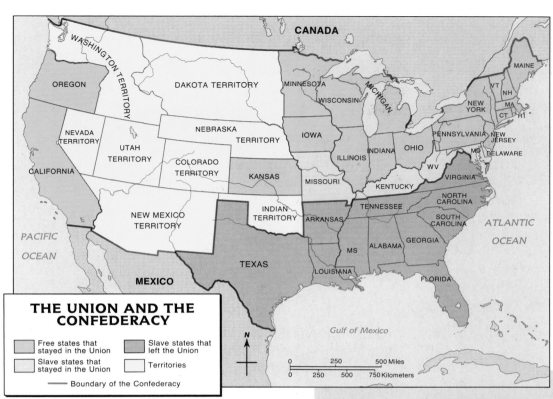

THE UNION AND THE CONFEDERACY

- Free states that stayed in the Union
- Slave states that stayed in the Union
- Slave states that left the Union
- Territories
- ▬▬ Boundary of the Confederacy

MAP SKILL: Locate Kentucky on the map. Was it part of the Union or the Confederacy?

In July 1861, 35,000 Union troops marched out of Washington, D.C., to invade Virginia. Along the way soldiers picked berries and joked with sightseers who had come along to watch the battle.

The Union army met a large Confederate force by a small stream called Bull Run. As the cannons boomed someone shouted, "I guess we will be in Richmond tomorrow."

Confederate General Thomas Jackson had other plans. He and his Virginians stood their ground "like a stone wall." By late afternoon Thomas "Stonewall" Jackson's soldiers had pushed back the Union attack.

Southerners were thrilled. A few more battles like Bull Run, they said, and the war will be over. Northerners were shocked. Their dreams of quick victory had ended.

THE NORTH AGAINST THE SOUTH

The Civil War began in 1861 with the Confederate attack on Fort Sumter. Northerners believed that they could quickly defeat the South. Southerners were just as sure that their army could outfight the North. As you will read, each side had misjudged the other.

Check Your Reading

1. Why did Northerners think the Union would win the Civil War?
2. Why did Southerners believe the Confederacy would win?
3. What happened at Bull Run?
4. **GEOGRAPHY SKILL:** Which western state left the Union in 1861?
5. **THINKING SKILL:** Compare the advantages of the North and South.

411

2 The Long Road to Victory

READ TO LEARN

Key Vocabulary

blockade
Anaconda Plan
Emancipation
  Proclamation
Gettysburg
  Address
total war

Key People

George McClellan
Clara Barton
Ulysses S. Grant
George Pickett
William Tecumseh
  Sherman

Key Places

Antietam
Vicksburg
Gettysburg
Appomattox

Read Aloud

In the early days of the Civil War, Union troops marched to battle singing Julia Ward Howe's "Battle Hymn of the Republic." Southerners' favorite marching song was "Dixie." But as the conflict dragged on, the songs of war changed. By 1863 tired troops were singing "When This Cruel War Is Over" and "Dear Mother, I've Come Home to Die." By then, the road to victory seemed endless.

Read for Purpose

1. **WHAT YOU KNOW:** What was the Confederacy fighting for? What was the Union fighting for?
2. **WHAT YOU WILL LEARN:** How did the North win the Civil War?

PLANNING FOR VICTORY

Before the Union defeat at Bull Run, President Abraham Lincoln and General Winfield Scott had made plans for winning the war. First, they called for a naval blockade of Southern ports. A blockade is the closing of an area to keep people and supplies from going in or out. The blockade was needed to keep the South from trading their cotton crops for military supplies from Europe.

Second, they planned to divide the South by gaining control of the Mississippi River. This would make it hard for Texas, Louisiana, and Arkansas to send soldiers and supplies to the other Confederate states. Finally, they planned to destroy the Confederate government by capturing Richmond.

Scott called this three-step approach the Anaconda Plan. Like a huge anaconda snake, the North would squeeze the life out of the South.

412

THE BLOCKADE

The Anaconda Plan got off to a slow start. The Union navy had fewer than 50 ships with which to patrol the South's long coastline. Fast Southern ships called "blockade runners" easily escaped capture.

In 1862 the South tried to destroy the Union's fleet of wooden ships. The Confederacy's secret weapon was the *Merrimac*, a large steamship that had been covered with thick iron plates. When the *Merrimac* chugged into Chesapeake Bay, Union ships opened fire. But their cannonballs bounced off the *Merrimac*'s thick sides. Then the guns of the iron monster ripped through the Union's wooden ships.

The Union, though, had its own secret weapon. The next day a small, strange-looking iron ship called the *Monitor* challenged the *Merrimac*. For hours the two iron ships pounded each other with cannon fire. Finally the *Merrimac* headed for safer waters, battered but not beaten.

More iron ships were built by both sides. But the North could build ships faster than the South. By 1865 the Union had over 650 ships blockading Confederate ports. Mountains of cotton piled up on Southern docks with nowhere to go.

The *Monitor*, with the Union flag flying from its stern, meets the *Merrimac* in battle. In both navies young sailors like the boy below carried powder to the guns.

ANTIETAM AND THE END OF SLAVERY

Another aim of the Anaconda Plan was to capture Richmond, Virginia, the Confederate capital. This task was given to General George McClellan. Day after day McClellan trained his men. But he showed no signs of going to war. Lincoln worried that the general had a case of "the slows." He even asked if he might "borrow" the army if McClellan was not going to use it.

In the spring of 1862 McClellan finally marched into Virginia. He was beaten back by General Robert E. Lee. That fall McClellan and Lee met again at Antietam (an tē' təm), Maryland.

Over 23,000 soldiers were killed or wounded in one terrible day. As Lee pulled back to Virginia, McClellan claimed victory. But the men who fought at Antietam called the battle "a defeat for both armies."

After the Battle of Antietam, President Lincoln gave the war a new purpose. The time had come, he said, "when slavery must die that the nation might live."

In September 1862, Lincoln issued the Emancipation Proclamation. To emancipate means to free someone. In his proclamation, or official announcement, Lincoln declared that on January 1, 1863, all slaves in the Confederacy would be "forever free." The Emancipation Proclamation turned the war into a fight for freedom.

MAP SKILL: Locate the Union and the Confederate states on the map. Did more battles take place in the Union or in the Confederacy?

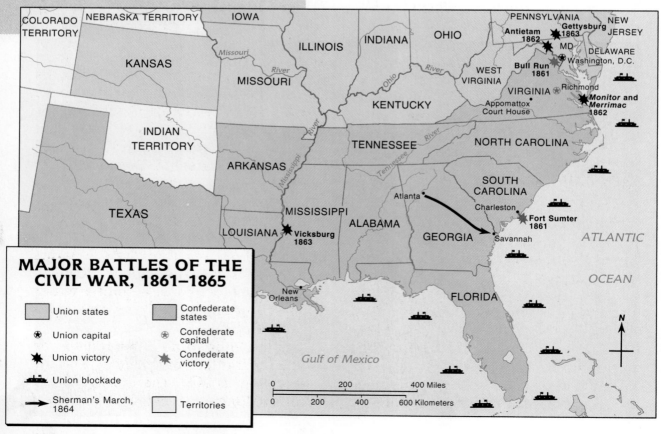

MAJOR BATTLES OF THE CIVIL WAR, 1861–1865

- Union states
- Union capital
- Union victory
- Union blockade
- Sherman's March, 1864
- Confederate states
- Confederate capital
- Confederate victory
- Territories

BLACKS AND WOMEN IN THE WAR

In 1861 African-American men who tried to join the Union army were told, "This is a white man's war," and were turned away. The Emancipation Proclamation made it a black man's war as well. In 1863 Lincoln ordered the Union army to allow blacks to join. Over 200,000 black soldiers served in the army and navy. More than half were former slaves.

When slaves became soldiers they lost their "plantation manners." No longer did they have to bow their heads or lower their eyes when around whites. When it was time to fight, they proved they were the equal of anyone in both courage and skill.

Women also joined the war effort. Some, like the abolitionist Harriet Tubman, served as spies or scouts. Both black and white women nursed the sick and wounded. Clara Barton risked her life to carry food and medicine to the wounded in battle areas. Soldiers called her the "Angel of the Battlefield." Later, Barton started the American Red Cross, an organization to help people in need.

VICKSBURG AND GETTYSBURG

Another part of the North's Anaconda Plan was to win control of the Mississippi River. By 1863 Union forces had taken control of most of the river. But the Confederacy still held the town of Vicksburg, Mississippi. Find Vicksburg on the map on page 414. Located on a cliff above the river, the guns of Vicksburg could destroy any passing boats.

Union troops led by General Ulysses S. Grant surrounded Vicksburg in May

The Granger Collection

After the **Emancipation Proclamation**, black soldiers were welcomed into the Union army. They fought bravely in many battles.

1863. As the town ran out of food, its people ate anything to survive—even mules. After six weeks, Vicksburg finally gave up. The Confederacy had been split in two. The Southern states west of the Mississippi River were now cut off from the rest of the South.

Meanwhile, Lee had invaded the North to try to cut off Washington, D.C., from the rest of the Union. On July 1, 1863, his army met a larger Union force near Gettysburg, Pennsylvania. For three days, a soldier wrote, "the slaughter [killing] on both sides was awful."

On the third day, Lee ordered the 15,000 men led by General George Pickett to charge the enemy lines. Union soldiers watched in silent terror as thousands of Confederate soldiers marched toward them. Then they opened fire. The Southerners were caught in a storm of bullets. Pickett's charge resulted in disaster. The next day, Lee led his battered army back to Virginia.

Four months later, in November 1863, Abraham Lincoln came to Gettysburg to honor the soldiers who had died there. In his **Gettysburg Address** Lincoln spoke about the purpose of the Civil War and the ideals of American democracy. You read the beginning of Lincoln's speech in the Chapter Opener on page 408. He ended with his promise:

> . . . that these dead shall not have died in vain; that this nation, under God, shall have a new birth of freedom . . . and that government of the people, by the people, for the people, shall not perish from the earth.

GRANT WAGES TOTAL WAR

In 1864 President Lincoln asked General Grant to take command of the Union army. Grant changed the way the Civil War was fought. No longer would it be a war between two armies. Grant wanted to wage **total war** against the South. Total war is an all-out war against an entire people. Its purpose is to destroy their ability and their will to fight.

The South got its first taste of total war in the Shenandoah Valley. Union troops marched in with orders from Grant to "let that valley be left so that crows flying over it will have to carry their rations [food] along with them." Union soldiers destroyed everything—crops, homes, and barns—and left a wasteland.

Grant then sent General **William Tecumseh Sherman** into Georgia with orders to do "all the damage you can." Sherman promised to "make Georgia howl." His troops cut a 60-mile-wide (90-km) path of destruction from

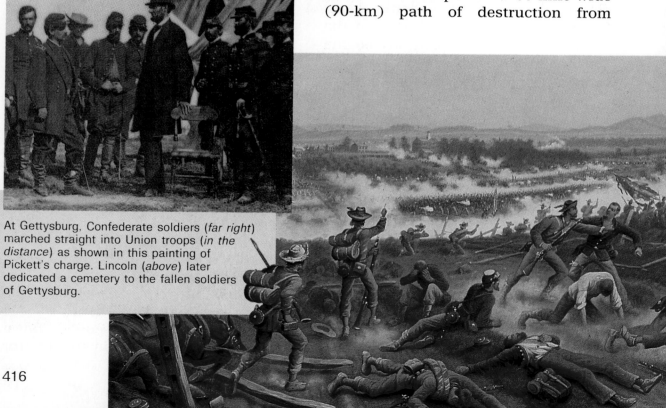

At Gettysburg, Confederate soldiers (*far right*) marched straight into Union troops (*in the distance*) as shown in this painting of Pickett's charge. Lincoln (*above*) later dedicated a cemetery to the fallen soldiers of Gettysburg.

Atlanta to Savannah. Wherever they went, they robbed plantations, tore up railroads, and burned cities.

SURRENDER AT APPOMATTOX

While Sherman was marching through Georgia, Grant was fighting Lee in Virginia. Grant's losses were so huge that people called him "The Butcher." Still, he pushed on. His motto was, "When in doubt, fight!"

In April 1865 Union troops invaded Richmond. Lee knew the war was over. "There is nothing left for me to do but go and see General Grant," he said, "and I would rather die a thousand deaths."

The two generals met on April 9 at Appomattox, Virginia. Grant agreed to let Lee's troops give up their guns and go home peacefully. When the surrender of the South was over, Grant's troops began to cheer. But Grant stopped them. "The war is over," he said, "the rebels are our countrymen again."

Generals Grant (*left*) and Lee (*right*) met to end the war at the little town of Appomattox, Virginia.

THE COST OF WAR

After four long years, our country's most destructive war was finally over. The Confederacy was gone and with it, slavery. The Union had survived. But the cost of the Civil War was huge. Over 600,000 Americans had died in the war, and the South lay in ruins.

Check Your Reading

1. How did the Union plan to defeat the Confederacy?
2. What was the Emancipation Proclamation? Why was it important?
3. How did General Grant change the way the war was fought?
4. **GEOGRAPHY SKILL:** Locate Vicksburg on the map in this lesson. Why was the Battle of Vicksburg important to the North?
5. **THINKING SKILL:** Based on your reading in this lesson, what can you conclude about the Anaconda Plan?

3 A Troubled Peace

READ TO LEARN

Key Vocabulary

Reconstruction impeach
Black Codes carpetbagger
Freedmen's Bureau scalawag
sharecropping segregation

Key People

John Wilkes Booth
Andrew Johnson
Hiram R. Revels
Blanche K. Bruce

Read Aloud

"The most terrible part of the war is now to come," wrote a young girl from Georgia upon learning of Robert E. Lee's surrender. Many Southerners shared her fears. They had begun the war with great hopes. Now they were left with burned towns and deserted plantations. Ahead, many Southerners could see only poverty, with no future and no hope. For the defeated South, the end of war brought a troubled peace.

Read for Purpose

1. **WHAT YOU KNOW:** How did the Civil War end?
2. **WHAT YOU WILL LEARN:** What changes took place in the South during Reconstruction?

THE DEATH OF LINCOLN

On April 14, 1865, five days after Lee's surrender, President Abraham Lincoln and his wife went to a play at Ford's Theater. As the audience was enjoying the performance, John Wilkes Booth slipped silently into the President's box. He drew a gun and fired. Lincoln slumped, a bullet in his brain. By morning the President was dead.

Booth blamed Lincoln for all the South's troubles. He believed he had struck down a tyrant. A few days later Booth was hunted down and trapped in a barn. As soldiers surrounded the building a gunshot rang out. Whether Booth was shot or whether he killed himself is not clear. But the man who had killed Abraham Lincoln was now dead. Booth's last words were said to be, "I thought I did [it] for the best."

Instead of helping the South, Booth had hurt it. Just a few weeks earlier, Lincoln had begun his second term as President. At that time he had called on all Americans to help him "bind up the nation's wounds." He wanted to build "a just and lasting peace." Now, as Northerners mourned their fallen leader, their hearts hardened against the South.

LINCOLN'S PLAN FOR RECONSTRUCTION

Before his death, President Lincoln had drawn up a plan for rebuilding the South. He knew that putting the country back together would take careful, thoughtful plans. When Lincoln died, Vice President Andrew Johnson became President. Johnson tried hard to carry out Lincoln's plan. This time of rebuilding that followed the Civil War is called Reconstruction.

Lincoln's plan for Reconstruction was simple. When 10 percent of a Confederate state's voters swore their loyalty to the Union, they could form a new state government. The new government had to approve the Thirteenth Amendment to the Constitution, which abolished slavery. Then that state could rejoin the Union.

By the end of 1865, every Confederate state but Texas had followed these steps to reenter the Union. President Johnson announced that Reconstruction was over.

Many members of Congress did not agree. They were upset about what was happening in the South. First, nothing had been done to punish Southerners who had rebelled against the Union. Those who had led the Confederacy were now running state governments.

Second, they objected to the way blacks were being treated. Across the South the new state governments had passed laws to control the newly freed blacks. These Black Codes made it unlawful for blacks to live in certain areas and hold certain jobs. Blacks without jobs could be arrested, fined, and jailed.

Not one Southern state allowed blacks the same rights as whites, including the right to vote. In the eyes of

Many Southern cities lay in ruins after the Civil War. Richmond (*above*) was once the capital of the Confederacy.

many Congressmen, this was all wrong. They began to develop their own plan for Reconstruction.

THE FREED SLAVES

While Congress and President Johnson argued over Reconstruction, 4 million freed slaves faced an uncertain future. Slavery was over at last. For the first time freed slaves could be legally married. Now their children belonged to them, not to a slave owner.

With freedom, though, came hunger and homelessness. After the war some slaves stayed on the plantations where they had lived and worked. However, many Southern planters sent their former slaves away with nothing to eat. "The Yankees [Northerners] freed you," the planters said. "Now let the Yankees feed you."

In March 1865 Congress set up the Freedmen's Bureau to help the freed slaves. The Freedmen's Bureau provided food and medical care to both blacks and whites after the war. It helped blacks find work at fair pay.

The **Freedmen's Bureau** provided an education for former slaves. Both children and adults, denied an education while slaves, were eager to attend school.

The Freedmen's Bureau also set up over 4,000 schools for former slaves. Blacks of all ages crowded into these schools. One observer saw "a child six years old, her mother, grandmother, and great-grandmother . . . all begin their alphabet together." Another person saw African-Americans "starve themselves, and go without clothes, in order to send their children to school."

BECOMING SHARECROPPERS

To survive, the freed slaves needed some way to earn a living. At the same time, planters needed workers to make their land productive. But the Civil War had left most Southerners penniless. Landowners had no money to pay farm workers.

To solve this problem, many planters divided up their land and rented it to farm workers. Since money was scarce, the planters agreed to accept part of the crop grown on their land as rent, instead of cash. Often the planter's share was as much as one half of the crop. This system of renting land for a share of the crop raised on it is called **sharecropping**.

Many freed slaves and poor whites became sharecroppers. It was a hard way of life. Sharecroppers often had to borrow money to buy seeds and supplies. If their crops were good and crop prices were high, they could make enough money to pay off their debts. But too often crops were poor and prices low. Every year, most sharecroppers slipped deeper into debt.

CONGRESS VERSUS PRESIDENT JOHNSON

For two years President Johnson and Congress fought bitterly over who would control Reconstruction. Then, in 1867, Congress passed its own plan for Reconstruction. Under Congress's plan, the South would be ruled by the Union army until new state governments were formed. This time, however, the governments would not be run by men who had rebelled. The new leaders would be blacks and whites who had been loyal to the Union.

At the same time, Congress passed laws limiting the President's power. In Johnson's view, these laws were not constitutional. He refused to obey any of them. The House of Representatives then voted to **impeach** him. To impeach means to charge the President with wrongdoing while in office.

The Constitution gives the Senate the power to hold impeachment trials. If two thirds of the senators find a President guilty of wrongdoing, the President is removed from office. President Johnson was saved by just one vote. He stayed in office, but he had lost his fight to control Reconstruction.

NEW SOUTHERN GOVERNMENTS

While the South was under military rule, it elected new leaders. Some were Northerners who had moved south after the Civil War to teach in black schools or to start businesses. Many came carrying a suitcase made of carpet scraps called a carpetbag. So these Northerners were called **carpetbaggers**. Most white Southerners believed carpetbaggers had come only to make money at the South's expense.

Other new leaders were Southerners who had stayed loyal to the Union. Many were poor whites who had never owned slaves. These white Southerners were called **scalawags**. A scalawag, said one Southern observer, was no better than a "mangy dog."

Under military rule, blacks voted and became political leaders. **Hiram R. Revels** and **Blanche K. Bruce** from Mississippi were the first African-Americans elected to the Senate. Other states elected blacks to the House of Representatives. Blacks served in the legislature of every Southern state. Blacks and whites worked together to write new state constitutions. They granted the right to vote to all men, black or white, rich or poor.

Once new governments were formed, these same leaders brought needed changes to their states. They repealed the Black Codes. They built the South's first public schools and hospitals. And

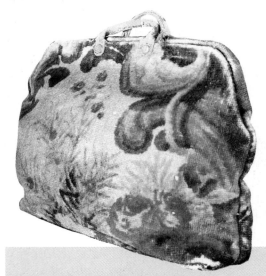

The carpetbag was an ordinary suitcase of the 1800s. To white Southerners, however, a Northerner coming South after the Civil War might be scorned as a **carpetbagger**

they rebuilt roads, bridges, and railroads damaged during the war.

The new state legislatures also approved two new amendments to the Constitution. The Fourteenth Amendment says that all people born in the United States are citizens. It also says that all citizens must be treated equally under the law. The Fifteenth Amendment states that no citizen can be denied the right to vote because of color or race.

BLACKS IN THE SOUTH

Most white Southerners were unhappy with the new governments. Taxes had gone up sharply to pay for new schools and roads. The high taxes hurt landowners, who needed money to rebuild their farms and plantations.

Many whites were also angered by seeing blacks holding public office. They still looked down on blacks, much as they had during slavery. It was time, they said, to put blacks "back in their place."

421

To stop blacks from voting and running for public office, a few people in the South turned to the use of violence and fear. Secret societies were formed throughout the South to bring back "white man's government."

The Ku Klux Klan was the most powerful of these secret groups. The Klan did its work at night. Dressed in white robes and hoods, Klan members warned blacks that voting could be dangerous. Those who did not listen were often beaten or even killed.

Threats and violence were not the only ways to keep blacks from voting. Blacks working for whites were told they would lose their jobs if they voted. Sometimes voting places were hidden from black voters.

Despite such pressure, blacks continued to vote. But they often found that their votes were not counted. As one black voter said, "A hole gets in the bottom of the [ballot] boxes some way and lets out our votes."

In 1877 the last Union soldiers left the South. Reconstruction was finally over. By then white Southerners had regained control of their state governments. They passed laws making it almost impossible for blacks to vote. They also moved the South toward the complete segregation, or separation, of blacks and whites.

Segregation laws were passed to keep blacks and whites separate in most public places. Blacks had to ride in segregated railroad cars. They went to separate black schools. Blacks were even buried in segregated graveyards.

THE END OF RECONSTRUCTION

As you have read, President Lincoln was killed in 1865 just as the Civil War ended. After Lincoln's death, President Andrew Johnson and Congress fought over who should control Reconstruction. Johnson lost. Under Congress's plan for Reconstruction, new leaders gained power in the South. For a few years blacks voted and held public office.

Reconstruction ended in 1877 when the Union army left the South. Soon the South returned to "white man's rule." Blacks lost many rights, including the right to vote. And segregation became a way of life in the South.

Check Your Reading

1. What was President Lincoln's plan for Reconstruction?
2. Why did some members of Congress disagree with Lincoln's plans?
3. What changes were made by the new Southern state governments during Reconstruction?
4. **THINKING SKILL:** Compare the life of a freed black person during Reconstruction with that of a slave before the Civil War.

During **Reconstruction** blacks got the right to vote in the South. What problems did blacks face in trying to vote?

The Friendly Supper Club

Americans are still dealing with the effects of slavery more than 100 years after Abraham Lincoln issued the Emancipation Proclamation. In many communities across the United States blacks and whites lead separate lives. Too often they do not take the time to get to know each other. This separation makes it hard to work out differences.

Nearly 300 people in Montgomery, Alabama, have found an enjoyable way to bring people together. They have formed The Friendly Supper Club. They meet every month for dinner at a local restaurant. They share a meal and get to know one another. There are no club officers, no official business, and no membership dues. Anyone can join. There is only one rule at The Friendly Supper Club—every member must bring a person of another color to dinner.

Mysteriously, the real name of the man who started The Friendly Supper Club has never been known. In 1983 there was a lot of anger between whites and blacks in Montgomery. Letters signed "Jack Smith" were sent to people of both groups suggesting that they all meet regularly at a local restaurant for dinner. His idea was that the supper club would offer a chance for blacks and whites to sit down and get to talk to one another. "Jack Smith's" letter said:

> Outright segregation has disappeared but . . . few blacks that I know visit socially with whites, or whites with blacks, in a way that builds understanding among friends.

Thirty-five people showed up for the first meeting. The club has kept on growing ever since. The idea of The Friendly Supper Club has spread to other towns and cities. Encouraging friendships among blacks and whites seems like a simple and pleasant way to bring a community together. As one member of the club said, "When people are friends, they're more likely to work things out."

Asking Questions

It is half-time at the championship game. The football coach has just reviewed with you and your teammates a new plan to win the game. Then the coach asks, "Are there any questions?"

Have you ever thought up a question when someone asked you to? How did you know what questions to ask? Asking good questions is one way to learn about things that *you* want to know. If you do not ask questions, you might learn only what someone else wants you to learn.

Trying the Skill

In this chapter you read that President Andrew Johnson was impeached by the House of Representatives but found not guilty by the Senate. List three questions you could ask to better understand what happened.

1. How did you decide what questions to ask?
2. What information would your questions provide?

HELPING YOURSELF

The steps on the left will help you ask questions on any topic. The example on the right shows one way to use these steps to learn more about the impeachment of Andrew Johnson.

One Way to Ask Questions	Example
1. Identify the topic that you want to find out about.	The topic is the impeachment of President Andrew Johnson.
2. Figure out what you want to know about the topic. Recall what you already know. Then ask yourself what else you could learn to understand the topic better.	In Lesson 3 you read that Congress and President Johnson fought for control of Reconstruction. Now try to find out what caused their conflict.
3. Remember the words that help you start a question. They are: • *who, what, where, when* and *how*—for finding facts • *why*—for finding cause and effect connections • *so what*—for finding the meaning or importance of the topic.	To find out more about the topic, you could ask *who* was involved or *when* did it happen. To learn about causes, you could ask *why* did it happen.
4. Arrange your questions in order from the easiest to the most difficult. You might start with fact-finding questions and then move to cause and effect-finding questions. End with questions that try to find out the meaning of something.	Fact-finding questions are the easiest. You should begin your list with these. Your list should end with questions that try to find out the importance of Johnson's impeachment.
5. Ask and then answer the questions that you came up with.	By asking and answering good questions, you will be able to find out what you want to know.

Applying the Skill

Another topic that you read about in this chapter is called "The New Southern Governments."

List three questions whose answers would help you to learn more about this subject.

1. This section is probably about
  a. Southern governments during Reconstruction
  b. control by the South of the carpet industry
  c. amendments to the Constitution

2. Which of the following questions would probably be hardest to answer?
  a. What changes took place in the South during Reconstruction?
  b. How did these changes affect the lives of people living in the South?
  c. Why were the new governments important?

Reviewing the Skill

1. What are some words you could use to come up with good questions?
2. How do you know what questions to ask?
3. Why is it useful to ask questions?

425

IMPORTANT EVENTS

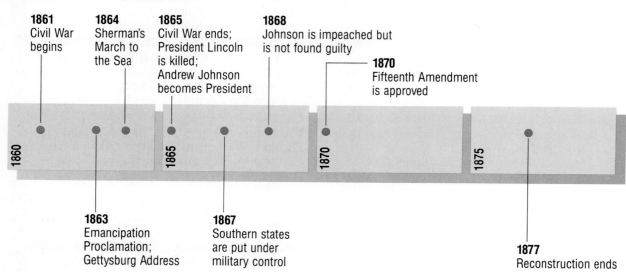

1861
Civil War begins

1864
Sherman's March to the Sea

1865
Civil War ends; President Lincoln is killed; Andrew Johnson becomes President

1868
Johnson is impeached but is not found guilty

1870
Fifteenth Amendment is approved

1860

1865

1870

1875

1863
Emancipation Proclamation; Gettysburg Address

1867
Southern states are put under military control

1877
Reconstruction ends

PEOPLE TO KNOW

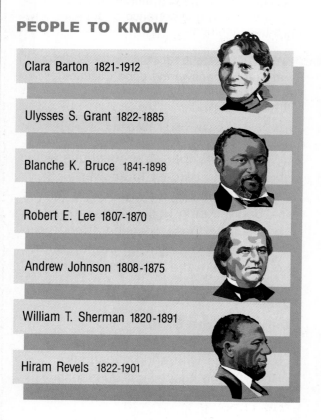

Clara Barton 1821-1912

Ulysses S. Grant 1822-1885

Blanche K. Bruce 1841-1898

Robert E. Lee 1807-1870

Andrew Johnson 1808-1875

William T. Sherman 1820-1891

Hiram Revels 1822-1901

IDEAS TO REMEMBER

■ When the Civil War began in 1861, the Union had the advantages of resources, factories, people, and transportation.

■ Union victories at Antietam, Vicksburg, and Gettysburg as well as Sherman's march through Georgia helped the North win the Civil War.

■ Although blacks were freed during the Civil War and gained rights during Reconstruction, they were denied many of their rights in the years after Reconstruction. Reconstruction introduced sharecropping, segregation, and terrorism to the South.

REVIEWING VOCABULARY

blockade   sharecropping
impeach   total war
segregation

Number a sheet of paper from 1 to 5. Beside each number write the word or term from the list above that best completes the sentence.

1. When Congress believes the President has done something wrong, they may vote to _____ the President.
2. When Grant decided to wage _____ against the South, his aim was to destroy more than the Confederate army.
3. After Reconstruction, _____ laws forced African-Americans to go to separate schools and churches.
4. During the Civil War the North used a _____ to try to keep the South from trading with other countries.
5. In _____, freed slaves rented farmland from planters. To pay the rent, they had to give much of their crop to the landowner.

REVIEWING FACTS

1. Name two strengths of the Union at the beginning of the Civil War. Name two strengths of the South.
2. What was the Anaconda Plan?
3. Name three battles of the Civil War. Where did each take place? Who won each battle?
4. What was Reconstruction?
5. Write two sentences about the way African-Americans in the South were treated during Reconstruction.

WRITING ABOUT MAIN IDEAS

1. **Writing a Paragraph:** Imagine that you lived in Georgia during Sherman's march from Atlanta to Savannah. Write a paragraph about Sherman's army. It should tell what the army did and what you learned from seeing their actions.
2. **Writing a Character Sketch:** Choose a military leader who fought in the Civil War. Then write a sketch describing that person's leadership qualities. Explain how his actions helped his side in the war.
3. **Writing a Paragraph:** List the Union's strengths at the beginning of the war. Then write a paragraph telling how these strengths actually helped the North win the war.
4. **Writing a Speech:** Write a speech on Reconstruction that might have been given in Congress in 1865. The speech should describe President Johnson's plan for Reconstruction. It should give at least one reason why you agree or disagree with Johnson's plan.
5. **Writing About a Time Line:** Make a time line of the events that affected Southern African-Americans after the Civil War. Then write a paragraph linking the events together.

BUILDING SKILLS: ASKING QUESTIONS

1. What steps could you follow to ask good questions?
2. List three questions you could ask to learn more about the Emancipation Proclamation.
3. Why should you ask questions?

REVIEWING VOCABULARY

abolitionist
blockade
Compromise of 1850
impeach
Missouri Compromise
secession

segregation
sharecropping
total war
Underground
    Railroad

Number a sheet of paper from 1 to 10. Beside each number write a sentence using one of the vocabulary words or terms from the list above. The sentence should show that you understand the meaning of the word or term.

◖◖⬟▷ WRITING ABOUT THE UNIT

1. **Writing a Paragraph:** Why do you think the Civil War took place? Write a paragraph that answers this question. Use specific facts to support your answer.
2. **Writing an Interview:** Imagine you are a newspaper reporter in the period before the Civil War. You are interviewing a conductor on the Underground Railroad and a Southern slaveowner. You ask each one: What did you think of *Uncle Tom's Cabin*? Describe what you think their answers would be.
3. **Writing a Paragraph:** Reread the section on Lee's surrender to Grant. Study the picture on page 417. Then imagine you are a Southern soldier at Appomattox. Write a paragraph that describes your thoughts at the time.
4. **Writing About a Picture:** Look closely at the picture on pages 416–417. Write a paragraph explaining the meaning of the picture.

ACTIVITIES

1. **Researching a Civil War Battle:** Use at least two sources to research a battle of the Civil War. Prepare a report about the battle. The report should include a map. Follow the guidelines in the skills lesson on page 397 while preparing your report.
2. **Writing a Book Report:** Read *Uncle Tom's Cabin*. Then write a book report telling about the story. Remember to include your opinion of the book.
3. **Planning an Exhibit of Photos:** Imagine that you are planning an exhibit of Civil War photos. Look in library books to find photographs taken during the Civil War. Then write your own caption for each photo.
4. **Writing a Letter:** Imagine that you are visiting the South during Reconstruction. Write a letter to a friend in New York describing what life is like there for the freed slaves.
5. **Working Together to Act Out the Women's Rights Convention:** Review the material in the book about the Seneca Falls Convention. Do extra research if necessary. Then, with a group of classmates, act out the convention. Some members of the group can play the parts of convention leaders. Others can act as people who took part in the convention. Still others might want to act as opponents of women's rights.

What was Nat Turner's childhood like?

Dorothy Sterling, *Forever Free*. Garden City, N.Y., Doubleday & Co., 1963.   p.105

taught himself to read and write

had an excellent memory

was interested in science

"All my time, not devoted to my master's service, was spent in making experiments."

BUILDING SKILLS: WRITING A REPORT

1. After taking notes for a report, what other steps should you follow?
2. Look closely at the note card above. Then answer these questions.
   a. What is the source?
   b. What direct quotation is included?
   c. Do the notes answer the question at the top of the card? Explain.
3. Why is it useful to use note cards when getting ready to write a report?

LINKING PAST, PRESENT, AND FUTURE

General Grant used a plan of total war to win the Civil War for the Union. It caused the loss of thousands of lives and much property. How would total war today be the same as Grant's total war? How would it be different? What can people do to avoid such a war in the future?

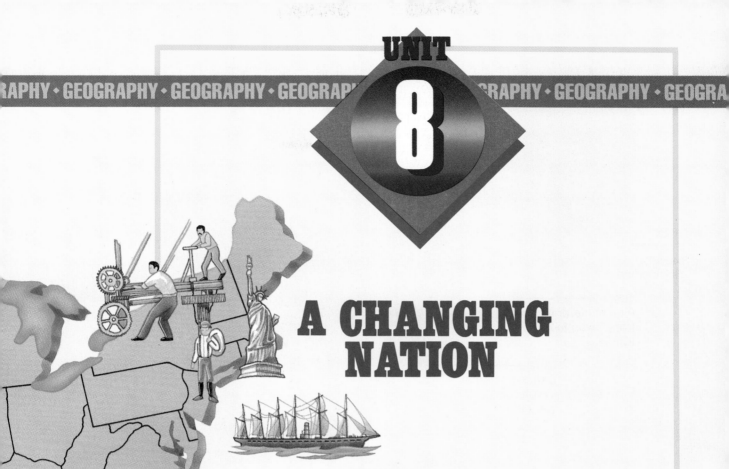

UNIT 8

A CHANGING NATION

WHERE WE ARE

In the years after the Civil War, America's frontier was moving farther and farther west. On the Great Plains, cattle ranchers drove their herds north from Texas. Other Americans came to the plains to start their own farms. In the western mountains, miners looked for silver and gold.

Once settlers had to use wagon trains to travel west. Now they could travel from New York to California on the railroad.

While some Americans traveled west, others moved from farms and small towns to the cities. After 1860, cities in America grew larger and larger. New inventions like the telephone, the electric light, and the motion picture made city life seem exciting. From east to west, America was changing.

431

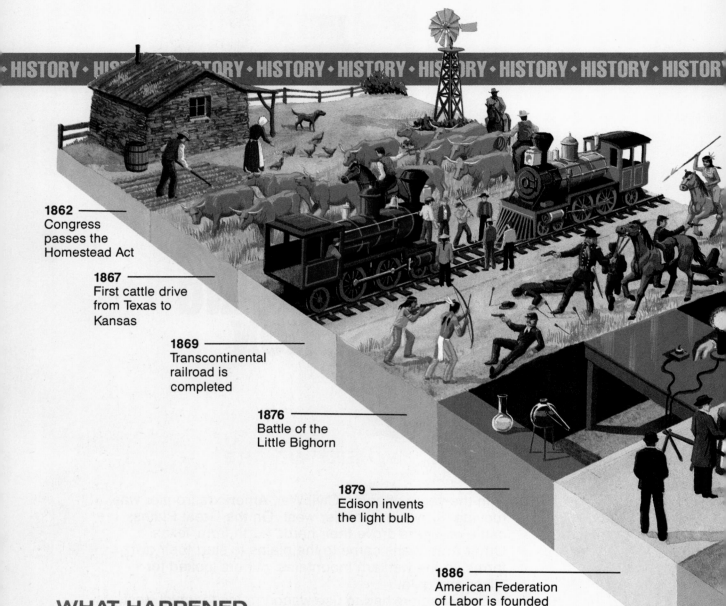

1862
Congress passes the Homestead Act

1867
First cattle drive from Texas to Kansas

1869
Transcontinental railroad is completed

1876
Battle of the Little Bighorn

1879
Edison invents the light bulb

1886
American Federation of Labor is founded

1889
Jane Addams starts Hull House

1890s
Immigrants begin coming from Eastern and Southern Europe

WHAT HAPPENED

The late 1800s was a time of rapid growth in the United States. As you can see from the time line, westward expansion continued until the frontier closed. While railroaders, ranchers, and farmers benefited from this growth, the Indians suffered. Their lives changed forever when they lost their hunting grounds.

Cities boomed in the late 1800s and workers sought new opportunities in these boom towns. New industries and new inventions gave jobs to thousands. Workers found new strength in unions at this time. The population of the nation changed as thousands of immigrants came to America seeking a better way of life.

CHAPTER 18

THE WESTWARD MOVEMENT

FOCUS

What was it the engines said,
Pilots touching, head to head,
Facing on a single track,
Half a world behind each back?

The writer Bret Harte wrote this to mark the event in 1869 when two trains met in the Utah desert. When the two rail lines met, Americans for the first time could cross the country from east to west by railroad. Railroads changed the West forever. The land would soon become the home of cattle ranchers and wheat farmers. It would also become the battleground for Indians trying to save their way of life.

1 Rails Across the West

READ TO LEARN

Key Vocabulary

transcontinental railroad

Key People

Grenville Dodge
Charles Crocker
Leland Stanford

Key Places

Promontory Point

Read Aloud

A railroad to the Pacific? Ridiculous! A railroad to the Pacific would have to cross 2,000 miles (3,200 km) of empty wilderness, a deadly desert, and two rugged mountain ranges—the Rockies and the Sierra Nevada. It seemed like an impossible dream.

Then, in 1862, Congress passed the Pacific Railroad Act which gave land and money to railroad companies to lay tracks across the West. The impossible dream was about to come true.

Read for Purpose

1. **WHAT YOU KNOW:** How might the geography of the West make building a railroad difficult?
2. **WHAT YOU WILL LEARN:** How was the first transcontinental railroad built?

A TRANSCONTINENTAL RAILROAD

Ever since gold was discovered in California in 1848, many Americans had dreamed of a transcontinental railroad. Such a railroad would stretch all the way across the continent, from the East Coast to the West Coast. Travel across the West by wagon train or stagecoach was slow and often dangerous. A transcontinental railroad would make this long journey faster, cheaper, and safer.

After the Civil War, Congress asked two companies to build a railroad across the West. The government gave them land and loaned them money. The Union Pacific Railroad began laying tracks westward from Omaha, Nebraska. At the same time the Central Pacific Railroad started building a line eastward from Sacramento, California. No one knew where the two lines would finally meet as each company raced to lay more track than the other.

THE UNION PACIFIC BUILDS WEST

A Union general named Grenville Dodge took charge of the Union Pacific Railroad. His work crew included former soldiers, freed slaves, and Irish and German immigrants.

The Union Pacific workers lived on a work train that followed them across the plains. The train had three barnlike cars, each lined with triple-decker bunks. The men slept here or in hammocks slung under the train.

Laying track was easy on the plains. First, workers used picks, shovels, and wheelbarrows to make a smooth roadbed. Then squared-off logs called "ties" were laid across the roadbed. Finally iron rails were set on the ties and held in place with large nails called "spikes."

In flat country Dodge's crew could lay 5 miles (8 km) of track a day. But when they reached the Rocky Mountains, their progress was sometimes just a few feet a day. Workers had to use blasting powder to carve a roadbed out of steep mountain slopes.

THE CENTRAL PACIFIC BUILDS EAST

A merchant from Sacramento named Charles Crocker was head of construction for the Central Pacific Railroad. Later, Crocker would boast, "I built the Central Pacific." But in 1865 it did not look like he would build anything. When his American and Irish workers reached the Sierra Nevada foothills, most of them took off to dig for gold.

Crocker then hired Chinese immigrants. Many people from China had come to California during the gold rush. The other workers made fun of the Chinese, with their pigtails and different-looking clothes. But the Chinese paid no attention. At the end of the day their roadbed was smoother and longer than that of any other workers.

The Central Pacific crew faced a backbreaking and often dangerous task. In some places workers had to lower themselves in baskets down steep cliff walls to blast a roadbed into the mountainside. They braved winter snowstorms to dig tunnels through mountains too tall to cross.

More than 12,000 Chinese immigrants helped build the transcontinental railroad. Workers cheer as a train comes through the Sierra Nevada Mountains.

THE LAST SPIKE

On May 10, 1869, the crews of the Central Pacific and Union Pacific met at Promontory Point, Utah. You can find Promontory Point on the map to the right. A great ceremony was held there to celebrate the "wedding of the rails." Nearby sat a telegraph operator. A telegraph is a machine that sends electrical messages by wire. The telegraph operator was waiting to tell the country when the last spike was driven into the last rail of the transcontinental railroad.

It was supposed to be a serious occasion. However, when workers picked up the last rail, someone shouted "Shoot!" to a photographer. The gunshy workers dropped the rail and ran for cover. Once the rail was finally in place, Leland Stanford, the president of the Central Pacific, picked up a silver hammer. He took a mighty swing to drive in the last, golden spike. He missed.

Even so, the telegraph officer flashed the message "Done." At that moment guns boomed in cities across the country. Chicago celebrated with a 4-mile-long (6-km) parade. San Franciscans danced in the streets.

BANDS OF IRON

In 1869 the dream of a railroad across the continent finally had come true. At last the country was bound together by bands of iron. During the next 25 years, four more transcontinental railroad lines crossed the West. Once it had taken pioneers months to travel by wagon to the Pacific. Now train travelers could make that same journey in just a week.

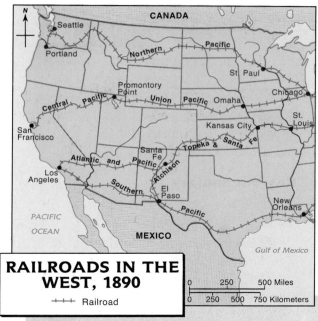

RAILROADS IN THE WEST, 1890

+++ Railroad

0   250   500 Miles

0   250   500   750 Kilometers

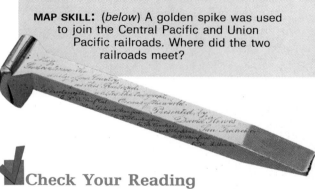

MAP SKILL: (below) A golden spike was used to join the Central Pacific and Union Pacific railroads. Where did the two railroads meet?

Check Your Reading

1. Why did building a transcontinental railroad seem like an impossible dream?

2. What problems did the companies have to solve in order to build a railroad across the West?

3. **GEOGRAPHY SKILL:** Use the map on this page to locate railroads to the West. Which railroad line most closely followed the southern border of the United States? The northern border?

4. **THINKING SKILL:** What could you do to check whether the following statement is true?: "Leland Stanford took a mighty swing to drive in the last, golden spike. He missed."

Reading Time Zone Maps

Key Vocabulary

time zone

Before the first transcontinental railroad was finished, most Americans did not travel long distances. After all, it took months to go from the Atlantic Coast to the Pacific Coast. But the railroad changed all that. A train traveler could go from New York City to San Francisco in just about seven days.

Understanding Time Zones

The problem with all this traveling was not knowing exactly what time it was. For thousands of years, people had kept time by the sun. According to sun time, noon occurs when the sun is directly overhead. But the sun is not overhead in all places at the same time. To understand how sun time works, suppose that the sun is directly overhead where you are. Because the earth turns from west to east, noon has already passed in places east of you. But it has yet to occur in places west of you. Therefore, when it is noon in the city of Chicago, Illinois, it is early afternoon in New York City and still morning in Los Angeles, California.

In the days when people used sun time, each city or town set its own time by the sun. You can imagine how hard it was to figure out a railroad timetable based on local times for places along the route. Train travelers had to ask, "Is the train going to arrive at 6:00 P.M. our time or their time?"

Finally, in 1884, the problem was solved. The world was divided into 24 time zones—one for each hour of the day. The time zones were laid out along every 15 degrees of longitude, starting at the prime meridian at Greenwich, England. It was decided that each time zone would be one hour different from the neighboring time zones. Every city and town in the same time zone would use the same time.

A Time Zone Map

The time zones set up in 1884 have since been changed to make them more practical. Today many time-zone boundaries follow national or state boundaries. The map on the next page shows the time zones in the United States. How many time zones are there in our country?

You can use the map to find out what time it is in different parts of the United States. But first you need to know a few simple rules.

The time in any zone *east* of you is always later than it is in your zone. The time in any zone *west* of you is always earlier than it is in your zone. As you move to the east, you must add an hour for each time zone that you cross. As you move to the west, you must subtract an hour for each time zone crossed.

For example, suppose it is 6:00 P.M. in New York City. To find the time in Chicago you have to subtract one hour. You can see from the map that Chicago is in the Central Time Zone while New York

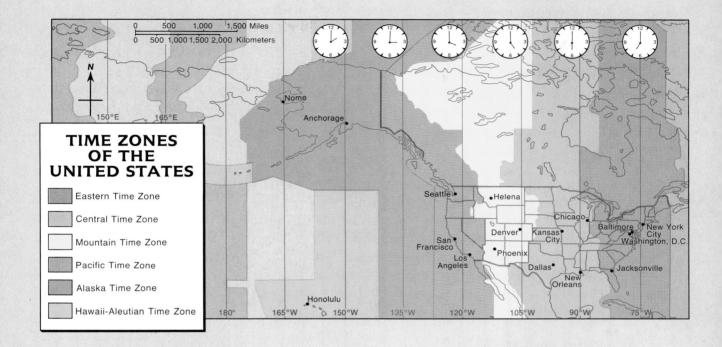

TIME ZONES OF THE UNITED STATES

- ▨ Eastern Time Zone
- ▨ Central Time Zone
- ▨ Mountain Time Zone
- ▨ Pacific Time Zone
- ▨ Alaska Time Zone
- ▨ Hawaii-Aleutian Time Zone

City is in the Eastern Time Zone. Now find Los Angeles on the map. It is in the Pacific Time Zone. It is two hours earlier in Los Angeles than it is in Chicago.

Sometimes the names of the time zones are abbreviated. For example, EST stands for Eastern Standard Time. CST stands for Central Standard Time. MST stands for Mountain Standard Time. What does PST stand for?

Suppose you want to watch a football game that is being played at 4:00 P.M. PST. But you live in Baltimore. You will have to figure out what time the game will be shown where you live.

Every year, on a Saturday in April, your newspaper probably has a headline that reads, "Remember to set your clocks ahead by one hour." Do you know why this is done? Clocks are pushed ahead so that there are more hours of light at the

end of each day. This is called daylight saving time. It lasts from the end of April to the end of October. When it is daylight saving time, the abbreviations for each time zone change. The *S* for standard is replaced with a *D* for daylight. The abbreviations in each time zone become EDT, CDT, MDT, and PDT.

Reviewing the Skill

1. What is a time zone?
2. In which time zone is Helena?
3. When it is 5:00 A.M. in Helena, what time is it in Jacksonville?
4. In which of the following cities is it 7:00 P.M. when it is 5:00 P.M. in Seattle: Dallas, New York City?
5. When it is 10:00 P.M. in Los Angeles, what time is it in Nome?
6. Why is it important to be able to use a time zone map?

439

2 The Indian Wars

READ TO LEARN

Key Vocabulary

reservation

Key People

Sitting Bull
Crazy Horse
George Custer
Chief Joseph

Key Places

Black Hills
Little Bighorn River

Read Aloud

The Cheyenne Indians watched from their hiding place as the train roared across the plains. By the time the engineer saw the stack of railroad ties that the Indians had piled on the tracks, it was too late to stop. The engine slammed into the barrier and flew off the tracks. To most Americans, the railroad was a sign of progress. But to many Indians, the "Iron Snake" crossing their lands was a threat to their way of life.

Read for Purpose

1. **WHAT YOU KNOW:** Why did most Americans want a transcontinental railroad?
2. **WHAT YOU WILL LEARN:** Why did Indians in the West go to war with American settlers?

PROBLEMS ON THE PLAINS

For hundreds of years the Plains Indians had hunted buffalo on the Great Plains. You read in Chapter 4 that the Plains Indians depended on the buffalo for food, clothing, and shelter. Then railroads began to be built across the plains, bringing farmers, miners, and ranchers. The Plains Indians tried to stop this invasion of settlers by attacking railroad workers. "We've got to clean the Indians out," warned General Grenville Dodge, "or give up building the Union Pacific Railroad."

In 1868 government officials tried to end the conflict between Indians and settlers moving west. Their plan was to send each group of western Indians to a reservation. A reservation is an area set aside for Indian use. Indians were supposed to stay on reservations. In exchange the government promised them food, supplies, and schools. Indians would be taught how to "live like the white man."

THE END OF A WAY OF LIFE

But few Indians wanted to "live like whites." The Kiowa chief Satanta said, "I don't want to settle. I love to roam over the prairies." To many Plains Indians, reservations felt like prisons. They longed to follow the buffalo again.

In 1865 millions of buffaloes roamed the plains. But as the railroads pushed into the West, these shaggy beasts began to disappear. Thousands of buffaloes were killed to feed railroad workers. William Cody hunted buffalo to feed the crew of the Kansas Pacific Railroad. He earned the nickname "Buffalo Bill" by shooting 4,000 buffaloes in a few months. The railroads also brought hunters who killed the buffalo for their hides and tourists who shot at them for sport.

The government encouraged the killing of the buffalo in order to force the Indians to settle on reservations. Without the buffalo, Indians would not have enough to eat. By 1890 fewer than 1,000 buffaloes were left on the plains.

As buffalo became scarce, Indians had to depend on the government for food. Often the food promised them never reached the reservations. Dishonest government agents sold it to the settlers instead. Sometimes the food was spoiled. A Cheyenne remembered when "great piles of [rotten] bacon were stacked on the prairie." The Indians used it for making fires.

Hungry and unhappy with reservation life, many Indians rebelled. They left the reservations to look for food or to attack settlers. When they did, they were hunted down by army troops. General George Crook hated this part of his job. He wrote:

I do not wonder that when these Indians see their wives and children starving . . . they go to war. And then we are sent out to kill. It is an outrage.

Railroad travelers in the West often shot at herds of buffalo for sport and fun. (*left*) "Buffalo Bill" Cody was a famous buffalo hunter.

The Granger Collection

Colonel George Custer was proud of his soldiers. "I could whip all the Indians on the continent with them," he bragged. What happened to Custer and his men?

CUSTER'S LAST STAND

From the Great Plains to the Pacific Ocean, Indians went to war to save their way of life. The most famous battle of the Indian wars was the Battle of the Little Bighorn, also known as Custer's Last Stand. It was fought by the Sioux (sü) Indians in 1876.

Two years earlier, gold had been discovered on Sioux land in the **Black Hills** of South Dakota. The government demanded that the Sioux sell the Black Hills. The Sioux refused and prepared to fight for their land. In June 1876 over 4,000 warriors camped beside Montana's **Little Bighorn River**. They were led by **Sitting Bull** and **Crazy Horse**. The United States army planned to trap the Indians along the river.

Colonel **George Custer** was sent with 600 soldiers to find the Indian camp. Custer's orders were to find the Indians and then wait for more troops

before attacking. As he set out, another officer called out, "Now, Custer, don't be greedy. Wait for us."

Custer was greedy—greedy for glory. On June 25 he spotted the Indian camp beside the Little Bighorn River. Custer decided to attack at once. He ordered Major Marcus Reno to charge one end of the camp. Custer rode off with about 215 men to attack the other end.

Major Reno never made it to the camp. His troops were stopped by hundreds of mounted Indian warriors. Reno's men found what shelter they could and fought until help came late the next day.

Meanwhile, Custer's ride for glory ended in disaster. His men were caught in a trap set by Crazy Horse. Custer and all of his men died. The Sioux celebrated with feasting and dancing, but this was their last victory dance. By the end of 1877 they had been driven onto reservations. No Indian group would ever again roam freely across the Great Plains.

THE NEZ PERCÉ'S LONG MARCH

A group of Nez Percé (nez pûrs') Indians was also at war in 1877. The Nez Percé lived in the Pacific Northwest where the present states of Idaho, Oregon, and Washington meet. Their leader, **Chief Joseph**, said, "I love that land more than all the rest of the world."

As much as he loved his land, he was not allowed to keep it. The United States government insisted that the Nez Percé make way for settlers. The Indians were ordered to leave their homeland and move to a reservation in Oregon.

CHIEF JOSEPH'S SPEECH OF SURRENDER

The following is part of Chief Joseph's speech of surrender to the United States Army in 1890:

"Tell General Howard I know his heart. What he told me before I have in my heart. I am tired of fighting. Our chiefs are killed. Looking Glass is dead. . . .The old men are all dead. It is the young men who say yes and no. He who led the young men is dead. It is cold and we have no blankets. The little children are freezing to death. My people, some of them, have run away to the hills, and have no blankets, no food; no one knows where they are—perhaps freezing to death. I want to have time to look for my children and see how many I can find. Maybe I shall find them among the dead. Hear me, my chiefs, I am tired; my heart is sick and sad. From where the sun now stands, I will fight no more forever."

The Granger Collection

Chief Joseph of the Nez Percé Indians described the Indians' heartbreak after losing their fight for freedom.

Chief Joseph's people had always been peaceful. But a few angry men rebelled, killing some settlers. Now the Nez Percé were outlaws. Their only hope for freedom was to escape north into Canada.

Chief Joseph's people knew little about fighting when they started their journey, but they learned quickly. In 13 battles the outnumbered Indians won all but the last one. After a 1,500-mile (2,400-km) march, they were finally captured only 40 miles (64 km) from freedom in Canada.

"I WILL FIGHT NO MORE FOREVER"

When settlers, hunters, and railroad builders moved into the West, conflict with Indians followed. As you have read, the United States government tried to bring peace by putting the Indians on reservations. Many Indians went to war to save the way of life they loved. It was a war they could not win,

however. The army always had more soldiers and more weapons.

By 1890 the Indian wars were over. The western Indian groups had been forced onto reservations. In the primary source on this page, Chief Joseph expressed the feelings of many of his people in his surrender speech.

Check Your Reading

1. How did the United States government plan to keep peace with the western Indians?
2. Why did the Indians object to living on reservations?
3. What happened at the Battle of the Little Bighorn?
4. THINKING SKILL: What alternatives might the United States government have considered to reach a peaceful settlement with the Indians?

3 Settling the West

READ TO LEARN

Key Vocabulary

Homestead Act
homesteader

Key People

Joseph McCoy
Joseph F. Glidden

Key Places

Pikes Peak
Abilene
Chisholm Trail

Read Aloud

"Go West, young man, and grow up with the country," advised newspaperman Horace Greeley in 1850. By then the eastern half of the country was settled, and more and more Americans were moving west. Some people built farms. Others started mines or large cattle ranches. To these Americans, the West seemed like a land of opportunity. But as you will read, it was also a land of hardship and heartbreak.

Read for Purpose

1. **WHAT YOU KNOW:** Why would the Plains Indians have been unhappy with Greeley's advice?
2. **WHAT YOU WILL LEARN:** What kinds of people settled the West after 1850?

THE MINERS' FRONTIER

You read in Chapter 15 that much of the West was first explored by miners. After gold was found in California, miners searched the western mountains for another "big strike."

In 1859 newspapers reported that gold had been discovered near **Pikes Peak** in what is now Colorado. "Gold is found everywhere you stick your shovel," promised one newspaper story. That spring 100,000 "Fifty-Niners" raced across the plains. On their wagons they painted the slogan "Pikes Peak or Bust."

The Fifty-Niners mined every stream and chipped every promising rock in the eastern Rockies. Most gold seekers found nothing, however. Many Fifty-Niners returned home with a new sign on their wagons—"Busted by gosh!"

A few lucky miners did find gold in Colorado. Valuable minerals were also found in present-day Nevada, Arizona, Idaho, Montana, and the Black Hills of South Dakota. Wherever miners found gold or silver in the West, mining camps sprang up like flowers after a desert rain.

CATTLE DRIVES

Texans found another kind of wealth on the western plains—cattle. The Spanish had first brought cattle to the grasslands in the 1600s. By 1865 about 4 million longhorn cattle roamed across Texas. There, longhorns sold for just $4 a head. In eastern cities, however, beef was in demand. Buyers there were willing to pay up to $40 for each animal.

Joseph McCoy figured out a way to get the Texas longhorns to eastern markets. He built large cattle pens in Abilene, Kansas, a sleepy town on the Kansas Pacific Railroad. All Texans had to do was drive their cattle across the plains to Abilene. From there McCoy would ship them east by rail.

In 1867 Texas cowhands rounded up huge herds of longhorns for the long cattle drive to Abilene. Their 1,000-mile (1,600-km) route was called the Chisholm (chiz′ əm) Trail. You can trace the Chisholm Trail on the map on this page.

Cowhands on the Chisholm Trail faced a long, dusty journey. But the price they got for their cattle in Abilene made the trip worth it. Soon there were cattle drives to other railroad towns dotting the plains.

A cowhand's life was tiring, boring, and lonely. Imagine what it was like to spend endless hours on horseback driving cattle across the plains. Most cowhands had bowed legs from long days in the saddle. Their faces were lined and leathery from the sun. For some cowhands, however, life on the open range was the only way to live. The song on page 446 tells something about life on the open range.

MAP SKILL: Cowhands had to know how to rope (*above*) and brand (*top left*). They led cattle drives from Texas to a number of railroad towns. In which state is Abilene located?

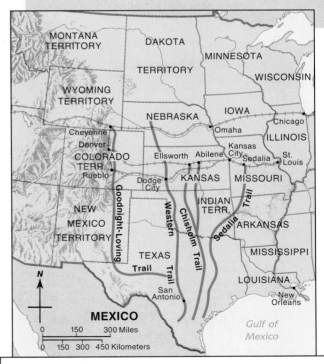

CATTLE TRAILS IN THE WEST

——— Cattle trail ++++ Railroad

Home On The Range

Cowboy Song

O give me a home where the buf - fa - lo roam, Where the

deer and the an - te - lope play, _____ Where

sel - dom is heard a dis - cour - ag - ing word, And the

skies are not cloud - y all day. _____

Home, home on the range, ___ where the deer and the an - te - lope

play, ___ Where sel - dom is heard a dis - cour - ag - ing word, And the

skies are not cloud - y all day. _____

THE CATTLE KINGDOM

By 1880 cattle and cowhands had taken the place of buffalo and Indians on the open plains. A huge cattle kingdom stretched from Texas all the way north to Canada. Large cattle herds roamed freely across the grasslands.

Then came the winters remembered as the "Big Die-ups." In both 1886 and 1887 blizzards killed millions of cattle.

After 1887 ranching changed. Ranchers built fences to keep their herds together. They raised hay to feed their animals when snow covered the ground. Many cowhands looked back fondly on the days "when we sat around the fire the winter through." Now there were fences to mend and cattle to feed all year round.

PLAINS FARMERS

Farmers followed ranchers onto the Great Plains. In 1862 Congress passed the Homestead Act. This law offered free farmland to anyone willing to work it for five years. The people who settled the land under the Homestead Act were called homesteaders.

Railroad companies also wanted people to settle on the plains. More people meant more business. So the railroads sold the land they owned along their routes. One company advertised the "Best Wheat Lands" where farmers could grow "large and sure crops every year."

Homesteaders found that there was nothing sure about life on the dry, treeless plains. Here they found soil so tangled with grass roots that wooden or iron plows were useless. They had to dig for water the way miners dug for gold. They had to build homes and fences without wood.

The plow problem was solved first. In 1868 James Oliver built a steel plow that could cut through tough prairie sod. Sod is the hard top layer of soil that is held together by the roots of grass and other plants.

Finding water was harder. Most farmers had to dig wells for water. Some wells were over 300 feet (90 m) deep. Pumps were needed to lift water from such depths. To power their pumps, farmers used windmills turned by the winds that blew constantly across the plains. In a normal day a pump could lift hundreds of gallons of water from the earth.

In this land without trees, settlers built homes from the earth itself. They used bricks of sod to build houses called soddies. Most farmers found they shared their sod houses with mice, snakes, and bedbugs. When it rained, soddies dripped mud everywhere. "Life is too short," wrote one woman, "to be spent under a sod roof."

Lacking wood, farmers had trouble building fences to keep cattle out of their fields. Then, in 1873, Joseph F. Glidden invented barbed, or pointed, wire. In a few years barbed-wire fences crisscrossed the plains.

Life on the plains meant hard work for everyone. This homesteader has collected fuel for a fire.

These Nebraska homesteaders had their photograph taken in front of their sod house.

AMERICA'S BREADBASKET

Farming on the plains was an endless struggle. In good years just enough rain fell to grow corn and wheat. In drought years, months went by with no rain, and hot winds blew across the land, killing crops.

Even worse than droughts were the blizzards that blew up suddenly out of a blue sky. Dakotans used to warn newcomers that there was "nothing between us and the North Pole except barbed-wire fence."

Plains farmers faced other problems, too. Prairie fires often swept across the grasslands, burning huge areas. Some years grasshoppers swarmed over the plains. "They came in untold millions," reported a Kansas newspaper in 1874, "in clouds upon clouds." The hungry insects ate crops, fence posts, and even boots. That year many farmers left this land "where it rains grasshoppers, fire, and destruction."

For every person who left the plains, there were more people who stayed.

The survivors were a mixed group of stubborn Easterners, freed slaves, and immigrants. But they all had one thing in common. They were as tough as the prairie sod they plowed. Together they turned the Great Plains into America's breadbasket.

THE END OF THE FRONTIER

By 1890 much of the West had been settled. In this lesson you read that miners led the way into the mountains and deserts. You saw how the Great Plains were settled first by ranchers and then by farmers. As more people spread across the West, the frontier disappeared. Only in the most rugged mountains and driest deserts was there land still untouched by the miner's pick or the settler's plow.

Check Your Reading

1. What attracted settlers to Colorado in 1859?
2. How did ranchers get their herds of cattle to eastern cities?
3. What problems did farmers face on the Great Plains?
4. **GEOGRAPHY SKILL:** Locate and name three cities in the West that were at the end of a cattle trail and also on a major railroad line.
5. **THINKING SKILL:** Suppose that you are asked to write a report about the homesteaders. The following sources are available in the library: a history of the United States written in 1830, a diary written by a plains farmer in 1870, and a novel about a present-day farm family. Which of these sources do you think would be the most credible? Explain your answer.

HOUSES FOR THE POOR

During the 1800s pioneer families came from miles around to help build a home or raise a barn. Today Millard Fuller of Georgia is making barn raising popular again. His "Habitat for Humanity" brings together people who need livable houses and volunteers who want to lend a helping hand. The volunteers are lawyers, teachers, construction workers, students, retired people—anyone willing to help build a house. One volunteer who works for a week every year is a former President of the United States.

Millard Fuller was a millionaire before he was 30 years old. But he and his wife decided to give their money away and live a simpler, more caring life. The Fullers were concerned about the lack of good housing available to the poor. Near his own town, Millard saw families living in shacks with no heat and no plumbing. These hard-working people just did not earn enough money to buy livable homes for their families.

Millard started Habitat for Humanity to provide low-cost shelter for the poor. He thought that a poor family could afford a home if the monthly payments were kept very low, and if volunteers helped the family to build it.

Families chosen by Habitat promise to make small, monthly payments over a period of 20 years. These payments cover the cost of the land and building materials. The families also promise to work 200 hours or more on their own house and on the houses of other Habitat members.

The proud home-owners work side by side with Habitat volunteers. Former President Jimmy Carter and his wife Rosalynn have been carpenters on many Habitat houses. They helped to turn old buildings into good homes in New York City. In Charlotte, North Carolina, the Carters worked with 350 other volunteers to build 14 new homes in just 5 days.

Millard Fuller's motto is "No More Shacks!" He wants to see Habitat houses in 1,000 American towns and 60 foreign countries by 1996. Millard hopes his example will bring back the pioneer tradition of neighbor helping neighbor.

IMPORTANT EVENTS

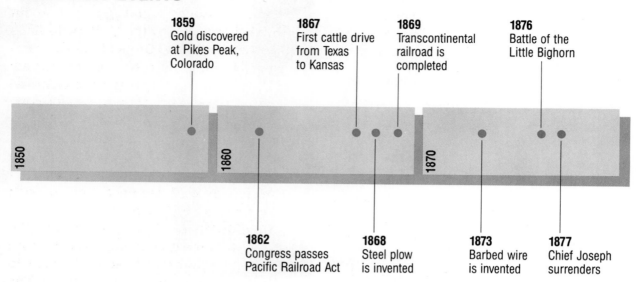

1859
Gold discovered at Pikes Peak, Colorado

1867
First cattle drive from Texas to Kansas

1869
Transcontinental railroad is completed

1876
Battle of the Little Bighorn

1850

1860

1870

1862
Congress passes Pacific Railroad Act

1868
Steel plow is invented

1873
Barbed wire is invented

1877
Chief Joseph surrenders

PEOPLE TO KNOW

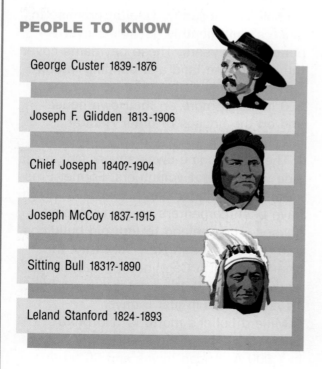

George Custer 1839-1876

Joseph F. Glidden 1813-1906

Chief Joseph 1840?-1904

Joseph McCoy 1837-1915

Sitting Bull 1831?-1890

Leland Stanford 1824-1893

IDEAS TO REMEMBER

■ When the transcontinental railroad linked the East and the West together, it opened up the West for settlement.

■ As settlers moved westward, Indians fought to save their way of life.

■ Miners, ranchers, and farmers all helped settle the Great Plains.

REVIEWING VOCABULARY

Homestead Act   transcontinental
homesteader   railroad
reservation

Number a sheet of paper from 1 to 5. Beside each number write the word or term from the list that matches the definition. One term is used twice.

1. An area set aside for Indians to use
2. A railroad that stretches across a whole continent

3. A law that gave free farmland in the Great Plains to anyone who promised to work it for five years
4. People living in the Great Plains who farmed land that was given to them by the government
5. In 1868 the government planned to send each group of western Indians to live on this kind of land

REVIEWING FACTS

1. What was the transcontinental railroad? Name three landforms that it crossed.
2. Name three ways that the railroad changed life for the Plains Indians.
3. Who were the Fifty-Niners?
4. Why were the plains known as the "cattle kingdom" in the 1880s?
5. Describe three inventions that helped farmers on the prairies.

WRITING ABOUT MAIN IDEAS

1. **Writing a Paragraph:** Review the information about the farmers of the Great Plains. Look at the pictures on pages 447 and 448. Then write a paragraph describing what life was like on the plains.
2. **Writing a Newspaper Story:** Imagine that you are a newspaper reporter in the 1860s and 1870s. Your job is to report on either the completion of the transcontinental railroad or the Battle of the Little Bighorn. Write the newspaper story. Tell the main facts and include some background information.

3. **Writing a Paragraph About the Nez Percé Indians:** You have read about what happened to the western Indians in the 1800s. The United States government passed laws that helped settlers move west. It set up reservations for the Indians to live on. Finally it sent troops to force the Indians to move. Write a paragraph about what happened to the Nez Percé. Give your opinion on the government action and the response of the Nez Percé. Were the actions of each side correct or incorrect?
4. **Writing About Cause and Effect:** Re-read the time line on page 450. Choose three of the events. Use each event to write a cause-and-effect statement. The event you choose can be a cause or an effect.

BUILDING SKILLS: READING TIME ZONE MAPS

Refer to the map on page 439 to answer the following questions.

1. How can you use a time zone map to help you figure out what time it is in Hawaii?
2. If it is 2:00 P.M. in Boston, what time is it in Denver?
3. If it is 9:00 A.M. in San Francisco, what time is it in Richmond?
4. In which time zone is Chicago located?
5. Why is it helpful to understand time zones?

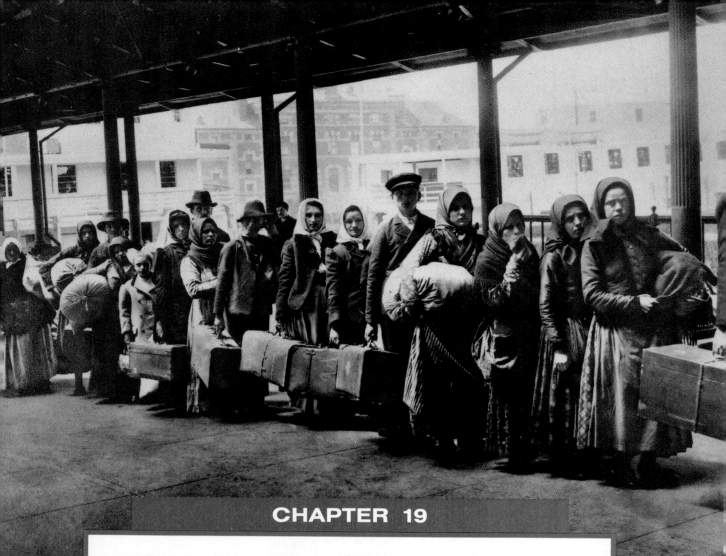

CHAPTER 19

THE RISE OF MODERN AMERICA

FOCUS

> . . . *Give me your tired, your poor,*
> *Your huddled masses yearning to breathe free,*
> *The wretched refuse of your teeming shore.*
> *Send these, the homeless, tempest-tost to me,*
> *I lift my lamp beside the golden door!*

If the Statue of Liberty could speak, thought poet Emma Lazarus, this is what she would say. When the "Lady with the Lamp" was unveiled in 1886, the United States was changing rapidly. Small towns were growing into cities. New inventions were changing the ways Americans lived and worked. And immigrants were pouring into America.

1 The Industrial Revolution

READ TO LEARN

🔲 Key Vocabulary

Industrial Revolution
technology
free enterprise system

Key People

Cyrus McCormick
Andrew Carnegie
Thomas Alva Edison
Alexander Graham Bell

🔲 Read Aloud

It talks!" shouted Don Pedro, the emperor of Brazil. Don Pedro had come to Philadelphia in 1876 to help celebrate our nation's 100th birthday. The United States had invited countries from all over the world to take part in a great World's Fair. In the back corner of one of the fair's exhibits, Don Pedro found Alexander Graham Bell showing his new invention, the telephone. The emperor put the telephone to his ear. To his astonishment, he could hear Bell talking through it. The telephone was one of many amazing inventions that would change American life forever.

🔲 Read for Purpose

1. **WHAT YOU KNOW:** Where were the first factories in the United States built?
2. **WHAT YOU WILL LEARN:** What happened during America's Industrial Revolution?

MACHINES REPLACE MUSCLES

When Don Pedro visited the United States in 1876, the country was in the middle of the Industrial Revolution. Machines were taking over jobs once done by hand. Products once made at home or in small workshops now were being produced in factories.

As you read in Chapter 15, America's Industrial Revolution began in New England. The country's first factories were built there to make cloth. Those early spinning and weaving machines were run by water power. Later, steam engines and electric motors would be used to run machines.

Machines helped farmers to harvest larger crops. In 1800 a farmer using hand tools could cut 1 acre (0.4 ha) of grain in a day. Then, in 1831, Cyrus McCormick invented a new cutting machine called a "reaper." With the reaper, a farmer could cut 5 acres (2 ha) of grain a day. By 1900 steam-powered machines could harvest 30 acres (12 ha) of wheat in one day.

Machines helped factory workers to produce goods faster than ever before. In 1865 a worker in a shoe factory could turn out 300 pairs of machine-made shoes a day. This was as many as a cobbler making shoes by hand might produce in an entire year.

ANDREW CARNEGIE

In the early days of the Industrial Revolution, most machines were made of iron. Iron is hard, but it breaks easily and wears out quickly. Iron rails, for example, last only three years. Steel, which is made from iron, is much

stronger. But steel was much too costly for most uses.

Then, in the late 1850s, Henry Bessemer, an English engineer, and William Kelly, an American inventor, both discovered a low-cost way to make steel. An American businessman named **Andrew Carnegie** decided to put this new steel-making **technology** to work. Technology is the use of new ideas, tools, and methods to solve practical problems.

In 1873 Carnegie built a steel mill in Pittsburgh, Pennsylvania. "The days of iron have passed," he told a friend, "steel is king." Carnegie was right. As the cost of steel came down, his steel business grew rapidly. By 1880 the railroads were buying every steel rail his company could make. Steel rails lasted 20 years, not 3. Farmers were using steel plows to cut through the thick prairie sod. Machines made of steel were humming in factories.

In 1900 Carnegie sold his steel business for over $250 million. Over the next 20 years he gave his fortune away. Carnegie built over 3,000 public libraries in towns and cities around the world. He also supported schools, parks, and hospitals.

THOMAS EDISON

Between 1860 and 1900 American inventors produced an amazing number of new inventions. The greatest inventor of this time was **Thomas Alva Edison**. Over 1,000 inventions, including the phonograph and motion pictures, came out of Edison's workshop in Menlo Park, New Jersey.

Edison's greatest invention was the electric light bulb. In the days before electric lights, most people used oil lamps to light their homes. But these

Andrew Carnegie used the fortune he earned from steel-making to help others. "The kept dollar," he once wrote, "is a stinking fish."

The Granger Collection

lamps did not give off much light. Working after dark was not easy.

To make his light bulb useful, Edison had to bring electricity into homes and workplaces. So he built a machine that produced electric power. Then he built the country's first electric power system to light up New York City.

In 1882 Edison proudly turned on his electric power system. Suddenly, New York City sparkled with light. By 1900 over 25 million electric light bulbs glowed across the country. Edison had brought the United States into the electric age.

THE FREE ENTERPRISE SYSTEM

Inventions like the light bulb led to the creation of new businesses. Why did this happen? One reason is that the United States has a **free enterprise system**. In this kind of economic system, people can start any business they want. They decide what to make, how much to produce, and what price to charge. If the enterprise, or business, fails, they will lose the money they put into it. If it succeeds, they are free to keep the profits.

A free enterprise system encourages people to invest in new ideas and inventions. To invest means to use money in the hope of making a profit. You already know that **Alexander Graham Bell** invented the telephone. But Bell did not have the cash to start a telephone business. He tried to sell his invention to a telegraph company. The company called his telephone a "toy" and said no.

Bell soon found people who were willing to invest in his invention. Bell and his investors started the American Bell Telephone Company. Their new

Two parts of the first telephone are shown above. The transmitter (*left*) changed sound into a pattern of waves that could travel over a wire. The receiver (*right*) reconverted the pattern of waves into sound.

business grew rapidly. By 1900 there were 1.3 million telephones in America.

AN INDUSTRIAL NATION

By 1900 the United States had become the world's leading industrial nation. Machines were doing jobs once done by hand. Inventions such as the electric light and the telephone were making darkness and distance disappear. America's Industrial Revolution came about because its system of free enterprise encouraged people to invest in new ideas and technology.

Check Your Reading

1. What changes came about during the Industrial Revolution?
2. Why was Andrew Carnegie able to sell all the steel he produced?
3. How does the free enterprise system encourage people to invest in new ideas and technology?
4. THINKING SKILL: How could you determine the accuracy of the following statement?: "Over 1,000 inventions, including the phonograph and motion pictures, came out of Edison's workshop in Menlo Park, New Jersey."

2 Workers and the Industrial Revolution

READ TO LEARN

Key Vocabulary

labor union
strike
American Federation of Labor

Key People

Samuel Gompers
Mary Harris Jones

Read Aloud

By 1900 the United States was producing a huge amount of goods each year. This was the bright side of the Industrial Revolution. But there was a dark side as well. In mills, mines, and factories across the country, workers toiled long hours for little pay. As one worker said, "Times are harder now than I ever knew them before."

Read for Purpose

1. **WHAT YOU KNOW:** How did new inventions such as the light bulb and the telephone improve life in the United States?
2. **WHAT YOU WILL LEARN:** How was life made better for workers in the United States during the Industrial Revolution?

CHANGING WORKING CONDITIONS

When the Industrial Revolution began in the early 1800s, most Americans worked on farms or in small workshops. By 1900 this had changed. Now there were more factory workers than farmers. Many people worked for large companies with hundreds or even thousands of workers.

On farms or in workshops, people worked at their own pace. In mills and factories, people had to work fast to keep up with the machines. They also had to work up to 16 hours a day. "Home is just the place where I eat and sleep," a steelworker said. "I live in the mills."

Many workplaces were uncomfortable and unsafe. Workers nearly froze in winter and then collapsed from the heat in summer. Many were injured by machines.

MAKING ENDS MEET

"My actual earnings last year were but $100," a worker said in 1884, "while the cost of living was $400." The wages paid most workers were too low to support a family. To make ends meet, both parents had to work. So did their children.

456

Children worked long hours for little pay in early industrial America. (*left*) A girl watches over a loom in a cotton mill. (*right*) A boy is covered with dust and dirt from working long hours in a coal mine.

Young boys worked ten hours a day, six days a week in coal mines. They earned just 50 cents a week for picking rocks out of coal as it tumbled down chutes. "The coal is hard," wrote one observer, "and accidents to the hand, such as cut, broken, or crushed fingers, are common among the boys."

Thousands of children also worked in textile mills. One woman wrote:

Tiny babies of 6 years with faces of 60 worked 8-hour shifts for 10 cents a day. If they fell asleep, cold water was dashed in their faces.

WORKERS ORGANIZED UNIONS

Across the country, workers joined labor unions to fight for better treatment. A labor union is a group of workers who join together to improve their lives. Unions bargain with employers, or business owners, for higher pay and safer workplaces. If an employer does not agree to the union's demands, its members may strike, or refuse to work. A strike lasts until an agreement is reached or workers give up and return to work.

At first most labor unions were made up of people who worked at the same craft. For example, carpenters were in one union and plumbers were in another. In 1886 leaders from several of these unions decided to work together. They formed the American Federation of Labor, or AFL. A federation is an organization made up of several groups that have a common goal.

In 1886 Samuel Gompers became president of the AFL. Gompers was a cigar maker who had grown up in England. As a union leader in the United States, his goal was "to improve the workingman's welfare year by year." Gompers encouraged union leaders to bargain with employers for better wages, hours, and working conditions. But when talks failed, the AFL used strikes as a weapon. Gompers urged AFL members to combine their money in order to help support striking workers.

The work of Mother Jones (*below*) led to thousands of children being sent home from the mills. She also aided workers on **strike**.

In the 1880s and 1890s there were hundreds of strikes. Some workers did win higher wages and shorter working hours. But most strikes failed despite Gompers's efforts. Strikers often ran out of money before their demands were met. Hunger forced them back to work. Many strikes ended when companies hired nonunion "strikebreakers" to replace striking workers.

A UNION ORGANIZER

Like Samuel Gompers, **Mary Harris Jones** was a famous union organizer. Most workers knew her simply as Mother Jones. For 50 years Mother Jones went wherever workers and unions needed help.

In 1900 coal miners went on strike in Pennsylvania. When the mining company tried to bring in strikebreakers, Mother Jones organized a group of women to drive them away. After that, women patrolled the mine both day and night to keep out strikebreakers.

In 1903 Jones led a "March of the Mill Children" from Philadelphia to New York City. Her young marchers carried signs saying "We Want to Go to School" and "We Want Time to Play." The children's march led Pennsylvania to pass a law forbidding child labor.

"THE CONCERN OF ALL"

For many Americans, as you have read, the Industrial Revolution meant long hours of work for low pay. Working conditions in mines, mills, and factories were often unsafe. Many workers joined labor unions to improve their lives. There they learned that "an injury to one is the concern of all."

 Check Your Reading

1. How did the Industrial Revolution change the way people worked?
2. Why did whole families have to go to work?
3. Why were unions formed?
4. THINKING SKILL: What conclusions can you draw about early labor unions from the facts in this lesson?

3 The Immigrants

READ TO LEARN

Key Vocabulary
sweatshop

Key Places
Ellis Island

Read Aloud

I was a man and stronger than most men. Yet my second childhood began the day I entered my new country. . . . I had to learn life over in a brand new world.

A Danish immigrant named Carl Jensen said these words after arriving in the United States. He was part of the greatest movement of people in history. Between 1860 and 1920, 28.5 million people left Europe and Asia to come to the United States. No matter where they came from, these immigrants found in America "a brand new world."

Read for Purpose

1. **WHAT YOU KNOW:** When did immigrants begin coming to the United States?
2. **WHAT YOU WILL LEARN:** What was life like for immigrants?

LEAVING HOME

People came to the United States for many reasons. "I want to leave my country because we are six children and we have very little land," wrote a young Polish farmer. All across Europe there was a lack of good farmland. The story was the same in Japan. As one Japanese boy wrote, "I saw little future in farm work."

Poverty caused many people to journey to America. A poor German girl decided to go when "I heard how easy it was to make money in America." A penniless Italian made the same choice because "I had heard things about America—that it was a far-off country where everybody was rich."

To the Jews of Eastern Europe, America meant freedom and safety. In Russia, Jews could not own land because of their religion. Many jobs were forbidden to Jews. In the 1880s Jewish villages in Russia were attacked by angry mobs. After that, wrote one Jewish immigrant, everyone talked about America.

To the poor and unwanted peoples of the world, the United States shone like a golden star. America, they had heard, was a land of opportunity. Here they could find land, work, and freedom. Here their children could go to free schools. Here, they believed, life would be better. Filled with such bright dreams, millions of immigrants left their homes for the United States.

STARTING A NEW LIFE

Immigrants traveled to the United States on crowded, smelly ships. "We were . . . like rotten sheep thrown into a pit," wrote one immigrant. "We were like silkworms [crowded] on a tray," said another weary traveler. The newcomers arrived in America dirty and worn out.

Most ships sailing to the United States landed in New York City. In 1892 the government set up an official inspection station on **Ellis Island** in New York Harbor. There, doctors checked newly arrived immigrants for illnesses. Other officials judged their ability to start a new life in a strange land.

Look at the bar graph on page 461. You can see that from 1861 to 1890, most immigrants came from Northwest Europe and Central Europe. Many headed west for the plains. By 1890, however, prairie farmers had reached the foothills of the Rockies. Good land was no longer easy to find.

After 1890 immigrants from Italy, Greece, Russia, and other parts of Eastern and Southern Europe poured into America. With the plains settled, these newcomers crowded into cities and began to search for work.

LONG HOURS, LOW PAY

The struggle to earn a living took many forms. You read in Chapter 18 that Irish, German, and Chinese workers helped build the transcontinental railroad. Many Hungarians, Poles, and Czechs worked in the steel mills. Most earned just $12 for one week of 12-hour days. Life was so hard that one steelworker wrote about life in the mills, "My people do not live in America. They live underneath America."

In San Francisco many Chinese immigrants started laundries and restaurants. In New York City many Jewish immigrants worked in **sweatshops** making clothes. A sweatshop is a small factory where people work long

The Lower East Side of New York City was a lively home to many immigrants. Newly arrived families lived, worked, shopped, and played on streets like this.

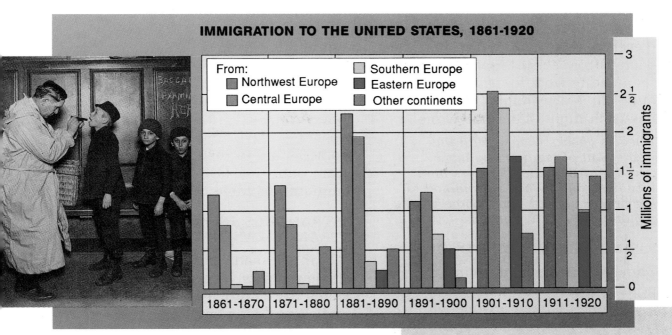

IMMIGRATION TO THE UNITED STATES, 1861-1920

From:
- Northwest Europe
- Central Europe
- Southern Europe
- Eastern Europe
- Other continents

Millions of immigrants

1861-1870 | 1871-1880 | 1881-1890 | 1891-1900 | 1901-1910 | 1911-1920

CHART SKILL: Immigrants had to have a medical exam before being admitted to the United States. According to the bar graph, how many immigrants came from Eastern Europe between 1881 and 1890?

hours for low pay in unhealthy conditions. Accidents were common in sweatshops.

By working hard, many immigrants were able to improve their lives. But as this poem by a Japanese newcomer says, starting a new life was not easy.

America . . . once
A dream of hope and longing.
Now a life of tears.

BECOMING AMERICANS

A Chinese immigrant named Lee Chew arrived in San Francisco nearly starved. The food on his ship seemed so strange to him that he could not eat it. Walking through the crowded city, Chew saw nothing that reminded him of China. Strange words and sounds confused his ear. Then, with a sigh of relief, he came to a street where he heard his own language. Here food tasted like it should, he thought. "A few days in the Chinese quarter," Chew wrote, "made me happy again."

Newcomers fought homesickness by living with others from their old coun-tries. Immigrant neighborhoods with names like Chinatown or Little Italy were found in every large city. Of his neighborhood, Stoyan Cristowe of Bulgaria said, "We had created a world of our own." In this world Cristowe could speak his own language and even buy newspapers written in Bulgarian.

While immigrants found comfort in sticking together, most wanted to become Americans. After long hours at their jobs, many went to night school to learn English and study American history.

Many immigrants saw education as the key to success in America for their children. Mary Antin was an immigrant from Russia. She had not been allowed to go to school there because she was Jewish. In the United States she found that "Education was free. . . . The [school] doors stood open for every one of us." While Mary attended public school, her older sister Frieda had to work to help support the family. So Mary taught her sister at home each night. Later she wrote:

> Frieda's cheeks flamed with the excitement of reading English . . . and her eyes shone like stars on a moonless night when I explained to her how she and I and George Washington were Fellow Citizens.

CLOSING THE GOLDEN DOOR

Some Americans had trouble accepting immigrants as "fellow citizens." Such people disliked anyone who was Catholic, Jewish, Asian, or in some other way not "just like us." Workers complained that immigrants took away their jobs and kept wages low.

In California some people stirred up hatred of the Chinese. Angry speeches usually ended with the cry, "The Chinese must go!" In 1882 Congress agreed. It passed a law that limited immigration from China. Later, immigration from Japan was also reduced.

For other immigrants, America's "golden door" remained open a while longer. Then, in 1924, Congress passed a law limiting immigration from Europe to just 165,000 people a year. With this law, 300 years of free immigration came to an end.

"STRANGERS IN A STRANGE LAND"

In this lesson you read that millions of newcomers came to the United States from Europe and Asia after the Civil War. Many settled in immigrant neighborhoods where they felt less like "strangers in a strange land."

The immigrants found new opportunities in the United States. In trying to create a better life, they helped build the new industrial America. Even so, anti-immigrant feeling grew. In 1924 America's "golden door" was closed. It was no longer open wide to the people Emma Lazarus called the "huddled masses yearning to breathe free."

A Chinese family takes an outing in San Francisco's Chinatown. When was Chinese immigration to the United States limited by law?

The Granger Collection

Check Your Reading

1. Why did many immigrants come to the United States?
2. What problems did some immigrants face once they reached the United States? How did they try to solve these problems?
3. Why did some people want to keep immigrants out of the United States?
4. **THINKING SKILL:** What was the point of view of many Americans toward immigrants before 1880? After 1880?

4 The Growing Cities

READ TO LEARN

Key Vocabulary

tenement
settlement house

Key People

Jane Addams

Key Places

Chicago

Read Aloud

"We cannot all live in cities," explained the newspaper reporter Horace Greeley in the late 1860s, "yet nearly all seem determined to do so." Between 1860 and 1900 cities in the United States doubled and even tripled in size. Many of the new city dwellers came from farms. As farmers used new machines like Cyrus McCormick's reaper, fewer workers were needed to raise crops. Americans who had once plowed and planted now looked for a new life in the cities. They were joined there by millions of immigrants.

Read for Purpose

1. **WHAT YOU KNOW:** Why did so many immigrants decide to live in cities?
2. **WHAT YOU WILL LEARN:** What was city life like after the Civil War?

THE HOUSING SHORTAGE

"Gentlemen will never consent to live on mere shelves under a common roof," said a New Yorker in the 1870s. Yet every day, more and more families arrived in New York City looking for places to live. The supply of houses could not keep up with the need for living space.

To solve this problem, Rutherford Stuyvesant built New York's first apartment building. Four families lived on each floor of the building. It seemed that New Yorkers were content to live on "mere shelves." By 1890 apartment living was part of city life.

Poor people had to settle for any housing they could find. Many lived crowded together in tenements. Most tenements were cheaply built apartment buildings divided into many tiny living units. Whole families lived in one or two small rooms with no heat or fresh air. One girl described her tenement home as "a place so dark it seemed as if there was no more sky."

Cities did not collect garbage or sweep streets in poor neighborhoods.

In 1871 most of the city of Chicago was destroyed by fire. Soon new buildings made from stone replaced the ash and rubble.

Disease spread quickly. In one poor, crowded section of **Chicago**, Illinois, three out of five babies born in 1900 died before they reached their third birthday.

CHICAGO

The river stinks. The air stinks. People's clothing . . . stinks. No other word expresses it so well as stink.

This was how the *Chicago Times* described Chicago in 1880. No other American city had grown so fast. In 1830 Chicago was a cluster of log huts beside Lake Michigan. By 1880 it was the country's second largest city. But with rapid growth came problems. Smelly garbage overflowed into the Chicago River. Factories filled the air with smoke and soot. Horse-drawn carriages clogged the streets.

Chicago was a railroad and shipping center. Every day trains brought the riches of the plains—cattle and wheat—to Chicago's flour mills and meat packing plants. Trains returned to the plains with reapers, barbed wire, and other factory goods. Meat and flour were shipped from Chicago to eastern cities and to Europe.

In 1871 there was a drought in Illinois. Barely an inch of rain fell all summer and fall. On October 8 a fire broke out in a crowded Chicago neighborhood. Hot winds spread the flames "as fast as a man could run."

The "Great Fire" burned out of control for 24 hours. The flames were so hot that wheels on streetcars melted. Train tracks turned into twisted steel snakes. Thousands fled to the shores of Lake Michigan. One man described what he saw to a newspaper.

Men buried their wives and children in the sand with a hole for air . . . then dashed into the water to stand chin-deep, breathing through handkerchiefs.

The fire left Chicago in ashes. At least 17,000 buildings were destroyed and 100,000 people were left homeless. But the city came roaring back. Soon new buildings made from stone lined Chicago's streets.

JANE ADDAMS AND HULL HOUSE

In 1889 a wealthy, well-educated young woman named Jane Addams moved into one of Chicago's poorest neighborhoods. She rented a large old home called Hull House. There she planned "to share the lives of the poor."

Addams turned Hull House into the country's first settlement house. It was a place where poor people could meet and get help with their problems. Hull House workers held classes in English, art, sewing, and cooking. There were clubs for children who had no place else to play but the streets. There was a nursery for young children of working mothers. For many poor people, Hull House was the only place where they could get a bath.

Settlement houses soon sprang up in other cities. But Jane Addams knew poor people needed government help as well. Settlement house workers urged cities to clean up poor neighborhoods. They worked to get parks built for poor children. In these and other ways, settlement workers improved life in America's cities.

Jane Addams (*left*) spent her life trying to improve the lives of the poor. She started the country's first **settlement house**.

A NATION OF CITIES

The Industrial Revolution had changed how and where Americans lived. The new jobs and opportunities were in cities. As you have read, the growing industrial cities were often dirty, smelly, unhealthy, and overcrowded. They also were exciting places to live and work. For it was here that Americans were building a new modern nation.

✔️ Check Your Reading

1. Why did apartment living become part of city life?
2. What problems did rapid growth bring in Chicago?
3. What was the purpose of Hull House?
4. **THINKING SKILL:** Do you think the source quoted on this page would be more credible or less credible than an encyclopedia account of the same topic? Explain why.

Reading Political Cartoons

Key Vocabulary
political cartoon
symbol

A cartoon is a drawing that makes you laugh. Cartoons come in many forms. You can find cartoons in comic books as well as in newspapers and magazines. One kind of cartoon is a **political cartoon**.

Political cartoons show how the cartoonist feels about a person, an event, or an issue. In their drawings cartoonists give their opinions. At the same time, they try to get other people to share their point of view.

Looking at Symbols in Cartoons

Cartoonists often use **symbols**. A symbol is a person or object that stands for something else. For example, the American flag is a symbol of our country.

Think about other symbols for our country. They include the Liberty Bell, the Statue of Liberty, and Uncle Sam. What do these symbols mean to Americans?

In the late 1800s a cartoonist named Thomas Nast created two symbols that are still used today. He drew an elephant to stand for the Republican Party and a donkey to stand for the Democratic Party.

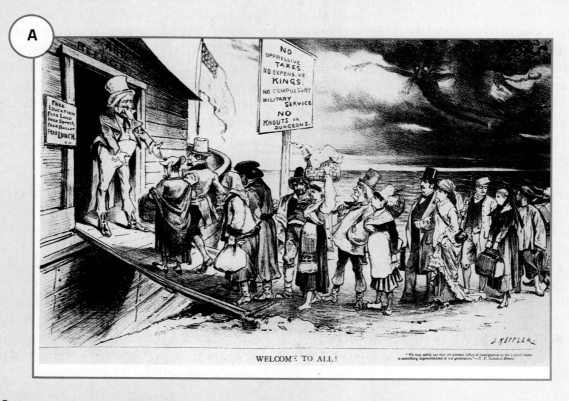

WELCOME TO ALL!

B

When you look at a political cartoon, look at all the people, animals, and objects in the drawing. See if the cartoonist has used any symbols. Think about what the symbols stand for. Look carefully at **Cartoon A** to see what symbols are used.

Finding the Cartoonist's Point of View

Cartoonists want to get their message across to their readers. Often they include captions to help readers understand their drawings. What does the caption say in **Cartoon A**?

Sometimes cartoonists make things seem larger than they really are to make a point. For example, they may show a rich man as being very fat. Often, however, cartoonists draw something bigger than it really is simply to be funny or to identify a person. If a President has large teeth or thick eyebrows, cartoonists may exaggerate that feature so that everyone can identify the person in the drawing. For example, Abraham Lincoln is often shown as *very* tall and *very* thin, with a dark beard.

Some cartoons find fault with what is going on. Others praise a person or event. The two cartoons in this lesson are about immigrants coming to the United States in the late 1800s. How are they being treated in **Cartoon A**?

As more and more immigrants arrived in the United States, some people looked down on the newcomers. Now study **Cartoon B**. What do you think the shadows behind the oldcomers represent? What are the oldcomers saying to the newcomer? What point is the cartoonist trying to make?

Reviewing the Skill

1. What is a political cartoon?
2. Why do cartoonists use symbols?
3. In your own words, what is the cartoonist saying in **Cartoon A** about the United States?
4. In **Cartoon B**, is the cartoonist for or against the oldcomers? How can you tell?
5. Do you think political cartoons are a good way to express an opinion? Why or why not?

IMPORTANT EVENTS

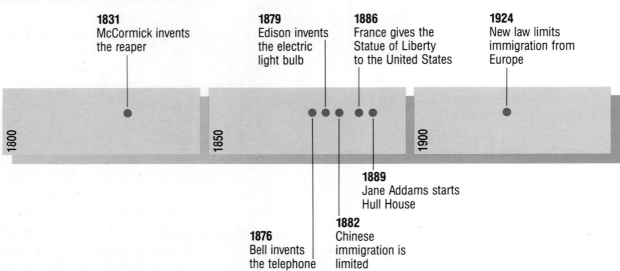

1831
McCormick invents the reaper

1879
Edison invents the electric light bulb

1886
France gives the Statue of Liberty to the United States

1924
New law limits immigration from Europe

1800

1850

1900

1889
Jane Addams starts Hull House

1876
Bell invents the telephone

1882
Chinese immigration is limited

PEOPLE TO KNOW

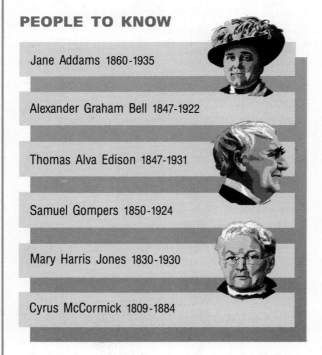

Jane Addams 1860-1935

Alexander Graham Bell 1847-1922

Thomas Alva Edison 1847-1931

Samuel Gompers 1850-1924

Mary Harris Jones 1830-1930

Cyrus McCormick 1809-1884

IDEAS TO REMEMBER

- The Industrial Revolution changed the United States from a nation of small towns and farms into a nation of cities and factories.
- Americans joined labor unions in order to improve their working conditions.
- Immigrants coming to the United States after the Civil War found new freedom and opportunity in our nation's cities.
- During the late 1800s America's cities became crowded and bustling as Americans moved to them from farms and small towns and immigrants arrived from Europe and Asia.

REVIEWING VOCABULARY

labor union   technology
strike   tenement
sweatshop

Number a sheet of paper from 1 to 5. Beside each number write the word or term from the list that completes the sentence.

1. New tools, such as the cotton gin and the steel plow, are examples of advances in ____.
2. The workers went on ____ in order to get a raise in pay.
3. An immigrant named Joe Schneider had to live in a crowded ____ in the city.
4. The workers joined together to form a ____.
5. Joe Schneider had to work long hours in a ____, making clothing.

REVIEWING FACTS

Number a sheet of paper from 1 to 5. Beside each number write whether the sentence is true or false. If it is false, explain why.

1. During the Industrial Revolution craft shops and hand tools took the place of factories and machines.
2. Railroad companies used steel rails because steel lasted longer than iron.
3. Andrew Carnegie is remembered for the coal mines he owned.
4. Thomas Edison invented the light bulb, the reaper, and the telephone.
5. The Industrial Revolution brought good times to everyone in the United States.

WRITING ABOUT MAIN IDEAS

1. **Writing a Paragraph:** What is the free enterprise system? Write a paragraph that would help a second grader understand this system.
2. **Writing a Character Sketch:** Choose one of the following people: Andrew Carnegie, Thomas A. Edison, Mother Jones, or Jane Addams. What kind of person was he or she? Write one or two paragraphs describing the person.
3. **Writing a Paragraph of Explanation by an Immigrant:** Imagine you are a new immigrant to the United States in the 1890s. Write a paragraph in which you explain your reasons for coming to America. Explain what you have found in your new country.
4. **Writing a Speech:** Workers trying to organize unions often hold meetings. Leaders give speeches telling why the workers should join the union. Write a speech that a union leader might give today.

BUILDING SKILLS: READING POLITICAL CARTOONS

1. Name two ways that a cartoonist helps readers understand the point of his or her cartoon.
2. Suppose you drew a political cartoon supporting a law to limit immigration. What might your cartoon look like?
3. Suppose you drew a political cartoon opposing a law limiting immigration. What might your cartoon look like?
4. Look again at the cartoons on pages 466 and 467. Give them new titles.

UNIT 8 · REVIEW

REVIEWING VOCABULARY

Number a sheet of paper from 1 to 5. Beside each number write the letter of the word or term that best completes each sentence.

1. A homesteader is a person who _____.
   a. leaves one country to settle in another
   b. settled on free farmland on the Great Plains after promising to work the land for at least five years
   c. kept up the family plantation after the Civil War
2. A labor union is made up of workers who _____.
   a. lay tracks for the railroad
   b. join together to improve their lives
   c. promise never to strike
3. A reservation is a place _____.
   a. set aside for Indian use
   b. where people are crowded together in a city
   c. that is reserved for immigrants to live in
4. Technology refers to the _____.
   a. Industrial Revolution
   b. production of steel
   c. machines, methods, and knowledge that are used to solve practical problems
5. A tenement is a _____.
   a. place set aside for Indian use
   b. large area reserved for immigrants
   c. crowded apartment building in a city

WRITING ABOUT THE UNIT

1. **Writing a Paragraph:** How did the Industrial Revolution help encourage the settling of the West? Write a paragraph that discusses at least two ways.
2. **Writing a Comparing Paragraph:** The immigrants left their homelands to move to the United States. The Plains Indians left their homes to move onto reservations. How were these situations alike? How were they different? Write a short paragraph in which you compare and contrast the two situations.
3. **Writing an Introduction:** Choose the person mentioned in this unit whom you admire the most. Then imagine that person is going to give a speech to a large group. Your job is to introduce him or her to the audience. As part of your introduction, tell some interesting or important things about the person's life. Also explain why the audience should pay attention to what the speaker has to say.

ACTIVITIES

1. **Writing a Book Report:** Read a book about life on the frontier, such as *Little House on the Prairie* by Laura Ingalls Wilder. Then write a book report.
2. **Reciting Indian Speeches:** Many Indian leaders of the 1880s gave moving speeches about the problems facing their people. Research and choose one of these speeches to recite to the class.

Before reciting, tell the class some facts about the Indian leader who made the speech.

3. **Working Together as a Group to Hold a Debate:** Divide into teams of two or three students. Each team should speak either for or against this statement: "The Industrial Revolution was good for the United States." Have the teams take turns presenting reasons why the statement is true or false.

BUILDING SKILLS: READING POLITICAL CARTOONS

1. What is a political cartoon?
2. Look at the cartoon below. What point do you think the cartoonist is trying to make?
3. Are political cartoons an effective way to express opinions? Why or why not?

 **LINKING PAST, PRESENT, AND FUTURE**

In the late 1800s thousands of immigrants came to the United States from Europe. Today many immigrants come to this country from Asia and Latin America. If an immigrant family moved into your community, what problems do you think it would face? What could you do to welcome the family?

North Pole

ARCTIC
OCEAN

Bering Strait

75°N

Baffin
Bay

Arctic Circle

Bering
Sea

Beaufort
Sea

Davis Strait

60°N

ALASKA

International Date Line

180°

Gulf
of Alaska

Labrador
Sea

Hudson
Bay

45°N

165°W

PACIFIC

OCEAN

150°W

Gulf of
St.
Lawrence

HAWAII

30°N

135°W

120°W

UNITED STATES

Washington, D.C.

60°W

75°W

Tropic of Cancer

15°N

Gulf of California

Gulf of Mexico

PUERTO RICO
(U.S.)

U.S. VIRGIN ISLANDS

0°

Equator

Caribbean
Sea

15°S

PACIFIC   OCEAN

105°W

90°W

UNIT 9

THE UNITED STATES IN THE TWENTIETH CENTURY

WHERE WE ARE

For most of this book, you have read about Americans developing their own land. With energy, skill, and practical know-how, they created a new, modern America. Then events in Europe and Asia drew the United States into world affairs. Our country became involved in two world wars. American soldiers fought in nations around the globe.

At the same time, Americans faced new challenges at home. They tried to end poverty and to achieve equality for all Americans. In this unit you will read about some of the events that shaped the lives of all Americans in the twentieth century.

473

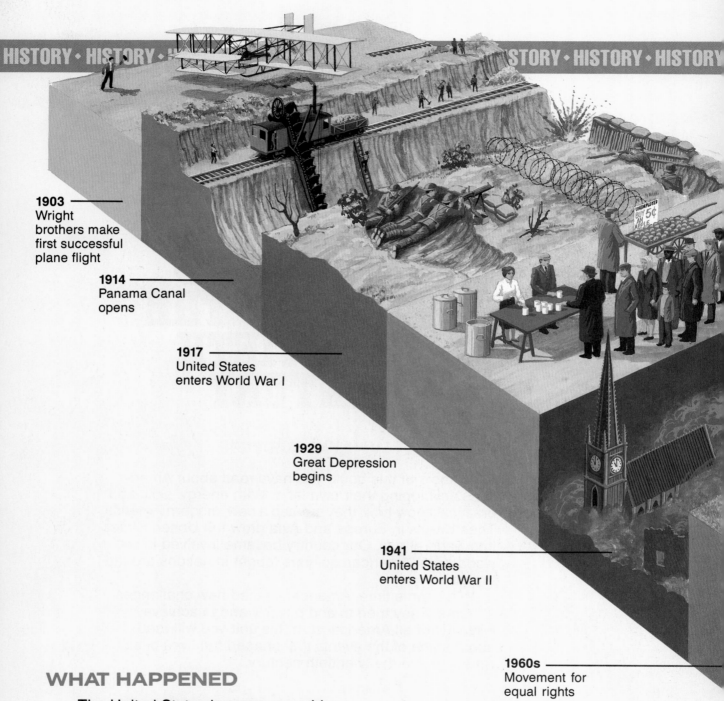

1903
Wright
brothers make
first successful
plane flight

1914
Panama Canal
opens

1917
United States
enters World War I

1929
Great Depression
begins

1941
United States
enters World War II

1960s
Movement for
equal rights

Late 1980s
Space shuttle
flights start
again

WHAT HAPPENED

The United States became a world
power in the 1900s. As the time line shows,
the country took part in two world wars—the
first in 1917 and the second in 1941. Great changes
took place in the way Americans lived during these years.
Women gained the right to vote. A great economic depression took place. As the century draws to a close, Americans
look forward to peace, equality, and well-being for all.

474

EQUALITY

EQUAL RIGHTS NOW

EQUAL RIGHTS FOR ALL

USA

CHAPTER 20

A NEW WORLD POWER

FOCUS

We have no choice as to whether or not we shall play a great part in the world. . . . All that we can decide is whether we shall play it well or ill.

President Theodore Roosevelt said these words in 1903. Never before had the United States seemed so strong. American factories led the world in making everything from steel to telephones. American ships traded in ports around the globe. The United States had one of the world's largest navies. It was clear to Roosevelt that the United States had become a world power.

1 The Geography of Alaska and Hawaii

READ TO LEARN

Key People

William Seward
James Cook
Queen Liliuokalani

Key Places

Alaska Panhandle
Alaskan Peninsula
Mount McKinley
Hawaiian Islands

Read Aloud

CASH! CASH! CASH!—Cash paid for cast-off territory. Best price given for old colonies, north or south.

This 1867 newspaper advertisement was printed as a joke. But as the United States grew more powerful, many Americans were looking for new territories. The first one they found was the huge Russian colony of Alaska. Then they turned to the Pacific Ocean and the warm and sunny islands of Hawaii.

Read for Purpose

1. **WHAT YOU KNOW:** To which region of the United States do Alaska and Hawaii belong?
2. **WHAT YOU WILL LEARN:** What landforms are found in Alaska and Hawaii?

ALASKA

"If you are young, stay away until you grow older," advised mapmaker Henry Gannett in 1899. After seeing the beauty of Alaska, he said, "all other scenery [will seem] flat."

Alaska is shaped something like a big dipper. The handle reaches south along the edge of Canada. This is the Alaska Panhandle, a long, narrow strip of land separated from Canada by steep mountains. Narrow inlets of the Pacific Ocean called fiords poke into the panhandle. Here trees grow as thick as hairs on a dog's back.

The Alaskan Peninsula forms the bowl of the dipper. Mountain ranges stretch over much of this region. The great Mount McKinley is found here. At 20,320 feet (6,194 m), it is the tallest mountain in North America. Volcanoes, mighty rivers, and huge glaciers left over from the Ice Age are also part of Alaska's landscape. A vast frozen plain called the tundra lines the region's north shore. In Russian *tundra* means "where the trees are not."

Russia claimed Alaska as a colony in the 1700s. In 1867 the American Secretary of State William Seward persuaded the Russians to sell Alaska to the United States for $7.2 million. Many critics called the Alaska purchase "Seward's Folly." They saw Alaska as a worthless land. But time has shown that Seward was right. Alaska is rich in minerals, lumber, and fish.

HAWAII

About 1,250 years ago, a group of Polynesian (pol i nē' zhən) people left their small, flat islands in the South Pacific. They sailed north in large canoes, searching for a new home. After crossing more than 2,000 miles (3,200 km) on the open sea, they finally saw land. Rising before them were islands of unbelievable size.

The first Hawaiians found eight islands lying in a gently curving line. You read in Chapter 2 that each island is the top of a volcano rising out of the ocean. The slopes of the volcanoes are covered with flowers and plants.

The Hawaiian Islands were discovered again by British explorer Captain James Cook in 1778. Soon Hawaii was a stopping place for American whaling and trading ships. Missionaries from New England came to the islands in the 1820s. They were followed by farmers who began huge sugar and pineapple plantations.

Over the years the American planters living in Hawaii gained more and more power. Then, in 1893, a new Hawaiian ruler named Queen Liliuokalani (li lē ə wō kə län' ē) tried to change things. She said that Hawaii should belong to the Hawaiian people. Unhappy with the queen's rule, the American planters decided to rebel. They took over the Hawaiian government and asked to become part of the United States. In 1898 Congress voted to make Hawaii an American territory.

TWO NEW TERRITORIES

After the Civil War, Americans began to look for new territories. In this lesson, you read how the United States purchased Alaska from Russia in 1867. Later, Hawaii was made a territory of the United States. The country seemed to be growing in all directions.

Check Your Reading

1. How did Alaska become part of the United States?
2. Why were Americans interested in the Hawaiian Islands?
3. **GEOGRAPHY SKILL:** What landforms are found in both Alaska and Hawaii?
4. **THINKING SKILL:** How could you determine the accuracy of the following statement: "In 1867 Secretary of State William Seward persuaded the Russians to sell Alaska for $7.2 million"?

Queen Liliuokalani was the last ruler of an independent Hawaii. She was overthrown in 1893.

2 The Spanish-American War

READ TO LEARN

Key Vocabulary

Spanish-American War
Rough Riders

Key People

George Dewey
Theodore Roosevelt

Key Places

Cuba
Puerto Rico
Philippines
Guam

Read Aloud

Blood on the roadsides, blood in the fields, blood on the doorsteps, blood, blood, blood! . . . Is there no nation wise enough, brave enough, and strong enough to restore peace in this blood-smitten land?

This report appeared in the New York newspaper the *World* in 1896. The story was about a rebellion in one of Spain's last American colonies. The *World*'s question would lead the United States into war.

Read for Purpose

1. **WHAT YOU KNOW:** What lands did the United States acquire after the Civil War?
2. **WHAT YOU WILL LEARN:** Why did the United States go to war with Spain?

A REVOLT IN CUBA

By 1896 Spain had only two colonies left in North America, Cuba and Puerto Rico. Both are islands that lie south of the United States, in the Caribbean Sea. A year earlier, Cubans had rebelled against Spain. Spanish soldiers in Cuba fought to put down the rebels.

Americans viewed the rebellion through the eyes of their newspapers. In New York City, the *Journal* and the *World* were battling for readers. Both used huge headlines, shocking pictures, and vivid stories to sell papers.

Reports of Spanish cruelty in Cuba, whether true or not, seemed perfect for the front page. Headlines such as "FEEDING PRISONERS TO SHARKS" sold papers. Other newspapers copied the style of the *Journal* and the *World*. Day after day Americans read about freedom-loving Cubans being killed by brutal Spanish troops.

In February 1898 the American battleship *Maine* blew up during a visit to Cuba. The twisted wreckage sank in Havana Harbor with 260 American sailors. The cause of the explosion was

The American battleship *Maine* blew up in Havana Harbor in 1898. Who was blamed for the explosion?

not known. But the *Journal* had no doubts. Giant headlines screamed "SPAIN GUILTY!"

War fever spread rapidly. The halls of Congress rang out with cries of "Remember the *Maine*" and "Free Cuba." In April 1898 Congress voted to go to war with Spain.

VICTORY IN THE PHILIPPINES

The first battle of the Spanish-American War was not fought in Cuba, but in a Spanish colony in Asia—the Philippines. At the time, a writer joked that few Americans knew whether the Philippines "were islands or canned goods." They soon found out.

On May 1, 1898, naval commander George Dewey led six American navy cruisers into Manila Bay in the Philippines. There he found a fleet of Spanish warships. Dewey gave the order to "fire when ready." The American guns blazed. By the end of the day, the Spanish ships were smoking ruins. Spain had lost nearly half its navy after a week of war.

After the victory in the Philippines, Americans went Dewey-crazy. They named babies, dogs, and towns after him. One company even called a new chewing gum Dewey's Chewies.

THEODORE ROOSEVELT

No one was happier about the war with Spain than Assistant Secretary of the Navy Theodore Roosevelt. For over a year he had been building up the American navy. Now the navy could show the world that the United States had become a powerful country.

Roosevelt was excited for another reason. "I was a sickly and timid boy," he wrote of his childhood. It was easy for stronger boys to "make life miserable for me." As a result, young Roosevelt admired "men who were fearless and who could hold their own in the world." He tried to become like them by learning to box, wrestle, and hunt.

The war with Spain gave Roosevelt a chance to prove that he was as brave as the men he had admired in his childhood dreams. He quickly quit his navy job and called for volunteers to fight the Spanish in Cuba. Some who volunteered were friends from the East and cowhands from the West. Newspapers called them "Roosevelt's **Rough Riders**."

VICTORY IN CUBA

In June 1898 about 17,000 American troops landed in Cuba. They were not well prepared. Despite Cuba's hot climate, they wore heavy woolen uniforms. Most of the Rough Riders' horses never made it to Cuba. They had been left in Florida by mistake. But that did not seem to matter to Roosevelt and his men, who sang:

Rough, rough, we're the stuff,
We want to fight, and can't get
*   enough. Whoopee!*

They did not have long to wait. The Rough Riders and the African-American troops of the Ninth and Tenth Cavalry were ordered to clear Spanish troops off San Juan Hill in Cuba. This was the moment Roosevelt had been waiting for. Leading the charge on horseback, Roosevelt was a perfect target. But he rode through a hail of Spanish bullets unharmed. Roosevelt's courage inspired his troops. Despite heavy losses, they took San Juan Hill.

Roosevelt and his Rough Riders were hailed as heroes. But part of the glory belonged to the African-American troops. One Rough Rider wrote of these soldiers:

I never saw braver men anywhere.
Some of those who rushed up the hill
will live in my memory forever.

In late July Spain surrendered. By then a disease called yellow fever was killing more Americans than were Spanish bullets. The men who had been so eager to fight were now just as eager to go home.

Of his charge up San Juan Hill, Theodore Roosevelt (*above*) wrote: "The instant I received the order, I sprang on my horse and then my (hour) began."

AMERICA'S NEW EMPIRE

The Spanish-American War ended in August 1898—just four months after it started. In December a peace treaty was signed that gave Cuba its independence. Spain also gave the Philippines, Puerto Rico, and the Pacific island of **Guam** to the United States.

Suddenly the United States controlled a chain of islands stretching from the Caribbean Sea across the Pacific Ocean to Asia. At the far end of that chain were the Philippine Islands.

During the war, rebels in the Philippines had helped American soldiers drive out the Spanish. The Filipinos expected the Americans to give their country its independence. But instead the Americans took control of the Philippines. In 1899 the same rebels rose up against their American rulers. It took the United States three years and

481

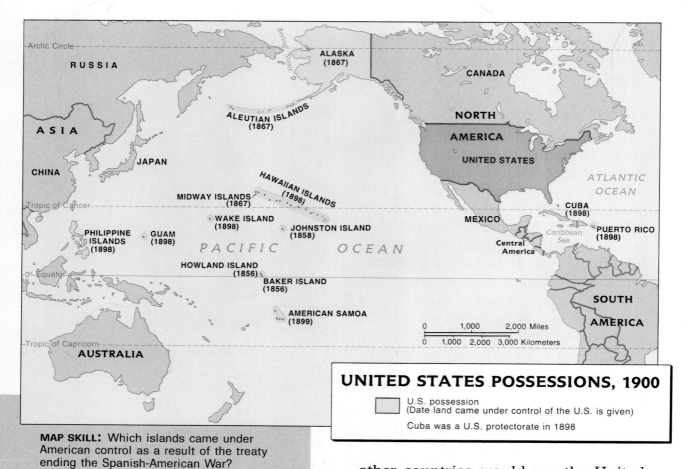

ALASKA
(1867)

RUSSIA

CANADA

ALEUTIAN ISLANDS
(1867)

NORTH
AMERICA

ASIA

UNITED STATES

JAPAN

ATLANTIC
OCEAN

CHINA

HAWAIIAN ISLANDS
(1898)

MIDWAY ISLANDS
(1867)

CUBA
(1898)

WAKE ISLAND
(1898)

MEXICO

PUERTO RICO
(1898)

PHILIPPINE
ISLANDS
(1898)

GUAM
(1898)

JOHNSTON ISLAND
(1858)

PACIFIC OCEAN

Caribbean
Sea

Central
America

HOWLAND ISLAND
(1856)

SOUTH
AMERICA

BAKER ISLAND
(1856)

AMERICAN SAMOA
(1899)

0   1,000   2,000 Miles
0   1,000   2,000   3,000 Kilometers

AUSTRALIA

UNITED STATES POSSESSIONS, 1900

U.S. possession
(Date land came under control of the U.S. is given)

Cuba was a U.S. protectorate in 1898

MAP SKILL: Which islands came under American control as a result of the treaty ending the Spanish-American War?

70,000 troops to end the rebellion. The Philippines did not become independent until 1946.

AN AMERICAN VICTORY

In 1898, as you have read, the United States went to war with Spain to free Cuba. The actual fighting lasted just ten weeks. When it was over, Spain had lost its last territories in the Western Hemisphere.

Theodore Roosevelt was pleased with the results of the Spanish-American War. Cuba had been freed. The American navy had proven that it was a powerful fighting force. The United States had come out of the war with a new empire of colonies. From now on,

other countries would see the United States as a major world power.

Check Your Reading

1. What event in 1898 caused the United States to declare war against Spain?
2. Who were the Rough Riders? What role did they play in America's victory over the Spanish?
3. What territories did the United States gain at the end of the Spanish-American War?
4. **GEOGRAPHY SKILL:** Why do you think Spain had difficulty fighting a war in Cuba?
5. **THINKING SKILL:** State two facts and one opinion in the section called "A Revolt in Cuba." Explain your choices.

482

3 The World of Theodore Roosevelt

READ TO LEARN

Key Vocabulary

conservation
national park
assembly line
suffrage

Key People

William Gorgas
Henry Ford
Orville Wright
Wilbur Wright
Carrie Chapman Catt

Key Places

Panama Canal
Kitty Hawk

Read Aloud

"It is a dreadful thing to come into the Presidency this way," said Theodore Roosevelt in September 1901. One year before, William McKinley had been elected President with Roosevelt as his Vice President. Now McKinley had been shot and killed. The Rough Rider became the new President.

Read for Purpose

1. **WHAT YOU KNOW:** Why were Roosevelt and his Rough Riders viewed as heroes?
2. **WHAT YOU WILL LEARN:** What changes took place in the United States while Theodore Roosevelt was President?

THE ROUGH RIDER PRESIDENT

Americans had never had a President like Theodore Roosevelt before. At age 42, he was the youngest man to hold this office. He was also one of the most energetic. "I always believe in going hard at everything," Roosevelt once wrote. His belief did not change when he became President.

Roosevelt moved into the White House with his wife Edith, their six children, and the family pets—dogs, rabbits, birds, squirrels, a black bear, and a short-tempered badger named Josiah. Roosevelt's children played football on the lawn, tag in the hallways, and had pillow fights at bedtime. More often than not, the President was at the center of all these activities.

Roosevelt faced the country's problems with equal energy. One example was the struggle of workers for better lives. In 1902 coal miners went on strike for higher pay and shorter hours. Mine owners called the strikers "outlaws" and would not hold talks with them. The President was outraged. "We demand that big business give the people a square [fair] deal," he said. With Roosevelt's help, the miners won a pay raise and a shorter workday.

THE PANAMA CANAL

The Spanish-American War had shown Roosevelt the need for a canal across the Isthmus of Panama. When the war began, the American battleship *Oregon* left San Francisco for Cuba. By the time it steamed around South America, the fighting was almost over. A canal linking the Atlantic and Pacific oceans would have cut 7,000 miles (11,200 km) from the trip.

At the time, Panama was part of Colombia. Roosevelt offered this South American country $10 million for a canal route through Panama. But the Colombian government refused, hoping to get much more money. After months of talks with the Colombians, Roosevelt was still unsuccessful.

Then, in 1903, the people of Panama rebelled against Colombia. Roosevelt knew that if Panama succeeded in forming its own country, he would not have to deal with Colombia any longer. He quickly sent warships to Panama to make sure the revolution there was successful. Within a week Panama declared its independence. Its new government agreed to sell to the United States a 10-mile (16-km) strip of land for a canal. This strip of land would be called the Canal Zone.

President Roosevelt then gave orders to "make the dirt fly in Panama." Instead American workers there began dropping like flies from yellow fever. Army doctor **William Gorgas** declared war on mosquitoes—the insects that spread the disease. Gorgas's workers drained the swamps and ponds in Panama where mosquitoes laid their eggs. In two years, yellow fever had disappeared from Panama.

It took ten years to build the **Panama Canal**. Huge mounds of dirt had to be

THE PANAMA CANAL ZONE

NICARAGUA

Central America

COSTA RICA

Canal Zone

Area shown on inset map

PACIFIC OCEAN

P A N A M A

0   150   300 Miles
0 150 300 450 Kilometers

Caribbean Sea

COLOMBIA

SOUTH AMERICA

N

Caribbean Sea

Colón

PANAMA

Gatún Lake

Canal Zone

N

PANAMA

Balboa

Panama City

0   2.5   5 Miles
0 2.5 5 7.5 Kilometers

PACIFIC OCEAN

MAP SKILL: President Theodore Roosevelt built a canal through Panama. Which countries border Panama?

moved. Mountains of solid rock had to be drilled and blasted. In 1914 the Panama Canal was opened at last. You can trace its route on the map on page 484. To Roosevelt, the canal was "one of the great feats of modern times."

CONSERVATION

In 1904 Theodore Roosevelt was elected to a second term as President. During his last four years in office, he often talked about conservation. By this, Roosevelt meant the protection and wise use of land and resources.

In the past, Americans had thought little about conservation. They had used up the country's resources with no thought about the future. In 1800 a squirrel could have traveled through the treetops from Texas to New England without ever touching the ground. By 1900 much of this forest was gone. Whole states, Roosevelt said, had been "stripped by the great lumber companies." Wildlife was also being destroyed. In 1800 huge buffalo herds blackened the plains. By 1890 less than 600 buffalo were left in the wild.

President Roosevelt told Americans about the need for conservation.

The time has come for a change. As a people we have the right and the duty to protect ourselves and our children against the wasteful development [use] of our natural resources.

To save the remaining woodlands, Roosevelt set aside 148 million acres (60 million ha) as national forest. In a national forest, the government limits the number of trees that can be cut down. This action helps protect the country's lumber supply.

President Roosevelt also set up 51 wildlife refuges to protect wild birds and animals. A wildlife refuge is an area where hunting is not allowed, so that birds and animals can live safely. As part of his conservation effort, Roosevelt created several national parks. National parks are areas of great beauty where nature has been preserved for all Americans to enjoy.

HENRY FORD AND THE MODEL "T"

In 1912 visitors to one of Roosevelt's national parks, the Grand Canyon, saw a surprising sight. Parked on the edge of the canyon was a Model "T" Ford. The car's driver had used explosives to blast a path through the desert to the canyon rim.

The car that conquered the Grand Canyon was built by automaker Henry Ford. When Ford started making cars in 1896, they were toys for the rich. Ford wanted to make a car "large enough for the family . . . but so low in price that no man making a good salary will be unable to own one." His Model "T" was that car.

A family gets ready for a ride in their new Model "T" automobile. The Model "T" was the creation of Henry Ford.

Ford's first cars were put together like houses. Factory workers carried parts to the car as they were building it. They often spent more time walking around than working.

In 1913 Ford tried "taking the work to the men instead of the men to the work." He set up an **assembly line** that moved cars slowly past the workers. Each person did one job. "The man who puts in a bolt does not put on the nut," Ford explained. "The man who puts on the nut doesn't tighten it."

Before the assembly line, it took about 14 hours to make one Model "T." A car rolling off Ford's assembly line was put together in only 93 minutes. As a result, the Model "T" dropped in price from $850 in 1908 to just $300 in 1925. Millions of Americans now had enough money to buy a Ford. The days of the horse and buggy were ending.

The Wright Brothers' airplane is just a few feet off the ground as it takes off from the sands at Kitty Hawk in 1903. Orville Wright was the pilot of the first flight. Wilbur Wright looks on.

THE WRIGHT BROTHERS FLY

While Henry Ford was developing his Model "T" car, some other Americans dreamed of travel by flight. One hot summer day in 1908, thousands of people gathered at Fort Myer, Virginia, to see if a person really could fly. They had read reports that two brothers, **Orville** and **Wilbur Wright**, had come to show their new flying machine. President Roosevelt sent his oldest son Teddy to see what the Wrights' airplane could do.

The Wright brothers had made their first flight at **Kitty Hawk**, North Carolina, in 1903. But early reports about their airplane seemed too fantastic to be true. Orville Wright found that "scarcely anyone believed in it until he actually saw it with his own eyes."

Now thousands of eyes watched as Orville Wright warmed up his *Flyer.* Teddy Roosevelt heard "a sound of complete surprise" from the crowd as the airplane rose slowly into the air. An amazing age of flight had begun.

Many women marched to get the right to vote. Carrie Chapman Catt (*above right*) was a leader of the American suffrage movement.

WOMEN WIN THE RIGHT TO VOTE

In 1908 Carrie Chapman Catt wrote a letter to President Roosevelt. Catt was a leader of the women's suffrage movement. Suffrage means the right to vote. Catt wanted Roosevelt to talk with Congress about women voting. The President turned her down.

Since the Seneca Falls Convention in 1848, women had been fighting for the right to vote. Ahead lay more hard years of struggle. Across the country women marched in suffrage parades. They fought for the vote in state legislatures. They carried signs in front of the White House asking "How Long Must Women Wait for Liberty?"

Finally, in 1920, the states approved the Nineteenth Amendment to the Constitution. This amendment gave American women the right to vote.

A TIME OF CHANGE

Theodore Roosevelt lived in a time of rapid change. By 1900 the United States had become a world power. As President, Roosevelt used that power to build a canal across Panama. Roosevelt was the first President to talk about conservation and the first to fly in an airplane. During his lifetime millions of Americans traded their buggies for cars. Women won the right to vote.

 Check Your Reading

1. Why did President Roosevelt call the Panama Canal "one of the great feats of modern times"?
2. How did Roosevelt help to protect America's natural resources?
3. How did Henry Ford make cars less expensive?
4. **GEOGRAPHY SKILL:** Why was Panama a good location for building a canal between the Atlantic and Pacific oceans?
5. **THINKING SKILL:** Based on your reading in this lesson, what can you conclude about Theodore Roosevelt as President?

Reading a Newspaper

Key Vocabulary

headline	editor
news article	classified ad
feature article	dateline
editorial	

Destruction of the Warship <u>Maine</u> Was the Work of an Enemy

MAINE EXPLOSION CAUSED BY BOMB OR TORPEDO

These headlines appeared in the New York newspapers the *World* and the *New York Journal* early in 1898. Headlines are sentences or phrases printed in large type across the top of a news story. Headlines are meant to catch the reader's attention and interest.

As you have read, newspapers played an important role in pushing the United States into war with Spain. Today most newspapers are more responsible about reporting events. Yet newspapers still use headlines to attract readers.

The Parts of a Newspaper

Most towns and cities in the United States have at least one newspaper. Many schools have their own newspapers. The major newspapers are sometimes called dailies because they are published every day.

All newspapers have a number of parts. The first part usually has news articles. A news article is a story about an important event that has just taken place. News articles can be about local, national, or international events.

Inside the paper, you might find feature articles. A feature article is a detailed report on a person, an issue, or an event. For example, a feature article might give the life story of a person who has won a major prize in science or literature.

Newspapers also have an editorial page. An editorial is an article in which the editors, or people who run the newspaper, give their opinion on an important issue. For example, the editors might support one candidate for President. In an editorial, the editors will tell why they support that candidate. What is an issue in your home town that might be the subject of an editorial?

The editorial page also has letters to the editor. Here you find letters written by the paper's readers telling how they feel on certain issues.

The Sunday Sentinel

MILWAUKEE, SUNDAY, JULY 3, 1898

AMERICANS ADVANCE ON SANTIAGO

On Board the Dispatch Boat Dandy, off Juragua, Friday, July 1, 4 p.m., via Port Antonio, Jamaica, Saturday, July 2, 5 a.m., and Kingston, Jamaica, 7:11 a.m.–[Copyright, 1898, by the Associated Press.]–The battle of Santiago has raged all day and at 4 o'clock this afternoon 15,000 American troops are thundering at the outer fortifications of the doomed city. Since daybreak, Gen. Shafter's army has fought its way across two and a half miles of bitterly contested and strongly fortified country; and the entire line from left to right is within gunshot of Santiago town.

The American loss thus far is estimated at hospital corps headquarters at twenty killed and fifty wounded, but it will be hours before the death roll can be accurately given.

Lieut.-Col. Patterson of the Twenty-second infantry is the only officer known to have been wounded and he is not fatally hurt.

The Spanish killed and wounded are undoubtedly numbered by hundreds.

Other parts of the newspaper are the sports pages and the **classified ads**. Classified ads are short advertisements that appear in small print. The ads might be for job openings, apartments for rent, or cars for sale. People place classified ads in a newspaper to let other people know that they want to buy or sell something.

Parts of a News Article

A news article always has a headline. Often a news article also has a **dateline**. A dateline tells when and where the story was written. What is the dateline on the news article above?

In the first paragraph of a news article, the reporter tries to get the reader interested in the story. Usually the first paragraph answers the questions *Who*? *What*? *When*? and *Where*? *Who* is the story about? *What* is it about? *When* did it take place? *Where* did it take place? The rest of the article gives more facts. A news article only gives facts. It does not give opinions.

Reviewing the Skill

1. What are four parts of a newspaper?
2. Does the first paragraph in the story above tell you *Who*? *What*? *When*? *Where*?
3. If you wrote to your local newspaper giving your opinion about a plan to cut the school budget, where would your letter appear?
4. What is one difference between an editorial and a news article?
5. What should the first paragraph of a news article do?
6. How can reading a newspaper help you in school?

1901: Should Women Work Outside the Home?

Many changes were taking place in the United States in the late 1800s and early 1900s. Cities grew rapidly as people began leaving family farms to work in factories. New machines made work easier in homes and in businesses. Many women left their homes to work in factories and offices. They formed groups to fight for better jobs and for the right to vote.

These changes upset many people. Some of them thought that women were naturally timid and delicate, and thus unfit for many kinds of jobs. A woman's place, they said, was in the home. Others believed that women should have the same opportunities to work as did men. They insisted that a woman could do anything that a man could do.

The Granger Collection

POINT ☆▷

Women Should Stay at Home

One person who thought that women should stay at home was Henry T. Finck. In April 1901 he wrote the following article in a magazine called *The Independent*.

One of the most important problems to be solved in the new century is this: Shall women be flowers or vegetables, pretty or useful? In other words, shall women work? Many troublemakers are telling women to make themselves self-supporting. They have tricked many of our girls into believing that they must go into the world to seek their fortunes.

But men still prefer the home girl to any other kind. They want a girl who has not marred [spoiled] her beauty and ruined her health by needless work.

Of course, some poor girls and women must work. But they should not be allowed to throw themselves blindly into nearly every kind of a job that men have performed. God made men and women, and men and women we want them to remain. This great principle cannot be ignored in the division of work to women and men.

● What does Finck mean by calling women "flowers" or "vegetables"?

COUNTERPOINT ▷☆

Women Should Be Free to Choose Where to Work

Ida Husted Harper disagreed with Finck. In May 1901 in the following article in *The Independent* she argued that opportunities for women should be increased.

Marriage should bear the same relation to a woman's life that it does to a man's. A wife should prepare to be a useful member of society. She should make a choice. She can run her home. She can be a nurse or a teacher. Or she can choose charity, typing, or factory work—whatever she is best suited for.

It is silly to draw a dividing line between the jobs which are right and those which are wrong for women. It is a mistaken kindness to think that a job like sitting at a sewing machine is better than a job that develops muscles. If, for the good of the world, it should become necessary to decide between "vegetables and flowers," between useful and pretty, the flowers would have to go. We do not mean that every woman should leave the home and go into business. We mean only that those who wish to do so shall have the chance.

● According to Harper, what should the role of a wife be?

UNDERSTANDING THE POINT/COUNTERPOINT

1. According to Henry Finck, how would work outside the home harm a woman?
2. Why does Ida Harper believe a woman should be able to choose her work?
3. Which writer do you think makes the stronger argument? Explain your answer.

IMPORTANT EVENTS

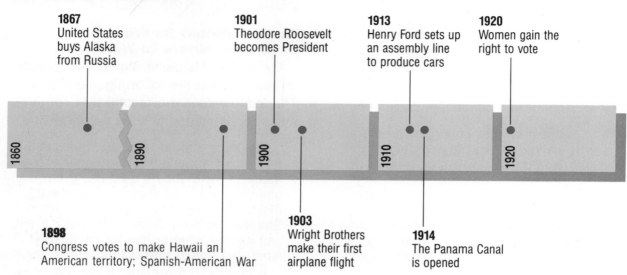

1867
United States
buys Alaska
from Russia

1901
Theodore Roosevelt
becomes President

1913
Henry Ford sets up
an assembly line
to produce cars

1920
Women gain the
right to vote

1860

1890

1900

1910

1920

1898
Congress votes to make Hawaii an
American territory; Spanish-American War

1903
Wright Brothers
make their first
airplane flight

1914
The Panama Canal
is opened

PEOPLE TO KNOW

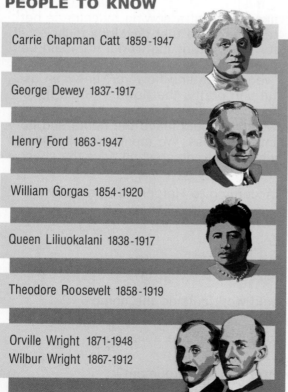

Carrie Chapman Catt 1859-1947

George Dewey 1837-1917

Henry Ford 1863-1947

William Gorgas 1854-1920

Queen Liliuokalani 1838-1917

Theodore Roosevelt 1858-1919

Orville Wright 1871-1948
Wilbur Wright 1867-1912

IDEAS TO REMEMBER

■ After the Civil War, Alaska and Hawaii
became territories of the United States.

■ The United States acquired an empire
after defeating Spain in the Spanish-
American War.

■ During the 1900s the United States
built the Panama Canal, gave women
the right to vote, and protected its natural resources for the first time.

REVIEWING VOCABULARY

Number a sheet of paper from 1 to 5. Beside each number write whether the underlined word or term in the sentence is used correctly. If it is not, write the word or term that would complete the sentence correctly.

1. The soldiers who fought with Theodore Roosevelt in the Spanish-American War were known as the <u>Rough Riders</u>.
2. The price of the Model "T" dropped when cars were made in <u>sweatshops</u>.
3. Beautiful areas set aside for all Americans to enjoy are called <u>conservation parks</u>.
4. Women worked hard to gain <u>liberty</u>, or the right to vote.
5. Protecting land and resources is called <u>protectionism</u>.

REVIEWING FACTS

1. Which event came first: the Spanish-American War broke out; Puerto Rico became a territory of the United States; Cuba became independent?
2. How did the United States acquire Alaska?
3. How did two New York newspapers, the *Journal* and the *World*, help lead the United States into war with Spain?
4. What was the *Maine*? Why was it important in American history?
5. Name three government jobs that were held by Theodore Roosevelt.
6. What were two problems that slowed down the building of the Panama Canal?
7. Why did President Roosevelt want to set aside national parks?
8. How did Henry Ford change the way cars were made?
9. Who was Carrie Chapman Catt?
10. Which event came first: Theodore Roosevelt became President; American women won the right to vote; the Panama Canal was built?

◀═▶ WRITING ABOUT MAIN IDEAS

1. **Writing a Paragraph of Contrast:** Imagine you grew up in the 1890s. Write a paragraph of contrast telling how the United States had changed by the 1920s. Mention specific changes such as the assembly line. Describe your feelings about these changes.
2. **Writing a Paragraph:** How do you think Queen Liliuokalani felt about the events that led to Hawaii becoming an American territory? Write a paragraph explaining your answer.
3. **Writing a Newspaper Story:** Choose one event discussed in this chapter. Write a newspaper story describing the event. Be sure to tell the most important facts at the beginning.

BUILDING SKILLS: READING A NEWSPAPER

1. Where in a newspaper would you look to find the most important news of the day? To find a job?
2. Write a short newspaper article about the purchase of Alaska. Remember that your story should answer the questions *Who? What? Where? When?* and *Why?*
3. Are newspaper articles primary or secondary sources? Explain your answer.

CHAPTER 21

IN PEACE AND WAR

FOCUS

It is a fearful thing to lead this great peaceful people into war. . . . But the right is more precious than peace, and we shall fight for the things which we have always carried nearest our hearts.

President Woodrow Wilson said these words in a speech to Congress on April 2, 1917. The nations of Europe had been at war since 1914. Now Wilson wanted the United States to join that bloody conflict. A year later Americans marched into battle thinking that World War I would be "the war to end all wars." Sadly, it was not.

1 World War I

READ TO LEARN

Key Vocabulary

World War I
Central Powers
Allied Powers
Treaty of Versailles
League of Nations

Key People

Woodrow Wilson

Read Aloud

We are in no peril [danger] *of being drawn into the European quarrel.*

An American magazine printed this statement when war broke out in Europe in 1914. Americans were thankful not to be part of the conflict. Never had the Atlantic Ocean seemed more wide. As you will read, the ocean was not broad enough to keep this country out of the first worldwide war.

Read for Purpose

1. **WHAT YOU KNOW:** Against which European country did the United States fight in 1898?
2. **WHAT YOU WILL LEARN:** Why did the United States enter World War I?

STAYING OUT OF WAR

When World War I began in 1914, President Woodrow Wilson asked Americans to "be neutral in thought as well as in action." He even told movie-goers not to cheer or boo either side while watching war films.

But staying neutral in thought was hard. The war had divided Europe into two enemy forces. On one side were the Central Powers, led by Germany, Austria-Hungary, and Turkey. On the other side were the Allied Powers, led by Great Britain, France, and Russia. The map on page 496 shows the division of Europe at the start of the war.

Many Americans who had come from Germany favored the Central Powers. Those from Great Britain rooted for the Allies. Still, no one wanted to send American troops to Europe. As a popular song title proclaimed, "I Didn't Raise My Boy to Be a Soldier."

Sending supplies was a different matter. Americans were happy to do

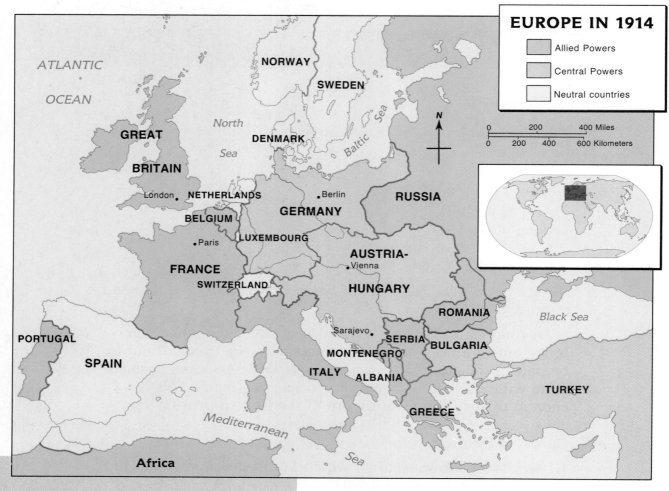

EUROPE IN 1914

- Allied Powers
- Central Powers
- Neutral countries

ATLANTIC OCEAN

NORWAY

SWEDEN

North Sea

DENMARK

Baltic Sea

GREAT BRITAIN

London

NETHERLANDS

Berlin

RUSSIA

BELGIUM

GERMANY

LUXEMBOURG

Paris

AUSTRIA-

Vienna

FRANCE

SWITZERLAND

HUNGARY

ROMANIA

Black Sea

Sarajevo

SERBIA

BULGARIA

PORTUGAL

MONTENEGRO

SPAIN

ITALY

ALBANIA

TURKEY

Mediterranean Sea

GREECE

Africa

MAP SKILL: Locate the Allied Powers and the Central Powers on the map. Which countries were neutral in 1914?

business with both sides. But early in the war a British naval blockade stopped American ships from reaching the Central Powers. Trade with the Allies, however, grew rapidly.

THE UNITED STATES AT WAR

In May 1915 a German submarine sank the British ocean liner *Lusitania* off the coast of Ireland. More than 1,000 passengers were killed, including 128 Americans. People in the United States were shocked.

By 1916 some Americans thought the United States should enter the war on the side of the Allies. Most people wanted to remain neutral. In 1916 President Wilson was elected to a second term. His winning slogan was "He Kept Us Out of War." But Wilson could not make this claim for long. Germany's leaders had decided that they had to stop American supplies from reaching the Allies.

In March 1917 German submarines began sinking American ships. A new wave of anti-German feeling swept the country. President Wilson asked Congress to declare war on Germany. American soldiers landed in Europe in 1918. There they found two lines of trenches stretching across France.

Trenches are long ditches that are dug in the ground to protect troops.

The American troops fought with the Allies to drive the Germans out of France. Faced with defeat, the Central Powers asked for an armistice, or an end to the fighting. On November 11, 1918, World War I was over.

MAKING PEACE

World War I was the largest, most destructive war the world had ever seen. More than 9 million people had been killed, including 116,000 Americans. President Wilson was determined that such a war should never happen again.

Early in 1919 Wilson went to Versailles, France, to help write a peace treaty. He wanted a treaty that would end the causes of war. Such a treaty would treat both sides fairly. Harsh terms, Wilson explained, would only cause Germany to seek revenge.

But the other Allies had very different ideas. They used the Treaty of Versailles to gain German territory and to make Germany pay for the damages it had caused. In the end President Wilson agreed to sign the treaty because it included his plan for an organization where countries could talk over their differences. Wilson hoped this League of Nations, as it was soon named, would settle future conflicts without war.

When Wilson returned home, he sent the Versailles Treaty to the Senate for approval. Many senators opposed the treaty. They were afraid the League of Nations might drag the United States into another war. The treaty was not approved. Much to Wilson's disappointment, the United States never joined the League of Nations.

American soldiers were welcomed home as heroes at the end of "the war to end all wars."

"THE WAR TO END ALL WARS"

When World War I began in 1914, Americans tried to remain neutral. But you have read how German submarine attacks made this impossible. With American help, the Allies defeated the Central Powers in 1918. Americans hoped that this terrible conflict had been "the war to end all wars."

Check Your Reading

1. What were the two opposing sides in World War I?
2. Why was the United States unable to remain neutral?
3. Why did President Wilson agree to the Treaty of Versailles?
4. **GEOGRAPHY SKILL:** Look at the map on page 496. Why did the location of the Central Powers make it difficult for them to win the war?
5. **THINKING SKILL:** What conclusions can you reach about the role of the United States in World War I?

Decision Making

Any time you choose to behave in a particular way you are making a decision. You read in Chapter 2 that decision making is selecting or choosing from among a number of alternatives to achieve a goal. Since every decision you make affects your life and the lives of people around you, it is important to know how to make good decisions. Use the chart below to review the steps in making a decision.

HELPING YOURSELF

The steps below show one way to make a decision.

1. Identify and clearly define the goal to be achieved.

2. Identify alternatives by which the goal can be achieved.

3. Predict the results of each alternative.

4. Judge each result by determining whether it helps or harms you and others.

5. Choose the best alternative.

Applying the Skill

Pretend you are an owner of an American trading company selling beef and grain to Europe at the start of World War I in 1914. Your grandparents still live in Germany. Most of your business has been with Germany. President Woodrow Wilson has asked Americans to "be neutral in thought as well as in action." Decide how you will meet the President's request as the British blockade stops your ships from reaching the Central Powers.

1. Which of the following would not be an alternative that you could choose?
   a. to continue selling goods to Germany
   b. to stop selling goods to Germany
   c. to increase trade with neutral countries in Europe
2. Name three groups of people who would be affected by your decision.
3. If you decide to remain completely neutral, which group would you help? Which group would you hurt?

Reviewing the Skill

1. What does it mean to make a decision?
2. Name some steps that can help you make a good decision.
3. When making a decision, why is it important to consider as many alternatives as possible?

2 Good Times

READ TO LEARN

Key Vocabulary

stock market

Key People

Charles Lindbergh
Herbert Hoover

Read Aloud

In 1924 two college teachers named Robert and Helen Lynd moved to a city in Indiana. They had come there to study how American life had changed since the Industrial Revolution. The Lynds called their new home "Middletown" because it was a middle-sized city in the middle part of the country. Soon after they arrived, an old-timer told them:

Why on earth do you need to study what's changing this country? I can tell you what's happening in just four letters: A-U-T-O!

Read for Purpose

1. **WHAT YOU KNOW:** How were automobiles made less expensive after 1913?
2. **WHAT YOU WILL LEARN:** What was life like for most Americans after World War I?

THE AGE OF THE A-U-T-O

The years after World War I were good times for many Americans. The United States was now the world's richest country. Its factories and mills were making more goods than all other nations combined. Businesses were growing fast, and profits and wages were going up.

For most people, the sign of good times was a car in the garage. By 1927 over half of all the families in America owned cars. A Middletown woman said, "We'd rather do without clothes than give up the car."

Cars were changing the way the country looked. Dusty, rutted country roads were being paved to make highways. These smooth new roads were soon lined with gas stations, diners, and tourist cabins that would later be called motels.

By the 1920s many workers were working just five-and-a-half days a week. In their free time they went for drives in their new cars. A Middletown minister complained to the Lynds about "automobilitis—the thing those people have who go off motoring on Sunday instead of going to church."

Some people even had paid vacations from work. In growing numbers they took to the road to see their vast country. One happy traveler noted that "for the first time in history the common ordinary folks of the North and South are meeting one another . . . mostly by means of the national chariot—the Ford car."

MOVIES AND RADIO

Soon after the Lynds came to Middletown, they saw this advertisement.

Go to a motion picture. . . . Before you know it you are living the story— laughing, loving, hating, struggling, winning! All the adventure, all the romance, all the excitement you lack in your daily life are in—PICTURES!

You read in Chapter 19 that motion pictures were invented by Thomas Edison. By 1920 movies were a big business. The first motion pictures had no sound. Even so, silent movies could make people laugh and cry. Then, in 1927, moviegoers heard Al Jolson speak and sing in the first talking motion picture, *The Jazz Singer*. The "talkies" were an instant hit. Americans in all parts of the country began going to the movies.

Another invention that created a new business was the radio. Radio broadcasting began in 1920. By 1929 nearly one third of all the families in America had "radio music boxes." Each night people gathered around their radios to listen to news, music, comedy shows, and sporting events.

On May 21, 1927, Americans were glued to their radios waiting for news of a daring young pilot named **Charles**

Charles Lindbergh (*left*) became a hero as a result of his solo flight across the Atlantic Ocean. Americans heard the news on their radios.

Lindbergh. The night before, Lindbergh had left New York City in his small plane, the *Spirit of St. Louis*. He landed in Paris, France, 33.5 hours later. Lindbergh was the first person to fly alone, nonstop across the Atlantic Ocean.

"Lucky Lindy" came home a hero. He was welcomed with huge parades, ceremonies, and speeches. Americans admired Charles Lindbergh for his skill and courage. They also honored him as a pioneer who had crossed a new frontier of flight.

THE STOCK MARKET CRASH

In 1929 **Herbert Hoover** became the country's President. By then many people thought the good times would go on forever. "We in America today," said President Hoover, "are nearer to the final triumph over poverty than ever before in the history of any land."

Making money seemed easy—just buy stocks today and sell them tomorrow at a profit. You read in Chapter 7 that stocks are shares of ownership in a business. Stocks are bought and sold on the **stock market**. If more people want to buy a stock than to sell, the price of the stock goes up. If more people want to sell than buy, the price of the stock goes down.

For most of the 1920s, stock prices went up. Then, in the fall of 1929, prices on the stock market began to drop. On October 29 stockholders panicked. Suddenly everyone wanted to sell. No one wanted to buy. Prices tumbled down. "It's the end of everything!" cried one man as the stock market crashed. And for some people it was. Just a few hours earlier they had felt rich. Now they had nothing.

THE END OF GOOD TIMES

For most Americans, the 1920s had brought good times. Business was booming. Workers had more money and free time. Then came the stock market crash of 1929. Suddenly the good times were over.

Worried people poured onto Wall Street in New York City on the day of the **stock market** crash, October 29, 1929.

Check Your Reading

1. What changes did cars bring to the United States?
2. How did some Americans spend their free time?
3. What happened when the stock market crashed?
4. **THINKING SKILL:** Is the quotation on page 500 an example of a fact or an opinion? Explain your answer.

3 Hard Times

Key Vocabulary

depression   unemployment
prejudice   Dust Bowl
Great Depression   New Deal

Key People

Franklin D. Roosevelt
Eleanor Roosevelt

Read Aloud

MARKET CRASHES—PANIC HITS NATION!

When Gordon Parks read this headline, he was not worried. He was an African-American teenager who had a job and was working his way through school. Only people with stocks would be hurt by the crash, he thought. "But by the first week in November I . . . knew differently," Parks later wrote. "Along with millions of others across the nation, I was without a job." Parks looked everywhere for work. All he heard was "We're firing, not hiring," and "Sorry, sonny, nothing doing here."

Read for Purpose

1. **WHAT YOU KNOW:** What event marked the end of the "good times" that followed World War I?
2. **WHAT YOU WILL LEARN:** What was life like during the Great Depression?

THE GREAT DEPRESSION

"The 1930 outlook for [Middletown] is bright. A boom is expected," said an Indiana newspaper after the stock market crash. But a business boom depends on people spending money to buy things. After the crash most people cut back on spending. A man in Lowell, Massachusetts, told a reporter:

Oh, quite a few working people in Lowell still have money . . . but they're holding onto it as if it was all there was in the world. . . . They're scared.

With fewer people buying things, stores fired salesclerks. Factories laid off workers. And since jobless workers had little money to spend, sales dropped even more. The result was a **depression**. A depression is a period when business is slow and many people are out of work.

Black workers were hit hardest by the depression. Over a million blacks had left the South between 1915 and 1930. Most had settled in northern cities where they found jobs in factories. But **prejudice** had followed them north. Prejudice is a negative opinion that has been formed in a hasty way, without careful thought. Sometimes people judge others unfavorably because of their race or religion. Because of prejudice black people were often treated unfairly. When times were hard, black workers were "the last hired and the first fired."

In the past, depressions in the United States had ended after a year or so. But the Great Depression of the 1930s dragged on year after year. By 1932, over 86,000 businesses had closed their doors. Over 4,000 banks had failed. People who had kept their savings in those banks lost all their money. And unemployment, or the number of people without jobs, reached an all-time high. Writer Will Rogers wrote:

Last year we said, "Things can't go on like this," and they didn't; they got worse.

HUNGRY AND HOMELESS

Many Americans were hungry and homeless by 1932. Across the country the unemployed waited in long bread lines for food. Hoping for a hot meal, they crowded into soup kitchens run by neighborhood churches.

In Chicago, teachers saw children faint from hunger. Many teachers used their own money to feed hungry students. A Chicago news reporter saw "hundreds of hungry workers . . . old and young, Negro and white" searching through trash for food. "Hunger and pride," he wrote, "do not go together."

Many people lost their homes when they could not pay rent. Some moved in with family or friends. Others found empty land where they built shacks out of old boxes, cans, and junk.

With **unemployment** at an all-time high during the **Great Depression**, many people had to line up for free food.

Thousands of Americans without homes took to the road. They traveled on freight trains from town to town. Their days were spent, wrote a wandering teenager, "always on the lookout for food, a place to sleep, and possible work." Usually they found only hunger and homelessness.

THE DUST BOWL

For farmers on the Great Plains, nature added its own disaster to the Great Depression. Years of drought during the 1930s turned many of the country's farms into dust. Day after day went by with no rain. Nothing grew to hold down the soil in farmers' fields. Winds picked up the powder-dry soil and carried it away in dark clouds. The map below shows this dry, dusty area, which became known as the Dust Bowl.

THE DUST BOWL, 1935-1940

☐ Dust Bowl

WYOMING

SD

UT

COLORADO

NEBRASKA

IA

AZ

KANSAS

MO

NEW
MEXICO

OKLAHOMA

AR

TEXAS

N

MEXICO

0 — 150 — 300 Mi
0 — 150 — 300 — 450 Km

Gulf of
Mexico

MAP SKILL: (below) An Oklahoma farmer and his children walk past a building that is half-buried by dust. What states were part of the Dust Bowl?

A farmer from Texas described a dust storm this way:

Flocks of crazed birds tumbled from the sky. The horizon was black, and soon the dust was so thick and everything was so black, that mothers holding their children couldn't see them.

At first farmers made grim jokes about the "black dusters." When asked how bad the dust was at his ranch, one man replied:

Well, I looked out the kitchen window about two o'clock and saw a prairie dog digging a hole ten feet in the air.

Jokes soon gave way to grief. Many farm families left the Dust Bowl to join the thousands of homeless people searching for better conditions.

FRANKLIN ROOSEVELT

In 1932 the Democratic Party chose Franklin D. Roosevelt to run for President. Roosevelt promised Americans a "new deal." What he meant by this was not clear. But Americans were ready to vote for anyone who promised to do something, do anything. Roosevelt was easily elected.

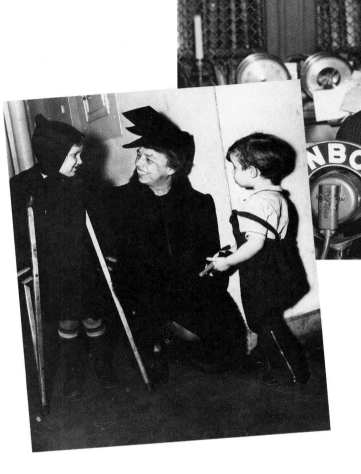

Franklin Roosevelt was the first President to speak regularly to the American people over the radio. His wife Eleanor toured the country to better understand the people's needs.

THE NEW DEAL

The new President acted swiftly. In his first 100 days in office, Roosevelt sent Congress one bill after another. Congress passed them all. New government programs were set up to help businesses, farmers, and the unemployed. The New Deal had begun.

The President depended on his wife, Eleanor Roosevelt, to find out what life was like for the people of the country. During her husband's first 15 months in office, the First Lady traveled over 50,000 miles (80,000 km). She talked with people everywhere about their lives, their hopes, and their fears.

What Eleanor Roosevelt saw and heard helped to shape the President's programs in the next few years. The First Lady took a special interest in the problems of the young, blacks, and women. She tried to make sure that they were not left out of the New Deal.

Roosevelt took office during the worst days of the Great Depression. Many were fearful about the country's future. Roosevelt wasn't. He told Americans, "This great nation will endure [last] as it has endured. . . . The only thing we have to fear is fear itself."

Despite the huge problems facing the country, President Roosevelt was not discouraged. Years before, he had been crippled by polio. This disease left him unable to use his legs. "Once I spent two years lying in bed, trying to move my big toe," he said. "That was the hardest job I ever had to do. After that, anything else seems easy."

505

New Deal programs gave work to many people during the Great Depression. Artists were even hired to create wall paintings.

During the New Deal the federal government grew rapidly and took on new roles. For the first time the government worked to feed the hungry. New Deal programs created jobs for millions of unemployed workers. These workers built roads and dams. They planted trees and cleared hiking trails. They were paid to create art works, write books, and put on plays.

For the first time the government worked with farmers to improve their lives. The government helped workers to form labor unions and improve wages and working conditions. The government worked to end child labor and close up sweatshops.

Older Americans were also helped by the government. The Social Security Act of 1935 created a system of regular payments to help people who were no longer working. For many older Americans, their social security payments helped them stay out of poverty.

These New Deal programs brought about a change in how Americans viewed their government. In 1929 most Americans believed that the government should not be in the business of helping people through hard times. People, they said, should take care of themselves.

The Great Depression changed this belief. Millions of people were not able to survive on their own. When they were helped by the New Deal, their thinking slowly changed. They began to believe that the federal government should be at least partly responsible for the well-being of all Americans.

HELP THROUGH HARD TIMES

In 1929 the United States entered the longest depression in its history. Hunger and homelessness spread across the land.

In this lesson, you read how Franklin Roosevelt was elected President in 1932 after promising Americans a "new deal." The New Deal did not end the Great Depression. In 1941, nearly 6 million workers were still unemployed. But the New Deal did help millions of Americans to at least survive.

Check Your Reading

1. Why did so many people lose their jobs during the Great Depression?
2. Why did farmers on the Great Plains suffer even more than most people in the United States during the Great Depression?
3. What did the New Deal do to help people get along during the Great Depression?
4. THINKING SKILL: List two questions you can ask to find out more about Franklin Roosevelt's presidency.

506

4 World War II

READ TO LEARN

Key Vocabulary

dictator
concentration camp
Axis Powers
World War II
Allies
Holocaust

Key People

Benito Mussolini
Adolf Hitler
Dwight D.
  Eisenhower
Harry S. Truman

Key Places

Pearl Harbor
Stalingrad
Berlin
Hiroshima
Nagasaki

Read Aloud

At 7:55 A.M. on December 7, 1941, the first of 363 Japanese warplanes flew low over Hawaii. Their target was Pearl Harbor, America's chief military base in the Pacific. A Japanese pilot saw the navy base below "asleep in the morning mist."

The Sunday morning calm was suddenly shattered. Japanese bombs rained down on American ships and planes. Dark clouds of smoke and the screams of dying men filled the air. A few minutes later President Roosevelt read the grim message: "AIR RAID, PEARL HARBOR—THIS IS NO DRILL." The United States was at war again.

Read for Purpose

1. **WHAT YOU KNOW:** Why was the United States drawn into World War I?
2. **WHAT YOU WILL LEARN:** What were the causes of World War II?

THE RISE OF THE DICTATORS

Americans had fought in World War I "to make the world safe for democracy." But after the war, democratic governments began to disappear in one country after another. Dictators with dreams of ruling the world came to power in Italy, Germany, and Japan. A dictator is a ruler who has complete control over a country.

Democracy failed first in Italy. World War I left Italy a poor country. Returning soldiers could not find jobs. The country soon was torn apart by strikes and riots.

Benito Mussolini (müs ə lē′ nē) promised to end these troubles. He talked of building a great Italian empire. In 1922 Mussolini made himself

507

dictator of Italy. Rights and freedoms disappeared. Mussolini defended his actions by saying, "The truth is . . . that men nowadays are tired of liberty."

Germans also faced problems after the war. You read in Lesson 1 that the Treaty of Versailles forced Germany to pay the Allies for damages that resulted from its part in World War I. These payments left Germany with no money to rebuild itself. To most Germans this seemed unfair.

The United States was not the only country to suffer from the Great Depression. The countries of Europe were also hit hard. By 1932 one third of Germany's workers were unemployed. Unhappy Germans turned to a new leader named Adolf Hitler. Hitler and his Nazi (nät' sē) Party promised to end their country's depression and build a mighty German empire.

Hitler made Germans feel good again. He told them that they were a "master race" who should rule the world. The main enemies of Germany, he said, were Jews. Hitler blamed all of

Adolf Hitler and his Nazi followers gained complete control of Germany in 1933.

Germany's problems on Jews, even its defeat in World War I. There was no truth to these charges. But many people believed Hitler's vicious lies.

In 1933 Hitler ended Germany's elected government and made himself a dictator. His Nazi followers ran Germany's military, police, schools, and industries. Hitler had Jewish men, women, and children arrested and put in prisons called concentration camps. There Jews and other "enemies of the master race" were starved and murdered. Most who entered concentration camps died in them.

Military leaders took control of Japan's government after World War I. Japan was then the only industrial country in Asia. But this island nation is poor in natural resources. To keep its machines running, Japan had to buy iron, copper, rubber, and oil from other countries. Japanese leaders dreamed of building a great Asian empire that would supply all of these needs.

THE ROAD TO WAR

These dreams of empire led to another world war. In 1931 Japan invaded Manchuria, a part of China. Four years later Italy attacked Ethiopia, a small country in Africa. The League of Nations protested these attacks but did nothing to stop them.

In 1936 Italy, Germany, and Japan signed a treaty of friendship. Each promised to help the others in time of war. These three countries were called the Axis Powers.

Now the dictators grew bolder. In 1938 Hitler sent troops into Austria. The next year Germans marched into Czechoslovakia. Again other nations protested these actions but did nothing. Then on September 1, 1939, the German army invaded Poland. Two days later France and Britain declared war on Germany. World War II had begun.

The attack on Poland was only the beginning. During the first half of 1940 Hitler's troops overran Norway, Denmark, the Netherlands, and Belgium. By July 1940 France had surrendered.

In 1941 Germany attacked the Soviet Union. As the Soviet army fell back, a German victory seemed certain.

PEARL HARBOR

Japan's leaders watched happily as German armies invaded most of Europe. Now only one nation could stop Japan from conquering Asia—the United States. With visions of power and glory, Japan's leaders planned a surprise attack on Pearl Harbor, Hawaii. They hoped to destroy America's entire Pacific fleet, which was docked there.

News of the attack on Pearl Harbor stunned the nation. In that early morning raid on December 7, 1941, the Japanese had damaged or destroyed 19 warships and over 150 airplanes. More than 2,400 Americans had been killed.

The Japanese attack on Pearl Harbor drew the United States into World War II. On December 8 Congress voted for war with Japan. Germany and Italy then declared war on the United States.

After Pearl Harbor, Japanese troops swept across Asia. American forces were driven out of the Philippines and Guam. There were rumors that California would be Japan's next target.

Californians panicked. Many began to fear that Japanese-Americans were spying for Japan. No Japanese spies were ever discovered. Even so, the government forced 120,000 Japanese-Americans to leave their West Coast homes in 1942. Whole families spent the rest of the war locked up in prison camps. Barbed wire and armed soldiers kept them from leaving.

Despite this unjust treatment, many Japanese-Americans obtained permission to join the United States army. They fought bravely for the United States. Many people believed that the Japanese-Americans were treated badly because of prejudice. Years later the United States apologized for unfairly putting them in prison camps.

Smoke rises from the ruined United States Pacific fleet at Pearl Harbor, Hawaii, moments after the Japanese attack. What was the result of this action?

Honolulu Star-Bulletin 1st EXTRA

SAN FRANCISCO, Dec. 7.—President Roosevelt announced this morning that Japanese planes had attacked Manila and Pearl Harbor.

WAR!
OAHU BOMBED BY JAPANESE PLANES

SIX KNOWN DEAD, 21 INJURED, AT EMERGENCY HOSPITAL

Attack Made On Island's Defense Areas

Hundreds See City Bombed

Both: The Granger Collection

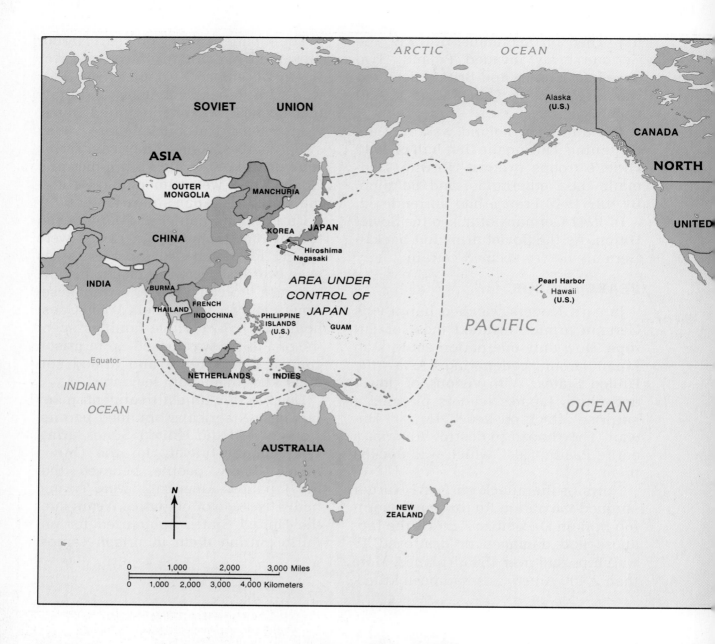

THE ALLIES FIGHT
BACK

On January 1, 1942, the United States joined Britain, the Soviet Union, China, and 22 other nations to form the Allies. Their goal was to defeat the Axis Powers. Americans united behind the war effort. Millions of men and women joined the armed forces. Factories began hiring again. People who had been unemployed for years went back to work. The United States was soon building more tanks, ships, and planes than Germany, Italy, and Japan combined. Slowly the tide of battle turned against the Axis Powers. In 1942 the Allies began to drive the Japanese out of areas they had captured earlier in the war.

In 1943 the Soviet Union stopped the Germans at Stalingrad. For the Soviet

510

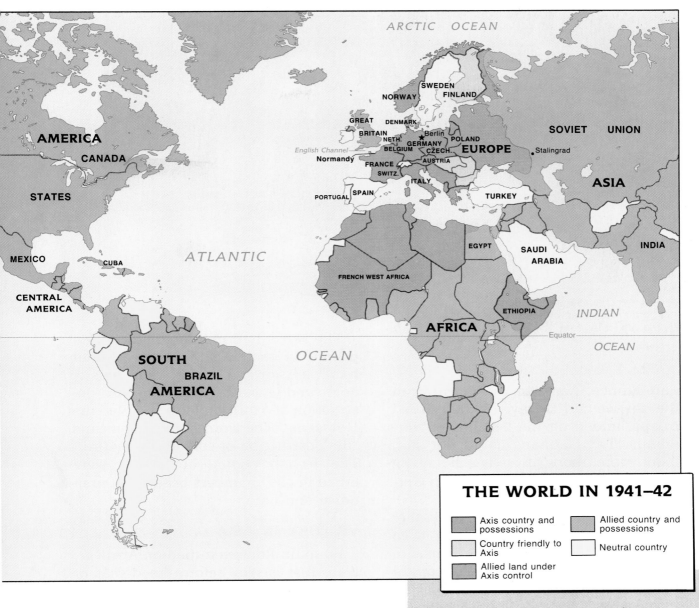

ARCTIC OCEAN

SWEDEN
FINLAND
NORWAY

GREAT
BRITAIN
DENMARK
NETH.
BELGIUM
Berlin
GERMANY
POLAND
CZECH.
AUSTRIA
EUROPE
SOVIET UNION
Stalingrad

English Channel
Normandy
FRANCE
SWITZ.
ITALY

ASIA

PORTUGAL
SPAIN
TURKEY
INDIA

MEXICO
CUBA
ATLANTIC
EGYPT
SAUDI
ARABIA

AMERICA
CANADA

STATES

CENTRAL
AMERICA
FRENCH WEST AFRICA
ETHIOPIA
INDIAN

SOUTH
BRAZIL
AMERICA
OCEAN
AFRICA
Equator
OCEAN

THE WORLD IN 1941–42

- Axis country and possessions
- Allied country and possessions
- Country friendly to Axis
- Neutral country
- Allied land under Axis control

MAP SKILL: Use the map to locate the area under Japanese control. How far east did this area extend?

Union this was a great, but costly, victory. They lost more soldiers at the siege of Stalingrad than the Americans lost in the entire war.

VICTORY IN EUROPE

In 1944 nearly 3 million Allied troops gathered in England. They were part of a plan to free Europe from German rule. The plan was organized by American general Dwight D. Eisenhower.

On June 6, 1944, General Eisenhower led the largest invasion force in history across the English Channel. You can see from the map above that this body of water separates Great Britain

511

Jewish men, women, and children were murdered in German **concentration camps** during the Holocaust.

and France. Early in the morning of the day we call D-Day, 130,000 Allied troops landed on the beaches of Normandy. The Germans could not stop them. More troops arrived each day. By September, France was free from German control.

In 1945 American, British, and other Allied forces invaded Germany from the west. At the same time, Russian troops approached the German capital of Berlin from the east. Knowing that all was lost, Hitler killed himself. On May 7, 1945, Germany surrendered.

THE HOLOCAUST

While marching through Germany and Poland, Allied troops entered Hitler's concentration camps. All the horrors of war had not prepared them for what they found. Bodies were stacked one on top of another. The prisoners who were still alive looked like living skeletons.

The Nazis had murdered 12 million people in their death camps. About half were Jews. The rest were mostly Poles and Gypsies. Today the Nazi destruction of 6 million Jews is called the Holocaust. The word *holocaust* means "the destruction of something by fire." The Jewish people of Europe were killed in gas chambers because of prejudice and hate.

VICTORY IN ASIA

Franklin Roosevelt died on April 12, 1945, just weeks before the defeat of Germany. The year before he had been elected to a fourth term as President. No other President had served his country for so long or led it through more difficult times. While the nation wept, Vice President Harry S. Truman took over, faced with the task of ending the war.

By the summer of 1945 the Japanese had been pushed back to their home islands. Bombing raids had left many Japanese cities in ruins. But Japan's leaders refused to give up.

The destruction caused by the atomic bomb in Hiroshima and Nagasaki (*above*) led to Japan's surrender.

Truman faced a terrible choice. He could order Allied troops to invade Japan. But he feared such an invasion might cost a million lives. Or he could use a new secret weapon called the atomic bomb against Japan. This bomb was more destructive than any weapon the world had ever known.

Truman made his choice. On August 6, 1945, the United States dropped an atomic bomb on the Japanese city of Hiroshima (hêr ō shē′ mə). Over 70,000 people were killed in a fiery flash. A survivor wrote that "Every living thing is blackened and dead."

Still Japan did not surrender. Three days later the United States dropped a second atomic bomb, leaving the city of Nagasaki (nä gə säk′ ē) in ruins. A child who watched the horrible explosion said, "I would rather blind myself than ever see such a sight again." On August 14, 1945, Japan surrendered. World War II was over.

A WORLD IN RUINS

After World War I, leaders who dreamed of ruling the world gained power in Italy, Germany, and Japan. Their dreams led the world to war. As you have read, the United States entered World War II in 1941 after Japan attacked Pearl Harbor.

In 1945 the Allies crushed the Axis Powers. The cost of this victory was staggering. Over 55 million men, women, and children died in the war, and much of the world lay in ruins.

 Check Your Reading

1. What were the goals of Adolf Hitler and Benito Mussolini? How did these goals lead to war?
2. What countries formed the Axis Powers? The Allies?
3. What caused Japan to surrender without being invaded?
4. **THINKING SKILL:** How did World War II help bring an end to the Great Depression?

IMPORTANT EVENTS

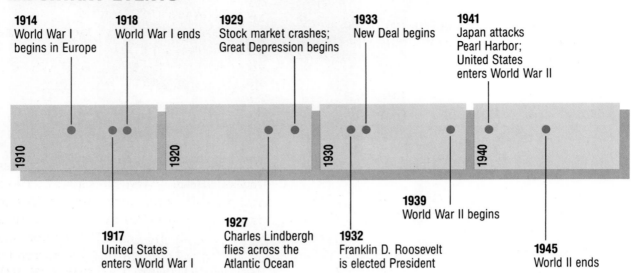

1914 World War I begins in Europe

1918 World War I ends

1929 Stock market crashes; Great Depression begins

1933 New Deal begins

1941 Japan attacks Pearl Harbor; United States enters World War II

1917 United States enters World War I

1927 Charles Lindbergh flies across the Atlantic Ocean

1932 Franklin D. Roosevelt is elected President

1939 World War II begins

1945 World II ends

PEOPLE TO KNOW

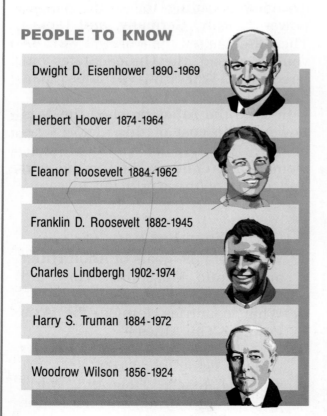

Dwight D. Eisenhower 1890-1969

Herbert Hoover 1874-1964

Eleanor Roosevelt 1884-1962

Franklin D. Roosevelt 1882-1945

Charles Lindbergh 1902-1974

Harry S. Truman 1884-1972

Woodrow Wilson 1856-1924

■ After trying to remain neutral, the United States entered World War I on the side of the Allied Powers.

■ Americans enjoyed good times after World War I as automobiles, movies, and radio changed their lives.

■ The country suffered a stock market crash in 1929, and many years of economic hardship followed.

■ Americans went to war again in 1941 and helped the Allies defeat Germany and Japan.

REVIEWING VOCABULARY

concentration camp	League of Nations
depression	New Deal
dictator	prejudice
Great Depression	stock market
Holocaust	unemployment

Number a sheet of paper from 1 to 10. Beside each number write the word or term from the list that matches the definition.

1. An organization set up after World War I where nations could talk over their differences
2. A prison where people were starved and murdered during World War II
3. People not having jobs
4. A period when business is slow and many people are out of work
5. The Nazi destruction of 6 million Jews during World War II
6. The dislike or hatred of a group because of their race or religion
7. A ruler who has complete control
8. The place where stocks are bought and sold
9. Government programs set up during the Great Depression to help businesses, farmers, and the unemployed
10. The time during the 1930s when business was slow and many people were out of work

REVIEWING FACTS

1. Which countries did the United States fight against in World War I? Which countries made up the Allies?
2. Why did the United States oppose the Treaty of Versailles?
3. Name three new forms of entertainment created in the 1920s.
4. Write four statements of fact about the Great Depression.
5. How did World War II begin? Why did the United States enter the war?

WRITING ABOUT MAIN IDEAS

1. **Writing a Radio News Story:** Choose one of the following events and write a radio news story about it: the United States' entry into World War I; the stock market crash and Great Depression; the bombing of Pearl Harbor; the surrender of Japan at the end of World War II.
2. **Making a Chart:** Make a chart comparing World War I and World War II. Include such information as: who fought on each side; when the war took place; why the United States entered the war; and how the war ended.
3. **Writing a Journal Entry:** Imagine that your family were farmers in the Dust Bowl during the Great Depression. Write a journal entry about your life.

BUILDING SKILLS: DECISION MAKING

1. Write a paragraph explaining the steps in good decision making.
2. Suppose you had been President Truman in 1945. Trace the steps you would have followed in deciding whether or not to use the atomic bomb.
3. What might happen if a person makes a hasty decision about an important issue?

CHAPTER 22

THE UNITED STATES LOOKS TO THE FUTURE

FOCUS

*That's one small step for a man,
one giant leap for mankind.*

These were the words of astronaut Neil Armstrong on July 20, 1969, as he became the first person to set foot on the moon. Landing Americans on the moon was just one of the challenges this country set for itself after World War II. Americans today face new challenges. With each one the nation moves forward, sometimes in small steps and sometimes in giant leaps.

1 The Cold War

READ TO LEARN

Key Vocabulary

United Nations
communism
iron curtain
cold war
Korean War
Peace Corps

Key People

Joseph Stalin
Dwight D. Eisenhower
John F. Kennedy

Key Places

North Korea
South Korea

Read Aloud

We seek peace—enduring [lasting] *peace. More than an end to war, we want an end to the beginnings of all wars.*

These were the last words written by President Franklin Roosevelt before he died. The search for peace, he knew, would not be easy. Still, as the guns of World War II finally fell silent, the United States faced no greater challenge.

Read for Purpose

1. **WHAT YOU KNOW:** What was the result of World War II?
2. **WHAT YOU WILL LEARN:** Why did a "cold war" develop after the end of World War II?

THE UNITED NATIONS

During World War II President Roosevelt began work on a new world organization. It was called the United Nations or UN. In April 1945 representatives of 50 nations met in San Francisco, California, to set up the United Nations. Its main purpose, they agreed, should be to prevent war. But it should also protect human rights and improve the lives of people around the world.

Once again the Senate had to decide whether the United States should join a world organization. In 1920 the answer had been no. As you read in Chapter 21, the United States did not join the League of Nations after World War I. Without American support, the League was too weak to prevent another world war.

The Senate did not want the same thing to happen again. Another world war, warned Senator Arthur Vandenberg of Michigan, was "too horrible" to think about. "Here is our chance to try to stop this disaster," he said, "before it starts." The Senate voted to join the United Nations.

MAP SKILL: Use the map to locate the European countries under **communist** control. Which of the countries border the Baltic Sea?

THE TWO SUPERPOWERS

When World War II ended, the United States and the Soviet Union were the two most powerful countries in the world. These superpowers were very different from one another. During the war they had put aside their differences to fight together against the Axis Powers. But when the fighting ended in 1945, those differences began to drive them apart.

As you read in Chapter 19, Americans live in a free enterprise system. They are free to run their own busi-

nesses and farms. They can choose their jobs and live where they want.

The Soviet Union is a communist country. Under **communism**, the government owns and runs most farms and businesses. The Soviet government also controls where people live, go to school, and work. In 1945 the Soviet Union was ruled by a dictator named Joseph Stalin. Stalin did not allow free speech or religious freedom.

STALIN'S IRON CURTAIN

After the war the Soviet Union tried to spread communism around the world. Soviet troops took control of the countries of Eastern Europe and set up communist governments there.

To many people it seemed as if an iron curtain had been drawn across Europe. West of the iron curtain Europeans were free. East of the iron curtain people were ruled by communist governments. Americans believed that communism should not be allowed to spread further.

The wartime allies now viewed each other as enemies. But neither country wanted to start another world war. The result was a cold war. In a cold war there is no shooting. Instead both sides fight with words and threats.

Early in the cold war the United States spent billions of dollars to help the nations of Western Europe rebuild. With this help, the spread of communism was stopped in Western Europe. It was not stopped in Asia. In 1949 China became a communist country.

THE KOREAN WAR

The cold war turned into a hot war in the Asian country of Korea. Both superpowers had freed Korea from Japan at the end of World War II. The Soviet Union set up a communist government in North Korea. The United States supported a democratic government in South Korea. Find North Korea and South Korea on the world map on pages 586–587 of your Atlas.

In 1950 troops from North Korea invaded South Korea. Their goal was to unite the country under communist rule. South Korea asked the United Nations for help. Sixteen members of the United Nations decided to send troops to fight the North Koreans. Most of the UN forces were American.

In a few months the UN troops drove the North Koreans out of South Korea. Then China sent soldiers to help North Korea. The war continued.

An American soldier in South Korea described the Korean War as "the war we can't win, we can't lose, we can't quit."

The Korean War finally ended in 1953. South Korea had been saved from communism. Today United Nations peacekeeping troops still help keep North and South Korea at peace with each other.

THE ARMS RACE

Peace came to Korea, but the cold war continued. Each superpower, fearful of the other, built up its military forces. Both also began working on new and more powerful weapons. The result was an arms race—a race to build the most powerful weapons the world has ever known.

When the arms race began, only the United States had atomic bombs. Then, in 1949, the Soviet Union exploded its own atomic bomb. By 1953 the superpowers were testing hydrogen bombs. These new nuclear weapons were far more powerful than the atomic bombs that were dropped on Japan.

In 1953 Dwight D. Eisenhower became President of the United States. As a general who had fought in World War II, he knew how destructive atomic weapons were. Thinking about the possibility of future nuclear warfare, Eisenhower said:

War has become not just tragic, but preposterous [senseless]. With modern weapons there can be no victory for anyone.

Still the arms race continued. By the late 1950s both sides were building rockets, or missiles, that could carry nuclear weapons. These missiles could hit targets halfway around the world.

President Eisenhower began looking for ways to control the arms race. In 1959 several nations agreed to keep nuclear weapons out of Antarctica. That frozen continent was set aside for peaceful purposes only.

Before leaving office in 1961, Eisenhower spoke to the United Nations. He asked all countries to agree to stop testing nuclear weapons above ground or underwater. In 1963 such an agreement was reached. One hundred nations signed a treaty that limited the testing of nuclear weapons.

THE PEACE CORPS

In 1960 John F. Kennedy became the youngest person ever to be elected President. Kennedy believed that one way to stop communism was to help the poor people of the world. People who have enough to eat and a decent place to live, he argued, will not turn to communism.

In early 1961 Kennedy set up the Peace Corps. Under this program, thousands of Americans volunteered to help countries in need. They built schools and hospitals. They taught new skills. Peace Corps volunteers spread American good will to people around the world.

POSTWAR PROBLEMS

At the end of World War II Americans dreamed of peace. Instead, as you have read, they found themselves in a cold war with the Soviet Union. The cold war led to an arms race between the two superpowers. As more and more powerful weapons were built, the American people worked hard to prevent war.

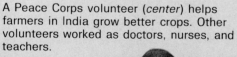

A Peace Corps volunteer (*center*) helps farmers in India grow better crops. Other volunteers worked as doctors, nurses, and teachers.

 Check Your Reading

1. What was the purpose of the United Nations?
2. Why did the United Nations decide to send troops to Korea?
3. Why is the arms race so dangerous?
4. **THINKING SKILL:** Compare and contrast democracy as it is practiced in the United States and communism as it is practiced in the Soviet Union.

2 The Struggle for Equal Rights

READ TO LEARN

Key Vocabulary

unconstitutional
integration
civil rights

Key People

Rosa Parks
Martin Luther King, Jr.
John F. Kennedy
Lyndon Johnson
Jesse Jackson

Key Places

Montgomery

Read Aloud

On December 1, 1955, a neatly dressed African-American woman named Rosa Parks was riding a bus home from work in Montgomery, Alabama. This bus, like almost everything in the South, was segregated. Whites sat in the front. Blacks sat in the back. If the bus became crowded, blacks had to stand so that whites could sit.

Rosa Parks knew the bus segregation laws. But when the driver shouted for her to give her seat to a white man, she did not move. She stayed seated until she was arrested and taken to jail. For Rosa Parks, the struggle for equal rights had begun.

Read for Purpose

1. **WHAT YOU KNOW:** When did segregation become a way of life in the South?
2. **WHAT YOU WILL LEARN:** What were some improvements brought about by the civil rights movement?

MARTIN LUTHER KING, JR.

After Rosa Parks was arrested, African-American people in Montgomery, Alabama, met at a neighborhood church. A young minister named Martin Luther King, Jr., spoke to them.

King did not have to tell the crowd how segregation hurt black people. They had grown up with segregated stores, restaurants, parks, and drinking fountains. They knew that segregated schools kept their children from getting a good education. They knew that most good jobs were closed to them because they were black.

They also knew about progress in the struggle for equal rights. In 1948 President Harry Truman had ended segregation in the armed forces and the government. In 1954 the Supreme Court ruled that segregated schools were unconstitutional, or not allowed by the Constitution. The Court ordered integration in the schools. Integration means making something open to all people. The court ordered that all schools be open to black and white students. Students, regardless of their color, were to go to school together.

While these victories were important, they had not changed life in Montgomery. Here life was still segregated. King spoke for all African-Americans when he said:

> There comes a time when people get tired . . . tired of being segregated and humiliated, tired of being kicked about.

Montgomery's 40,000 black citizens decided to take up Rosa Parks's cause. They protested segregation by not riding the buses. The boycott would go on until the city's buses were integrated.

The action of Rosa Parks (*below*) in 1955 inspired many of the civil rights marchers of the 1960s.

THE MONTGOMERY BUS BOYCOTT

For the next year, no blacks rode Montgomery's buses. Most black people were too poor to own cars. But those who did drove other blacks to and from work. One elderly woman drove from dawn to dark month after month until her car wore out.

Most blacks walked each day to jobs or school. King asked one old woman, "Aren't your feet tired?" She answered, "Yes, my feet [are] tired, but my soul is rested."

Some whites supported the bus boycott by giving blacks rides. Others tried to scare blacks into giving up. King and other leaders of the boycott were put in jail. African-American homes and churches were bombed by whites. King told blacks to "use the weapon of love" against their enemies. "Don't let anyone pull you so low as to hate them," he said.

A year after Rosa Parks had been arrested, the Supreme Court ruled that bus segregation was unconstitutional. The boycott ended. Blacks and whites rode the buses as equals.

THE CIVIL RIGHTS MOVEMENT

The Montgomery bus boycott made Martin Luther King, Jr., the leader of a growing civil rights movement. Civil

EXCERPTS FROM MARTIN LUTHER KING, JR.'S, "I HAVE A DREAM" SPEECH

I say to you today, my friends, even though we face the difficulties of today and tomorrow, I still have a dream. It is a dream deeply rooted in the American dream. I have a dream that one day this nation will rise up and live out the true meaning of its creed: "We hold these truths to be self-evident: that all men are created equal . . . ."

From every mountainside, let freedom ring. And when we allow freedom to ring, when we let it ring from every village, from every hamlet, from every state and every city, we will be able to speed up that day when all of God's children, black men and white men, Jews and Gentiles, Protestants and Catholics, will be able to join hands and sing in the words of the old Negro spiritual: "Free at last! Free at last! Thank God almighty, we are free at last!"

Martin Luther King, Jr., gave his "I Have a Dream" speech in Washington, D.C., in 1963.

rights are the rights of all people to be treated equally under the law. King's goal was to see that black Americans had the same rights, freedoms, and opportunities as did white Americans.

King taught civil rights workers to fight segregation with peaceful protests. One kind of protest was the sit-in. The first sit-in began when black students sat down at a lunch counter that served only whites. The students refused to leave until they were served. They were dragged out by police and arrested. But the students came back day after day until blacks were treated the same as whites.

In 1961 black and white civil rights workers began "freedom rides" across the South. The freedom riders rode buses from town to town. At each stop they tried to end segregation in bus stations. Many freedom riders were arrested or beaten by angry white crowds. But they did not give up.

Soon after John F. Kennedy became President, he asked Congress to pass a civil rights law to end unfair treatment of blacks. "This nation," said Kennedy, "will not be fully free until all its citizens are free."

In August 1963, 250,000 civil rights supporters marched to Washington, D. C. They wanted Congress to pass a civil rights law. As the marchers stood before the Lincoln Memorial, King told them, "I have a dream." He dreamed of a nation in which people "will not be judged by the color of their skin." Read the rest of King's stirring words in the box on this page.

President Kennedy never saw his civil rights law passed. On November 22, 1963, he was shot and killed in Dallas, Texas.

Vice President Lyndon Johnson became President. Johnson was a Southerner who did not believe in segregation. As President he pushed strong civil rights laws through Congress. One law outlawed segregation in public places. It also said people could not be denied jobs because of race, age, or sex. Another law protected the right of blacks to vote.

The civil rights laws ended segregation in the South. But many problems remained. In 1968 Martin Luther King, Jr., made plans for a new march on Washington. His goal was to get Congress to pass laws to help all poor people. But King died before the march took place. The man who had so hated violence was murdered by a gunman.

NEW POWER FOR AFRICAN-AMERICANS

The civil rights movement opened new opportunities for black Americans. Many more black students began to go to college. New jobs opened up for black workers. Cities began to hire black police officers and firefighters. Black performers and news reporters began to appear on television screens.

Blacks also gained political power. As more and more black people be-

Jesse Jackson campaigned throughout the United States in 1988. He was seeking the Democratic Party's nomination for President.

came voters, the number of blacks elected to public office grew. Before 1965 not one American city had a black mayor. Since then many of our largest cities such as Chicago, Los Angeles, Atlanta, and Washington, D.C., have elected black mayors. Since 1965 the number of blacks elected to Congress has more than tripled.

In 1984 and 1988 an African-American political leader, Jesse Jackson, campaigned to become the Democratic Party candidate for President. Jackson was not successful, but his ideas about justice and fairness appealed to a growing number of voters of all colors and backgrounds. Jackson urged that Americans whose ancestors came from Africa be called "African-Americans" rather than "black."

THE STRUGGLE CONTINUES

The Declaration of Independence says that "all men are created equal." But for many years black Americans were treated as less than equal. In this lesson you read how blacks began to demand the same rights and opportunities as whites.

Martin Luther King, Jr., the leader of the civil rights movement, was killed in 1968. But his dream of a nation in which all people are treated as equals did not die. Americans are still working to make King's dream come true.

Check Your Reading

1. Why was Rosa Parks arrested?
2. How did civil rights workers try to bring an end to segregation?
3. What was the purpose of the March on Washington in 1963?
4. **THINKING SKILL:** What was Martin Luther King, Jr.'s, view of violence?

READ TO LEARN

Key Vocabulary

Vietnam War
Watergate
pardon

Key People

Richard Nixon
Gerald Ford
Jimmy Carter
Ronald Reagan
Mikhail Gorbachev

Key Places

Vietnam
Cambodia

Read Aloud

In 1964 Lyndon Johnson was elected President by a huge number of votes. The new President declared a "war on poverty." He talked of building a "Great Society" in which all people would have enough to eat, a decent home, and a good education. The nation united behind the President's goals.

Four years later Americans were deeply divided. There were angry protest marches in cities across the country. So many people opposed Johnson that he decided not to run for President again in 1968. What was tearing the country apart? The answer begins in a distant land during the early days of the cold war.

Read for Purpose

1. **WHAT YOU KNOW:** When did the cold war begin?
2. **WHAT YOU WILL LEARN:** How did the United States become involved in the Vietnam War?

A DIVIDED VIETNAM

Vietnam is a small country in Southeast Asia. World War II left Vietnam divided into two parts. A communist government ruled North Vietnam. The government was supported by the Soviet Union and China. South Vietnam's leaders opposed communism. Their government was supported by the United States. Find North and South Vietnam on the map on page 526.

President Dwight D. Eisenhower wanted to keep communism from spreading across Southeast Asia. If one country fell to communism, he said, the rest would topple like "a row of dominoes." Eisenhower sent military advisers to South Vietnam to help that country train its army.

President John Kennedy continued to help South Vietnam. When Kennedy

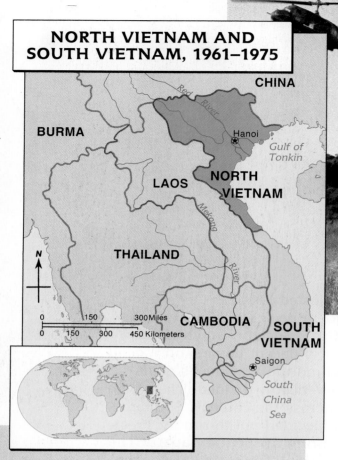

NORTH VIETNAM AND SOUTH VIETNAM, 1961–1975

CHINA

BURMA

Red River

Hanoi

Gulf of Tonkin

LAOS

NORTH VIETNAM

THAILAND

Mekong River

N

0   150   300 Miles
0   150   300   450 Kilometers

CAMBODIA

SOUTH VIETNAM

Saigon

South China Sea

MAP SKILL: Helicopters were used to drop off and pick up American troops during the Vietnam War. Name the capitals of each part of Vietnam.

was killed in 1963, there were 16,000 Americans giving military advice in that small country.

President Lyndon Johnson expanded the Vietnam War rapidly. By the end of 1966 there were 385,000 Americans fighting in South Vietnam. American bombers were dropping more bombs on North Vietnam than had been dropped on Germany in World War II.

THE "LIVING ROOM WAR"

In the 1950s Americans had fallen in love with a new invention called television. Television brought the world into people's homes. It also made the Viet-

nam War America's first "living room war." Night after night people watched the war on television newscasts. They were shown the courage of American troops. They also saw the death and destruction caused by the war.

President Johnson kept telling Americans that victory was near. But the enemy that people saw on television did not look beaten. Many people began to believe that the Vietnam War was becoming a no-win, no-end war.

As the Vietnam War dragged on, opposition to it grew. By 1968 the country was deeply divided between "hawks" and "doves." Hawks wanted the United States to stay in the war until it was won. They believed that defeating North Vietnam was the only way to stop the spread of communism.

Doves were against the war. Vietnam's problems, they said, should be solved by the people of Vietnam. Doves believed that American troops should not be fighting there. They saw the war as a terrible waste of human life, both American and Vietnamese.

THE UNITED STATES PULLS OUT

In 1969 Richard Nixon became President of the United States. Nixon wanted to end the Vietnam War without losing it. His goal was to "bring an honorable end to the war." President Nixon began bringing American troops home from South Vietnam. But at the same time he increased the bombing of North Vietnam. He also sent American troops into another country in Southeast Asia—Cambodia. It was the army's job to capture communist headquarters there.

The invasion of Cambodia set off a storm of protests in the United States. Angry students closed 250 colleges. Police and National Guard troops were called in to keep order. At Kent State University, in Ohio, National Guardsmen, who were trying to keep order, shot and killed four students.

In 1973 President Nixon signed a peace agreement with the leaders of North and South Vietnam. America's longest war was over. Over 57,000 Americans had died in Vietnam. Another 300,000 came home wounded.

In 1975 North Vietnam defeated South Vietnam. The country was united under a communist government based in North Vietnam.

THE WATERGATE SCANDAL

By this time, Richard Nixon was no longer President of the United States. He had been forced to leave office because of the Watergate scandal. A scandal is an action that shocks people because it is wrong.

The Watergate scandal began in 1972. One night five "burglars" were arrested for breaking into the Watergate Hotel in Washington, D. C. They had been sent to spy on Nixon's politi-

These statues in Washington, D.C., are part of the nation's memorial to those who fought and died in Vietnam.

cal opponents. Soon Americans learned that the Watergate "burglars" had ties to people who worked for President Nixon.

At first Nixon said he knew nothing about the break-in. But the evidence later showed that he was lying. He even had arranged for the "burglars" to be paid to keep them from telling the truth. This was a crime.

In the summer of 1974 the United States House of Representatives planned to vote to impeach President Nixon for abusing his power. Just as the House of Representatives was about to vote on his impeachment, Richard Nixon announced that he was resigning from the presidency. Nixon was the first President to step down from office before the end of his term.

Vice President Gerald Ford took over as President as soon as Nixon resigned. President Ford told Americans that "the long national nightmare is over." One of his first acts as President was to **pardon** Richard Nixon. That meant that Nixon could not be brought to trial. Ford, like most Americans, wanted to leave the scandal of Watergate behind.

CONTROLLING THE ARMS RACE

Soon after taking office, President Ford visited the Soviet Union. He went to talk about the arms race. By 1970 the superpowers had enough nuclear weapons to destroy all life on earth. Still the arms race continued. In 1972 the United States and the Soviet Union finally agreed to slow down the arms race. President Ford worked to strengthen that agreement.

In 1977 **Jimmy Carter** became President. Two years later he reached an agreement with the Soviet Union to put limits on some kinds of nuclear weap-

Mikhail Gorbachev and Ronald Reagan met several times as part of their attempt to bring the Soviet Union and the United States closer together.

ons. This agreement, said Carter, "will not end the arms competition, but it does make that competition safer."

In 1980 and again in 1984, American voters chose **Ronald Reagan** for President. Reagan insisted that "real arms control" meant having fewer nuclear weapons. A new leader of the Soviet Union named **Mikhail Gorbachev** (myik ə ēl′ gôr′ bə chôf) agreed.

The United States and the Soviet Union signed a new arms control treaty in 1987. For the first time both superpowers agreed to destroy some of their nuclear weapons.

FROM WAR TO PEACE

In this lesson, you read how the cold war turned hot again during the 1960s. American troops went to South Vietnam to try to stop the spread of communism. But millions of Americans opposed the Vietnam War. They argued that the United States should be making peace, not war.

Since the Vietnam War the superpowers have taken steps toward controlling the arms race. Ahead lies the challenge of ending the cold war and building a more peaceful world. For as President John Kennedy once warned, "mankind must put an end to war or war will put an end to mankind."

Check Your Reading

1. Why did the United States send troops to Vietnam?
2. What was the result of the Watergate scandal?
3. What progress did the superpowers make in controlling the arms race?
4. **THINKING SKILL:** How did President Carter view the 1977 arms agreement with the Soviet Union?

4 Our Country Today

READING TO LEARN

Key People

Neil Armstrong   Sandra Day O'Connor
Christa McAuliffe   Geraldine Ferraro
George Bush

Read Aloud

The year 1976 was a special one for Americans. That year the United States celebrated the bicentennial, or 200th birthday, of the Declaration of Independence.

More celebrations followed. The year 1987 was the 200th birthday of our Constitution. And in 1989 Americans celebrated the bicentennial of our first President, George Washington. What if Washington could have returned for this celebration? What changes do you think he would have seen? What things would have seemed the same to him even after 200 years?

Read for Purpose

1. **WHAT YOU KNOW:** What was one problem that our country faced after the Vietnam War?
2. **WHAT YOU WILL LEARN:** How has our country changed since George Washington was President?

A NEW FRONTIER—SPACE

The first thing George Washington might have noticed is how much the United States has grown in 200 years. When he was President there were just 13 states hugging the Atlantic Coast. Today the United States is a superpower of 50 states. It stretches from the Atlantic Coast to the Pacific Coast and beyond to Hawaii and Alaska.

Even though Americans have spread across the continent, the old frontier spirit that George Washington found in the Virginia backcountry is still alive. Today's pioneers are exploring a new frontier—space.

America's space program began in the late 1950s. Space scientists used rockets to carry weather and communication satellites into space. Satellites are objects that circle the earth in space.

In 1961 President John F. Kennedy set a new goal for America's space program. He challenged the nation to land

529

an American on the moon before 1970. That goal was reached in the summer of 1969. As millions of people watched on television, Neil Armstrong stepped out onto the dusty surface of the moon. Humans had made their first journey to another world.

The space program has seen tragedy as well as triumphs. In 1986 the space shuttle *Challenger* exploded one minute after lifting off from Cape Canaveral. The seven crew members on board were killed. One of them was schoolteacher Christa McAuliffe, the first person to go into space who was not a professional astronaut. Space flights were stopped until the shuttle could be made safer.

Late in 1988 Americans held their breaths as the shuttle *Discovery* took off in a cloud of smoke. Four days later the shuttle returned safely to earth. The United States was back in space.

IMPROVING THE ENVIRONMENT

George Washington would have surely been amazed by the great changes in our nation's environment. Washington lived in a nation of farms, small villages, and wilderness. Today most Americans live in huge cities and sprawling suburbs.

As the United States changed, so did its environment. In some cities blue skies turned brown as factory smoke and car exhaust filled the air. Many factories and towns dumped poisonous waste materials and sewage into waterways. Nearby lakes and rivers were poisoned with chemicals. Fish and ducks could not survive in these deadly waters.

On April 22, 1970, Americans who were worried about the environment celebrated the first Earth Day. Across the country there were festivals, parades, and projects in support of a clean environment. A girl in New York carried a sign warning, "We treat this

In the future, American astronauts might travel on the shuttle *Discovery* to a space station like the one in this artist's picture (*right*).

world of ours as if we had a spare one in our back pocket." But we don't.

As concern about the environment grew, Congress took action. Since 1970 it has passed several laws to clean up our nation's air and water. Today skies are blue again over most cities. Some lakes and rivers have been cleaned up. There is still much work to be done to improve our environment, however.

AMERICA'S NEW FACES

George Washington might have been surprised by the number of Americans today. In 1789 there were about 4 million people in the United States. By 1989 there were almost 250 million Americans. In Washington's time 95 people out of 100 lived on farms. Today only 25 out of every 100 Americans live in rural areas.

One thing has not changed in 200 years. The United States is still a nation of immigrants. The faces of recent immigrants, however, are different from those that Washington knew. In 1789 most newcomers were from Europe. Today's immigrants come mostly from Asia, Mexico, the Caribbean, and Central and South America.

The largest group of newcomers are the Hispanics, or Spanish-speaking immigrants. They come from many countries in Latin America. Together they make up about 6 percent of the population of the United States.

Like earlier immigrants, the new immigrants face poverty and prejudice. But they are working hard to improve their lives.

The reasons immigrants come to the United States have not changed in 200 years. Many are driven from their homelands by poverty and hunger.

Newly arrived immigrants take the oath of allegiance and become citizens of the United States. Where do most of today's immigrants come from?

Some are fleeing from war and harsh governments. Others come seeking better opportunities for themselves and their children. As a newcomer from the Caribbean country of Jamaica says:

I think the United States is the best place for going as far as you are going to go. And it doesn't matter whether you're black, white, brown, yellow or green.

OUR LIVING CONSTITUTION

If Washington were to have come back in 1989, he might have seen our 41st President, George Bush, take the oath of office. Washington would have recognized that oath as the same one he took when he became President. The Constitution that Washington promised to "preserve, protect, and defend" in 1789 is still "the supreme law of the land."

531

The decade of the 1980s opened with the swearing in of the first woman Supreme Court Justice, Sandra Day O'Connor. The decade came to a close as George Bush became the country's 41st President.

Our Constitution has survived for over 200 years for two reasons. First, it set up a strong, workable system of government. Second, it is a living constitution. It can be changed as the nation changes.

Since Washington left office, the Constitution has been amended 16 times. One amendment ended slavery forever. Other important amendments gave civil rights to African-Americans and the right to vote to women.

These changes have made our government more democratic. When Washington was President, the government was run only by white men. If Washington could visit Congress today, he would find men and women of different colors and backgrounds working as our country's lawmakers. In 1981 Sandra Day O'Connor became the first woman to serve on the Supreme Court.

Women and members of minority groups can also be found today working in the executive branch. In 1984 the Democratic Party chose New York Representative Geraldine Ferraro as its first woman candidate for Vice President. The Democrats lost the election. But Ferraro proved that a woman could handle a tough campaign.

AMERICA'S UNFINISHED STORY

As you have read, the United States has faced many challenges in its first 200 years. But the story of this great nation is far from over. The future will bring challenges we cannot begin to imagine. How you help meet those challenges will become part of America's unfinished story.

 Check Your Reading

1. What success did America's space program celebrate in 1969?
2. How has America's environment changed since George Washington's time?
3. How has our nation become more democratic since 1789?
4. **THINKING SKILL:** Based on your reading in this lesson, what can you conclude about the changes our country has experienced since Washington became President?

This year you read about some people who have made a difference in their communities. You read about the two police officers who started the Fort Apache Youth Center. Beginning as a boxing club, the Youth Center now provides a variety of activities for teenagers in the neighborhood. You also met Julie Leirich, who started The Loving Cup program. With the help of other volunteers and local supermarkets, The Loving Cup distributes tons of food to poor people in Los Angeles.

Beatrice Gallego has made a difference in her community too. She worked hard to improve the lives of people in San Antonio, Texas, by heading a voter registration drive. When it came time for the people to vote, they chose leaders who understood their problems.

The members of The Friendly Supper Club of Montgomery, Alabama, also saw a problem and tried to solve it. Through their monthly dinners they have brought hundreds of black people and white people together. They know that even one friendship among people of different groups can lead to greater understanding among all Americans.

Finally, you read about Millard Fuller, the man who started Habitat for Humanity. He found a way for poor families to have livable housing. Working together, new homeowners and Habitat volunteers turn rundown buildings into comfortable places to live.

In your textbook this year you read about only a few people who have tried to make a difference. Maybe you know someone in your own community who saw a problem and tried to solve it.

Helping other people in your community, state, or country is not a job for adults only. A young person like you can help too. Maybe there is a park or street that needs cleaning up. Or perhaps there are senior citizens who can no longer mow their lawns or carry their groceries. You might be able to help with a problem like one of these. Or you might think of other ways to help. The important thing to remember is that *you* can make a difference.

Comparing Maps

Life in the United States has changed greatly in the late 1900s. Maps can help you see some of these changes.

There are hundreds of different kinds of maps. Most of the time you can find a map that tells you just what you want to know or that helps you answer a particular question. Sometimes, however, you want information that is not provided by any single map. In such cases, you can use two or more maps and compare them. By comparing maps, you can learn things that you cannot learn from any one of the maps by itself. Comparing maps can help you understand relationships and changes.

Look at the maps on these pages. The titles tell you that both maps provide information about women in state legislatures. The map below is for 1977. Look at the map key to find out what the different colors used on the maps stand for. You can see that green shows states in which women made up 18 percent or more of the legislature in 1977. What color shows states in which women made up from 9 to 18 percent of the legislature? In how many states did women make up 4 percent or more of the legislature in 1977? In what states was the percent of women in the legislature 4 percent or less?

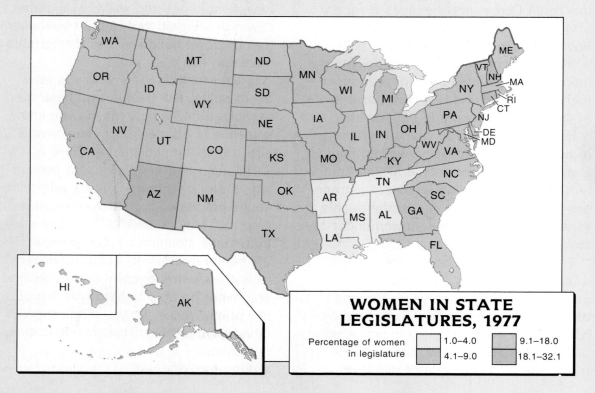

WOMEN IN STATE LEGISLATURES, 1977

Percentage of women in legislature

| 1.0–4.0 | 9.1–18.0 |
| 4.1–9.0 | 18.1–32.1 |

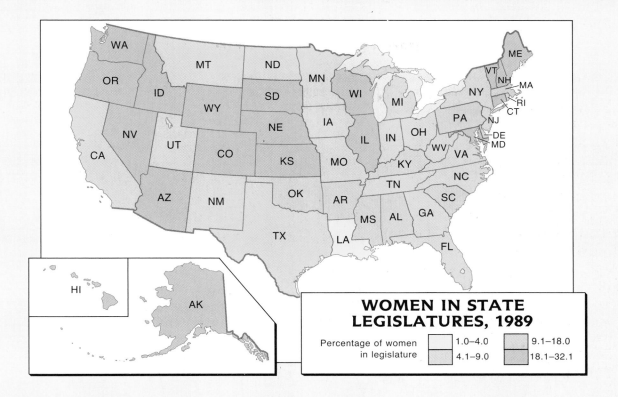

WOMEN IN STATE LEGISLATURES, 1989

Percentage of women in legislature

1.0–4.0	9.1–18.0
4.1–9.0	18.1–32.1

The map on this page gives information about women in state legislatures in 1989. You can see from the key that the colors used for percents are the same as those used on the map on page 534. In how many states did women make up from 18 to 32 percent of the legislature in 1989? In what states did women make up from 9 to 18 percent of the legislature?

Now suppose you are asked this question: Did the number of states in which women made up 18 percent or more of the legislature increase or decrease between 1977 and 1989? You will have to use both maps to answer this question. The map on page 534 shows that there were three states in which women made up 18 percent or more of the legislature in 1977. The map on this page shows that there were 19 states in which women

made up 18 percent or more of the legislature in 1989.

Reviewing the Skill

Compare the maps to answer these questions.

1. What do you do when you compare maps?
2. Did the number of states in which women made up 4 percent or more of the legislature increase or decrease between 1977 and 1989?
3. In which state did the percent of women in the legislature stay the same between the years 1977 and 1989?
4. On the whole, did the percent of women in state legislatures in the United States increase or decrease from 1977 to 1989?
5. When is it helpful to compare maps?

IMPORTANT EVENTS

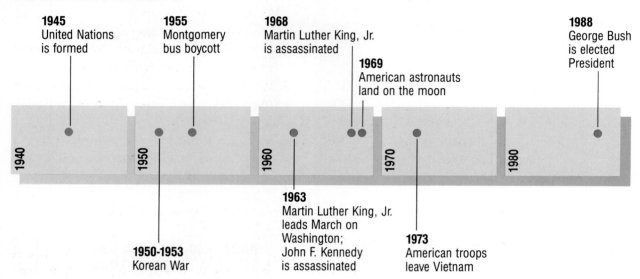

1945
United Nations
is formed

1955
Montgomery
bus boycott

1968
Martin Luther King, Jr.
is assassinated

1969
American astronauts
land on the moon

1988
George Bush
is elected
President

1940
1950
1960
1970
1980

1950-1953
Korean War

1963
Martin Luther King, Jr.
leads March on
Washington;
John F. Kennedy
is assassinated

1973
American troops
leave Vietnam

PEOPLE TO KNOW

George Bush 1924-

John F. Kennedy 1917-1963

Martin Luther King, Jr. 1929-1968

Richard Nixon 1913-

Sandra Day O'Connor 1930-

Rosa Parks 1913-

Ronald Reagan 1911-

IDEAS TO REMEMBER

■ The cold war between the United States and the Soviet Union led to a war in Korea and an intense arms race between the two superpowers.

■ During the 1950s and 1960s black Americans struggled to gain their civil rights.

■ The United States sent troops to South Vietnam during the 1960s to prevent a communist takeover.

■ The changes the United States has seen since 1776 have made our country a more democratic place in which to live.

REVIEWING VOCABULARY

civil rights   integration
cold war   unconstitutional
communism

Number a sheet of paper from 1 to 5. Beside each number write a sentence using one of the vocabulary words or terms from the list above. The sentence should show that you understand the meaning of the word or term.

REVIEWING FACTS

Number a sheet of paper from 1 to 10. Beside each number write whether the statement is true or false. If it is false, explain why.

1. The United States never joined the UN because it did not want to be drawn into another world war.
2. The Korean War started when North Korean communists invaded South Korea.
3. An arms race is a race in which different American companies try to build weapons as quickly as possible.
4. All of the following people have been President of the United States since 1950: Dwight D. Eisenhower; Martin Luther King, Jr.; Lyndon Johnson; and Geraldine Ferraro.
5. In 1954 the Supreme Court hurt the civil rights movement by deciding that segregated schools were legal under the Constitution.
6. Civil rights laws passed in the 1960s outlawed segregation in public places and protected the right of blacks to vote.

7. During the Vietnam War the United States sent only a small number of advisers to help South Vietnam.
8. Gerald Ford is the only President ever to have resigned from office.
9. After the space shuttle *Challenger* exploded, the United States ended its space program.
10. Earth Day is a day set aside for people to think of specific ways to clean up the environment.

WRITING ABOUT MAIN IDEAS

1. **Writing a Journal Entry:** Write a journal entry that Rosa Parks might have written the day she refused to give up her seat on the bus. Describe what happened. Also tell what Parks might have been feeling at the time.
2. **Writing a Letter About Peace with the Soviet Union:** Write a letter to the President of the United States. Tell the President what you think are the best ways to achieve lasting peace with the Soviet Union. Suggest something the country should do to make peace a reality.

BUILDING SKILLS: COMPARING MAPS

1. Why is it sometimes useful to compare two or more maps?
2. Turn to the Atlas maps of the United States on pages 590–591 and 592–593. Locate your state and write a paragraph about it.
3. How would your paragraph be different if you had used only the map on pages 590–591? Why?

537

REVIEWING VOCABULARY

assembly line	dictator
civil rights	integration
communism	prejudice
conservation	suffrage
depression	unconstitutional

Number a sheet of paper from 1 to 10. Beside each number write the word or term from the list above that best completes the sentence.

1. Setting aside land for national parks is one kind of _____.
2. A law that is not in keeping with the Constitution is _____.
3. The _____ of Germany, Adolf Hitler, had complete control of the country.
4. Cars built on an _____ can be made faster and more cheaply.
5. Black Americans have often been treated unfairly because of _____.
6. The right to vote and to have an equal chance for an education are examples of _____.
7. Under _____ the government decides what type of work each person will do.
8. Carrie Chapman Catt was a leader of the women's _____ movement that wanted to give women the right to vote.
9. In 1954 the Supreme Court ruled that there should be _____ in all public schools.
10. During a _____, business slows down and many people lose their jobs.

WRITING ABOUT THE UNIT

1. **Writing a Paragraph:** How has the United States become more democratic in the twentieth century? Write a paragraph explaining your answer.
2. **Writing an Opinion Paragraph:** How do you think Theodore Roosevelt would have felt about the clean air and water laws of the 1970s? Write a paragraph as if you were President Roosevelt. Tell "your" opinion of these laws.
3. **Writing an Editorial:** Choose one of the Presidents discussed in this unit. Then write a newspaper editorial that gives your opinion of one of the President's actions. Remember to give reasons for your opinion.

ACTIVITIES

1. **Making an Illustrated Report About National Parks:** Do some research about America's national parks. Gather information about the parks in general. Then choose one park that interests you. Prepare an illustrated report based on your research. Your report should include at least one map.
2. **Working Together to Learn About the Space Program:** Work with three or four classmates to find out about the history and achievements of the United States space program. Then prepare a bulletin board display. Your display might include a time line, diagrams, a map of space travel, stories about specific astronauts, or other topics that interest your group.

BUILDING SKILLS: READING A NEWSPAPER

1. What are the parts of a newspaper?
2. Read the news article on this page. What event is being reported?

3. Where was the news reporter when he wrote the story?
4. In which newspaper did the story appear?

The Sunday Sentinel

MILWAUKEE, SUNDAY, JULY 3, 1898

AMERICANS ADVANCE ON SANTIAGO

On Board the Dispatch Boat Dandy, off Juragua, Friday, July 1, 4 p.m., via Port Antonio, Jamaica, Saturday, July 2, 5 a.m., and Kingston, Jamaica, 7:11 a.m.–[Copyright, 1898, by the Associated Press.]–The battle of Santiago has raged all day and at 4 o'clock this afternoon 15,000 American troops are thundering at the outer fortifications of the doomed city. Since daybreak, Gen. Shafter's army has fought its way across two and a half miles of bitterly contested and strongly fortified country; and the entire line from left to right is within gunshot of Santiago town.

The American loss thus far is estimated at hospital corps headquarters at twenty killed and fifty wounded, but it will be hours before the death roll can be accurately given.

Lieut.-Col. Patterson of the Twenty-second infantry is the only officer known to have been wounded and he is not fatally hurt.

The Spanish killed and wounded are undoubtedly numbered by hundreds.

LINKING PAST, PRESENT, AND FUTURE

During World War II, millions of innocent people were killed. In the Holocaust six million Jewish men, women, and children were sent to their deaths. Millions of other civilians were worked to death or were killed in concentration camps and in bombing raids. Do you think it is right for young people to study about such horrible things? Can learning about the Holocaust help the people of the world today and in the future? Explain your answer.

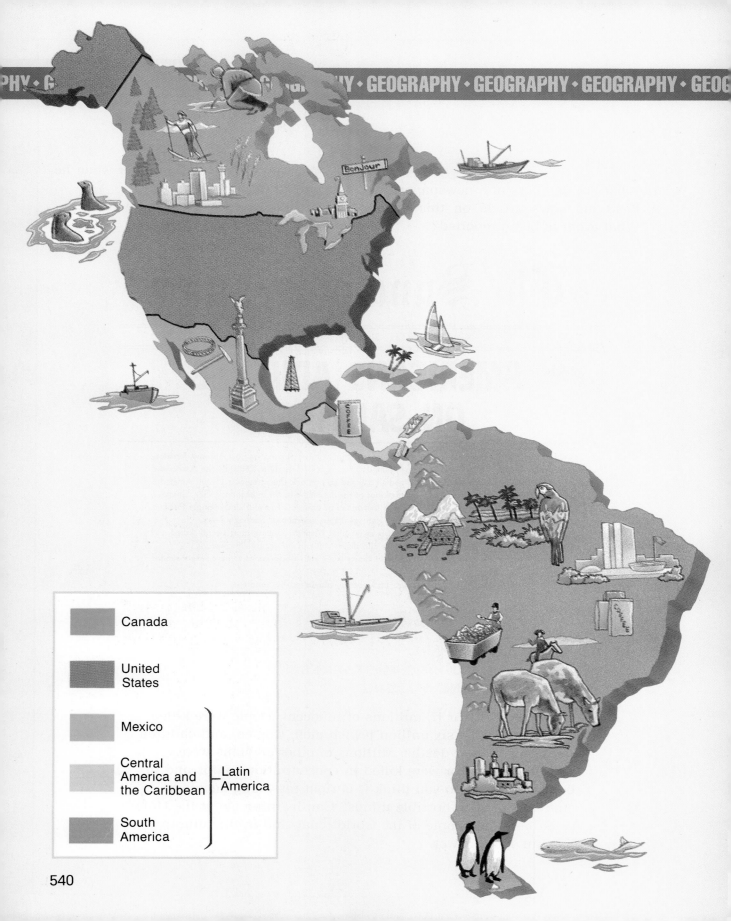

Bonjour

Canada

United
States

Mexico

Central
America and
the Caribbean

Latin
America

South
America

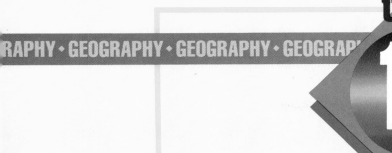

UNIT
10

CANADA
AND
LATIN AMERICA

WHERE WE ARE

This is a map of the Western Hemisphere. Canada borders the United States on the north. It is the largest country in the Western Hemisphere. Mexico is our neighbor directly to the south. Mexico and the land south of the United States make up a region known as Latin America.

Like the people of the United States, the people of Canada and Latin America and the Caribbean live in many different environments. Over the years trade and travel with our neighbors to the north and south have increased.

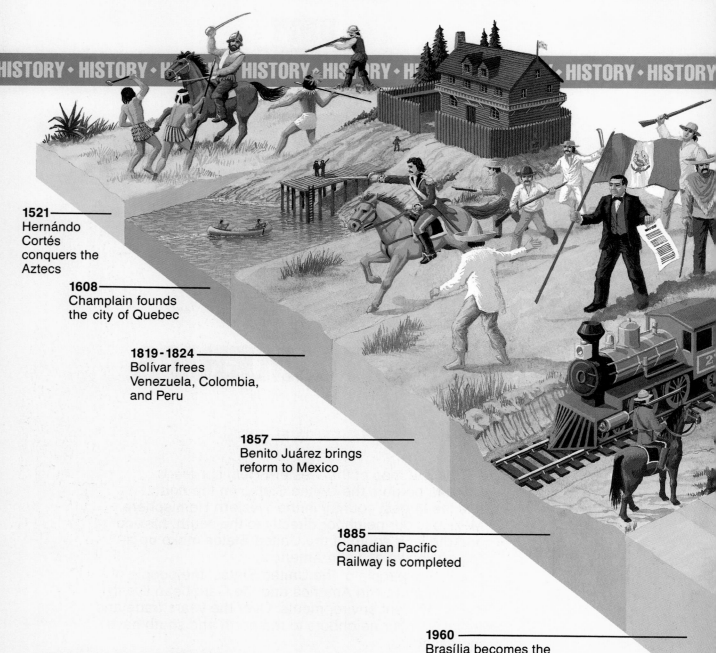

1521
Hernándo Cortés conquers the Aztecs

1608
Champlain founds the city of Quebec

1819-1824
Bolívar frees Venezuela, Colombia, and Peru

1857
Benito Juárez brings reform to Mexico

1885
Canadian Pacific Railway is completed

1960
Brasília becomes the new capital of Brazil

1982
Canada approves a new Constitution

WHAT HAPPENED

As you read about Canada and the countries of Latin America, you will see that they have much in common with the United States. All were once European colonies. All struggled to achieve their independence. In this unit, you will read the story of many countries and their people. Some parts of their story, like the building of the Canadian Pacific Railway, will remind you of events in our nation's past. Other parts will show you what makes the people and places of Canada and Latin America unique.

542

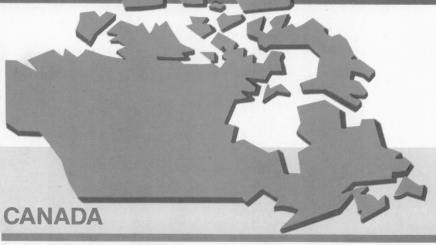

CANADA

CANADA
Capital ★ Ottawa
Population: 26,087,536
Area: 3,851,798 sq mi;
9,976,140 sq km

MEXICO, CENTRAL AMERICA, AND THE CARIBBEAN

ANTIGUA AND BARBUDA
Capital ★ St. John's
Population: 70,925
Area: 170 sq mi;
440 sq km

THE BAHAMAS
Capital ★ Nassau
Population: 242,983
Area: 5,382 sq mi;
13,940 sq km

BARBADOS
Capital ★ Bridgetown
Population: 256,784
Area: 166 sq mi;
430 sq km

BELIZE
Capital ★ Belmopan
Population: 171,735
Area: 8,865 sq mi;
22,960 sq km

COSTA RICA
Capital ★ San Jose
Population: 2,888,227
Area: 19,652 sq mi;
50,900 sq km

CUBA
Capital ★ Havana
Population: 10,353,932
Area: 42,803 sq mi;
110,860 sq km

DOMINICA
Capital ★ Roseau
Population: 97,763
Area: 290 sq mi;
750 sq km

DOMINICAN REPUBLIC
Capital ★ Santo Domingo
Population: 7,136,748
Area: 18,816 sq mi;
48,730 sq km

EL SALVADOR
Capital ★ San Salvador
Population: 5,388,644
Area: 8,124 sq mi;
21,040 sq km

GRENADA
Capital ★ St. George's
Population: 84,455
Area: 131 sq mi;
340 sq km

GUATEMALA
Capital ★ Guatemala City
Population: 8,831,148
Area: 42,042 sq mi;
108,890 sq km

HAITI
Capital ★ Port-au-Prince
Population: 6,295,570
Area: 10,714 sq mi;
27,750 sq km

HONDURAS
Capital ★ Tegucigalpa
Population: 4,972,287
Area: 43,277 sq mi;
112,090 sq km

JAMAICA
Capital ★ Kingston
Population: 2,458,102
Area: 4,243 sq mi;
10,990 sq km

544

MEXICO
Capital ★ Mexico City
Population: 83,527,567
Area: 761,604 sq mi;
1,972,550 sq km

NICARAGUA
Capital ★ Managua
Population: 3,407,183
Area: 49,998 sq mi;
129,494 sq km

PANAMA
Capital ★ Panama City
Population: 2,323,622
Area: 30,193 sq mi;
78,200 sq km

PUERTO RICO
Capital ★ San Juan
Population: 3,196,520
Area: 3,515 sq mi;
9,104 sq km

ST. CHRISTOPHER AND NEVIS
Capital ★ Basseterre
Population: 36,738
Area: 139 sq mi; 360 sq km

ST. LUCIA
Capital ★ Castries
Population: 136,564
Area: 239 sq mi;
620 sq km

ST. VINCENT & THE GRENADINES
Capital ★ Kingstown
Population: 107,425
Area: 131 sq mi; 340 sq km

TRINIDAD AND TOBAGO
Capital ★ Port-of-Spain
Population: 1,279,920
Area: 1,980 sq mi;
5,130 sq km

SOUTH AMERICA

ARGENTINA
Capital ★ Buenos Aires
Population: 31,532,538
Area: 1,068,299 sq mi;
2,766,890 sq km

BOLIVIA
Capital ★ Sucre (legal)
Population: 6,448,297
Area: 424,163 sq mi;
1,098,580 sq km

BRAZIL
Capital ★ Brasília
Population: 150,685,145
Area: 3,286,480 sq mi;
8,511,970 sq km

CHILE
Capital ★ Santiago
Population: 12,638,046
Area: 292,259 sq mi;
756,950 sq km

COLOMBIA
Capital ★ Bogotá
Population: 31,298,803
Area: 439,734 sq mi;
1,138,910 sq km

ECUADOR
Capital ★ Quito
Population: 10,231,630
Area: 109,483 sq mi;
283,560 sq km

FRENCH GUIANA
Capital ★ Cayenne
Population: 91,641
Area: 35,135 sq mi;
91,000 sq km

GUYANA
Capital ★ Georgetown
Population: 765,796
Area: 83,000 sq mi;
214,970 sq km

PARAGUAY
Capital ★ Asunción
Population: 4,386,024
Area: 157,047 sq mi;
406,750 sq km

PERU
Capital ★ Lima
Population: 21,269,074
Area: 496,225 sq mi;
1,285,220 sq km

SURINAME
Capital ★ Paramaribo
Population: 394,999
Area: 63,039 sq mi;
163,270 sq km

URUGUAY
Capital ★ Montevideo
Population: 2,976,138
Area: 68,039 sq mi;
176,220 sq km

VENEZUELA
Capital ★ Caracas
Population: 18,775,780
Area: 352,143 sq mi;
912,050 sq km

CHAPTER 23

CANADA

FOCUS

O Canada!
Our home and native land!

These words begin the national anthem of Canada, our neighbor to the north. Snow-capped mountains, dense forests, frozen plains, and shining lakes make Canada a land of great beauty. But it also is a challenging place to live. This far north, summers are short and winters are long and cold. For these reasons Canada has grown far more slowly than the United States. Today about 26 million people call Canada "our home and native land."

1 The Geography of Canada

READS TO LEARN

🔲 Key Places

Canadian Shield
Appalachian Highlands
Great Lakes–St. Lawrence Lowlands

Interior Plains
Western Mountain Region
Arctic North

🔲 Read Aloud

Many thousands of years ago Ice Age hunters came to North America from Asia. In Canada they found a frozen world. You read in Chapter 3 how glaciers, or mile-thick sheets of ice, covered most of the land. The glaciers inched slowly toward the sea. As they moved, the ice wore away mountains and scooped out the basins of future lakes. About 15,000 years ago the ice began to melt. As sunshine warmed the land, trees and grass grew and covered huge areas. Birds, animals, and fish moved into this new wilderness. So did people. In each region they learned how to use the resources of this large and lovely land.

🔲 Read for Purpose

1. **WHAT YOU KNOW:** Where did the first people in North America come from?
2. **WHAT YOU WILL LEARN:** What are the six physical regions in Canada?

CANADA'S PHYSICAL REGIONS

Canada is a vast country, second in size only to the Soviet Union. Canada stretches for over 3,200 miles (5,120 km) from the Atlantic to the Pacific coasts. Its northernmost land reaches nearly to the North Pole.

Given its size, it is not surprising to learn that Canada is a varied country with six quite different physical regions. Physical regions are large areas that have similar landforms, climate, and resources. As you read about each

of Canada's physical regions, find it on the map on page 548.

THE CANADIAN SHIELD

The largest of the six physical regions, the Canadian Shield covers about half of Canada. It lies like a huge horseshoe around Hudson Bay.

The Canadian Shield is the oldest part of North America. Its core, or center, of solid rock was formed over 2 billion years ago. Some of the rocks are

547

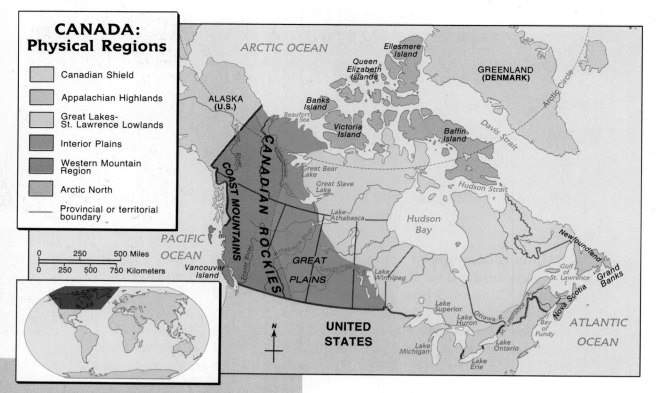

CANADA: Physical Regions

- Canadian Shield
- Appalachian Highlands
- Great Lakes–St. Lawrence Lowlands
- Interior Plains
- Western Mountain Region
- Arctic North
- Provincial or territorial boundary

0   250   500 Miles
0   250   500   750 Kilometers

ARCTIC OCEAN
Ellesmere Island
Queen Elizabeth Islands
GREENLAND (DENMARK)
ALASKA (U.S.)
Banks Island
Beaufort Sea
Victoria Island
Baffin Island
Arctic Circle
Davis Strait
Yukon River
COAST MOUNTAINS
CANADIAN ROCKIES
Great Bear Lake
Great Slave Lake
Hudson Strait
PACIFIC OCEAN
Vancouver Island
Fraser River
Athabasca River
Lake Athabasca
Saskatchewan River
GREAT PLAINS
Lake Winnipeg
Hudson Bay
Newfoundland
Gulf of St. Lawrence
Grand Banks
Nova Scotia
Lake Superior
Lake Huron
Lake Michigan
Ottawa R.
St. Lawrence
Bay of Fundy
ATLANTIC OCEAN
Lake Ontario
Lake Erie
UNITED STATES
N

MAP SKILL: Use the map to locate Canada's physical regions. Which region is shown by the color yellow?

rich in minerals. Today copper, iron, gold, nickel, and uranium are mined in this region.

Glaciers once covered the Shield. When the earth warmed, water from the melting ice flowed into thousands of lakes and rivers. Today those rivers turn machines that make electricity.

Most of the Canadian Shield is covered with dense forests. Mixed with the forests are flat, swampy areas called muskegs. *Muskeg* is an Indian word for wet, spongy ground.

With its tangled forests, soggy muskegs, and cold climate, the Canadian Shield has never been an easy place in which to live. But after the Ice Age, hardy groups of Indians made their home here. They lived by hunting and trapping woodland animals, such as beaver and moose. Today the Canadian Shield is the scene of much logging by lumber and paper companies.

THE APPALACHIAN HIGHLANDS

East of the Canadian Shield are the Appalachian Highlands. This region of wooded hills, peninsulas, and islands is the northernmost part of the Appalachian Mountains. Glaciers have left the Appalachian Highlands with plenty of rocks but with little soil.

While most land in the Appalachian Highlands is not good for farming, the nearby sea provides plenty of food. The coastal waters are alive with porpoises, whales, swordfish, sharks, and tuna. Millions of codfish feed in the Grand Banks off the coast of Newfoundland. Lobsters cover the ocean floor off Nova Scotia.

Today most people in the Appalachian Highlands live near the sea and make their living from its riches.

THE GREAT LAKES– ST. LAWRENCE LOWLANDS

South of the Canadian Shield lies one of Canada's smallest physical regions—the Great Lakes–St. Lawrence Lowlands. This region is named for its most important waterways—the Great Lakes and the St. Lawrence River. Together they form a water highway going from the Atlantic Ocean deep into the heart of North America.

The St. Lawrence River is sometimes called the "Mother of Canada." The first Europeans followed its route to explore and settle Canada. The towns the Europeans founded—Quebec, Montreal, Ottawa, and Toronto—have grown into large industrial cities.

The land in the Lowlands is flat and fertile. This area is also the most southern part of Canada. The growing season is long enough and warm enough for many crops.

The first people to farm in the Lowlands were the Hurons and the Iroquois. The Indians cleared patches of land in the forest and planted corn, beans, squash, and sunflowers.

Today fruit orchards, tobacco fields, vegetable gardens, and dairy farms are found throughout the Great Lakes–St. Lawrence Lowlands.

THE INTERIOR PLAINS

Between the western edge of the Canadian Shield and the Rocky Mountains lie the Interior Plains. This broad flat region reaches from the Great Plains in the United States all the way north to the Arctic Ocean.

The Interior Plains region has some of the best farmland in Canada. Its deep, fertile soil was a gift of the glaciers. These moving sheets of ice stripped dirt off the surrounding hills and carried it down onto the plains. When the ice melted, thick, rich soil was left behind.

The first Indians to settle on the plains found a grassy world stretching as far as the eye could see. Huge herds of buffalo and antelope roamed across this wilderness. The Plains Indians were buffalo hunters. As you read in Chapter 4, the buffalo provided them with food, clothing, and shelter.

Today the grass and buffalo are gone. Wheat farms and cattle ranches have taken their place.

THE WESTERN MOUNTAIN REGION

The **Western Mountain Region** lies between the Interior Plains and the Pacific Ocean. The Canadian Rockies and the Coast Mountains stretch south into the United States from this region. Another mountain range lies mostly underwater just off the Pacific Coast. Only the highest peaks rise above the sea to form a chain of coastal islands.

This region of rugged mountains has always been thinly settled. Most areas are too hilly to farm. The winters here are long and harsh. The climate of the Pacific Coast, however, is milder than in other parts of Canada. In winter, winds blowing from the Pacific Ocean warm the land. As a result, rain is as likely as snow.

Here the Northwest Coast Indians lived in a land of plenty. As you read in Chapter 4, the land and sea provided so much food that the Indians could settle in permanent villages. They did not have to move from place to place in search of food to eat. Do you remember how these wealthy coastal Indians held ceremonies called potlatches to show off their wealth?

Today most people in the Western Mountain Region still live off the land and sea. Valuable minerals and timber are found in the mountains. And the coastal waters provide an abundant supply of fish.

Each year thousands of tourists marvel at the beauty of the Canadian Rockies. Banff National Park in Alberta is a popular attraction.

THE ARCTIC NORTH

North of the Canadian Shield lie the frozen plains and ice-covered islands of the **Arctic North**. Here the Ice Age never ended. Glaciers still blanket the hills. The treeless plain, or tundra, along the Arctic Ocean has never thawed. The ground is frozen as deep as 2,000 feet (600 m) below the surface. Near the North Pole the sea is frozen all year-round. This great floating island of ice is called the polar icecap.

During the long northern winter, the Arctic North is a dark, frozen world. For months the sun does not shine. It is no more than a faint glow on the horizon. Snow covers the tundra, and the ocean waters freeze. Winter temperatures can drop to −50°F. (−46°C). At such low temperatures water poured from a cup will freeze before it hits the ground.

Musk oxen (*left*), arctic foxes (*center*) and polar bears (*right*) thrive in the cold environment of Canada's Arctic North. What other animals live in or visit this region?

Summer brings days when the sun never sets. The sea ice breaks up, creating large rafts of ice called ice floes. Polar bears often ride from island to island on floating ice floes. Whales, sea otters, walruses, and seals come north to feed on fish in the arctic waters.

In summer the top few inches of tundra thaw and come to life. Moss and grass thrive in the warming sun. Over 700 kinds of flowers burst into bloom. Huge herds of caribou arrive to feed and raise their calves.

People also live in this harsh environment. In Chapter 4 you read about the Eskimos. For thousands of years they have built villages along the Arctic shore. Today the discovery of oil, coal, natural gas, and other minerals in this region is drawing more people to the Arctic North.

A VAST AND VARIED LAND

Canada clearly is a huge land of many varied regions. If you could travel from coast to coast, you would see rugged mountains, dense forests, flat grasslands, and frozen plains. You would discover a land that is full of riches—from furry animals to valuable minerals. As you have read, each of Canada's regions has something special to offer those who have settled in this beautiful and challenging land.

Check Your Reading

1. Describe Canada's physical regions.
2. Where do most people in Canada live? Why do they live there?
3. Why is the Interior Plains a good region for farming?
4. **GEOGRAPHY SKILL:** Which three oceans surround Canada?
5. **THINKING SKILL:** What are three questions you could ask to find out specific facts about Canada's geography?

2 The History of Canada

READ TO LEARN

Key Vocabulary

province

Key People

Jacques Cartier
Samuel de Champlain
Lord Durham
John A. Macdonald

Key Places

Ottawa

Read Aloud

Canadian history is the history of a people building a nation in spite of geography.

These words of a Canadian historian remind us that Canada is a country divided by geography. Canadians have always lived in widely scattered settlements. These settled areas are cut off from each other by mountains, forests, muskegs, plains, and stormy seas. As you will read, uniting Canada's people into a nation was not an easy task.

Read for Purpose

1. **WHAT YOU KNOW:** Who were the first Europeans to settle Canada?
2. **WHAT YOU WILL LEARN:** How did Canada win its independence from Great Britain?

THE FRENCH SETTLE CANADA

You read in Chapter 6 that French explorer Jacques Cartier first reached Canada in 1534. Cartier was looking for a sea route to Asia. Instead he found a land rich in fish, forests, and fur.

The Europeans' demand for beaver fur brought the French back to Canada. In 1608 Samuel de Champlain started the colony of New France in the Great Lakes–St. Lawrence Lowlands.

Champlain quickly made friends with the Huron Indians. He even sided with them against their old enemies, the Iroquois. After that the Iroquois tried to drive the French colonists out of Canada.

One French fur trading post, Fort Verchres (vâr shar'), was attacked by a band of Iroquois when most of the men at the fort were away. The two soldiers left behind were about to surrender. But then a 14-year-old girl named Madeleine de Verchres took command.

For a week Madeleine defended the fort with this tiny army. Day and night she had the men shouting orders. Whenever they spotted an Iroquois, the men yelled a signal to Madeleine. With a steady hand, she fired a cannon from the fort. The Iroquois decided that the fort was well defended and gave up their attack.

The colony of New France not only survived but also grew wealthy from the fur trade. But with success came conflict with Great Britain's American colonies.

THE BRITISH CONQUER CANADA

As you know, France and Britain went to war for control of the Ohio River Valley in 1754. When the French and Indian War ended in 1763, France had lost almost all the lands it controlled in Canada. For many years to come, this vast area would be ruled by Great Britain.

The French colonists in Canada were uneasy with their new rulers. Britain tried to gain their loyalty by letting them keep their language and laws. But when the American colonies rebelled in 1776, few French Canadians fought for Britain.

After the American Revolution many Loyalists—American colonists who had remained loyal to Britain—moved to Canada. About 30,000 Loyalists sailed to Nova Scotia. Later some left this island and settled on the nearby mainland where they built the new colony of New Brunswick. Others went farther north to settle on Prince Edward Island or on Newfoundland.

More Loyalists settled in the Great Lakes–St. Lawrence Lowlands. These English-speaking newcomers did not

The Granger Collection

Many Loyalists fled to Canada after the American Revolution. Where in Canada did they settle?

like living with French Canadians. As a result, Britain divided this region into two new colonies in 1791. The colony of Quebec was mostly French. The colony of Ontario was mostly English.

THE ROAD TO INDEPENDENCE

A group of Americans known as the War Hawks helped put Canada on the road to independence. In 1812 the War Hawks persuaded the United States Congress to declare war on Great Britain. One of the goals of the War Hawks was to add Canada to the United States.

In 1812 the French and English colonists of Canada agreed on one thing. They did not want their homeland to become part of the United States. During the War of 1812 United States soldiers invaded Canada several times. Each time French and English Canadians fought together to drive them back.

The Canadians' success in defending their homeland gave them a new sense of pride and confidence. They began to demand more power to govern themselves. In 1838 Britain sent Lord Durham to talk with the Canadians. Durham wrote a report urging more self-government for the Canadian colonies. This was the best way, he argued, to keep the Canadians loyal to Britain.

Slowly Britain acted on Lord Durham's ideas. One by one the colonies became self-governing provinces. In Canada a province is similar to a state in the United States. Each Canadian province elects its own leaders to run its affairs.

THE DOMINION OF CANADA

During the 1860s the provinces began to talk about forming a national government. Britain's Parliament approved of this idea by passing the Constitution Act of 1867. This law united Ontario, Quebec, New Brunswick, and Nova Scotia into one nation. The city of Ottawa in Ontario was chosen as the capital of Canada.

John A. Macdonald was the new nation's first leader. He dreamed of a Canada that would stretch from the Atlantic to the Pacific. Already a few Canadians were living on the plains and along the Pacific Coast. But they

MAP SKILL: Locate Canada's provinces Which province borders Ontario to the west?

CANADA: Political

✪ National capital
★ Provincial or territorial capital
• Other city
+++ Canadian Pacific Railway

were cut off from the rest of Canada by the Canadian Shield and the peaks and valleys of the Western Mountain Region.

Macdonald saw only one way to bring these distant settlements into the new nation. That was to promise to build a railroad across all of Canada. Only a railroad, he believed, could tie Canadians together from sea to sea.

Macdonald's talk of a railroad encouraged more provinces to become part of Canada. Manitoba became the nation's first plains province in 1870. A year later the Western Mountain province of British Columbia joined Canada. Tiny Prince Edward Island became the seventh province in 1873.

THE CANADIAN PACIFIC RAILWAY

The Canadian Pacific Railway got off to a slow start. Finally in 1881 an American engineer named William Van Horne was hired to start construction. Van Horne promised to lay 500 miles (800 km) of track in 1882. "Impossible!" people said. "Nothing is impossible," replied Van Horne.

By the end of 1885 the railroad was finished. You can trace its route on the map on page 554. As Macdonald had hoped, the new railroad tied eastern and western Canada together. In 1905 two new plains provinces, Alberta and Saskatchewan (sas kach' ə won), joined Canada. Newfoundland became Canada's tenth province in 1949.

FROM SEA TO SEA

As you have read, Canada began as a French colony. In 1763 Great Britain won this vast land from France. Twenty years later thousands of Loyalists left the United States for Canada.

Five thousand workers built the Canadian Pacific Railway. They blasted through the Rockies and then built tracks on the steep mountain sides.

In 1867 the British Parliament passed a law that united Canada into one nation. In order to expand, the new government had to overcome barriers of distance and geography. The Canadian Pacific Railway helped to unite the growing country. Today Canada has ten provinces and two territories that together stretch from sea to sea.

Check Your Reading

1. What attracted French colonists to Canada?
2. What happened to the colony of New France at the end of the French and Indian War?
3. What was John A. Macdonald's dream? How did he bring it about?
4. **THINKING SKILL:** Why did Canada decide to fight the United States during the War of 1812? What goal was Canada trying to achieve?

READ TO LEARN

Key Places

Vancouver
Yukon Territory
Northwest Territories

Read Aloud

Canadians often describe their country as a "mosaic." In art a mosaic is a picture made up of different colored stones or tiles. The Canadian mosaic is made up of people from more than 50 different countries. This mixture of people and cultures makes Canada a colorful and interesting country.

Read for Purpose

1. **WHAT YOU KNOW:** What group of people settled in Canada at the end of the American Revolution?
2. **WHAT YOU WILL LEARN:** What groups of people live in Canada today?

A NATION OF IMMIGRANTS

Canada, like the United States, is a nation of immigrants. At first most Canadians traced their roots back to France or Britain. Then in 1881 thousands of Chinese workers came to Canada. You read in Chapter 18 that many Chinese immigrants worked for the Central Pacific Railroad in California. In Canada the Chinese helped build the Canadian Pacific Railway. Later many of them settled in the city of Vancouver in British Columbia. Today visitors enjoy the interesting shops and restaurants in Vancouver's Chinatown.

The first immigrants to settle on the Interior Plains were Mennonites from Russia. The Mennonites are a religious

people. Like Quakers, they do not believe in fighting wars. When Russia tried to force the Mennonites to become soldiers, they left their homeland.

The Mennonites found religious freedom and rich land to farm in Canada. They were soon followed onto the plains by other religious groups. Jews came from Russia, and Mormons came from the United States.

The fertile land of the plains also attracted poor farmers from all across Europe. Swedes, Finns, Icelanders, Germans, Italians, Ukrainians, Poles, Czechs, Slovaks, and others filled the plains, bringing a variety of languages and cultures.

These newcomers faced a hard life. Like the homesteaders on the Great Plains, most families lived in sod houses. They often found little to eat but wild rabbit. In time the newcomers turned the Great Plains into Canada's breadbasket.

Today most Canadian immigrants are from Asia, Africa, and Latin America. Like earlier immigrants they come seeking freedom and a better life.

THE CANADIAN INDIANS

The oldest members of Canada's mosaic are the Canadian Indians. When European explorers and fur traders first came to Canada, the Indians taught them how to survive in the wilderness. But before long the Indians were fighting for their own survival.

Most Canadian Indians were hunters. As the European settlers cleared the forests and plowed the plains, the animals that the Indians hunted disappeared. Suddenly to rely on hunting meant to starve. Canada's Indians were forced to give up a way of life that their people had followed for thousands of years.

Today about two thirds of Canada's Indians live on reservations. In recent years many Indians have moved to Canada's busy cities. Wherever they live, Indians are working to save their old ways while learning to live in a modern, industrial nation. Making this change has not been easy. One Indian has written:

It is hard, very hard, to know that the land that once was ours will never ever be again our hunting grounds. . . . We understand that we must change—and we are changing. But remember, it once was our land, our life, and it is hard.

Canadian Indians practice their customs at many Indian gatherings throughout Canada. These gatherings help the Indians keep their heritage alive.

BRITISH AND FRENCH CANADIANS

The two largest groups in the Canadian mosaic are the British and French Canadians. About 44 percent of Canadians are of British descent, or have British ancestors. Their first language is English. About 28 percent of Canadians speak French as their first language. Most French Canadians still live in the province of Quebec.

There has always been tension between British and French Canadians. During the French and Indian War, British soldiers forced 10,000 French settlers from their homes in Nova Scotia. Many who were forced to leave went to the state of Louisiana. Their descendants are known as the Cajuns.

The Scots bagpiper, Ukrainian girl, and Chinese dancers reflect Canada's cultural "mosaic." People from more than 50 countries have made Canada their home.

After Britain took over New France, French Canadians in Quebec found themselves surrounded by English-speaking colonists. To keep their French culture and identity, they clung tightly to their language, their customs, and their land.

You read in Lesson 2 that the French and British Canadians viewed each other with distrust for many years. When Lord Durham visited Canada in 1838 he found "two nations warring within . . . a single state." Like most British Canadians, Durham looked down on the French. He called them "a people with no history." Naturally the French resented British prejudice against them.

The Industrial Revolution had little effect on the lives of most French Canadians. While the British were earning money by building railroads and factories, the French remained on their land and farmed. When factories did come to Quebec, it was because French Canadians needed jobs and often were willing to work for low wages. As a result, most French workers were poor.

In the 1960s the French in Quebec began a "Quiet Revolution" to improve their lives. They demanded more freedom to preserve their culture and more power to control Quebec's economy. There was even talk of making Quebec a separate country.

In 1980 Quebec voted to remain part of Canada. But French Canadians made it clear that they were no longer willing to feel like foreigners in their own country. It was time for change.

THE CONSTITUTION OF 1982

Change came in 1982 when the Canadian government approved a new constitution. This constitution gave Canada two languages—English and French. Every province was required to make both languages available in schools and courts.

Canada's Parliament made English and French the country's two official languages. Road signs and laws must appear in both languages.

The 1982 constitution also gave Canada a federal system of government that is similar to the system in the United States. Power is divided between the central government and the provinces. Provincial governments control local matters, such as natural resources and schools. The central government controls areas that affect the entire nation, such as defense and foreign affairs. It also governs the Yukon Territory and the Northwest Territories. These thinly settled lands lie north of the provinces in the Arctic North.

ONE NATION, MANY PEOPLES

Canada is one nation with many groups of people. You have read that the Indians were the first Canadians. Later, immigrants from many lands settled in Canada. Together these many different peoples make up the Canadian mosaic.

In the past, language and customs have separated British and French Canadians. But this is changing. Today both groups are learning to speak each other's language and work together. The future of Canada is bright and full of promise.

 Check Your Reading

1. Why have immigrants from many countries come to Canada?
2. What happened to the Indians living in Canada?
3. What are Canada's two official languages?
4. **THINKING SKILL:** How does the Canadian system of government compare with that of the United States?

Understanding Map Projections

Key Vocabulary
projection   distortion

One of the ways you learned about Canada in this chapter was by studying the maps on pages 548 and 554. Another way to learn about Canada is by looking at the globe in your classroom.

Projection and Distortion

Globes and maps are ways of showing the earth. A globe, like the earth, is a sphere. Globes show size, shape, distance, and direction correctly because a globe is an exact model of the earth.

Maps are drawings that show all or part of the earth. They are drawn on a flat surface, such as paper. The way mapmakers show the round earth on a flat sheet of paper is called a **projection**. There is no perfect way to show a sphere on a flat surface. Parts of the sphere must be cut or stretched. These changes cause the map to be distorted in some way. Map **distortion** is an error in size, shape, distance, or direction.

There are many different projections. Since none gives a completely accurate picture of the earth, mapmakers use different projections to show different things.

The Mercator Projection

The map below is drawn on a Mercator projection. On this projection, all lines of latitude and all lines of longitude appear as straight lines. These lines and all straight lines drawn accurately on the map show compass direction. From any

MERCATOR PROJECTION

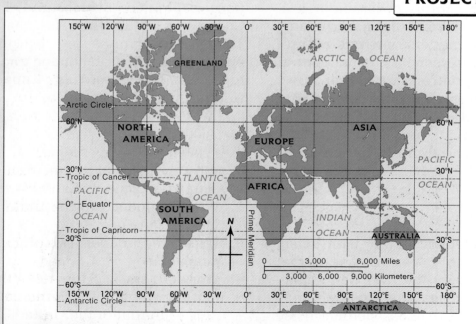

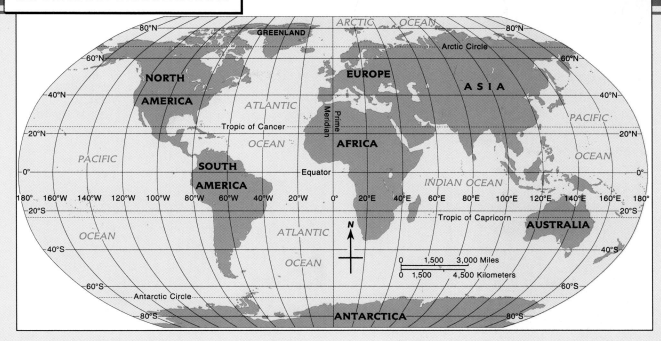

point on the map, north is directly toward the top of the map. East is directly to the right. Where is south? Where is west?

On the Mercator projection size, shape, and distance are quite accurate in the tropics. However, all three are badly distorted near the poles. To understand why this is, compare the map with your classroom globe. The globe shows that the equator is the longest line of latitude. Other lines of latitude become shorter and shorter as they get closer to the poles. On the map all lines of latitude are the same length. The globe shows that Greenland is smaller than South America. But on the map Greenland looks larger.

The Robinson Projection

The map above is drawn on a Robinson projection. Here size, shape, and distance are shown quite accurately in the tropics. You can see that all three are much less distorted near the poles than they are on the Mercator map. Look again at Greenland. On this map it appears smaller than

South America. Because the Robinson projection shows sizes fairly accurately, it is useful for comparing the sizes of places.

On the Robinson projection all lines of latitude are shown as straight lines. North is directly toward the top of the map along only one line of longitude. What line of longitude is this?

Reviewing the Skill

1. What is a map projection?
2. Which map projection—Mercator or Robinson—would be more useful to a sailor? Why?
3. On which projection are east–west distances near the poles more distorted? On which projection are north–south distances near the tropics more distorted?
4. Would a Mercator projection or a Robinson projection be better for comparing the size of countries? Why?
5. Why do mapmakers use different projections?

561

IMPORTANT EVENTS

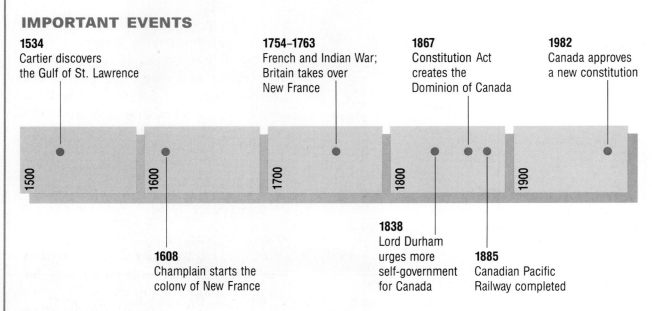

1534
Cartier discovers
the Gulf of St. Lawrence

1754–1763
French and Indian War;
Britain takes over
New France

1867
Constitution Act
creates the
Dominion of Canada

1982
Canada approves
a new constitution

1500 1600 1700 1800 1900

1608
Champlain starts the
colony of New France

1838
Lord Durham
urges more
self-government
for Canada

1885
Canadian Pacific
Railway completed

PEOPLE TO KNOW

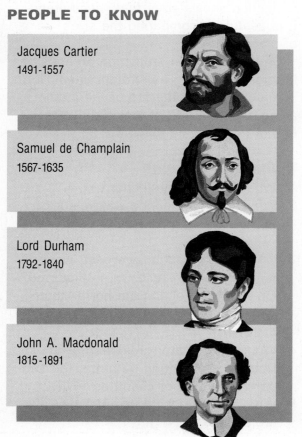

Jacques Cartier
1491-1557

Samuel de Champlain
1567-1635

Lord Durham
1792-1840

John A. Macdonald
1815-1891

IDEAS TO REMEMBER

- Canada is a huge country that is made up of six different physical regions.
- Canada's history has been influenced in part by its geography.
- The people of Canada come from all parts of the world.

REVIEWING VOCABULARY

province

Write a sentence using the vocabulary word above. The sentence should show that you understand the meaning of the word.

REVIEWING FACTS

1. Where in Canada can each be found: fishing villages, glaciers, muskeg, wheat farms, and large cities.
2. How is Samuel de Champlain important to the history of Canada? How is Lord Durham important?
3. Why do Canadians describe their country as a mosaic?
4. Which region of Canada is known as the country's breadbasket?
5. What were two features of the Constitution of 1982?

✏️ WRITING ABOUT MAIN IDEAS

1. **Making a List:** Make a list of the events that have caused problems between French and English Canadians. Write a paragraph describing the problems and explaining why they happened.
2. **Writing a Paragraph of Facts About Canada:** If you were moving to Canada, where would you like to live? Write a paragraph of facts that describes the geography of the region that you selected. Why would you like to live there?

BUILDING SKILLS: UNDERSTANDING MAP PROJECTIONS

1. What is a map projection?
2. Look at the Robinson projection below. Why is this kind of projection useful for comparing the sizes of places?
3. Through which three continents does the prime meridian pass?
4. Why do mapmakers use different projections?

ROBINSON PROJECTION

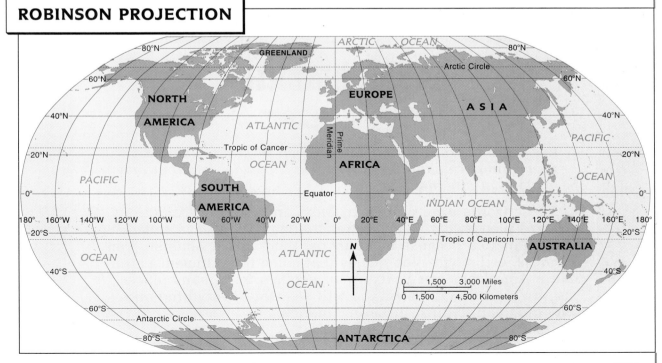

CHAPTER 24

LATIN AMERICA

FOCUS

Everything and anything can happen in Latin America. . . .
Everything seems to rest lightly on a powder keg that may
explode at any moment.

These words were written by Mexican historian Daniel
Cosío Villegas. Latin America is a huge region. It is called
Latin America because most people there speak Spanish, Por-
tuguese, or French—languages that come from ancient Latin.
Latin Americans are a mixture of peoples from many places.
As you read this chapter, you will see why "Everything and
anything can happen in Latin America."

1 Mexico

READE TO LEARN

Key Vocabulary

mestizo

Key People

Hernándo Cortés
Montezuma
Miguel Hidalgo
Agustín de Iturbide
Benito Juárez
Diego Rivera
José Clemente Orozco

Key Places

Baja Peninsula
Gulf of California
Sierra Madres
Mexico City
Yucatán Peninsula
Central Highlands
Tenochtitlán

Read Aloud

In Mexico City, the capital of Mexico, there is a square known as the Plaza of the Three Cultures. It was given this name because the buildings here symbolize, or stand for, the cultures and peoples that have shaped the Mexican nation.

The oldest culture—Mexico's Indian heritage—is represented by the ruins of an Aztec temple. Nearby stands an old, thick-walled church. It represents the culture of Mexico's Spanish conquerors. Glass and concrete office buildings also line the plaza. They represent modern Mexico. As you will read, these three cultures live side by side in Mexico today.

Read for Purpose

1. **WHAT YOU KNOW:** What country borders Mexico on the north?
2. **WHAT YOU WILL LEARN:** Why is Mexico called a land of three cultures?

A MOUNTAINOUS LAND

On a map our southern neighbor is shaped like a giant, curving horn. At the wide end of the horn, Mexico shares a 1,900 mile (3,040 km) border with the United States. At its narrow southern end, Mexico borders Central America. A long, narrow piece of land juts out from the northwest corner of Mexico. This piece of land is the Baja (bä' hä) Peninsula. It is separated from the Mexican mainland by the Gulf of California.

When Hernándo Cortés returned to Spain after conquering Mexico, King Charles V asked him to describe his new Spanish colony. Cortés crumpled a piece of paper in his fist and placed it

565

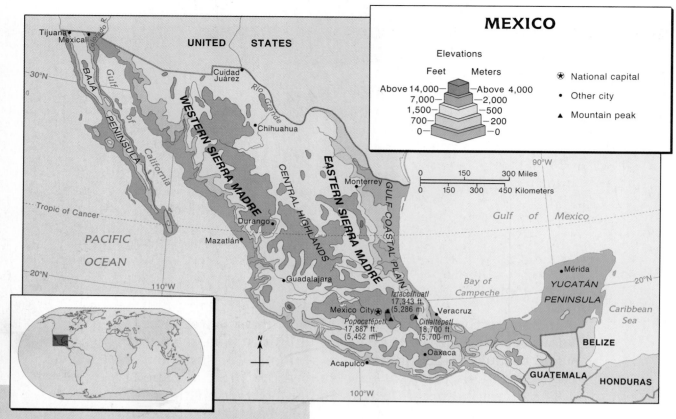

MEXICO

Elevations

Feet	Meters
Above 14,000	Above 4,000
7,000	2,000
1,500	500
700	200
0	0

✯ National capital
• Other city
▲ Mountain peak

MAP SKILL: Use the map to identify Mexico's physical regions. What is the elevation of Mexico City?

before the king saying, "This is your map of Mexico." The conquistador had seen only part of Mexico. But his description was amazingly accurate.

As Cortés discovered, most of Mexico is mountainous. Dry, steep hills line the eastern shore of Baja California. Two towering mountain ranges stretch along the coastlines of the Mexican mainland. These mountains are called the Eastern and Western **Sierra Madres** (sē âr′ ə mä′ drāz), which means "mother mountains" in Spanish. Today most Mexicans live between these two large mountain ranges.

Look at the map of Mexico on this page. You can see how the Eastern and Western Sierra Madres meet south of

Mexico City to form a gigantic *V.* Below the base of this *V* lie the hot, humid lowlands of southern Mexico. Forests cover most of this area. However, the northern tip of the **Yucatán** (ū kə tan′) **Peninsula**, which juts into the Caribbean Sea like a thumb, is dry enough for cactus. Oil has been discovered in these lowlands and in the waters of the Gulf of Mexico.

Between the Eastern and Western Sierra Madres lies a hilly plateau. The northern half of this plateau is low, hot, and dry. But hidden below the desert sands are rich deposits of silver, gold, lead, zinc, and iron.

To the south the plateau rises. The **Central Highlands** around Mexico City are cooler and wetter than the northern desert. Fertile soil and plenty of rainfall make this a good region for farming.

THE CONQUEST OF MEXICO

The first people to live in Mexico were Indians. You read in Chapter 3 that long before Christopher Columbus came to America, the Mayas were building stone temples in Mexico's lowlands. Later, Aztec armies marched out of the Central Highlands to create a great empire.

In 1519 Hernándo Cortés stood face-to-face with the mighty Aztec emperor Montezuma (mon tə zü′ mə) in the city of Tenochtitlán (tā nôch′ tē tlän). At first their meeting was friendly. But within two years Montezuma was dead, and Tenochtitlán lay in ruins.

To the conquerors from Spain this was a great victory. But Mexicans have a different view. In the Plaza of the Three Cultures there is a plaque marking the fall of Tenochtitlán. It reads:

It was neither a victory nor a defeat. It was the painful birth of the mestizo people, who are the Mexico of today.

Later in this lesson you will read more about the mestizos (mes tē′ zōz). They are people of mixed Indian and Spanish ancestry.

MEXICO UNDER SPANISH RULE

For the next 300 years Mexico was a Spanish colony. The king of Spain gave large grants of land to Spanish soldiers, colonists, and Catholic priests. He also gave them Indians to work the land. The colonists did not govern themselves. Instead the king sent a viceroy to Mexico to rule his colony for him.

From the early days of Spanish rule, there was a mixing of peoples in Mexico. Many of Cortés's soldiers married Indian women. Their children were the

The Spanish conquistador Cortés conquered Mexico. Which group did he defeat?

first mestizos. Today eight out of ten Mexicans are mestizos.

Spanish and Indian cultures also mixed. Spanish priests taught Indians the Catholic religion. The stones of Aztec temples were used to build churches. On the outside the churches looked like Spanish buildings. But inside they were painted with Indian designs.

The Spaniards brought European plants, animals, and tools to Mexico. They taught Indians how to use the wheel, farm with a plow, and make things out of iron. The Indians, in turn, taught the Spaniards how to use plants and foods native to America. Today's Mexican taco combines Indian corn, beans, chilies, tomatoes, and avocados with Spanish onions, beef, olives, and cheese.

While the two peoples and cultures mixed, they were never treated as equals. The Spanish controlled Mexico's land and wealth. They alone sent their children to school.

The Indians were forced to work for the Spanish for little or no pay. The work of the Indians made Mexico wealthy. But none of that wealth belonged to them. As a result, Mexico was, in the words of Daniel Cosío Villegas, "a powder keg" ready to "explode at any moment."

AN INDEPENDENT MEXICO

The explosion came in 1810 when a priest named Miguel Hidalgo led a rebellion of Indians and mestizos against Spanish rule. The War of Independence went on for 11 years and cost many lives. Finally, in 1821, Mexico won its freedom. Agustín de Iturbide (a güs tēn' dā ē tür bē' dā), the new nation's first leader, told his people, "Mexicans, you are now free. It is for you to find happiness."

Few people found happiness in the new nation. The war had left much of Mexico in ruins. Setting up a strong, central government was difficult because Mexicans had no experience at governing themselves. The country was also divided between a few thousand families who owned most of the land and millions of poor Indians and mestizos.

Father Miguel Hidalgo (*center*) raises the cry for Mexico's independence in this painting by Juan O'Gorman. When did Mexico's revolution begin?

For the next 100 years Mexico was torn apart by revolutions and civil wars. During that troubled time the nation lost half of its territory to the United States. A few leaders, like President Benito Júarez (be nē' tō wär' ez), a Zapotec Indian, worked hard to improve life for all Mexicans. Others were more interested in gaining wealth and power for themselves.

Mexico's last revolution ended in 1917 with a new constitution. That constitution is still in effect today. Under it, Mexico has been ruled by leaders who are elected. The government is headed by a president who serves just one six-year term.

Under the 1917 constitution many large farms have been broken up to give land to poor farmers. New industries have been built and new jobs have been created. But poverty remains a difficult problem.

MEXICO TODAY

Mexico today is a land of three cultures. There are still Indians in the mountains and lowlands who follow their traditional ways of life. Indian arts and crafts are still important in Mexico. Mexican artists such as Diego Rivera (dyā' gō ri vâr' ə) and José Clemente Orozco (klā mān' tā ō rōs' kō) used Indian designs in their work.

Mexico City has many beautiful and historic buildings such as those decorated by Juan O'Gorman (*left*). The Plaza of the Three Cultures (*above*) contains examples of Mexico's three cultures—Indian, Spanish, and present-day.

Many of Mexico's public buildings are covered with dramatic paintings done by the country's artists.

The culture of Spain also survives. Most Mexicans speak Spanish and follow the Catholic religion. Mexican towns, which are built around a church and central plaza, look much like towns in Spain. Bullfighting, which came from Spain, is still popular in Mexico.

A third culture has grown out of Mexico's Indian and Spanish roots. This is the culture of modern Mexico—a culture of cities, factories, computers, and television.

Education is the key to this modern culture. Since 1930 the Mexican government has built schools at an amazing rate. Between 1960 and 1970 a new classroom was completed about every two hours. Today most Mexican children go to school. This new generation of educated Mexicans will shape the Mexico of tomorrow.

MEXICO'S THREE CULTURES

As you can see, Mexico is a nation rich in cultures and traditions. The Indians created Mexico's first culture. Its second culture came from Spain with the conquistadors. Today Mexicans are shaping a new modern culture that blends the past with the future.

Check Your Reading

1. Name three landforms that are found in Mexico.
2. What did the Spanish conquerors learn from the Indians of Mexico? What did the Indians learn from the Spanish?
3. Why was it difficult for the people of Mexico to establish a strong central government?
4. **GEOGRAPHY SKILL:** Why did Cortés compare Mexico to a crumpled piece of paper?
5. **THINKING SKILL:** Based on your reading, what can you conclude about the people who live in Mexico?

569

2 Central America and the Caribbean

READ TO LEARN

Key Vocabulary

hurricane

Key Places

Caribbean Sea
West Indies

Key People

Fidel Castro

Read Aloud

Daniel Cosío Villegas wrote that in Latin America "nothing is firm and stable." When he wrote this, he might have been thinking about Central America and the Caribbean. Few countries in this area have been able to build stable governments. Wars and revolutions have been common. Even nature seems shaky here. Earthquakes, volcanoes, and violent storms can destroy in minutes what took a lifetime to build. Yet for many people, there is no lovelier place on earth to live or visit.

Read for Purpose

1. **WHAT YOU KNOW:** Who was the first European explorer to reach the islands of the Caribbean?
2. **WHAT YOU WILL LEARN:** Why have few countries in Central America and the Caribbean been able to set up stable governments?

A BRIDGE BETWEEN CONTINENTS

Central America is an isthmus. You read in Chapter 5 that an isthmus is a narrow bridge of land linking two larger areas. You can see from the map on page 571 that Central America links North and South America. It is formed by a mountain range that runs from Mexico to South America. The Pacific Ocean pounds on the western shore of the isthmus. The Caribbean Sea washes its eastern shore.

Millions of years ago another mountain range formed a bridge between the two Americas. Today the tops of these sunken peaks form a long chain of islands across the Caribbean Sea. These islands are called the West Indies.

Because Central America and the Caribbean Islands lie close to the equator, the climate can be warm all year round. At sea level days can be uncomfortably hot and humid. But temperatures drop with altitude. Most people live in the mountains where the air is cool and fresh.

There are only two seasons in this region. The rainy season lasts from about May to November. During these months rainfall can be heavy. Then comes the dry season when the sun shines brightly day after day. This is when tourists from North America, tired of winter snow and ice, flock to sunny Caribbean beaches.

The tourists see the beauty of this region, its blue seas, sandy beaches, and high green mountains. It is easy for them to forget the natural dangers of this area. In late summer and early fall hurricanes—violent storms with powerful winds and enormous waves—often race across the Caribbean. Hurricanes flatten trees, sink ships, and destroy homes. In 1988 a fierce hurricane named Joan left thousands of people homeless in the Central American country of Nicaragua.

Volcanoes are also a danger here. In 1903 a volcano erupted on the island of Martinique. Hot gases from the volcano smothered 30,000 people in just seconds. Where there are volcanoes there are also earthquakes. Guatemala City in the Central American country of Guatemala has been destroyed by earthquakes nine times. Each time, the city has been rebuilt.

A MIXTURE OF PEOPLE

When Christopher Columbus sailed into the Caribbean Sea in 1492, he described the land he found as "the best and most fertile . . . in the world." The Spanish colonists who settled in the Caribbean and Central America agreed

MAP SKILL: Use the map to locate the West Indies. Which are the largest islands in this region?

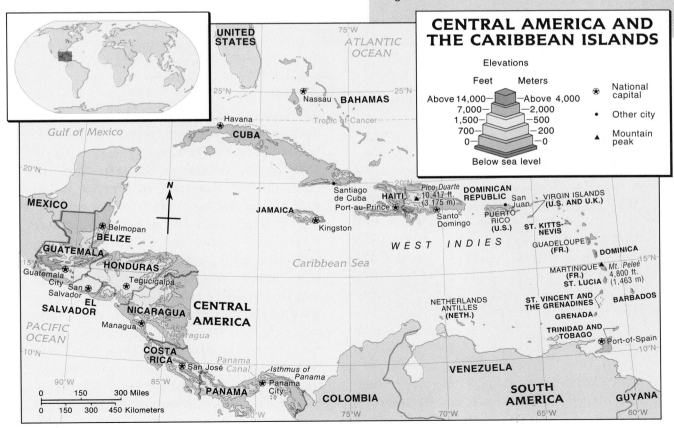

with him. This was a perfect place for growing tropical crops. Sugar, coffee, and cacao beans—which are used to make chocolate—brought high prices in Europe.

Spanish colonists raised these crops on large plantations. At first they forced Indians to work for them. But the Indians soon died from disease or overwork. The Spaniards then forced Africans to work as slaves on their plantations. Today large numbers of people in the Caribbean can trace their roots to Africa.

In the 1600s Britain, France, the Netherlands, and Denmark took over many Caribbean islands. Planters from these countries also depended on slaves from Africa to raise their crops. Slavery was finally ended in most of the Caribbean in the early 1800s. After that the planters brought farm workers from China, India, and other parts of Asia to work on their plantations.

The result is a mixture of people and languages in the region. Some Indians still speak their traditional languages.

These schoolchildren reflect the mixture of people who live in the Caribbean region.

Spanish is spoken in most of Central America and on the islands of Cuba and Puerto Rico. English is the language of Belize and of islands such as Trinidad and Tobago.

A POOR REGION

Today all of Central America and most of the Caribbean islands have become independent nations. Haiti was the first Latin American colony to gain its freedom. In 1791 Haitian slaves rebelled against their French owners, burning houses and crops. After many years of bloody warfare, blacks took control of Haiti in 1804.

The Spanish colonies of Central America became independent in 1821. But as you learned in Chapter 20, Cuba and Puerto Rico were ruled by Spain until the Spanish-American War in 1898.

The British colonies were slower to break their ties with the ruling country. The island of Jamaica was a colony until 1962. The Bahamas became independent in 1973.

While most colonies are now independent countries, many problems still remain. In the past the wealth of this region came from the land and the cash crops grown on it. During colonial times the best land belonged to a few rich planters. Most of the Central American country of El Salvador, for example, was once owned by 14 families. When independence came, the wealthy held on to their land.

While a few families were very rich, most people were very poor. The poor had little or no land. They had no schools. There were no factories where they could find jobs. They survived mainly by working on plantations or fishing. But such work paid little.

Life for the poor has improved in some countries in the last 50 years. New industries such as tourism have created new jobs, but many countries remain very poor. Every year thousands of people come to the United States from Central America and the Caribbean Islands hoping to find a brighter future.

SHAKY GOVERNMENTS IN THE REGION

In 300 years of Spanish rule, the colonies in the region had never been allowed to govern themselves. When the Spanish colonies gained their independence, they tried to set up democratic governments. Only the Central American country of Costa Rica made democracy work.

Elsewhere, elected presidents were soon replaced by military leaders and dictators. Most of these leaders governed badly. But there was no way to vote unpopular rulers out of power. They could only be driven out by war or revolution. In some countries, such as the Dominican Republic and Panama, governments seemed to change constantly. Panama has had more presidents since it became independent in 1903 than the United States has had in over 200 years.

A history of shaky governments has hurt this region. Dictators were more interested in getting rich and keeping power than in making reforms. Foreigners gained control of the economies of some nations. As a result, few efforts were made to improve life for the poor. Few schools were built. Poor farmers, without land of their own, had to work on the plantations as they had in the past.

CONTINUING CONFLICT

Political conflict is still a problem in Central America and the Caribbean. Today people differ over what kinds of changes are needed. Some wealthy businesspeople and landowners want to keep the old system. Many other people favor democratic governments. They believe that people should be free to choose their leaders. They also believe that the best hope for ending poverty lies in the free enterprise system. Free enterprise, they say, encourages people to start businesses and create jobs for the poor.

Other people favor a communist-style government like that of the Soviet Union. The best way to end poverty, they say, is to create a powerful government that controls all land and wealth.

Over the years differences among these groups of people have led to bloody conflicts. In 1959 communist rebels led by Fidel Castro took over Cuba. Since then Castro has supported other communist rebellions throughout Latin America with troops, money, and weapons. A revolution brought

Fidel Castro has led a communist government in Cuba since 1959. Use the map on page 571 to locate the island of Cuba.

Central American voters prepare to cast their vote in an election. What challenges face the region?

communists to power in Nicaragua in 1979. Communist rebels have also been fighting to overthrow the government of El Salvador.

Supporters of democracy also saw gains. During the 1980s elected governments replaced dictators in El Salvador, Guatemala, and Honduras, but democracy remains shaky there. Democracy seems more firmly rooted in Costa Rica and in some Caribbean islands.

AN UNCERTAIN FUTURE

The countries of Central America and the Caribbean have had a troubled past. You have read that centuries of colonial rule and slavery left these countries badly divided between rich and poor. Today this area is caught in a struggle between supporters of democracy and supporters of communism. Until these conflicts end, the future of this region remains uncertain.

Check Your Reading

1. Why do tourists enjoy visiting the Caribbean Islands?
2. How did peoples from many parts of the world come to live in Central America and the Caribbean?
3. What problems did many of the countries of this region face after they gained independence?
4. **GEOGRAPHY SKILL:** Locate Haiti on the map on page 571. What other nation shares its island?
5. **THINKING SKILL:** List three questions you could ask to learn more about the governments of Central America and the Caribbean.

3 South America

READ TO LEARN

Key Vocabulary
river basin
rain forest

Key People
Francisco Pizarro
Atahualpa
Simón Bolívar
José de San
    Martín

Key Places
Andes Mountains   Gran Chaco
Atacama Desert   Pampas
Guiana Highlands   Patagonia
Brazilian
    Highlands
Amazon Basin
Amazon River
Rio de la Plata

Read Aloud

South America is a vast continent stretching south from the Caribbean Sea almost to Antarctica. It is also a land of surprises. The wettest and driest places on earth are found on its Pacific shore. South America's forests are home to giant trees, snakes, and insects. One spider called the "bird eater" grows to be 10 inches (25 cm) wide. As historian Daniel Cosío Villegas says, this is a place where "everything and anything can happen."

Read for Purpose

1. **WHAT YOU KNOW:** Which group of Indians built a great empire in South America?
2. **WHAT YOU WILL LEARN:** Why is life difficult for many people who live in South America today?

A CONTINENT OF CONTRASTS

On a map, South America looks like a rough triangle. A chain of snow-capped mountains lines the continent's western edge. These are the Andes Mountains, the longest mountain chain in the world. The Andes are the highest mountains in the Western Hemisphere. There are 50 peaks that rise over 20,000 feet (6,100 m) above sea level.

The narrow strip of land between the Andes Mountains and the Pacific Ocean is hot and humid near the equator. Some places get as much as 350 inches (889 cm) of rain a year. Further south lies the Atacama Desert. Parts of this desert have not had rain for 100 years! South of the desert lies a narrow strip of forests, lakes, and fertile valleys.

| CENTRAL AMERICA | | |
| 80°W | 70°W | 60°W |

Caribbean Sea

Cartagena

Caracas

VENEZUELA

PANAMA

GUYANA Georgetown

SURINAME Paramaribo

GUIANA HIGHLANDS Cayenne
FRENCH GUIANA (FR.)

Bogotá

COLOMBIA

40°W

Quito

ECUADOR

Equator

Guayaquil

Iquitos

AMAZON

Manaus

BASIN

Amazon River

Belém

Recife

PERU

A N D E S

Huascarán
22,205 ft.
(6,768 m)

Lima

Cuzco

Lake Titicaca

BOLIVIA

La Paz

BRAZIL

BRAZILIAN

HIGHLANDS

Brasília

M T S.

Sajama
21,391 ft.
(6,520 m)

Sucre

ATACAMA DESERT

Antofagasta

Tropic of Capricorn

PACIFIC

OCEAN

GRAN CHACO

PARAGUAY

Asunción

São Paulo

Rio de Janeiro

ATLANTIC

OCEAN

Ojos del Salado
22,572 ft.
(6,880 m)

Paraná River

Pôrto Alegre

ARGENTINA

Rosario

URUGUAY

Valparaíso
Santiago

Aconcagua
22,834 ft.
(6,960 m)

Buenos
Aires

Montevideo
Rio de la Plata

CHILE

PAMPAS

A N D E S   M T S.

PATAGONIA

| 0 | 300 | 600 Miles |
| 0 | 300 | 600 | 900 Kilometers |

N

Strait of
Magellan

Tierra
del
Fuego

| 100°W | 90°W | 80°W | 70°W | Cape Horn | 60°W |

SOUTH AMERICA

Elevations

Feet	Meters
Above 14,000	Above 4,000
7,000	2,000
1,500	500
700	200
0	0

Below sea level

✪ National capital

• Other city

▲ Mountain peak

MAP SKILL: Locate the Amazon Basin, Brazilian Highlands, and Andes Mountains on the map. Which region is the area of highest elevation?

576

Low hills mark the other two sides of the South American triangle. On the north are the Guiana (gē än' ə) Highlands. The Brazilian Highlands line the continent's eastern edge.

Between the Guiana and Brazilian highlands lies the Amazon Basin. A river basin is all the land drained by a river and its tributaries. Thousands of streams tumble down the Andes and the highlands into this huge river basin. There they flow together to form the world's second-longest river, the Amazon River. The Amazon Basin is covered by a vast rain forest. A rain forest is a warm, wet region where trees and plants grow closely together.

South of the Brazilian Highlands lie the plains drained by the Rio de la Plata, or "River of Silver." The northern plains, known as the Gran Chaco, are forested.

The southern plains are grasslands much like the Great Plains of the United States. This region is known as the Pampas from an Indian word meaning "flatland." South of the Pampas lies a cold, dry plateau called Patagonia. This lonely land forms the southern tip of South America.

THE COLONIZERS

Tales of gold brought Spanish conquistadors to South America. In 1531 Francisco Pizarro invaded the land of the Incas with 200 men. You read in Chapter 5 that the Incas ruled a huge empire on the western side of the Andes Mountains.

Pizarro defeated the ruler of the Incas, Atahualpa (ät ə wäl' pə), and won a fortune in silver and gold. The Incan empire became the new Spanish colony of Peru.

The Amazon Basin is home to thousands of kinds of wildlife, like this toucan.

Soon Spaniards were pushing across South America. Some went north from Peru to conquer Colombia and Venezuela. Others marched south where they founded Chile. A few crossed the Andes and claimed the Gran Chaco and the Pampas for Spain. This region later became the countries of Paraguay, Uruguay, and Argentina.

Meanwhile Portuguese colonists were founding the largest colony in South America—Brazil. The Portuguese colony slowly expanded to take in most of the Amazon Basin and the Brazilian Highlands. Today Brazil includes about half of South America's land and people.

Other European countries tried to start colonies in South America. Usually Spain or Portugal drove them out. North of Brazil, however, the Netherlands, Great Britain, and France each started a colony in a hot swampy region that no one else wanted. The Dutch and British colonies became the nations of Suriname and Guyana. French Guiana still belongs to France.

THE PEOPLE OF SOUTH AMERICA

Few Spanish and Portuguese wanted to settle in South America. Those who did settle here were given most of the land. In Peru, as in Mexico, the Spanish colonists forced Indians to plant their crops and work in their mines. As the two groups mixed, many mestizos were added to the colony.

Colonists in Colombia, Brazil, and other hot, lowland areas could not find enough Indians to work for them. Like the planters in the Caribbean, they imported slaves from Africa to grow sugar and other tropical crops. Later many Asians were hired to work on lowland plantations.

After 300 years of colonial rule, South Americans began to dream of independence. A small group of wealthy, white landowners wanted to run the colonies themselves. The much larger group of poor Indians, Africans, and mestizos dreamed of freedom and equality with whites.

Simón Bolívar was determined to win independence for South Americans. Which countries did he free?

Brazil gained its independence peacefully in 1822. But in the rest of South America, freedom was won only with bloodshed.

THE LIBERATORS

In the north the fight for independence was started by Simón Bolívar (sē mōn′ bə lē′ vär) of Venezuela. Bolívar began a long, bloody war against Spain in 1810. He inspired his soldiers with the cry, "Spaniards, you will receive death at our hands! Americans, you will receive life!"

At first Bolívar saw defeat after defeat. But his losses made him more determined. In 1819 Bolívar's army defeated a larger Spanish force in Colombia. Venezuela and Colombia were at last freed from Spanish rule.

Meanwhile, another rebel army was fighting for freedom in the south. It was led by José de San Martín (sän mär tēn′) of Argentina. San Martín won several victories in Argentina. But he did not stop there. He believed that no part of South America could be free until all of it was free.

From Argentina, San Martín went to Chile. To get there, he had to cross the towering Andes. Early in 1817 San Martín led an army of 4,000 men through a maze of icy peaks, steep canyons, and high mountain passes. Three weeks later San Martín was in Chile, where his troops quickly defeated the Spanish forces.

San Martín tried to liberate Peru but failed. Then in 1824 Simón Bolívar marched his army from Colombia into Peru. There he defeated the last Spanish army in South America. From that time on Bolívar has been honored throughout South America as "The Liberator."

South America's rich soil and mineral resources provide jobs for large numbers of people.

A LAND RICH IN RESOURCES

South America is rich in natural resources. But despite this wealth, most of the people are very poor.

One of South America's most valuable resources is farmland. Today one of every five South American workers has a job on a farm, ranch, or plantation. Bananas and cacao beans are grown in Ecuador. Brazil produces much of the world's coffee. Argentina raises wheat and cattle.

Below the ground lie other riches. During colonial times the Spanish mined silver in Peru while the Portuguese dug gold in Brazil. Since then many other minerals have been discovered in South America. Chile is the world's largest producer of copper. Bolivia has many tin mines.

Perhaps the greatest challenge facing South America today is to decide how best to use these resources. Will they be used to make a few people rich? Or will they be used to help end widespread poverty?

PROBLEMS AND PROMISE

South America is a large and varied continent. You have read that it was colonized mainly by Spain and Portugal. The colonies were liberated after years of conflict. Independence did not solve the problem of poverty, however. But South America is a land rich in resources. If those resources are used wisely, the future holds the promise of better times.

 Check Your Reading

1. Why is South America described as a continent of contrasts?
2. Which European countries once ruled most of South America?
3. Why is Simón Bolívar known as "The Liberator"?
4. **GEOGRAPHY SKILL:** Which South American countries do you think are the hottest? The coldest? Explain your answers.
5. **THINKING SKILL:** How was Canada's struggle for independence similar to or different from the fight for independence in many South American countries?

Reading Climographs

Key Vocabulary
climograph

You have learned that Latin America includes many countries. The landforms and natural resources of each country are very different. The climates, too, vary from place to place.

You should remember from Chapter 1 that the two most important parts of climate are temperature and precipitation. You should also remember that latitude, altitude, and distance from the ocean affect the climate of a place.

Look at the map in your Atlas on page 594. You can see that some Latin American countries lie north and south of the equator and that some lie right on the equator. You can also see that some cities in Latin America lie along the coast, while others are many miles from the ocean.

One way to see what the climate of a place is like is to look at a climograph. A climograph is a graph that shows information about the temperature and precipitation of a place over time.

Parts of a Climograph

A climograph is useful because it gives a picture of the weather for each month. Look at **Climograph A**. Notice that it includes two graphs—a bar graph in blue and a line graph in red. The bar graph shows the average monthly precipitation. The line graph shows the average monthly temperature.

Read a climograph the same way you read other kinds of graphs. First look at the title. Next read the labels on the sides and along the bottom of the graph. What city is shown in **Climograph A**? What information do the labels along the bottom tell you?

Notice the labels and scales of measurement on the sides of the climograph. The left side of **Climograph A** tells you the average monthly precipitation. The right side measures average monthly temperature.

You can see that the bar graph is made up of vertical bars. Each bar shows the average amount of precipitation. In which month does Mexico City get the least precipitation?

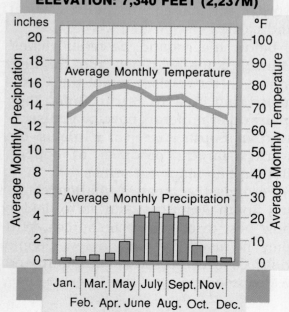

CLIMOGRAPH A:
MEXICO CITY, MEXICO
ELEVATION: 7,340 FEET (2,237M)

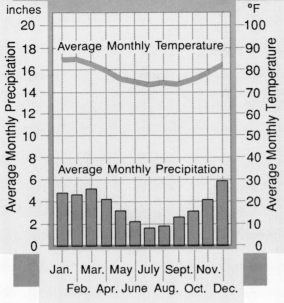

**CLIMOGRAPH B:
RIO DE JANEIRO, BRAZIL
ELEVATION: 201 FEET (61M)**

Average Monthly Precipitation

Average Monthly Temperature

Average Monthly Precipitation

Average Monthly Temperature

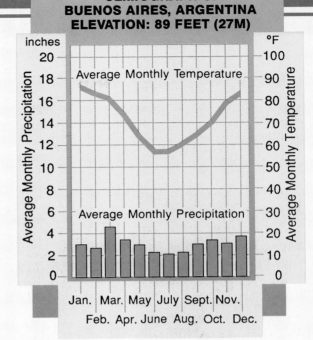

**CLIMOGRAPH C:
BUENOS AIRES, ARGENTINA
ELEVATION: 89 FEET (27M)**

Average Monthly Precipitation

Average Monthly Temperature

Average Monthly Precipitation

Average Monthly Temperature

Now look at the line graph for Mexico City's temperature. What is the average temperature there in December?

Interpreting Climographs

By looking at a climograph you can see in which months the temperature and precipitation are highest and lowest. Remember that if the temperature is above freezing, the precipitation will be rain. In which month(s) does Mexico City have the most precipitation? Is it rain or snow? In which month does Mexico City have the lowest temperatures?

Climographs are useful when you want to compare the climates of different places. Study **Climographs B** and **C** on this page. In which month does Rio de Janeiro have the least rain? In which month does Buenos Aires have the least rain? Which city has generally higher temperatures?

Find Buenos Aires on the map on page 594. Notice that it is south of the equator.

The climate in countries south of the equator is the opposite of the climate in the United States. For example, which months are the warmest in Buenos Aires? When do most parts of the United States have their warmest temperatures?

By looking at a climograph, you can tell if the climate of a place is warm, cold, wet, dry, or perhaps something in-between.

Reviewing the Skill

1. What is a climograph?
2. In which city does the rainfall in March reach more than 5 inches?
3. Which city has average temperatures in June of about 63°F.?
4. Which city gets the most rainfall?
5. Which city's rainiest months are from June through September?
6. What months would people living in Buenos Aires call winter?
7. When would it be most helpful to be able to read a climograph?

581

CHAPTER 24 · SUMMARY AND REVIEW

EVENTS TO REMEMBER

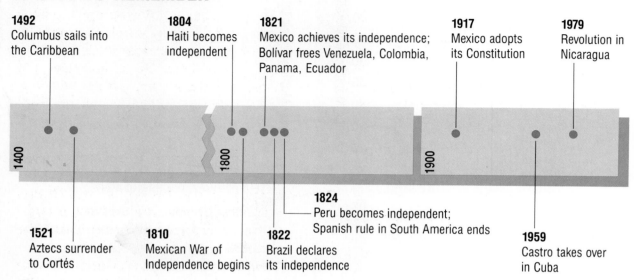

1492
Columbus sails into
the Caribbean

1804
Haiti becomes
independent

1821
Mexico achieves its independence;
Bolívar frees Venezuela, Colombia,
Panama, Ecuador

1917
Mexico adopts
its Constitution

1979
Revolution in
Nicaragua

1400

1800

1900

1521
Aztecs surrender
to Cortés

1810
Mexican War of
Independence begins

1824
Peru becomes independent;
Spanish rule in South America ends

1822
Brazil declares
its independence

1959
Castro takes over
in Cuba

PEOPLE TO KNOW

Simón Bolívar 1783-1830

Fidel Castro 1926-

Hernándo Cortés 1485?-1547

Agustín de Iturbide 1783-1824

Benito Juárez 1806-1872

Francisco Pizarro 1471?-1541

José de San Martín 1778-1850

IDEAS TO REMEMBER

- The people and culture of Mexico represent a blend of Indian and Spanish cultures.
- Central America and the Caribbean are lands of great beauty.
- Few countries in Central America and the Caribbean have been able to set up strong democratic governments.
- South America is a continent rich in natural resources, but it must use these resources wisely in order to lessen the problem of widespread poverty.

582

REVIEWING VOCABULARY

hurricane
mestizo
rain forest
river basin

Number a sheet of paper from 1 to 5. After each number write the word or term from the list that matches the definition. One of the words is used more than once.

1. A warm, wet area where many trees and plants grow closely together
2. A violent storm with powerful winds and enormous waves
3. A person of mixed Indian and Spanish ancestry
4. All the land drained by a river and its tributaries
5. Thousands of streams tumble down the Andes Mountains into this huge, forested lowland.

REVIEWING FACTS

1. In what part of Mexico do most people live?
2. Why is Miguel Hidalgo important to the history of Mexico?
3. Which political views are in conflict in Central America and the Caribbean today?
4. What are three landforms found in South America? What are three natural resources?
5. How did most South American countries become independent?

WRITING ABOUT MAIN IDEAS

1. **Writing a Book Introduction:** Imagine you have written a book about Simón Bolívar. Write a paragraph about Bolívar that would serve as an introduction.
2. **Writing a Gazetteer:** A gazetteer is a kind of dictionary of geographic places and terms. It describes places and tells where they are located. It also defines terms. The items in a gazetteer are listed in alphabetical order. Choose five geographic places or terms mentioned in this chapter. Then write a gazetteer using them.
3. **Writing a Paragraph of Comparison:** How is the history of Latin America similar to the history of the United States? How is it different? Write a paragraph comparing and contrasting the two. Use at least two examples.
4. **Writing a Paragraph:** A German visitor once said that South America was like "a beggar sitting on a bench of gold." Write a paragraph explaining what you think he meant.

BUILDING SKILLS: READING CLIMOGRAPHS

Use the climographs on pages 580–581 to answer the following questions.

1. Which part of the year is the rainy season in Mexico City? In Rio de Janeiro?
2. Which city has an average temperature of 64°F in May?
3. In which month does Buenos Aires have the most rain?
4. Do you think it ever snows in Mexico City? If so, when?
5. Write three sentences describing the climate of Rio de Janeiro.
6. Why is a climograph more helpful than a temperature chart?

REVIEWING VOCABULARY

hurricane   province   river basin
mestizo   rain forest

Number a paper from 1 to 5. Beside each number write the word or term from the list above that best completes the sentence.

1. The ____ man looked like both his Indian and Spanish ancestors.
2. A ____ is land that is drained by a river and its tributaries.
3. Each ____ in Canada has a government that shares power with the national government.
4. Because of a warm, wet climate trees and plants grow close together in a ____.
5. The winds of the ____ blew so hard that many houses were knocked down.

 ## WRITING ABOUT THE UNIT

1. **Writing a Comparing Paragraph:** Choose two people, one from Canada and one from Latin America, who you think did the most for his or her country. Then write a paragraph comparing and contrasting the two people.
2. **Writing a Skit:** Write a skit in which people from Canada meet people from Latin America. Have them discuss their homelands with each other.

ACTIVITIES

1. **Researching a City in the Americas:** Choose one city in Canada or Latin America. Find out about its geography, history, people, and economy. Then prepare a report about the city.
2. **Writing a Travel Brochure:** Plan a trip through one or more areas in Canada or Latin America. Then write a travel brochure describing the trip.
3. **Working Together to Play "What Am I?"** With the class, play the game "What Am I?" about people, places, and events in Canada and Latin America. Take turns having a secret word or name taped on your back. The rest of the class gives hints until you can guess what is written on your back.

BUILDING SKILLS: READING CLIMOGRAPHS

1. What is a climograph?
2. Look at the climographs on pages 580 and 581. Which city—Mexico City, Rio de Janeiro, or Buenos Aires—receives the most rain during the year?
3. According to the climographs, which city experiences the greatest change in temperature during the year?

LINKING PAST, PRESENT, AND FUTURE

The United States, Canada, and Latin America share the Western Hemisphere. What else do these vast lands have in common? Name at least three things. Then think about why you should be interested in the future of Canada and Latin America. Write a paragraph explaining why.

REFERENCE SECTION

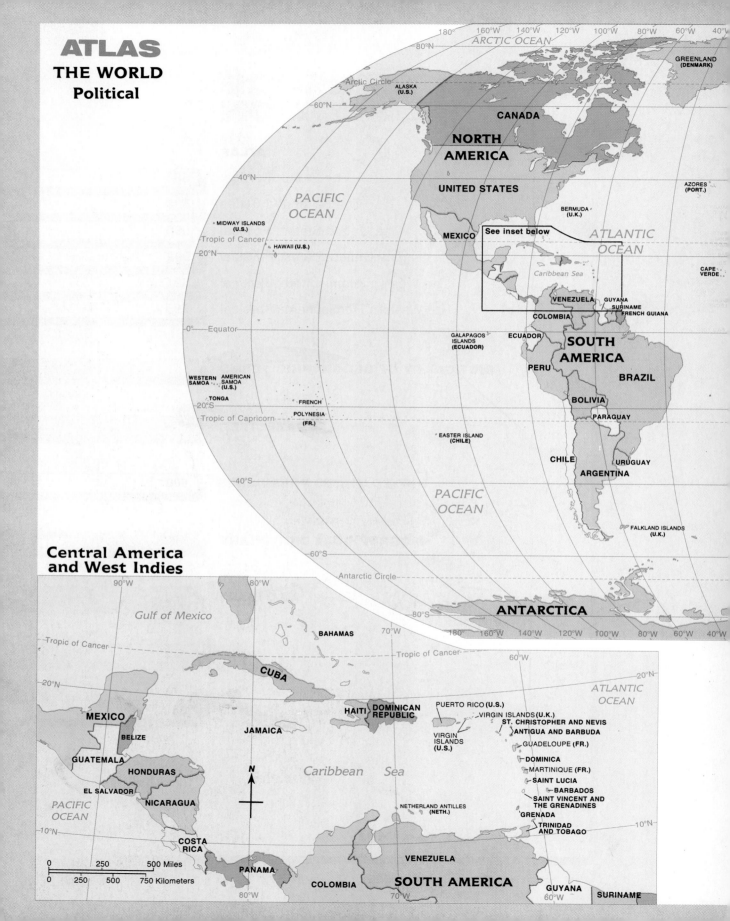

ATLAS
THE WORLD
Political

ARCTIC OCEAN

180° 160°W 140°W 120°W 100°W 80°W 60°W 40°W

80°N

GREENLAND
(DENMARK)

Arctic Circle

ALASKA
(U.S.)

60°N

CANADA

**NORTH
AMERICA**

40°N

UNITED STATES

AZORES
(PORT.)

PACIFIC
OCEAN

BERMUDA
(U.K.)

ATLANTIC
OCEAN

MIDWAY ISLANDS
(U.S.)

Tropic of Cancer

MEXICO

See inset below

CAPE
VERDE

20°N

HAWAII (U.S.)

Caribbean Sea

VENEZUELA   GUYANA
SURINAME
COLOMBIA   FRENCH GUIANA

0°—Equator

GALAPAGOS
ISLANDS
(ECUADOR)

ECUADOR

**SOUTH
AMERICA**

PERU

BRAZIL

WESTERN
SAMOA

AMERICAN
SAMOA
(U.S.)

TONGA

20°S

FRENCH
POLYNESIA
(FR.)

Tropic of Capricorn

BOLIVIA

PARAGUAY

EASTER ISLAND
(CHILE)

CHILE

URUGUAY

ARGENTINA

40°S

PACIFIC
OCEAN

FALKLAND ISLANDS
(U.K.)

60°S

Antarctic Circle

80°S

ANTARCTICA

180° 160°W 140°W 120°W 100°W 80°W 60°W 40°W

Central America
and West Indies

90°W   80°W

Gulf of Mexico

BAHAMAS

70°W

Tropic of Cancer

Tropic of Cancer

60°W

20°N

CUBA

20°N

ATLANTIC
OCEAN

MEXICO

HAITI
DOMINICAN
REPUBLIC

PUERTO RICO (U.S.)

VIRGIN ISLANDS (U.K.)
ST. CHRISTOPHER AND NEVIS
ANTIGUA AND BARBUDA

BELIZE

JAMAICA

VIRGIN
ISLANDS
(U.S.)

GUADELOUPE (FR.)

GUATEMALA

N

Caribbean   Sea

DOMINICA

MARTINIQUE (FR.)

HONDURAS

SAINT LUCIA

EL SALVADOR

BARBADOS
SAINT VINCENT AND
THE GRENADINES

NICARAGUA

NETHERLAND ANTILLES
(NETH.)

GRENADA

PACIFIC
OCEAN

TRINIDAD
AND TOBAGO

10°N

10°N

COSTA
RICA

0   250   500 Miles

PANAMA

VENEZUELA

0 250 500 750 Kilometers

COLOMBIA

SOUTH AMERICA

GUYANA

SURINAME

80°W   70°W   60°W

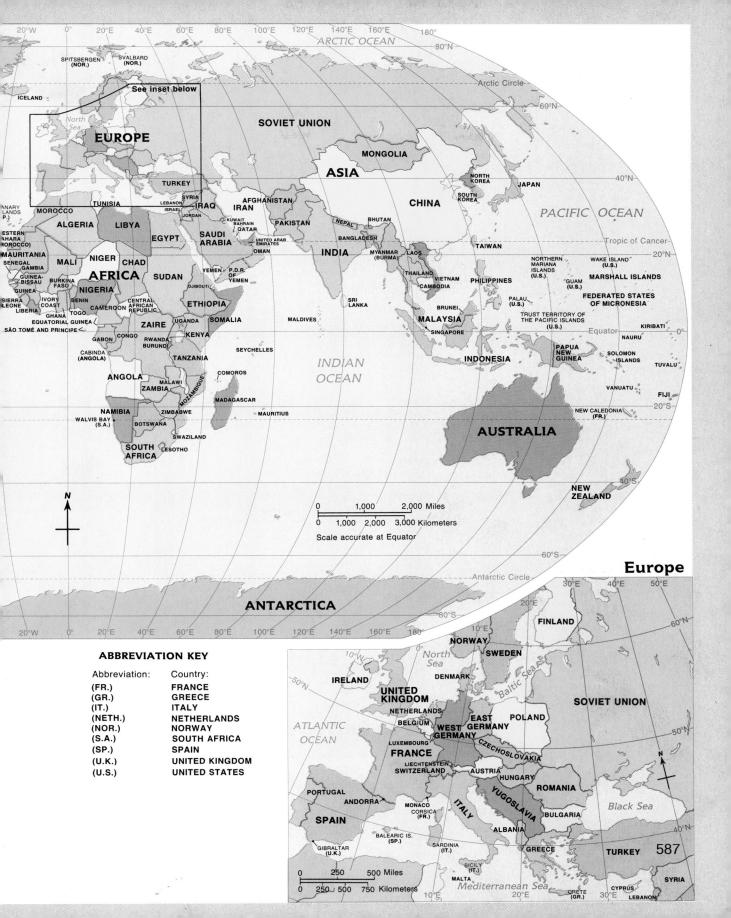

ARCTIC OCEAN

SPITSBERGEN (NOR.) SVALBARD (NOR.)

ICELAND

See inset below

North Sea

EUROPE

SOVIET UNION

MONGOLIA

ASIA

TURKEY

NORTH KOREA

JAPAN

CANARY ISLANDS (SP.)

MOROCCO

TUNISIA

SYRIA
LEBANON
ISRAEL
JORDAN

IRAQ IRAN

AFGHANISTAN

CHINA

SOUTH KOREA

PACIFIC OCEAN

ESTERN AHARA OROCCO)

ALGERIA

LIBYA

EGYPT

SAUDI ARABIA

KUWAIT
BAHRAIN
QATAR

PAKISTAN

NEPAL

BHUTAN

Tropic of Cancer

MAURITANIA

MALI

NIGER

CHAD

UNITED ARAB EMIRATES

OMAN

BANGLADESH

INDIA

MYANMAR (BURMA)

LAOS

TAIWAN

WAKE ISLAND (U.S.)

20°N

SENEGAL
GAMBIA
GUINEA-BISSAU
GUINEA
SIERRA LEONE
LIBERIA

AFRICA

SUDAN

YEMEN

P.D.R. OF YEMEN

NORTHERN MARIANA ISLANDS (U.S.)

MARSHALL ISLANDS

BURKINA FASO

NIGERIA

BENIN
TOGO
GHANA

IVORY COAST

CAMEROON

CENTRAL AFRICAN REPUBLIC

DJIBOUTI

ETHIOPIA

THAILAND

VIETNAM

CAMBODIA

PHILIPPINES

GUAM (U.S.)

FEDERATED STATES OF MICRONESIA

EQUATORIAL GUINEA

SÃO TOMÉ AND PRINCIPE

GABON CONGO

ZAIRE

UGANDA

RWANDA
BURUNDI

SOMALIA

KENYA

SRI LANKA

MALDIVES

BRUNEI

MALAYSIA

SINGAPORE

TRUST TERRITORY OF THE PACIFIC ISLANDS (U.S.)

Equator

KIRIBATI

NAURU

CABINDA (ANGOLA)

TANZANIA

SEYCHELLES

INDIAN OCEAN

INDONESIA

PAPUA NEW GUINEA

SOLOMON ISLANDS

TUVALU

ANGOLA

ZAMBIA

MALAWI

COMOROS

MADAGASCAR

VANUATU

FIJI

20°S

NAMIBIA

WALVIS BAY (S.A.)

ZIMBABWE

BOTSWANA

MOZAMBIQUE

MAURITIUS

NEW CALEDONIA (FR.)

SOUTH AFRICA

SWAZILAND

LESOTHO

AUSTRALIA

N

0   1,000   2,000 Miles
0   1,000 2,000 3,000 Kilometers
Scale accurate at Equator

NEW ZEALAND

40°S

60°S

Antarctic Circle

ANTARCTICA

80°S

ABBREVIATION KEY

Abbreviation:	Country:
(FR.)	FRANCE
(GR.)	GREECE
(IT.)	ITALY
(NETH.)	NETHERLANDS
(NOR.)	NORWAY
(S.A.)	SOUTH AFRICA
(SP.)	SPAIN
(U.K.)	UNITED KINGDOM
(U.S.)	UNITED STATES

Europe

FINLAND

NORWAY

SWEDEN

North Sea

Baltic Sea

IRELAND

DENMARK

SOVIET UNION

UNITED KINGDOM

NETHERLANDS

BELGIUM

EAST GERMANY

POLAND

ATLANTIC OCEAN

WEST GERMANY

CZECHOSLOVAKIA

LUXEMBOURG

FRANCE

LIECHTENSTEIN
SWITZERLAND

AUSTRIA

HUNGARY

ROMANIA

PORTUGAL

ANDORRA

MONACO
CORSICA (FR.)

ITALY

YUGOSLAVIA

Black Sea

SPAIN

BALEARIC IS. (SP.)

BULGARIA

ALBANIA

GIBRALTAR (U.K.)

SARDINIA (IT.)

GREECE

TURKEY

587

SICILY (IT.)

0   250   500 Miles
0   250 500 750 Kilometers

MALTA

Mediterranean Sea

CRETE (GR.)

CYPRUS

SYRIA

LEBANON

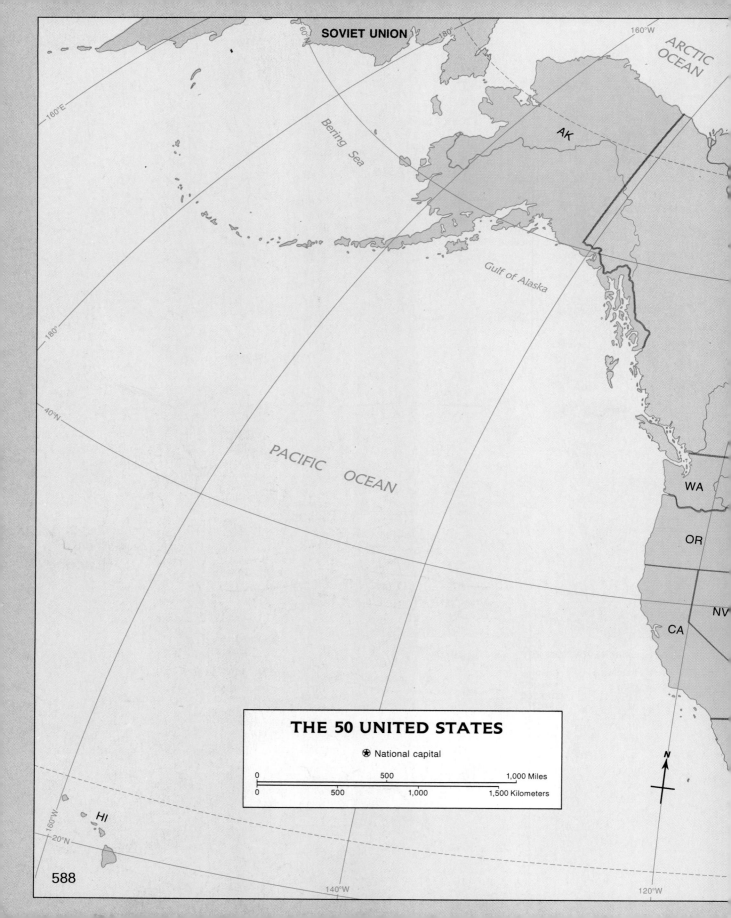

SOVIET UNION

ARCTIC
OCEAN

160°W

160°E

Bering Sea

AK

180°

Gulf of Alaska

40°N

180°

PACIFIC OCEAN

WA

OR

NV

CA

THE 50 UNITED STATES

✪ National capital

0		500		1,000 Miles
0	500	1,000		1,500 Kilometers

N

160°W

HI

20°N

140°W

120°W

CANADA

Greenland
(DENMARK)

Arctic Circle

Hudson Bay

Great Lakes

ATLANTIC
OCEAN

MT | ND | MN | ME
ID | SD | WI | MI | VT | NH
WY | | IA | MI | NY | MA
| NE | | IL | IN | OH | PA | CT | RI
UT | CO | KS | MO | | KY | WV | NJ | Washington, D.C. | MD | DE
AZ | NM | OK | AR | TN | VA | NC
| | | MS | AL | GA | SC
TX | LA | | FL

MEXICO

Gulf of Mexico

Tropic of Cancer

CUBA

589

THE UNITED STATES: Political

⊛ National capital   ★ State capital   • Other city

0   100   200   300 Miles
0   100 200 300   400 Kilometers

591

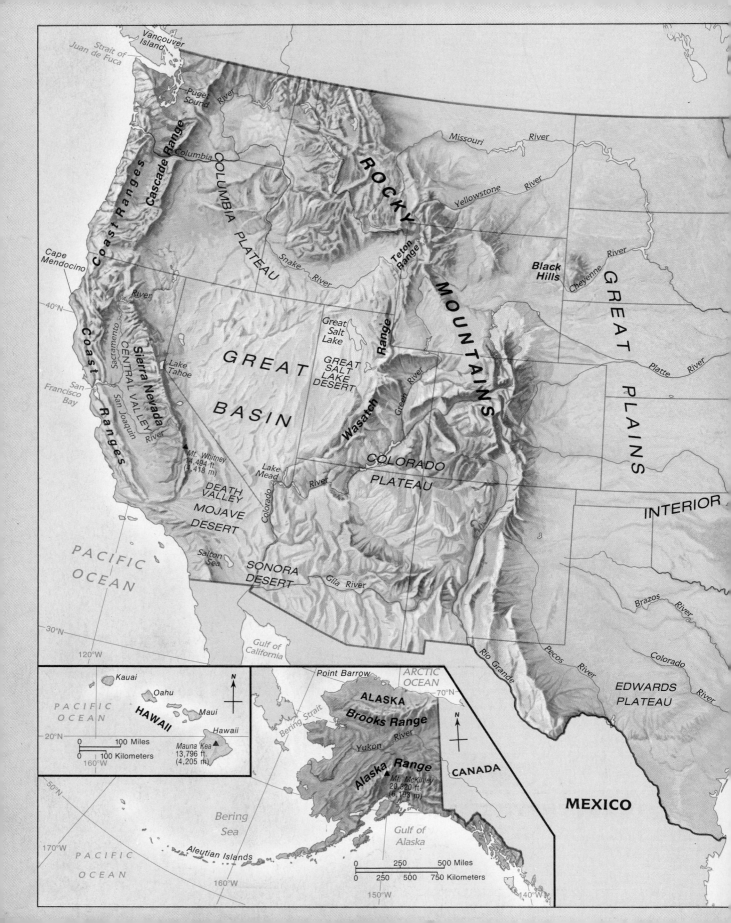

Vancouver Island
Strait of Juan de Fuca
Puget Sound
Columbia River
CASCADE RANGE
Coast Range
Columbia
COLUMBIA PLATEAU
ROCKY
Missouri River
Yellowstone River
Cape Mendocino
Coast Ranges
River
40°N
Snake River
Teton Range
MOUNTAINS
Black Hills
Cheyenne River
GREAT
Sacramento
CENTRAL VALLEY
Sierra Nevada
Lake Tahoe
San Francisco Bay
San Joaquin River
GREAT
SALT
LAKE
DESERT
Great Salt Lake
Range
GREAT
BASIN
Wasatch
Green River
PLAINS
Platte River
Mt. Whitney 14,494 ft. (4,418 m)
Lake Mead
COLORADO PLATEAU
Colorado River
INTERIOR
DEATH VALLEY
MOJAVE DESERT
PACIFIC OCEAN
Salton Sea
SONORA DESERT
Gila River
Brazos River
30°N
Gulf of California
120°W
Rio Grande
Pecos River
Colorado River
EDWARDS PLATEAU

Kauai
Oahu
Maui
Hawaii
HAWAII
N
PACIFIC OCEAN
20°N
0 100 Miles
0 100 Kilometers
160°W
Mauna Kea 13,796 ft. (4,205 m)

Point Barrow
ARCTIC OCEAN
70°N
ALASKA
Brooks Range
Bering Strait
Yukon River
Alaska Range
Mt. McKinley 20,320 ft. (6,193 m)
CANADA
N
MEXICO

50°N
Bering Sea
Aleutian Islands
Gulf of Alaska
170°W
PACIFIC OCEAN
160°W
150°W
140°W
0 250 500 Miles
0 250 500 750 Kilometers

THE UNITED STATES
Physical

Lake of
the Woods

CANADA

Lake Superior

GREAT

LAKES

Mesabi Range

St. Lawrence River

White Mts.

Bay of
Fundy

Mississippi

Lake Michigan

Lake Huron

Lake Ontario

Adirondack
Mts.

Green Mts.

CENTRAL   PLAINS

River

Lake Erie

ALLEGHENY
PLATEAU

Hudson River

Cape
Cod

40°N

Long Island

Wabash River

Susquehanna

Delaware R.

Missouri

Ohio   River

Allegheny Mountains

Potomac R.

ATLANTIC   COASTAL   PLAIN

Delaware Bay

70°W

River

APPALACHIAN   MOUNTAINS

Chesapeake Bay

PLAINS

OZARK
PLATEAU

Kentucky
Lake

PIEDMONT

Cape Hatteras

Arkansas

River

Tennessee

River

ATLANTIC

OCEAN

Ouachita
Mountains

Mississippi River

River

Savannah River

30°N

Alabama River

Chattahoochee River

Red

River

GULF COASTAL PLAIN

Mobile Bay

Mississippi Delta

Lake
Okeechobee

Galveston Bay

Gulf of Mexico

90°W

80°W

N

Florida Keys

Straits of Florida

WEST INDIES

0   100   200   300 Miles

0   100   200   300   400 Kilometers

593

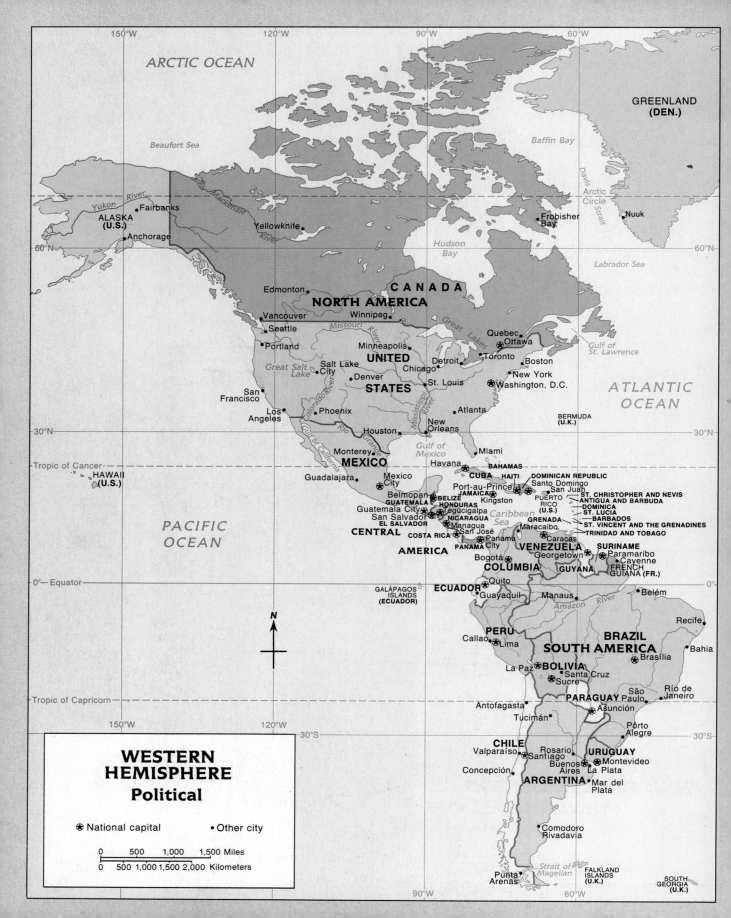

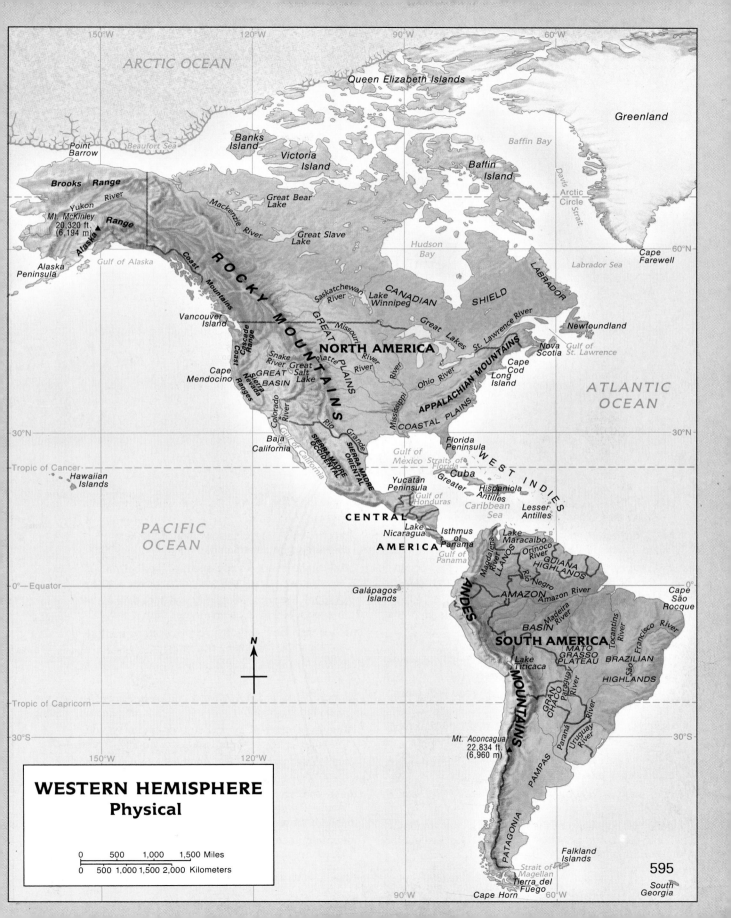

ARCTIC OCEAN

Point
Barrow

Beaufort Sea

Queen Elizabeth Islands

Greenland

Banks
Island

Victoria
Island

Baffin Bay

Baffin
Island

Arctic
Circle

Davis Strait

Cape
Farewell

Brooks   Range

Yukon
Mt. McKinley
20,320 ft.
(6,194 m)

River

Alaska   Range

Great Bear
Lake

Mackenzie River

Great Slave
Lake

Hudson
Bay

Labrador Sea

60°N

Alaska
Peninsula

Gulf of Alaska

Coast Mountains

ROCKY   MOUNTAINS

Saskatchewan
River

Lake
Winnipeg

CANADIAN

SHIELD

LABRADOR

Newfoundland

Vancouver
Island

GREAT

Missouri
River

Great Lakes

St. Lawrence River

Nova
Scotia

Gulf of
St. Lawrence

Cascade
Range

Coast
Ranges

Snake
River

Platte
River

NORTH AMERICA

Ohio River

APPALACHIAN MOUNTAINS

Cape
Cod
Long
Island

ATLANTIC
OCEAN

Cape
Mendocino

Sierra
Nevada

GREAT
BASIN

Great
Salt
Lake

PLAINS

River

Mississippi

COASTAL PLAINS

30°N

Colorado River

Rio

Grande

Florida
Peninsula

WEST INDIES

30°N

Baja
California

Gulf of California

SIERRA MADRE OCCIDENTAL

SIERRA MADRE ORIENTAL

Gulf of
Mexico

Straits of
Florida

Cuba

Greater

Hispaniola
Antilles

Tropic of Cancer

Hawaiian
Islands

Yucatán
Peninsula

Gulf of
Honduras

Caribbean
Sea

Lesser
Antilles

PACIFIC
OCEAN

CENTRAL

AMERICA

Lake
Nicaragua

Isthmus
of
Panama

Gulf of
Panama

Lake
Maracaibo

Magdalena River

LLANOS

Orinoco
River

GUIANA
HIGHLANDS

Galápagos
Islands

ANDES

Rio Negro

AMAZON

Amazon River

0°   Equator

Cape
São
Rocque

0°

Madeira River

BASIN

Tocantins River

São Francisco River

SOUTH AMERICA

MATO
GROSSO
PLATEAU

BRAZILIAN

Lake
Titicaca

HIGHLANDS

N

MOUNTAINS

GRAN
CHACO

Paraguay River

Tropic of Capricorn

Mt. Aconcagua
22,834 ft.
(6,960 m)

Paraná River

Uruguay River

30°S

30°S

PAMPAS

WESTERN HEMISPHERE
Physical

PATAGONIA

Falkland
Islands

595

0   500   1,000   1,500 Miles

0   500 1,000 1,500 2,000 Kilometers

Strait of
Magellan

Tierra del
Fuego

Cape Horn

South
Georgia

150°W

120°W

90°W

60°W

150°W

120°W

90°W

60°W

DICTIONARY OF
GEOGRAPHIC TERMS

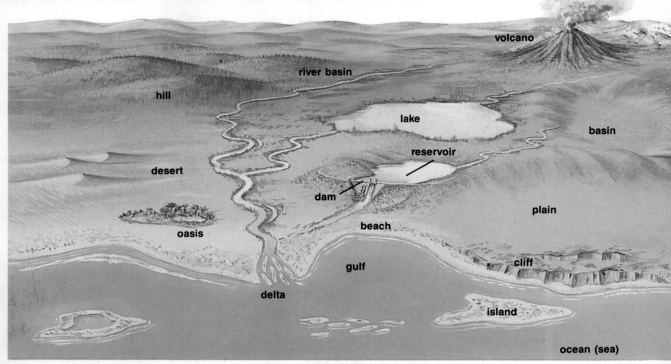

volcano

river basin

hill

lake

basin

reservoir

desert

dam

plain

oasis

beach

cliff

gulf

delta

island

ocean (sea)

basin (bā′ sin) A low, bowl-shaped landform surrounded by higher lands. *See also* **river basin.**

bay (bā) Part of an ocean, sea, or lake that extends
into the land. A bay is usually smaller than a gulf.

beach (bēch) The gently sloping shore of an ocean
or other body of water, especially that part covered by sand or pebbles.

butte (būt) A small, flat-topped hill. A butte is
smaller than a plateau or mesa.

canal (kə nal′) A waterway built to carry water for
navigation or irrigation. Navigation canals usually
connect two other bodies of water.

canyon (kan′ yən) A deep, narrow valley with steep
sides.

cape (kāp) A projecting part of a coastline that extends into an ocean, sea, gulf, bay, or lake.

cliff (klif) A high, steep face of rock or earth.

coast (kōst) Land along an ocean or sea.

dam (dam) A wall built across a river to hold back
the flowing water.

delta (del′ tə) Land at the mouth of a river, made of
silt, sand, and pebbles. A delta is usually shaped
like a triangle.

desert (dez′ ərt) A very dry area where few plants
grow.

fjord (fyôrd) A deep, narrow inlet of the sea
between high, steep cliffs.

glacier (glā′ shər) A large sheet of ice that moves
slowly over some land surface or down a valley.

gulf (gulf) Part of an ocean or sea that extends into
the land. A gulf is usually larger than a bay.

harbor (här′ bər) A protected place along a shore
where ships can safely anchor.

hill (hil) A rounded, raised landform, not as high as
a mountain.

island (ī′ lənd) A body of land completely surrounded by water.

isthmus (is′ məs) A narrow strip of land bordered
by water that connects two larger bodies of land.

lake (lāk) A body of water completely surrounded
by land.

mesa (mā′ sə) A high, flat landform rising steeply
above the surrounding land. A mesa is smaller
than a plateau and larger than a butte.

mountain (mount′ ən) A high, rounded, or pointed
landform with steep sides, higher than a hill.

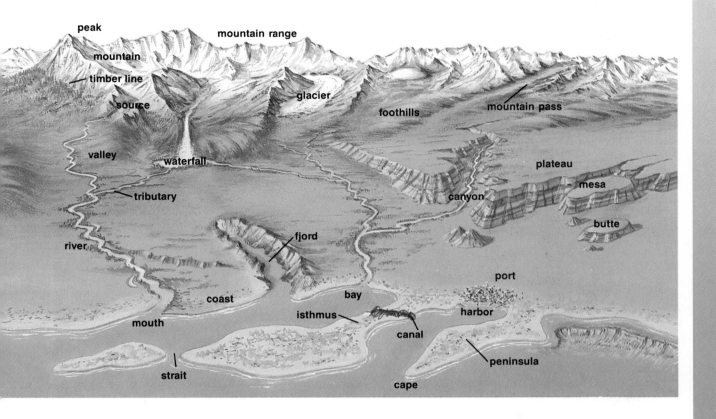

The illustration is labeled with the following geographic terms: peak, mountain range, mountain, timber line, glacier, source, foothills, mountain pass, valley, waterfall, plateau, mesa, tributary, canyon, butte, fjord, river, port, coast, bay, mouth, isthmus, harbor, canal, peninsula, strait, cape.

mountain pass (mount′ ən pas) An opening or gap through a mountain range.

mountain range (mount′ ən rānj) A row or chain of mountains.

mouth (mouth) The place where a river empties into another body of water.

oasis (ō ā′ sis) A place in the desert where there is a supply of water.

ocean (ō′ shən) One of the earth's four largest bodies of water. The four oceans are really a single connected body of salt water that covers about three fourths of the earth's surface.

peak (pēk) The pointed top of a mountain or hill.

peninsula (pə nin′ sə lə) A body of land nearly surrounded by water.

plain (plān) A large area of flat or nearly flat land.

plateau (pla tō′) A high, flat landform that rises steeply above the surrounding land. A plateau is larger than a mesa and a butte.

port (pôrt) A place where ships load and unload goods.

reservoir (rez′ ər vwär′) A natural or artificial lake used to store water.

river (riv′ ər) A large stream of water that flows across the land and usually empties into a lake, ocean, or other river.

river basin (riv′ ər bās′ in) All the land drained by a river and its tributaries.

sea (sē) A large body of water partly or entirely surrounded by land; another word for *ocean*.

source (sôrs) The place where a river or stream begins.

strait (strāt) A narrow waterway or channel connecting two larger bodies of water.

timber line (tim′ bər līn′) An imaginary line on mountains and in arctic regions, above which trees do not grow.

tributary (trib′ yə târ ē) A small river or stream that flows into a larger river or stream.

valley (val′ ē) An area of low land between hills or mountains.

volcano (vol kā′ nō) An opening in the earth through which lava, rock, gases, and ash are forced out.

waterfall (wô′ tər fôl′) A flow of water falling from a high place to a lower place.

GAZETTEER

This Gazetteer is a geographical dictionary that will help you to pronounce and locate the places discussed in this book. Latitude and longitude are given for cities and some other places. The page number tells you where each place appears on a map.

PRONUNCIATION KEY

a	cap	êr	clear	oi	coin	ü	moon
ā	cake	hw	where	ôr	fork	ū	cute
ä	father	i	bib	ou	cow	ûr	term
är	car	ī	kite	sh	show	ə	about, taken,
âr	dare	ng	song	th	thin		pencil, apron,
ch	chain	o	top	th	those		helpful
e	hen	ō	rope	u	sun	ər	letter, dollar,
ē	me	ô	saw	ù	book		doctor

A

Abilene (ab′ ə lēn) A town in central Kansas, at the northern end of the old Chisholm Trail; 39°N, 97°W. (p. 445)

Africa (af′ ri kə) One of the earth's seven continents. (pp. 586–587)

Alaska Range (ə las′ kə rānj) A mountain range in southern Alaska. (p. 21)

Albany (ôl′ bə nē) Capital of New York State; 43°N, 74°W. (p. 38)

Alberta (al bûr′ tə) A province of Canada, in the southwestern part of the country. (p. 554)

Allegheny Mountains (al ə gā′ nē mount′ ənz) Mountains extending from Pennsylvania into Virginia and West Virginia. (p. 38)

Amazon River (am′ ə zon riv′ ər) The longest river in South America, flowing from the Andes Mountains across Brazil into the Atlantic Ocean. (p. 576)

Anchorage (ang′ kər ij) A city in southern Alaska, the largest city in the state and an important port; 61°N, 150°W. (p. 57)

Andes Mountains (an′ dēz mount′ ənz) The mountains extending along the west coast of South America, the longest chain of mountains in the world. (p. 576)

Annapolis (ə nap′ ə lis) Capital of Maryland; 39°N, 76°W. (p. 38)

Antarctica (ant ärk′ ti kə) One of the earth's seven continents. (pp. 586–587)

Antarctic Circle (ant ärk′ tik sûr′ kəl) An imaginary line around the earth; 66°33′S. (p. 29)

Antietam (an tē′ təm) A town in north-central Maryland, site of a major battle of the Civil War; 39°N, 78°W. (p. 414)

Appalachian Mountains (ap ə lā′ chē ən mount′ enz) Chain of mountains that stretch from Alabama into Canada. (p. 21)

Appomattox (ap ə mat′ əks) A town in central Virginia, where General Lee surrendered to General Grant, ending the Civil War; 37°N, 79°W. (p. 414)

Arctic North (ärk′ tik nôrth) A region of frozen plains and ice-covered islands lying north of the Canadian Shield, in Canada. (p. 548)

Arctic Ocean (ärk′ tik ō′ shən) The smallest of the earth's four largest bodies of water. (pp. 586–587)

Argentina (är jən tē′ nə) A country in southern South America. (p. 576)

Asia (ā′ zhə) The largest of the earth's seven continents. (pp. 586–587)

Atlanta (at lan′ tə) Capital and largest city of Georgia; 34°N, 84°W. (p. 43)

Atlantic Coastal Plain (at lan′ tik kōst′ əl plān) The flat or gently sloping land that stretches from Maine to Florida along the Atlantic Ocean. (p. 21)

Atlantic Ocean (at lan′ tik ō′ shən) One of the earth's four largest bodies of water. (pp. 586–587)

Augusta (ô gus′ tə) Capital of Maine; 44°N, 70W. (p. 38)

Austin (ôs′ tin) Capital of Texas; 30°N, 98°W. (p. 51)

Australia (ôs trāl′ yə) The smallest of the earth's seven continents. (pp. 586–587)

B

Baltimore (bôl′ tə môr) A city in Maryland, on Chesapeake Bay. It is the largest city in the state; 39°N, 77°W. (p. 38)

Baton Rouge (bat′ ən rüzh′) Capital of Louisiana; 30°N, 91°W. (p. 43)

Bering Strait (bâr′ ing strāt) A narrow waterway connecting the Bering Sea and the Arctic Ocean. (pp. 592–593)

Birmingham (bûr′ ming ham) A city in north-central Alabama, the largest city in the state and an important steel-manufacturing center; 34°N, 87°W. (p. 43)

Bismark (biz′ märk) Capital of North Dakota; 47°N, 101°W. (p. 47)

Blue Ridge Mountains (blü rij mount′ ənz) Mountains extending from West Virginia to Georgia that are part of the Appalachians. (p. 242)

Boise (boi′ sē) Capital and largest city of Idaho; 44°N, 116°W. (p. 57)

Bolivia (bə liv′ ē ə) A country in west-central South America. (p. 576)

Boonesborough (bünz′ bər ə) A town in east-central Kentucky, now **Boonesboro**, site of a fort founded by Daniel Boone; 38°N, 84°W. (p. 340)

Boston (bôs′ tən) Capital and largest city of Massachusetts; 42°N, 71°W. (p. 38)

Brazil (brə zil′) The largest country in South America, in the northeastern part of the continent. (p. 576)

British Columbia (brit′ ish kə lum′ bē ə) A province of Canada, in the southwestern part of the country. (p. 554)

Brooks Range (brúks rānj) A mountain range extending across the northern part of Alaska. (p. 21)

Bull Run (búl run) A stream in northeastern Virginia, flowing into the Potomac River, site of a major battle of the Civil War; 39°N, 77°W. (p. 414)

Bunker Hill (bung′ kər hil) A small hill on Charlestown Peninsula in Massachusetts, near Breed's Hill, where an important battle of the American Revolution was fought; 42°N, 71°W. (p. 300)

C

Canada (kan′ ə də) A country in northern North America, bordering the United States. Canada, the second-largest country in the world, is made up of ten provinces and two territories. (p. 554).

Canadian Shield (kə nā′ dē ən shēld) A low-lying plateau of ancient rocks that covers more than half of Canada, extending from Labrador southwest around Hudson Bay and northwest to the Arctic Ocean. (p. 548)

Cape Canaveral (kāp kə nav′ ər əl) A point of land on the east-central coast of Florida; the city located near this point, the site of the Kennedy Space Center; 29°N, 80°W. (p. 43)

Cape Cod (kāp kod) A peninsula in southeastern Massachusetts, enclosing Cape Cod Bay. (p. 38, p. 194)

Cape of Good Hope (kāp əv gúd hōp) The southernmost tip of Africa, on the Atlantic Ocean; 34°S, 18°E. (p. 132)

Caribbean Sea (kâr ə bē′ ən sē) An arm of the Atlantic Ocean. (p. 571)

Carson City (kär′ sən sit′ ē) Capital of Nevada; 39°N, 120°W. (p. 57)

Cascade Range (kas kād′ rānj) A mountain range in the northwestern United States and southwestern Canada. The Cascades extend from northern California into British Columbia. (p. 57)

Catskill Mountains (kats′ kil mount′ ənz) Mountains in New York that are part of the Appalachians. (p. 38)

Central America (sen′ trəl ə mâr′ i kə) The southern part of North America, lying south of Mexico between the Pacific Ocean and the Caribbean Sea. Central America includes Guatemala, Belize, Honduras, El Salvador, Nicaragua, Costa Rica, and Panama. (p. 571)

Central Plains (sen′ trəl plānz) The eastern part of the Interior Plains, the flat or gently rolling land that makes up much of the central United States. (p. 47)

Charleston (chärl′ stən) Capital and largest city of West Virginia; 38°N, 82°W (p. 43). A city in southeastern South Carolina, originally Charles Town; 33°N 80°W. (p. 43)

Charles Town (chärlz toun) The original name of Charlestown, South Carolina, a city in the southeastern part of the state; 33°N, 80°W. (p. 242)

Chesapeake Bay (ches′ ə pēk bā) A long arm of the Atlantic Ocean, on the coast of Maryland and Virginia. (p. 21)

Cheyenne (shī en′) Capital of Wyoming; 41°N, 105°W. (p. 57)

Chicago (shi kä′ gō) A city in northeastern Illinois, the largest city in the state, and a port and steel-manufacturing center; 42°N, 88°W. (p. 47)

Chile (chil′ ē) A country in southwestern South America. (p. 576)

GAZETTEER

Cleveland (klēv′ lənd) A city in northeastern Ohio, and an important port and steel-manufacturing center; 42°N, 82°W. (p. 47)

Coast Ranges (kōst rānj′ ez) The mountain ranges along the western coast of North America. (p. 21)

Colombia (kə lum′ bē ə) A country in northwestern South America. (p. 576)

Colorado River (kol ə rad′ ō riv′ ər) A river in the southwestern United States, flowing from Colorado to northern Mexico, where it empties into the Gulf of California. (p. 21)

Columbia (kə lum′ bē ə) Capital and largest city in South Carolina; 34°N, 81°W. (p. 43)

Columbus (kə lum′ bəs) Capital of Ohio; 40°N, 83°W. (p. 47)

Concord (kong′ kərd) Capital of New Hampshire; 43°N, 72°W. (p. 38); A town in eastern Massachusetts, site of one of the first battles of the American Revolution; 42°N, 71°W. (p. 281, p. 300)

Continental Divide (kon tə nent′ əl di vīd′) In North America, the high peaks of the Rocky Mountains that separate the waters flowing into the Pacific Ocean from those flowing into the Atlantic and Arctic Oceans. (p. 21)

Costa Rica (kos′ tə rē′ kə) A country in the southern part of Central America. (p. 571)

Cuba (kū′ bə) An island country in the Caribbean, the largest and westernmost island of the West Indies; 22°N, 79°W. (p. 571).

Cumberland Gap (kum′ bər lənd gap) A pass, or low place providing easy passage, across the high ridge of the Appalachian Mountains, in northeastern Tennessee; 37°N, 84°W. (p. 340)

Cuzco (kü′ skō) A city in southern Peru, in the Andes Mountains. It was the capital of the ancient Incan empire; 14°S, 72°W. (p. 78)

D

Denver (den′ vər) Capital and largest city of Colorado; 40°N, 105°W. (p. 57)

Des Moines (də moin′) Capital and largest city of Iowa; 42°N, 94°W. (p. 47)

Detroit (di troit′) A city in southeastern Michigan. The largest city in the state and an important manufacturing center; 42°N, 83°W. (p. 47)

Dominican Republic (də min′ i kən ri pub′ lik) A country in the West Indies, occupying the eastern part of the island of Hispaniola. (p. 571)

Dust Bowl (dust bōl) The area of dry, dusty land with irregular rainfall and frequent dust storms that developed in the Great Plains in the 1930s. (p. 504)

E

Eastern Hemisphere (ēs′ tərn hem′ is fêr) The half of the earth that lies east of the prime meridian (0° longitude) and west of 180° longitude. (p. 5)

Ecuador (ek′ wə dôr) A country in the northwestern part of South America. (p. 576)

El Salvador (el sal′ və dôr) A country in the middle part of Central America. (p. 571)

England (ing′ glənd) Part of the United Kingdom of Great Britain and Northern Ireland. England occupies the southern part of the island of Great Britain. (p. 132)

equator (i kwā′ tər) An imaginary line encircling the earth halfway between the North Pole and the South Pole. (p. 28)

Erie Canal (êr′ ē kə nal′) A waterway across New York, connecting the Hudson River with Lake Erie, now part of the New York State Barge Canal. (p. 366)

Europe (yür′ əp) The smallest of the earth's seven continents. (pp. 586–587)

F

Fort Christina (fôrt kris tē′ nə) An early Swedish settlement in New Sweden, on the site of present-day Wilmington, Delaware; 40°N, 76°W. (p. 197)

Fort Orange (fôrt ôr′ inj) An early Dutch settlement in New Netherland, on the site of present-day Albany, New York; 43°N, 74°W. (p. 197)

Fort Sumter (fôrt sum′ tər) A fort at the entrance of Charleston Harbor, South Carolina, the site of the opening battle of the Civil War; 33°N, 80°W. (p. 414)

Fort Ticonderoga (fôrt tī kon də rō′ gə) A historic fort on Lake Champlain, in New York, site of important battles in the American Revolution; 44°N, 74°W. (p. 300)

Fort Vincennes (fôrt vin senz′) An early fort on the site of present-day Vincennes, Indiana, on the Wabash River; 39°N, 88°W. (p. 300)

Frankfort (frangk′ fərt) Capital of Kentucky; 38°N, 85°W. (p. 43)

French Guiana (french gē ä′ nə) An overseas department of France, in north central South America. (p. 576)

G

Gettysburg (get′ iz bûrg) A town in south-central Pennsylvania, site of a major battle of the Civil War; 40°N, 77°W. (p. 414)

Grand Canyon (grand kan′ yən) A spectacular canyon on the Colorado River in northwestern Arizona. (p. 21)

GAZETTEER

Great Basin (grāt bā′ sin) A large arid or semiarid area in the western United States. (p. 21)

Great Lakes (grāt lāks) A group of five large fresh-water lakes in North America, along the border between the United States and Canada. The Great Lakes include Lake Superior, Lake Michigan, Lake Huron, Lake Erie, and Lake Ontario. (p. 21)

Great Lakes-St. Lawrence Lowlands (grāt lāks sānt lôr′ əns lō′ ləndz) The low-lying plains around the Great Lakes and the St. Lawrence River. (p. 548)

Great Plains (grāt plānz) The western part of the Interior Plains, the flat or gently rolling land that makes up much of the central United States. (p. 21)

Greenland (grēn′ lənd) An island in the North Atlantic Ocean, the largest island in the world. (p. 128)

Grenada (grə nā′ də) An island country in the West Indies. (p. 571)

Guam (gwäm) An island in the western Pacific Ocean; 14°N, 143°E. (pp. 586–587)

Guatemala (gwä tə mä′ lə) A country in the northern part of Central America. (p. 571)

Gulf Coastal Plain (gulf kōst′ əl plān) The flat or gently sloping land that borders the Gulf of Mexico. (p. 21)

Gulf of Mexico (gulf əv mek′ si kō) An arm of the Atlantic Ocean that extends the southeastern part of North America. (p. 21)

Gulf of St. Lawrence (gulf əv sānt lôr′ əns) A deep gulf of the Atlantic Ocean off the east coast of Canada, between Newfoundland and the Canadian mainland. (p. 154)

Guyana (gī an′ ə) A country in north-central South America. (p. 576)

H

Haiti (hā′ tē) A country in the West Indies, occupying the western part of the island of Hispaniola. (p. 571)

Harrisburg (hâr′ is bûrg) Capital of Pennsylvania; 40°N, 77°W. (p. 38)

Hartford (härt′ fərd) Capital of Connecticut; 42°N, 73°W. (p. 38)

Helena (hel′ ə nə) Capital of Montana; 47°N, 112°W. (p. 57)

Hiroshima (hêr ō shē′ mə) A port city in southwestern Japan, on the island of Honshu. It was the first city to be devastated by an atomic bomb; 34°N, 132°E. (pp. 510–511)

Honduras (hon dùr′ əs) A country in northern Central America. (p. 571)

Honolulu (hon ə lü′ lü) Capital and largest city of Hawaii; 21°N, 158°W. (p. 57)

Hudson Bay (hud′ sən bā) A large inland sea in northeastern Canada, connected with the Atlantic Ocean by Hudson Strait. (p. 548)

Hudson River (hud′ sən riv′ ər) A river in eastern New York that empties into the Atlantic Ocean. (p. 38)

I

Iceland (īs′ lənd) An island country in the North Atlantic Ocean, between Greenland and Norway. (p. 128, pp. 586–587)

Indianapolis (in dē ə nap′ ə lis) Capital and largest city of Indiana; 40°N, 86°W. (p. 47)

Indian Ocean (in′ dē ən ō′ shən) One of the earth's four largest bodies of water. It lies south of Asia, between Africa and Australia. (p. 5)

Interior Plains (in tēr′ ē ər plānz) The large area of flat or gently rolling land that makes up much of the interior of North America. In the United States, the Interior Plains are divided into the Central Plains and the Great Plains (pp. 592–593)

J

Jackson (jak′ sən) Capital and largest city of Mississippi; 32°N, 90°W. (p. 43)

Jamaica (jə mā′ kə) An island country in the West Indies, south of Cuba. (p. 571)

Jamestown (jāmz′ toun) A town in southeastern Virginia, the first permanent English settlement in America, founded in 1607; 37°N, 77°W. (p. 194)

Japan (jə pan′) An island country in the North Pacific, off the eastern coast of Asia. (pp. 586–587)

Jefferson City (jef′ ər sən sit′ ē) Capital of Missouri; 39°N, 92°W. (p. 47)

---

a cap; ā cake; ä father; är car; âr dare; ch chain; e hen; ē me; êr clear; hw where; i bib; ī kite; ng song; o top; ō rope; ô saw; oi coin; ôr fork; ou cow; sh show; th thin; th those; u sun; ù book; ü moon; ū cute; ûr term; ə about, taken, pencil, apron, helpful; ər letter, dollar, doctor

GAZETTEER

Juneau (jü′ nō) Capital of Alaska; 58°N, 135°W. (p. 57)

K

Kansas Territory (kan′ zəs târ′ ə tôr ē) Formerly, a territory of the United States that included present-day Kansas and part of present-day Colorado. (p. 401)

L

Lake Erie (lāk êr′ ē) Southernmost of the Great Lakes, on the border between the United States and Canada. (p. 21)

Lake Huron (lāk hūr′ ən) Second-largest of the Great Lakes, on the border between the United States and Canada. (p. 21)

Lake Michigan (lāk mish′ ə gən) Third-largest of the Great Lakes, lying between Michigan and Wisconsin. (p. 21)

Lake Ontario (lāk on târ′ ē ō) Smallest and east-ernmost of the Great Lakes, on the border between the United States and Canada. (p. 21)

Lake Superior (lāk sə pêr′ ē ər) Largest and north-ernmost of the Great Lakes, on the border between the United States and Canada. (p. 21)

Lansing (lan′ sing) Capital of Michigan; 43°N, 85°W. (p. 47)

Latin America (lat′ in ə mâr′ i kə) The part of the Western Hemisphere south of the United States that includes Mexico, Central America, the West Indies, and South America. (p. 594)

Lexington (lek′ sing tən) A town in eastern Massa-chusetts, site of one of the first battles of the American Revolution; 42°N, 71°W. (p. 281, p. 300)

Lincoln (ling′ kən) Capital of Nebraska; 41°N, 97°W. (p. 47)

Little Rock (lit′ əl rok) Capital and largest city of Arkansas; 35°N, 92°W. (p. 43)

Los Angeles (lôs an′ jə ləs) A city in southwestern California, the largest city in the state and an important port; 34°N, 118°W. (p. 57)

Louisiana Purchase (lü ē zē an′ ə pûr′ chəs) The largest tract of land lying between the Mississippi River on the east and the Rocky Mountains on the west, and between Canada on the north and the Gulf of Mexico on the south; bought by the United States from France in 1803. (p. 346)

M

Madison (mad′ ə sən) Capital of Wisconsin; 43°N 89°W. (p. 47)

Manitoba (man ə tō′ bə) A province of Canada in the south-central part of the country. (p. 554)

Massachusetts Bay Colony (mas ə chü′ sits bā kol′ ə nē) The colony founded by English Puritans in 1630 in the area around Massachusetts Bay. It included the settlements of Boston and Salem. (p. 194)

Mexico (mek′ si kō) A country in southern North America, lying south of the 48 United States and north of Central America. (p. 566)

Mexico City (mek′ si kō sit′ ē) Capital and largest city of Mexico; 19°N, 99°W. (p. 566)

Miami (mī am′ ē) a resort and port city in south-eastern Florida; 26°N, 80°W. (p. 43)

Mississippi River (mis′ ə sip′ ē riv′ ər) A river in the central United States, flowing from Minnesota to southern Louisiana, where it empties into the Gulf of Mexico. The Mississippi is the longest river in the United States. (p. 21)

Missouri River (mi zur′ ē riv′ ər) A river in the north-central United States, flowing from Montana to St. Louis, Missouri, where it joins the Missis-sippi River. (p. 21)

Montgomery (mont gum′ ər ē) Capital of Alabama; 32°N, 86°W. (p. 43)

Montpelier (mont pēl′ yər) Capital of Vermont; 44°N, 73°W. (p. 38)

Montreal (mon trē ôl′) A port city in southern Que-bec, the largest city in Canada; 46°N, 74°W. (p. 154)

Mount McKinley (mount mə kin′ lē) The highest mountain in North America, elevation 20,320 feet (6,194 m), located in the Alaska Range in south-central Alaska; 63°N, 153°W. (p. 21)

N

Nashville (nash′ vil) Capital of Tennessee; 36°N, 87°W. (p. 43)

New Amsterdam (nü am′ stər dam) An early Dutch settlement in New Netherland, on the site of present-day New York City; 41°N, 74°W. (p. 197)

New Brunswick (nü brunz′ wik) A province of Can-ada, in the southeastern part of the country. (p. 554)

New England (nü ing′ glənd) Part of the Northeast region of the United States. The New England states are Maine, Vermont, New Hampshire, Mas-sachusetts, Connecticut, and Rhode Island. (p. 38)

Newfoundland (nü′ fənd lənd) An island off the east coast of Canada; a province of Canada, in the eastern part of the country, made up of the island of Newfoundland and Labrador. (p. 554)

New France (nü frans) French possessions in North America in colonial times. New France included large parts of present-day Canada and the United States. (p. 271)

New Netherland (nü neth′ ər lənd) A former Dutch colony in North America, from 1609 to 1664. It included parts of present-day New York, New Jersey, and Connecticut. (p. 197)

New Orleans (nü ôr′ lē ənz) A city in southern Louisiana, the largest city in the state; 30°N, 90°W. (p. 43)

New Spain (nü spān) Formerly, lands held by Spain, mainly in North America. New Spain included parts of the present-day United States, Mexico, Central America, islands in the West Indies, and the Philippine Islands. (p. 144)

New Sweden (nü swēd′ ən) Formerly, a Swedish colony in North America, from 1638 to 1655, along the Delaware River in present-day New Jersey, Pennsylvania, and Delaware. (p. 197)

New York City (nü yôrk sit′ ē) A city in southeastern New York, a major port and the largest city in the United States; 41°N, 74°W. (p. 38)

Nicaragua (nik ə rä′ gwə) A country in the middle part of Central America. (p. 571)

North America (nôrth ə mâr′ i kə) One of the earth's seven continents. (pp. 586–587)

Northern Hemisphere (nôr′ thərn hem′ is fêr) The half of the earth that lies north of the equator (0° latitude). (p. 5)

North Pole (nôrth pōl) The northwestern point on earth; the northern end of the earth's axis; 90°N. (p. 28)

Northwest Territory (nôrth′ west târ′ ə tôr ē) Formerly, a territory of the United States bounded by the Ohio River, the Great Lakes, and the Mississippi River. The states of Ohio, Indiana, Illinois, Michigan, Wisconsin, and part of Minnesota were formed from the Northwest Territory. (p. 318)

Northwest Territories (nôrth′ west târ′ ə tôr ēz) An administrative division of Canada, in the northern part of the country. (p. 554)

Nova Scotia (nō′ və skō′ shə) A province of Canada, in the southeastern part of the country. (p. 554)

Nueces River (nü ā′ səs riv′ ər) A river in southern Texas, flowing into the Gulf of Mexico near Corpus Christi. (p. 51)

O

Oklahoma City (ō klə hō′ mə sit′ ē) Capital and largest city of Oklahoma; 35°N, 98°W. (p. 51)

Olympia (ō lim′ pē ə) Capital of Washington; 47°N, 123°W. (p. 57)

Omaha (ō′ mə hô) A city in east-central Nebraska, the largest city in the state; 41°N, 96°W. (p. 47)

Ontario (on târ′ ē ō) A province of Canada, in the southeastern part of the country (p. 554). The smallest of the Great Lakes. (p. 548)

Ottawa (ot′ ə wə) The capital of Canada, in the province of Ontario; 45°N, 76°W. (p. 554)

P

Pacific Ocean (pə sif′ ik o′ shən) The largest of the earth's four largest bodies of water. (pp. 586–587)

Pampas (pam′ pəz) A vast, treeless plain covering much of the central part of Argentina between the Atlantic Ocean and the Andes Mountains. (p. 576)

Panama (pan′ ə mä) The southernmost country in Central America. (p. 571)

Panama Canal (pan′ ə mä kə nal′) A ship canal across the Isthmus of Panama, connecting the Atlantic Ocean (through the Caribbean Sea) and the Pacific Ocean. (p. 484)

Paraguay (pâr′ ə gwā) A country in south-central South America. (p. 576)

Pearl Harbor (pûrl här′ bər) A principal United States naval base near Honolulu, on the island of Oahu, Hawaii. The bombings of Pearl Harbor by the Japanese on December 7, 1941, caused the United States to enter World War II; 21°N, 158°W. (pp. 510–511)

Peru (pə rü′) A country in northwestern South America (p. 576). Lands held by Spain in colonial times that included large parts of western South America. (p. 144)

Philadelphia (fil ə del′ fē ə) A city in southeastern Pennsylvania, the largest city in the state. Philadelphia was the capital of the United States from 1790 to 1800; 40°N, 75°W. (p. 38)

Philippine Islands (fil′ ə pēn ī′ ləndz) A group of more than 7,000 islands off the coast of southeast Asia, making up the country of the Philippines. (p. 141)

a cap; ā cake; ä father; är car; âr dare; ch chain; e hen; ē me; êr clear; hw where; i bib; ī kite; ng song; o top; ō rope; ô saw; oi coin; ôr fork; ou cow; sh show; th thin; th those; u sun; u̇ book; ü moon; ū cute; ûr term; ə about, taken, pencil, apron, helpful; ər letter, dollar, doctor

GAZETTEER

Phoenix (fē′ niks) Capital and largest city of Arizona; 34°N, 112°W. (p. 51)

Piedmont (pēd′ mont) The rolling hills extending from New Jersey to Alabama and sloping gently seaward from the Appalachian Mountains to the Atlantic Coastal Plain. (p. 38)

Pierre (pêr) Capital of South Dakota; 44°N, 100°W. (p. 47)

Pittsburgh (pits′ bûrg) A city in southwestern Pennsylvania, an important iron- and steel-manufacturing center; 40°N, 80°W. (p. 38)

Plymouth (plim′ əth) A town in southeastern Massachusetts, settled by the Pilgrims in 1620; 42°N, 71°W. (p. 194)

Portsmouth (pôrts məth) A town in southeastern Rhode Island, settled in 1637; 42°N, 71°W. (p. 202)

Prime Meridian (prīm mə rid′ ē ən) The meridian, or line of longitude, that passes through Greenwich, England, from which longitude east and west is measured; 0° longitude. (p. 29)

Prince Edward Island (prins ed′ wərd ī′ lənd) The smallest province of Canada, in the southeastern part of the country (p. 554). The island that makes up this province.

Promontory Point (prom′ ən tôr ē point) A place in northwestern Utah where the tracks of the Union Pacific Railroad and those of the Central Pacific Railroad met in 1869, completing the first transcontinental railroad in the United States; 41°N, 113°W. (p. 437)

Providence (prov′ ə dəns) Capital and largest city of Rhode Island; 42°N, 71°W. (p. 38)

Pueblo Bonito (pweb′ lō bə nēt′ ō) An Anasazi village that flourished from 950 to 1300 A.D., now in ruins, located in what is now northwestern New Mexico; 36°N, 108°W. (p. 83)

Puerto Rico (pwâr′ tō rē′ kō) An island in the West Indies, a commonwealth of the United States. (p. 571)

Q

Quebec (kwi bek′) The largest province of Canada, in the eastern part of the country; the city that is the capital of this province; 47°N, 71°W. (p. 554)

R

Raleigh (rô′ lē) Capital of North Carolina; 36°N, 79°W. (p. 43)

Richmond (rich′ mənd) Capital of Virginia (p. 43). Richmond was the capital of the Confederacy and the site of a major battle of the Civil War; 38°N, 78°W. (p. 414)

Rio Grande (rē′ ō grand) A river in the southwestern North America, flowing from Colorado into the Gulf of Mexico and forming the border between Texas and Mexico. (p. 21)

Rocky Mountains (rok′ ē mount′ ənz) High, rugged mountains stretching through the western part of North America from Alaska into Mexico. (p. 21)

S

Sacramento (sak rə men′ tō) Capital of California; 39°N, 122°W. (p. 57)

St. Lawrence River (sānt lôr′ əns riv′ ər) A river in eastern North America, flowing from Lake Ontario into the Gulf of St. Lawrence. It is the chief outlet of the Great Lakes and forms part of the boundary between the United States and Canada. (p. 38)

St. Louis (sānt lü′ is) A city in eastern Missouri, near the place where the Missouri River flows into the Mississippi River. St. Louis is the largest city in the state; 39°N, 90°W. (p. 47)

St. Paul (sānt pôl) Capital of Minnesota; 45°N, 93°W. (p. 47)

Salem (sā′ ləm) Capital of Oregon; 45°N, 123°W. (p. 57). A city in northeastern Massachusetts; 43°N, 71°W. (p. 202)

Salt Lake City (sôlt lāk sit′ ē) Capital and largest city of Utah; 41°N, 112°W. (p. 57)

San Antonio (san an tō′ nē ō) A city in central Texas; 29°N, 99°W. (p. 51)

San Diego (san dē ā′ gō) A port city in southern California; 33°N, 117°W. (p. 57)

San Francisco (san frən sis′ kō) A port city in western California; 38°N, 122°W. (p. 57)

San Salvador (san sal′ və dôr) Capital and largest city of El Salvador, in the central part of the country; 14°N, 89°W. (p. 571). Also, an island in the central Bahamas, also known as Watling Island, where Columbus may have landed in the New World; 24°N, 75°W. (p.137)

Santa Fe (san′ ta fā) Capital of New Mexico; 35°N, 106°W. (p. 51)

Saratoga (sâr ə tō′ gə) A city in east-central New York, site of an important battle in the American Revolution; 43°N, 75°W. (p. 300)

Saskatchewan (sas kach′ ə won) A province of Canada in the south-central part of the country. (p. 554)

Savannah (sə van′ ə) A port city in southeastern Georgia, site of important battles in the American Revolution and the Civil War; 32°N, 81°W. (p. 43)

Seattle (sē at′ əl) A city in northwestern Washington, the largest city in the state and an important port; 48°N, 122°W. (p. 57)

Sierra Madres (sē âr′ ə mä′ dräz) A mountain system in eastern and western Mexico. (p. 566)

Sierra Nevada (sē âr′ ə nə vad′ ə) A mountain range in eastern California. (p. 21)

South America (south ə mâr′ i kə) One of the earth's seven continents. It lies between the Atlantic Ocean on the east and the Pacific Ocean on the west. It is connected to North America by the Isthmus of Panama. (pp. 586–587)

Southern Hemisphere (suth′ ərn hem′ is fêr) The half of the earth that lies south of the equator; 0° latitude. (p. 5)

South Pole (south pōl) The southernmost point on the earth; 90°S. (p. 28)

Soviet Union (sō′ vē et ūn′ yən) The largest country in the world occupying the northern part of Asia and the eastern part of Europe. (pp. 586–587)

Springfield (spring′ fēld) Capital of Illinois; 40°N, 90°W. (p. 47)

Strait of Magellan (strāt uv mə jel′ ən) The narrow waterway between the southern tip of South America and Tierra del Fuego, that links the Atlantic Ocean with the Pacific Ocean. (p. 141)

Suriname (sür ə näme′) A country in north-central South America. (p. 576)

T

Tallahassee (tal ə has′ ē) Capital of Florida; 30°N, 84°W. (p. 43)

Tenochtitlán (tā nôch′ tē tlän) Capital of the ancient Aztec empire, on the site of present-day Mexico City; 19°N, 99°W. (p. 78)

Topeka (tə pē′ kə) Capital of Kansas; 39°N, 96°W. (p. 47)

Toronto (tə ron′ tō) The capital of the province of Ontario, Canada; 44°N, 79°W. (p. 554)

Trenton (trent′ ən) Capital of New Jersey, site of an important battle in the American Revolution; 40°N, 75°W. (p. 38)

Trinidad and Tobago (trin′ ə dad and tə bā′ gō) A country in the West Indies, made up of the islands of Trinidad and Tobago. (p. 571)

Tropic of Cancer (trop′ ik əv kan′ sər) An imaginary line around the earth, parallel to the equator; 23°27′N. (p. 29)

Tropic of Capricorn (trop′ ik əv kap′ rə kôrn) An imaginary line around the earth, parallel to the equator; 23°27′S. (p. 29)

U

Uruguay (yür′ ə gwā) A country in southeastern South America. (p. 576)

V

Valley Forge (val′ ē fôrj) A town in southeastern Pennsylvania, the place Washington camped during the winter of 1777–1778; 40°N, 75°W. (p. 300)

Venezuela (ven ə zwā′ lə) A country in northwestern South America. (p. 576)

Vicksburg (viks′ bûrg) A city in west-central Mississippi, site of a major battle of the Civil War; 32°N, 91°W. (p. 43)

Vietnam (vē et näm′) A country in southeastern Asia. (p. 526)

Vinland (vin′ lənd) The Viking name for a part of the northeastern coast of North America. (p. 128)

W

Washington, D.C. (wô′ shing tən dē sē) Capital of the United States; 39°N, 77°W. (p. 38)

Western Hemisphere (wes′ tərn hem′ is fêr) The half of the earth that lies west of the Prime Meridian and east of 180° longitude. (p. 5)

West Indies (west in′ dēz) The islands stretching from Florida in North America to Venezuela in South America. (p. 137)

Wilderness Road (wil′ dər nis rōd) An early road across the Appalachians, between western Virginia and eastern Kentucky. (p. 340)

Williamsburg (wil′ yəmz bûrg) An early colonial settlement in Virginia; 37°N, 77°W. (p. 43)

Y

Yorktown (yôrk′ toun) A town in southeastern Virginia, the site of the last major battle of the American Revolution; 37°N, 77°W. (p. 300)

Yucatán Peninsula (ū kə tan′ pə nin′ sə lə) A peninsula in southeastern Mexico and northeastern Central America. (p. 566)

Yukon Territory (ū′ kon târ′ ə tôr ē) A territory in northwestern Canada. (p. 554)

---

a cap; ā cake; ä father; är car; âr dare; ch chain; e hen; ē me; êr clear; hw where; i bib; ī kite; ng song; o top; ō rope; ô saw; oi coin; ôr fork; ou cow; sh show; th thin; <u>th</u> those; u sun; u̇ book; ü moon; ū cute; ûr term; ə about, taken, pencil, apron, helpful; ər letter, dollar, doctor

GAZETTEER

UNITED STATES PRESIDENTS

George Washington (1732–1799)
Years in Office: 1789–1797
Home State: Virginia
Vice President: J. Adams

John Adams (1735–1826)
Years in Office: 1797–1801
Home State: Massachusetts
Vice President: T. Jefferson

Thomas Jefferson (1743–1826)
Years in Office: 1801–1809
Home State: Virginia
Vice Presidents: A. Burr, G. Clinton

James Madison (1751–1836)
Years in Office: 1809–1817
Home State: Virginia
Vice Presidents: G. Clinton, E. Gerry

James Monroe (1758–1831)
Years in Office: 1817–1825
Home State: Virginia
Vice President: D. D. Tompkins

John Quincy Adams (1767–1848)
Years in Office: 1825–1829
Home State: Massachusetts
Vice President: J. C. Calhoun

Andrew Jackson (1767–1845)
Years in Office: 1829–1837
Home State: Tennessee
Vice Presidents: J. Calhoun, M. Van Buren

Martin Van Buren (1782–1862)
Years in Office: 1837–1841
Home State: New York
Vice President: R. M. Johnson

William Henry Harrison (1773–1841)
Years in Office: 1841–1841
Home State: Ohio
Vice President: J. Tyler*

John Tyler (1790–1862)
Years in Office: 1841–1845
Home State: Virginia

James K. Polk (1795–1849)
Years in Office: 1845–1849
Home State: Tennessee
Vice President: G. M. Dallas

Zachary Taylor (1784–1850)
Years in Office: 1849–1850
Home State: Louisiana
Vice President: M. Fillmore*

Millard Fillmore (1800–1874)
Years in Office: 1850–1853
Home State: New York

Franklin Pierce (1804–1869)
Years in Office: 1853–1857
Home State: New Hampshire
Vice President: W. R. King

James Buchanan (1791–1868)
Years in Office: 1857–1861
Home State: Pennsylvania
Vice President: J. C. Breckinridge

Abraham Lincoln (1809–1865)
Years in Office: 1861–1865
Home State: Illinois
Vice Presidents: H. Hamlin, A. Johnson*

Andrew Johnson (1808–1875)
Years in Office: 1865–1869
Home State: Tennessee

Ulysses S. Grant (1822–1885)
Years in Office: 1869–1877
Home State: Illinois
Vice Presidents: S. Colfax, H. Wilson

Rutherford B. Hayes (1822–1893)
Years in Office: 1877–1881
Home State: Ohio
Vice President: W. A. Wheeler

James A. Garfield (1831–1881)
Years in Office: 1881–1881
Home State: Ohio
Vice President: C. A. Arthur*

Chester A. Arthur (1830–1886)
Years in Office: 1881–1885
Home State: New York

Franklin D. Roosevelt (1882–1945)
Years in Office: 1933–1945
Home State: New York
Vice Presidents: Garner, Wallace, Truman*

Grover Cleveland (1837–1908)
Years in Office: 1885–1889, 1893–1897†
Home State: New York
Vice Presidents: T. Hendricks, A. Stevenson

Harry S Truman (1884–1972)
Years in Office: 1945–1953
Home State: Missouri
Vice President: A. Barkley

Benjamin Harrison (1833–1901)
Years in Office: 1889–1893
Home State: Indiana
Vice President: L. P. Morton

Dwight D. Eisenhower (1890–1969)
Years in Office: 1953–1961
Home State: New York
Vice President: R. M. Nixon

William McKinley (1843–1901)
Years in Office: 1897–1901
Home State: Ohio
Vice Presidents: G. A. Hobart, T. Roosevelt*

John F. Kennedy (1917–1963)
Years in Office: 1961–1963
Home State: Massachusetts
Vice President: L. B. Johnson*

Theodore Roosevelt (1858–1919)
Years in Office: 1901–1909
Home State: New York
Vice President: C. W. Fairbanks

Lyndon B. Johnson (1908–1973)
Years in Office: 1963–1969
Home State: Texas
Vice President: H. Humphrey

William Howard Taft (1857–1930)
Years in Office: 1909–1913
Home State: Ohio
Vice President: J. S. Sherman

Richard M. Nixon (1913–   )
Years in Office: 1969–1974
Home State: California
Vice Presidents: S. Agnew, G. R. Ford**

Woodrow Wilson (1856–1924)
Years in Office: 1913–1921
Home State: New Jersey
Vice President: T. R. Marshall

Gerald R. Ford (1913– *1990*)
Years in Office: 1974–1977
Home State: Michigan
Vice President: N. Rockefeller

Warren G. Harding (1865–1923)
Years in Office: 1921–1923
Home State: Ohio
Vice President: C. Coolidge*

Jimmy Carter (1924– *1990*)
Years in Office: 1977–1981
Home State: Georgia
Vice President: W. F. Mondale

Calvin Coolidge (1872–1933)
Years in Office: 1923–1929
Home State: Massachusetts
Vice President: C. G. Dawes

Ronald Reagan (1911–   )
Years in Office: 1981–1989
Home State: California
Vice President: G. Bush

Herbert Hoover (1874–1964)
Years in Office: 1929–1933
Home State: California
Vice President: C. Curtis

George Bush (1924–   )
Years in Office: 1989– *1993*
Home State: Texas
Vice President: D. Quayle

†Cleveland was elected for a second term after Benjamin Harrison.
*Succeeded from the Vice Presidency on the death of the President.
**Succeeded from the Vice Presidency on the resignation of the President.

BIOGRAPHICAL DICTIONARY

The Biographical Dictionary will help you to pronounce and identify the people discussed in this book. The page number tells you where each person first appears in the text.

PRONUNCIATION KEY

a	cap	êr	clear	oi	coin	ü	moon
ā	cake	hw	where	ôr	fork	ū	cute
ä	father	i	bib	ou	cow	ûr	term
är	car	ī	kite	sh	show	ə	about, taken,
âr	dare	ng	song	th	thin		pencil, apron,
ch	chain	o	top	th	those		helpful
e	hen	ō	rope	u	sun	ər	letter, dollar,
ē	me	ô	saw	ů	book		doctor

A

Adams, Abigail (ad′ əmz), 1744–1818 Wife of John Adams and mother of John Quincy Adams. She wrote many letters about the role of women in society. (p. 317)

Adams, John (ad′ əmz), 1735–1826 Massachusetts lawyer who was a member of the Continental Congress and the Constitutional Convention. Adams became the second President of the United States. (p. 279)

Addams, Jane (ad′ əmz), 1860–1935 Reformer who started Hull House in Chicago. (p. 465)

Arnold, Benedict (är′ nəld), 1741–1801 American army leader who helped defeat the British at Fort Ticonderoga. He later fought for the British and is remembered as a traitor to his country. (p. 287)

Atahualpa (ät ə wäl′ pə), (1502–1533) Incan ruler defeated by Spanish conquistador Francisco Pizarro in 1531. (p. 577)

Attucks, Crispus (at′ əks), 1723?–1770 A former slave who was killed during the "Boston Massacre." (p. 277)

Austin, Stephen (ôs′ tin), 1793–1836 Pioneer who led a group of American settlers to Texas in 1822. (p. 374)

B

Balboa, Vasco Núñez de (bal bō′ ə väs′ kō nu′ ñez), 1475?–1517 Spanish explorer who reached the Pacific Ocean by crossing the Isthmus of Panama. (p. 140)

Banneker, Benjamin (ban′ ə kər), 1731–1806 A mathematician and surveyor who helped plan Washington, D.C. Banneker was the first African-American to be appointed by a President to work for the government. (p. 344)

Barton, Clara (bärt′ ən), 1821–1912 Nurse who aided wounded soldiers during the Civil War. Barton later started the American Red Cross. (p. 415)

Bell, Alexander Graham (bel), 1847–1922 Invented the telephone and later started the American Bell Telephone Company. (p. 455)

Berkeley, Lord John (burk′ lē), ?–1678 English army officer who started the colony of New Jersey with Sir George Carteret. (p. 223)

Bolívar, Simón (bə lē′ vär, sē mōn′), 1783–1830 Leader of the struggle for independence in South America. Known as "The Liberator," his armies freed Colombia, Venezuela, and Peru from Spanish rule. (p. 578)

Boone, Daniel (bün), 1734–1820 Explorer and pioneer who blazed the trail to Kentucky that was later known as the Wilderness Road. (p. 339)

Braddock, Edward (brad′ ək), 1695–1755 British general who led British and American troops against the French and Indians at Fort Duquesne in 1755. Braddock died in the battle. (p. 269)

Bradford, William (brad′ fərd), 1590?–1657 Leader of the Pilgrims who came to Plymouth on the *Mayflower* in 1620. (p. 188)

Brown, John (broun), 1800–1859 Abolitionist who led a raid on Harper's Ferry, Virginia, in 1859. (p. 402)

Burgoyne, John (bûr goin′), 1722–1792 British general who was defeated by American troops at the Battle of Saratoga during the American Revolution. (p. 299)

Bush, George (bush), 1924– Became the 41st President of the United States in 1989. (p. 531)

C

Cabot, John (kab′ ət), 1450?–1498 Italian explorer sailing for England who reached Newfoundland. (p. 153)

Calhoun, John C. (kal hün′), 1782–1850 Senator from South Carolina who warned that slavery was pulling the United States apart. (p. 398)

Calvert, George (kal′ vərt), 1580–1632 An English noble who started the colony of Maryland as a place where Catholics could worship in peace. (p. 243)

Carnegie, Andrew (kär nā′ gē), 1835–1919 Businessman who helped develop the steel industry. (p. 454)

Carter, Jimmy (kär′ tər), 1924– President of the United States from 1977 to 1981. (p. 528)

Carteret, Sir George (kär′ tər et), 1613?–1680 English naval officer who started the colony of New Jersey with Lord John Berkeley. (p. 223)

Cartier, Jacques (kär tē a′, zhäk), 1491–1557 French explorer who searched for the Northwest Passage and found the St. Lawrence River. Cartier started the city that became Montreal. (p. 154)

Catt, Carrie Chapman (kat), 1859–1947 Women's suffrage leader in the early 1900s. (p. 487)

Champlain, Samuel de (sham′ plān′), 1567–1635 Known as ''the Father of New France,'' Champlain built the first successful French settlement in America at Quebec. (p. 164)

Clark, George Rogers (klärk), 1752–1818 Frontier fighter who defeated the British at Fort Vincennes and gained control of the Northwest Territory for the United States during the American Revolution. (p. 303)

Clark, William (klärk), 1770–1838 Frontier scout chosen by President Thomas Jefferson to explore the Louisiana Territory with Meriwether Lewis. (p. 346)

Clay, Henry (clā), 1777–1852 Senator from Kentucky who helped work out the Missouri Compromise and the Compromise of 1850. (p. 336)

Columbus, Christopher (kə lum′ bəs) 1451?– 1506 Italian explorer, sailing for Spain, who reached America while sailing west to Asia in 1492. (p. 134)

Cooper, Peter (kü′ per), 1791–1883 Inventor who built one of the early steam-driven railroad trains, the *Tom Thumb*. (p. 366)

Cornwallis, Charles (kôrn wô′ lis) 1738–1805 British general who surrendered to the Continental Army at Yorktown in 1781. This was the last major battle of the American Revolution. (p. 305)

Coronado, Francisco (kôr ə nä′ dō), 1500?–1544 Spanish explorer of the Southwest. (p. 145)

Cortés, Hernándo (kôr tez′, er nän′ dō), 1485–1547 Spanish conquistador who conquered the Aztecs in 1521. (p. 143)

Crazy Horse (krā′ zē hôrs), 1849?–1877 Sioux chief whose warriors defeated General Custer at the Battle of the Little Big Horn. (p. 442)

Crockett, Davy (krok′ ət), 1786–1836 Bear hunter, frontiersman, and congressman who helped defend the Alamo in 1836. (p. 375)

Custer, George (kus′ tər), 1839–1876 Army colonel who was defeated by the Sioux Indians at the Battle of the Little Big Horn. This battle is known as ''Custer's Last Stand.'' (p. 442)

D

Da Gama, Vasco (də gä′ mə, väs′ kō), 1469?–1524 Portuguese sea captain who sailed all the way from Europe to Asia by sea. (p. 133)

Davis, Jefferson (dā′ vis), 1808–1889 President of the Confederacy during the Civil War. (p. 403)

De Soto, Hernando (də sō′ tō, er nän′ dō), 1500?–1542 Spanish explorer who found the Mississippi River while searching for the Seven Cities of Gold. (p. 144)

Deganawida (di gan ə wē′ də), 1500s Iroquois holy man who, together with Hiawatha, helped persuade the Iroquois to stop fighting among themselves. (p. 107)

Dewey, George (dü′ ē), 1837–1917 American naval commander who defeated the Spanish in the Philippines during the Spanish-American War. (p. 480)

Dias, Bartholomeu (dē′ əs, bär tù lù mā′ ù), 1450–1500 Portuguese ship captain who discovered the Cape of Good Hope at the southern tip of Africa. Dias paved the way for the discovery of a sea route from Europe to Asia. (p. 133)

Douglass, Frederick (dug′ ləs), 1817–1895 Abolitionist leader who was an escaped slave. (p. 394)

E

Edison, Thomas Alva (ed′ i sən), 1847–1931 Inventor of the light bulb, the phonograph, and over 1,000 other inventions. (p. 454)

Eisenhower, Dwight D. (ī′ zən hou ər), 1890–1969 American general during World War II who organized the Allied invasion of Europe. Eisenhower was elected President of the United States in 1952. (p. 511)

Eric the Red (er′ ik), 950?–1000? Viking leader who explored Greenland around the year 980. (p. 127)

Ericson, Leif (er' ik sən, lēf), died 1020?   Son of Eric the Red who landed in North America around the year 1000. Ericson named the land that he explored *Vinland*. (p. 128)

F

Ferraro, Geraldine (fə rar' ō), 1935–   New York Representative who was the Democratic candidate for Vice President in 1984. (p. 532)

Ford, Gerald (fôrd), 1913–   President of the United States following the resignation of Richard M. Nixon in 1974. (p. 527)

Ford, Henry (fôrd), 1863–1947 Automaker who first used the assembly line to produce cars. (p. 485)

Franklin, Benjamin (frangk' lin), 1706–1790 American colonial leader, writer, and scientist. (p. 232)

Fulton, Robert (fûlt' ən), 1765–1815   Inventor who built the first successful steamboat, the *Clermont*, in 1807. (p. 364)

G

Garrison, William Lloyd (gar' ə sən), 1805–1879 Abolitionist who started a newspaper in 1831 called *The Liberator*. (p. 394)

George III (jorj), 1738–1820   King of England during the American Revolution. (p. 274)

Gompers, Samuel (gom' pərz), 1850–1924 Cigar maker and labor union leader who became the first president of the American Federation of Labor in 1886. (p. 457)

Gorbachev, Mikhail (gôr' bə chôf), 1931–   Leader of the Soviet Union in the 1980s. (p. 528)

Grant, Ulysses S. (grant), 1822–1885   Commander of the Union army during the Civil War. In 1868 he was elected President of the United States. (p. 415)

Grimké, Angelina (grim' kē), 1805–1879 Southerner who moved north with her sister Sarah to work against slavery. (p. 395)

Grimké, Sarah (grim' kē), 1792–1873   Southerner who moved north with her sister Angelina to become an abolitionist speaker. (p. 395)

H

Hale, Nathan (hāl, na' thən), 1755–1776   American patriot who was hanged as a spy by the British. (p. 298)

Hamilton, Alexander (ham' əl tən), 1757–1804 New York lawyer who served as the first Secretary of the Treasury under President George Washington. (p. 319)

Hays, Mary Ludwig (hāz), 1754–1832   Called "Molly Pitcher," she helped American soldiers during the Revolution by bringing them pitchers of water during battles. (p. 302)

Henry, Patrick (hen' rē), 1736–1799   American patriot who encouraged colonists to fight for their independence from Great Britain. (p. 275)

Hiawatha (hī ə woth' ə), 1500s   An Iroquois warrior who worked with Deganawida to create the Iroquois League. (p. 107)

Hidalgo, Miguel (hi däl' gō), 1753–1811   Priest and leader of the Indian and mestizo revolt that started the Mexican War of Independence against Spain. (p. 568)

Hitler, Adolf (hit' lər, ād' olf), 1889–1945   Nazi dictator of Germany during World War II. (p. 508)

Hooker, Thomas (hù' kər), 1586–1647   Puritan preacher who started the colony of Connecticut. (p. 206)

Hoover, Herbert (hù' vər), 1874–1964   President of the United States at the beginning of the Great Depression. (p. 501)

Houston, Sam (hūs' tən), 1793–1863   Leader of the Texas army in its rebellion against Mexico. Houston later was elected the first President of the Republic of Texas. (p. 375)

Howe, Julia Ward (hou), 1819–1875   Author and reformer who wrote the "Battle Hymn of the Republic." (p. 412)

Howe, William (hou), 1729–1814   British general who fought at the Battle of Bunker Hill. (p. 288)

Hudson, Henry (hud' sən), died 1611   English explorer who searched for the Northwest Passage. Hudson explored New York Harbor, the Hudson River, and northern Canada. (p. 156)

Hutchinson, Anne (huch' ən sən), 1591–1643 Puritan woman who was brought to trial because of her beliefs. Forced to leave Massachusetts, Hutchinson moved to Rhode Island and started the settlement of Portsmouth. (p. 205)

I

Isabella, Queen (iz ə bel' ə), 1451–1504 Queen of Spain who sponsored the voyages of Christopher Columbus. (p. 135)

Iturbide, Agustín de (ē tür bē' dā, a güs tēn' dā), 1783–1824   First leader of Mexico after it won its independence from Spain in 1821. (p. 568)

J

Jackson, Andrew (jak' sən), 1767–1845   General who defeated the British at the Battle of New Orleans at the end of the War of 1812. Known as Old Hickory, Jackson was later elected the seventh President of the United States. (p. 352)

Jackson, Jesse (jak' sən), 1941–   Black political leader who unsuccessfully campaigned to become the Democratic candidate for President in 1984 and 1988. (p. 524)

Jackson, Thomas "Stonewall" (jak´ sən), 1824–1863 Confederate general during the Civil War who defeated the Union army in the Battle of Bull Run. (p. 411)

Jefferson, Thomas (jef´ ər sən), 1743–1826 Writer of the Declaration of Independence and third President of the United States. (p. 292)

Johnson, Andrew (jon´ sən), 1808–1875 President of the United States during Reconstruction. Johnson was the first American President to be impeached. (p. 419)

Johnson, Lyndon (jon´ sən), 1908–1973 President of the United States following the assassination of John F. Kennedy in 1963. (p. 523)

Joliet, Louis (jō´ lē et, lü´ ē), 1645–1700 French explorer who, together with Jacques Marquette, sailed across the Great Lakes and down the Mississippi River as far south as the mouth of the Arkansas River. (p. 166)

Jones, John Paul (jōnz), 1747–1792 American seaman whose ship the *Bonhomme Richard* defeated the British warship *Serapis* in a battle fought during the American Revolution. (p. 304)

Jones, Mary Harris (jōnz), 1830–1930 Known as "Mother Jones," this labor union organizer worked to protect workers and unions. (p. 458)

Joseph, Chief (jō´ səf), 1832–1904 Nez Percé chief who led his people on a long march to escape being sent to an Indian reservation. Chief Joseph and his people were captured within 40 miles (64 km) of the Canadian border. (p. 442)

Júarez, Benito (wär´ ez, be nē´ tō), 1806–1872 President of Mexico from 1858 to 1865 and again from 1867 to 1872. (p. 568)

K

Kennedy, John F. (ken´ ə dē), 1917–1963 Youngest elected President of the United States, serving from 1961 to 1963. Kennedy was killed in 1963. (p. 520)

Key, Francis Scott (kē), 1799–1843 Wrote "The Star-Spangled Banner" during the War of 1812. This poem was later set to music and became our national anthem. (p. 350)

King, Martin Luther, Jr. (king), 1928–1968 Major civil rights leader of the 1950s and 1960s. King was murdered in 1968. (p. 521)

Kosciuszko, Thaddeus (käs ē əs´ kō, thad´ ē əs), 1746–1817 Polish patriot who helped the Continental Army during the American Revolution. (p. 302)

L

La Salle, Robert (lə sal´), 1643–1687 French fur trapper who reached the mouth of the Mississippi in 1682 and claimed the entire Mississippi River Valley for France. (p. 167)

Lafayette, Marquis de (läf ē et´), 1757–1834 French officer who fought with the Americans during the Revolution. (p. 302)

Lee, Robert E. (lē), 1807–1870 Commander of the Confederate army during the Civil War. (p. 410)

Lewis, Meriwether (lü´ is), 1774–1809 Frontier scout chosen by President Jefferson to explore the Louisiana Territory with William Clark. (p. 346)

Liliuokalani, Queen (li lē ə wō kə län´ ē), 1838–1917 Last queen of Hawaii, who was forced from her throne by American planters in the 1890s. (p. 478)

Lincoln, Abraham (ling´ kən), 1809–1865 President of the United States during the Civil War. (p. 401)

Lindbergh, Charles (lind´ burg´), 1902–1974 First person to fly solo nonstop across the Atlantic Ocean. In the *Spirit of St. Louis*, Lindberg flew from New York to Paris in 33.5 hours. (p. 501)

Lord Baltimore (bôl´ tə môr), ?–1675 First proprietor of the colony of Maryland. (p. 243)

M

Macdonald, John A. (mək don´ əld), 1815–1891 First leader of the nation of Canada. Macdonald promoted the building of the railroad across Canada. (p. 554)

Madison, James (mad´ ə sən), 1751–1836 Virginia planter who is known as the Father of the Constitution because of his influence at the Constitutional Convention. Madison later was elected the fourth President of the United States. (p. 322)

Magellan, Ferdinand (mə jel´ ən), 1480?–1521 Portuguese explorer who led the first sea voyage around the world. (p. 140)

Marion, Francis (mâr´ ē ən), 1732?–1795 Known as the "Swamp Fox," Marion led a band of guerrilla fighters against the British in South Carolina during the American Revolution. (p. 305)

a cap; ā cake; ä father; är car; âr dare; ch chain; e hen; ē me; êr clear; hw where; i bib; ī kite; ng song; o top; ō rope; ô saw; oi coin; ôr fork; ou cow; sh show; th thin; <u>th</u> those; u sun; ù book; ü moon; ū cute; ûr term; ə about, taken, pencil, apron, helpful; ər letter, dollar, doctor

BIOGRAPHICAL DICTIONARY

Marquette, Jacques (mär ket′, zhäk), 1637–1675 French priest who, together with Louis Joliet, sailed across the Great Lakes and down the Mississippi River as far south as the mouth of the Arkansas River. (p. 166)

Massasoit (mas ə soit′), 1580?–1661 Wampanoag chief who made peace with the Pilgrims at Plymouth. (p. 191)

McClellan, George (mə klel′ ən), 1826–1885 General in the Union army during the Civil War. (p. 414)

McCormick, Cyrus (mə kôr′ mək), 1809–1884 Invented a cutting machine called a reaper in 1831. (p. 453)

Metacom (met′ ə kom), ?–1676 Son of Massasoit, known as King Philip by the colonists in New England. Metacom led a war against the colonists, which ended in 1676 when the Indian leader was killed. (p. 207)

Monroe, James (mən rō′), 1758–1831 Fifth President of the United States. (p. 345)

Montezuma (mon tə zü′ mə), 1480?–1520 Aztec emperor defeated by the Spanish conquistador Hernándo Cortés in 1520. (p. 567)

Mott, Lucretia (mot), 1793–1880 Abolitionist and leader in the women's rights movement. (p. 396)

N

Nixon, Richard (nik′ sən), 1913– President who resigned from office as a result of the Watergate scandal. (p. 527)

O

O'Connor, Sandra Day (ō kon′ ər), 1930– First woman to serve on the Supreme Court. O'Connor was appointed in 1981. (p. 532)

Oglethorpe, James (ō′ gəl thôrp), 1696–1785 British military officer who started the colony of Georgia in 1733. (p. 245)

Osceola (os ē ō′ lə), 1804–1838 Leader of the Seminole Indians who resisted Andrew Jackson's Indian removal policy. (p. 355)

P

Paine, Thomas (pān), 1737–1809 American patriot who wrote *Common Sense*. This pamphlet convinced many colonists to join the fight for independence. (p. 292)

Parks, Rosa (pärks), 1913– Black woman whose refusal to give up her seat on a public bus led to the Montgomery, Alabama, bus boycott of 1955. (p. 521)

Penn, William (pen), 1644–1718 Quaker leader who started the colony of Pennsylvania in 1681. (p. 225)

Perry, Oliver Hazard (pâr′ ē, haz′ ərd), 1785–1819 American naval captain during the War of 1812. (p. 349)

Pizarro, Francisco (pi zär′ ō), 1471?–1541 Spanish conquistador who conquered the Incas in 1533. (p. 144)

Pocahontas (pō kə hon′ təs), 1595?–1617 Daughter of Powhatan, who saved John Smith and helped Jamestown to survive. Pocahontas later married John Rolfe. (p. 181)

Ponce de León, Juan (pons′ də le′ ən, wän), 1460?–1521 Spanish explorer who reached Florida in 1513. (p. 144)

Powhatan (pau ə tan′), 1550?–1618 Chief of the Powhatan Indians who lived near the English settlement at Jamestown. (p. 180)

Printz, Johan (printz, yō′ hän), 1592–1663 Governor of New Sweden until that colony became part of New Netherland in 1655. (p. 196)

R

Raleigh, Sir Walter (rô′ lē), 1552?–1618 English adventurer who started the Roanoke colony in America. (p. 160)

Reagan, Ronald (rā′ gən), 1911– President of the United States from 1981 to 1989. (p. 528)

Revere, Paul (ri vēr′), 1735–1818 Boston silversmith who, on the night of April 18, 1775, warned the people of Concord that the British army was coming. (p. 281)

Rolfe, John (rolf), 1585–1622 Jamestown leader who developed a type of tobacco that sold for a high price in England. Rolfe was the husband of Pocahontas. (p. 184)

Roosevelt, Eleanor (rō′ zə velt), 1884–1962 Wife of Franklin D. Roosevelt who talked with people all across the country during the Great Depression. Her ideas and impressions helped shape the President's New Deal programs. (p. 505)

Roosevelt, Franklin D. (rō′ zə velt), 1882–1945 President of the United States during the Great Depression and World War II. (p. 504)

Roosevelt, Theodore (rō′ zə velt), 1858–1919 Leader of the Rough Riders during the Spanish-American War, and President of the United States from 1901 to 1909. (p. 480)

S

Sacajawea (sak ə jə wē′ ə), 1784?–1884 Shoshone Indian who helped the Lewis and Clark expedition by serving as a translator. (p. 346)

Salomon, Haym (sol′ ə mən), 1740–1785 Polish-American who raised money for the Continental Army during the American Revolution. (p. 302)

San Martín, José de (sän mär tēn′), 1778–1850 Leader of the armies that freed Argentina and Chile from Spanish rule. (p. 578)

Scott, Winfield (skot), 1786–1866 Commander of the Union army at the beginning of the Civil War. (p. 410)

Sequoyah (si kwoi′ ə), 1770?–1843 Indian chief who invented the Cherokee alphabet. (p. 355)

Serra, Junípero (ser′ rə, hū nē′ pə rō), 1713–1784 Spanish priest who built missions in California in the 1700s. (p. 147)

Shays, Daniel (shāz), 1747?–1825 A soldier in the American Revolution who led a rebellion of Massachusetts farmers against the state courts. (p. 319)

Sitting Bull (sit′ ing bùl), 1834?–1890 Sioux chief who defeated General George Custer at the Battle of the Little Big Horn. (p. 442)

Slater, Samuel (slā′ tər), 1768–1835 Englishman who built the first water-powered spinning mill in the United States. (p. 369)

Smith, John (smith), 1580–1631 English colonist in America whose strict discipline helped the settlement at Jamestown to survive. (p. 179)

Squanto (skwän′ tō), ?–1622 Wampanoag Indian who helped the Pilgrims in Plymouth. (p. 191)

Stanton, Elizabeth Cady (stan′ tən), 1815–1902 Abolitionist and women's rights leader. (p. 396)

Steuben, Friedrich von (stü′ bən), 1730–1794 German officer who trained American soldiers at Valley Forge during the Revolution. (p. 302)

Stowe, Harriet Beecher (stō), 1811–1896 Author of *Uncle Tom's Cabin*. (p. 399)

Stuyvesant, Peter (stī′ və sənt), 1592–1672 Dutch governor of the colony of New Netherland. (p. 196)

T

Truman, Harry S. (trü′ mən), 1884–1972 President of the United States following the death of Franklin D. Roosevelt in 1945. (p. 512)

Truth, Sojourner (trüth), 1797?–1883 Former slave who was an abolitionist and spoke out for women's rights. (p. 396)

Tubman, Harriet (tub′ mən), 1821?–1913 Escaped slave who helped other blacks reach freedom on the Underground Railroad. (p. 395)

V

Verrazano, Giovanni da (vâr rät sän′ ō, jō vän′ nē da), 1485?–1528 Italian explorer who searched for the Northwest Passage. (p. 154)

Vespucci, Amerigo (ves pü′ chē, ə mâr′ ə gō), 1454–1512 Italian explorer who realized that Christopher Columbus had found a new continent. A German mapmaker named the new land after Vespucci. (p. 137)

W

Washington, George (wô′ shing tən), 1732–1799 Virginia planter who led the Continental Army during the American Revolution and who later became the first President of the United States. (p. 254)

Washington, Martha (wô′ shing tən), 1731–1802 Wife of George Washington who assisted the Continental Army during the Revolution. (p. 301)

White, John (wīt), 1500s Leader of the Roanoke colony in America. (p. 160)

Whitman, Marcus (hwit′ mən), 1802–1847 Missionary who traveled to Oregon with his wife Narcissa in 1836. (p. 377)

Whitman, Narcissa (hwit′ mən), 1808–1847 Missionary who traveled to Oregon in 1836 with her husband Marcus. (p. 377)

Whitney, Eli (hwit′ nē), 1765–1825 Inventor of the cotton gin. (p. 368)

Williams, Roger (wil′ yəmz), 1603?–1684 Puritan preacher who founded the colony of Rhode Island in 1636. (p. 204)

Wilson, Woodrow (wil′ sən), 1865–1924 President of the United States during World War I. (p. 495)

Winthrop, John (win′ thrəp), 1588–1649 First leader of the Massachusetts Bay Colony. (p. 194)

Wright, Orville (rīt), 1871–1948 Inventor who, with his brother Wilbur, made the first successful airplane flight in 1903. (p. 486)

Wright, Wilbur (rīt), 1867–1912 Inventor who, with his brother Orville, made the first successful airplane flight in 1903. (p. 486)

Y

Young, Brigham (yung), 1801–1877 Leader of the Mormons who brought about the Mormon settlement at Salt Lake City. (p. 379)

Z

Zenger, John Peter (zeng′ ər), 1697–1746 Newspaper publisher, whose trial in 1734 helped establish the idea of freedom of the press. (p. 224)

BIOGRAPHICAL DICTIONARY

a cap; ā cake; ä father; är car; âr dare; ch chain; e hen; ē me; êr clear; hw where; i bib; ī kite; ng song; o top; ō rope; ô saw; oi coin; ôr fork; ou cow; sh show; th thin; <u>th</u> those; u sun; ù book; ü moon; ū cute; ûr term; ə about, taken, pencil, apron, helpful; ər letter, dollar, doctor

GLOSSARY

This glossary will help you to pronounce and understand the meanings of the Key Vocabulary in this book. The page number at the end of the definition tells where the word first appears.

A

abolitionist (ab ə lish′ ə nist) A person who wanted to end slavery. (p. 394)

accuracy (ak′ yər ə sē) Truth; correctness. (p. 272)

A.D. (ā dē) "*Anno Domini*"; a way of naming the year of an event that took place after the birth of Christ. (p. 91)

agriculture (ag′ rə kul chər) Farming. (p. 42)

Allied Powers (ə līd′ pou′ ərz) The name given to the side led by Great Britain, France, and Russia during World War I. The United States joined the Allied Powers in 1917. (p. 495)

Allies (al′ īz) Name given to the side led by the United States, Great Britain, the Soviet Union, and China during World War II. (p. 510)

almanac (ôl′ mə nak) A reference book of facts on many subjects. (p. 233)

alternative (ôl tûr′ nə tiv) A choice between two or more things; one of the many things that may be chosen. (p. 54)

altitude (al′ tə tüd) The height of a place above sea level. (p. 26)

amendment (ə mend′ mənt) An addition to the Constitution. (p. 327)

American Federation of Labor (ə mâr′ i kən fed ə rā′ shən əv lā′ bər) An organization of labor unions, formed in 1886, to work together to meet common goals. (p. 457)

Anaconda Plan (an ə kon′ də plan) The North's three-part plan for defeating the South in the Civil War. (p. 412)

aqueduct (ak′ wə dukt) A pipe or canal that is used to carry water long distances from lakes and rivers. (p. 51)

archaeologist (är kē ol′ ə jist) A scientist who looks for and studies artifacts. (p. 89)

armada (är mä′ də) A large fleet of ships. (p. 161)

Articles of Confederation (är′ ti kəlz əv kən fed ə rā′ shən) The plan of government set up by the Continental Congress. Under the Articles, Congress ran the national government, but most power remained with the states. (p. 318)

artifact (är′ tə fakt) An object, such as a tool, weapon, or clay pot, that was left behind by people long ago. (p. 88)

assembly (ə sem′ blē) A lawmaking body. (p. 224)

assembly line (ə sem′ blē līn) A system in which a conveyor belt brings parts of a product to workers who then add other parts to it. (p. 486)

atlas (at′ ləs) A book of maps. (p. 372)

Axis Powers (ak′ sis pou′ ərz) Name given to the side led by Germany, Italy, and Japan during World War II. (p. 508)

B

bar graph (bär graf) A type of graph that uses bars to present numerical information. (p. 247)

basin (bā′ sin) A low region surrounded by higher land. (p. 22)

B.C. (bē sē) "Before Christ"; a way of naming the year of an event that took place before the birth of Christ. (p. 91)

GLOSSARY

bibliography (bib lē og′ rə fē) A list of the sources used in preparing a report. (p. 397)

Big Dipper (big dip′ ər) A star pattern whose pointer stars are always in a line with the North Star. (p. 138)

Bill of Rights (bil əv rīts) The first ten amendments to the United States Constitution. (p. 328)

Black Codes (blak cōdz) Laws passed in the South during Reconstruction that controlled the lives of the newly freed blacks. (p. 419)

blockade (blo kād′) The closing of an area to keep people and supplies from going in or out. (p. 412)

Boston Tea Party (bôs′ tən tē pär′ tē) Event in 1773 in which colonists opposing the British tea tax dressed as Indians and dumped chests of tea into Boston Harbor. (p. 280)

boycott (boi′ kot) To refuse to buy something. (p. 276)

C

Cabinet (kab′ ə nit) Government officials chosen by the President to be advisors and to head government departments. (p. 328)

call number (kôl num′ bər) A number that tells where to find a book in the library. (p. 373)

canal (kə nal′) A narrow waterway dug for boat travel. (p. 364)

canyon (kan′ yən) A valley with steep sides. (p. 22)

cape (kāp) A pointed piece of coastline. (p. 133)

card catalog (kärd kat′ əl og) A collection of cards in a library that tell where to find each book in the library. The card catalog is organized by author, title, and subject of books. (p. 373)

carpetbagger (kär′ pit bag ər) Name given to Northern whites who moved South after the Civil War. (p. 421)

cash crop (kash krop) A crop grown to be sold for a profit. (p. 244)

cause (kôz) Something that makes something else happen. (p. 100)

Central Powers (sen′ trəl pou′ ərz) The name given to the side led by Germany, Austria-Hungary, and Turkey during World War I. (p. 495)

century (sen′ chər ē) A 100-year period. (p. 90)

checks and balances (cheks and bal′ əns əz) The system in which the power of each branch of government is balanced by the powers of the other branches. (p. 326)

circle graph (sûr′ kəl graf) A graph that shows how something can be divided into parts. (p. 246)

civil rights (siv′ əl rīts) The rights of all people to be treated equally under the law. (p. 522)

Civil War (siv′ əl wôr) Armed fight between northern and southern states; also called the War between the States, fought between 1861 and 1865. (p. 409)

civilization (siv ə li zā′ shən) A community that has developed special skills in farming, building, trade, government, art, and science. (p. 77)

classified ad (klas′ ə fīd ad) Short advertisement in a newspaper that appears in small print and might list such things as a job opening, an apartment for rent, or a car for sale. (p. 489)

climate (klī′ mit) The weather that a place has over many years. (p. 25)

climograph (klī′ mə graf) A graph that shows information about the climate and precipitation of a place. (p. 580)

cold war (kōld wôr) A war fought with words, money, and threats. (p. 519)

colony (kol′ ə nē) A place that is ruled by another country. (p. 143)

Committee of Correspondence (kə mit′ ē əv kôr′ ə spon′ dəns) Group organized to inform colonists in other places of important events. (p. 279)

communism (kom′ yə niz′ əm) System in which the government owns and runs most farms and businesses. (p. 518)

compass (kum′ pəs) An instrument with a magnetic needle that always points north when the compass is held level. (p. 139)

Compromise of 1850 (kom′ prə mīz) Laws passed by Congress providing that California would enter the union as a free state; that people living in other territories would be allowed to decide whether or not they wanted slavery; and that everyone would have to obey the Fugitive Slave Law. (p. 399)

concentration camp (kon sən trā′ shən kamp) Prison camp where the Germans murdered millions of people during World War II. (p. 508)

conclusion (kən klü′ zhən) A statement that results from pulling together pieces of information so that they mean something. (p. 342)

Confederate States of America (kən fed′ ər it stāts) The country formed by the Southern states during the Civil War. (p. 403)

conquistador (kon kēs′ tə dôr) Name for a Spanish conqueror who came to America in the hope of finding new lands, gold, and glory. (p. 143)

conservation (kon sər vā′ shən) The protection and wise use of land and natural resources. (p. 485)

constitution (kon stə tü′ shən) A plan of government. (p. 323)

cotton gin (kot′ ən jin) A machine used to separate cotton from its seeds. (p. 368)

credibility (kred ə bil′ ət ē) Believability; reliability. (p. 216)

culture (kul′ chər) Way of life of a group of people, including their beliefs, crafts, religion, and customs. (p. 82)

D

dateline (dāt′ līn) The words at the beginning of a news article that tell where and when the story was written. (p. 489)

decade (dek′ ād) A ten-year period. (p. 90)

decision (di sizh′ ən) Choice. (p. 54)

Declaration of Independence (dek lə rā′ shən əv in di pen′ dəns) An official document issued by the Second Continental Congress explaining to the world why the American colonies had to break away from Great Britain. (p. 293)

degrees (di grēz′) Units of measurement for latitude and longitude. (p. 28)

delegate (del′ ə gāt) A person chosen by people to represent them. (p. 322)

democracy (di mok′ rə sē) Rule by the people. (p. 212)

depression (di presh′ ən) A period when business is slow and many people are out of work. (p. 502)

dictator (dik′ tā tər) A ruler who has complete control over a country. (p. 507)

dictionary (dik′ shə nâr ē) A reference book that gives the definitions of words and their pronunciation. (p. 372)

distortion (dis tôr′ shən) On a map, an error in size, shape, distance, or direction. (p. 560)

Dred Scott Decision (dred skot) Supreme Court decision of 1857 that said that slavery was legal in any part of the United States. (p. 402)

Dust Bowl (dust bōl) The dry, rainless land in the Great Plains during the 1930s. (p. 504)

E

economy (i kon′ ə mē) The way people use resources to make and sell goods and services. (p. 44)

editor (ed′ ə tər) One of the people who runs a newspaper. (p. 488)

editorial (ed ə tôr′ ē əl) An article in a newspaper in which the editors give their opinion. (p. 488)

effect (i fekt′) What happens as the result of a cause. (p. 100)

elevation (el ə vā′ shən) Height of land above sea level. (p. 236)

Emancipation Proclamation (i man sə pā′ shən prok lə mā′ shən) An official announcement issued by President Lincoln in 1862 that proclaimed the freedom of all slaves in the Confederacy. (p. 414)

empire (em′ pīr) Lands and people ruled by one group or leader. (p. 78)

encyclopedia (en sī klə pē′ dē ə) A book or set of books that gives information on a number of subjects. (p. 372)

environment (en vī′ rən mənt) Everything that surrounds you, including plants, animals, climate, and soil. (p. 95)

executive branch (eg zek′ yə tiv) The part of the government that carries out the laws and runs the government. (p. 323)

expedition (eks pə dish′ ən) A journey made for a special purpose. (p. 134)

F

fact (fakt) Something that is known for certain. (p. 162)

fall line (fôl līn) The boundary between rolling hills and low coastal plains, marked by waterfalls and rapids. (p. 221)

feature article (fē′ chər är′ ti kəl) A detailed report in a newspaper on a person, issue, or event. (p. 488)

federal system (fed′ ər əl sis′ təm) A system of government in which power is shared between the national government and the state governments. The United States has a federal system of government. (p. 325)

fiction book (fik′ shən bùk) A book with a make-believe story. (p. 372)

First Continental Congress (kon tə nent′ əl kong′ gris) A meeting in 1774 in which representatives from every colony except Georgia met together in Philadelphia. (p. 280)

flatboat (flat′ bōt) A large raft used to travel down rivers. (p. 363)

Forty-Niners (fôr′ tē nī′ nərz) People who left their homes to search for gold in 1849. (p. 381)

fossil fuel (fos′ əl fū′ əl) A fuel, such as oil, natural gas, and coal, that is formed from the remains of plants and animals that lived long ago. (p. 31)

free enterprise system (frē en′ tər prīz) An economic system where people are free to make their own decisions about what to produce and how to use their money. (p. 455)

Freedmen's Bureau (frēd′ mənz bùr′ ō) A program set up by Congress in 1865 to provide food and medical care to freed blacks in the South. (p. 419)

frontier (frun tēr′) The edge of a settled area. (p. 230)

Fundamental Orders of Connecticut (fun də ment′ əl ôr′ dərz əv kə net′ i kit) A written plan of government drawn up by Connecticut settlers in 1639. (p. 206)

GLOSSARY

G

geography (jē og′ rə fē) Study of the earth and the way people live on it and use it. (p. 19)

Gettysburg Address (get′ iz bûrg ə dres′) A speech given by President Lincoln in 1863 after the Battle of Gettysburg, explaining the purpose of the Civil War. (p. 416)

glacier (glā′ shər) A thick sheet of ice. (p. 71)

gold rush (gold rush) The great effort by large numbers of people to find gold, as in California in 1849. (p. 381)

government (guv′ ərn mənt) The group of people in charge of ruling a country, state, or city. (p. 40)

graph (graf) A diagram that allows you to compare different facts and figures. (p. 246)

Great Depression (grāt di presh′ ən) The period of hard times during the 1930s. (p. 503)

grid (grid) A set of squares on a map or globe formed by lines of latitude and longitude. (p. 29)

H

headline (hed′ līn) An attention-getting sentence or phrase printed in large type across the top of a news story. (p. 488)

historian (his tôr′ ē ən) A person who studies the past. (p. 87)

historical map (his tôr′ i kəl map) A map that shows something about the past or where past events took place. (p. 182)

history (his′ tər ē) The study or record of what happened in the past. (p. 87)

Holocaust (hol′ ə kôst) The Nazi murder of 6 million Jews during World War II. (p. 512)

Homestead Act (hōm′ sted) An 1862 law that offered free farmland on the Great Plains to anyone who agreed to work it for five years. (p. 447)

homesteader (hom′ sted ər) A person who settled on the Great Plains under the Homestead Act of 1862. (p. 447)

House of Burgesses (bur′ jis iz) The lawmaking body established in Jamestown in 1619. (p. 185)

House of Representatives (rep ri zen′ tə tivz) House of Congress in which each state is represented according to its population. (p. 324)

hurricane (hur′ ə kān′) A violent storm. (p. 571)

I

Ice Age (īs āj) A period of time that began more than 70,000 years ago when thick sheets of ice covered most of the earth. (p. 71)

immigrant (im′ ə grənt) A person who leaves one country to come and live in another. (p. 229)

impeach (im pēch′) To charge a public official with wrongdoing while in office. (p. 420)

indentured servant (in den′ chərd sur′ vənt) A person who agreed to work for a period of time in America in exchange for ocean passage. (p. 186)

independence (in di pen′ dəns) Freedom. (p. 289)

Industrial Revolution (in dus′ trē əl rev ə lü′ shən) A change from hand-made to machine-made goods and a change from home workshops to factories. (p. 453)

industry (in′ dəs trē) A branch of business or manufacturing that makes a product or service; all the companies that make a certain product or service. (p. 44)

integration (in tə grā′ shən) The act of making something open to people of all races. (p. 522)

Intolerable Acts (in tol′ ər ə bəl) British acts that closed Boston Harbor, dissolved the Massachusetts assembly, and required colonists in Boston to quarter British troops. (p. 280)

iron curtain (ī′ ərn kur′ tin) An imaginary division of Europe into communist and noncommunist countries. (p. 519)

irrigation (ir ə gā′ shən) Method in which water is brought to dry fields from rivers or lakes by means of ditches. (p. 82)

isthmus (is′ məs) A narrow strip of land that connects two larger pieces of land. (p. 140)

J

judicial branch (jü dish′ əl) The part of the government that decides the meaning of laws. (p. 323)

K

kachina (kä chē′ nə) According to the Pueblo Indians, the living spirit of an ancestor. (p. 102)

a cap; ā cake; ä father; är car; âr dare; ch chain; e hen; ē me; êr clear; hw where; i bib; ī kite; ng song; o top; ō rope; ô saw; oi coin; ôr fork; ou cow; sh show; th thin; th those; u sun; ů book; ü moon; ū cute; ûr term; ə about, taken, pencil, apron, helpful; ər letter, dollar, doctor

GLOSSARY

Kansas-Nebraska Act (kan′ zəs ni bras′ kə) A law passed by Congress in 1854 that allowed the people who settled in Kansas and Nebraska to decide for themselves whether they would allow slavery in their territories. (p. 400)

Korean War (kô rē′ ən wôr) War fought between North Korea, aided by China, and South Korea, aided by the United States and other United Nations members, over the spread of communism. It lasted from June 1950 until July 1953. (p. 519)

L

labor union (lā′ bər ūn′ yən) A group of workers who join together to improve their lives. (p. 457)

land bridge (land brij) An area of land connecting two larger land masses. During the Ice Age a land bridge connected Asia and North America. (p. 73)

landform (land′ form) A shape on the earth's surface, such as a mountain or a valley. (p. 19)

latitude (lat′ ə tüd) Imaginary line that measures distance north or south of the equator. (p. 28)

league (lēg) A union of people who join together for a common purpose. (p. 107)

League of Nations (lēg əv nā′ shənz) World organization, set up after World War I, to encourage countries to talk over their differences and settle conflicts without war. (p. 497)

legislative branch (lej′ is lā tiv) The lawmaking part of the government. (p. 323)

line graph (līn graf) A type of graph that uses a line or lines to present numerical information. A line graph shows changes over time. (p. 246)

Little Dipper (lit′ əl dip′ ər) A star pattern of which the North Star is a part. (p. 138)

lock (lok) A kind of water elevator that moves boats to higher or lower levels. (p. 365)

longitude (lon′ jə tüd) Imaginary line that measures distance east or west of the prime meridian. (p. 28)

Louisiana Purchase (lü ē zē an′ ə pur′ chəs) The buying of Louisiana by the United States from France in 1803. (p. 345)

Loyalist (loi′ ə list) A colonist who remained loyal to Britain and opposed the Revolution. (p. 290)

M

manufacturing (man yə fak′ chər ing) Making things by machinery. (p. 39)

mass production (mas prə duk′ shən) The making of large amounts of goods by machine. (p. 371)

Mayflower Compact (mā′ flou ər kom′ pakt) An agreement in which the Pilgrims decided to set up a government and make fair laws. (p. 190)

megalopolis (meg ə lop′ ə lis) A group of cities that have grown so close together they seem to form one city. (p. 40)

mercenary (mûr′ sə nâr ē) A soldier hired to fight in another country's war. (p. 291)

meridians (mə rid′ ē ənz) Lines of longitude. (p. 28)

mestizo (mes tē′ zō) A person of mixed Indian and Spanish ancestry. (p. 567)

militia (mi lish′ ə) A group of volunteers who fight in times of emergency. (p. 269)

mineral (min′ ər əl) A substance found in the earth that is neither plant nor animal. (p. 32)

minutemen (min′ it men) An army of citizens at the time of the American Revolution who claimed to be ready to fight the British on a moment's notice. (p. 281)

mission (mish′ ən) A settlement built by missionaries. (p. 147)

missionary (mish′ ə nâr ē) A person who teaches his or her religion to others with different beliefs. (p. 147)

Missouri Compromise (mi zur′ ē kom′ prə mīz) A law passed by Congress in 1820 that created an imaginary line between territories in the West where slavery would be allowed and territories where it would not be allowed. (p. 398)

Mountain Men (mount′ ən men) Fur trappers who crossed the Great Plains to hunt for beaver in the Rocky Mountains during the early 1800s. (p. 361)

mountain range (mount′ ən rānj) A series of many mountains. (p. 20)

N

national park (nash′ ən əl pärk) An area of great beauty that is set aside for everyone to enjoy. (p. 485)

natural resource (nach′ ər əl rē′ sôrs) A material found in nature that people need and use, such as water, soil, and air. (p. 30)

navigable (nav′ i gə bəl) Wide and deep enough for ships to use. (p. 222)

navigation (nav i gā′ shən) The science of determining a ship's direction and location. (p. 131)

neutral (nü′ trəl) Not taking sides. (p. 348)

New Deal (nü dēl) Government programs begun by President Franklin Roosevelt to help businesses, farmers, and the unemployed during the Great Depression. (p. 505)

news article (nüz är′ ti kəl) A story in a newspaper about an important event. (p. 488)

nomad (nō′ mad) A wanderer with no permanent home who lives by moving from place to place in search of food. (p. 109)

nonfiction book (non fik′ shən bùk) A book about real people, places, and events. (p. 372)

North Star (nôrth stär) A star that always shines from the direction of the North Pole. The North Star can be used in the Northern Hemisphere to find north. (p. 138)

Northwest Ordinance (nôrth west′ ôrd′ ən əns) Law passed in 1787 that provided a way to divide and settle the Northwest Territory. (p. 318)

Northwest Passage (nôrth west′ pas′ ij) A waterway through North America that would link the Atlantic and Pacific oceans. (p. 154)

O

opinion (ə pin′ yən) A personal view or belief. (p. 162)

overseer (ō′ vər sē ər) A person hired by a planter to make sure the slaves did their work. (p. 252)

P

parallels (par′ ə lelz) Lines of latitude. (p. 28)

pardon (pärd′ ən) To free a person from going to trial for wrong doings. (p. 528)

Parliament (par′ lə mənt) Great Britain's lawmaking body. (p. 275)

Patriot (pā′ trē ət) An American colonist who supported the fight against Great Britain. (p. 290)

Peace Corps (pēs côr) Program set up in 1961 by President John Kennedy in which Americans volunteered to help countries in need. (p. 520)

petition (pə tish′ ən) A written request signed by many people. (p. 280)

pilgrim (pil′ grəm) A person who makes a journey for religious reasons. (p. 188)

pioneer (pī ə nēr′) One of the first people to explore or settle a region. (p. 337)

plain (plān) An area of flat or sloping land. (p. 19)

plantation (plan tā′ shən) A very large farm in the South. (p. 248)

plateau (pla tō′) An area of flat land that is higher than the surrounding land. (p. 20)

point of view (point əv vū) The way a person looks at or feels about something. (p. 320)

political cartoon (pə lit′ i kəl kär tün′) A drawing that shows how the cartoonist feels about a person, an event, or an issue. (p. 466)

political party (pə lit′ i kəl) A group of people who share similar ideas about government. (p. 329)

population (pop yə lā′ shən) The number of people living in a place. (p. 265)

potlatch (pot′ läch) A feast among the Northwest Coast Indians, in which the chief of a village showed off his wealth by giving it all away. (p. 115)

prairie (prer′ ē) A gently rolling plain covered with tall, thick grass. (p. 337)

Preamble (prē′ am bəl) Introduction to the Constitution of the United States. (p. 325)

precipitation (pri sip ə tā′ shən) The moisture that falls to the earth as rain or snow. (p. 25)

prejudice (prej′ ə dis) The unfair dislike or hatred of a group because of their race or religion. (p. 502)

President (prez′ ə dənt) The head of the executive branch of the United States government. (p. 323)

primary source (prī′ mâr ē sôrs) Information that comes from the time that is being studied. (p. 87)

prime meridian (prīm mə rid′ ē ən) The starting line for measuring longitude. The longitude of the prime meridian is 0°. (p. 28)

proclamation (prok lə mā′ shən) An official announcement. (p. 274)

projection (prə jek′ shən) The way the earth is shown on a flat sheet of paper. (p. 560)

proprietor (prə prī′ ə tər) A person who owns property or a business. (p. 244)

province (prov′ ins) A division of Canada, similar to a state in the United States. (p. 554)

R

rain forest (rān fôr′ ist) A warm, wet area where many trees and plants grow closely together. (p. 577)

rain shadow (rān shad′ ō) An area on a mountain that does not get much rain because clouds passing over it have lost much of their moisture. (p. 58)

rebel (reb′ əl) Someone who will not obey those in charge because he or she has different beliefs about what is right. (p. 205)

Reconstruction (rē kən struk′ shən) A time in American history after the Civil War when laws were passed to rebuild the nation and bring the Southern states back into the Union. (p. 419)

---

a cap; ā cake; ä father; är car; âr dare; ch chain; e hen; ē me; êr clear; hw where; i bib; ī kite; ng song; o top; ō rope; ô saw; oi coin; ôr fork; ou cow; sh show; th thin; <u>th</u> those; u sun; ù book; ü moon; ū cute; ûr term; ə about, taken, pencil, apron, helpful; ər letter, dollar, doctor

GLOSSARY

reference book (ref′ ər əns buk) A book that gives information about a subject. (p. 372)

region (rē′ jən) A large area that has common features, such as landforms and climate. (p. 33)

relief (ri lēf′) The difference in height between highlands and lowlands. (p. 237)

repeal (ri pēl′) To withdraw or cancel. (p. 276)

representative (rep ri zen′ tə tiv) Someone chosen by a group to speak and act for them. (p. 185)

republic (ri pub′ lik) A type of government in which people elect representatives to run the country. (p. 323)

reservation (rez ər vā′ shən) An area set aside for Indian use. (p. 440)

revolution (rev ə lü′ shən) A sudden, complete change in government. (p. 293)

river basin (riv′ ər bā′ sin) All the land drained by a river and its tributaries. (p. 577)

Rough Riders (ruf rī′ dərz) Group of volunteers who fought with Theodore Roosevelt in the Spanish-American War. (p. 481)

S

saga (sä′ gə) Long story about the great deeds of the Vikings. (p. 127)

scalawag (skal′ ə wag) Name given to Southern whites who helped carry out Congress's plan for Reconstruction. (p. 421)

secession (si sesh′ ən) Breaking away from the Union. (p. 403)

Second Continental Congress (kon tə nent′ əl kong′ gris) A meeting in Philadelphia in 1775 attended by delegates from all 13 colonies. It decided to set up an army to fight the British and issued the Declaration of Independence. (p. 289)

secondary source (sek′ ən dâr ē sôrs) An account of the past written by someone who was not an eyewitness to those events. (p. 88)

segregation (seg rə gā′ shən) The separation of blacks and whites. (p. 422)

self-sufficient (self sə fish′ ənt) Able to take care of one's needs without help from others. (p. 230)

Senate (sen′ it) House of Congress in which each state has two members regardless of the state's population. (p. 324)

Seneca Falls Convention (sen′ ə kə fôlz kən ven′ shən) The world's first women's rights meeting, held in Seneca Falls, New York, in 1848. (p. 396)

settlement house (set′ əl mənt hous) A place in a city where poor people could meet to get help with their problems in the form of classes, child care services, and so on. (p. 465)

sharecropping (shâr′ krop ing) A system where a farmer rents land by paying a share of the crop raised on the land. (p. 420)

slave (slāv) Someone who is owned by another person. (p. 145)

slave trade (slāv trād) The buying and selling of slaves. (p. 214)

source (sôrs) Something that gives information or evidence, such as a book or letter. (p. 307)

Spanish-American War (span′ ish ə mâr′ i kən wôr) War fought between Spain and the United States in 1898. (p. 480)

specialize (spesh′ ə līz) To spend most of one's time doing one kind of job. (p. 77)

Stamp Act (stamp akt) A law passed by Parliament in 1765 which put a tax on documents purchased in Britain's American colonies. (p. 275)

steamboat (stēm′ bōt) A boat powered by a steam engine. (p. 364)

stock (stok) Share of ownership in a company. (p. 179)

stock market (stok mär′ kit) A place where stocks are bought and sold. (p. 501)

strait (strāt) A narrow waterway that connects two larger bodies of water. (p. 73)

strike (strīk) To refuse to work. (p. 457)

suffrage (suf′ rij) The right to vote. (p. 487)

Supreme Court (sə prēm′ kôrt) The head of the judicial branch of the national government. (p. 323)

surplus (sûr′ plus) An amount greater than what is needed. (p. 77)

sweatshop (swet shop) A small factory where people work in unhealthy conditions. (p. 460)

symbol (sim′ bəl) A person or object that stands for something else. (p. 466)

T

technology (tek nol′ ə jē) The use of new tools, ideas, and methods to solve problems. (p. 454)

temperate zone (tem′ pər it zōn) One of the areas of the earth where the climate is not as hot as near the equator nor as cold as at the North and South poles. (p. 26)

temperature (tem′ pər ə chər) The amount of heat or cold in the air. (p. 25)

tenement (ten′ ə mənt) An apartment building divided into many cramped living units. (p. 463)

territory (târ′ ə tôr ē) An area of government land. (p. 304)

tidewater (tīd′ wô tər) A low-lying coastal plain that is full of waterways. (p. 241)

time line (tīm′ līn) A diagram that shows when important events took place. (p. 90)

GLOSSARY

time zone (tīm zōn) One of the 24 areas into which the earth is divided for measuring standard time. (p. 438)

tolerate (tol′ ə rāt) To allow people to hold beliefs even if you disagree. (p. 204)

total war (tōt′ əl wôr) An all-out war against an entire people to destroy their ability and will to fight. (p. 416)

totem pole (tō′ təm pōl) A carved pole showing the history of a family, and placed in front of a house as a sign of wealth. (p. 114)

town meeting (toun mē′ ting) A meeting held in New England in which villagers discussed their needs and voted on what to do. (p. 212)

Townshend Acts (toun′ zhund akts) Laws passed by Parliament in 1767 that taxed many goods brought into the colonies from Britain. (p. 276)

Trail of Tears (trāl əv tērz) Name given to the long journey made by the Cherokees from Georgia to the Indian Territory after they had been forced off their land. (p. 356)

traitor (trā′ tər) A person who turns against his or her country and gives aid to its enemies. (p. 304)

transcontinental railroad (trans kon tə nent′ əl) A railroad that stretches across a continent. (p. 435)

treason (trē′ zən) The betrayal of one's country by giving help to an enemy. (p. 275)

treaty (trē′ tē) A formal agreement. (p. 380)

Treaty of Versailles (trē′ tē əv vâr sī′) Peace treaty that was signed at the end of World War I. (p. 497)

triangular trade (trī ang′ gyə lər trād) Three-sided trade route between Africa, the West Indies, and New England, which involved the buying and selling of slaves as well as goods such as molasses and sugar. (p. 213)

tributary (trib′ yə târ ē) A stream or river that flows into a larger river. (p. 20)

tundra (tun′ drə) A huge frozen plain. (p. 117)

U

Uncle Tom's Cabin (ung′ kəl tomz kab′ in) An 1852 novel by Harriet Beecher Stowe that attacked slavery. (p. 399)

unconstitutional (un kon stə tü′ shən əl) Not allowed by the Constitution. (p. 522)

Underground Railroad (un′ dər ground rāl′ rōd) The network of people and places that helped runaway slaves to escape to freedom in the North or Canada. (p. 395)

unemployment (un em ploi′ mənt) The number of people without jobs. (p. 503)

United Nations (ū nīt′ əd nā′ shənz) World organization set up in 1945 whose main purpose is to prevent war; also called the UN. (p. 517)

V

veto (vē′ tō) To refuse to approve. (p. 326)

Vietnam War (vē et näm′ wôr) War fought between North Vietnam, aided by the Soviet Union and China, and South Vietnam, aided by the United States, over the spread of communism. It lasted from 1954 until 1975. (p. 526)

village common (vil′ ij kom′ ən) An open field located in the center of a New England town. (p. 208)

volcano (vol kā′ nō) An opening in the earth through which melted rock, ashes, and gas are forced out. (p. 57)

W

War Hawks (wôr hôks) People in the early 1800s who wanted the United States to go to war against Great Britain. (p. 348)

Watergate (wô′ tər gāt) Political scandal in which several people were arrested for spying on President Richard Nixon's political opponents. (p. 527)

World War I (wûrld wôr) War that broke out in Europe in 1914 between the Central Powers and the Allied Powers. (p. 495)

World War II (wûrld wôr) War that involved most countries in the world, fought between 1939 and 1945. The two sides were known as the Axis Powers and the Allies. (p. 509)

---

a cap; ā cake; ä father; är car; âr dare; ch chain; e hen; ē me; êr clear; hw where; i bib; ī kite; ng song; o top; ō rope; ô saw; oi coin; ôr fork; ou cow; sh show; th thin; <u>th</u> those; u sun; ù book; ü moon; ū cute; ûr term; ə about, taken, pencil, apron, helpful; ər letter, dollar, doctor

GLOSSARY

INDEX

Page references in italic type which follow an *m* indicate maps. Those following a *p* indicate photographs, artwork, or charts.

A

Abilene, Kansas, 445
Abolitionists, 394–396, 401
Adams, Abigail, 281, 317
Adams, John, 279–281, 289, 317
Adams, Samuel, 276–277, 279–280, *p276*
Addams, Jane, 465, *p465*
Africa, 5, 132–133
African-Americans. *See* Black Americans
Agriculture. *See* Farming
Alabama, 423, 521–522
Alamo, 375, *p375*
Alaska
  climate of, 25–26, *m35*
  Eskimos in, 116–117
  geography of, 60, 477–478
Alaska Range, 24
Albany, New York, 195
Alberta, Canada, 555
Allen, Ethan, 287
Allied Powers, 495–497, 510–513, *m511*
Almanac, 233, 372
Alternatives, 54–55
Altitude, 26–27
Amazon Basin, 576
Amazon River, 576, *m577*
Amendments, 327–328, as part of the Constitution, 331, 487
American Federation of Labor (AFL), 457
American Revolution
  battles of, *m300*
  beginning of, 279–283
  Bunker Hill battle, 288–289, *p288*
  debate over, 296–297
  and Declaration of Independence, 293–295, *p295*
  Fort Ticonderoga battle, 287
  at frontier, 303–304
  and independence, 306
  Long Island battles, 298–299
  Saratoga battle, 299, 301
  at sea, 304–305, *p304*
  in Southern colonies, 305, *p305*
  surrender at Yorktown, 306, *p306*
  traitors in, 304–305
  Trenton victory, 299, *p299*
  Valley Forge, 301
"America, the Beautiful," 18, 23
Anaconda Plan, 412–413
Anasazi, 82–84

Anchorage, Alaska, 25
Andes Mountains, 80, 575
Antarctica, 5
Antietam, Maryland, 414
Apache Indians, 95, 102
Appalachian Highlands, 548, 550
Appalachian Mountains, 19–20, 32, 38, 43–44, 144, 236, 242, 337, *m340*
Appomattox, Virginia, 417
Archaeologists, 89, 129
Arctic North, 550–551
Arctic Plains, 116–117
Argentina, 577, 578, *m576*
Arid America, 27, 50
Arizona, 52–53
Arkansas, 42–43
Armada, Spanish, 160–161, *p161*
Arms race, 519–520, 528
Armstrong, Neil, 530
Arnold, Benedict, 287, 304–305
Articles of Confederation, 318, 323
Artifacts, 88–89, 129
Asia
  continent of, 5
  immigrants from, to U.S., 462
  Marco Polo's travels to, 130–131
  in World War II, 508, 512–513
Asian hunters, 71–73
Assembly, 224, 266–267, *p267*
Assembly lines, 486
Astronauts, 529–530, *p516*
Atacama Desert, 575
Atahualpa, 577
Atlanta, Georgia, 416–417
Atlantic Coastal Plain, 19, 27
Atlantic Ocean, 134–136
Atlas, 372, *m586–595*
Atomic bomb, 513, 519–520
Attucks, Crispus, 277
Austin, Stephen, 374
Australia, 5
Author card, 373
Axis Powers, 508–509, 513, *m511*
Aztecs, 78–79, 143

B

Balboa, Vasco Núñez de, 140
Baltimore, Lord, 243
Baltimore, Maryland, 350
Banneker, Benjamin, 344, *p345*
Bar graphs, 246–247
Barton, Clara, 415

Basins, 22
Battles. *See* specific names
Bell, Alexander Graham, 455
Beringia, 73, *m72*
Bering Strait, 73
Berkeley, Lord John, 223
Berkshire Mountains, 201
Berlin, Germany, 512
Bibliography, 397
Bill of Rights, 327–328
Biography, 608–613
Black Americans
  in the American Revolution, 277, 301
  and civil rights of, 420–421, 524
  and civil rights movement, 521–523, 524
  in the Civil War, 415
  in colonies, 186, 250, 252–253
  in postwar South, 419, 420–421, 422
  women, 395, 396
Black Codes, 419
Blackfoot Indians, 111
Black Hills, 442
Blockades, 412–413
Blue Ridge Mountains, 242
Bolívar, Simón, 578, *p578*
Bolivia, 576, 579
Bonhomme Richard, 304, *p304*
Boone, Daniel, 339–341, *p341*
Boonesborough, Kentucky, 340
Booth, John Wilkes, 418
Boston, Massachusetts, 40, 194, 277
Boston Massacre, 277
Boston Tea Party, 280
Boswash, 40
Bowie, Jim, 375
Boycott, 276–277, 522
Braddock, General Edward, 269, *p270*
Bradford, William, 188–190
Brazil, 576, 578–579
Brazilian Highlands, 576
Breadbasket, U.S., 48
Breed's Hill battle, 288
British. *See* England
British Canadians, 557–558
Brown, John, 402
Buffalo, 22, 109, 441
Bull Run battle, 410–411
Bunker Hill battle, 288–289
Burgoyne, General John, 299, 301
Bush, George, 531, *p532*
Byrd, William II, 250, 253

C

Cabinet, Presidential, 328
Cabot, John, 153–154
Cahokia, Mississippi, 85–86
Cahokians, 85–86
California
  Central Valley, 24, 57
  farming in, 61
  Gold Rush in, 380–381
  immigrants to, 462
  Indians in, 113
  Los Angeles, 61
  prison camps in, during World War II, 509–510
  Spanish missionaries in, 146–147
California Indians, 113
California Trail, 378
Call number, 373
Calvert, George, 243
Canada
  climate of, 548–551
  Constitution of, 558
  and England, 553
  exploration of, 155–156
  farming in, 549
  and France, 552
  future of, 559
  geography of, 547–551
  history of, 552–555
  immigrants to, 556–557
  independence of, 553
  Indians in, 548–550, 552–553, 557
  Industrial Revolution in, 558–559
  modern, 556–559
  people in, 556–559
  provinces in, *m554*
Canadian Pacific Railway, 555, *m554*, *p555*
Canadian Rockies, 555
Canadian Shield, 547–548
Canals, 47, 364–366, 484–485, *p484*
Canyons, 22, 50
Cape, 132–133, 190–191
Cape Cod, 190–191
Cape of Good Hope, 132–133
Capital, 39
Capitol, 40, *p40*
Card catalog, 372–373
Caribbean Sea, 136, 570
Carnegie, Andrew, 454, *p454*
Carpetbaggers, 421
Cars, 485–486, 499
Carter, Jimmy, 449, 528
Carteret, Sir George, 223
Cartier, Jacques, 154–155, 552, *p155*
Cartoons, political, 466–467, *p466–467*

INDEX

INDEX

CREDITS